A Quick Guide to Working with Primary Sources

This quick guide provides some basic steps for analyzing the documents and visual sources in this book. For more detailed help in working with primary sources, see pp. xxxvii–xli.

Reading and Analyzing a Written Document

The following questions will help you understand and analyze a written document:

- Who wrote the document?

- When and where was it written?

- What type of document is it (for example, a letter to a friend, a political decree, an exposition of a religious teaching)?

- Why was the document written? Under what circumstances was it composed?

- What point of view does it reflect?

- Who was its intended audience?

- What about the document is believable and what is not?

- What can the document tell us about the individual that produced it and the society from which he or she came?

Viewing and Analyzing a Visual Source

These questions will help you to understand and analyze a visual source:

- When and where was the image or artifact made?

- Who made the image or artifact? How was it made?

- Who paid for or commissioned it?

- Where might the image or artifact have originally been displayed or used?

- For what audience(s) was it intended?

- What message(s) is it trying to convey?

- How could it be interpreted differently depending on who viewed or used it?

- What can this image tell us about the individual that produced it and the society from which he or she came?

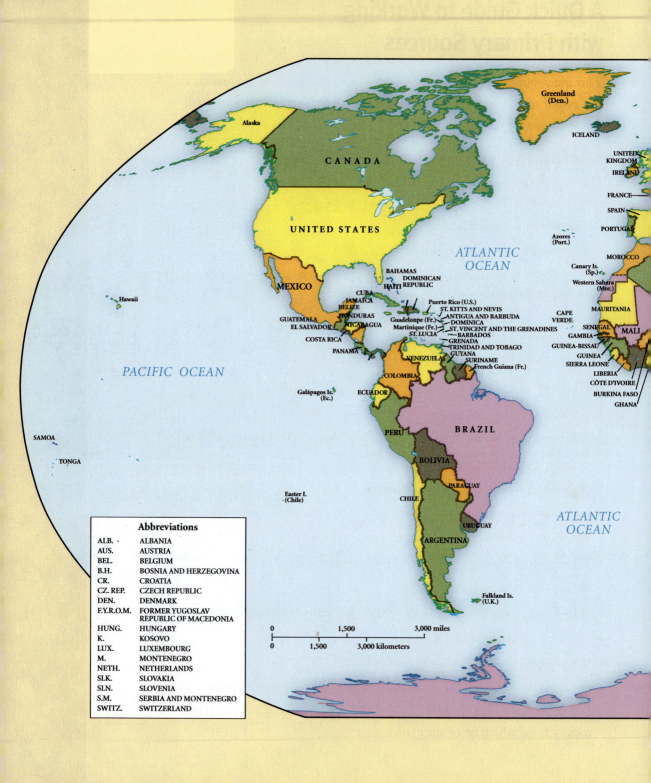

A Brief Guide to Working with Primary Sources

CANADA

UNITED STATES

Alaska

Hawaii

Greenland
(Den.)

ICELAND

UNITED
KINGDOM

IRELAND

FRANCE

SPAIN

PORTUGAL

Azores
(Port.)

MOROCCO

Canary Is.
(Sp.)

Western Sahara
(Mor.)

CAPE
VERDE

MAURITANIA

SENEGAL

GAMBIA

MALI

GUINEA-BISSAU

GUINEA

SIERRA LEONE

LIBERIA

CÔTE D'IVOIRE

BURKINA FASO

GHANA

ATLANTIC
OCEAN

BAHAMAS
DOMINICAN
REPUBLIC
HAITI
CUBA
JAMAICA
BELIZE
HONDURAS

Puerto Rico (U.S.)
ST. KITTS AND NEVIS
ANTIGUA AND BARBUDA
Guadeloupe (Fr.)
DOMINICA
Martinique (Fr.)
ST. VINCENT AND THE GRENADINES
ST. LUCIA
BARBADOS
GRENADA
TRINIDAD AND TOBAGO

MEXICO

GUATEMALA
EL SALVADOR
COSTA RICA

NICARAGUA

PANAMA

VENEZUELA

GUYANA
SURINAME
French Guiana (Fr.)

COLOMBIA

ECUADOR

Galápagos Is.
(Ec.)

PERU

BRAZIL

BOLIVIA

PACIFIC OCEAN

SAMOA

TONGA

Easter I.
(Chile)

CHILE

PARAGUAY

URUGUAY

ARGENTINA

ATLANTIC
OCEAN

Falkland Is.
(U.K.)

0	1,500	3,000 miles
0	1,500	3,000 kilometers

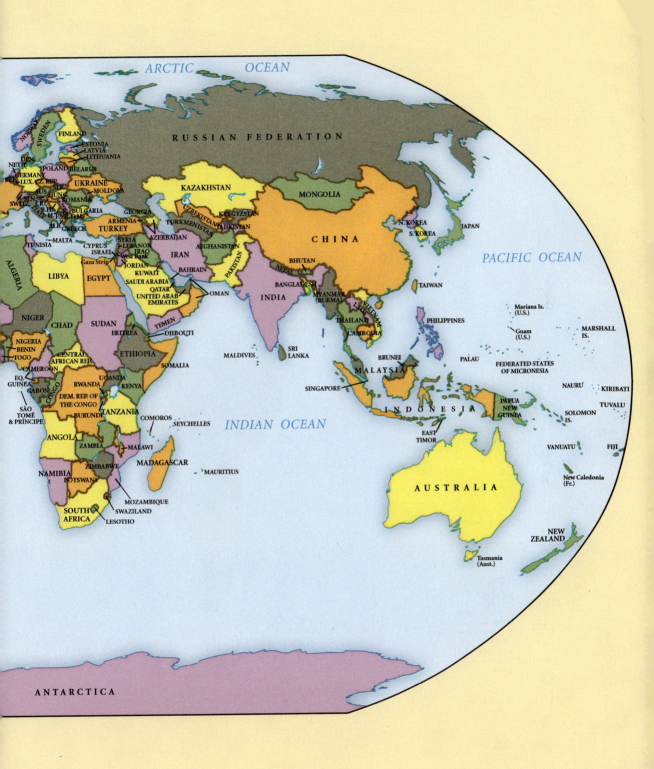

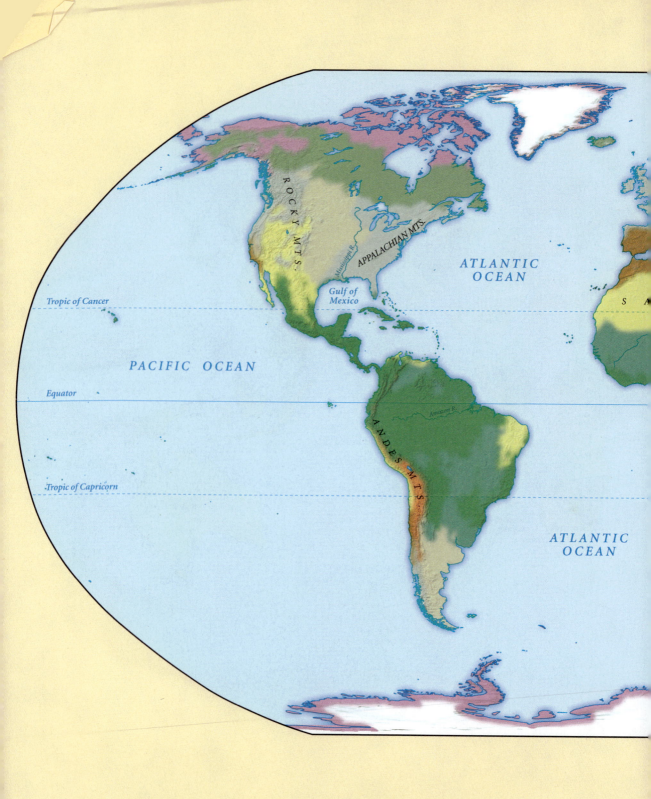

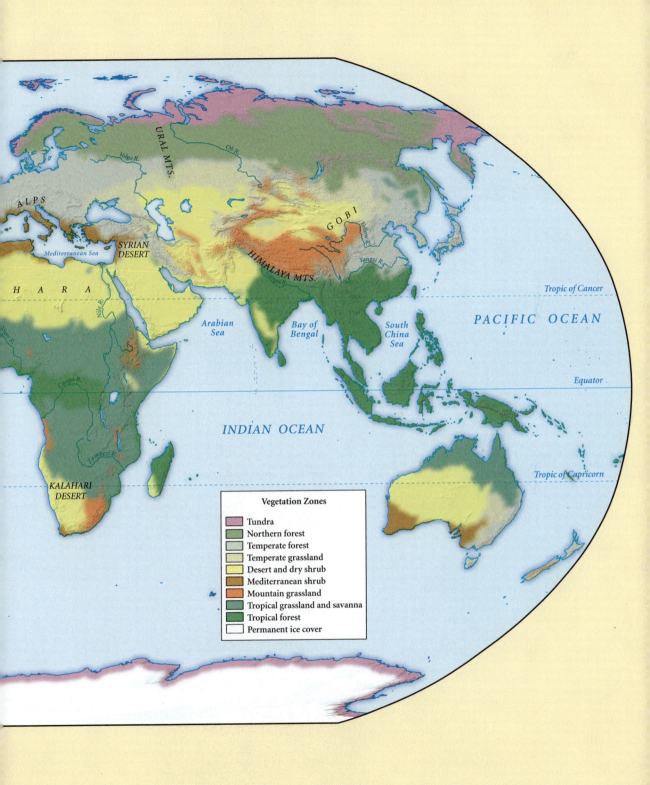

ALPS

URAL MTS.

Volga R.

Ob R.

GOBI

Yellow R.

SYRIAN
DESERT

Mediterranean Sea

HIMALAYA MTS.

Yangzi R.

Ganges R.

H A R A

Nile R.

Niger R.

Tropic of Cancer

PACIFIC OCEAN

Arabian
Sea

Bay of
Bengal

South
China
Sea

Congo R.

Equator

INDIAN OCEAN

Zambezi R.

Tropic of Capricorn

KALAHARI
DESERT

Vegetation Zones

- Tundra
- Northern forest
- Temperate forest
- Temperate grassland
- Desert and dry shrub
- Mediterranean shrub
- Mountain grassland
- Tropical grassland and savanna
- Tropical forest
- Permanent ice cover

Ways of the World

A Brief Global History

with Sources

VOLUME 2: SINCE 1500

Ways of the World

A Brief Global History with Sources

ROBERT W. STRAYER

California State University, Monterey Bay

Bedford/St. Martin's
Boston • New York

For Bedford/St. Martin's

Executive Editor for History: Mary Dougherty

Director of Development for History: Jane Knetzger

Executive Editor for History: Traci Mueller Crowell

Developmental Editor: Kathryn Abbott

Senior Production Editor: Bridget Leahy

Senior Production Supervisor: Joe Ford

Executive Marketing Manager: Jenna Bookin Barry

Editorial Assistant: Robin Soule

Production Assistant: Lidia MacDonald-Carr

Copyeditor: Janet Renard

Editorial Consultant: Eric W. Nelson, Missouri State University

Text and Cover Design: Joyce Weston

Photo Research: Carole Frohlich, The Visual Connection Image Research, Inc.

Indexer: Leoni Z. McVey

Cover Art: Codex Duran: Fol. 208v. Meeting between Hernán Cortés and Moctezuma. Bridgeman Art Library.

Frontispiece: Imperial Indian durbar (detail). 1903. Topham/The Image Works

Cartography: Mapping Specialists Limited

Composition: NK Graphics

Printing and Binding: RR Donnelley and Sons

President: Joan E. Feinberg

Editorial Director: Denise B. Wydra

Director of Marketing: Karen R. Soeltz

Director of Editing, Design, and Production: Susan W. Brown

Assistant Director of Editing, Design, and Production: Elise S. Kaiser

Managing Editor: Elizabeth M. Schaaf

Library of Congress Control Number: 2010920404

Manufactured in the United States of America.

4   5   6   14   13   12   11

For information, write: Bedford/St. Martin's, 75 Arlington Street, Boston, MA 02116 (617-399-4000)

ISBN-10: 0-312-48916-1   ISBN-13: 978-0-312-48916-8   (combined edition)
ISBN-10: 0-312-48917-X   ISBN-13: 978-0-312-48917-5   (Vol. 1)
ISBN-10: 0-312-48918-8   ISBN-13: 978-0-312-48918-2   (Vol. 2)
ISBN-10: 0-312-64466-3   ISBN-13: 978-0-312-64466-6   (high school edition)

For Gina, Nicole, Alisa, and their generation

Preface

WAYS OF THE WORLD FIRST APPEARED in September 2008 and was warmly welcomed by students and teachers, who seemed to like its brevity, clarity, and accessibility. Among the responses that the book provoked, however, was the call for a set of primary sources keyed to its narrative. This version of *Ways of the World* addresses that need in what Bedford/St. Martin's calls a "docutext" format. Each chapter narrative is now followed by a group of related documents and, separately, a collection of visual sources, both of which are organized around particular themes or questions from the chapter. Thus this docutext version of *Ways of the World* presents an integrated package of text and sources that offers instructors a wide range of pedagogical possibilities. For students, it provides a "laboratory" experience, enabling them to engage the evidence directly and to draw conclusions from sources—in short to "do history" rather than simply read history.

The history that students encounter in *Ways of the World* is now widely known as world or global history, a rather new and remarkably ambitious field of study that has come of age during my own career in the academy and particularly during the past quarter of a century. Those of us who practice world history, as teachers or textbook authors, are seldom specialists in the particulars of what we study and teach. Rather we are "specialists of the whole," seeking to find the richest, most suggestive, and most meaningful contexts in which to embed those particulars. We look for the big-picture processes and changes that have marked the human journey; we are alert to the possibilities for comparison across cultural boundaries; and we pay special attention to the multiple interactions among human communities. Our task, fundamentally, is to teach contextual thinking. The documents and visual sources presented here frequently add a personal dimension to these big-picture themes by evoking the words and images of particular historical actors who lived, worked, played, suffered, triumphed, and interacted over the many centuries of the human journey.

What's in a Title?

The title of a book should evoke something of its character and outlook. The main title of *Ways of the World* is intended to suggest at least three dimensions of this text.

The first is **diversity** or **variation**, for the "ways of the world," or the ways of being human in the world, have been many and constantly changing. World history was conceived in part to counteract a Eurocentric perspective on the human past, deriving from several centuries of Western dominance on the world stage. This book seeks to embrace the experience of humankind in its vast diversity, while noticing the changing location of particular centers of innovation and wider influence.

Second, the title *Ways of the World* invokes major **panoramas**, **patterns**, or **pathways** in world history, as opposed to highly detailed narratives. Many world history instructors have found that students often feel overwhelmed by the sheer quantity of data that a course in global history can require of them. In the narrative sections of this book, the larger patterns or the "big pictures" of world history appear in the foreground on center stage, while the still plentiful details, data, and facts occupy the background, serving in supporting roles.

A third implication of the book's title lies in a certain **reflective** or **musing quality** of *Ways of the World*, which appears especially in the Big Picture essays that introduce each part of the book and in a Reflections section at the end of each chapter. This dimension of the text is a product of my own growing appreciation that history of any kind, and world history in particular, offers endless raw material for contemplating large questions. Here are some of the issues that are addressed in this fashion:

- How can we tell when one period of history ends and another begins? What marks off the classical era, for example, or the early modern period of world history? Does the twentieth century deserve to be considered a separate period of time?

- In what ways and why do historians and religious believers sometimes rub each other the wrong way?

- How can we, or should we, make moral judgments in the face of the vast ambiguity of most historical phenomena?

- Are there clear "lessons" to be learned from the past? And does history really repeat itself, as so many students seem to believe?

- How can we avoid Eurocentrism when dealing with recent centuries, in which Europeans were in fact increasingly central to the human story?

- How can we retain a sense of surprise, unexpectedness, contingency, or luck in our telling of the human story, particularly when we know the outcomes of those stories?

None of these questions have clear or easy answers, but the opportunity to contemplate them is among the great gifts that the study of history offers to us all.

Integrating Narrative and Sources: The Docutext Approach

The subtitle of this book, *A Brief Global History with Sources*, refers to its docutext format. Following the narrative portion of each chapter are a set of written primary sources and then another set of visual primary sources. Each collection is organized around a particular theme, issue, or question that derives from the chapter narrative. As the title of these features suggests, they enable students to "consider the evidence" and thus begin to understand the craft of historians as well as their conclusions. All of them are thoroughly cross-referenced with the text, are furnished with brief head-notes providing context for the sources, and are accompanied by a series of prob-ing Using the Evidence questions appropriate for in-class discussion and writing assignments.

Many of these Considering the Evidence features are broadly comparative or cross-cultural. For example, the Documents feature for Chapter 5 invites students to consider the nature of the good life and good society in the thinking of Confucius, the *Bhagavad Gita*, Socrates, and Jesus. Likewise the Visual Sources feature for Chapter 15 raises questions about the display of status derived from items acquired in the transregional commerce of the early modern era, with examples from Europe, the Ottoman Empire, colonial Mexico, and the West African kingdom of Dahomey. Other features are regionally focused, providing a more in-depth look at certain elements of specific societies. In Chapter 7, for example, the Documents feature allows students to explore the history of Axum through a series of texts from the early centuries of the Common Era, while the Visual Sources feature of Chapter 22 examines the commu-nist vision of the future in Mao's China via its poster art.

Achieving Coherence

The great virtue of world history lies in its inclusiveness, for it allows us to see the world and to see it whole. But that virtue is also the source of world history's greatest difficulty—telling a coherent story. How can we meaningfully present the planet's many and distinct peoples and their intersections with one another in the confines of a single book or a single term? What prevents that telling from bogging down in the endless detail of various civilizations or cultures, from losing the forest for the trees, from implying that history is just "one damned thing after another"?

Less Can Be More

Ways of the World seeks to cope with that fundamental conundrum of world history—the tension between inclusion and coherence—in several ways. The first is the rela-tive brevity of the narrative and a corresponding selectivity. This means, of course, leaving some things out or treating them more succinctly than some instructors might expect. But the docutext format allows for exploration of particular topics in greater depth via the Documents and Visual Sources features. The positive side of narrative brevity is that the textbook need not overwhelm students or dominate the pedagogy of the course. It allows for more professorial creativity in constructing indi-vidual world history courses and in mixing and matching text and sources.

Narrative brevity also encourages a "themes and cases" rather than a "civilization-by-civilization" approach to the global past. Thus most chapters in this book focus on a broad theme, explored on a global or transregional scale: agricultural revolutions in Chapter 2; classical-era empires in Chapter 4; axial-age religions in Chapter 5; long-distance commerce in Chapters 8 and 15; the colonial experience of the long nineteenth century in Chapter 20; the Communist experiment in Chapter 22; twentieth-century globalization in Chapter 24. Docutext features add substantially to the "themes and cases" dimension of the book.

The Three Cs of World History: Change, Comparison, Connection

As a further aid to achieving coherence on a global scale, *Ways of the World* refers repeatedly to what I call the "**three Cs**" of world history. They represent some of the distinctive perspectives of world history as an academic discipline and are introduced more extensively in the prologue.

The first "C" emphasizes large-scale **changes**, both within and especially across major regions of the world. Change, of course, is a central theme in all historical study and serves to challenge "essentialist" descriptions of particular cultures or peoples. Among the macrochanges highlighted in *Ways of the World* are the peopling of the planet in Chapter 1; the emergence of "civilization" in Chapter 3; the rise of universal religions in Chapter 5; the changing shape of the Islamic world in Chapter 11; the breakthrough of industrialization in Chapter 18; the development of European global dominance in Chapters 19 and 20; the rise and fall of world communism in Chapter 22; the acceleration of globalization in Chapter 24.

The second "C" involves frequent **comparison**. It is a technique of integration through juxtaposition, of bringing several regions or cultures into our field of vision at the same time. It encourages reflection both on the common elements of the human experience and on its many variations. Such comparisons are pervasive throughout the book, informing both the chapter narratives and many of the docutext features. We examine the difference, for example, between the Agricultural Revolution in the Eastern and Western Hemispheres in Chapter 2; between the beginnings of Buddhism and the early period of Christianity in Chapter 5; between patriarchy in Athens and in Sparta in Chapter 6; between European and Asian empires of the early modern era in Chapter 14; between the Chinese and the Japanese response to European intrusion in Chapter 19; between postures toward Islam in twentieth-century Turkey and in Iran in Chapter 23; and many more.

The final "C" emphasizes **connections**, networks of communication and exchange that increasingly shaped the character of those societies that participated in them. For world historians, cross-cultural interaction becomes one of the major motors of historical change. Such connections are addressed in nearly every chapter narrative and many docutext features. For example, Chapter 3 explores the clash of the Greeks and the Persians during the classical era; Chapter 8 highlights the long-distance commercial networks that linked the Afro-Eurasian world, while its Visual Sources feature illustrates Central Asia as a cultural crossroads; Chapter 11 focuses attention on the numerous cross-cultural encounters spawned by the spread of Islam; Chapters 14 and 15 explore various facets of the transhemispheric Columbian exchange of the early modern era; Chapter 17 probes the linkages among the Atlantic revolutions of the late eighteenth and early nineteenth centuries, and its Documents feature displays the interplay of the idea of "rights" across the region; Chapter 24 concludes the book with an examination of globalization, highlighting its economic, feminist, religious, and environmental dimensions.

Organizing World History: Chronology, Theme, and Region

Organizing a world history textbook or a world history course is, to put it mildly, a daunting task. How should we divide up the seamless stream of human experience into manageable and accessible pieces, while recognizing always that such divisions are both artificial and to some extent arbitrary? Historians, of course, debate the issue endlessly. In structuring *Ways of the World*, I have drawn on my own sense of "what works" in the classroom, on a personal penchant for organizational clarity, and on established practice in the field. The outcome has been an effort to balance three principles of organization—chronology, theme, and region—in a flexible format that can accommodate a variety of teaching approaches and organizational strategies.

The chronological principle is expressed most clearly in the overall structure of the book, which divides world history into six major periods. Each of these six "parts" begins with a brief **Big Picture essay** that introduces the general patterns of a particular period and raises questions about the problems historians face in dividing up the human past into meaningful chunks of time.

Part One (to 500 B.C.E.) deals in three separate chapters with beginnings—of human migration and social construction in the Paleolithic era, of agriculture, and of civilization. Each of them pursues an important theme on a global scale and illustrates that theme with regional examples treated comparatively.

Part Two, on the classical era (500 B.C.E. to 500 C.E.), likewise employs the thematic principle in exploring the major civilizations of Eurasia (Chinese, Indian, Persian, and Mediterranean), with separate chapters focusing on their empires (Chapter 4), cultural traditions (Chapter 5), and social organization (Chapter 6). This structure represents a departure from conventional practice, which usually treats the classical era on a civilization-by-civilization basis, but it allows for more effective and pointed comparison. These Eurasian chapters are followed by a single chapter (Chapter 7) that examines regionally the classical era in sub-Saharan Africa and the Americas, while asking whether their histories largely follow Eurasian patterns or depart from them.

Part Three embraces the thousand years between 500 and 1500 C.E., often known simply, and not very helpfully, as the "postclassical" era. The Big Picture essay for Part Three spotlights and seeks to explain a certain vagueness in our descriptions of this period of time, pointing out the various distinctive civilizational patterns of that millennium as well as the accelerating interactions among them. The six chapters of Part Three reflect a mix of thematic and regional principles. Chapter 8 focuses topically on commercial networks, while Chapters 9, 10, and 11 deal regionally with the Chinese, Christian, and Islamic worlds respectively. Chapter 12 treats pastoral societies as a broad theme and the Mongols as the most dramatic illustration of their impact on the larger stage of world history. Chapter 13, which bridges the two volumes of the book, presents an around-the-world tour in the fifteenth century, which serves both to conclude Volume 1 and to open Volume 2.

In considering the early modern era (1450–1750), **Part Four** treats each of its three constituent chapters thematically. Chapter 14 compares European and Asian empires; Chapter 15 lays out the major patterns of global commerce and their consequences (trade in spices, silver, furs, and slaves); and Chapter 16 focuses on cultural patterns, including the globalization of Christianity and the rise of modern science.

Part Five takes up the era of maximum European influence in the world, from 1750 to 1914. Here the Big Picture essay probes how we might avoid Eurocentrism, while describing a period of time in which Europeans were in fact increasingly central to the global story. Part Five, which charts the emergence of a distinctively modern society in Europe, devotes separate chapters to the Atlantic revolutions (Chapter 17) and the Industrial Revolution (Chapter 18). Then it turns to the growing impact of those societies on the rest of humankind—on China, the Ottoman Empire, and Japan, which are treated comparatively in Chapter 19; and on the world of formal colonies in Chapter 20.

The most recent century (1914–2010), which is treated in **Part Six**, is perhaps the most problematic for world historians, given the abundance of data and the absence of time to sort out what is fundamental and what is peripheral. The Big Picture essay that opens Part Six explores this difficulty, asking whether that century deserves the status of a separate period in the human story. Chapters 21, 22, and 23 examine respectively three major regions of the world in that century—the Western or industrial world, the communist world, and the third or developing world—while Chapter 24 explores the multiple processes of globalization, which have both linked and divided the human community in new ways.

Promoting Active Learning

As all instructors know, students can often "do the assignment" or read the required chapter and yet have nearly no understanding of it when they come to class. The problem, frequently, is passive studying—a quick once-over, perhaps some highlighting of the text—but little sustained involvement with the material. A central pedagogical problem in all teaching at every level is how to encourage more active, engaged styles of learning. How can we push students to articulate in their own words the major ideas of a particular chapter or section of the text? How can we encourage them to recognize arguments, even in a textbook, and to identify and evaluate the evidence on which those arguments are based? Active learning seeks to enable students to manipulate the information of the book, using its ideas and data to answer questions, to make comparisons, to draw conclusions, to criticize assumptions, and to infer implications that are not explicitly disclosed in the book itself. This ability to use and rearrange the material of a text, not simply to recall it, lies at the heart of active college-level learning.

This docutext version of *Ways of the World* incorporates a wealth of opportunities to promote active learning, to assist students in reading the book, and to generate livelier classroom exchanges.

- Chief among those opportunities are the docutext **Considering the Evidence features**. Both written and visual sources call for interpretation and imagination, an understanding of context, and consideration of point of view. Working with those sources virtually requires active engagement. A series of prompts for each document or image and the integrative Using the Evidence questions at the end of every feature serve to guide that engagement.

- The part-opening **Big Picture essays** preview for students what follows in the subsequent chapters. In doing so, they provide a larger context for those chapters; they enable students to make comparisons with greater ease; they facilitate making connections across several chapters; and they raise questions about periodization.

- Each Big Picture essay is followed by a **Landmarks timeline**, providing a chronological overview of what follows in that particular part of the book. Each of these Landmarks is organized in a series of parallel regional timelines, allowing students to see at a glance significant developments in various regions of the world during the same time.

- A **contemporary vignette** opens each chapter with a story that links the past and the present. Chapter 1, for example, presents Gudo Mahiya, a twenty-first-century member of a gathering and hunting society in Tanzania, who rejects an opportunity to become a settled farmer or herder. Chapter 15, which describes the Atlantic slave trade, opens with a brief account of an African American woman who in 2002 visits what had been a slave port in Ghana. These vignettes seek to show the continuing resonance of the past in the lives of contemporary people.

- To encourage active learning explicitly, a series of **questions in the margins** provides students with "something to look for" as they read particular sections. Those notations also indicate what kind of question is being asked—about change, comparison, or connection, for example.

- The **Reflections** section at the end of each chapter raises provocative, sometimes quasi-philosophical questions about the craft of the historian and the unfolding of the human story. It provides grist for the mill of vigorous class discussions and personal pondering.

- To further foster active learning, the **Second Thoughts** section at the end of each chapter provides a list of particulars (people, places, events, processes, concepts) under the heading "**What's the Significance?**" inviting students to check their grasp of that chapter's material. The next part of the Second

Thoughts section is a set of **Big Picture Questions**. Unlike the marginal questions, which are keyed specifically to the adjacent material, these Big Picture Questions are not directly addressed in the text. Instead, they provide opportunities for integration, comparison, analysis, and sometimes speculation. Such questions might well become the basis for engaging writing assignments, class discussions, or exam items. Finally, a limited **list of suggested readings**—books, articles, and Web sites-invites further exploration of the material in the chapter.

- **Snapshots** appear in every chapter and present succinct glimpses of particular themes, regions, or time periods, adding some trees to the forest of world history.

- As is always true of books published by Bedford/St. Martin's, a **rich program of maps and images** accompanies the narrative. Because history and geography are so closely related, more than 100 maps have been included in the two volumes of the book. About 150 images, most of them contemporary to the times and places they illustrate, punctuate the narrative text, while dozens of others in the various Visual Sources features provide multiple occasions for students to assess visual sources as historical evidence.

Supplements

A comprehensive collection of print and electronic resources for students and instructors accompanies this book. Developed with my collaboration, they are designed to provide a host of practical learning and teaching aids. You can learn more about the accompanying materials by visiting bedfordstmartins.com/strayersources/catalog.

For Students

Ways of the World: A Brief Global History with Sources **e-Book.** This easy-to-use, searchable e-book integrates the narrative, maps, and images from *Ways of the World* with resources from the Online Study Guide, making it a dynamic learning and study tool. Instructors can share annotations as well as add documents, images, and other materials to customize the text. The e-book can be packaged free with the print text or purchased stand-alone at a discount.

FREE **Student Center at bedfordstmartins.com/strayer.** The Student Center is a free resource to help students master themes and information presented in the textbook and improve their historical skills. **The Online Study Guide** provides students with self-review quizzes and activities for each chapter, including a multiple-choice self-test that focuses on important conceptual ideas; an identification quiz that helps students remember key people, places, and events; a flashcard activity that tests students' knowledge of key terms; and two interactive map activities intended to strengthen students' geography skills. Instructors can monitor students' progress through an online Quiz Gradebook or receive e-mail updates. The Student Center also features **History Research and Writing Help**, which includes *History Research and Reference Sources*, with links to history-related databases, indexes, and journals, plus contact information for state, provincial, local, and professional history organizations; *More Sources and How to Format a History Paper*, with clear advice on how to integrate primary and secondary sources into research papers, how to cite sources correctly, and how to format in MLA, APA, *Chicago*, or CBE style; *Build a Bibliography*, a simple but powerful Web-based tool that addresses the process of collecting sources and generates bibliographies in four commonly used documentation styles; and *Tips on Avoiding Plagiarism*, an online tutorial that reviews the consequences of plagiarism and explains what sources to acknowledge, how to keep good notes, how to organize research, and how to integrate sources appropriately and includes exercises to help students practice integrating sources and recognize acceptable summaries.

For Instructors

HistoryClass for *Ways of the World: A Brief Global History with Sources.* Bedford/St. Martin's online learning space for history gives you the right tools and the rich content to create your course, your way. An interactive e-book enables you to easily assign relevant textbook sections. Additional primary sources supplement the textbook and provide more options for class discussion and assignments. Other resources include guidelines for analyzing primary materials, avoiding plagiarism, and citing sources. Access to the acclaimed content library Make History provides unlimited access to thousands of maps, images, documents, and Web links. Online Study Guide content offers a range of activities to help students assess their progress, study more effectively, and improve their critical thinking skills. Customize the provided content and mix in your own with ease—everything in HistoryClass is integrated to work together in the same space.

Instructor's Resource Manual at bedfordstmartins.com/strayersources/ catalog. This extensive manual by Eric W. Nelson (Missouri State University) and Phyllis G. Jestice (University of Southern Mississippi) offers both experienced and first-time instructors tools for presenting the book's material in exciting and engaging ways. Introductory essays cover teaching with the docutext and analyzing primary written and visual sources. Also included are chapter learning objectives; annotated chapter outlines; lecture strategies; tips for helping students with common misconceptions and difficult topics; a list of key terms and definitions; answer guidelines for in-text chapter questions; and suggestions for in-class activities (including using film, video, and literature), ways to start discussions, topics for debate, and analyzing primary sources. For the Documents and Visual Sources features in each textbook chapter, the instructor's manual includes answers to headnote questions and to the Considering the Evidence comparative questions. The manual also provides suggestions for in-class and out-of-class activities for the Documents and Visual Sources features. Each chapter concludes with a guide to all the chapter-specific supplements available with *Ways of the World*. A guide for first-time teaching assistants, two sample syllabi, a list of useful books for the first-time world history professor, and a list of books that form the basis of a world history reference library are also included.

Instructor's Resource CD-ROM. This disc provides instructors with ready-made and customizable PowerPoint multimedia presentations built around chapter outlines, maps, figures, and all images from the docutext, plus jpeg versions of these maps, figures, and images. Also included are chapter questions formatted in PowerPoint and MS Word for use with i<clicker, a classroom response system, and blank outline maps in PDF format. Many of these resources are also available for download at bedfordstmartins.com/strayersources/catalog.

Computerized Test Bank. Written by Eric W. Nelson (Missouri State University) and Phyllis G. Jestice (University of Southern Mississippi), the test bank provides more than thirty exercises per chapter, including multiple-choice, fill-in-the-blank, short-answer, and full-length essay questions. The answer key includes textbook page numbers, correct answers, and essay outlines. Instructors can customize quizzes, add or edit both questions and answers, and export questions and answers to a variety of formats, including WebCT and Blackboard.

FREE Student Center with Instructor Resources at bedfordstmartins.com/strayer. The Student Center for *Ways of the World* gathers not only all the electronic resources for students but also those for instructors in one easy-to-use site. Instructors can keep track of their students' progress in the Online Study Guide by using the Quiz Gradebook and can also gain access to lecture, assignment, and research materials; PowerPoint chapter outlines and images; and the digital libraries at Make History.

Make History at bedfordstmartins.com/makehistory. Free and open to instructors and students, Make History combines the best Web resources with hundreds of maps and images, to make finding source material simple. Users can browse the collection of thousands of resources by course or by topic, date, and type. Each item has been carefully chosen and helpfully annotated. Instructors can also create collections to share with students or for use in lectures and presentations.

Content for Course Management Systems. A variety of student and instructor resources developed for this textbook is ready for use in course management systems such as Blackboard, WebCT, and other platforms. This e-content includes the book's Online Study Guide, online instructor's resources, and the book's test bank.

Videos and Multimedia. A wide assortment of videos and multimedia CD-ROMs on various topics in world history is available to qualified adopters. Contact your Bedford/St. Martin's representative for more information.

Packaging Opportunities

In addition to using book-specific supplements, instructors have numerous options for packaging other Bedford/St. Martin's titles with *Ways of the World* for free or at a discount. Visit bedfordstmartins.com/strayer/catalog for more information.

Rand McNally Historical Atlas of the World. This collection of almost seventy full-color maps illustrates the eras and civilizations in world history from the emergence of human societies to the present. *Available for $3.00 when packaged with the text.*

The Bedford Glossary for World History. This handy supplement for the survey course gives students historically contextualized definitions for hundreds of terms—from *abolitionism* to *Zoroastrianism*—that students will encounter in lectures, reading, and exams. *Free when packaged with the text.*

World History Matters: A Student Guide to World History Online. Based on the popular World History Matters Web site produced by the Center for History and New Media, this unique resource, edited by Kristin Lehner (The Johns Hopkins University), Kelly Schrum (George Mason University), and T. Mills Kelly (George Mason University), combines reviews of 150 of the most useful and reliable world history Web sites with an introduction that guides students in locating, evaluating, and correctly citing online sources. *Free when packaged with the text.*

The Bedford Series in History and Culture. More than 100 titles in this highly praised series combine first-rate scholarship, historical narrative, and important primary documents for undergraduate courses. Each book is brief, inexpensive, and focused on a specific topic or period. *Package discounts are available.*

Trade Books. Titles published by sister companies Farrar, Straus and Giroux; Henry Holt and Company; Hill and Wang; Picador; St. Martin's Press; and Palgrave Macmillan are *available at a 50 percent discount* when packaged with Bedford/St. Martin's textbooks. For more information, visit bedfordstmartins.com/tradeup.

"It Takes a Village"

In any enterprise of significance, "it takes a village," as they say. Bringing *Ways of the World* to life, it seems, has occupied the energies of several villages.

The largest of these villages consists of those many people who read the manuscript at various stages, and commented on it, sometimes at great length. I continue to be surprised at the power of this kind of collaboration. Frequently, passages I had regarded as polished to a gleaming perfection benefited greatly from the collective wisdom and experience of these thoughtful reviewers. Reviewers in the early phases of this project provided detailed and invaluable advice on the Documents and Visual

Sources features for this docutext. Reviewers commissioned by Bedford/St. Martin's are listed here in alphabetical order, with my great thanks:

Sanjam Ahluwalia, *Northern Arizona University*
Abel Alves, *Ball State University*
Cynthia Bisson, *Belmont University*
Deborah Buffton, *University of Wisconsin–La Crosse*
Brian D. Bunk, *University of Massachusetts–Amherst*
Allen Dieterich-Ward, *Shippensburg University*
Jonathan Dresner, *Pittsburg State University*
Deborah Gerish, *Emporia State University*
Nicholas Germana, *Keene State College*
Terrell Goddard, *Northwest Vista College*
L. Dana Goodrich, *Northwest Vista College*
Andrew Goss, *University of New Orleans*
Candace Gregory-Abbott, *California State University–Sacramento*
Jeanne Harrie, *California State University–Bakersfield*
Stephen Hernon, *Notre Dame Academy (NY)*
Marianne Holdzkom, *Southern Polytechnic State University*
Bryan Jack, *Winston–Salem State University*
Theresa Jordan, *Washington State University*
Jared Brent Krebsbach, *University of Memphis*
John LaValle, *Western New Mexico University*
Otto W. Mandahl Jr., *Skagit Valley College*
Kathryn Mapstone, *Bunker Hill Community College*
John Maunu, *Grosse Ile High School*
Mario D. Mazzarella, *Christopher Newport University*
Mark W. McLeod, *University of Delaware*
Eben Miller, *Southern Maine Community College*
Theodore A. Nitz, *Gonzaga University*
Kenneth Osgood, *Florida Atlantic University*
John Pinheiro, *Aquinas College*
Anthony R. Santoro, *Christopher Newport University*
Alyssa Goldstein Sepinwall, *California State University–San Marcos*
David Simonelli, *Youngstown State University*
Helene Sinnreich, *Youngstown State University*
Steven Stofferahn, *Indiana State University*
Lisa Tran, *California State University–Fullerton*
Wendy Turner, *Augusta State University*
Elaine C. P. Turney, *University of Texas–San Antonio*
Michael Vann, *California State University–Sacramento*
Kurt J. Wertmuller, *Azusa Pacific University*
Nathaniel P. Weston, *Seattle Central Community College*
James Wood, *North Carolina A&T State University*.

Others in the village of reviewers have been friends, family, and colleagues who graciously agreed to read portions of the manuscript and offer helpful counsel: Kabir Helminski, James Horn, Elisabeth Jay, David Northrup, Lynn Parsons, Katherine Poethig, Kevin Reilly, and Julie Shackford–Bradley.

The "Bedford village" has been a second community supporting this enterprise and the one most directly responsible for the book's appearance in print. It would be difficult for any author to imagine a more encouraging and professional publishing team. Developmental editor Kathryn Abbott, herself an experienced professor of history, has been my primary point of contact with the Bedford village as this docutext version of *Ways of the World* unfolded. She has helped to conceptualize the entire project, masterfully summarized and analyzed the numerous reviews of the manuscript, added her own thoughtful suggestions to the mix, and generally kept the project on track—all with grace and courtesy. In a similar role, Jim Strandberg guided the development of the original text with the sensitivity of a fine historian as well as the skill of an outstanding editor. Eric Nelson of Missouri State University has served as a general consultant for the docutext, as well as the co-author of the fine instructor's manual that accompanies the book. A number of the ideas for Considering the Evidence features came from him, and his careful reading of all the features in draft form was extremely helpful. To all of these close collaborators, I acknowledge a debt of gratitude that I am unable to adequately repay.

Publisher Mary Dougherty first broached the idea of my writing a world history text for Bedford and later surprised me with the suggestion for a docutext version of the book. With a manner as lovely as it is professional, she has provided overall editorial leadership and a calming balm to authorial anxieties. More recently these tasks have passed to executive editor Traci Mueller, who has undertaken them with a similar combination of kindness and competence. Jane Knetzger, director of development, has overseen the project from its beginning, bore my many questions with forbearance, and, even better, provided timely answers. Company president Joan Feinberg has, to my surprise and delight, periodically kept her own experienced hand in this pot, while executive editor Beth Welch, though fully engaged in her own projects, has served as counselor from the sidelines. Photo researcher Carole Frohlich identified and acquired the many images that grace *Ways of the World: A Brief Global History with Sources* and did so with amazing efficiency and courtesy. Working with her has been an aesthetic education for me and a personal delight.

Operating more behind the scenes in the Bedford village, a series of highly competent and always supportive people have shepherded this book along its way. Lynn Sternberger and Robin Soule provided invaluable assistance in handling the manuscript, contacting reviewers, and keeping on top of the endless details that such an enterprise demands. Bridget Leahy served as project editor during the book's production and, often under considerable pressure, did so with both grace and efficiency. Copy editor Janet Renard polished the prose and sorted out my inconsistent usages with a seasoned and perceptive eye.

Jenna Bookin Barry and Sally Constable have overseen the marketing process, while history specialist John Hunger and a cadre of humanities specialists and sales representatives have introduced the book to the academic world. Jack Cashman supervised the development of ancillary materials to support the book, and Donna Dennison ably coordinated research for the lovely covers that mark *Ways of the World*.

Yet another "village" that contributed much to *Ways of the World* consists in that group of distinguished scholars and teachers who worked with me on an earlier world history text, *The Making of the Modern World*, published by St. Martin's Press (1988, 1995). They include Sandria Freitag, Edwin Hirschmann, Donald Holsinger, James Horn, Robert Marks, Joe Moore, Lynn Parsons, and Robert Smith. That collective effort resembled participation in an extended seminar, from which I benefited immensely. Their ideas and insights have shaped my own understanding of world history in many ways and greatly enriched *Ways of the World*.

A final and much smaller community sustained this project and its author. It is that most intimate of villages that we know as a marriage. Here I pay wholly inadequate tribute to its other member, my wife, Suzanne Sturn. She knows how I feel, and no one else needs to.

To all my fellow villagers, I offer deep thanks for perhaps the richest intellectual experience of my professional life. I am grateful beyond measure.

Robert Strayer
La Selva Beach, California

Brief Contents

Contents

16. Religion and Science, 1450–1750 *721*

Maps

Special Features

Landmarks

Snapshots

Working with Primary Sources

Introduction

Historians interpret the past by examining what they refer to as "primary" or "original" sources—documents, images, or objects produced by the very people we are studying and at the time of or soon after the events that they describe or depict. These sources—the "raw material" of the historian's craft—can take many forms: recorded versions of oral traditions, handed down over many centuries; an endless variety of written materials; images and artifacts such as paintings and pottery. Such sources are precious windows into the past. Their survival in large part determines what history can be recovered and what is forever lost. For instance, only the chance survival of the well-preserved agricultural settlement at Çatalhüyük that is among the subjects of Chapter 2's Visual Sources feature allows us to examine what may be the first surviving map in human history.

Using primary sources effectively is no easy task. Unlike textbooks, which are written explicitly for twenty-first-century students, the sources that historians work with were not aimed at you. They were produced in circumstances and with cultural assumptions that are often quite unfamiliar to contemporary readers. And so they require effort: critical reading and observation, systematic analysis, and historical imagination. Working with them is like listening in on conversations from the past, eavesdropping, as it were, on our ancestors. Each source potentially provides a valuable glimpse into the past, but all sources must be analyzed carefully because, like ourselves, our ancestors' understandings of their own lives and time were subject to distortions, fabrications, misunderstandings, and ambiguity.

Working with Written Documents

Written documents are the most common type of primary source that historians use. Typical written sources include personal records, such as diaries, memoirs, business account books, and private correspondence; and public records, including sacred texts, autobiographies, travelers' accounts, newspaper articles, legislation and law codes, court rulings, and wills. Indeed, nearly every written record is potentially a useful primary source depending on the questions that historians are trying to answer. Usually historians are able to draw stronger conclusions when they can locate and examine sources on the same topic from a number of different perspectives. For example, in the Documents feature of Chapter 15, the Atlantic slave trade is explored from the perspective of a slave, a European slave trader, and several African rulers, building up a more complex picture of the trade than any one of these documents could convey on its own. However, even a single source, when analyzed effectively, can provide a window into the past.

Reading a Document

Reading a document requires careful analysis and an understanding of the context in which the document was produced. The following questions provide the basis for understanding and analyzing any primary document:

- Who wrote the document?
- When and where was it written?
- What type of document is it (for example, a letter to a friend, a political decree, an exposition of a religious teaching)?
- Why was the document written? Under what circumstances was it composed? What point of view does it reflect? What other views or opinions is the document arguing against?
- Who was its intended audience?
- What about the document is believable, and what is not?
- What might historians learn from this document?
- What can the document tell us about the individual who produced it and the society from which he or she came from?

Many documents do not answer the first three questions directly. In *Ways of the World: A Brief Global History with Sources*, questions that cannot be answered directly are addressed in the introductory headnote to the document. These headnotes may help you to establish a context for understanding the document and to identify its point of view or potential biases and the larger discourse of which it is a part.

Once these three basic questions are answered, a historian is then likely to consider the next two questions, which often shape what is written and how ideas are presented—why the document was written and who the intended audience was. The document itself and sometimes its headnote will provide information essential for answering these questions. Inspiration and intention are crucial factors that shape the form and content of a source. For instance, one might examine a document differently depending on whether it was intended for a private or a public readership or whether it was intended to be read by a small elite or a wider audience.

Finally, through both establishing the context in which the document was written and carefully reading the document, historians seek to come to some conclusions about the document by asking whether the document is believable, in what ways it sheds light on the past, and what the document tells us about the person who produced it and the time period in which it was generated. In answering these more complex questions, historical imagination is essential. Your imagination, informed by knowledge of the context, enables you to read the document through the eyes of its author and its audience. How might this document have been understood at the time it was written? But in using your imagination, you must take care not to read into the documents your own assumptions and understandings. It is a delicate balance, a kind of dance that historians constantly undertake. Even documents that contain material that historians find unbelievable can be useful, for we seek not only to know the "truth" about what happened in the past but also to grasp the world as our ancestors understood it. Historians sometimes even speak about reading documents "against the grain," seeking understandings that authors certainly did not intend to convey. For example, the Law Code of Hammurabi in Chapter 3's Documents feature depicts an impressive system of justice in ancient Mesopotamia, but it can also be read as an account of the numerous problems or conflicts that that society had to confront.

Reading Documents Together

While each document must be read and understood individually, historians typically draw their strongest conclusions when they analyze a number of documents together. The essays in the Documents features in *Ways of the World* are designed to explore sets of primary sources that address a central theme of the chapter and frequently include several related documents. When considered together, these sources from different perspectives allow the historian to understand the issue or event more fully. A good example of this approach can be found in the Documents feature for Chapter 11, which explores the emergence of Islam through both holy texts such as the Quran and later interpretations of these texts by Sharia legal scholars and Sufi mystics.

The broad theme and approach introduced at the opening of each essay is further defined by the Using the Evidence questions at its conclusion. For instance, Chapter 13's Documents feature, "The Aztecs and Incas through Spanish Eyes," explores the advantages and disadvantages of using sources written by conquerors to reconstruct conquered societies that left few written records of their own.

Working with Visual Sources

Artifacts that derive from the material culture of the past, religious icons or paintings that add to our understanding of belief systems, a family portrait that provides insight into presentations of self in a particular time and place, a building whose layout reveals how power and authority were displayed in a specific empire—all of these visual sources represent another category of primary sources that historians can use to re-create and understand the past. However, visual evidence can be more difficult to interpret than written documents because most people are not trained in visual analysis. Furthermore, it may be more difficult to discern what meanings animated the creators of particular images or artifacts and what understandings they conveyed to those who viewed or used them.

To use visual sources, we must be able to see these pieces of evidence through the eyes of the societies that produced them and to decode the symbols and other features that imbue these visual sources with meaning. The values of past cultures are often far removed from our own; thus the symbols in these images and artifacts are often unfamiliar to our eyes. Nevertheless, interpreting visual sources effectively can provide insights not offered by written documents. Indeed, for some preliterate societies, archeological and artistic evidence is all that remains of their history.

Analyzing an Image or Artifact

Just as with written documents, context is crucial for analyzing visual evidence. Context provides critical information needed to see the visual source through the eyes of its creator and of those for whom it was created. Sometimes the image or artifact will provide this information, but more often in *Ways of the World: A Brief Global History with Sources*, the Visual Sources essay will provide essential context for your interpretation, as in Chapter 16's Visual Sources feature, where the specific contexts in which Christian images were created are critical to their interpretation and analysis.

Once again, a set of fundamental questions, similar to those you would ask a written document, will help you understand and analyze a visual source:

- When and where was the image or artifact made?
- Who made the image or artifact? How was it made?
- Who paid for or commissioned it?
- Where might the image or artifact have originally been displayed or used?
- Where is it now, and how did it get there?
- For what audience(s) was it intended?
- What message(s) is it trying to convey?
- How could it be interpreted differently depending on who viewed or used it?
- What are the meanings of the symbols or other abstract features in the visual source?

While these questions do not always have a single, clear answer, being aware of the possibilities will shape your examination of the source.

Once you have established the context in which the piece of visual evidence was produced, you should then focus on a careful examination of the source itself, asking the following questions:

- If the source is an image, who or what is depicted?
- What information can be gleaned from the positioning of figures, their clothing, hairstyles, and other visual cues?
- What activities are depicted?
- If it is a specifically religious image, what is depicted, and what likely purpose did the image serve?
- If it is an artifact, what function did it serve?

- What can the image tell us about the society that produced it and the time period in which it was created?

Addressing this question can take a historian down many different lines of inquiry. Depending on the visual sources under examination, additional questions arise, such as the following:

- What types of technology or techniques were used to produce the visual source?

- What was the relationship between those who made the visual source and those who used or viewed it?

Considering Visual Evidence Collectively

As with written documents, each piece of visual evidence must be examined and understood in its own right, although historians draw their strongest conclusions when they analyze a number of visual sources together rather than relying on a single source. The Visual Sources essays in *Ways of the World* explore sets of visual sources that address a central theme in the chapter and frequently include several related images that, when considered together, allow the historian to become aware of how multiple perspectives on a single topic can enhance understanding. Moreover, these essays often explore the strengths and weaknesses of a type of visual source for answering questions posed by historians.

The broad theme and approach are introduced at the opening of each essay and are further defined by the Using the Evidence questions at its conclusion. For instance, the Visual Sources feature for Chapter 13, "Sacred Places in the World of the Fifteenth Century," explores the intersections between sacred sites and political authority in fifteenth-century Africa and Eurasia. While each source considered individually speaks to a specific region and has distinctive characteristics, collectively the sources show that these sorts of sites across Africa and Eurasia were frequently set apart from the profane or ordinary world and were linked to a wider sacred geography.

Finally, as you begin to explore the Documents and Visual Sources features in *Ways of the World*, you might think of the experience as a kind of "history laboratory." In working with these materials, you are "doing history," much like lab experiments in chemistry courses represent "doing science." Furthermore, you will probably recognize connections between particular documents and visual sources. When that happens, the work of "doing history" has truly begun, as most historians use visual sources in conjunction with written documents to create an even more complete picture of the past. Enjoy!

Prologue

Considering World History

THE HISTORY OF THE HUMAN SPECIES HAS occupied roughly the last 250,000 years, conventionally divided into three major phases, based on the kind of technology that was most widely practiced. The enormously long Paleolithic age, with its gathering and hunting way of life, accounts for 95 percent or more of the time that humans have occupied the planet. People utilizing a Paleolithic technology initially settled every major landmass on the planet and constructed the first human societies. Then beginning with the first Agricultural Revolution, about 12,000 years ago, the domestication of plants and animals increasingly became the primary means of sustaining human life and societies. In giving rise to farming village societies, to pastoral communities depending on their herds of animals, and to state- and city-based civilizations, this agrarian way of life changed virtually everything and fundamentally shaped the human experience ever since. Finally around 1750, a quite sudden spurt in the rate of technological change, which we know as the Industrial Revolution, took hold. That vast increase in productivity, wealth, and human control over nature once again reshaped virtually every aspect of human life and gave rise to new kinds of societies that we call "modern."

Here then, in a single paragraph, is the history of humankind—the Paleolithic era, the age of agricultural civilizations, and, most recently and briefly, the modern industrial era. Clearly this is a world history perspective, based on the notion that the human species as a whole has a history that transcends any of its particular and distinctive cultures. Volume 2 of *Ways of the World* turns the spotlight on the final several centuries of the age of agriculture and then on the modern industrial era. This perspective—known variously as planetary, global, or world history—has become increasingly prominent among those who study the past. Why should this be so?

Why World History?

Not long ago—in the mid-twentieth century, for example—virtually all college-level history courses were organized in terms of particular civilizations or nations. In the United States, it was Western Civilization or some version of American History that served to introduce students to the study of the past. Since then, however, a set of profound changes has pushed the historical profession in a different direction.

The world wars of the twentieth century, revealing as they did the horrendous consequences of unchecked nationalism, persuaded some historians that a broader view of the past might contribute to notions of global citizenship. Economic and cultural globalization has highlighted both the interdependence of the world's peoples and their very unequal positions within the global network. Moreover, we are aware as never before that our problems—whether they involve economic well-being, environmental deterioration, disease, or terrorism—respect no national boundaries. To many thoughtful people, a global present seemed to call for a global past. Furthermore, as colonial empires shrank and newly defined third-world peoples asserted themselves on the world stage, these peoples also insisted that their histories be accorded equivalent treatment with those of Europe. An explosion of new knowledge about the histories of Asia, Africa, and pre-Columbian America erupted from the research of scholars around the world. All of this has generated a "world history movement," reflected in college and high school curricula, in numerous conferences and specialized studies, and in a proliferation of textbooks, of which this is one.

This world history movement has attempted to create a global understanding of the human past that highlights broad patterns cutting across particular civilizations and countries, while acknowledging in an inclusive fashion the distinctive histories of its many peoples. This is, to put it mildly, a tall order. How is it possible to encompass within a single book or course the separate stories of the world's various peoples? Surely it must be something more than just recounting the history of one civilization or culture after another. How can we distill a common history of humankind as a whole from the distinct trajectories of particular peoples? Because no world history book or course can cover everything, what criteria should we use for deciding what to include and what to leave out? Such questions have ensured no end of controversy among students, teachers, and scholars of world history, making it one of the most exciting fields of historical inquiry.

Comparison, Connection, and Change: The Three Cs of World History

Despite much debate and argument, one thing is reasonably clear: in world history, nothing stands alone. Every event, every historical figure, every culture, society, or civilization gains significance from its inclusion in some larger context. Most world historians would probably agree on three such contexts that define their field of study. Each of them confronts a particular problem in our understanding of the past.

The first is constant **comparison**. Whatever else it may be, world history is a comparative discipline, seeking to identify similarities and differences in the experience of the world's peoples. In what respects did European empires in the Americas differ from the Ottoman Empire in the Middle East or the Russian Empire across northern Asia or Chinese expansion into Central Asia? Why did the Scientific and Industrial Revolutions and a modern way of life evolve first in Western Europe rather than somewhere else? What distinguished the French, Haitian, Russian, and Chinese revolutions? How might we compare the modern transformation of capitalist, communist, and colonial societies? Did feminist movements in the developing countries resemble those of the industrial West? Describing and, if possible, explaining such similarities and differences are among the major tasks of world history.

Comparison has proven an effective tool in countering Eurocentrism, the notion that Europeans or people of European descent have long been the primary movers and shakers of the historical process. That notion arose in recent centuries when Europeans were in fact the major source of innovation in the world and did in fact exercise something close to world domination. But this temporary preeminence decisively shaped the way Europeans thought and wrote about their own histories and those of other people. In their own eyes, Europeans alone were progressive people, thanks to a cultural or racial superiority. Everyone else was to some degree stagnant, backward, savage, or barbarian. The unusual power of Europeans allowed them for a time to act on those beliefs and to impose such ways of thinking on much of the world. But comparative world history sets European achievements in a global and historical context, helping us to sort out what was distinctive about its development and what similarities it bore to other major regions of the world. Puncturing the pretensions of Eurocentrism has been high on the agenda of world history.

The art of comparison is a learned skill, entailing several steps. It requires, first of all, asking explicitly comparative questions and determining what particular cases will be involved. If you want to compare revolutions, for example, you would need to decide which ones you are considering—American, French, Russian, Chinese, Cuban. Defining categories of comparison is a further step. Precisely which characteristics of those revolutions will you compare—their origins, their ideologies, the social classes involved, their outcomes? Finally, how will you present your comparison? You might choose a case-by-case analysis in which you would describe, say, the American Revolution first, followed by an account of the Cuban Revolution, which makes explicit comparisons with the former. Or you might choose a thematic approach in which you would consider first the origins of both revolutions, followed by a comparison of their ideologies, and so on. You will find examples of both approaches in the chapters that follow.

A second context that informs world history involves the interactions, encounters, and **connections** among different and often distant peoples. What happened when representatives of distinct civilizations or cultures met? Focusing on cross-cultural connections represents an effort to counteract a habit of thinking about particular peoples, states, or cultures as self-contained or isolated communities. Despite the historical emergence of separate and distinct societies, none of them developed alone. Each was embedded in a network of relationships with both near and more distant peoples. The growing depth and significance of such cross-cultural relationships has been a distinguishing feature of the modern era. The voyages of Columbus brought the peoples of the Eastern and Western hemispheres into sustained contact for the first time, and several centuries later Europeans took advantage of their industrial power to bring much of the world under their control. Particularly during the past five centuries, the encounter with strangers, or at least with strange ideas and practices, was everywhere among the most powerful motors of change in human societies.

And here lies a third context in which the particulars of world history can be situated. It is that perennial issue with which historians of every kind are concerned: what changes, what persists, and why. In world history, it is the "big picture" **changes**—those that impact large segments of humankind—that are of greatest interest. What generated the amazing transformations of the "revolution of modernity" in recent centuries? What lay behind the emergence of a new balance of global power after 1500, one that featured the growing prominence of Europe on the world stage? Why did the ancient civilizations of Russia and China explode in revolution during the twentieth century? What led to the rapid collapse of Europe's global empires after World War II? How might we explain the emergence of Islamic radicalism during the final third of the twentieth century?

Both change and comparison provide an antidote to a persistent tendency of human thinking that historians call "essentialism." A more common term is "stereotyping." It refers to our inclination to define particular groups of people with an unchanging or essential set of characteristics. Women are nurturing; peasants are conservative; Americans are aggressive; Hindus are religious. Serious students of history soon become aware that every significant category of people contains endless divisions and conflicts and that human communities are constantly in flux. Peasants may often accept the status quo, except of course when they rebel, as they frequently have. Americans have experienced periods of official isolationism and withdrawal from the world as well as times of aggressive engagement with it. Things change.

But some things persist, even if they also change. We should not allow an emphasis on change to blind us to the continuities of human experience. A recognizably Chinese state has operated for more than 2,000 years. Slavery and patriarchy persisted as human institutions for thousands of years until they were challenged in recent centuries, and in various forms they exist still. The teachings of Buddhism, Christianity, and Islam have endured for centuries, though with endless variations and transformations.

Comparisons, connections, and changes—all of them operating on a global scale—represent three contexts or frameworks that can help us bring some coherence to the multiple and complex stories of world history. They will recur repeatedly in the pages that follow.

About the Author

ROBERT W. STRAYER (Ph.D., University of Wisconsin) brings wide experience in world history to the writing of this text. His teaching career began with two years of high school instruction in Ethiopia as part of the Peace Corps. At the university level, he taught African, Soviet, and world history for many years at Suny College at Brockport, where he received Chancellor's Awards for Excellence in Teaching and for Excellence in Scholarship. In 1998 he was visiting professor of world and Soviet history at the University of Canterbury in Christchurch, New Zealand. Since moving to California in 2002, he has taught world history at the University of California, Santa Cruz; California State University, Monterey Bay; and Cabrillo College. He is a long-time member of the World History Association and served on its Executive Committee.

His publications include *Kenya: Focus on Nationalism* (1975), *The Making of Mission Communities in East Africa* (1978), *The Making of the Modern World* (1988, 1995), *Why Did the Soviet Union Collapse* (1998), and *The Communist Experiment* (2007). He has also published in a number of academic journals, including the *Journal of World History*.

Ways of the World

A Brief Global History

with Sources

The Worlds of the Fifteenth Century

During 2005, Chinese authorities marked the 600th anniversary of the initial launching of their country's massive maritime expeditions in 1405. Some eighty-seven years before Columbus sailed across the Atlantic with three small ships and a crew of about ninety men, the Chinese admiral Zheng He had captained a fleet of more than 300 ships and a crew numbering some 27,000 people, which brought a Chinese naval presence into the South China Sea and the Indian Ocean as far as the East African coast. Now in 2005, China was celebrating. Public ceremonies, books, magazine articles, two television documentaries, an international symposium, a stamp in honor of Zheng He—all of this and more was part of a yearlong remembrance of these remarkable voyages.

Given China's recent engagement with the larger world, Chinese authorities sought to use Zheng He as a symbol of their country's expanding, but peaceful, role on the international stage. Until recently, however, his achievement was barely noticed in China's collective memory, and for six centuries Zheng He had been largely forgotten or ignored. Columbus, on the other hand, had long been highly visible in the West, celebrated as a cultural hero and more recently harshly criticized as an imperialist, but certainly remembered. The voyages of both of these fifteenth-century mariners were pregnant with meaning for world history. Why were they remembered so differently in the countries of their origin?

THE FIFTEENTH CENTURY, DURING WHICH BOTH ZHENG HE and Columbus undertook their momentous expeditions, proved in

---

The Meeting of Two Worlds: This famous sixteenth-century engraving by the Flemish artist Theodore de Bry shows Columbus landing in Hispaniola (Haiti), where the Taino people bring him presents, while the Europeans claim the island for God and queen. In light of its long-range consequences, this voyage was arguably the most important single event of the fifteenth century. (Bildarchiv Preussischer Kulturbesitz/Art Resource, NY)

Snapshot **Major Developments around the World in the Fifteenth Century**

Region	Major Developments
Central, East, and Southeast Asia	Ming dynasty China, 1368–1644 Conquests of Timur, 1370–1406 Zheng He's maritime voyages, 1405–1433 Spread of Islam into Southeast Asia Rise of Malacca Civil war among competing warlords in Japan
South Asia/India	Timur's invasion of India, 1398 Various Muslim sultanates in northern India Rise of Hindu state of Vijayanagar in southern India Founding of Mughal Empire, 1526
Middle East	Expansion of Ottoman Empire Ottoman seizure of Constantinople, 1453 Founding of Safavid Empire in Persia, 1501 Ottoman siege of Vienna, 1529
Christendom/Europe	European Renaissance Portuguese voyages of exploration along West African coast Completion of reconquest of Spain, ending Muslim control End of the Byzantine Empire, 1453 End of Mongol rule in Russia; reign of Ivan the Great, 1462–1505
Africa	Songhay Empire in West Africa, 1464–1591 Kingdom of the Kongo in West Central Africa Expansion of Ethiopian state in East Africa Kingdom of Zimbabwe/Mwene Mutapa in southern Africa
The Americas/Western Hemisphere	Aztec Empire in Mesoamerica, 1345–1521 Inca Empire along the Andes, 1438–1533 Iroquois confederacy (New York State) "Complex" Paleolithic societies along west coast of North America
Pacific Oceania	Paleolithic persistence in Australia Chiefdoms and stratified societies on Pacific islands Yap as center of oceanic trading network with Guam and Palau

retrospect to mark a major turning point in the human story. At the time, of course, no one was aware of it. No one knew in 1405 that the huge armada under Zheng He's command would be recalled in 1433, never to sail again. And no one knew in 1492 that Columbus's minuscule fleet of three ships would utterly transform the world, bringing the people of two "old worlds" and two hemispheres permanently together, with enduring consequences for them all. The outcome of the processes set in motion by those three small ships included the Atlantic slave trade, the decimation of the native population of the Americas, the massive growth of world population, the Industrial Revolution, and the growing prominence of Europeans on the world stage. But none of these developments were even remotely foreseeable in 1492.

Thus the fifteenth century, as a hinge of major historical change, provides an occasion for a bird's-eye view of the world through a kind of global tour. This excursion around the world will serve to briefly review the human saga thus far and to establish a baseline from which the transformations of the modern era might be measured. How then might we describe the world, and the worlds, of the fifteenth century?

The Shapes of Human Communities

One way to describe the world of the fifteenth century is to identify the various types of societies that it contained. Bands of hunters and gatherers, villages of agricultural peoples, newly emerging chiefdoms or small states, nomadic/pastoral communities, established civilizations and empires—all of these social or political forms would have been apparent to a widely traveled visitor in the fifteenth century. They represented alternative ways of organizing human communities and responded to differences in the environment, in the historical development of various regions, and in the choices made by particular peoples. All of them were long established by the fifteenth century, but the balance among these distinctive kinds of societies at the end of the postclassical millennium (1500) was quite different than it had been at the beginning (500).

Paleolithic Persistence

Despite millennia of agricultural advance, substantial areas of the world still hosted gathering and hunting societies, known to scholars as Paleolithic (old stone-age) peoples. All of Australia, much of Siberia, the arctic coastlands, and parts of Africa and the Americas fell into this category. These peoples were not simply relics of a bygone age, however. They too had changed over time, though more slowly than their agricultural counterparts, and they too interacted with their neighbors. In short, they had a history, although most history books largely ignore them after the age of agriculture arrived. Nonetheless, this most ancient way of life still had a sizable and variable presence in the world of the fifteenth century.

Consider, for example, Australia. That continent's many separate groups, some 250 of them, still practiced a gathering and hunting way of life in the fifteenth century, a pattern that continued well after Europeans arrived in the late eighteenth century.

■ **Comparison**

In what ways did the gathering and hunting people of Australia differ from those of the northwest coast of North America?

Over many thousands of years, these people had assimilated various material items or cultural practices from outsiders—outrigger canoes, fish hooks, complex netting techniques, artistic styles, rituals, and mythological ideas—but despite the presence of farmers in nearby New Guinea, no agricultural practices penetrated the Australian mainland. Was it because large areas of Australia were unsuited for the kind of agriculture practiced in New Guinea? Or did the peoples of Australia, enjoying an environment of sufficient resources, simply see no need to change their way of life?

Despite the absence of agriculture, Australia's peoples had mastered and manipulated their environment, in part through the practice of "firestick farming," a pattern of deliberately set fires, which they described as "cleaning up the country." These controlled burns served to clear the underbrush, thus making hunting easier and encouraging the growth of certain plant and animal species. In addition, native Australians exchanged goods among themselves over distances of hundreds of miles, created elaborate mythologies and ritual practices, and developed sophisticated traditions of sculpture and rock painting. They accomplished all of this on the basis of an economy and technology rooted in the distant Paleolithic past.

A very different kind of gathering and hunting society flourished in the fifteenth century along the northwest coast of North America among the Chinookan, Tulalip, Skagit, and other peoples. With some 300 edible animal species and an abundance of salmon and other fish, this extraordinarily bounteous environment provided the foundation for what scholars sometimes call "complex" or "affluent" gathering and hunting cultures. What distinguished the northwest coast peoples from those of Australia were permanent village settlements with large and sturdy houses, considerable economic specialization, ranked societies that sometimes included slavery, chiefdoms dominated by powerful clan leaders or "big men," and extensive storage of food.

Although these and other gathering and hunting peoples persisted still in the fifteenth century, both their numbers and the area they inhabited had contracted greatly as the Agricultural Revolution unfolded across the planet. That relentless advance of the farming frontier continued in the centuries ahead as the Russian, Chinese, and European empires encompassed the lands of the remaining Paleolithic peoples. By the early twenty-first century, what was once the only human way of life had been reduced to minuscule pockets of people whose cultures seemed doomed to a final extinction.

Agricultural Village Societies

■ Change

What kinds of changes were transforming West African agricultural village societies and those of the Iroquois as the fifteenth century dawned?

Far more numerous than hunters and gatherers were those many peoples who, though fully agricultural, had avoided incorporation into larger empires or civilizations and had not developed their own city- or state-based societies. Living usually in small village-based communities and organized in terms of kinship relations, such people predominated during the fifteenth century in much of North America and in parts of the Amazon River basin, Southeast Asia, and Africa south of the equator. They had created societies largely without the oppressive political authority, class inequalities, and seclusion of women that were so common in civilizations. Historians have largely relegated such societies to the periphery of world history, marginal to their overwhelming focus on large-scale civilizations. Viewed from within their own circles, though, these societies were of course at the center of things, each with its own history of migration, cultural transformation, social conflict, incorporation of new people, political rise and fall, and interaction with strangers. In short, they too changed as their histories unfolded.

In the forested region of what is now southern Nigeria in West Africa, for example, three quite different patterns of change emerged in the centuries between 1000 and 1500 (see Map 13.3, p. 582). Each of them began from a base of farming village societies whose productivity was generating larger populations.

Among the Yoruba-speaking people, a series of rival city-states emerged, each within a walled town and ruled by an *oba*, or "king" (some of whom were women), who performed both religious and political functions. As in ancient Mesopotamia or classical Greece, no single state or empire encompassed all of Yorubaland. Nearby lay the kingdom of Benin, a small, highly centralized territorial state that emerged by the fifteenth century and was ruled by a warrior king named Ewuare, said to have conquered 201 towns and villages in the process of founding the new state. His administrative chiefs replaced the heads of kinship groups as major political authorities, while the ruler sponsored extensive trading missions and patronized artists who created the remarkable brass sculptures for which Benin is so famous.

East of the Niger River lay the lands of the Igbo peoples, where dense population and extensive trading networks might well have given rise to states, but the deliberate Igbo preference was to reject the kingship and state-building efforts of their neighbors, boasting on occasion that "the Igbo have no kings." Instead they relied on other institutions—title societies in which wealthy men received a series of prestigious ranks, women's associations, hereditary ritual experts serving as mediators, a balance of power among kinship groups—to maintain social cohesion beyond the level of the village. It was a "stateless society," famously described in Chinua Achebe's *Things Fall Apart*, the most widely read novel to emerge from twentieth-century Africa.

The Yoruba, Bini, and Igbo peoples did not live in isolated, self-contained societies, however. They traded actively among themselves and with more distant peoples, such as the large African kingdom of Songhay far to the north. Cotton cloth, fish, copper and iron goods, decorative objects, and more drew neighboring peoples into networks of exchange. Common artistic traditions reflected a measure of cultural unity in a politically fragmented region, and all of these peoples seem to have changed from a matrilineal to a patrilineal system of tracing their descent. Little of this registered in the larger civilizations of the Afro-Eurasian world, but to the peoples of the West African forest during the fifteenth century, these processes were central to their history and their daily lives. Soon, however, all of them would be caught up in the transatlantic slave trade and would be changed substantially in the process.

Benin Bronzes
With the patronage of the royal court, Benin's artists produced an array of wood, ivory, and most famously exquisite brass or bronze sculptures, most of which celebrated the royal family and decorated their palaces. Here is a sixteenth-century representation of the Queen Mother of Benin. (National Museum, Lagos, Nigeria/The Bridgeman Art Library)

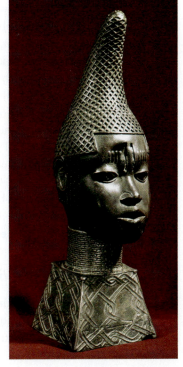

Across the Atlantic in what is now central New York State, other agricultural village societies were also in the process of substantial change during the several centuries preceding their incorporation into European trading networks and empires. The Iroquois-speaking peoples of that region had only recently become fully agricultural, adopting maize- and bean-farming techniques that had originated long ago in Mesoamerica. As this productive agriculture took hold by 1300 or so, the population grew, the size of settlements increased, and distinct peoples emerged, such as the Onondaga, Seneca, Cayuga, Oneida, and Mohawk. Frequent warfare also erupted among them. Some scholars have speculated that as agriculture, largely seen as women's work, became the primary economic activity, "warfare replaced successful food getting as the avenue to male prestige."[1]

Whatever caused it, this increased level of conflict among Iroquois peoples triggered a remarkable political innovation—a loose alliance or confederation among five Iroquois peoples based on an agreement known as the Great Law of Peace (see Map 13.5, p. 589). It was an agreement to settle their differences peacefully through a confederation council of clan leaders, some fifty of them altogether, who had the authority to adjudicate disputes and set reparation payments. Operating by consensus, the Iroquois League of Five Nations effectively suppressed the blood feuds and tribal conflicts that had only recently been so widespread. It also coordinated their peoples' relationship with outsiders, including the Europeans, who arrived in growing numbers in the centuries after 1500.

The Iroquois League also gave expression to values of limited government, social equality, and personal freedom, concepts that some European colonists found highly attractive. One British colonial administrator declared in 1749 that the Iroquois had "such absolute Notions of Liberty that they allow no Kind of Superiority of one over another, and banish all Servitude from their Territories."[2] Such equality extended to gender relationships, for among the Iroquois, descent was matrilineal (reckoned through the woman's line), married couples lived with the wife's family, and women controlled agriculture. While men were hunters, warriors, and the primary political officeholders, women selected and could depose those leaders.

Wherever they lived in 1500, over the next several centuries independent agricultural peoples such as the Iroquois, Yoruba, and Igbo were increasingly encompassed in expanding economic networks and conquest empires based in Western Europe, Russia, China, or India. In this respect, they repeated the experience of many other village-based farming communities that had much earlier found themselves forcibly included in the powerful embrace of Egyptian, Mesopotamian, Roman, Indian, Chinese, and other civilizations.

■ **Significance**
What role did Central Asian and West African pastoralists play in their respective regions?

Herding Peoples

Nomadic pastoral peoples impinged more directly and dramatically on civilizations than did hunting and gathering or agricultural village societies. The Mongol incursion, along with the enormous empire to which it gave rise, was one in a long series of challenges from the steppes, but it was not the last. As the Mongol Empire disintegrated, a brief attempt to restore it occurred in the late fourteenth and early fifteenth centuries under the leadership of a Turkic warrior named Timur, born in what is now Uzbekistan and known in the West as Tamerlane (see Map 13.1, p. 576).

With a ferocity that matched or exceeded that of his model, Chinggis Khan, Timur's army of nomads brought immense devastation yet again to Russia, Persia, and India. Timur himself died in 1405, while preparing for an invasion of China. Conflicts among his successors prevented any lasting empire, although his descendants retained control of the area between Persia and Afghanistan for the rest of the fifteenth century. That state hosted a sophisticated elite culture, combining Turkic and Persian elements, particularly at its splendid capital of Samarkand, as its rulers patronized artists, poets, traders, and craftsmen. Timur's conquest proved to be the last great military success of nomadic peoples from Central Asia. In the centuries that followed, their homelands were swallowed up in the expanding Russian and Chinese empires, as the balance of power between steppe nomads of inner Eurasia and the civilizations of outer Eurasia turned decisively in favor of the latter.

In Africa, pastoral peoples stayed independent of established empires several centuries longer than the nomads of Inner Asia, for not until the late nineteenth century were they incorporated into European colonial states. The experience of the Fulbe, West Africa's largest pastoral society, provides a useful example of an African herding people with a highly significant role in the fifteenth century and beyond. From their homeland in the western fringe of the Sahara along the upper Senegal River, the Fulbe migrated gradually eastward in the centuries after 1000 C.E. (see Map 13.3, p. 582). Unlike the pastoral peoples of Inner Asia, they generally lived in small communities among agricultural peoples and paid various grazing fees and taxes for the privilege of pasturing their cattle. Relations with their farming hosts often were tense because the Fulbe resented their subordination to agricultural peoples, whose way of life they despised. That sense of cultural superiority became even more pronounced as the Fulbe, in the course of their eastward movement, slowly adopted Islam. Some of them in fact dropped out of a pastoral life and settled in towns, where they became highly respected religious leaders. In the eighteenth and nineteenth centuries, the Fulbe were at the center of a wave of religiously based uprisings, or jihads, that greatly expanded the practice of Islam and gave rise to a series of new states, ruled by the Fulbe themselves.

Civilizations of the Fifteenth Century: Comparing China and Europe

Beyond the foraging, farming, and herding societies of the fifteenth-century world were its civilizations, those city-centered and state-based societies that were far larger and more densely populated, more powerful and innovative, and much more unequal in terms of class and gender than other forms of human community. Since the First Civilizations had emerged between 3500 and 1000 B.C.E., both the geographic space they encompassed and the number of people they embraced had grown substantially. By the fifteenth century, a considerable majority of the world's population lived within one or another of these civilizations, although most of these people no doubt identified more with local communities than with a larger civilization. What might an imaginary global traveler notice about the world's major civilizations in the fifteenth century?

Ming Dynasty China

■ **Description**

How would you define the major achievements of Ming dynasty China?

Such a traveler might well begin his or her journey in China, heir to a long tradition of effective governance, Confucian and Daoist philosophy, a major Buddhist presence, sophisticated artistic achievements, and a highly productive economy. That civilization, however, had been greatly disrupted by a century of Mongol rule, and its population had been sharply reduced by the plague. During the Ming dynasty (1368–1644), however, China recovered (see Map 13.1). The early decades of that dynasty witnessed an effort to eliminate all signs of foreign rule, discouraging the use

Map 13.1   Asia in the Fifteenth Century
The fifteenth century in Asia witnessed the massive Ming dynasty voyages into the Indian Ocean, the last major eruption of nomadic power in Timur's empire, and the flourishing of the maritime city of Malacca.

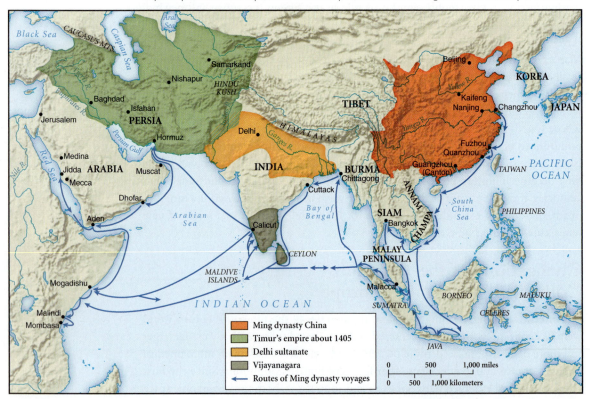

of Mongol names and dress, while promoting Confucian learning based on earlier models from the Han, Tang, and Song dynasties. Emperor Yongle (reigned 1402–1422) sponsored an enormous *Encyclopedia* of some 11,000 volumes. With contributions from more than 2,000 scholars, this work sought to summarize or compile all previous writing on history, geography, ethics, government, and more. Yongle also relocated the capital to Beijing, ordered the building of a magnificent imperial residence known as the Forbidden City, and constructed the Temple of Heaven, where subsequent rulers performed Confucian-based rituals to ensure the well-being of Chinese society (see Visual Source 13.1, p. 610). Culturally speaking, China was looking to its past.

Politically, the Ming dynasty reestablished the civil service examination system that had been neglected under Mongol rule and went on to create a highly centralized government. Power was concentrated in the hands of the emperor himself, while a cadre of eunuchs (castrated men) personally loyal to the emperor exercised great authority, much to the dismay of the official bureaucrats. The state acted vigorously to repair the damage of the Mongol years by restoring millions of acres to cultivation; rebuilding canals, reservoirs, and irrigation works; and planting, according to some estimates, a billion trees in an effort to reforest China. As a result, the economy rebounded, both international and domestic trade flourished, and the population grew. During the fifteenth century, China had recovered and was perhaps the best-governed and most prosperous of the world's major civilizations.

China also undertook the largest and most impressive maritime expeditions the world had ever seen. Since the eleventh century, Chinese sailors and traders had been a major presence in the South China Sea and in Southeast Asian port cities, with much of this activity in private hands. But now, after decades of preparation, an enormous fleet, commissioned by Emperor Yongle himself, was launched in 1405, followed over the next twenty-eight years by six more such expeditions. On board more than 300 ships of the first voyage was a crew of some 27,000, including 180 physicians, hundreds of government officials, 5 astrologers, 7 high-ranking or grand eunuchs, carpenters, tailors, accountants, merchants, translators, cooks, and thousands of soldiers and sailors. Visiting many ports in Southeast Asia, Indonesia, India, Arabia, and East Africa, these fleets, captained by the Muslim eunuch Zheng He, sought to enroll distant peoples and states in the Chinese tribute system (see Map 13.1). Dozens of rulers accompanied the fleets back to China, where they presented tribute, performed the required rituals of submission, and received in return abundant gifts, titles, and trading opportunities. Chinese officials were amused by some of the exotic products to be found abroad—ostriches, zebras, and giraffes, for

Comparing Chinese and European Ships
Among the largest vessels in Zheng He's early-fifteenth-century fleet were "treasure ships" such as this vessel measuring more than 400 feet long and carrying a crew of perhaps 1,000 men. The figure at the bottom right represents one of Columbus's ships. (© Dugald Stermer)

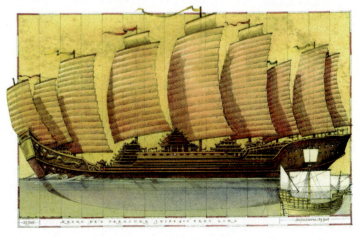

example. Officially described as "bringing order to the world," Zheng He's expeditions served to establish Chinese power and prestige in the Indian Ocean and to exert Chinese control over foreign trade in the region. The Chinese, however, did not seek to conquer new territories, establish Chinese settlements, or spread their culture, though they did intervene in a number of local disputes. On one of the voyages, Zheng He erected on the island of Ceylon (Sri Lanka) a tablet honoring alike the Buddha, Allah, and a Hindu deity.

The most surprising feature of these voyages was how abruptly and deliberately they were ended. After 1433, Chinese authorities simply stopped such expeditions and allowed this enormous and expensive fleet to deteriorate in port. "In less than a hundred years," wrote a recent historian of these voyages, "the greatest navy the world had ever known had ordered itself into extinction."[3] Part of the reason involved the death of the emperor Yongle, who had been the chief patron of the enterprise. Many high-ranking officials had long seen the expeditions as a waste of resources because China, they believed, was the self-sufficient "middle kingdom," requiring little from the outside world. In their eyes, the real danger to China came from the north, where nomadic barbarians constantly threatened. Finally, they viewed the voyages as the project of the court eunuchs, whom these officials despised. Even as these voices of Chinese officialdom prevailed, private Chinese merchants and craftsmen continued to settle and trade in Japan, the Philippines, Taiwan, and Southeast Asia, but they did so without the support of their government. The Chinese state quite deliberately turned its back on what was surely within its reach—a large-scale maritime empire in the Indian Ocean basin.

European Comparisons: State Building and Cultural Renewal

■ Comparison

What political and cultural differences stand out in the histories of fifteenth-century China and Western Europe? What similarities are apparent?

At the other end of the Eurasian continent, similar processes of demographic recovery, political consolidation, cultural flowering, and overseas expansion were under way. Western Europe, having escaped Mongol conquest but devastated by the plague, began to regrow its population during the second half of the fifteenth century. As in China, the infrastructure of civilization proved a durable foundation for demographic and economic revival.

Politically too Europe joined China in continuing earlier patterns of state building. In China, however, this meant a unitary and centralized government that encompassed almost the whole of its civilization, while in Europe a decidedly fragmented system of many separate, independent, and highly competitive states made for a sharply divided Christendom (see Map 13.2). Many of these states—Spain, Portugal, France, England, the city-states of Italy (Milan, Venice, and Florence), various German principalities—learned to tax their citizens more efficiently, to create more effective administrative structures, and to raise standing armies. A small Russian state centered on the city of Moscow also emerged in the fifteenth century as Mongol rule faded away. Much of this state building was driven by the needs of war, a frequent occurrence in such a fragmented and competitive political environment. England and

Map 13.2   Europe in 1500

By the end of the fifteenth century, Christian Europe had assumed its early modern political shape as a system of competing states threatened by an expanding Muslim Ottoman Empire.

France, for example, fought intermittently for more than a century in the Hundred Years' War (1337–1453) over rival claims to territory in France. Nothing remotely similar disturbed the internal life of Ming dynasty China.

A renewed cultural blossoming, known in European history as the Renaissance, likewise paralleled the revival of all things Confucian in Ming dynasty China. In Europe, however, that blossoming celebrated and reclaimed a classical Greek tradition that earlier had been obscured or viewed through the lens of Arabic or Latin translations. Beginning in the vibrant commercial cities of Italy between roughly 1350 and 1500, the Renaissance reflected the belief of the wealthy elite that they were living in a wholly new era, far removed from the confined religious world of feudal Europe. Educated citizens of these cities sought inspiration in the art and literature of ancient Greece and Rome; they were "returning to the sources," as they put it. Their purpose was not so much to reconcile these works with the ideas of Christianity, as the twelfth- and thirteenth-century university scholars had done, but to use them as a cultural standard to imitate and then to surpass. The elite patronized great Renaissance artists such as Leonardo da Vinci, Michelangelo, and Raphael, whose paintings and sculptures were far more naturalistic, particularly in portraying the human body, than those of their medieval counterparts.

Although religious themes remained prominent, Renaissance artists now included portraits and busts of well-known contemporary figures and scenes from ancient mythology. In the work of scholars, known as "humanists," reflections on secular topics such as grammar, history, politics, poetry, rhetoric, and ethics complemented more religious matters. For example, Niccolò Machiavelli's (1469–1527) famous work *The Prince* was a prescription for political success based on the way politics actually operated in a highly competitive Italy of rival city-states rather than on idealistic and religiously based principles. To the question of whether a prince should be feared or loved, Machiavelli replied:

> One ought to be both feared and loved, but as it is difficult for the two to go together, it is much safer to be feared than loved.... For it may be said of men in general that they are ungrateful, voluble, dissemblers, anxious to avoid danger, and covetous of gain.... Fear is maintained by dread of punishment which never fails.... In the actions of men, and especially of princes, from which there is no appeal, the end justifies the means.[4]

Heavily influenced by classical models, Renaissance figures were more interested in capturing the unique qualities of particular individuals and in describing the world as it was than in portraying or exploring eternal religious truths. In its focus on the affairs of this world, Renaissance culture reflected the urban bustle and commercial preoccupations of the Italian cities. Its secular elements challenged the other-worldliness of Christian culture, and its individualism signaled the dawning of a more capitalist economy of private entrepreneurs. A new Europe was in the making, rather more different from its own recent past than Ming dynasty China was from its pre-Mongol glory.

European Comparisons: Maritime Voyaging

■ Comparison

In what ways did European maritime voyaging in the fifteenth century differ from that of China? What accounts for these differences?

A global traveler during the fifteenth century might be surprised to find that Europeans, like the Chinese, were also launching outward-bound maritime expeditions. Initiated in 1415 by the small country of Portugal, those voyages sailed ever farther down the west coast of Africa, supported by the state and blessed by the pope (see Map 13.3). As the century ended, two expeditions marked major breakthroughs, although few suspected it at the time. In 1492, Christopher Columbus, funded by Spain, Portugal's neighbor and rival, made his way west across the Atlantic hoping to arrive in the East and, in one of history's most consequential mistakes, ran into the Americas. Five years later, in 1497, Vasco da Gama launched a voyage that took him

Snapshot   **Key Moments in European Maritime Voyaging**

Portuguese seize Ceuta in Morocco	1415
Prince Henry the Navigator launches Portuguese exploration of the West African coast	1420
Portuguese settle the Azores	1430s
Chinese fleets withdrawn from Indian Ocean	1433
Portuguese reach the Senegal River; beginning of Atlantic slave trade	1440s
Portuguese contact with Kongo; royal family converts to Christianity	1480s
Sugar production begins in Atlantic islands (Canaries, São Tomé)	1480s
Establishment of trading station at Elmina (in present-day Ghana)	1480s
First transatlantic voyage of Columbus	1492
John Cabot sails across North Atlantic to North America	1496
Vasco da Gama enters Indian Ocean and reaches India	1497–1498
Portuguese attacks on various Swahili cities; establishment of Fort Jesus at Mombasa; Portuguese contacts with Christian Ethiopia	1497–1520s
Magellan's voyage to Asia via the Americas; first circumnavigation of the globe	1520–1523

around the tip of South Africa, along the East African coast, and, with the help of a Muslim pilot, across the Indian Ocean to Calicut in southern India.

The differences between the Chinese and European oceangoing ventures were striking, most notably perhaps in terms of size. Columbus captained three ships and a crew of about 90, while da Gama had four ships, manned by perhaps 170 sailors. These were minuscule fleets compared to Zheng He's hundreds of ships and a crew in the many thousands. "All the ships of Columbus and da Gama combined," according to a recent account, "could have been stored on a single deck of a single vessel in the fleet that set sail under Zheng He."[5]

Motivation as well as size differentiated the two ventures. Europeans were seeking the wealth of Africa and Asia—gold, spices, silk, and more. They also were in search of Christian converts and of possible Christian allies with whom to continue their long crusading struggle against threatening Muslim powers. China, by contrast, faced no equivalent power, needed no military allies in the Indian Ocean basin, and required little that these regions produced. Nor did China possess an impulse to convert foreigners to Chinese culture or religion as the Europeans surely did. Furthermore, the confident and overwhelmingly powerful Chinese fleet sought neither conquests nor colonies, while the Europeans soon tried to monopolize by force the commerce of the Indian Ocean and violently carved out huge empires in the Americas.

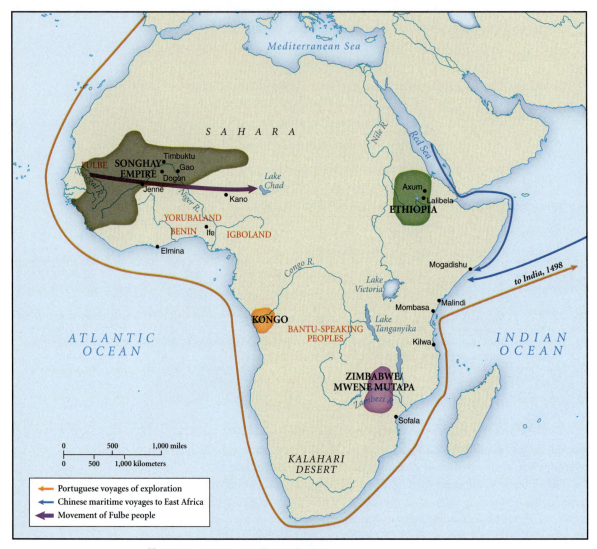

Map 13.3   Africa in the Fifteenth Century
By the 1400s, Africa was a virtual museum of political and cultural diversity, encompassing large empires, such as Songhay; smaller kingdoms, such as Kongo; city-states among the Yoruba, Hausa, and Swahili peoples; village-based societies without states at all, as among the Igbo; and nomadic pastoral peoples, such as the Fulbe. Both European and Chinese maritime expeditions touched on Africa during that century, even as Islam continued to find acceptance in the northern half of the continent.

The most striking difference in these two cases lay in the sharp contrast between China's decisive ending of its voyages and the continuing, indeed escalating, European effort, which soon brought the world's oceans and growing numbers of the world's people under its control. This is the reason that Zheng He's voyages were so long neglected in China's historical memory. They led nowhere, whereas the initial European expeditions, so much smaller and less promising, were but the first steps on a journey to world power. But why did the Europeans continue a process that the Chinese had deliberately abandoned?

In the first place, of course, Europe had no unified political authority with the power to order an end to its maritime outreach. Its system of competing states, so unlike China's single unified empire, ensured that once begun, rivalry alone would drive the Europeans to the ends of the earth. Beyond this, much of Europe's elite had an interest in overseas expansion. Its budding merchant communities saw opportunity for profit; its competing monarchs eyed the revenue that could come from taxing overseas trade or from seizing overseas resources; the Church foresaw the possibility of widespread conversion; impoverished nobles might imagine fame and fortune abroad. In China, by contrast, support for Zheng He's voyages was very shallow in official circles, and when the emperor Yongle passed from the scene, those opposed to the voyages prevailed within the politics of the court.

Finally, the Chinese were very much aware of their own antiquity, believed strongly in the absolute superiority of their culture, and felt with good reason that, should they desire something from abroad, others would bring it to them. Europeans too believed themselves unique, particularly in religious terms as the possessors of Christianity, the "one true religion." In material terms, though, they were seeking out the greater riches of the East, and they were highly conscious that Muslim power blocked easy access to these treasures and posed a military and religious threat to Europe itself. All of this propelled continuing European expansion in the centuries that followed.

The Waldseemüller Map of 1507
Just fifteen years after Columbus landed in the Western Hemisphere, this map, which was created by the German cartographer Martin Waldseemüller, reflected a dawning European awareness of the planet's global dimensions and location of the world's major landmasses. (Bildarchiv Preussischer Kulturbesitz/Art Resource, NY)

The Chinese withdrawal from the Indian Ocean actually facilitated the European entry. It cleared the way for the Portuguese to enter the region, where they faced only the eventual naval power of the Ottomans. Had Vasco da Gama encountered Zheng He's massive fleet as his four small ships sailed into Asian waters in 1498, world history may well have taken quite a different turn. As it was, however, China's abandonment of oceanic voyaging and Europe's embrace of the seas marked different responses to a common problem that both civilizations shared—growing populations and land shortage. In the centuries that followed, China's rice-based agriculture was able to expand production internally by more intensive use of the land, while the country's territorial expansion was inland toward Central Asia. By contrast, Europe's agriculture, based on wheat and livestock, expanded primarily by acquiring new lands in overseas possessions, which were gained as a consequence of a commitment to oceanic expansion.

Civilizations of the Fifteenth Century: The Islamic World

■ Comparison

What differences can you identify among the four major empires in the Islamic world of the fifteenth and sixteenth centuries?

Beyond the domains of Chinese and European civilization, our fifteenth-century global traveler would surely have been impressed with the transformations of the Islamic world. Stretching across much of Afro-Eurasia, the enormous realm of Islam experienced a set of remarkable changes during the fifteenth and early sixteenth centuries, as well as the continuation of earlier patterns. The most notable change lay in the political realm, for an Islamic civilization that had been severely fragmented since at least 900 now crystallized into four major states or empires (see Map 13.4). At the same time, a long-term process of conversion to Islam continued the cultural transformation of Afro-Eurasian societies both within and beyond these new states.

In the Islamic Heartland: The Ottoman and Safavid Empires

The most impressive and enduring of the new Islamic states was the Ottoman Empire, which lasted in one form or another from the fourteenth to the early twentieth century. It was the creation of one of the many Turkic warrior groups that had earlier migrated into Anatolia. By the mid-fifteenth century, these Ottoman Turks had already carved out a state that encompassed much of the Anatolian peninsula and had pushed deep into southeastern Europe (the Balkans), acquiring in the process a substantial Christian population. In the two centuries that followed, the Ottoman Empire extended its control to much of the Middle East, coastal North Africa, the lands surrounding the Black Sea, and even farther into Eastern Europe.

The Ottoman Empire was a state of enormous significance in the world of the fifteenth century and beyond. In its huge territory, long duration, incorporation of many diverse peoples, and economic and cultural sophistication, it was

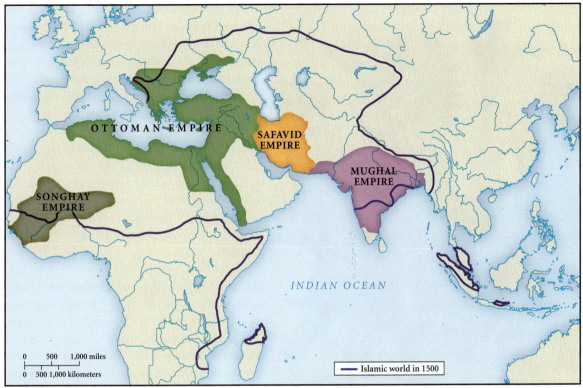

Map 13.4   Empires of the Islamic World
The most prominent political features of the vast Islamic world in the fifteenth and sixteenth centuries
were four large states: the Songhay, Ottoman, Safavid, and Mughal empires.

one of the great empires of world history. In the fifteenth century, only Ming
dynasty China and the Incas matched it in terms of wealth, power, and splendor.
The empire represented the emergence of the Turks as the dominant people of
the Islamic world, ruling now over many Arabs, who had initiated this new faith
more than 800 years before. In adding "caliph" (successor to the Prophet) to their
other titles, Ottoman sultans claimed the legacy of the earlier Abbasid Empire.
They sought to bring a renewed unity to the Islamic world, while also serving as
protector of the faith, the "strong sword of Islam."

The Ottoman Empire also represented a new phase in the long encounter between
Christendom and the world of Islam. In the Crusades, Europeans had taken the
aggressive initiative in that encounter, but the rise of the Ottoman Empire reversed
their roles. The seizure of Constantinople in 1453 marked the final demise of Christian Byzantium and allowed Ottoman rulers to see themselves as successors to the
Roman Empire. In 1529, a rapidly expanding Ottoman Empire laid siege to Vienna
in the heart of Central Europe. The political and military expansion of Islam, at the
expense of Christendom, seemed clearly under way. Many Europeans spoke fearfully
of the "terror of the Turk."

Des obristen kamerling
Vnd Truchses

Ottoman Janissaries
Originating in the fourteenth century, the Janissaries became the elite infantry force of the Ottoman Empire. Complete with uniforms, cash salaries, and marching music, they were the first standing army in the region since the days of the Roman Empire. When gunpowder technology became available, Janissary forces soon were armed with muskets, grenades, and handheld cannon. This image dates from the seventeenth century. (Austrian National Library, picture archive, Vienna: Cod. 8626, fol. 15r)

In the neighboring Persian lands to the east of the Ottoman Empire, another Islamic state was also taking shape in the late fifteenth and early sixteenth centuries—the Safavid Empire. Its leadership was also Turkic, but in this case it had emerged from a Sufi religious order founded several centuries earlier by Safi al-Din (1252–1334). The long-term significance of the Safavid Empire, which was established in the decade following 1500, was its decision to forcibly impose a Shia version of Islam as the official religion of the state. Over time, this form of Islam gained popular support and came to define the unique identity of Persian (Iranian) culture.

This Shia empire also introduced a sharp divide into the political and religious life of heartland Islam, for almost all of Persia's neighbors practiced a Sunni form of the faith. For a century (1534–1639), periodic military conflict erupted between the Ottoman and Safavid empires, reflecting both territorial rivalry and sharp religious differences. In 1514, the Ottoman sultan wrote to the Safavid ruler in the most bitter of terms:

You have denied the sanctity of divine law…you have deserted the path of salvation and the sacred commandments…you have opened to Muslims the gates of tyranny and oppression…you have raised the standard of irreligion and heresy.…[Therefore] the *ulama* and our doctors have pronounced a sentence of death against you, perjurer and blasphemer.[6]

This Sunni/Shia hostility has continued to divide the Islamic world into the twenty-first century.

On the Frontiers of Islam: The Songhay and Mughal Empires

While the Ottoman and Safavid empires brought both a new political unity and a sharp division to the heartland of Islam, two other states performed a similar role on the expanding African and Asian frontiers of the faith. In the West African savannas, the Songhay Empire rose in the second half of the fifteenth century. It was the most recent and the largest in a series of impressive states that operated at a crucial intersection of the trans-Saharan trade routes and that derived much of their revenue from taxing that commerce. Islam was a growing faith in Songhay but was limited largely to urban elites. This cultural divide within Songhay largely accounts for the religious behavior of its fifteenth-century monarch Sonni Ali (reigned 1465–1492), who gave alms and fasted during Ramadan in proper Islamic style but also enjoyed a reputation as a magician and possessed a charm thought to render his soldiers invisible to their enemies. Nonetheless, Songhay had become a major center of Islamic learning and commerce by the early sixteenth century. A North African traveler known as Leo Africanus remarked on the city of Timbuktu:

> Here are great numbers of [Muslim] religious teachers, judges, scholars, and other learned persons who are bountifully maintained at the king's expense. Here too are brought various manuscripts or written books from Barbary [North Africa] which are sold for more money than any other merchandise....Here are very rich merchants and to here journey continually large numbers of negroes who purchase here cloth from Barbary and Europe....It is a wonder to see the quality of merchandise that is daily brought here and how costly and sumptuous everything is.[7]

Sonni Ali's successor made the pilgrimage to Mecca and asked to be given the title "Caliph of the Land of the Blacks." Songhay then represented a substantial Islamic state on the African frontier of a still-expanding Muslim world.

The Mughal Empire in India bore similarities to Songhay, for both governed largely non-Muslim populations. Much as the Ottoman Empire initiated a new phase in the interaction of Islam and Christendom, so too did the Mughal Empire continue an ongoing encounter between Islamic and Hindu civilizations. Established in the early sixteenth century, the Mughal Empire was the creation of yet another Islamized Turkic group, which invaded India in 1526. Over the next century, the Mughals (a Persian term for Mongols) established unified control over most of the Indian peninsula, giving it a rare period of political unity and laying the foundation for subsequent British colonial rule. During its first several centuries, the Mughal Empire, a land of great wealth and imperial splendor, was the location of a remarkable effort to blend many Hindu groups and a variety of Muslims into an effective partnership. The inclusive policies of the early Mughal emperors showed that Muslim rulers could accommodate their overwhelmingly Hindu subjects in somewhat the same fashion as Ottoman authorities provided religious autonomy for their Christian peoples. In southernmost India, however, the distinctly Hindu kingdom of Vijayanagara flourished in the fifteenth century, even as it borrowed architectural styles from the Muslim states of northern India and sometimes employed Muslim mercenaries in its military forces.

Together these four Muslim empires—Ottoman, Safavid, Songhay, and Mughal—brought to the Islamic world a greater measure of political coherence, military power, economic prosperity, and cultural brilliance than it had known since the early centuries of Islam. This new energy, sometimes called a "second flowering of Islam," impelled the continuing spread of the faith to yet new regions. The most prominent of these was oceanic Southeast Asia, which for centuries had been intimately bound up in the world of Indian Ocean commerce. By the fifteenth century, that trading network was largely in Muslim hands, and the demand for Southeast Asian spices was mounting as the Eurasian world recovered from the devastation of Mongol conquest and the plague. Growing numbers of Muslim traders, many of them from India, settled in Java and Sumatra, bringing their faith with them. Thus, unlike the Middle East and India, where Islam was established in the wake of Arab or Turkic conquest, in Southeast Asia, as in West Africa, it was introduced by traveling merchants and solidified through the activities of Sufi holy men.

The rise of Malacca, strategically located on the waterway between Sumatra and Malaya, was a sign of the times (see Map 13.1, p. 576). During the fifteenth century, it was transformed from a small fishing village to a major Muslim port city. A Portuguese visitor in 1512 observed that Malacca had "no equal in the world.... Commerce between different nations for a thousand leagues on every hand must come to Malacca."[8] That city also became a springboard for the spread of Islam throughout the region. The Islam of Malacca, however, demonstrated much blending with local and Hindu/Buddhist traditions, while the city itself, like many port towns, had a reputation for "rough behavior." An Arab Muslim pilot in the 1480s commented critically:

> They have no culture at all.... You do not know whether they are Muslim or not.... They are thieves, for theft is rife among them and they do not mind.... They appear liars and deceivers in trade and labor.[9]

Nonetheless, Malacca, like Timbuktu, became a center for Islamic learning, and students from elsewhere in Southeast Asia were studying there in the fifteenth century. As the more central regions of Islam were consolidating politically, the frontier of the faith continued to move steadily outward.

Civilizations of the Fifteenth Century: The Americas

■ **Comparison**

What distinguished the Aztec and Inca empires from each other?

Across the Atlantic, centers of civilization had long flourished in Mesoamerica and in the Andes. The fifteenth century witnessed new, larger, and more politically unified expressions of those civilizations in the Aztec and Inca empires. Both were the work of previously marginal peoples who had forcibly taken over and absorbed older cultures, giving them new energy, and both were decimated in the sixteenth century at the hands of Spanish conquistadores and their diseases. To conclude this global tour of world civilizations, we will send our weary traveler to the Western Hemisphere for a brief look at these American civilizations (see Map 13.5).

The Aztec Empire

The empire known to history as the Aztec state was largely the work of the Mexica people, a seminomadic group from northern Mexico who had migrated southward and by 1325 had established themselves on a small island in Lake Texcoco. Over the

Map 13.5 The Americas in the Fifteenth Century

The Americas before Columbus represented a world almost completely separate from Afro-Eurasia. It featured similar kinds of societies, though with a different balance among them, but it completely lacked the pastoral economies that were so important in the Eastern Hemisphere.

589

next century, the Mexica developed their military capacity, served as mercenaries for more powerful people, negotiated elite marriage alliances with them, and built up their own capital city of Tenochtitlán. In 1428, a Triple Alliance between the Mexica and two other nearby city-states launched a highly aggressive program of military conquest, which in less than 100 years brought more of Mesoamerica within a single political framework than ever before. Aztec authorities, eager to shed their rather undistinguished past, now claimed descent from earlier Mesoamerican peoples such as the Toltecs and Teotihuacán.

With a core population recently estimated at 5 to 6 million people, the Aztec Empire was a loosely structured and unstable conquest state that witnessed frequent rebellions by its subject peoples. Conquered peoples and cities were required to regularly deliver to their Aztec rulers impressive quantities of textiles and clothing, military supplies, jewelry and other luxuries, various foodstuffs, animal products, building materials, rubber balls, paper, and more. The process was overseen by local imperial tribute collectors, who sent the required goods on to Tenochtitlán, a metropolis of 150,000 to 200,000 people, where they were meticulously recorded.

That city featured numerous canals, dikes, causeways, and bridges. A central walled area of palaces and temples included a pyramid almost 200 feet high. Surrounding the city were "floating gardens," artificial islands created from swamplands that supported a highly productive agriculture. Vast marketplaces reflected the commercialization of the economy. A young Spanish soldier who beheld the city in 1519 described his reaction:

> Gazing on such wonderful sights, we did not know what to say, or whether what appeared before us was real, for on one side, on the land there were great cities, and in the lake ever so many more, and the lake was crowded with canoes, and in the causeway were many bridges at intervals, and in front of us stood the great city of Mexico.[10]

Beyond tribute from conquered peoples, ordinary trade, both local and long-distance, permeated Aztec domains. The extent of empire and rapid population growth stimulated the development of markets and the production of craft goods, particularly in the fifteenth century. Virtually every settlement, from the capital city to the smallest village, had a marketplace that hummed with activity during weekly market days. The largest was that of Tlatelolco, near the capital city, which stunned the Spanish with its huge size, its good order, and the immense range of goods available. Hernán Cortés, the Spanish conquistador who defeated the Aztecs, wrote that "every kind of merchandise such as can be met with in every land is for sale there, whether of food and victuals, or ornaments of gold and silver, or lead, brass, copper, tin, precious stones, bones, shells, snails and feathers."[11] Professional merchants, known as *pochteca*, were legally commoners, but their wealth, often exceeding that of the nobility, allowed them to rise in society and become "magnates of the land." (See Document 13.1, pp. 601–04, for another Spanish view of the Aztec realm.)

■ **Description**
How did Aztec religious thinking support the empire?

Among the "goods" that the pochteca obtained were slaves, many of whom were destined for sacrifice in the bloody rituals so central to Aztec religious life. Long a part of Mesoamerican and many other world cultures, human sacrifice assumed an unusually prominent role in Aztec public life and thought during the fifteenth century. Tlacaelel (1398–1480), who was for more than half a century a prominent official of the Aztec Empire, is often credited with crystallizing the ideology of state that gave human sacrifice such great importance.

In that cyclical understanding of the world, the sun, central to all of life and identified with the Aztec patron deity Huitzilopochtli, tended to lose its energy in a constant battle against encroaching darkness. Thus the Aztec world hovered always on the edge of catastrophe. To replenish its energy and thus postpone the descent into endless darkness, the sun required the life-giving force found in human blood. Because the gods had shed their blood ages ago in creating humankind, it was wholly proper for people to offer their own blood to nourish the gods in the present. The high calling of the Aztec state was to supply this blood, largely through its wars of expansion and

Aztec Women

Within the home, Aztec women cooked, cleaned, spun and wove cloth, raised their children, and undertook ritual activities. Outside the home, they served as officials in palaces, priestesses in temples, traders in markets, teachers in schools, and members of craft workers' organizations. This domestic image comes from the sixteenth-century Florentine Codex, which was compiled by the Spanish but illustrated by Aztec artists. (Templo Mayor Library Mexico/Gianni Dagli Orti/The Art Archive)

from prisoners of war, who were destined for sacrifice. The victims were "those who have died for the god." The growth of the Aztec Empire therefore became the means for maintaining cosmic order and avoiding utter catastrophe. This ideology also shaped the techniques of Aztec warfare, which put a premium on capturing prisoners rather than on killing the enemy. As the empire grew, priests and rulers became mutually dependent, and "human sacrifices were carried out in the service of politics."[12] Massive sacrificial rituals, together with a display of great wealth, served to impress enemies, allies, and subjects alike with the immense power of the Aztecs and their gods.

Alongside these sacrificial rituals was a philosophical and poetic tradition of great beauty, much of which mused on the fragility and brevity of human life. Such an outlook characterized the work of Nezahualcoyotl (1402–1472), a poet and king of the city-state of Texcoco, which was part of the Aztec Empire:

Truly do we live on Earth?
Not forever on earth; only a little while here.
Be it jade, it shatters.
Be it gold, it breaks.
Be it a quetzal feather, it tears apart.
Not forever on earth; only a little while here.

Like a painting, we will be erased.
Like a flower, we will dry up here on earth.
Like plumed vestments of the precious bird,
That precious bird with an agile neck,
We will come to an end.[13]

The Inca Empire

While the Mexica were constructing an empire in Mesoamerica, a relatively small community of Quechua-speaking people, known to us as the Inca, was building the Western Hemisphere's largest imperial state along the spine of the Andes Mountains, which run almost the entire length of the west coast of South America. Much as the Aztecs drew upon the traditions of the Toltecs and Teotihuacán, the Incas incorporated the lands and cultures of earlier Andean civilizations: the Chavín, Moche, Nazca, and Chimu. The Inca Empire, however, was much larger than the Aztec state; it stretched some 2,500 miles along the Andes and contained perhaps 10 million subjects. Although the Aztec Empire controlled only part of the Mesoamerican cultural region, the Inca state encompassed practically the whole of Andean civilization during its short life in the fifteenth and early sixteenth centuries.

Both the Aztec and Inca empires represent rags-to-riches stories in which quite modest and remotely located people very quickly created by military conquest the largest states ever witnessed in their respective regions, but the empires themselves were quite different. In the Aztec realm, the Mexica rulers largely left their conquered people alone, if the required tribute was forthcoming. No elaborate administrative system arose to integrate the conquered territories or to assimilate their people to Aztec culture.

■ **Description**
In what ways did Inca authorities seek to integrate their vast domains?

The Incas, on the other hand, erected a rather more bureaucratic empire, though with many accommodations for local circumstances. At the top reigned the emperor, an absolute ruler regarded as divine, a descendant of the creator god Viracocha and the son of the sun god Inti. In theory, the state owned all land and resources, and each of the some eighty provinces in the empire had an Inca governor. At least in the central regions of the empire, subjects were grouped into hierarchical units of 10, 50, 100, 500, 1,000, 5,000, and 10,000 people, each headed by local officials, who were appointed and supervised by an Inca governor or the emperor. A separate set of "inspectors" provided the imperial center with an independent check on provincial officials. Births, deaths, marriages, and other population data were carefully recorded on *quipus*, the knotted cords that served as an accounting device. A resettlement program moved one-quarter or more of the population to new locations, in part to disperse conquered and no doubt resentful people.

Efforts at cultural integration required the leaders of conquered peoples to learn Quechua. Their sons were removed to the capital of Cuzco for instruction in Inca culture and language. Even now, millions of people from Ecuador to Chile still speak Quechua, and it is the official second language of Peru after Spanish. While the Incas required their subject peoples to acknowledge major Inca deities, these peoples were then largely free to carry on their own religious traditions. Human sacrifice took place on great public occasions or at times of special difficulty, but nothing remotely on the scale of the Aztec practice.

Like the Aztec Empire, the Inca state represented an especially dense and extended network of economic relationships within the "American web," but these relationships took shape in quite a different fashion. Inca demands on their conquered people were expressed, not so much in terms of tribute, but as labor service, known as *mita*, which was required periodically of every household.[14] What people produced at home usually stayed at home, but almost everyone also had to work for the state. Some labored on large state farms or on "sun farms," which supported temples and religious institutions; others herded, mined, served in the military, or toiled on state-directed construction projects. Those with particular skills were put to work manufacturing textiles, metal goods, ceramics, and stonework. The most well known of these specialists were the "chosen women," who were removed from their homes as young girls, trained in Inca ideology, and set to producing corn beer and cloth at state centers. Later they were given as wives to men of distinction or sent to serve as priestesses in various temples, where they were known as "wives of the Sun." In return for such labor services, Inca ideology, expressed in terms of family relationships, required the state to provide elaborate feasts at which large quantities of food and drink were consumed. Thus the authority of the state penetrated and directed the Incas' society and economy far more than did that of the Aztecs. (See Document 13.2, pp. 605–07, for an early Spanish account of Inca governing practices.)

If the Inca and Aztec civilizations differed sharply in their political and economic arrangements, they resembled each other more closely in their gender

Machu Picchu
Machu Picchu, high in the Andes Mountains, was constructed by the Incas in the 1400s on a spot long held sacred by local people. Its 200 buildings stand at some 8,000 feet above sea level, making it truly a "city in the sky." According to scholars, it was probably a royal retreat or religious center, rather than serving administrative, commercial, or military purposes. The outside world became aware of Machu Picchu only in 1911, when it was discovered by a Yale University archeologist. (Crispin Rodwell/Alamy)

systems. Both societies practiced what scholars call "gender parallelism," in which "women and men operate in two separate but equivalent spheres, each gender enjoying autonomy in its own sphere."[15]

In both Mesoamerican and Andean societies, such systems had emerged long before their incorporation into the Aztec and Inca empires. In the Andes, men reckoned their descent from their fathers and women from their mothers, while Mesoamericans had long viewed children as belonging equally to their mothers and fathers. Parallel religious cults for women and men likewise flourished in both societies. Inca men venerated the sun, while women worshipped the moon, with matching religious officials. In Aztec temples, both male and female priests presided over rituals dedicated to deities of both sexes. Particularly among the Incas, parallel hierarchies of male and female political officials governed the empire, while in Aztec society, women officials exercised local authority under a title that meant "female person in charge of people." Social roles were clearly defined and different for men and women, but the domestic concerns of women—childbirth, cooking, weaving, cleaning—were not regarded as inferior to the activities of men. Among the Aztec, for example, sweeping was a powerful and sacred act with symbolic significance as "an act of purification and a preventative against evil elements penetrating the center of the Aztec universe, the home."[16] In the Andes, men broke the ground, women sowed, and both took part in the harvest.

None of this meant gender equality. Men occupied the top positions in both political and religious life, and male infidelity was treated more lightly than was women's unfaithfulness. As the Inca and Aztec empires expanded, military life, limited to men, grew in prestige, perhaps skewing an earlier gender parallelism. In other ways, the new Aztec and Inca rulers adapted to the gender systems of the people they had conquered. Among the Aztecs, the tools of women's work, the broom and the weaving spindle, were ritualized as weapons; sweeping the home was believed to assist men at war; and childbirth for women was regarded as "our kind of war."[17] Inca rulers did not challenge the gender parallelism of their subjects but instead replicated it at a higher level, as the *sapay Inca* (the Inca ruler) and the *coya* (his female consort) governed jointly, claiming descent respectively from the sun and the moon.

Webs of Connection

■ Connection

In what different ways did the peoples of the fifteenth century interact with one another?

Few people in the fifteenth century lived in entirely separate and self-contained communities. Almost all were caught up, to one degree or another, in various and overlapping webs of influence, communication, and exchange. Such interactions represent, of course, one of the major concerns of world history. What kinds of webs or networks linked the various societies and civilizations of the fifteenth century?[18]

Perhaps most obvious were the webs of empire, large-scale political systems that brought together a variety of culturally different people. Christians and Muslims encountered each other directly in the Ottoman Empire, as did Hindus and Muslims in the Mughal Empire. No empire tried more diligently to integrate its diverse peoples than the fifteenth-century Incas.

Religion too linked far-flung peoples, and divided them as well. Christianity provided a common religious culture for peoples from England to Russia, although the great divide between Roman Catholicism and Eastern Orthodoxy endured, and in the sixteenth century the Protestant Reformation would shatter permanently the Christian unity of the Latin West. Although Buddhism had largely vanished from its South Asian homeland, it remained a link among China, Korea, Tibet, Japan, and parts of Southeast Asia, even as it splintered into a variety of sects and practices. More than either of these, Islam actively brought together its many peoples. In the hajj, the pilgrimage to Mecca, Africans, Arabs, Persians, Turks, Indians, and many others joined as one people as they rehearsed together the events that gave birth to their common faith. And yet divisions and conflicts persisted within the vast realm of Islam, as the violent hostility between the Sunni Ottoman Empire and the Shia Safavid Empire so vividly illustrates.

Long-established patterns of trade among peoples occupying different environments and producing different goods were certainly much in evidence during the fifteenth century, as they had been for millennia. Hunting societies of Siberia funneled furs and other products of the forest into the Silk Road trading network traversing the civilizations of Eurasia. In the fifteenth century, some of the agricultural peoples in southern Nigeria were receiving horses brought overland from the drier regions to the north, where those animals flourished better. The Mississippi River in North America and the Orinoco and Amazon rivers in South America facilitated a canoe-borne commerce along those waterways. Coastal shipping in large seagoing canoes operated in the Caribbean and along the Pacific coast between Mexico and Peru. In the Pacific, the Micronesian island of Yap by the fifteenth century was the center of an oceanic trading network, which included the distant islands of Guam and Palau and used large stone disks as money. Likewise the people of Tonga, Samoa, and Fiji intermarried and exchanged a range of goods, including mats and canoes.

The great long-distance trading patterns of the Afro-Eurasian world, in operation for a thousand years or more, likewise continued in the fifteenth century, although the balance among them was changing (see Map 13.6). The Silk Road overland network, which had flourished under Mongol control in the thirteenth and fourteenth centuries, contracted in the fifteenth century as the Mongol Empire broke up and the devastation of the plague reduced demand for its products. The rise of the Ottoman Empire also blocked direct commercial contact between Europe and China, but oceanic trade from Japan, Korea, and China through the islands of Southeast Asia and across the Indian Ocean picked up considerably. Larger ships made it possible to trade in bulk goods such as grain as well as luxury products, while more sophisticated partnerships and credit mechanisms greased the wheels of commerce. A common Islamic culture over much of this vast region likewise smoothed the passage of goods among very different peoples, as it also did for the trans-Saharan trade.

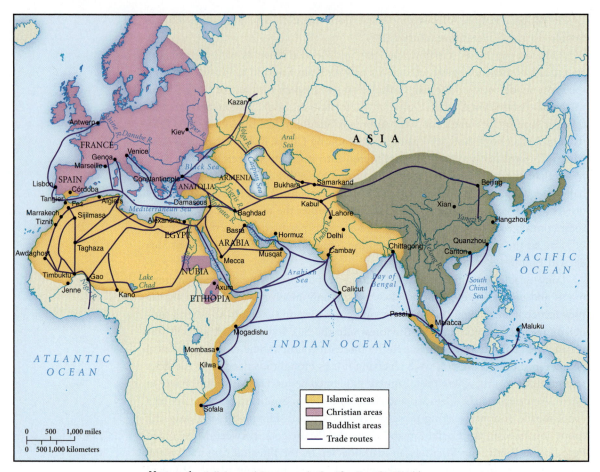

Map 13.6   Religion and Commerce in the Afro-Eurasian World

By the fifteenth century, the many distinct peoples and societies of the Eastern Hemisphere were linked to one another by ties of religion and commerce. Of course, not everyone was involved in long-distance trade, and many people in areas shown as Buddhist or Islamic on the map practiced other religions.

A Preview of Coming Attractions: Looking Ahead to the Modern Era, 1500–2010

While ties of empire, culture, and commerce surely linked many of the peoples in the world of the fifteenth century, none of those connections operated on a genuinely global scale. Although the densest webs of connection had been woven within the Afro-Eurasian zone of interaction, this huge region had no sustained ties with the Americas, and neither of them had meaningful contact with the peoples of Pacific Oceania. That situation was about to change as Europeans in the sixteenth century and beyond forged a set of genuinely global relationships that generated sustained interaction among all of these regions. That huge process and the many outcomes that flowed from it marked the beginning of what historians commonly call the modern age—the more than five centuries that followed the voyages of Columbus starting in 1492.

Over those five centuries, the previously separate worlds of Afro-Eurasia, the Americas, and Pacific Oceania became inextricably linked, with enormous consequences for everyone involved. Global empires, a global economy, global cultural exchanges, global migrations, global disease, global wars, and global environmental changes have made the past 500 years a unique phase in the human journey. Those webs of communication and exchange have progressively deepened, so much so that by the end of the twentieth century few people in the world lived beyond the cultural influences, economic ties, or political relationships of a globalized world.

A second distinctive feature of the past five centuries involves the emergence of a radically new kind of human society, also called "modern," which took shape first in Europe during the nineteenth century and then in various forms elsewhere in the world. The core feature of such societies was industrialization, rooted in a sustained growth of technological innovation. The human ability to create wealth made an enormous leap forward in a very short period of time, at least by world history standards. Accompanying this economic or industrial revolution was an equally distinctive and unprecedented jump in human numbers, a phenomenon that has affected not only human beings but also many other living species and the earth itself (see the Snapshot).

Moreover, these modern societies were far more urbanized and much more commercialized than ever before, as more and more people began to work for wages, to produce for the market, and to buy the requirements of daily life rather than

Snapshot   World Population Growth, 1000–2000[19]

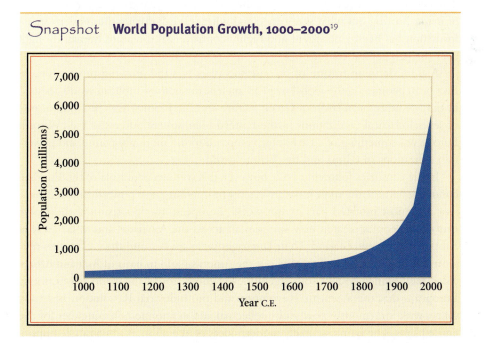

growing or making those products for their own use. These societies gave prominence and power to holders of urban wealth—merchants, bankers, industrialists, educated professionals—at the expense of rural landowning elites, while simultaneously generating a substantial factory working class and diminishing the role of peasants and handicraft artisans.

Modern societies were generally governed by states that were more powerful and intrusive than earlier states and empires had been, and they offered more of their people an opportunity to play an active role in public and political life. Literacy in modern societies was far more widespread than ever before, while new national identities became increasingly prominent, competing with more local loyalties. To the mix of established religious ideas and folk traditions were now added the challenging outlook and values of modern science, with its secular emphasis on the ability of human rationality to know and manipulate the world. Modernity has usually meant a self-conscious awareness of living and thinking in new ways that deliberately departed from tradition.

This revolution of modernity, comparable in its pervasive consequences only to the Agricultural Revolution of some 10,000 years ago, introduced new divisions and new conflicts into the experience of humankind. The ancient tensions between rich and poor within particular societies were now paralleled by new economic inequalities among entire regions and civilizations and a much-altered global balance of power. The first societies to experience the modern transformation—those in Western Europe and North America—became both a threat and a source of envy to much of the rest of the world. As modern societies emerged and spread, they were enormously destructive of older patterns of human life, even as they gave rise to many new ways of living. Sorting out what was gained and what was lost during the modern transformation has been a persistent and highly controversial thread of human thought over the past several centuries.

A third defining feature of the last 500 years was the growing prominence of European peoples on the global stage. In ancient times, the European world, focused in the Mediterranean basin of Greek culture and the Roman Empire, was but one of several classical civilizations in the Eastern Hemisphere. After 500 C.E., Western Europe was something of a backwater, compared to the more prosperous and powerful civilizations of China and the Islamic world.

In the centuries following 1500, however, this western peninsula of the Eurasian continent became the most innovative, most prosperous, most powerful, most expansive, and most imitated part of the world. European empires spanned the globe. European peoples created new societies all across the Americas and as far away as Australia and New Zealand. Their languages were spoken and their Christian religion was widely practiced throughout the Americas and in parts of Asia and Africa. Their businessmen bought, sold, and produced goods around the world. It was among Europeans that the Scientific Revolution and the Industrial Revolution first took shape, with enormously powerful intellectual and economic consequences for the entire planet. The quintessentially modern ideas of liberalism, nationalism, feminism, and socialism all bore the imprint of their European origin. By the beginning of the twentieth century, Europeans or peoples of European descent exercised unprecedented influence and control over the earth's many other peoples, a wholly novel experience in human history.

For the rest of the world, growing European dominance posed a common task. Despite their many differences, the peoples of Asia, Africa, the Middle East, the Americas, and Pacific Oceania all found themselves confronted by powerful and intrusive Europeans. The impact of this intrusion and how various peoples responded to it—resistance, submission, acceptance, imitation, adaptation—represent critically important threads in the world history of the past five centuries.

Reflections: What If? Chance and Contingency in World History

Seeking meaning in the stories they tell, historians are inclined to look for deeply rooted or underlying causes for the events they recount. And yet, is it possible that, at least on occasion, history turns less on profound and long-term causes than on coincidence, chance, or the decisions of a few that might well have gone another way?

Consider, for example, the problem of explaining the rise of Europe to a position of global power in the modern era. What if the Great Khan Ogodei had not died in 1241, requiring the forces then poised for an assault on Germany to return to Mongolia? It is surely possible that Central and Western Europe might have been overrun by Mongol armies as so many other civilizations had been, a prospect that could have drastically altered the trajectory of European history. Or what if the Chinese had decided in 1433 to continue their huge maritime expeditions, creating an empire in the Indian Ocean basin and perhaps moving on to "discover" the Americas and Europe? Such a scenario suggests a wholly different future for world history than the one that in fact occurred. Or what if the forces of the Ottoman Empire had taken the besieged city of Vienna in 1529? Might they then have incorporated even larger parts of Europe into their expanding domain, requiring a halt to Europe's overseas empire-building enterprise?

None of this necessarily means that the rise of Europe was merely a fluke or an accident of history, but it does raise the issue of "contingency," the role of unforeseen or small events in the unfolding of the human story. An occasional "what if" approach to history reminds us that alternative possibilities existed in the past and that the only certainty about the future is that we will be surprised.

Second Thoughts

What's the Significance?

Paleolithic persistence	Iroquois	Ming dynasty China	To assess your mastery of the material in this chapter, visit the **Student Center** at bedfordstmartins.com/strayer
Benin	Timur	Zheng He	
Igbo	Fulbe	European Renaissance	

Ottoman Empire   Songhay Empire   Aztec Empire
seizure of Constantinople   Timbuktu   Inca Empire
  (1453)   Mughal Empire
Safavid Empire   Malacca

Big Picture Questions

1. Assume for the moment that the Chinese had *not* ended their maritime voyages in 1433. How might the subsequent development of world history have been different? What value is there in asking this kind of "what if" or counterfactual question?

2. How does this chapter distinguish among the various kinds of societies that comprised the world of the fifteenth century? What other ways of categorizing the world's peoples might work as well or better?

3. What would surprise a knowledgeable observer from 500 C.E., were he or she to make a global tour in the fifteenth century? What features of that earlier world might still be recognizable?

4. What predictions about the future might a global traveler of the fifteenth century reasonably have made? To what extent would it depend on precisely when and where those predictions were made?

Next Steps: For Further Study

For Web sites and additional documents related to this chapter, see **Make History** at bedfordstmartins.com/strayer.

Terence N. D'Altroy, *The Incas* (2002). A history of the Inca Empire that draws on recent archeological and historical research.

Edward L. Dreyer, *Zheng He: China and the Oceans in the Early Ming Dynasty* (2006). The most recent scholarly account of the Ming dynasty voyages.

Halil Inalcik and Donald Quataert, *An Economic and Social History of the Ottoman Empire, 1300–1914* (1994). A classic study of the Ottoman Empire.

Robin Kirkpatrick, *The European Renaissance, 1400–1600* (2002). A beautifully illustrated history of Renaissance culture as well as the social and economic life of the period.

Charles Mann, *1491: New Revelations of the Americas before Columbus* (2005). A review of Western Hemisphere societies and academic debates about their pre-Columbian history.

J. R. McNeill and William H. McNeill, *The Human Web* (2003). A succinct account of the evolving webs or relationships among human societies in world history.

Michael Smith, *The Aztecs* (2003). A history of the Aztec Empire, with an emphasis on the lives of ordinary people.

"Ming Dynasty," http://www.metmuseum.org/toah/hd/ming/hd_ming.htm. A sample of Chinese art from the Ming dynasty from the collection of the Metropolitan Museum of Art.

"Renaissance Art in Italy," http://witcombe.sbc.edu/ARTHrenaissanceitaly.html. An extensive collection of painting and sculpture from the Italian Renaissance.

Documents

Considering the Evidence:
The Aztecs and the Incas
through Spanish Eyes

During the fifteenth century, the Western Hemisphere hosted human communities of many kinds—gathering and hunting peoples, agricultural village societies, chiefdoms, and two major state-based agrarian civilizations. Most of the population of the Americas was concentrated in those two societies— the Aztec and Inca empires (see Map 13.5, p. 589). Since neither had an extensive literary tradition, historians seeking to understand their history and culture have depended heavily on the records and observations of the Spanish who conquered them in the sixteenth century. This raises obvious questions about the credibility of such accounts. Can writers from a conquering power and a completely different culture accurately describe the life and history of those they have recently defeated? At least some of those Spanish observers were able to draw on the local knowledge and experience of native peoples. What follows are accounts of the Aztec and Inca empires as seen through the eyes of two remarkable Spanish observers, both of whom at least tried to understand the people of these American civilizations.

Document 13.1

Diego Duran on the Aztecs

Coming to Mexico with his family as a young boy, Diego Duran (1537–1588) subsequently became a Dominican friar, learned to speak fluently the native Nahuatl language of the Aztecs, and began a lifelong enterprise of studying their history and culture. His research often involved extensive interviewing of local people in the rural areas where he worked and resulted in three books published between 1574 and 1581. The first excerpt records a series of laws or decrees, which Duran attributes to the Aztec ruler Moctezuma I, who governed the empire between 1440 and 1469. They reveal something of the court practices and social hierarchy of the Aztec realm as the empire was establishing itself in the middle decades of the fifteenth century. The second excerpt touches on various aspects of Aztec culture—religion, human sacrifice, social mobility, commercial markets, and slavery.

- What do Moctezuma's laws tell us about the social and moral values of the Aztecs?

- Based on these two excerpts, how would you describe Aztec society? What distinct social groups or classes can you identify? How were they distinguished from one another? What opportunities for social mobility were available? How might people fall into slavery?

- What impressed Duran about the markets operating within the Aztec Empire?

- How was human sacrifice related to war, to market activity, to slavery, and to religious belief and practice?

- Duran's accounts of Aztec life and history were written more than fifty years after the Spanish conquest of the Aztec Empire. To what extent do you think this compromises his efforts to describe preconquest Aztec society?

King Moctezuma I
Laws, Ordinances, and Regulations
ca. 1450

The following laws were decreed:

1. The king must never appear in public except when the occasion is extremely important and unavoidable.

2. Only the king may wear a golden diadem in the city, though in war all the great lords and brave captains may wear this (but on no other occasion)....

3. Only the king and the prime minister Tlacaelel may wear sandals within the palace.... [N]oblemen are the only ones to be allowed to wear sandals in the city and no one else, also under pain of death, with the exception of men who have performed some great feat in war....

4. Only the king is to wear the final mantles of cotton brocaded with designs and threads of different colors and adorned with featherwork....

5. The great lords, who are twelve, may wear special mantles of certain make and design, and the minor lords, according to their valor and accomplishments, may wear others.

6. The common soldiers are permitted to wear only the simplest type of mantle. They are prohibited from using any special designs that might set them off from the rest....

7. The commoners will not be allowed to wear cotton clothing, under pain of death, but can use only garments of maguey fiber....

8. Only the great noblemen and valiant warriors are given license to build a house with a second story; for disobeying this law a person receives the death penalty....

9. Only the great lords are to wear labrets, ear plugs, and nose plugs of gold and precious stones, except for commoners who are strong men, brave captains, and soldiers, but their labrets, ear plugs, and nose plugs must be of bone, wood, or other inferior material of little value....

Source: Fray Diego Duran, *The History of the Indies of New Spain*, translated by Doris Heyden (Norman: University of Oklahoma Press, 1994), 208–10.

11. In the royal palace there are to be diverse rooms where different classes of people are to be received, and under pain of death no one is to enter that of the great lords or to mix with those men [unless of that class himself]....

12. An order of judges is to be established, beginning with the judges of the supreme council. After these would come regular court judges, municipal judges, district officials, constables, and councilmen, although none of them may give the death sentence without notifying the king. Only the sovereign can sentence someone to death or pardon him....

13. All the barrios will possess schools or monasteries for young men where they will learn religion and correct comportment. They are to do penance, lead hard lives, live with strict morality, practice for warfare, do physical work, fast, endure disciplinary measures, draw blood from different parts of the body, and keep watch at night. There are to be teachers and old men to correct them and chastise them and lead them in their exercises and take care that they are not idle, do not lose their time. All of these youth must observe chastity in the strictest way, under pain of death.

14. There is to be a rigorous law regarding adulterers. They are to be stoned and thrown into the rivers or to the buzzards.

15. Thieves will be sold for the price of their theft, unless the theft be grave, having been committed many times. Such thieves will be punished by death.

16. Great privileges and exemptions are to be given those who dedicate themselves to religion, to the temples and the gods. Priests will be awarded great distinction, reverence, and authority.

Diego Duran

Book of the Gods and Rites

1574–1576

I wish to tell of the way in which the natives sacrificed....

So ended the ceremony of the blessing of the pieces of dough in the form of the bones and the flesh of the god. They were revered and honored in the name of Huitzilopochtli with all the respectful veneration that we ourselves hold for the Divine Sacrament of the Altar. To exalt the occasion further, the sacrificers of men were also present....

Smeared with black, the six sacrificers appeared.... Seeing them come out with their ghastly aspect filled all the people with dread and terrible fear! The high priest carried in one hand a large stone knife, sharp and wide. Another carried a wooden yoke carved in the form of a snake. They humbled themselves before the idol and then stood in order next to a pointed stone, which stood in front of the door of the idol's chamber....

All the prisoners of war who were to be sacrificed upon this feast were then brought forth.... They seized the victims one by one, one by one foot, another by the other, one priest by one hand, another by the other hand. The victim was thrown on his back, upon the pointed stone, where the wretch was grabbed by the fifth priest, who placed the yoke upon his throat. The high priest then opened the chest and with amazing swiftness tore out the heart, ripping it out with his own hands. Thus steaming, the heart was lifted toward the sun, and the fumes were offered up to the sun. The priest then turned toward the idol and cast the heart in its face. After the heart had been extracted, the body was allowed to roll down the steps of the pyramid....

All the prisoners and captives of war brought from the towns we have mentioned were sacrificed in this manner, until none were left. After they had been slain and cast down, their owners—those who

Source: Fray Diego Duran, *Book of the Gods and Rites and the Ancient Calendar*, translated by Fernando Horcasitas and Doris Heyden (Norman: University of Oklahoma Press, 1971), 90–92, 137–38, 273–76, 279, 281–82.

had captured them—retrieved the bodies. They were carried away, distributed, and eaten, in order to celebrate the feast. There were at least forty or fifty captives, depending upon the skill which the men had shown in seizing and capturing men in war....

[M]any strove, in every possible way, to lift their names on high, to obtain glory, to procure greater honors, to found lineages and titles, and [to gain] good fame for their persons. There were three established and honored ways in all the nations [for obtaining these rewards]. The first and principal path which the kings designated was soldiery—to make oneself known in war through valiant feats, to be outstanding in killing, taking prisoners, to destroy armies and squadrons, to have directed these things. These [warriors] were given great honors, rewards, weapons, and insignia which were proof of their splendid deeds and valor....

The second way in which men rose was through religion, entering the priesthood. After having served in the temples in a virtuous, penitential, and cloistered way of life, in their old age they were sent out to high and honorable posts.... They were present when the government councils were held, their opinions and advice were listened to, and they were part of the ruling boards and juntas. Without their council and opinion kings did not dare act....

The third and least glorious manner of [rising in the world] was that of becoming a merchant or trader, that of buying and selling, going forth to all the markets of the land, bartering cloth for jewels, jewels for feathers, feathers for stones, and stones for slaves, always dealing in things of importance, of renown, and of high value. These [men] strengthened their social position with their wealth.... They acquired wealth and obtained slaves to sacrifice to this their god [Quetzalcoatl]. And so they were considered among the magnates of the land, just as the valorious soldier brought sacrificial captives from war, gaining fame as a brave....

[I]n olden times there was a god of markets and fairs....

The gods of these market places threatened terrible ills and made evil omens and auguries to the neighboring villages which did not attend their market places....

The markets were so inviting, pleasurable, appealing, and gratifying to these people that great crowds attended, and still attend, them, especially during the big fairs, as is well known to all....

The markets in this land were all enclosed by walls and stood either in front of the temples of the gods or to one side. Market day in each town was considered a main feast in that town or city. And thus in that small shrine where the idol of the market stood were offered ears of corn, chili, tomatoes, fruit, and other vegetables, seeds, and breads—in sum, everything sold in the *tianguiz*....

Furthermore, a law was established by the republic prohibiting the selling of goods outside the market place. Not only were there laws and penalties connected with this, but there was a fear of the supernatural, of misfortune, and of the ire and wrath of the god of the market. No one ventured, therefore, to trade outside [the market limits]....

There were many ways of becoming a slave within the law of the Indian nations....

First, he who stole the number of pieces of cloth or ears of corn, jewels, or turkeys which the laws of the republic had determined and set a penalty for was himself sold for the same amount in order to satisfy the owner of the purloined goods....

Second, another way in which a native could become a slave was that of the gambler who risked all his possessions on the dice or in any other game which the natives played....

Third, if the father of a family had many sons and daughters and among them was one [who was] incorrigible, disobedient, shameless, dissolute, incapable of receiving counsel or advice, the law... permitted [the father] to sell him in the public market place as an example and lesson to bad sons and daughters....

Fourth, one became a slave if he borrowed valuable things, such as cloth, jewels, featherwork, and did not return them on the appointed date....

In times of famine a man and wife could agree to a way of satisfying their needs and rise from their wretched state. They could sell one another, and thus husband sold wife and wife sold husband, or they sold one of their children.

Document 13.2

Pedro de Cieza de Léon on the Incas

Like Duran, Pedro de Cieza de Léon (1520–1554), a Spanish chronicler of the Inca Empire, came to the Americas as a boy. But unlike Duran, he came alone at the age of thirteen, and he followed a very different career. For the next seventeen years Cieza took part as a soldier in a number of expeditions that established Spanish rule in various parts of South America. Along the way, he collected a great deal of information, especially about the Inca Empire, which he began to publish upon his return to Spain in 1550. Despite a very limited education, Cieza wrote a series of works that have become a major source for historians about the workings of the Inca Empire and about the Spanish conquest of that land. The selection that follows focuses on the techniques that the Inca used to govern their huge empire.

■ How would you describe Cieza's posture toward the Inca Empire? What in particular did he seem to appreciate about it?

■ Based on this account, what difficulties did the Inca rulers face in governing their large and diverse realm?

■ What policies or practices did the Inca authorities follow in seeking to integrate their empire? How do these compare with other empires that you have studied?

■ Some modern observers have described the Inca Empire as "totalitarian" or "socialist." Do such terms seem appropriate? How else might you describe the Inca state?

PEDRO DE CIEZA DE LÉON

Chronicles of the Incas

ca. 1550

The Incas had the seat of their empire in the city of Cuzco, where the laws were given and the captains set out to make war.... As soon as one of these large provinces was conquered, ten or twelve thousand of the men and their wives, or six thousand, or the number decided upon, were ordered to leave and remove themselves from it. These were transfered to another town or province of the same climate and nature as that which they left.... And they had another device to keep the natives from hating them, and this was that they never divested the natural chieftains of their power. If it so happened that one of them committed a crime or in some way deserved to be stripped of his power, it was vested in his sons or brothers, and all were ordered to obey them....

Source: *The Incas of Pedro de Cieza de Leon*, translated by Harriet de Onis (Norman: University of Oklahoma Press, 1959), 56–57, 158–60, 165–73, 177–78.

★ ★ ★

One of the things most to be envied these rulers is how well they knew to conquer such vast lands....

[T]hey entered many lands without war, and the soldiers who accompanied the Inca were ordered to do no damage or harm, robbery or violence. If there was a shortage of food in the province, he ordered supplies brought in from other regions so that those newly won to his service would not find his rule and acquaintance irksome....

In many others, where they entered by war and force of arms, they ordered that the crops and houses of the enemy be spared.... But in the end the Incas always came out victorious, and when they had vanquished the others, they did not do them further harm, but released those they had taken prisoner, if there were any, and restored the booty, and put them back in possession of their property and rule, exhorting them not to be foolish and try to compete with his royal majesty nor abandon his friendship, but to be his friends as their neighbors were. And saying this, he gave them a number of beautiful women and fine pieces of wool or gold....

They never deprived the native chieftains of their rule. They were all ordered to worship the sun as God, but they were not prohibited from observing their own religions and customs....

It is told for a fact of the rulers of this kingdom that in the days of their rule they had their representatives in the capitals of all the provinces.... They served as head of the provinces or regions, and from every so many leagues around the tributes were brought to one of these capitals, and from so many others, to another. This was so well organized that there was not a village that did not know where it was to send its tribute. In all these capitals the Incas had temples of the sun, mints, and many silversmiths who did nothing but work rich pieces of gold or fair vessels of silver.... The tribute paid by each of these districts where the capital was situated, and that turned over by the natives, whether gold, silver, clothing, arms, and all else they gave, was entered in the accounts of the [quipu-] camayocs, who kept the quipus and did everything ordered by the governor in the matter of finding the soldiers or supplying whomever the

Inca ordered, or making delivery to Cuzco; but when they came from the city of Cuzco to go over the accounts, or they were ordered to go to Cuzco to give an accounting, the accountants themselves gave it by the quipus, or went to give it where there could be no fraud, but everything had to come out right. Few years went by in which an accounting of all these things was not made....

When the Incas set out to visit their kingdom, it is told that they traveled with great pomp, riding in rich litters set upon smooth, long poles of the finest wood and adorned with gold and silver....

So many people came to see his passing that all the hills and slopes seemed covered with them, and all called down blessings upon him....

He [the Inca] traveled four leagues each day, or as much as he wished; he stopped wherever he liked to inquire into the state of his kingdom; he willingly listened to those who came to him with complaints, righting wrongs and punishing those who had committed an injustice....

[T]hese rulers, as the best measure, ordered and decreed, with severe punishment for failure to obey, that all the natives of their empire should know and understand the language of Cuzco, both they and their women.... This was carried out so faithfully that in the space of a very few years a single tongue was known and used in an extension of more than 1,200 leagues; yet, even though this language was employed, they all spoke their own [languages], which were so numerous that if I were to list them it would not be credited....

[The Inca] appointed those whose duty it was to punish wrongdoers, and to this end they were always traveling about the country. The Incas took such care to see that justice was meted out that nobody ventured to commit a felony or theft. This was to deal with thieves, ravishers of women, or conspirators against the Inca; however, there were many provinces that warred on one another, and the Incas were not wholly able to prevent this.

By the river [Huatanay] that runs through Cuzco justice was executed on those who were caught or brought in as prisoners from some other place.

There they had their heads cut off, or were put to death in some other manner which they chose. Mutiny and conspiracy were severely punished, and, above all, those who were thieves and known as such; even their wives and chidren were despised and considered to be tarred with the same brush....

[I]n each of the many provinces there were many storehouses filled with supplies and other needful things; thus, in times of war, wherever the armies went they draw upon the contents of these storehouses, without ever touching the supplies of their confederates or laying a finger on what they had in their settlements. And when there was no war, all this stock of supplies and food was divided up among the poor and the widows. These poor were the aged, or the lame, crippled, or paralyzed, or those afflicted with some other diseases.... If there came a lean year, the storehouses were opened and the provinces were lent what they needed in the way of supplies; then, in a year of abundance, they paid back all they had received.

Using the Evidence:
The Aztecs and the Incas
through Spanish Eyes

1. **Assessing documents:** Both Duran and Cieza were outsiders to the societies they described, and they were part of the conquering Spanish forces. In what ways did these conditions affect their descriptions of the Aztec and Inca empires?

2. **Considering the subtext of documents:** In what ways might these authors have been using their observation of Aztec or Inca society to praise or to criticize their own European homeland?

3. **Evaluating the credibility of documents:** Which statements in these documents do you find most credible and which ones might you be inclined to question or challenge? What criteria might you use to assess the evidence in these documents?

4. **Relating primary documents and text narrative:** How might you use the information in these documents to support the descriptions of the Aztec and Inca empires that are contained in this chapter? Are there ways the documents might challenge statements in the text?

5. **Making comparisons:** What similarities and differences between Aztec and Inca societies can you glean from these documents?

6. **Seeking more data:** What additional primary sources about the Aztec and Inca empires of the fifteenth century would you like to have? What other perspectives on those states would be useful for historians?

Visual Sources

Considering the Evidence: Sacred Places in the World of the Fifteenth Century

Virtually every human community throughout history has designated certain places and certain structures as particularly sacred or holy, even if they understand all of creation to partake in that sacredness. Such sites represent intersections between the ordinary world and the world beyond. Many such places were private—the Chinese family altars displaying ancestral tablets and the "house churches" of early Christians, for example—but the most visible and prominent were public spaces such as shrines, cathedrals, temples, and mosques.

Sometimes the holiness of such sites derived from the burial of a highly respected figure, such as the tomb of Abraham in Israel, sacred to Jews and Muslims alike, or Lenin's tomb in Moscow, virtually a shrine to faithful communists. Particular historical or religious events, such as the birth of Jesus or the enlightenment of the Buddha, have contributed to the sacred status of structures erected in those places. Formal rites of consecration, the presence of relics, and rituals of devotion such as the Muslim pilgrimage to Mecca add to the extraordinary character of particular buildings. So too did distinctive architectural styles as well as the sensory stimulus of bells, calls to prayer, and the burning of incense or candles.[20] Still other buildings acquired a sacred character because they were gathering places for prayer or worship.

Such sacred sites, however, did not function exclusively in the spiritual realm; they often operated as well in the more secular domains of commerce and politics. The New Testament records that Jesus angrily drove the money changers from the temple in Jerusalem, while Buddhist monasteries on the Silk Road and elsewhere often became wealthy centers of trade. Furthermore, sacred places played important political roles as rulers sought the blessing and support of religious leaders and the aura of legitimacy that derived from some association with the realm of the holy. State authorities and wealthy elites often patronized the construction of sacred buildings and contributed to their upkeep. Sacred sites have sometimes spawned violence as rivalries erupted among competing sects or between political and religious authorities.

The four sacred sites shown in this section might well have been on the itinerary of an imaginary global traveler in the fifteenth century. Together they illustrate something of the diversity of such places in terms of their physical setting and architectural styles, the sources of their sacredness, their intended function, and their relationship to those who exercised political power. Yet they also bore similarities to one another. All of them were deliberately set apart from the profane or ordinary world, were linked to a wider sacred geography, and were commissioned and funded by a ruler.

Perhaps not surprisingly, the largest sacred site in the world of the fifteenth century lay in China. Known as the Temple of Heaven, it was constructed during the early fifteenth century in the Ming dynasty capital of Beijing by the ambitious emperor Yongle (reigned 1402–1424), who likewise ordered the building of the magnificent imperial residence of the Forbidden City. (He also sent Zheng He on his immense maritime voyages in the Indian Ocean; see pp. 577–78.)

Set in a forest of more than 650 acres, the Temple of Heaven was, in Chinese thinking, the primary place where Heaven and earth met. From his residence in the Forbidden City, the Chinese emperor led a procession of thousands twice a year to this sacred site, where he offered sacrifices, implored the gods for a good harvest, and performed those rituals that maintained the cosmic balance. These sacred ceremonies, from which commoners were barred even from watching, demonstrated the emperor's respect for the age-old source of his imperial authority, the Mandate of Heaven, from which Chinese emperors derived their legitimate right to rule. As the emperor bowed to Heaven, he was modeling in good Confucian fashion the respect required of all subordinates to their social superiors and especially to the emperor himself.

The temple complex was laced with ancient symbolism. The southern part of the wall that enclosed the complex was square, symbolizing the earth, while the northern wall was rounded or semicircular, suggesting Heaven in Daoist thinking. Major buildings were likewise built in the round while being situated within a square enclosure, also symbolizing the intersection of Heaven and earth. The most prominent building was the Hall of Prayer for Good Harvest (Visual Source 13.1), constructed by 1420. There the emperor prayed and conducted rituals to ensure a successful agricultural season on which the country's well-being and his own legitimacy depended. The emperor and others approached the hall from the south on a gradually ascending 360-meter walkway symbolizing progression from earth to Heaven. The walkway divides into three parallel paths: the center one for the gods; the left for the emperor; and the right for the empress and court officials. Originally the three roofs of the structure were of different colors: the top was blue, suggesting Heaven; the middle was yellow, the color of the emperor; and the lowest was green, indicating commoners or the earth. Later all three roofs were painted blue.

Visual Source 13.1 The Hall of Prayer for Good Harvest at the Temple of Heaven, Beijing, China (AP Images)

- Which symbolic features can you identify in Visual Source 13.1?

- What did the original color scheme of the roofs suggest?

- What was the role of the emperor within the Temple of Heaven and in the larger religious or cosmological framework of Chinese thinking?

- What impressions or understandings might those who observed the ceremonies or learned about them take away from that experience?

About the same time as the Temple of Heaven was taking shape in China, another sacred site was under construction in Kyoto, Japan: a Buddhist temple known as Kinkakuji, or the "Temple of the Golden Pavilion" (Visual Source 13.2). Like the Chinese structure, Kinkakuji was a project of the Japanese ruler of the time, the *shogun* (military leader) Yoshimitsu Ashikaga (1358–1408), rather than the emperor. Unlike his Chinese counterpart, the Japanese emperor functioned more as a symbol of Japan's historical tradition rather than its effective ruler. Initially, Kinkakuji was constructed as part of a villa to which Yoshimitsu retired when he gave up his formal political role in 1394 to devote himself to Buddhist practice and the arts. After his death it was converted into a Zen Buddhist temple, as he had wished.

The building itself reflects the strong influence of Chinese culture on Japan. Yoshimitsu, well known as a lover of all things Chinese, modeled Kinkakuji on the lakeside villas of earlier Chinese emperors and collected in the Golden Pavilion thousands of Chinese paintings. He also accepted the title "King of Japan" from a Ming dynasty emperor and reopened trade relations with China.

As a Buddhist temple, Kinkakuji is situated in a garden setting at the edge of a "mirror lake," suggesting, some have said, a position between heaven and earth. The lake contained a series of rocks and small islands representing the eight oceans and nine mountains of the Buddhist creation story. Inside were statues of the Amida Buddha, the benevolent bodhisattva of compassion known as Kannon, and dozens of other sacred figures. It also became known as one of the few Buddhist temples housing relics of the historical Buddha himself.

While Buddhism has a reputation as a religion of peace and tranquillity, in Japan from the tenth century on, various Buddhist sects organized private armies, fought among themselves, and contested both imperial and samurai authorities. Kinkakuji itself was burned several times in the fifteenth century amid the wars that racked Japan and left Kyoto in ruins.

- How might you compare the purposes that Kinkakuji served with those of the Temple of Heaven?

Thus, while the Dome of the Rock physically occupied an already sacred site in Jerusalem, the rock churches of Lalibela sought to symbolically re-create the Holy City in the highlands of Ethiopia. They have been both a monastic site and a pilgrimage destination ever since.

These belowground churches represent an enormously impressive architectural achievement, said by local people to have been assisted by angels. But well before the coming of Christianity, the local Agaw-speaking people had long incorporated rock shrines into their religious practice. And the architecture of the churches shows a clear connection to earlier Axumite styles.

While this sacred site clearly had indigenous roots, these churches were certainly distinctive as Christian structures. Unlike almost all other religious architecture—Christian or otherwise—they were virtually invisible from a distance, becoming apparent only when the observer was looking down on them from ground level. In fact these eleven churches were not really constructed at all, but rather excavated, using only hammers and chisels. Underground, they were connected to one another by a series of "hidden tunnels, dark twisting passages, and secret chambers," while the whole complex abounded with "columns and arches, shafts and galleries, courts and terraces."[23] The first European observer to see them, the Portuguese priest Francisco Alvarez in the 1520s, was stunned. "I weary of writing more about these buildings," he declared, "because it seems to me that I shall not be believed if I write more."[24] Visual Source 13.4 shows one of these structures, the Church of St. George, the patron saint of Ethiopia.

■ How might our imaginary traveler, a pilgrim who had toured the grand Christian cathedrals of Europe, have responded to these Ethiopian churches? How might he or she understand their belowground construction? What might strike such a traveler as distinctive about Lalibela as a sacred site in comparison to the others presented here?

■ What do these churches disclose about the outlook of the Zagwe monarchs who ordered their creation?

■ What might you infer about the labor and social organization required to create these churches?

Using the Evidence:
Sacred Places in the World of the Fifteenth Century

1. **Comparing experiences of the sacred:** What do these visual sources and the documents for this chapter (see pp. 601–07) suggest about the experience of the sacred? What common features and what differences

characterize that experience? In particular, how might our global traveler have responded to sacred places among the Aztecs after visiting the various sites shown here?

2. **Considering the construction of the sacred:** What historical circumstances and what motivations contributed to the creation of each site? What factors rendered them holy in the eyes of believers? What evidence of cultural borrowing can you see in these sites?

3. **Defining purpose:** How would you compare the purposes for which each of these sacred places was intended?

4. **Thinking about religion and politics:** In what ways were these sacred sites embedded in the political circumstances of their societies? How might people of the fifteenth century have understood the connection between the religious and the political as evidenced in these images? To what extent did those understandings differ from more modern views?

Notes

Prologue

1. Adapted from Carl Sagan, *The Dragons of Eden* (New York: Random House, 1977), 13–17.
2. See David Christian, *Maps of Time* (Berkeley: University of California Press, 2004).
3. Voltaire, *Treatise on Toleration*, chap. 22.
4. See David Christian, "World History in Context," *Journal of World History* 14, no. 4 (December 2003), 437–58.

Part One

Chapter 1

1. Richard Rainsford, "What Chance, the Survival Prospects of East Africa's Last Hunting and Gathering Tribe," 1997, http://www.ntz.info/gen/n00757.html.
2. What follows comes from Sally McBreatry and Alison S. Brooks, "The Revolution That Wasn't: A New Interpretation of the Origin of Modern Human Behavior," *Journal of Human Evolution* 39 (2000): 453–563.
3. Peter Bogucki, *The Origins of Human Society* (Oxford: Blackwell, 1999), 94–95.
4. Paul G. Bahn and Jean Vertut, *Images of the Ice Age* (New York: Facts on File, 1988), chap. 7.
5. John Mulvaney and Johan Kaminga, *Prehistory of Australia* (Washington, D.C.: Smithsonian Institution Press, 1999), 93–102.
6. For a recent summary of this debate, see Charles C. Mann, *1491: New Revelations of the Americas before Columbus* (New York: Alfred Knopf, 2005), chap. 5.
7. Brian M. Fagan, *Ancient North America* (London: Thames and Hudson, 1995), 77–87.
8. Ben Finney, "The Other One-Third of the Globe," *Journal of World History* 5, no. 2 (Fall 1994): 273–85.
9. David Christian, *Maps of Time* (Berkeley: University of California Press, 2004), 143.
10. Richard B. Lee, *The Dobe Ju/'hoansi* (New York: Harcourt Brace, 1993), 58.
11. J. C. Beaglehole, *The Journals of Captain James Cook* (Cambridge: Hakluyt Society, 1968), 1:399.
12. Inga Clendinnen, *Dancing with Strangers* (Cambridge: Cambridge University Press, 2005), 159–67.
13. Marshall Sahlins, *Stone Age Economics* (London: Tavistock, 1972), 1–39.
14. Christopher Ehret, *The Civilizations of Africa* (Charlottesville: University of Virginia Press, 2002), chap. 2.
15. Marija Gimbutas, *The Language of the Goddess* (San Francisco: HarperCollins, 1989), 316–18.
16. Derived from Christian, *Maps of Time*, 208.
17. D. Bruce Dickson, *The Dawn of Belief* (Tucson: University of Arizona Press, 1990), 210.
18. Brian Fagan, *People of the Earth* (New York: HarperCollins, 1992), 200–201.
19. Jan Platvoet, "At War with God: Ju/'hoan Curing Dances," *Journal of Religion in Africa* 29, no. 1 (1999): 5.
20. J. David Lewis-Williams, *Believing and Seeing: Symbolic Meaning in Southern San Rock Paintings* (London: Academic Press, 1981).
21. Lee, *The Dobe Ju/'hoansi*. Unless otherwise noted, all information and quotes about the Ju/'hoansi come from this book.
22. Elizabeth Marshall Thomas, *The Harmless People* (New York: Vintage Books, 1989), 180.
23. For a contemporary account of a curing dance, see Bradford Keeney, "Ropes to God: Experiencing the Bushman Spiritual Universe," *Parabola* 27, no. 3 (2002): S1–S16.
24. Platvoet, "At War with God."
25. Brian Fagan, *Before California* (New York: Rowman and Littlefield, 2003), 153–55, 341–44.
26. Jeanne E. Arnold, *The Origins of a Pacific Coast Chiefdom* (Salt Lake City: University of Utah Press, 2001), 14.
27. Chester King, "Chumash Inter-Village Economic Exchange," in *Native Californians*, edited by Lowell John Bean and Thomas C. Blackburn (Menlo Park: Ballena Press, 1976), 289–318. The quote is on p. 297.
28. http://www.lonker.net/art_aboriginal_1.htm (accessed April 1, 2009).
29. Elaine Godden and Jutta Malnic, *Rock Paintings of Aboriginal Australia* (London: New Holland Publishers, 2001), preface.

Chapter 2

1. "Population 1: The Town That's Been Reclaimed by the Prairie," *International Observer*, November 20, 2005, http://observer.guardian.co.uk/international/story/0,6903,1646659,00.html?gusrc=rss.
2. Peter Bellwood, *First Farmers* (London: Blackwood, 2005), 7.

3. Mark Nathan Cohen, *The Food Crisis in Prehistory* (New Haven: Yale University Press, 1977).

4. Bruce Smith, *The Emergence of Agriculture* (New York: Scientific American Library, 1995), 206–14.

5. Jared Diamond, *Guns, Germs, and Steel* (New York: Vintage, 1997), 132, 157–75.

6. Bellwood, *First Farmers*, 54–55.

7. Steven Mithen, *After the Ice: A Global Human History, 20,000–50,000 B.C.* (Cambridge, Mass.: Harvard University Press, 2004), 87.

8. Neil Roberts, *The Holocene: An Environmental History* (Oxford: Blackwell, 1998), 116.

9. Nina V. Federoff, "Prehistoric GM Corn," *Science* 302 (November 2003): 1158.

10. Diamond, *Gun, Germs, and Steel*, 367.

11. The most recent summary of an immense literature on the spread of languages is found in Bellwood, *First Farmers*.

12. Many of these dates are much debated. See John Staller et al., *Histories of Maize* (Boston: Academic Press, 2006).

13. John A. Mears, "Agricultural Origins in Global Perspective," in *Agricultural and Pastoral Societies in Ancient and Classical History*, edited by Michael Adas (Philadelphia: Temple University Press, 2001), 63–64.

14. Elizabeth Wayland Barber, *Women's Work: The First 20,000 Years* (New York: W. W. Norton, 1994), chap. 3.

15. Andrew Sherrat, "The Secondary Exploitation of Animals in the Old World," *World Archeology* 15, no. 1 (June 1983): 90–104.

16. Clive Ponting, *A Green History of the World* (New York: St. Martin's Press, 1991), 69.

17. Anatoly M. Khazanov, *Nomads and the Outside World* (Madison: University of Wisconsin Press, 1994), 15.

18. Ian Hodder, "Women and Men at Catalhoyuk," *Scientific American* 15, no. 1 (2005): 35–41.

19. Allen W. Johnson and Timothy Earle, *The Evolution of Human Societies* (Stanford, Calif.: Stanford University Press, 2000), 281–94.

20. Ian Hodder, "Discussions with the Goddess Community," Catalhöyük: Excavations of a Neolithic Anatolian Höyük, http://www.catalhoyuk.com/library/goddess.html (accessed April 1, 2009).

21. Ian Hodder, "A Journey to 9,000 Years Ago," January 17, 2008, http://sci.tech-archive.net/Archive/sci.archaeology/2008-01/msg00519.html (accessed April 1, 2009).

22. http://www.reuters.com/article/scienceNews/idUSLM62397220080922 (accessed April 15, 2009).

23. Reuters, "Stonehenge May Have Been Pilgrimage Site for Sick," September 22, 2008, http://uk.reuters.com/article/scienceNews/idUKTRE48M0R320080923 (accessed April 15, 2009).

Chapter 3

1. Utah Outventures, http://www.utahoutventures.com/multiactivity/raftoffroadtours.htm (accessed April 1, 2009).

2. Charles C. Mann, 1491: *New Revelations of the Americas before Columbus* (New York: Alfred A. Knopf, 2005), 174–91; Proyecto Arqueológico Norte Chico, Project Description, 2005, http://www.fieldmuseum.org/research_collections/anthropology/anthro_sites/PANC/proj_desc.htm.

3. Jonathan Mark Kenoyer, *Ancient Cities of the Indus Valley Civilization* (Oxford: Oxford University Press, 1998), 83–84.

4. For a summary of many theories, see Stephen K. Sanderson, *Social Transformations* (Oxford: Blackwell, 1995), chap. 3.

5. Robert Carneiro, "A Theory of the Origin of the State," *Science* 169 (1970): 733–38.

6. Susan Pollock, *Ancient Mesopotamia* (Cambridge: Cambridge University Press, 1999), 48.

7. *The Epic of Gilgamesh*, translated and edited by Benjamin R. Foster (New York: W. W. Norton, 2001), 10, Tablet 1:226–32.

8. Samuel Noah Kramer, *History Begins at Sumer* (Philadelphia: University of Pennsylvania Press, 1981), 3–4.

9. James Legge, trans., *The Chinese Classics* (London: Henry Frowde, 1893), 4:171–72.

10. Marija Gimbutas, *The Living Goddess* (Berkeley: University of California Press, 1999).

11. Margaret Ehrenberg, *Women in Prehistory* (London: British Museum Publications, 1989), 107.

12. David Christian, *Maps of Time* (Berkeley: University of California Press, 2004), 256–57, 263–64.

13. Sherry Ortner, "Is Female to Male as Nature Is to Culture?" in *Women, Culture, and Society*, edited by Michelle Rosaldo and Louise Lamphere (Stanford, Calif.: Stanford University Press, 1974), 67–88.

14. Gerda Lerner, *The Creation of Patriarchy* (New York: Oxford University Press, 1986), 70.

15. Miriam Lichtheim, *Ancient Egyptian Literature* (Berkeley: University of California Press, 1975), 2:184–85.

16. Ibid., 2:168–75.

17. Prologue to *The Code of Hammurabi*, http://www.wsu.edu/~dee/MESO/CODE.HTM.

18. Gary Urton, "From Knots to Narratives: Reconstructing the Art of Historical Record-Keeping in the Andes from Spanish Transcriptions of Inka Khipus," *Ethnohistory* 45, no. 3 (1998): 409–38.

19. Adolf Erman, *The Literature of the Ancient Egyptians*, translated by Aylward M. Blackman (London: Methuen, 1927), 136–37.

20. Henri Frankfort, H. A. Frankfort, John A. Wilson, and Thorkild Jacobsen *Before Philosophy: The Intellectual Adventure of Ancient Man* (Baltimore: Penguin Books, 1963), 39, 138.

21. Quoted in Peter Stearns et al., *World Civilizations* (New York: Longman, 1996), 1:30.

22. See Clive Ponting, *A Green History of the World* (New York: St. Martin's Press, 1991), chap. 5.

23. Samuel Kramer, *The Sumerians* (Chicago: University of Chicago Press, 1963), 142.

24. Cyril Aldred, *The Egyptians* (London: Thames and Hudson, 1998), 138.

25. For a recent summary of a long debate about the relationship of Egypt and Africa, see David O'Connor and Andrew Reid, eds., *Ancient Egypt in Africa* (London: UCL Press, 2003).

26. James B. Pritchard, ed., *Ancient Near Eastern Texts Relating to the Old Testament* (Princeton: Princeton University Press, 1969), 647–48.

27. Lichtheim, *Ancient Egyptian Literature*, 1:25–27.

28. Joan Oates, *Babylon* (London: Thames and Hudson, 1986), 91.

29. Marvin Harris, ed., *Cannibals and Kings* (New York: Vintage, 1978), 102.

30. Lichtheim, *Ancient Egyptian Literature*, 2:177.

31. Jonathan M. Kenoyer, *Ancient Cities of the Indus Valley Civilization* (Karachi: Oxford University Press, 1998), 84.

32. Ibid., 100.

33. Gregory L. Possehl, *The Indus Civilization: A Contemporary Perspective* (Walnut Creek, Calif.: AltaMira Press, 2002), 114.

Part Two

1. Stephen K. Sanderson, *Social Transformation* (Oxford: Blackwell, 1995), chap. 4.

2. From ibid., 103.

3. Colin Ronan and Joseph Needham, *The Shorter Science and Civilization in China* (Cambridge: Cambridge University Press, 1978), 58.

4. Sidney W. Mintz, *Sweetness and Power* (New York: Penguin Books, 1985), chap. 2.

5. William H. McNeill, *Plagues and Peoples* (New York: Doubleday, 1977), 94.

6. See world population estimates by region in Paul Adams et al., *Experiencing World History* (New York: New York University Press, 2000), 334.

Chapter 4

1. Cullen Murphy, *Are We Rome? The Fall of an Empire and the Fate of America* (Boston: Houghton Mifflin, 2007).

2. J. M. Cook, *The Persian Empire* (London: J. M. Dent & Sons, 1983), 76.

3. George Rawlinson, trans., *The Histories of Herodotus* (London: Dent, 1910), 1:131–40.

4. Erich F. Schmidt, *Persepolis I: Structures, Reliefs, Inscriptions*, OIP 68 (Chicago: University of Chicago Press, 1953), 63.

5. Quoted in Thomas R. Martin, *Ancient Greece from Prehistoric to Hellenistic Times* (New Haven: Yale University Press, 1996), 86.

6. Christian Meier, *Athens* (New York: Metropolitan Books, 1993), 93.

7. Arrian, *The Campaigns of Alexander*, translated by Aubrey de Selincourt, revised by J. R. Hamilton (London: Penguin, 1971), 395–96.

8. Stanley Burstein, *The Hellenistic Period in World History* (Washington, D.C.: American Historical Association, 1996), 12.

9. Norman F. Cantor, *Antiquity* (New York: HarperCollins, 2003), 25.

10. Greg Woolf, "Inventing Empire in Ancient Rome," in *Empires: Perspectives from Archeology and History*, edited by Susan Alcock et al. (Cambridge: Cambridge University Press, 2001), 314.

11. S. A. M. Adshead, *China in World History* (London: McMillan Press, 1988), 4–21.

12. See Padma Manian, "Harappans and Aryans: Old and New Perspectives on Ancient Indian History," *The History Teacher* 32, no. 1 (November 1998): 17–32.

13. Roger Boesche, *The First Great Political Realist: Kautilya and His Arthashastra* (Lanham, Md.: Lexington Books, 2002), 17.

14. Stanley Wolpert, *A New History of India* (New York: Oxford University Press, 1993), chap. 5.

15. Zhengyuan Fu, *Autocratic Tradition and Chinese Politics* (New York: Cambridge University Press, 1993), 188.

16. Jane Portal, ed., *The First Emperor: China's Terracotta Army* (London: The British Museum Press, 2007), 110.

17. Quoted in Anders Blixt, "Qin Shi Huang Di, 'The Tiger Emperor': The First Emperor of China," http://biphome.spray.se/coif/history/qin/shie09.html (accessed Feb. 1, 2009).

18. Portal, *First Emperor*, 21.

Chapter 5

1. S. N. Eisenstadt, ed., *The Origins and Diversity of Axial Age Civilizations* (Albany: SUNY Press, 1986), 1–4; Karen Armstrong, *The Great Transformation* (New York: Alfred A. Knopf, 2006).

2. Quoted in Arthur Waley, *Three Ways of Thought in Ancient China* (Garden City, N.Y.: Doubleday, 1956), 159–60.

3. Nancy Lee Swann, trans., *Pan Chao: Foremost Woman Scholar of China* (New York: Century, 1932), 111–14.

4. Quoted in Huston Smith, *The Illustrated World's Religions* (San Francisco: HarperCollins, 1994), 123.

5. Lao Tsu, *Tao Te Ching*, translated by Gia-Fu Feng and Jane English (New York: Vintage Books, 1972), 80.

6. George Bühler, trans., *The Laws of Manu*, 5:148, http://www.sacred-texts.com/hin/manu/manu05.htm (accessed Feb. 1, 2009).

7. Quoted in Karen Andrews, "Women in Theravada Buddhism," http://www.enabling.org/ia/vipassana/Archive/A/Andrews/womenTheraBudAndrews.html (accessed Feb. 1, 2009).

8. A. L. Basham, *The Wonder That Was India* (London: Sidgwick and Jackson, 1967), 309.

9. S. A. Nigosian, *The Zoroastrian Faith: Tradition and Modern Research* (Montreal: McGill–Queen's University Press, 1993), 95–97.

10. Isaiah 1:11–17.

11. Plato, *Apologia*.

12. Hippocrates, *On the Sacred Disease*, http://classics.mit.edu/Hippocrates/sacred.html.

13. Thanissaro Bhikkhu, trans., "Karaniya Metta Sutta, 2004," http://www.accesstoinsight.org/tipitaka/kn/snp/snp.1.08.than.html (accessed Feb. 1, 2009).

14. Matthew 5:43–44.

15. See Marcus Borg, ed., *Jesus and Buddha: The Parallel Sayings* (Berkeley, Calif.: Ulysses Press, 1997).

16. For a popular summary of the voluminous scholarship on Jesus, see Stephen Patterson et al., *The Search for Jesus: Modern Scholarship Looks at the Gospels* (Washington, D.C.: Biblical Archeological Society, 1994).

17. Galatians 3:28.

18. Ephesians 5:22; 1 Corinthians 14:35.

19. Ekkehard W. Stegemann and Wolfgang Stegemann, *The Jesus Movement: A History of Its First Century* (Minneapolis: Fortress Press, 1999), 291–96.

20. Ramsay MacMullen, *Christianizing the Roman Empire* (New Haven: Yale University Press, 1984), chap. 4.

21. Peter Brown, *The Rise of Western Christendom* (London: Blackwell, 2003), 69–71.

22. Mary Ann Rossi, "Priesthood, Precedent, and Prejudice: On Recovering the Women Priests of Early Christianity," *Journal of Feminist Studies* 7, no. 1 (1991): 73–94.

23. Chai-Shin Yu, *Early Buddhism and Christianity* (Delhi: Motilal Banarsidass, 1981), 211.

24. "Footprints of the Buddha," http://www.sacred-texts.com/shi/igj/igj09.htm.

Chapter 6

1. Po Chu-I, "After Passing the Examination," in Arthur Waley, *More Translations from the Chinese* (New York: Alfred A. Knopf, 1919), 37.

2. Quoted in Michael Lowe, *Everyday Life in Early Imperial China* (New York: Dorset, 1968), 38.

3. Selected Poems from Tang Dynasty: http://shixuewang.com/xlib/lingshidao/hanshi/tang1.htm.

4. A. L. Basham, *The Wonder That Was India* (London: Sidgwick and Jackson, 1967), 138.

5. Karl Jacoby, "Slaves by Nature: Animals and Human Slaves," *Slavery and Abolition* 15 (1994): 89–97.

6. Orlando Patterson, *Slavery and Social Death* (Cambridge, Mass.: Harvard University Press, 1982).

7. Basham, *The Wonder That Was India*, 152.

8. Sarah Pomeroy et al., *Ancient Greece* (New York: Oxford University Press, 1999), 63, 239.

9. R. Zelnick-Abramovitz, *Not Wholly Free* (Leiden: Brill, 2005), 337, 343.

10. Keith Bradley, *Slavery and Society at Rome* (Cambridge: Cambridge University Press, 1994), 30.

11. 1 Peter 2:18.

12. Milton Meltzer, *Slavery: A World History* (New York: Da Capo Press, 1993), 189.

13. Quoted in Bret Hinsch, *Women in Early Imperial China* (Oxford: Rowman and Littlefield, 2002), 155.

14. Nancy Lee Swann, trans., *Pan Chao: Foremost Woman Scholar of China* (New York: Century, 1932), 111–14.

15. Lisa Raphals, *Sharing the Light: Representations of Women and Virtue in Early China* (Albany: SUNY Press, 1998).

16. Valerie Hansen, *The Open Empire* (New York: Norton, 2000), 183–84; Thomas Barfield, *The Perilous Frontier* (Cambridge: Blackwell, 1989), 140.

17. Vivian-Lee Nyitray, "Confucian Complexities," in *A Companion to Gender History* edited by Teresa A. Meade and Merry E. Weisner-Hanks (Oxford: Blackwell, 2004), 278.

18. Aristotle, *Politica*, ed. Loeb Classical Library, 1254b10–14.

19. Quoted in Pomeroy et al., *Ancient Greece*, 146.

20. "The Destruction of Pompeii, 79 AD," EyeWitness to History, www.eyewitnesstohistory.com/pompeii.htm (accessed April 1, 2009).

21. August Mau, *Pompeii: Its Life and Art* (New Rochelle: Caratzas Brothers, 1982), 16.

22. "Graffiti from Pompeii," http://www.pompeiana.org/Resources/Ancient/Graffiti%20from%20Pompeii.htm (accessed April 1, 2009).

Chapter 7

1. Rethinking Schools *Online*, Fall 1999, http://www.rethinkingschools.org/archive/14_01/poor141.shtml.

2. Thomas Benjamin, "A Time of Reconquest: History, the Maya Revival, and the Zapatista Rebellion in Chiapas," *American Historical Review* 105, no. 2 (April 2000): 417.

3. Population figures are taken from Paul Adams et al., *Experiencing World History* (New York: New York University Press, 2000), 334.

4. Roderick J. McIntosh, *Ancient Middle Niger* (Cambridge: Cambridge University Press, 2005), 10.

5. Roderick J. McIntosh, *The Peoples of the Middle Niger* (Oxford: Blackwell, 1998), 177.

6. Kairn A. Klieman, *"The Pygmies Were Our Compass": Bantu and Batwa in the History of West Central Africa, Early Times to C. 1900 C.E.* (Portsmouth, N.H.: Heinemann, 2003), chaps. 4, 5.

7. Christopher Ehret, *The Civilizations of Africa* (Charlottesville: University of Virginia Press, 2002), 175.

8. See Jan Vansina, *Paths in the Rainforest* (Madison: University of Wisconsin Press, 1990), 95–99.

9. Richard E. W. Adams, *Prehistoric Mesoamerica* (Norman: University of Oklahoma Press, 2005), 16.

10. Richard E. W. Adams, *Ancient Civilizations of the New World* (Boulder, Colo.: Westview Press, 1997), 53–56; T. Patrick Culbert, "The New Maya," Archeology 51, no. 5 (September–October 1998): 47–51.

11. William Haviland, "State and Power in Classic Maya Society," *American Anthropologist* 94, no. 4 (1992):937.

12. Jared Diamond, *Collapse: How Societies Choose to Fail or Succeed* (New York: Viking, 2005), chap. 5.

13. Esther Pasztory, *Teotihuacan: An Experiment in Living* (Norman: University of Oklahoma Press, 1997), 193.

14. George L. Cowgill, "The Central Mexican Highlands . . . ," in *The Cambridge History of the Native Peoples of the Americas*, vol. 2, part 1, Mesoamerica, edited by Richard E. W. Adams and Murdo J. MacLeod (Cambridge: Cambridge University Press, 2000), 289.

15. Karen Olsen Bruhns, *Ancient South America* (Cambridge: Cambridge University Press, 1994), 126–41; Sylvia R. Kembel and John W. Rick, "Building Authority at Chavín de Huántar," in *Andean Archeology*, edited by Helaine Silverman (Oxford: Blackwell, 2004), 59–76.

16. Garth Bawden, *The Moche* (Oxford: Blackwell, 1996), chaps. 9, 10.

17. John E. Kicza, *The Peoples and Civilizations of the Americas before Contact* (Washington, D.C.: American Historical Association, 1998), 43–44.

18. Much of this section draws on Brian M. Fagan, *Ancient North America* (London: Thames and Hudson, 2005), chaps. 14, 15. The quote is on p. 345.

19. George R. Milner, *The Moundbuilders: Ancient Peoples of Eastern North America* (London: Thames and Hudson, 2004).

20. David Hurst Thomas, *Exploring Ancient Native America* (New York: Routledge, 1999), 137–42.

21. Stephen H. Lekson and Peter N. Peregrine, "A Continental Perspective for North American Archeology," *The SAA Archeological Record* 4, no. 1 (January 2004): 15–19.

22. Fagan, *Ancient North America*, 475.

23. Quoted in Lynda Norene Shaffer, *Native Americans before 1492* (Armonk, N.Y.: M. E. Sharpe, 1992), 70.

24. See Stanley Burstein, *Ancient African Civilizations: Kush and Axum* (Princeton: Markus Weiner Publishers, 1998), 14–20. I am grateful to Professor Burstein and this book for references to many of the documents in this section.

25. Mary Ellen Miller, *Maya Art and Architecture* (London: Thames & Hudson, 1999), 8–11.

26. Linda Schele and Mary Ellen Miller, *The Blood of Kings* (London: Thames & Hudson, 1992), 176.

27. Mary Miller and Simon Martin, *Courtly Art of the Ancient Maya* (New York: Thames & Hudson, 2004), 63.

Part Three

1. Marshall G. S. Hodgson, *The Venture of Islam* (Chicago: University of Chicago Press, 1974), 1:71.

2. Lynda Shaffer, "Southernization," *Journal of World History* 5, no. 1 (Spring 1994): 7.

Chapter 8

1. Somini Sengupta, "Sahara Journal," *New York Times*, November 25, 2003.

2. Seneca the Younger, *Declamations*, vol. 1.

3. Liu Xinru, "Silks and Religion in Eurasia, A.D. 600–1200," *Journal of World History* 6, no. 1 (Spring 1995): 25–48.

4. Jerry Bentley, "Hemispheric Integration, 500–1500 C.E.," *Journal of World History* 9, no. 2 (Fall 1998): 241–44.

5. See Jerry Bentley, *Old World Encounters* (New York: Oxford University Press, 1993), 42–53, 69–84.

6. Liu Xinru, *The Silk Road* (Washington, D.C.: American Historical Association, 1998), 10.

7. See William H. McNeill, *Plagues and Peoples* (New York: Doubleday, 1977), chaps. 3, 4.

8. Boccaccio, *The Decameron*, translated by M. Rigg (London: David Campbell, 1921), 1:5–11.

9. Kenneth McPherson, *The Indian Ocean* (Oxford: Oxford University Press, 1993), 15.

10. Janet L. Abu-Lughod, *Before European Hegemony* (Oxford: Oxford University Press, 1989), 269.

11. Nigel D. Furlonge, "Revisiting the Zanj and Revisioning Revolt," *Negro History Bulletin* 62 (December 1999).

12. Patricia Risso, *Merchants and Faith: Muslim Commerce and Culture in the Indian Ocean* (Boulder, Colo.: Westview, 1995), 54.

13. McPherson, *The Indian Ocean*, 97.

14. Kenneth R. Hall, *Maritime Trade and State Development in Early Southeast Asia* (Honolulu: University of Hawaii Press, 1985), 101.

15. Lynda Norene Shaffer, *Maritime Southeast Asia to 1500* (Armonk, N.Y.: M. E. Sharpe, 1996), 37, 46.

16. M. C. Horton and T. R. Burton, "Indian Metalwork in East Africa: The Bronze Lion Statuette from Shanga," *Antiquities* 62 (1988): 22.

17. Ross Dunn, *The Adventures of Ibn Battuta* (Berkeley: University of California Press, 1986), 124.

18. Christopher Ehret, *The Civilizations of Africa* (Charlottesville: University of Virginia Press, 2002), 255.

19. Ibid., 227–32.

20. Nehemia Levtzion and Jay Spaulding, eds., *Medieval West Africa: Views from Arab Scholars and Merchants* (Princeton, N.J.: Marcus Wiener, 2003), 5.

21. Quoted in John Iliffe, *Africans: The History of a Continent* (Cambridge: Cambridge University Press, 1995), 75–76.

22. J. R. McNeill and William McNeill, *The Human Web* (New York: W. W. Norton, 2003), 160.

23. Lauren Ristvet, *In the Beginning* (New York: McGraw-Hill, 2007), 165.

24. Maria Rostworowski de Diez Canseco, *History of the Inca Realm* (Cambridge: Cambridge University Press, 1999), 209–12.

25. Michael Haederle, "Mystery of Ancient Pueblo Jars Is Solved," *New York Times*, February 4, 2009.

26. Anthony Andrews, "America's Ancient Mariners," *Natural History*, October 1991, 72–75.

27. Richard Blanton and Gary Feinman, "The Mesoamerican World System," *American Anthropologist* 86, no. 3 (September 1984): 677.

28. Li Rongxi (trans.), *A Biography of the Tripitaka Master of the Great Ci'en Monastery of the Great Tang Dynasty* (Berkeley: Numata Center for Buddhist Translation, 1995), 31.

29. For a brief account of Xuanzang's life and travels, see Stephen S. Gosch and Peter N. Stearns, *Premodern Travel in World History* (New York: Routledge, 2008), 75–101.

30. Craig Benjamin, "The Kushans in World History," *World History Bulletin*, XXV:1 (Spring 2009), 30.

31. Xinru Liu and Lynda N. Shaffer, *Connections across Eurasia* (Boston: McGraw-Hill, 2007), 56–63.

32. Quoted in David Christian, *Inner Eurasia from Prehistory to the Mongol Empire* (Oxford: Blackwell Publishers, 1998), 267.

33. Hans-Joachim Klimkeit, *Manichaean Art and Calligraphy* (Leiden: E. J. Brill, 1982), 38

34. Carter Findley, *The Turks in World History* (Oxford: Oxford University Press, 2005), 61–64.

35. Bahodir Sidikov, "Sufism and Shamanism" in Eva Fridman and Mariko Walter (eds), *Shamanism* (ABC-Clio, 2004), 241.

Chapter 9

1. *The Guardian*, June 15, 2006.

2. John K. Fairbank, ed., *The Chinese World Order* (Cambridge, Mass.: Harvard University Press, 1968).

3. Quoted in Mark Elvin, *The Retreat of the Elephants* (New Haven: Yale University Press, 2004), chap. 1. The quote is on p. 19.

4. Mark Elvin, *The Pattern of the Chinese Past* (London: Eyre Methuen, 1973), 55.

5. Samuel Adshead, *T'ang China: The Rise of the East in World History* (New York: Palgrave, 2004), 30.

6. Elvin, *The Pattern of the Chinese Past*, part 2; William McNeill, *The Pursuit of Power* (Chicago: University of Chicago Press, 1984), 50.

7. See "The Attractions of the Capital," in *Chinese Civilization: A Sourcebook* edited by Patricia B. Ebrey (New York: Free Press, 1993), 178–85.

8. Marco Polo, "The Glories of Kinsay," *Medieval Sourcebook*, http://www.fordham.edu/halsall/source/polo-kinsay.html.

9. John K. Fairbank, *China: A New History* (Cambridge, Mass.: Harvard University Press, 1992), 89.

10. J. R. McNeill and William H. McNeill, *The Human Web* (New York: W. W. Norton, 2003), 123.

11. Francesca Bray, *Technology and Gender: Fabrics of Power in Late Imperial China* (Berkeley: University of California Press, 1997), 116.

12. Patricia Ebrey, *The Inner Quarters* (Berkeley: University of California Press, 1993), 207.

13. Ibid., 37–43.

14. Ibid., 6.

15. See Nicolas DiCosmo, *Ancient China and Its Enemies* (Cambridge: Cambridge University Press, 2002), chap. 6.

16. Ibid., 94.

17. Quoted in Thomas J. Barfield, "Steppe Empires, China, and the Silk Route," in *Nomads in the Sedentary World*, edited by Anatoly M. Khazanov and Andre Wink (Richmond: Kurzon Press, 2001), 237.

18. Quoted in Edward H. Shafer, *The Golden Peaches of Samarkand* (Berkeley: University of California Press, 1963), 28.

19. Susan Mann, "Women in East Asia," in *Women's History in Global Perspective*, edited by Bonnie Smith (Urbana: University of Illinois Press, 2005), 2:53–56.

20. Joseph Buttinger, *A Dragon Defiant: A Short History of Vietnam* (New York: Praeger, 1972), 32–34; Jerry Bentley, *Old World Encounters* (New York: Oxford University Press, 1993), 85–86.

21. Cited in "Trung Trac and Trung Nhi," http://www.viettouch .com/trungsis.

22. Liam C. Kelley, *Beyond the Bronze Pillars: Envoy Poetry and the Sino-Vietnamese Relationship* (Honolulu: University of Hawai'i Press, 2005).

23. H. Paul Varley, "Japan, 550–838," in *Asia in Western and World History*, edited by Ainslee T. Embrey and Carol Gluck (Armonk, N.Y.: M. E. Sharpe, 1997), 353.

24. Quoted in McNeill, *The Pursuit of Power*, 40.

25. John K. Fairbank et al., *East Asia: Tradition and Transformation* (Boston: Houghton Mifflin, 1978), 353.

26. Arnold Pacey, *Technology in World Civilization* (Cambridge, Mass.: MIT Press, 1991), 50–53.

27. McNeill, *The Pursuit of Power*, 24–25.

28. Hugh Clark, "Muslims and Hindus in the Culture and Morphology of Quanzhou from the Tenth to the Thirteenth Century," *Journal of World History* 6, no. 1 (Spring 1995): 49–74.

29. Quoted in Arthur F. Wright, *Studies in Chinese Buddhism* (New Haven: Yale University Press, 1990), 16.

30. Arthur F. Wright, *Buddhism in Chinese History* (Stanford, Calif.: Stanford University Press, 1959), 36–39.

31. Quoted in Wright, *Buddhism in Chinese History*, 67.

32. Quoted in Eric Zurcher, *The Buddhist Conquest of China* (Leiden: E. J. Brill, 1959), 1:262.

33. Jacquet Gernet, *A History of Chinese Civilization* (Cambridge: Cambridge University Press, 1996), 291–96.

34. Edwin O. Reischauer, *Ennin's Travels in T'ang China* (New York: Ronald Press, 1955), 221–24.

35. William Theodore de Bary et al., *Sources of Japanese Tradition* (New York: Columbia University Press, 2001), 1:42.

36. Kenneth Henshall, *A History of Japan* (New York: Palgrave Macmillan, 2004), 17.

37. Donald Keene, *Seeds in the Heart* (New York: Henry Holt, 1993), 477–78.

38. Quoted in China History Forum, http://www.chinahistoryforum.com/index.php ?showtopic=17789&st=30&start=30.

39. I Lo-fen, "Dialogue Between the 'Fatuous Emperor' and the 'Treacherous Minister': Song Hui Zong's 'Literary Gathering' Painting (Wen-Hui Tu) and Its Poetic Inscriptions," *Literature and Philosophy* 8 (June 2006): 253–78.

40. Quoted at Charles Hartman's site for SUNY–Albany students in his Chinese Painting course, http://www.albany .edu/faculty/hartman/eac280/25.html.

Chapter 10

1. "East and West Churches Reconcile," http://chi.gospelcom .net/DAILYF/2002/12/daily-12-07-2002.shtml.

2. Paul R. Spickard and Kevin M. Cragg, *A Global History of Christians* (Grand Rapids, Mich.: Baker Academic, 1994), chap. 6.

3. Leonora Neville, *Authority in Byzantine Provincial Society, 950–1100* (Cambridge: Cambridge University Press, 2004), 2.

4. Quoted in Deno John Geanakoplos, *Byzantium: Church, Society, and Civilization Seen through Contemporary Eyes* (Chicago: University of Chicago Press, 1984), 389.

5. Quoted in ibid., 143.

6. Quoted in A. A. Vasiliev, *History of the Byzantine Empire* (Madison: University of Wisconsin Press, 1978), 79–80.

7. Quoted in Geanakoplos, *Byzantium*, 362.

8. Quoted in ibid., 369.

9. Rowena Loverance, *Byzantium* (Cambridge, Mass.: Harvard University Press, 2004), 43.

10. Daniel H. Kaiser and Gary Marker, *Reinterpreting Russian History* (Oxford: Oxford University Press, 1994), 63–67.

11. Quoted in Patrick J. Geary, *Before France and Germany* (New York: Oxford University Press, 1988), 79.

12. Quoted in Stephen Williams, *Diocletian and the Roman Recovery* (London: Routledge, 1996), 218.

13. Peter Brown, *The Rise of Western Christendom* (London: Blackwell, 1996), 305.

14. Quoted in John M. Hobson, *The Eastern Origins of Western Civilization* (New York: Cambridge University Press, 2004), 113.

15. Clive Ponting, *A Green History of the World* (New York: St. Martin's, 1991), 121–23.

16. Christopher Tyerman, *Fighting for Christendom: Holy Wars and the Crusades* (Oxford: Oxford University Press, 2004), 16.

17. Edward Peters, "The Firanj Are Coming—Again," *Orbis* 48, no. 1 (Winter 2004), 3–17.

18. Quoted in Peter Stearns, *Western Civilization in World History* (New York: Routledge, 2003), 52.

19. Quoted in Jean Gimple, *The Medieval Machine* (New York: Holt, 1976), 178.

20. Quoted in Stuart B. Schwartz, ed., *Victors and Vanquished* (Boston: Bedford/St. Martins, 2000), 147.

21. Quoted in Carlo Cipolla, *Before the Industrial Revolution* (New York: Norton, 1976), 207.

22. Quoted in S. Lilley, *Men, Machines, and History* (New York: International, 1965), 62.

23. See Toby Huff, *The Rise of Early Modern Science* (Cambridge: Cambridge University Press, 1993).

24. Quoted in Edward Grant, *Science and Religion from Aristotle to Copernicus* (Westport, Conn.: Greenwood Press, 2004), 158.

25. Quoted in L. Thorndike, *A History of Magic and Experimental Science* (New York: Columbia University Press, 1923), 2:58.

26. Quoted in Edward Grant, *God and Reason in the Middle Ages* (Cambridge: Cambridge University Press, 2001), 70.

27. Grant, *Science and Religion*, 228–29.

28. Marcia L. Colish, *Medieval Foundations of the Western Intellectual Tradition* (New Haven: Yale University Press, 1997), 128.

29. Charles G. Herbermann, ed., *The Catholic Encyclopedia* (New York: The Encyclopedia Press, 1913), 7:668.

30. Simon Morsink, *The Power of Icons* (Ghent: Snoek, 2006), 12; Robin Cormack, *Icons* (London: The British Museum Press, 2007), 29.

Chapter 11

1. Al-Hajj Malik El-Shabazz (Malcolm X), "The Pilgrimage to Mecca," Islam Online, http://www.islamonline.net/English/hajj/2002/01/Experience/article2.shtml.

2. Reza Aslan, *No God but God* (New York: Random House, 2005), 14.

3. Quoted in Karen Armstrong, *A History of God* (New York: Ballantine Books, 1993), 146.

4. Quran 1:5.

5. Quran 3:110.

6. Quran 9:71.

7. "The Prophet's Farewell Sermon," Islam Online, http://www.islamonline.net/English/In_Depth/mohamed/1424/kharitah/article02.shtml.

8. Quoted in Patricia Crone, "The Rise of Islam in the World," in *Cambridge Illustrated History of the Islamic World*, edited by Francis Robinson (Cambridge: Cambridge University Press, 1996), 11.

9. Richard Bulliet, *Conversion to Islam in the Medieval Period* (Cambridge, Mass.: Harvard University Press, 1979), 33.

10. Nehemiah Levtzion, ed., *Conversion to Islam* (New York: Holmes and Meier, 1979), chap. 1.

11. Jerry Bentley, *Old World Encounters* (New York: Oxford University Press, 1993), 93.

12. Bernard Lewis, *Islam and the West* (New York: Oxford University Press, 1993), 157.

13. Quoted in Crone, "The Rise of Islam in the World," 14.

14. Quoted in Margaret Smith, *Readings from the Mystics of Islam* (London: Luzac, 1972), 11.

15. Aslan, *No God but God*, 201.

16. Quran 33:35.

17. Quran 4:34.

18. Quoted in Judith Tucker, "Gender and Islamic History," in *Islamic and European Expansion*, edited by Michael Adas (Philadelphia: Temple University Press, 1993), 46.

19. Nikki R. Keddie, "Women in the Middle East since the Rise of Islam," in *Women's History in Global Perspective*, edited by Bonnie G. Smith (Urbana: University of Illinois Press, 2005), 74–75.

20. Quoted in William T. de Bary, ed., *Sources of Indian Tradition* (New York: Columbia University Press, 1958), 2:355–57.

21. V. L. Menage, "The Islamization of Anatolia," in *Conversion to Islam*, edited by Nemehia Levtzion (New York: Holmes and Meier, 1979), chap. 4.

22. Ira M. Lapidus, *A History of Islamic Societies* (Cambridge: Cambridge University Press, 1988), 304–6.

23. Quoted in Keddie, "Women in the Middle East," 81.

24. Ross Dunn, *The Adventures of Ibn Battuta* (Berkeley: University of California Press, 1986), 300.

25. Jane I. Smith, "Islam and Christendom," in *The Oxford History of Islam*, edited by John L. Esposito (Oxford: Oxford University Press, 1999), 317–21.

26. Richard Eaton, "Islamic History as Global History," in *Islamic and European Expansion*, edited by Michael Adas (Philadelphia: Temple University Press, 1993), 12.

27. Francis Robinson, "Knowledge, Its Transmission and the Making of Muslim Societies," in *Cambridge Illustrated History of the Islamic World*, edited by Francis Robinson (Cambridge: Cambridge University Press, 1996), 230.

28. Janet L. Abu-Lughod, *Before European Hegemony* (Oxford: Oxford University Press, 1989), 216–24.

29. Andrew Watson, *Agricultural Innovation in the Early Islamic World* (Cambridge: Cambridge University Press, 1983); Michael Decker, "Plants and Progress: Rethinking the Islamic Agricultural Revolution," *Journal of World History* 20; no. 2 (June 2009): 187–206.

30. Arnold Pacey, *Technology in World History* (Cambridge, Mass.: MIT Press, 1991), 8, 74.

31. Robinson, "Knowledge, Its Transmission," 215.

32. Ahmad Dallal, "Science, Medicine, and Technology: The Making of a Scientific Culture," in *The Oxford History of Islam*, edited by John Esposito (Oxford: Oxford University Press, 1999), chap. 4.

33. David W. Tschanz, "The Arab Roots of European Medicine," *Aramco World*, May–June 1997, 20–31.

34. Bertold Spuler. *The Muslim World*, vol. 1, *The Age of the Caliph* (Leiden: E. J. Brill, 1960), 29.

35. Oleg Grabar, *Mostly Miniatures: An Introduction to Persian Painting* (Princeton: Princeton University Press, 2000), 2.

36. The commentary on both Visual Sources 11.1 and 11.2 draws on Oleg Grabar and Mika Natif, "Two Safavid

Paintings: An Essay in Interpretation," *Muqarnas* 18 (2001): 173–202.

Chapter 12

1. Jack Weatherford, *Genghis Khan and the Making of the Modern World* (New York: Crown, 2004), xv.

2. Data derived from Thomas J. Barfield, "Pastoral Nomadic Societies," in *Berkshire Encyclopedia of World History* (Great Barrington: Berkshire, 2005), 4:1432–37.

3. Giovanni Carpini, *The Story of the Mongols*, translated by Erik Hildinger (Boston: Braden, 1996), 54.

4. Quoted in Peter B. Golden, "Nomads and Sedentary Societies in Eurasia," in *Agricultural and Pastoral Societies in Ancient and Classical History*, edited by Michael Adas (Philadelphia: Temple University Press, 2001), 73.

5. Thomas J. Barfield, *The Nomadic Alternative* (Englewood Cliffs, N.J.: Prentice Hall, 1993), 12.

6. Anatoly Khazanov, "The Spread of World Religions in Medieval Nomadic Societies of the Eurasian Steppes," in *Nomadic Diplomacy, Destruction and Religion from the Pacific to the Adriatic*, edited by Michael Gervers and Wayne Schlepp (Toronto: Joint Center for Asia Pacific Studies, 1994), 11.

7. Quoted in Gregory Guzman, "Were the Barbarians a Negative or Positive Factor in Ancient and Medieval History?" *The Historian* 50 (August 1988): 558–72.

8. Carter Finley, *The Turks in World History* (Oxford: Oxford University Press, 2005), 28–37.

9. Ibid., 40.

10. Thomas Spear and Richard Waller, eds., *Being Maasai* (London: James Curry, 1993), 6, 12.

11. Richard Waller, ""Ecology, Migration, and Expansion in East Africa," *African Affairs* 84 (1985): 347–70; Thomas Spear, *Kenya's Past* (London: Longman, 1981), 107.

12. Godfrey Muriuki, *A History of the Kikuyu* (Nairobi: Oxford University Press, 1974), chap. 4.

13. David Christian, *A History of Russia, Central Asia, and Mongolia* (London: Blackwell, 1998), 1:385.

14. Quoted in ibid., 389.

15. David Morgan, *The Mongols* (Oxford: Blackwell, 1986), 63–67.

16. Weatherford, *Genghis Khan*, 86.

17. Chinggis Khan, "Letter to Changchun" in E. Bretschneider, *Mediaeval Researches from Eastern Asiatic Sources* (London: Kegan, Paul, Trench, Trübner, 1875), 37–39.

18. Thomas T. Allsen, *Mongol Imperialism* (Berkeley: University of California Press, 1987), 6.

19. Chinggis Khan, "Letter to Changchun."

20. Quoted in Weatherford, *Genghis Khan*, 111.

21. Barfield, *The Nomadic Alternative*, 166.

22. Peter Jackson, "The Mongols and the Faith of the Conquered," in *Mongols, Turks, and Others*, edited by Reuven Amitai and Michael Biran (Leiden: Brill, 2005), 262.

23. Quoted in Christian, *A History of Russia*, 425.

24. Quoted in David Morgan, *Medieval Persia* (London: Longman, 1988), 79.

25. Morgan, *Medieval Persia*, 82.

26. Charles J. Halperin, *Russia and the Golden Horde* (Bloomington: Indiana University Press, 1985), 126.

27. Charles H. Halperin, "Russia in the Mongol Empire in Comparative Perspective," *Harvard Journal of Asiatic Studies* 43, no. 1 (June 1983): 261.

28. Quoted in Kevin Reilly, ed., *Worlds of History* (Boston: Bedford, 2004), 1:420.

29. Thomas Allsen, *Culture and Conquest in Mongol Eurasia* (Cambridge: Cambridge University Press, 2001), 211.

30. Quoted in ibid., 121.

31. John Aberth, *From the Brink of the Apocalypse* (New York: Routledge, 2000), 122–131.

32. Quoted in John Aberth, *The Black Death: The Great Mortality of 1348–1350* (Boston: Bedford/St. Martin's, 2005), 84–85.

33. Michael Dols, *The Black Death in the Middle East* (Princeton: Princeton University Press, 1977), 212, 223.

34. Quoted in John Aberth, *A Knight at the Movies: Medieval History on Film* (New York: Routledge, 2003), 225.

35. Aberth, *The Black Death*, 72.

36. Quoted in Dols, *The Black Death in the Middle East*, 67.

37. Andre Gunder Frank, *ReOrient* (Berkeley: University of California Press, 1998), 256.

38. Arnold Pacey, *Technology in World Civilization* (Cambridge, Mass.: MIT Press, 1990), 62.

39. Quoted in Golden, "Nomads and Sedentary Societies," 72–73.

40. Quoted in Guzman, "Were the Barbarians a Negative or Positive Factor?" 558–72.

41. Quoted in Barfield, *The Nomadic Alternative*, 3.

42. Quoted in Aberth, *The Black Death*, 99.

43. Quoted in David Herlihy, *The Black Death and the Transformation of the West* (Cambridge: Harvard University Press, 1997), 65.

44. Quoted in ibid., 62.

45. Quoted in Aberth, *The Black Death*, 79.

46. Quoted in ibid., 174.

47. "Lübeck's Dance of Death," http://www.dodedans.com/Etext2.htm.

48. Quoted in Norman Cantor, *In the Wake of the Plague* (New York: The Free Press, 2001), 6.

49. Quoted in Aberth, *The Black Death*, 73–74.

Chapter 13

1. Brian Fagan, *Ancient North America* (London: Thames and Hudson, 2005), 503.

2. Quoted in Charles C. Mann, *1491: New Revelations of the Americas before Columbus* (New York: Alfred A. Knopf, 2005), 334.

3. Louise Levanthes, *When China Ruled the Seas* (New York: Simon and Schuster, 1994), 175.

4. Niccolò Machiavelli, *The Prince* (New York: New American Library, 1952), 90, 94.

5. Frank Viviano, "China's Great Armada," *National Geographic*, July 2005, 34.

6. Quoted in John J. Saunders, ed., *The Muslim World on the Eve of Europe's Expansion* (Englewood Cliffs, N.J.: Prentice Hall, 1966), 41–43.

7. Leo Africanus, *History and Description of Africa* (London: Hakluyt Society, 1896), 824–25.

8. Quoted in Craig A. Lockhard, *Southeast Asia in World History* (Oxford: Oxford University Press, 2009), 67.

9. Quoted in Patricia Risso, *Merchants and Faith* (Boulder, Colo.: Westview Press, 1995), 49.

10. Quoted in Stuart B. Schwartz, ed., *Victors and Vanquished* (Boston: Bedford/St. Martin's, 2000), 8.

11. Quoted in Michael E. Smith, *The Aztecs* (London: Blackwell, 2003), 108.

12. Smith, *The Aztecs*, 220.

13. Miguel Leon-Portilla, *Aztec Thought and Culture*, translated from the Spanish by Jack Emory Davis (Norman: University of Oklahoma Press, 1963), 7; Miguel Leon-Portilla, *Fifteen Poets of the Aztec World* (Norman: University of Oklahoma Press, 1992), 80–81.

14. Terence N. D'Altroy, *The Incas* (London: Blackwell, 2002), chaps. 11, 12.

15. For a summary of this practice among the Aztecs and Incas, see Karen Vieira Powers, *Women in the Crucible of Conquest* (Albuquerque: University of New Mexico Press, 2005), chap. 1.

16. Ibid., 25.

17. Louise Burkhart, "Mexica Women on the Home Front," in *Indian Women of Early Mexico*, edited by Susan Schroeder et al. (Norman: University of Oklahoma Press, 1997), 25–54.

18. The "web" metaphor is derived from J. R. McNeill and William H. McNeill, *The Human Web* (New York: W. W. Norton, 2003).

19. Graph from David Christian, *Map of Time* (Berkeley: University of California Press, 2004), 343.

20. Andrew Spicer and Sarah Hamilton, eds., *Defining the Holy: Sacred Space in Medieval and Early Modern Europe* (Farnham, U.K.: Ashgate Publishing, 2006), Chap. 1.

21. Oleg Grabar, "The Umayyad Dome of the Rock in Jerusalem," in Eva R. Hoffman, ed., *Late Antique and Medieval Art of the Mediterranean World* (London: John Wiley and Sons, 2007), 166.

22. Ibid., 161.

23. Trudy Ring, ed., *International Dictionary of Historic Places*, vol. 4, *Middle East and Africa* (Chicago: Fitzroy Dearborn, 1994–96), 444.

24. Francisco Alvarez, *The Prester John of the Indies* (Cambridge: Hakluyt Society, 1961), 226.

Acknowledgments

Chapter 3

Benjamin R. Foster. "Come then, Enkidu, to ramparted Uruk." Excerpt (7 lines) from *The Epic of Gilgamesh*, translated by Benjamin R. Foster, p. 10. Tablet 1: 226–232. Copyright © 2001 by W. W. Norton & Company. Used by permission of W. W. Norton & Company, Inc.

Miriam Lichtheim. "Seven days to yesterday, I have not seen the 'sister.'" As appears in *Ancient Egyptian Literature*, volume 2, pp. 184–185 by Miriam Lichtheim, translator. Copyright © 1976 by University of California Press. Reproduced with permission of University of California Press, in the format Textbook via Copyright Clearance Center.

Miriam Lichtheim. "Now the scribe lands on the shore." From *Ancient Egyptian Literature*, volume 2, translated by Miriam Lichtheim, pp. 168–175. As appears in *A Book of Readings: the New Kingdom* by Miriam Lichtheim, translator. Copyright © 1976 by University of California Press. Reproduced with permission of University of California Press, in the format textbook via Copyright Clearance Center.

N. K. Sandars. "You will never find that life for which you are looking…." Excerpts from *The Epic of Gilgamesh*, translated with an introduction by N. K. Sandars (Penguin Classics 1960, Third Edition 1972). Copyright © N.K. Sandars, 1960, 1964, 1972. Reproduced by permission of Penguin Books, Ltd.

Miriam Lichtheim. "The gatekeeper comes out to you." From *Ancient Egyptian Literature*, volume 2, translated by Miriam Lichtheim, pp. 124–126. As appears in *A Book of Readings: the New Kingdom* by Miriam Lichtheim, translator. Copyright © 1976 by University of California Press. Reproduced with permission of University of California Press, in the format textbook via Copyright Clearance Center.

Samuel Kramer. "After your city had been destroyed, how now can you exist!" From *The Sumerians*, translated by Samuel Kramer, p. 142. Copyright © 1963 by University of Chicago Press. Used by permission of University of Chicago Press.

Samuel Kramer. "In those days the dwellings of Agade were filled with gold." Translated by Samuel Kramer. As appears in *Ancient Near Eastern Texts Relating to the Old Testament* by James Pritchard, ed., pp. 647–648. Copyright © 1969 Princeton University Press. Used by permission of Princeton University Press.

Chapter 5

Lao Tsu. "A small country has few people." From *Tao Te Ching* by Lau Tsu, translated by Gia-Fu Feng and Jane English, p. 80. Copyright © 1972 by Gia-Fu Feng and Jane English. Translation copyright © 1997 by Jane English. Used by permission of Alfred A. Knopf, a division of Random House, Inc.

Sappho. "If you will come, I shall put out new pillows for you to rest on." From *Sappho: A New Translation* by Mary Bernard, translator. Copyright © 1958 by University of California Press. Reproduced with permission of University of California Press, in the format Textbook via Copyright Clearance Center.

Ovid. "Add gifts of mind to bodily language…." From *The Art of Love and Other Poems*, translated by H. H. Mozley. Published by William Heinemann, 1929, pp. 73, 75.

Chapter 9

Yuan Chen. "Ever since the Western horsemen began raising smut and dust." Quoted in *The Golden Peaches of Samarkand: A Study of T'ang Exotics*, by Edward H. Shafer, translator. Copyright © 1963 by University of California Press. Reproduced by permission of University of California Press in the format Textbook via Copyright Clearance Center.

Chapter 11

Visual Source 11.1. Attributed to Mir Sayyid 'Ali, *Nomadic Encampment*, folio from a manuscript of the *Khamsa* (quintet) of Nizami, mid-16th century. Opaque watercolor, gold, and silver on paper, 28.4 x 20 cm. Harvard Art Museum, Arthur M. Sackler Museum, Gift of John Goelet, formerly in the collection of Louis J. Cartier, 1958.75. Photo: Katya Kallsen. © President and Fellows of Harvard College.

Visual Source 11.2. Attributed to Mir Sayyid 'Ali, *Nighttime in a Palace*, folio from a manuscript, c. 1539–1543. Opaque watercolor, gold, and silver on paper; 28.6 x 20 cm. Harvard Art Museum, Arthur M. Sackler Museum, Gift of John Goelet, formerly in the collection of Louis J. Cartier, 1958.76. Photo: Katya Kallsen. © President and Fellows of Harvard College.

Chapter 13

Miguel Leon-Portilla. "Like a painting, we will be erased." From *Fifteen Poets of the Aztec World* by Miguel Leon-Portilla, editor and translator. Copyright © 1992 by the University of Oklahoma Press, Norman. Reprinted by permission.

Index

Note: Names of individuals are in **boldface** and: (f) figures, including charts and graphs; (i) illustrations, including photographs and artifacts in the narrative portion of the book only, not in the docutext sections; (m) maps; (t) tables; (v) visual sources, including all illustrations in the docutext portion of the book; (d) documents in the docutext portion of the book

demanded an oath of allegiance by which native peoples swore "eternal submission to the grand tsar," the monarch of the Russian Empire. They also demanded *yasak*, or "tribute," paid in cash or in kind. In Siberia, this meant enormous quantities of furs, especially the extremely valuable sable, which Siberian peoples were compelled to produce. As in the Americas, devastating epidemics accompanied conquest, particularly in the more remote regions of Siberia, where local people had little immunity to smallpox or measles. Also accompanying conquest was an intermittent pressure to convert to Christianity. Tax breaks, exemptions from paying tribute, and the promise of land or cash provided incentives for conversion, while the destruction of many mosques and the forced resettlement of Muslims added to the pressures. Yet the Russian state did not pursue conversion with the single-minded intensity that Spanish authorities exercised in Latin America, particularly if missionary activity threatened political and social stability. The empress Catherine the Great, for example, established religious tolerance for Muslims in the late eighteenth century and created a state agency to oversee Muslim affairs.

The most profoundly transforming feature of the Russian Empire was the influx of Russian settlers, whose numbers by the end of the eighteenth century overwhelmed native peoples, thus giving their lands a distinctively Russian character. By 1720, some 700,000 Russians lived in Siberia, thus reducing the native Siberians to 30 percent of the total population, a figure that dropped to 14 percent in the nineteenth century. The loss of hunting grounds and pasturelands to Russian agricultural settlers undermined long-standing economies and rendered local people dependent on Russian markets for grain, sugar, tea, tobacco, and alcohol. Pressures to encourage pastoralists to abandon their nomadic ways included the requirement to pay fees and to obtain permission to cross agricultural lands. Kazakh herders responded with outrage: "The grass and the water belong to Heaven, and why should we pay any fees?"[17] Intermarriage, prostitution, and sexual abuse resulted in some mixed-race offspring, but these were generally absorbed as Russians rather than identified as distinctive communities, as in Latin America.

Over the course of three centuries, both Siberia and the steppes were incorporated into the Russian state. Their native peoples were not driven into reservations or eradicated as in the

A Cossack Jail

In the vanguard of Russian expansion across Siberia were the Cossacks, bands of fiercely independent warriors consisting of peasants who had escaped serfdom as well as criminals and other adventurers. This seventeenth-century jail was part of an early Cossack settlement on the Kamchatka Peninsula at the easternmost end of Siberia. It illustrates Russian wooden architecture. (Sovfoto/Eastfoto)

Americas. Many of them, though, were Russified, adopting the Russian language and converting to Christianity, even as their traditional ways of life—hunting and herding—were much disrupted. The Russian Empire represented the final triumph of an agrarian civilization over the hunting societies of Siberia and over the pastoral peoples of the grasslands.

Russians and Empire

If the empire transformed the conquered peoples, it also fundamentally changed Russia itself. As it became a multiethnic empire, Russians diminished as a proportion of the overall population, although they remained politically dominant. Among the growing number of non-Russians in the empire, Slavic-speaking Ukrainians and Belorussians predominated, while the vast territories of Siberia and the steppes housed numerous separate peoples, but with quite small populations.[18] The wealth of empire—rich agricultural lands, valuable furs, mineral deposits—played a major role in making Russia one of the great powers of Europe by the eighteenth century, and it has enjoyed that position ever since. This European and Christian state also became an Asian power, bumping up against China, India, Persia, and the Ottoman Empire. It was on the front lines of the encounter between Christendom and the world of Islam.

This straddling of Asia and Europe was the source of a long-standing identity problem that has troubled educated Russians for 300 years. Was Russia a backward European country, destined to follow the lead of more highly developed Western European societies? Or was it different, uniquely Slavic or even Asian, shaped by its Mongol legacy and its status as an Asian power? It is a question that Russians have not completely answered even in the twenty-first century. Either way, the very size of that empire, bordering on virtually all of the great agrarian civilizations of outer Eurasia, turned Russia, like many empires before it, into a highly militarized state, "a society organized for continuous war," according to one scholar.[19] It also reinforced the highly autocratic character of the Russian Empire because such a huge state arguably required a powerful monarchy to hold its vast domains and highly diverse peoples together.

Clearly the Russians had created an empire, similar to those of Western Europe in terms of conquest, settlement, exploitation, religious conversion, and feelings of superiority. Nonetheless, the Russians had acquired their empire under different circumstances than did the Western Europeans. The Spanish and the British had conquered and colonized the New World, an ocean away and wholly unknown to them before 1492. They acquired those empires only after establishing themselves as distinct European states. The Russians, on the other hand, entered adjacent territories with which they had long interacted, and they did so *at the same time* that a modern Russian state was taking shape. "The British had an empire," wrote historian Geoffrey Hosking. "Russia *was* an empire."[20] Perhaps this helps explain the unique longevity of the Russian Empire. Whereas the Spanish, Portuguese, and British colonies in the Americas long ago achieved independence, the Russian Empire remained intact until the collapse of the Soviet Union in 1991. So thorough was Russian coloniza-tion that Siberia and much of the steppes remain still an integral part of the Russian state. But many internal administrative regions, which exercise a measure of auton-omy, reflect the continuing presence of some 160 non-Russian peoples who were earlier incorporated into the Russian Empire.

Asian Empires

Even as Europeans were building their empires in the Americas and across Siberia, other imperial projects were likewise under way. The Chinese pushed deep into cen-tral Eurasia; Turko-Mongol invaders from Central Asia created the Mughal Empire, bringing much of Hindu South Asia within a single Muslim-ruled political system; and the Ottoman Empire brought Muslim rule to a largely Christian population in southeastern Europe and Turkish rule to largely Arab populations in North Africa and the Middle East. None of these empires had the global reach or worldwide impact of Europe's American colonies; they were regional rather than global in scope. Nor did they have the same devastating and transforming impact on their conquered peoples, for those peoples were not being exposed to new diseases. Nothing remotely approaching the catastrophic population collapse of Native American peoples occurred in these Asian empires. Moreover, the process of building these empires did not trans-form the imperial homeland as fundamentally as did the wealth of the Americas and to a lesser extent Siberia for European imperial powers. Nonetheless, these expand-ing Asian empires reflected the energies and vitality of their respective civilizations in the early modern era, and they gave rise to profoundly important cross-cultural encounters, with legacies that echoed for many centuries.

Making China an Empire

In the fifteenth century, China had declined an opportunity to construct a mar-itime empire in the Indian Ocean, as Zheng He's massive fleet was withdrawn and left to wither away (see pp. 580–84). In the seventeenth and eighteenth centuries, however, China built another kind of empire on its northern and western frontiers that vastly enlarged the territorial size of the country and incorporated a number of non-Chinese peoples. Undertaking this enormous project of imperial expansion was China's Qing, or Manchu, dynasty (1644–1912). (See Document 14.1, pp. 653–54, for Chinese state building during the Qing dynasty.) Strangely enough, the Qing dynasty was itself of foreign and nomadic origin, hailing from Manchuria, north of the Great Wall. Having conquered China, the Qing rulers sought to maintain their ethnic distinctiveness by forbidding intermarriage between themselves and Chinese. Nonetheless, their ruling elites also mastered the Chinese language and Confucian teachings and used Chinese bureaucratic techniques to govern the empire.

For many centuries, the Chinese had interacted with the nomadic peoples, who inhabited the dry and lightly populated regions now known as Mongolia, Xinjiang, and Tibet. Trade, tribute, and warfare ensured that these ecologically and culturally

■ **Description**
What were the major features of Chinese empire building in the early modern era?

China's Qing Dynasty Empire

different worlds were well known to each other, quite unlike the New World "discoveries" of the Europeans. Chinese authority in the area had been intermittent and actively resisted. Then, in the early modern era, Qing dynasty China undertook an eighty-year military effort (1680–1760) that brought these huge regions solidly under Chinese control. It was largely security concerns that motivated this aggressive posture. During the late seventeenth century, the creation of a substantial state among the western Mongols, known as the Zunghars, revived Chinese memories of an earlier Mongol conquest. As in so many other cases, Chinese expansion was viewed as a defensive necessity. The eastward movement of the Russian Empire likewise appeared potentially threatening, but this danger was resolved diplomatically, rather than militarily, in the Treaty of Nerchinsk (1689), which marked the boundary between Russia and China.

Although undertaken by the non-Chinese Manchus, the Qing dynasty campaigns against the Mongols marked the evolution of China into a Central Asian empire. The Chinese, however, have seldom thought of themselves as an imperialist power. Rather they spoke of the "unification" of the peoples of central Eurasia within a Chinese state. Nonetheless, historians have seen many similarities between Chinese expansion and other cases of early modern empire building, while noting some clear differences as well.

Clearly the Qing dynasty takeover of central Eurasia was a conquest, making use of China's more powerful military technology and greater resources. Furthermore, the area was ruled separately from the rest of China through a new office called the Court of Colonial Affairs. Like other colonial powers, the Chinese made active use of local notables—Mongol aristocrats, Muslim officials, Buddhist leaders—as they attempted to govern the region as inexpensively as possible. Sometimes these native officials abused their authority, demanding extra taxes or labor service from local people and thus earning their hostility. In places, those officials imitated Chinese ways by wearing peacock feathers, decorating their hats with gold buttons, or adopting a Manchu hairstyle that was much resented by many Chinese who were forced to wear it.

More generally, however, Chinese or Qing officials did not seek to assimilate local people into Chinese culture and showed considerable respect for the Mongolian, Tibetan, and Muslim cultures of the region. People of noble rank, Buddhist monks, and those associated with monasteries were excused from the taxes and labor service required of ordinary people. Nor was the area flooded with Chinese settlers. In parts of Mongolia, for example, Qing authorities sharply restricted the entry of Chinese merchants and other immigrants in an effort to preserve the area as a source of recruitment for the Chinese military. They feared that the "soft" and civilized Chinese ways might erode the fighting spirit of the Mongols.

The long-term significance of this new Chinese imperial state was tremendous. It greatly expanded the territory of China and added a small but important minority of non-Chinese people to the empire's vast population. The borders of contemporary China are essentially those created during the Qing dynasty. Some of those peoples, particularly those in Tibet and Xinjiang, have retained their older identities and in recent decades have actively sought greater autonomy or even independence from China.

Even more important, Chinese conquests, together with the expansion of the Russian Empire, utterly transformed Central Asia. For centuries, that region had been the cosmopolitan crossroads of Eurasia, hosting the Silk Road trading network, welcoming all of the major world religions, and generating an enduring encounter between the nomads of the steppes and the farmers of settled agricultural regions. Now under Russian or Chinese rule, it became the backward and impoverished region known to nineteenth- and twentieth-century observers. Land-based commerce across Eurasia increasingly took a backseat to oceanic trade. Indebted Mongolian nobles lost their land to Chinese merchants, while nomads, no longer able to herd their animals freely, fled to urban areas, where many were reduced to begging. The incorporation of the heartland of Eurasian nomads into the Russian and Chinese empires "eliminated permanently as a major actor on the historical stage the nomadic pastoralists, who had been the strongest alternative to settled agricultural society since the second millennium B.C.E."[21] It was the end of a long era.

Muslims and Hindus in the Mughal Empire

If the creation of a Chinese imperial state in the early modern era provoked a final clash of nomadic pastoralists and settled farmers, India's Mughal Empire hosted a different kind of encounter—a further phase in the long interaction of Islamic and Hindu cultures in South Asia. That empire was the product of Central Asian warriors, who were Muslims in religion and Turkic in culture and who claimed descent from Chinggis Khan and Timur (see pp. 587–88). Their brutal conquests in the sixteenth century provided India with a rare period of relative political unity (1526–1707), as Mughal emperors exercised a fragile control over a diverse and fragmented subcontinent, which had long been divided into a bewildering variety of small states, principalities, tribes, castes, sects, and ethnolinguistic groups.

■ **Change**
How did Mughal attitudes and policies toward Hindus change from the time of Akbar to that of Aurangzeb?

The central division within Mughal India was religious. The ruling dynasty and perhaps 20 percent of the population were Muslims; most of the rest practiced some form of Hinduism. Mughal India's most famous emperor, Akbar (ruled 1556–1605), clearly recognized this fundamental reality and acted deliberately to accommodate the Hindu majority. After conquering the warrior-based and Hindu Rajputs of northwestern India, Akbar married several of their princesses but did not require them to convert to Islam. He incorporated a substantial number of Hindus into the political-military elite of the empire and supported the building of Hindu temples as well as mosques, palaces, and forts. (See Document 14.2, pp. 655–57, for Mughal state-building under Akbar and his son Jahangir.)

The Mughal Empire

In directly religious matters, Akbar imposed a policy of toleration, deliberately restraining the more militantly Islamic ulama (religious scholars) and removing the special tax (jizya) on non-Muslims. He constructed a special House of Worship where he presided over intellectual discussion with representatives of many religions—Muslim, Hindu, Christian, Buddhist, Jewish, Jain, and Zoroastrian. His son Jahangir wrote proudly of his father: "He associated with the good of every race and creed and persuasion.... The professors of various faiths had room in the broad expanse of his incomparable sway."[22] Akbar went so far as to create his own state cult, a religious faith aimed at the Mughal elite. This cult drew on Islam, Hinduism, and Zoroastrianism and emphasized loyalty to the emperor himself. The overall style of the Mughal Empire was that of a blended elite culture in which both Hindus and various Muslim groups could feel comfortable. Thus Persian artists and writers were welcomed into the empire, and the Hindu epic *Ramayana* was translated into Persian, while various Persian classics appeared in Hindi and Sanskrit. In short, Akbar and his immediate successors downplayed a distinctly Islamic identity for the Mughal Empire in favor of a cosmopolitan and hybrid Indian-Persian-Turkic culture.

Such policies fostered sharp opposition among some Muslims. The philosopher Shayk Ahmad Sirhindi (1564–1624), claiming to be a "renewer" of authentic Islam in his time, strongly objected to this cultural synthesis. The worship of saints, the sacrifice of animals, and support for Hindu religious festivals all represented impure intrusions of Sufi Islam or Hinduism that needed to be rooted out. It was the duty of Muslim rulers to impose the sharia (Islamic law), to enforce the jizya, and to remove non-Muslims from high office. This strain of Muslim thinking found a champion in the emperor Aurangzeb (1658–1707), who reversed Akbar's policy of accommodation and sought to impose Islamic supremacy. He forbade the Hindu practice of *sati*, in which a widow followed her husband to death by throwing herself on his funeral pyre. Music and dance were now banned at court, and previously tolerated vices such as gambling, drinking, prostitution, and narcotics were actively suppressed. Some Hindu temples were destroyed, and the jizya was reimposed. "Censors of public morals," posted to large cities, enforced Islamic law.

Aurangzeb's religious policies, combined with intolerable demands for taxes to support his many wars of expansion, antagonized Hindus and prompted various movements of opposition to the Mughals. "Your subjects are trampled underfoot," wrote one anonymous protester. "Every province of your empire is impoverished.... God is the God of all mankind, not the God of Mussalmans [Muslims] alone."[23] These opposition movements, some of them self-consciously Hindu, fatally fractured the Mughal Empire, especially after Aurangzeb's death in 1707, and opened the way for a British takeover in the second half of the eighteenth century.

Thus the Mughal Empire was the site of a highly significant encounter between two of the world's great religious traditions. It began with an experiment in multicultural empire building and ended in growing antagonism between Hindus and Muslims. In the centuries that followed, both elements of the Mughal experience would be repeated.

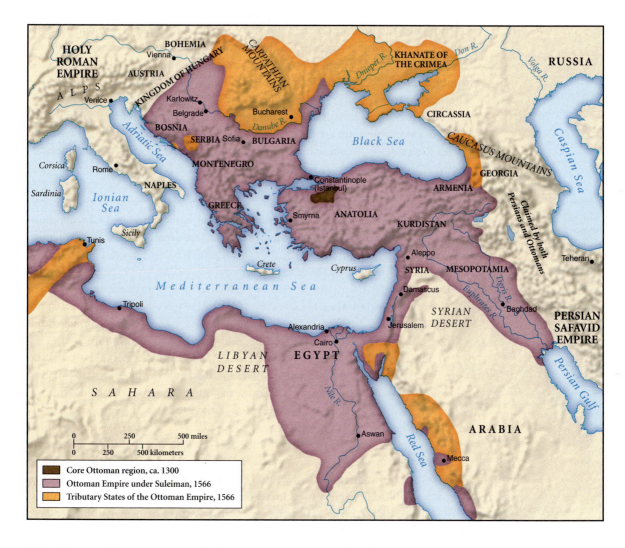

Map 14.3 The Ottoman Empire
At its high point in the mid-sixteenth century, the Ottoman Empire encompassed a vast diversity of peoples; straddled Europe, Africa, and Asia; and battled both the Austrian and Safavid empires.

Muslims, Christians, and the Ottoman Empire

Like the Mughal state, the Ottoman Empire was also the creation of Turkic warrior groups, whose aggressive raiding of agricultural civilization was now legitimized in Islamic terms. Beginning around 1300 from a base area in northwestern Anatolia, these Ottoman Turks over the next three centuries swept over much of the Middle East, North Africa, and southeastern Europe to create the Islamic world's most significant empire (see Map 14.3). During those centuries, the Ottoman state was transformed from a small frontier principality to a prosperous, powerful, cosmopolitan empire, heir to both the Byzantine Empire and to leadership within the Islamic world. Its sultan combined the roles of a Turkic warrior prince, a Muslim caliph, and a conquering emperor, bearing the "strong sword of Islam" and serving as chief defender of the faith.

Within the Islamic world, the Ottoman Empire represented the growing prominence of Turkic people, for their empire now incorporated a large number of Arabs, among whom the religion had been born. The responsibility and the prestige of protecting Mecca, Medina, and Jerusalem—the holy cities of Islam—now fell to the Ottoman Empire. A century-long conflict (1534–1639) between the Ottoman Empire, espousing the Sunni version of Islam, and the Persian Safavid Empire, holding fast to the Shia form of the faith, expressed a deep and enduring division within the Islamic world. Nonetheless, Persian culture, especially its poetry, painting, and traditions of imperial splendor, occupied a prominent position among the Ottoman elite.

■ **Significance**

In what ways was the Ottoman Empire important for Europe in the early modern era?

The Ottoman Empire, like its Mughal counterpart, was the site of a highly significant cross-cultural encounter in the early modern era, adding yet another chapter to the long-running story of interaction between the Islamic world and Christendom. As the Ottoman Empire expanded across Anatolia, its largely Christian population converted in large numbers to Islam as the Byzantine state visibly weakened and large numbers of Turks settled in the region. By 1500, some 90 percent of Anatolia's inhabitants were Muslims and Turkic speakers. The climax of this Turkic assault on the Christian world of Byzantium occurred in 1453, when Constantinople fell to the invaders. Renamed Istanbul, that splendid Christian city became the capital of the Ottoman Empire. Byzantium, heir to the glory of Rome, was no more.

In the empire's southeastern European domains, known as the Balkans, the Ottoman encounter with Christian peoples unfolded quite differently than it had in Anatolia. In the Balkans, Muslims ruled over a large Christian population, but the scarcity of Turkish settlers and the willingness of the Ottoman authorities to accommodate the region's Christian churches led to far less conversion. By the early sixteenth century, only about 19 percent of the area's people were Muslims, and 81 percent were Christians.

Many of these Christians had welcomed Ottoman conquest because taxes were lighter and oppression less pronounced than under their former Christian rulers. Christian communities such as the Eastern Orthodox and Armenian churches were granted considerable autonomy in regulating their internal social, religious, educational, and charitable affairs. A substantial number of these Christians—Balkan landlords, Greek merchants, government officials, and high-ranking clergy—became part of the Ottoman elite, without converting to Islam. Jewish refugees, fleeing Christian persecution in a Spain recently "liberated" from Islamic rule, likewise found greater opportunity in the Ottoman Empire, where they became prominent in trade and banking circles. In these ways, Ottoman dealings with the Christian and Jewish populations of their empire broadly resembled Akbar's policies toward the Hindu majority of Mughal India.

In another way, however, Turkish rule bore heavily on Christians. Through a process known as the *devshirme* (the collecting or gathering), Balkan Christian communities were required to hand over a quota of young boys, who were then removed from their families, required to learn Turkish, usually converted to Islam, and trained for either civil administration or military service in elite Janissary units. Although it was a terrible blow for families who lost their children, the *devshirme* also represented a means of upward mobility within the Ottoman Empire. Nonetheless, this social gain occurred at a high price.

Even though Ottoman authorities were relatively tolerant toward Christians within their borders, the empire itself represented an enormous threat to Christendom generally. The seizure of Constantinople, the conquest of the Balkans, Ottoman naval power in the Mediterranean, and the siege of Vienna in 1529 and again in 1683 raised anew "the specter of a Muslim takeover of all of Europe."[24] (See Document 14.3, pp. 657–59.) One European ambassador reported fearfully in 1555 from the court of the Turkish ruler Suleiman:

> He tramples the soil of Hungary with 200,000 horses, he is at the very gates of Austria, threatens the rest of Germany, and brings in his train all the nations that extend from our borders to those of Persia.[25]

Indeed, the "terror of the Turk" inspired fear across much of Europe and placed Christendom on the defensive, even as Europeans were expanding aggressively across the Atlantic and into the Indian Ocean.

The Ottoman encounter with Christian Europe spawned admiration and cooperation as well as fear and trembling. The sixteenth-century French philosopher Jean

The Ottoman Siege of Vienna, 1683
In this late-seventeenth-century painting by artist Frans Geffels, the last Ottoman incursion into the Austrian Empire was pushed back with French and Polish help, marking the end of a serious Muslim threat to Christian Europe. (Historisches Museum der Stadt Wien/Gianni Dagli Orti/The Art Archive)

Bodin praised the religious tolerance of the Ottoman sultan in contrast to Christian intolerance: "The King of the Turks who rules over a great part of Europe safeguards the rites of religion as well as any prince in this world. Yet he constrains no-one, but on the contrary permits everyone to live as his conscience dictates."[26] The French government on occasion found it useful to ally with the Ottoman Empire against their common enemy of Habsburg Austria, while European merchants willingly violated a papal ban on selling firearms to the Turks. In the early eighteenth century, the wife of an English diplomat posted to Istanbul praised the morality of Ottoman women as well as their relative freedom: "It is easy to see they have more liberty than we do."[27] Cultural encounter involved more than conflict.

Reflections: Countering Eurocentrism... or Reflecting It?

With an emphasis on empires and cross-cultural encounters, this chapter deliberately places the more familiar account of European colonization in the Americas alongside the less well-known stories of Russian, Chinese, Mughal, and Ottoman empire building. The chief purpose in doing so is to counteract a Eurocentric understanding of the early modern age, in which European initiatives dominate our view of this era. It reminds us that Western Europe was not the only center of vitality and expansion and that the interaction of culturally different peoples, so characteristic of the modern age, derived from multiple sources. How often do we notice that a European Christendom creating empires across the Atlantic was also the victim of Ottoman imperial expansion in the Balkans?

A critic of this chapter, however, might well argue that it is nonetheless a Eurocentric narrative, for it allots rather more space to the Western European empires than to the others, and it tells the European story first. What led to such an ordering of this material?

Underlying the organization of this chapter is the notion that Western European empires in the Americas were in some ways both different from and more significant than the others. They represented something wholly new in human history, an interacting Atlantic world, while the Russian, Chinese, Mughal, and Ottoman empires continued older patterns of historical development. Furthermore, the European empires had a far heavier impact on the peoples they incorporated than did the others. After all, the great tragedies of the early modern era—the population collapse of Native American societies and the Atlantic slave trade—both grew out of these European empires. Moreover, they had, arguably, a far wider impact on the world as a whole, as they extended European civilization to the vast areas of the Americas, laid the nutritional foundation for the global population explosion of modern times, and contributed to both the Scientific Revolution and the Industrial Revolution.

Counteracting Eurocentrism, while acknowledging the unique role of Europe, continues to generate controversy among both scholars and students of modern world history. It is an issue that will recur repeatedly in the chapters that follow.

Second Thoughts

What's the Significance?

the great dying
Columbian exchange
peninsulares
mestizo
mulattoes
plantation complex

settler colonies
Siberia
yasak
Qing dynasty empire
Mughal Empire
Akbar

Aurangzeb
Ottoman Empire
Constantinople, 1453
devshirme

To assess your mastery of the material in this chapter, visit the **Student Center** at bedfordstmartins.com/strayer.

Big Picture Questions

1. In comparing the European empires in the Americas with the Russian, Chinese, Mughal, and Ottoman empires, should world historians emphasize the similarities or the differences? What are the implications of each approach?

2. In what different ways was European colonial rule expressed and experienced in the Americas?

3. Why did the European empires in the Americas have such an enormously greater impact on the conquered people than did the Chinese, Mughal, and Ottoman empires?

4. In what ways did the empires of the early modern era continue patterns of earlier empires? In what ways did they depart from those patterns?

Next Steps: For Further Study

Jorge Canizares-Esguerra and Erik R. Seeman, eds., *The Atlantic in Global History* (2007). A collection of essays that treats the Atlantic basin as a single interacting region.

Alfred W. Crosby, *The Columbian Voyages, the Columbian Exchange, and Their Historians* (1987). A brief and classic account of changing understandings of Columbus and his global impact.

John Kicza, *Resilient Cultures: America's Native Peoples Confront European Colonization, 1500–1800* (2003). An account of European colonization in the Americas that casts the native peoples as active agents rather than passive victims.

Peter Perdue, *China Marches West: The Qing Conquest of Central Eurasia* (2005). Describes the process of China becoming an empire as it incorporated the non-Chinese people of Central Asia.

John F. Richards, *The Mughal Empire* (1996). A well-regarded summary by a major scholar in the field.

David R. Ringrose, *Expansion and Global Interaction, 1200–1700* (2001). A world history perspective on empire building that bridges the postclassical and early modern eras.

Willard Sutherland, *Taming the Wild Fields: Colonization and Empire on the Russian Steppe* (2004). An up-to-date account of Russian expansion in the steppes.

"1492: An Ongoing Voyage," http://www.ibiblio.org/expo/1492.exhibit/Intro.html. An interactive Web site based on an exhibit from the Library of Congress that provides a rich context for exploring the meaning of Columbus and his voyages.

For Web sites and additional documents related to this chapter, see **Make History** at bedfordstmartins.com/strayer.

Documents

Considering the Evidence:
State Building in the Early Modern Era

The empires of the early modern era were the projects of states, though these states often made use of various private groups—missionaries, settlers, merchants, mercenaries—to achieve the goals of empire. Such imperial states, Qing-dynasty China, Mughal India, the Ottoman Empire, and France, for example, were invariably headed by monarchs—kings or emperors who were the source of ultimate political authority in their lands. Each of those rulers sought to govern societies divided by religion, region, ethnicity, or class.

During the three centuries between 1450 and 1750, all of these states, and a number of non-imperial states as well, moved toward greater political integration and centralization. In all of them, more effective central bureaucracies curtailed, though never eliminated, entrenched local interests; royal courts became more elaborate; and the role of monarchs grew more prominent. The growth of empire accompanied this process of political integration, and perhaps helped to cause it. However, the process of state building differed considerably across the early modern world, depending on variations in historical backgrounds, the particular problems and circumstances that each state faced, the cultural basis of political authority, and the policies that individual leaders followed.

The documents that follow allow us to examine this state-building effort in several distinct settings through the writings of monarchs, the edicts they issued, or outsiders who observed them. Pay attention to both the similarities and the variations in this process of state building as you study the documents. You may also want to consider how these early modern states differed from the states of later centuries. To what extent was government personal rather than institutional? In what ways was power exercised—through coercion and violence, through accommodation with established elites, through the operation of new bureaucratic structures, or by persuading people that the central authority was in fact legitimate?

Document 14.1

The "Self-Portrait" of a Chinese Emperor

Of all the early modern states, China had the longest tradition of centralized rule and political integration. By the time the Qing dynasty came to power in 1644, China could look back on many centuries of effective unity. Although interrupted periodically by peasant upheaval, external invasion, or changes in dynasties, cultural expectations nonetheless defined a unified state, headed by an emperor, as the norm. The Qing dynasty, although of Manchurian origin and proud of its military skills, generally accepted Chinese conceptions of state-craft, based on literary learning and a long-established system of civil service examinations designed to recruit scholar-officials into official positions. During the long reign of Kangxi (reigned 1661–1722), that dynasty initiated a vast imperial project extending Chinese control deep into inner Asia. (See the map on p. 644, and see pp. 643–45.) Document 14.1 contains a number of Kangxi's personal reflections on the management of this huge imperial state and its bureaucracy. Drawn from his own writings, this "self-portrait" of the Chinese emperor was compiled by the highly regarded historian Jonathan Spence.

- What major challenges to the effective exercise of state authority does Kangxi identify in this document?

- How would you describe Kangxi's style of governance or his posture toward imperial rule?

- Look carefully at the second paragraph of the document. Why did Kangxi impose a harsher penalty on Hu Chien-ching than the one originally given?

- What does this document suggest about the sources of Kangxi's authority?

THE EMPEROR KANGXI

Reflections

1671–1722

Giving life to people and killing people—those are the powers that the emperor has.... He knows that sometimes people have to be persuaded into morality by the example of an execution....

Hu Chien-ching was a subdirector of the Court of Sacrificial Worship whose family terrorized their native area in Kiangsu, seizing people's lands and wives and daughters, and murdering people after falsely accusing them of being thieves. When a commoner finally managed to impeach him, the Governor was slow to hear the case and the Board of Punishment recommended that Hu be dismissed

Source: Jonathan D. Spence, *Emperor of China* (New York: Alfred A. Knopf, 1974), 29–58.

and sent into exile for three years. I ordered instead that he be executed with his family, and in his native place, so that all the local gentry might learn how I regarded such behavior....

I have been merciful where possible. For the ruler must always check carefully before executions and leave room for the hope that men will get better if they are given the time....

Of all the things that I find distasteful, none is more so than giving a final verdict on the death sentences that are sent to me for ratification.... Each year we went through the lists, sparing sixteen out of sixty-three at one session, eighteen out of fifty-seven at another....

There are too many men who claim to be *ju*—pure scholars—and yet are stupid and arrogant; we'd be better off with less talk of moral principles and more practice of it.... This is one of the worst habits of the great officials, that if they are not recommending their teachers or their friends for high office, then they recommend their relatives....

There is no way the emperor can know every official in the country, so he has to rely on the officials themselves for evaluation, or on censors to impeach the wicked. But when they are in cliques, he has to make his own inquiries as well; for no censor impeached the corrupt army officers Cho-ts'e and Hsu-sheng until I heard how they were hated by their troops and people and had them dismissed....

The emperor can get extra information in audience, on tours, and in palace memorials. From the beginning of my reign, I sought ways to guarantee that discussion among the great officials be kept confidential. The palace memorials were read by me in person, and I wrote rescripts on them myself.... [R]egular audiences are crucial with military men, especially when they have held power for a long time. There might have been no rebellion if Wu San-kuei, Keng Ching-chung, and Shang Chih-hsin had been summoned for regular audiences and made properly fearful. And army officers on the frontiers tend to obey only their own commander, acknowledging him as the ruler....

On tours I learned about the common people's grievances by talking with them, or by accepting their petitions. I asked peasants about their officials, looked at their houses and discussed their crops. I heard pleas from a woman whose husband had been wrongfully enslaved, from a traveling trader complaining about high customs dues, from a monk whose temple was falling down, and from a man who was robbed on his way to town....

In 1694 I noted that we were losing talent because of the way the exams were being conducted: even in the military *chin-shih* exams, most of the successful candidates were from Cheikiang and Chiangnan, while there was only one from Honan and one from Shansi. The successful ones had often done no more than memorize old examination books, whereas the best should be selected on the basis of riding and archery....

Even among the examiners, there are those who are corrupt, those who do not understand basic works, those who ask detailed questions about practical matters of which they know nothing, those who insist entirely on memorization of the *Classics*... those who put candidates from their own geographical area at the top of the list....

My divines have often been tempted to pass over bad auguries, but I have double-checked their calculations and warned them not to distort the truth: the Bureau of Astronomy once reported that a benevolent southeast wind was blowing, but I myself calculated the wind's direction with the palace instruments and found it to be, in fact, an inauspicious northeast wind; I told the Bureau that ours was not a dynasty that shunned bad omens; I also warned the Bureau not to guess or exaggerate in interpreting the omens that they observed, but simply to state their findings.... And being precise about forecasting the motions of the sun, moon, and planets, the winter and summer festivals, the eclipses of the sun and moon—all that is relevant to regulating spring planting, summer weeding, and autumn harvest....

I have never tired of the *Book of Changes*, and have use it in fortune-telling and as a source of moral principles; the only thing you must not do, I told my court lecturers, is to make this book appear simple, for there are meanings here that lie beyond words.

Document 14.2

The Memoirs of Emperor Jahangir

The peoples of India, unlike those of China, had only rarely experienced a political system that encompassed most of the subcontinent. Its vast ethnic and cultural diversity and the division between its Hindu and Muslim peoples usually generated a fragmented political order of many competing states and principalities. But in the early modern era, the Mughal Empire gave to South Asia a rare period of substantial political unity. Document 14.2 offer excerpts from the memoirs of Jahangir, who ruled the Mughal state from 1605 to 1627, following the reign of his more famous father Akbar (see pp. 645–46). Written in Persian, the literary language of the eastern Islamic world, Jahangir's account of his reign followed the tradition of earlier Mughal emperors in noting major events of his lifetime, but it departed from that tradition in reflecting personally on art, politics, family life, and more.

- Why do you think Jahangir mounted such an elaborate coronation celebration for himself?

- In what ways did Jahangir seek to ensure the effective authority of the state he led?

- In what ways was Jahangir a distinctly Muslim ruler? In what respects did he and his father depart from Islamic principles?

- How would you compare the problems Jahangir faced with those of Kangxi? Notice, among other things, that each of them had to adjust to a long-established cultural tradition—Kangxi to Chinese Confucianism and Jahangir to Hinduism. In what ways did they do so?

JAHANGIR

Memoirs

1605–1627

At the age of thirty-eight, I became Emperor, and under auspices the most felicitous, took my seat on the throne of my wishes....

As at the very instant that I seated myself on the throne, the sun rose from the horizon; I accepted this as the omen of victory, and as indicating a reign of unvarying prosperity. Hence I assumed the titles of...the world-subduing emperor, the world-subduing king. I ordained that the following legend should be stamped on the coinage of the empire: "Stricken at Agrah by that...safeguard of the world, the sovereign splendor of the faith, Jahangir, son of the imperial Akbar."

On this occasion I made use of the throne prepared by my father, and enriched at an expense without parallel for the celebration of the festival of the

Source: *The Memoirs of the Emperor Jahangir*, translated from the Persian by Major David Price (London: Oriental Translation Committee, 1829), 1–3, 5–8, 15.

new year.... Having thus seated myself on the throne of my expectations and wishes, I caused also the imperial crown, which my father had caused to be made after the manner of that which was worn by the great kings of Persia, to be brought before me, and then, in the presence of the whole assembled Emirs, having placed it on my brows, as an omen auspicious to the stability and happiness of my reign, kept it there for the space of a full astronomical hour....

For forty days and forty nights I caused the... great imperial state drum, to strike up, without ceasing, the strains of joy and triumph; and... around my throne, the ground was spread by my directions with the most costly brocades and gold embroidered carpets. Censers° of gold and silver were disposed in different directions for the purpose of burning odoriferous drugs, and nearly three thousand camphorated wax lights... illuminated the scene from night till morning. Numbers of blooming youths, beautiful as young Joseph in the pavilions of Egypt, clad in dresses of the most costly materials... awaited my commands, rank after rank, and in attitude most respectful. And finally, the Emirs of the empire... covered from head to foot in gold and jewels, and shoulder to shoulder, stood round in brilliant array, also waiting for the commands of their sovereign. For forty days and forty nights did I keep open to the world these scenes of festivity and splendor, furnishing altogether an example of imperial magnificence seldom paralleled in this stage of earthly existence....

I instituted... special regulations... as rules of conduct, never to be deviated from in their respective stations.

1. I remitted [canceled] altogether to my subjects three sources of revenue taxes or duties....

2. I directed, when the district lay waste or destitute of inhabitants, that towns should be built.... I charged the Jaguir-daurs,° or feudatories of the empire, in such deserted places to erect mosques and

---

°**Censers:** containers for burning incense.

°**Jaguir-daurs:** local rulers granted a certain territory by the Emperor.

substantial... stations for the accommodation of travelers, in order to render the district once more an inhabited country, and that wayfaring men might again be able to pass and repass in safety.

3. Merchants traveling through the country were not to have their bales or packages of any kind opened without their consent. But when they were perfectly willing to dispose of any article of merchandise, purchasers were permitted to deal with them, without, however, offering any species of molestation....

5. No person was permitted either to make or sell either wine or any other kind of intoxicating liquor. I undertook to institute this regulation, although it is sufficiently notorious that I have myself the strongest inclination for wine, in which from the age of sixteen I have liberally indulged....

6. No person [official] was permitted to take up his abode obtrusively in the dwelling of any subject of my realm....

7. No person was to suffer, for any offense, the loss of a nose or ear. If the crime were theft, the offender was to be scourged with thorns, or deterred from further transgression by an attestation on the Koran.

8. [High officials] were prohibited from possessing themselves by violence of the lands of the subject, or from cultivating them on their own account....

10. The governors in all the principal cities were directed to establish infirmaries or hospitals, with competent medical aid for the relief of the sick....

11. During the month of my birth... the use of all animal food was prohibited both in town and country; and at equidistant periods throughout the year a day was set apart, on which all slaughtering of animals was strictly forbidden.

[H]aving on one occasion asked my father [Akbar] the reason why he had forbidden any one to prevent or interfere with the building of these haunts of idolatry [Hindu temples], his reply was in the following terms: "My dear child," said he, "I find myself a powerful monarch, the shadow of God upon earth. I have seen that he bestows the blessings of his gracious providence upon all his creatures without distinction. Ill should I discharge the duties of my exalted station, were I to withhold my compassion and indulgence from any of those entrusted to my charge. With all of the human race, with all of God's creatures, I am at peace: why then should I permit myself, under any consideration, to be the cause of molestation or aggression to any one? Besides, are not five parts in six of mankind either Hindus or aliens to the faith; and were I to be governed by motives of the kind suggested in your inquiry, what alternative can I have but to put them all to death!

I have thought it therefore my wisest plan to let these men alone. Neither is it to be forgotten, that the class of whom we are speaking…are usefully engaged, either in the pursuits of science or the arts, or of improvements for the benefit of mankind, and have in numerous instances arrived at the highest distinctions in the state, there being, indeed, to be found in this city men of every description, and of every religion on the face of the earth."

Document 14.3

An Outsider's View of Suleiman I

Under Suleiman I (1520–1566), the Ottoman Empire reached its greatest territorial extent and perhaps its "golden age" in terms of culture and economy (see Map 14.3, p. 647). A helpful window into the life of this most powerful of Muslim states comes from the writings of Ogier Ghiselin de Busbecq, a Flemish nobleman who served as a diplomat for the Austrian Empire, which then felt under great threat from Ottoman expansion into central Europe. For six years in the mid-sixteenth century, Busbecq represented Austria in the Ottoman Empire, from which he sent a stream of letters to a friend. The excerpts in Document 14.3 present his view of the Ottoman court and his reflections on Ottoman military power.

■ How do you think Busbecq's outsider status shaped his perceptions of Ottoman political and military life? To what extent does his role as a foreigner enhance or undermine the usefulness of his account for historians?

■ How did he define the differences between Ottoman Empire and Austria? What do you think he hoped to accomplish by highlighting these differences?

■ What sources of Ottoman political authority are apparent in Busbecq's account?

■ What potential problems of the Ottoman Empire does this document imply or state?

OGIER GHISELIN DE BUSBECQ

The Turkish Letters

1555–1562

On his [Suleiman's] arrival we were admitted to an audience; but the manner and spirit in which he listened to our address, our arguments, and our message, was by no means favorable. The Sultan was seated on a very low ottoman, not more than a foot from the ground, which was covered with a quantity of costly rugs and cushions of exquisite workmanship; near him lay his bow and arrows. His air, as I said, was by no means gracious, and his face wore a stern, though dignified, expression. On entering we were separately conducted into the royal presence by the chamberlains, who grasped our arms. This has been the Turkish fashion of admitting people to the Sovereign ever since a Croat, in order to avenge the death of his master . . . asked Amurath [an earlier Sultan] for an audience, and took advantage of it to slay him. After having gone through a pretense of kissing his hand, we were conducted backward to the wall opposite his seat, care being taken that we should never turn our backs on him. . . .

The Sultan's hall was crowded with people, among whom were several officers of high rank. Besides these there were all the troopers of the Imperial guard and a large force of Janissaries; but there was not in all that great assembly a single man who owed his position to aught save his valor and his merit. No distinction is attached to birth among the Turks. . . . In making his appointments the Sultan pays no regard to any pretensions on the score of wealth or rank, nor does he take into consideration recommendations or popularity. . . . It is by merit that men rise in the service, a system which ensures that posts should only be assigned to the competent. . . . Those who receive the highest offices from the Sultan are for the most part the sons of shepherds or herdsmen, and so far from being ashamed of their parentage, they actually glory in it, and consider it a matter of boasting that they owe nothing to the accident of birth. . . .

Among the Turks, therefore, honors, high posts, and judgeships are the rewards of great ability and good service. If a man be dishonest, or lazy, or careless, he remains at the bottom of the ladder, an object of contempt; for such qualities there are no honors in Turkey! This is the reason that they are successful in their undertakings, that they lord it over others, and are daily extending the bounds of their empire. These are not our ideas, with us [Europeans] there is no opening left for merit; birth is the standard for everything; the prestige of birth is the sole key to advancement in the public service. . . .

[T]ake your stand by my side, and look at the sea of turbaned heads, each wrapped in twisted folds of the whitest silk; look at those marvelously handsome dresses of every kind and every color; time would fail me to tell how all around is glittering with gold, with silver, with purple, with silk, and with velvet; words cannot convey an adequate idea of that strange and wondrous sight: it was the most beautiful spectacle I ever saw.

With all this luxury, great simplicity and economy are combined; every man's dress, whatever his position may be, is of the same pattern; no fringes or useless points are sewn on, as is the case with us, appendages which cost a great deal of money, and are worn out in three days. . . . I was greatly struck with the silence and order that prevailed in this great crowd. There were no cries, no hum of voices, the usual accompaniments of a motley gathering, neither was there any jostling; without the slightest disturbance each man took his proper place according to his rank. . . .

On leaving the assembly we had a fresh treat in the sight of the household cavalry returning to their quarters; the men were mounted on splendid horses, excellently groomed, and gorgeously accoutred. And so we left the royal presence, taking with us but little hope of a successful issue to our embassy.

Source: Charles Thornton Forester and F. H. Blackburne Daniell, *The Life and Letters of Ogier Ghiselin de Busbecq* (London: C. Kegan Paul and Co., 1881), 114–15, 152–56, 219–22.

The Turkish monarch going to war takes with him over 40,000 camels and nearly as many baggage mules, of which a great part, when he is invading Persia, are loaded with rice and other kinds of grain.... The invading army carefully abstains from encroaching on its magazines° at the outset.... The Sultan's magazines are opened, and a ration just sufficient to sustain life is daily weighed out to the Janissaries and other troops of the royal household.

From this you will see that it is the patience, self-denial, and thrift of the Turkish soldier that enable him to face the most trying circumstances.... What a contrast to our men! Christian soldiers on a campaign refuse to put up with their ordinary food, and call for thrushes, beccaficos,° and such like dainty dishes! If these are not supplied they grow mutinous and work their own ruin; and, if they are supplied, they are ruined all the same. For each man is his own worst enemy, and has no foe more deadly than his own intemperance, which is sure to kill him, if the enemy be not quick.

It makes me shudder to think of what the result of a struggle between such different systems must be; one of us must prevail and the other be destroyed.... On their side is the vast wealth of their empire, unimpaired resources, experience and practice in arms, a veteran soldiery, an uninterrupted series of victo-

ries, readiness to endure hardships, union, order, discipline, thrift, and watchfulness. On ours are found an empty exchequer, luxurious habits, exhausted resources, broken spirits, a raw and insubordinate soldiery, and greedy generals; there is no regard for discipline, license runs riot, the men indulge in drunkenness and debauchery, and, worst of all, the enemy are accustomed to victory, we, to defeat. Can we doubt what the result must be? The only obstacle is Persia, whose position on his rear forces the invader to take precautions. The fear of Persia gives us a respite, but it is only for a time. When he has secured himself in that quarter, he will fall upon us with all the resources of the East. How ill prepared we are to meet such an attack it is not for me to say.

[In the following passage, Busbeq reflects on a major problem of the Ottoman state, succession to the throne.]

The sons of Turkish Sultans are in the most wretched position in the world, for, as soon as one of them succeeds his father, the rest are doomed to certain death. The Turk can endure no rival to the throne, and, indeed, the conduct of the Janissaries renders it impossible for the new Sultan to spare his brothers; for if one of them survives, the Janissaries are forever asking largesses. If these are refused, forthwith the cry is heard, "Long live the brother!" "God preserve the brother!"—a tolerably broad hint that they intend to place him on the throne. So that the Turkish Sultans are compelled to celebrate their succession by imbruing their hands in the blood of their nearest relatives.

°**magazines:** supplies.

°**beccafico:** a small bird.

Documents 14.4 and 14.5

French State Building and Louis XIV

Like their counterparts in the Middle East and Asia, a number of European states in the early modern era also pursued the twin projects of imperial expansion abroad and political integration at home. But consolidating central authority was a long and difficult task. Obstacles to the ambitions of kings in Europe were many—the absence of an effective transportation and communication infrastructure; the difficulty of acquiring information about the population and resources; the entrenched interests of privileged groups such as the nobility, church, town councils, and guilds; and the division between Catholics and Protestants.

Perhaps the most well-known example of such European state-building efforts is that of France under the rule of Louis XIV (reigned 1643–1715). Louis and other European monarchs, such as those in Spain and Russia, operated under a set of assumptions known as "absolutism," which held that kings ruled by "divine right" and could legitimately claim sole and uncontested power in their realms. Louis's famous dictum *"L'etat, c'est moi"* ("I am the state") summed up the absolutist ideal. Documents 14.4 and 14.5 illustrate several ways in which Louis attempted to realize this ideal.

Document 14.4, written by Louis himself, focuses on the importance of "spectacle" and public display in solidifying the exalted role of the monarch. The "carousel" described in the document was an extravagant pageant, held in Paris in June of 1662. It featured various exotic animals, slaves, princes, and nobles arrayed in fantastic costumes representing distant lands, together with much equestrian competition. Unifying this disparate assembly was King Louis himself, dressed as a Roman emperor, while on the shields of the nobles was that grand symbol of the monarchy, the sun.

- What posture does Louis take toward his subjects in this document?

- How does he understand the role of spectacle in general and the carousel in particular?

- What does the choice of the sun as a royal symbol suggest about Louis's conception of his role in the French state and empire?

Document 14.5 explores yet another effort at French state building, expanding the power of *intendants*, royal officials appointed by the king. They differed from other officials in that they were not native to the regions they administered and did not own the offices they held. Thus they were instruments of royal authority and more centralized control. Document 14.5, written in 1680 by Jean-Baptiste Colbert, Louis's famous minister of finance, instructs these intendants on their duties.

- What was the main purpose of the intendants according to this document?

- What kind of opposition do you expect the intendants experienced?

Louis XIV
Memoirs
1670

It was necessary to conserve and cultivate with care all that which, without diminishing the authority and the respect due to me, linked me by bonds of affection to my peoples and above all to the people of rank, so as to make them see by this very means that it was neither aversion for them nor affected severity, nor harshness of spirit, but simply reason and duty, that made me more reserved and more exact toward them in other matters. That sharing of pleasures, which gives people at court a respectable familiarity with us, touches them and charms them more than can be expressed. The common people, on the other hand, are delighted by shows in which, at bottom, we always have the aim of pleasing them; and all our subjects, in general, are delighted to see that we like what they like, or what they excel in. By this means we hold on to their hearts and their minds, sometimes more strongly perhaps than by recompenses and gifts; and with regard to foreigners, in a state they see flourishing and well ordered, that which is spent on expenses and which could be called superfluous, makes a very favorable impression on them, of magnificence, of power, of grandeur....

The carousel, which has furnished me the subject of these reflections, had only been conceived at first as a light amusement; but little by little, we were carried away, and it became a spectacle that was fairly grand and magnificent, both in the number of exercises, and by the novelty of the costumes and the variety of the [heraldic] devices. It was then that I began to employ the one that I have always kept since and which you see in so many places. I believed that, without limiting itself to something precise and lessening, it ought to represent in some way the duties of a prince, and constantly encourage me to fulfill them. For the device they chose the sun, which, according to the rules of this art, is the most noble of all, and which, by its quality of being unique, by the brilliance that surrounds it, by the light that it communicates to the other stars which form for it a kind of court, by the just and equal share that the different climates of the world receive of this light, by the good it does in all places, ceaselessly producing as it does, in every sphere of life, joy and activity, by its unhindered movement, in which it nevertheless always appears calm, by its constant and invariable course, from which it never departs nor wavers, is the most striking and beautiful image of a great monarch.

Those who saw me governing with a good deal of ease and without being confused by anything, in all the numerous attentions that royalty demands, persuaded me to add the earth's globe, and for motto, *nec pluribus impar* (not unequal to many things): by which they meant something that flattered the aspirations of a young king, namely that, being sufficient to so many things, I would doubtless be capable of governing other empires, just as the sun was capable of lighting up other worlds if they were exposed to its rays.

Source: Robert Campbell, *Louis XIV* (London: Longmans, 1993), 117–18.

JEAN-BAPTISTE COLBERT
Instructions for Intendants
1680

The King has instructed me to repeat most strongly to you the orders which His Majesty has given you, in every preceding year, about the inspection of the generality in which you serve. He wants you to apply yourself to this task even more vigorously than you have in the past, because he wishes there to be equality in the allocation of taxes and a reduction in all kinds of abuses and expenses, thus bringing further relief to his peoples in addition to that which they have received from the lowering of taxation.

The King intends that, as soon as you have read this letter, you should begin your visit to each of the elections in your generality:

That, during this tour, you should examine with the utmost care the extent of landed wealth, the quality of livestock, the state of industries and in fact everything in each election [district] which helps to attract money there; that you should seek out, with the same diligence, anything which might help to increase animal foodstuffs, to expand industrial production or even to establish new manufactures. At the same time, His Majesty wants you to journey to three or four of the main towns in each election, excluding those which you have chosen in earlier years, and in these places to call before you a large number of the tax-collectors and leading inhabitants from the surrounding parishes; to take pains to find out all that has taken place concerning the receipt of the King's orders, the nomination of collectors, and the allocation and payment of the *taille*;° to ferret out all the malpractices in these procedures; try to remedy them yourself; and, in case you find some which can be treated

°**taille:** land tax.

Source: Roger R. Mettan, *Government and Society in Louis XIV's France* (Basingstoke: Macmillan, 1977), 18–21.

only by a royal judgment or decree, to send me a report in order that I may inform His Majesty....

Listen to all the complaints which are brought to you about inequalities in allocation on the rolls of the *tailles*, and do everything which you consider appropriate to stamp out these iniquities and to make the allocation as fair as possible. Examine with the same thoroughness the expenses which are incurred, both by the receivers in relation to the collectors and by the collectors in relation to the taxpayers.... One of the most effective methods which His Majesty wishes you to use in repressing these abuses is to suspend the receiver of the *tailles* who seems the most culpable in your generality, and to entrust his duties to someone else for the next year. This punishment will assuredly cause the disappearance of many of these evil practices. His Majesty will also offer a reward to the receiver who has run his election the most effectively, and who has incurred the least expenses.

His Majesty likewise requires that you should report every three months, without fail, on the number of prisoners who have been arrested concerning the *taille* or the various indirect taxes....

You must also inspect in each election the amount of the taxes collected to date, both for last year and for this, giving all the necessary orders for hurrying up the whole process....

He also requires you to keep watch over everything involving the coinage throughout your generality, which is to say that only coins authorized by royal edict and decree may be in circulation. On this same subject, His Majesty wants you continually to ascertain that there are no mints producing false coins; and, if you should find one, to send word immediately, so that His Majesty may issue the necessary orders for bringing the culprits to trial without delay, because there is no crime which is more prejudicial to the interests of the people than this one.

Using the Evidence:
State Building in the Early Modern Era

1. **Making comparisons:** To what extent did these four early modern states face similar problems and devise similar solutions? How did they differ? In particular, how did the rulers of these states deal with subordinates? How did they use violence? What challenges to imperial authority did they face?

2. **Assessing spectacle:** In what different ways was spectacle, royal splendor, or public display evident in the documents? How would you define the purpose of such display? How effective do you think spectacle has been in consolidating state authority?

3. **Distinguishing power and authority:** Some scholars have made a distinction between "power," the ability of a state to coerce its subjects into some required behavior, and "authority," the ability of a state to persuade its subjects to do its bidding voluntarily by convincing them that it is proper, right, or natural to do so. What examples of power and authority can you find in these documents? How were they related? What are the advantages and disadvantages of each, from the viewpoint of ambitious rulers?

4. **Comparing past and present:** It is important to recognize that early modern states differed in many ways from twentieth or twenty-first century states. How would you define those differences? Consider, among other things, the personal role of the ruler, the use of violence, the means of establishing authority, and the extent to which the state could shape the lives of its citizens.

Visual Sources

Considering the Evidence:
The Conquest of Mexico
Through Aztec Eyes

Among the sagas of early modern empire building, few have been more dramatic, more tragic, or better documented than the Spanish conquest of Mexico during the early sixteenth century (see Map 14.1, p. 627). In recounting this story, historians are fortunate in having considerable evidence—both documentary and visual—from the Aztec side of the encounter.

The peoples of central Mexico had long used a type of book called a codex to record their history. Codices included drawings and symbols (glyphs) painted by carefully trained high-status persons known as *tlacuilo* (artist-scribes). Although Spanish invaders destroyed most of these codices, the codex tradition continued in a modified form in the century following conquest. These new codices, often assembled under the supervision of European missionaries, were largely composed by native peoples, many of them new converts to Christianity and some of them literate in both Spanish and Latin. These codices included numerous paintings by local artists as well as written texts in a variety of Mesoamerican languages using the Roman alphabet.

The *Florentine Codex*, for example, was compiled under the leadership of Fray Bernardino de Sahagun, a Franciscan missionary who felt that an understanding of Aztec culture was essential to the task of conversion. Because Sahagun relied on Aztec informants and artists, many scholars believe that the Florentine and other codices represent indigenous understandings of the conquest. However, they require a critical reading. They date from several decades after the events they describe. Many contributors to the codices had been influenced by the Christian and European culture of their missionary mentors, and they were writing in a society thoroughly dominated by Spanish colonial rule. Furthermore, the codices reflect the ethnic and regional diversity of Mesoamerica rather than a single Aztec perspective. Despite such limitations, these codices represent a unique window into Mesoamerican understandings of the conquest.

In the Aztec telling of the Spanish conquest, accounts of earlier warnings or omens of disaster abound. One of these was described as follows in the *Florentine Codex*: "Ten years before the arrival of the Spaniards an omen first

Visual Source 14.1 Disaster Foretold (Biblioteca Nacional Madrid/Gianni Dagli Orti/The Art Archive)

appeared in the sky like a flame or tongue of fire.... For a full year it showed itself.... People were taken aback, they lamented."[28] That ominous appearance was illustrated in the *Duran Codex*, presented here in Visual Source 14.1 showing the Aztec ruler Moctezuma observing this omen of death from the rooftop of his palace. Some scholars suggest that such stories reflect a postconquest understanding of the traumatic defeat the Aztecs suffered, for other evidence indicates that the Aztecs were not initially alarmed by the coming of the Spanish and that, instead, they viewed the Europeans as "simply another group of powerful and dangerous outsiders who needed to be controlled or accommodated."[29]

■ Why might Aztec contributors to the codices have included accounts of such supernatural events preceding the arrival of the Spanish?

■ Why do you think the Spanish frequently incorporated such accounts into their own descriptions of the conquest?

■ Why might the artist have chosen to show Moctezuma alone rather than in the company of his supposedly fearful people?

Visual Source 14.2 Moctezuma and Cortés (The Granger Collection, New York)

In February of 1519 Hernán Cortés, accompanied by some 350 Spanish soldiers, set off from Cuba with a fleet of eleven ships, stopping at several places along the Gulf of Mexico before proceeding to march inland toward Tenochtitlán, the capital of the Aztec Empire. Along the way, he learned something about the fabulous wealth of this empire and about the fragility of its political structure. Through a combination of force and astute diplomacy, Cortés was able to negotiate alliances with a number of the Aztecs' restive subject peoples and with the Aztecs' many rivals or enemies, especially the Tlaxcala. With his modest forces thus greatly reinforced, Cortés arrived in Tenochtitlán on November 8, 1519, where he met with Moctezuma. Visual Source 14.2 presents an image of that epic encounter, drawn from the Lienzo de Tlaxcala, a series of paintings completed by 1560. They reflect generally the viewpoint of the Tlaxcala people.

- How does this painting present the relationship between Cortés and Moctezuma? Are they meeting as equals, as enemies, as allies, as ruler and subject? Notice that both sit on European-style chairs, which had come to suggest authority in the decades following Spanish conquest.

- What do the items at the bottom of the image represent?

- Does this image support or challenge the perception that the Aztecs viewed the Spanish newcomers, at least initially, in religious terms as gods?

- What might the painter have tried to convey by placing three attendants behind Moctezuma, while Cortés appears alone, except for his translator?

The woman standing behind Cortés in Visual Source 14.2 is Doña Marina (sometimes called La Malinche), a Nahuatl-speaking woman who had been a slave in Maya territory and was given as a gift to Cortés's forces in April 1519. She subsequently became an interpreter for the Spanish, as well as Cortés's mistress. Doña Marina appears frequently and prominently in many of the paintings of the era. Cortés himself wrote that "after God we owe this conquest of New Spain to Doña Marina." But in Mexico, some have condemned her as a traitor to her people, while others have praised her as the beginning of European and Native American cooperation and mixing.

- What impression of Doña Marina does this image suggest?

Whatever the character of their initial meeting, the relationship of the Spanish and Aztecs soon deteriorated amid mutual suspicion. Within a week, Cortés had seized Moctezuma, holding him under a kind of house arrest in his own palaces. For reasons not entirely clear, this hostile act did not immediately trigger a violent Aztec response. Perhaps Aztec authorities were concerned for the life of their ruler, or perhaps their factional divisions inhibited coordinated resistance.

But in May 1520, while Cortés was temporarily away at the coast, an incident occurred that set in motion the most violent phase of the encounter. During a religious ceremony in honor of Huitzilopochtli, the Aztec patron deity of Tenochtitlán, the local Spanish commander, apparently fearing an uprising, launched a surprise attack on the unarmed participants in the celebration, killing hundreds of the leading warriors and nobles. An Aztec account from the *Florentine Codex* described the scene:

Visual Source 14.3 The Massacre of the Nobles (Bridgeman-Giraudon/Art Resource, NY)

[W]hen the dance was loveliest and when song was linked to song, the Spaniards were seized with an urge to kill the celebrants. They all ran forward, armed as if for battle. They closed the entrances and passageways...then [they] rushed into the Sacred Patio to slaughter the inhabitants....They attacked the man who was drumming and cut off his arms. Then they cut off his head, and it rolled across the floor. They attacked all the celebrants stabbing them, spearing them, striking them with swords....Others they beheaded...or split their heads to pieces....The blood of the warriors flowed like water and gathered into pools...[T]hey invaded every room, hunting and killing.[30]

Visual Source 14.3 shows a vivid depiction of this "massacre of the nobles," drawn from the *Codex Duran*, first published in 1581.

- What elements of the description above are reflected in this painting?

- What image of the Spanish does this painting reflect?

- What do the drums in the center of the image represent?

The massacre of the nobles prompted a citywide uprising against the hated Spanish, who were forced to flee Tenochtitlán on June 30, 1520, across a causeway in Lake Texcoco amid ferocious fighting. Some 600 Spaniards and several thousand of their Tlaxcala allies perished in the escape, many of them laden with gold they had collected in Tenochtitlán. For the Spaniards it was La Noche Triste (the night of sorrow), while for the Aztecs it was no doubt a fitting revenge and a great triumph. Visual Source 14.4, from a Tlaxcala codex, depicts the scene. Cortés and his Tlaxcala allies to the left of the image are shown on the causeway, while many others are drowning in the lake, pursued by Aztec warriors in canoes.

■ Whose perspective do you think is represented in this image—that of the Spanish, their Tlaxcala allies, or the Aztecs? How might each of them have understood this retreat differently?

■ In neither Visual Source 14.3 or 14.4 are the Spanish portrayed with their firearms. How might you understand this omission?

■ Notice the blending of artistic styles in this image. The water, the boats, and shields of the warriors are shown in traditional Mesoamerican fashion, while the Spanish are portrayed in European stereotypes. What does this blending suggest about the cultural processes at work in the codices?

Visual Source 14.4 The Spanish Retreat from Tenochtitlán (The Rout of La Noche Triste [June 30, 1520], Lienzo de Tlaxcala, Pl 18. Library of Congress)

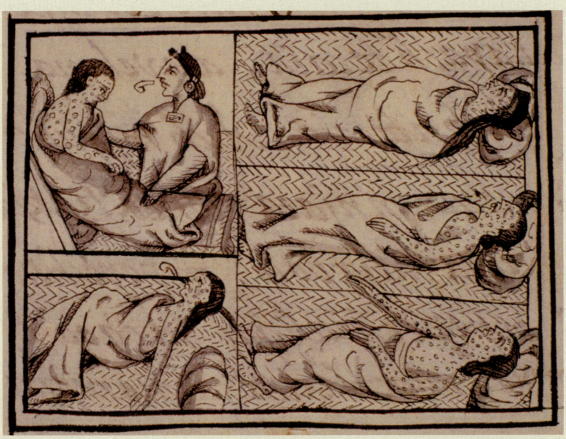

Visual Source 14.5 Smallpox: Disease and Defeat (Biblioteca Medicea Laurenziana, Florence)

While the Aztecs may well have thought themselves permanently rid of the Spanish, La Noche Triste offered only a temporary respite from the European invaders. Cortés and his now diminished forces found refuge among their Tlaxcala allies, where they regrouped and planned for yet another assault on Tenochtitlán. Meanwhile, smallpox had begun to ravage the Aztec population, which lacked any immunity to this Old World disease. The *Florentine Codex* described the situation: "[A]n epidemic broke out, a sickness of pustules.... [The disease] brought great desolation; a great many died of it. They could no longer walk about... no longer able to move or stir.... Starvation reigned, and no one took care of others any longer.... And when things were in this state, the Spaniards came." Visual Source 14.5, likewise from the *Florentine Codex*, is an Aztec portrayal of the disease.

In mid-1521, Cortés returned, strengthened with yet more Mesoamerican allies, and laid siege to the Aztec capital. Bitter fighting ensued, often in the form of house-to-house combat, ending with the surrender of the last Aztec emperor on August 13, 1521. In Tenochtitlán, all was sorrow and lamentation, as reflected in some of the poetry of the time:

> Nothing but flowers and songs of sorrow are left in Mexico and Tlateloco
> where once we saw warriors and wise men....
> We wander here and there in our desolate poverty.
> We are mortal men.
> We have seen bloodshed and pain where once we saw beauty and valor.
> We are crushed to the ground; we lie in ruins....
> Have you grown weary of your servants?
> Are you angry with your servants, O giver of Life?[31]

■ How does Visual Source 14.5 represent the impact of the smallpox epidemic and Aztec response to it?

Using the Evidence:
The Conquest of Mexico through Aztec Eyes

1. **Evaluating images as evidence:** What are the strengths and the limitations of these images as sources for understanding the colonial conquest of Mexico? How well did the native artists who created them understand the Spanish?

2. **Analyzing perspectives:** How might you define the perspective from which these visual sources approach their subjects? Keep in mind that they were drawn by native artists who had been clearly influenced by Spanish culture and religion. In what ways are they criticizing the Spanish conquest, celebrating it, or simply describing it?

3. **Portraying the Spanish:** In what ways do these visual sources portray the Spanish? How might the Spanish themselves present a different account of the conquest?

4. **Describing the conquest:** Based on the information in this section, write a brief description of the conquest from the Aztec point of view.

Global Commerce

1450–1750

"I have come full circle back to my destiny: from Africa to America and back to Africa. I could hear the cries and wails of my ancestors. I weep with them and for them."[1] This is what an African American woman from Atlanta wrote in 2002 in the guest book of the Cape Coast Castle, one of the many ports of embarkation for slaves located along the coast of Ghana in West Africa. There she no doubt saw the whips and leg irons used to discipline the captured Africans as well as the windowless dungeons in which hundreds of them were crammed while waiting for the ships that would carry them across the Atlantic to the Americas. Almost certainly she also caught sight of the infamous "gate of no return," through which the captives departed to their new life as slaves.

THIS VISITOR'S EMOTIONAL ENCOUNTER WITH THE LEGACY OF THE ATLANTIC SLAVE TRADE reminds us of the enormous significance of this commerce in human beings for the early modern world and of its continuing echoes even at the beginning of the twenty-first century. The slave trade, however, was only one component of those international trading networks that shaped human interactions during the centuries between 1450 and 1750. Europeans now smashed their way into the ancient spice trade of the Indian Ocean, developing new relationships with Asian societies as a result. Silver, obtained from mines in Spanish America, enriched Western Europe, even as much of it made its way to China, where it allowed Europeans

The Atlantic Slave Trade: Among the threads of global commerce during the early modern era, none has resonated more loudly in historical memory than the Atlantic slave trade. This eighteenth-century French painting shows the sale of slaves at Goree, a major slave trading port in what is now Dakar in Senegal. A European merchant and an African authority figure negotiate the arrangement, while the shackled victims themselves wait for their fate to be decided. (Bibliothèque des Arts Décoratifs, Paris/Archives Charmet/The Bridgeman Art Library)

to participate more fully in the rich commerce of East Asia. Furs from North America and Siberia found a ready market in Europe and China, while the hunting and trapping of those fur-bearing animals transformed both natural environments and human societies. Despite their growing prominence in long-distance exchange, Europeans were far from the only active traders. Southeast Asians, Chinese, Indians, Armenians, Arabs, and Africans likewise played major roles in the making of the world economy of the early modern era.

Thus commerce joined empire as the twin drivers of globalization during these centuries. Together they created new relationships, disrupted old patterns, brought distant peoples into contact with one another, enriched some, and impoverished or enslaved others. From the various "old worlds" of the premodern era, a single "new world" emerged—slowly, with great pain, and accompanied by growing inequalities. What was gained and what was lost in the transformations born of global commerce have been the subject of great controversy ever since.

Europeans and Asian Commerce

Schoolchildren everywhere know that European empires in the Western Hemisphere grew out of an accident—Columbus's unknowing encounter with the Americas—and that new colonial societies and new commercial connections across the Atlantic were the result. In Asia, it was a very different story. The voyage (1497–1499) of the Portuguese mariner Vasco da Gama, in which Europeans sailed to India for the first time, was certainly no accident. It was the outcome of a deliberate, systematic, century-long Portuguese effort to explore a sea route to the East, by creeping slowly down the West African coast, around the tip of South Africa, up the East African coast, and finally to Calicut in southern India in 1498. There Europeans encountered an ancient and rich network of commerce that stretched from East Africa to China. They were certainly aware of the wealth of that commercial network, but largely ignorant of its workings.

■ Causation
What drove European involvement in the world of Asian commerce?

The most immediate motivation for this massive effort was the desire for tropical spices—cinnamon, nutmeg, mace, cloves, and, above all, pepper—which were widely used as condiments and preservatives and were sometimes regarded as aphrodisiacs. Other products of the East, such as Chinese silk, Indian cottons, rhubarb for medicinal purposes, emeralds, rubies, and sapphires, also were in great demand.

Underlying this growing interest in Asia was the more general recovery of European civilization following the disaster of the Black Death in the early fourteenth century. During the fifteenth century, Europe's population was growing again, and its national monarchies—in Spain, Portugal, England, and France—were learning how to tax their subjects more effectively and to build substantial military forces equipped with gunpowder weapons. Its cities were growing too. Some of them—in England, the Netherlands, and northern Italy, for example—were becoming centers of international commerce, giving birth to a more capitalist economy based on market exchange, private ownership, and the accumulation of capital for further investment.

For many centuries, Eastern goods had trickled into the Mediterranean through the Middle East from the Indian Ocean commercial network. From the viewpoint of an increasingly dynamic Europe, several major problems accompanied this pattern of commerce. First, of course, the source of supply for these much-desired goods lay solidly in Muslim hands. Most immediately, Muslim Egypt was the primary point of transfer into the Mediterranean basin and its European customers. The Italian commercial city of Venice largely monopolized the European trade in Eastern goods, annually sending convoys of ships to Alexandria in Egypt. Venetians resented the Muslim monopoly on Indian Ocean trade, and other European powers disliked relying on Venice as well as on Muslims. Circumventing these monopolies was yet another impetus—both religious and political—for the Portuguese to attempt a sea route to India that bypassed both Venetian and Muslim middlemen. In addition, many Europeans of the time were persuaded that a mysterious Christian monarch, known as Prester John, ruled somewhere in Asia or Africa. Joining with his mythical kingdom to continue the Crusades and combat a common Islamic enemy was likewise a goal of the Portuguese voyages.

A final problem lay in paying for Eastern goods. Few products of an economically less developed Europe were attractive in Eastern markets. Thus Europeans were required to pay cash—gold or silver—for Asian spices or textiles. This persistent trade deficit contributed much to the intense desire for precious metals that attracted early modern European explorers, traders, and conquerors. Portuguese voyages along the West African coast, for example, were seeking direct access to African goldfields. The enormously rich silver deposits of Mexico and Bolivia provided at least a temporary solution to this persistent European problem.

First the Portuguese and then the Spanish, French, Dutch, and British found their way into the ancient Asian world of Indian Ocean commerce (see Map 15.1). How they behaved in that world and what they created there differed considerably among the various European countries, but collectively they contributed much to the new regime of globalized trade.

A Portuguese Empire of Commerce

The arena of Indian Ocean commerce into which Vasco da Gama and his Portuguese successors sailed was a world away from anything they had known. It was a vast world, both in geographic extent and in the diversity of those who participated in it. East Africans, Arabs, Persians, Indians, Malays, Chinese, and others traded freely. Most of them were Muslims, though hailing from many separate communities, but Hindus, Christians, Jews, and Chinese likewise had a role in this commercial network. Had the Portuguese sought simply to participate in peaceful trading, they certainly could have done so, but it was quickly apparent that European trade goods were crude and unattractive in Asian markets and that Europeans would be unable to compete effectively. Moreover, the Portuguese soon learned that most Indian Ocean merchant ships were not heavily armed and certainly lacked the onboard cannons that Portuguese ships carried. Since the withdrawal of the Chinese fleet from the Indian

■ **Connection**
To what extent did the Portuguese realize their own goals in the Indian Ocean?

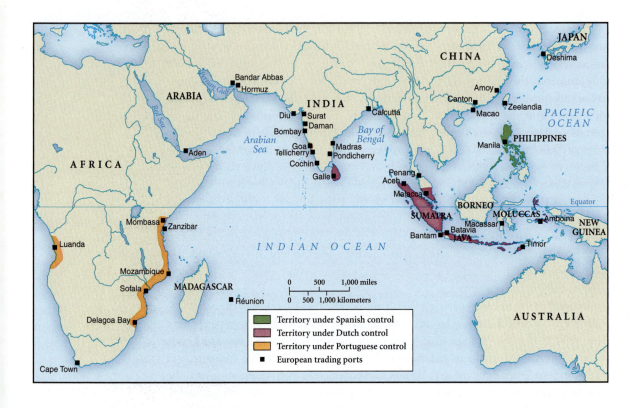

Map 15.1   Europeans in Asia in the Early Modern Era The early modern era witnessed only very limited territorial control by Europeans in Asia. Trade, rather than empire, was the chief concern of the Western newcomers, who were not, in any event, a serious military threat to major Asian states.

Ocean early in the fifteenth century, no major power was in a position to dominate the sea-lanes, and the many smaller-scale merchants generally traded openly, although piracy was sometimes a problem.

Given these conditions, the Portuguese saw an opening, for their ships could outgun and outmaneuver competing naval forces, while their onboard cannons could devastate coastal fortifications. Although their overall economy lagged behind that of Asian producers, Europeans had more than caught up in the critical area of naval technology and naval warfare. This military advantage enabled the Portuguese to quickly establish fortified bases at several key locations within the Indian Ocean world—Mombasa in East Africa, Hormuz at the entrance to the Persian Gulf, Goa on the west coast of India, Malacca in Southeast Asia, and Macao on the south coast of China. With the exception of Macao, which had been obtained through bribery and negotiations with Chinese authorities, these Portuguese bases were obtained forcibly against small and weak states. In Mombasa, for example, the commander of a Portuguese fleet responded to local resistance in 1505 by burning and sacking the city, killing some 1,500 people, and seizing large quantities of cotton and silk textiles and carpets. The king of Mombasa wrote a warning to a neighboring city:

This is to inform you that a great lord has passed through the town, burning it and laying it waste. He came to the town in such strength and was of such a cruelty that he spared neither man nor woman, or old nor young—nay, not even the smallest child. . . . Nor can I ascertain nor estimate what wealth they have taken from the town.[2]

What the Portuguese created in the Indian Ocean is commonly known as a "trading post empire," for they aimed to control commerce, not large territories or populations, and to do so by force of arms rather than by economic competition. Seeking to monopolize the spice trade, the Portuguese king grandly titled

himself "Lord of the Conquest, Navigation, and Commerce of Ethiopia, Arabia, Persia, and India." Portuguese authorities in the East tried to require all merchant vessels to purchase a *cartaz*, or pass, and to pay duties of 6 to 10 percent on their cargoes. They partially blocked the traditional Red Sea route to the Mediterranean and for a century or so monopolized the highly profitable route around Africa to Europe. Even so, they never succeeded in controlling much more than half of the spice trade to Europe.[3]

Failing to dominate Indian Ocean commerce as they had hoped, the Portuguese gradually assimilated themselves to its ancient patterns. They became heavily involved in carrying Asian goods to Asian ports, selling their shipping services because they were largely unable to sell their goods. Even in their major settlements, the Portuguese were outnumbered by Asian traders, and many married Asian women. Hundreds of Portuguese escaped the control of their government altogether and settled in Asian or African ports, where they learned local languages, sometimes converted to Islam, and became simply one more group in the diverse trading culture of the East.

By 1600, the Portuguese trading post empire was in steep decline. This small European country was overextended, and rising Asian states such as Japan, Burma, Mughal India, Persia, and the sultanate of Oman actively resisted Portuguese commercial control. Unwilling to accept a dominant Portuguese role in the Indian Ocean, other European countries also gradually contested Portugal's efforts to monopolize the rich spice trade to Europe.

Spain and the Philippines

Spain was the first to challenge Portugal's position. As precious and profitable spices began to arrive in Europe on Portuguese ships in the early sixteenth century, the Spanish soon realized that they were behind in the race to gain access to the riches of the East. In an effort to catch up, they established themselves on what became the Philippine Islands, named after the Spanish king Philip II. The Spanish first

■ **Comparison**
How did the Portuguese, Spanish, Dutch, and British initiatives in Asia differ from one another?

Snapshot   **Key Moments in the European Encounter with Asia**

Vasco da Gama's arrival in India	1498
Portuguese trading post empire established	early 1500s
Spanish takeover of Philippines begins	1565
China establishes taxes payable in silver	1570s
Beginning of silver shipments from Mexico to Manila	1570s
British and Dutch East India companies begin operation in Asia	1601–1602
Missionaries expelled from Japan	early 1600s
Dutch conquest of nutmeg-producing Banda Islands	1620
French East India Company established	1664
British begin military conquest of India	1750s

encountered the region during the famous round-the-world voyage (1519–1521) of Ferdinand Magellan, a Portuguese mariner sailing on behalf of the Spanish Crown. There they found an archipelago of islands, thousands of them, occupied by cultur-ally diverse peoples and organized in small and highly competitive chiefdoms. One of the local chiefs later told the Spanish: "There is no king and no sole authority in this land; but everyone holds his own view and opinion, and does as he prefers."[4] Some were involved in tribute trade with China, and a small number of Chinese settlers lived in the port towns. Nonetheless, the region was of little interest to the governments of China and Japan, the major powers in the area.

These conditions—proximity to China and the spice islands, small and militarily weak societies, the absence of competing claims—encouraged the Spanish to establish outright colonial rule on the islands, rather than to imitate a Portuguese-style trading post empire. Small-scale military operations, gunpowder weapons, local alliances, gifts and favors to chiefs, and the pageantry of Catholic ritual all contributed to a relatively easy and often bloodless Spanish takeover of the islands in the century or so after 1565. They remained a Spanish colonial territory until the end of the nineteenth century, when the United States assumed control following the Spanish-American War of 1898.

Accompanying Spanish rule was a major missionary effort, which turned Filipino society into the only major outpost of Christianity in Asia. That effort also opened up a new front in the long encounter of Christendom and Islam, for on the southern island of Mindanao, Islam was gaining strength and provided an ideology of resistance to Spanish encroachment for 300 years. Indeed Mindanao remains a contested part of the Philippines into the twenty-first century.

Beyond the missionary enterprise, other features of Spanish colonial practice in the Americas found expression in the Philippines. People living in scattered settlements were persuaded or forced to relocate into more concentrated Christian communities. Tribute, taxes, and unpaid labor became part of ordinary life. Large landed estates emerged, owned by Spanish settlers, Catholic religious orders, or prominent Filipinos. Women who had played a major role as ritual specialists, healers, and midwives were now displaced by male Spanish priests, and their ceremonial instruments were deliberately defiled and disgraced. Short-lived revolts and flight to interior mountains were among the Filipino responses to colonial oppression.

Yet others fled to Manila, the new capital of the colonial Philippines. By 1600, it had become a flourishing and culturally diverse city of more than 40,000 inhabitants and was home to many Spanish settlers and officials and growing numbers of Filipino migrants. Its rising prosperity also attracted some 3,000 Japanese and more than 20,000 Chinese. Serving as traders, artisans, and sailors, the Chinese in particular became an essential element in the Spanish colony's growing economic relationship with China; however, their economic prominence and their resistance to conversion earned them Spanish hostility and clearly discriminatory treatment. Periodic Chinese revolts, followed by expulsions and massacres, were the result. On one occasion in 1603, the Spanish killed about 20,000 people, nearly the entire Chinese population of the island.

The East India Companies

Far more important than the Spanish as European competitors for the spice trade were the Dutch and English, both of whom entered Indian Ocean commerce in the early seventeenth century. Together they quickly overtook and displaced the Portuguese, often by force, even as they competed vigorously with each other as well. These rising Northern European powers were both militarily and economically stronger than the Portuguese. For example, during the sixteenth century, the Dutch had become a highly commercialized and urbanized society, and their business skills and maritime shipping operations were the envy of Europe. Around 1600, both the British and the Dutch, unlike the Portuguese, organized their Indian Ocean ventures through private trading companies, which were able to raise money and share risks among a substantial number of merchant investors. The British East India Company and the Dutch East India Company received charters from their respective governments granting them trading monopolies and the power to make war and to govern conquered peoples. Thus they established their own parallel and competing trading post empires, with the Dutch focused on the islands of Indonesia and the English on India. Somewhat later, a French company also established settlements in the Indian Ocean basin.

Operating in a region of fragmented and weak political authority, the Dutch acted to control not only the shipping but also the production of cloves, cinnamon, nutmeg, and mace. With much bloodshed, the Dutch seized control of a number of small spice-producing islands, forcing their people to sell only to the Dutch and destroying the crops of those who refused. On the Banda Islands, famous for their

■ **Change**
To what extent did the British and Dutch trading companies change the societies they encountered in Asia?

A European View of Asian Commerce
The various East India companies (British, French, and Dutch) represented the major vehicle for European commerce in Asia during the early modern era. This wall painting, dating from 1778 and titled *The East Offering Its Riches to Britannia*, hung in the main offices of the British East India Company. (© British Library Board)

nutmeg, the Dutch killed, enslaved, or left to starve virtually the entire population of some 15,000 people and then replaced them with Dutch planters, using a slave labor force to produce the nutmeg crop. For a time in the seventeenth century, the Dutch were able to monopolize the trade in nutmeg, mace, and cloves and to sell these spices in Europe and India at fourteen to seventeen times the price they paid in Indonesia.[5] While Dutch profits soared, the local economy of the Spice Islands was shattered, and their people were impoverished.

The British East India Company operated differently than its Dutch counterpart. Less well financed and less commercially sophisticated, the British were largely excluded from the rich Spice Islands by the Dutch monopoly. Thus they fell back on India, where they established three major trading settlements during the seventeenth century: Bombay, on India's west coast, and Calcutta and Madras, on the east coast. Although British naval forces soon gained control of the Arabian Sea and the Persian Gulf, largely replacing the Portuguese, on land they were no match for the powerful Mughal Empire, which ruled most of the Indian subcontinent. Therefore, the British were unable to practice "trade by warfare," as the Dutch did in Indonesia.[6] Rather they secured their trading bases with the permission of Mughal authorities or local rulers, with substantial payments and bribes as the price of admission to the Indian market. When some independent English traders plundered a Mughal ship in 1636, local authorities detained British East India Company officials for two months and forced them to pay a whopping fine. Although pepper and other spices remained important in British trade, British merchants came to focus much more heavily on Indian cotton textiles, which were becoming widely popular in England and its American colonies. Hundreds of villages in the interior of southern India became specialized producers for this British market.

Like the Portuguese before them, both the Dutch and English became heavily involved in trade within Asia. The profits from this "carrying trade" enabled them to purchase Asian goods without paying for them in gold or silver from Europe. Dutch and English traders also began to deal in bulk goods for a mass market—pepper, textiles, and later tea and coffee—rather than just luxury goods for an elite market. In the second half of the eighteenth century, both the Dutch and British trading post empires slowly evolved into a more conventional form of colonial domination, in which the British came to rule India and the Dutch controlled Indonesia.

Asian Commerce

Although European commerce in the Indian Ocean and the South China Sea created new linkages between East and West, historians have sometimes exaggerated their impact on Asian societies during the early modern era. Certainly the European presence was far less significant in Asia than it was in the Americas or Africa during these centuries. European political control was limited to the Philippines and a few of the Spice Islands. To the great powers of South and East Asia—Mughal India, China, and Japan—Europeans represented no real military threat and played minor roles in their large and prosperous economies. Japan provides a fascinating case study in the ability of major Asian powers to control the European intruders.

When Portuguese traders and missionaries first arrived on that island nation in the mid-sixteenth century, soon followed by Spanish, Dutch, and English merchants, Japan was plagued by endemic conflict among numerous feudal lords, known as *daimyo*, each with his own cadre of *samurai* warriors. In these circumstances, the European newcomers found a hospitable welcome, for their military technology, shipbuilding skills, geographic knowledge, commercial opportunities, and even religious ideas proved useful or attractive to various elements in Japan's fractious and competitive society. The second half of the sixteenth century, for example, witnessed the growth of a substantial Christian movement, with some 300,000 converts and a Japanese-led church.

By the early seventeenth century, however, a series of remarkable military figures had unified Japan politically, under the leadership of a supreme military commander known as the *shogun*, who hailed from the Tokugawa clan. With the end of Japan's civil wars, successive shoguns came to view Europeans as a threat to the country's newly established unity rather than an opportunity. They therefore expelled Christian missionaries and violently suppressed the practice of Christianity. This policy included the execution, often under torture, of some sixty-two missionaries and thousands of Japanese converts. Shogunate authorities also forbade Japanese from traveling abroad and banned most European traders altogether, permitting only the Dutch, who appeared less interested in spreading Christianity, to trade at a single site. Thus, for two centuries (1650–1850), Japanese authorities of the Tokugawa shogunate largely closed their country off from the emerging world of European commerce, although they maintained their trading ties to China and Korea.

Despite the European naval dominance in Asian waters, Asian merchants did not disappear. Arab, Chinese, Javanese, Malay, and other traders benefited from the upsurge in seaborne commerce. Chinese merchants, for example, continued to carry most of the spice trade from Southeast Asia to China. Overland trade within Asia remained wholly in Asian hands and grew considerably. Christian merchants from Armenia were particularly active in the overland commerce linking Europe, the Middle East, and Central Asia. Tens of thousands of Indian merchants and moneylenders, mostly Hindus representing sophisticated family firms, lived throughout Central Asia, Persia, and Russia, thus connecting this vast region to markets in India. These commercial networks, equivalent in their sophistication to those of Europe, continued to operate successfully even as Europeans militarized the seaborne commerce of the Indian Ocean.

Silver and Global Commerce

■ **Significance**
What was the world historical importance of the silver trade?

Even more than the spice trade of Eurasia, it was the silver trade that gave birth to a genuinely global network of exchange (see Map 15.2). As one historian put it, silver "went round the world and made the world go round."[7] The mid-sixteenth-century discovery of enormously rich silver deposits in Bolivia, and simultaneously in Japan, suddenly provided a vastly increased supply of that precious metal. Spanish America alone produced perhaps 85 percent of the world's silver during the early modern era. Spain's sole Asian colony, the Philippines, provided a critical link in this emerging network of global commerce. Manila, the colonial capital of the Philippines, was the destination of annual Spanish shipments of silver, which were drawn from the rich mines of Bolivia, transported initially to Acapulco in Mexico, and from there shipped across the Pacific to the Philippines. This trade was the first direct and sustained link between the Americas and Asia, and it initiated a web of Pacific commerce that grew steadily over the centuries.

Map 15.2 The Global Silver Trade
Silver was one of the first major commodities to be exchanged on a genuinely global scale.

At the heart of that Pacific web, and of early modern global commerce generally, was China's huge economy, and especially its growing demand for silver. In the

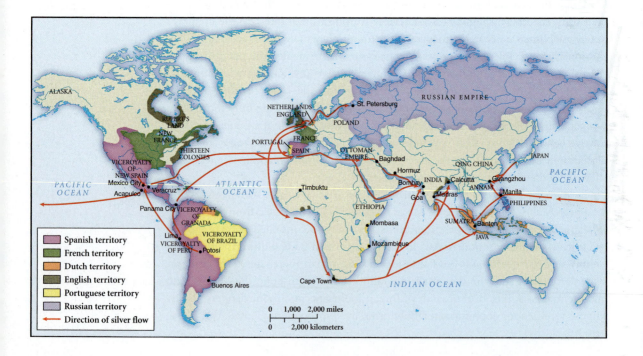

1570s, Chinese authorities consolidated a variety of tax levies into a single tax, which its huge population was now required to pay in silver. This sudden new demand for the white metal caused its value to skyrocket. It meant that foreigners with silver could now purchase far more of China's silks and porcelains than before.

This demand set silver in motion around the world, with the bulk of the world's silver supply winding up in China and much of the rest elsewhere in Asia. The routes by which this "silver drain" operated were numerous. Chinese, Portuguese, and Dutch traders flocked to Manila to sell Chinese goods in exchange for silver. European ships carried Japanese silver to China. Much of the silver shipped across the Atlantic to Spain was spent in Europe generally and then used to pay for the Asian goods that the French, British, and Dutch so greatly desired. Silver paid for some African slaves and for spices in Southeast Asia. The standard Spanish silver coin, known as a "piece of eight," was used by merchants in North America, Europe, India, Russia, and West Africa as a medium of exchange. By 1600, it circulated widely in southern China. A Portuguese merchant in 1621 noted that silver "wanders throughout all the world…before flocking to China, where it remains as if at its natural center."[8]

In its global journeys, silver transformed much that it touched. At the world's largest silver mine in what is now Bolivia, the city of Potosí arose from a barren landscape high in the Andes, a ten-week mule trip away from Lima. "New people arrive by the hour, attracted by the smell of silver," commented a Spanish observer in the 1570s. With 160,000 people, Potosí became the largest city in the Americas and equivalent in size to London, Amsterdam, or Seville. Its wealthy European elite lived in luxury, with all the goods of Europe and Asia at their disposal. Meanwhile, the city's Native American miners worked in conditions so horrendous that some families held funeral services for men drafted to work the mines. One Spanish priest referred to Potosí as a "portrait of hell."[9]

In Spain itself, which was the initial destination for much of Latin America's silver, the precious metal vastly enriched the Crown, making Spain the envy of its European rivals during the sixteenth century. Spanish rulers could now pursue military and political ambitions in both Europe and the Americas far beyond the country's own resource base. "New World mines," concluded one scholar, "supported the Spanish empire."[10] Nonetheless, this vast infusion of wealth did not fundamentally transform the Spanish economy, because it generated more inflation of prices than real economic

Potosí

This colonial-era painting shows the enormously rich silver mines of Potosí, then a major global source of the precious metal and the largest city in the Americas. Brutally hard work and poisonous exposure to mercury, which was used in the refining process, led to the deaths of many thousands of workers, even as the silver itself contributed to European splendor in the early modern era. (Courtesy, The Hispanic Society of America)

growth. A rigid economy laced with monopolies and regulations, an aristocratic class that preferred leisure to enterprise, and a crusading insistence on religious uniformity all prevented the Spanish from using their silver windfall in a productive fashion. When the value of silver dropped in the early seventeenth century, Spain lost its earlier position as the dominant Western European power.

Japan, another major source of silver production in the sixteenth century, did better. Its military rulers, the Tokugawa shoguns, used silver-generated profits to defeat hundreds of rival feudal lords and unify the country. Unlike their Spanish counterparts, the shoguns allied with the country's vigorous merchant class to develop a market-based economy and to invest heavily in agricultural and industrial enterprises. Japanese state and local authorities alike acted vigorously to protect and renew Japan's dwindling forests, while millions of families in the eighteenth century took steps to have fewer children by practicing late marriages, contraception, abortion, and infanticide. The outcome was the dramatic slowing of Japan's population growth, the easing of an impending ecological crisis, and a flourishing, highly commercialized economy. These were the foundations for Japan's remarkable nineteenth-century Industrial Revolution.

In China, silver deepened the already substantial commercialization of the country's economy. In order to obtain the silver needed to pay their taxes, more and more people had to sell something—either their labor or their products. Communities that devoted themselves to growing mulberry trees, on which silkworms fed, had to buy their rice from other regions. Thus the Chinese economy became more regionally specialized. Particularly in southern China, this surging economic growth resulted in the loss of about half the area's forest cover as more and more land was devoted to cash crops. No Japanese-style conservation program emerged to address this growing problem. An eighteenth-century Chinese poet, Wang Dayue, gave voice to the fears that this ecological transformation wrought:

> Rarer, too, their timber grew, and rarer still and rarer
> As the hills resembled heads now shaven clean of hair.
> For the first time, too, moreover, they felt an anxious mood
> That all their daily logging might not furnish them with fuel.[11]

China's role in the silver trade is a useful reminder of Asian centrality in the world economy of the early modern era. Its large and prosperous population, increasingly operating within a silver-based economy, fueled global commerce, vastly increasing the quantity of goods exchanged and the geographic range of world trade. Despite their obvious physical presence in the Americas, Africa, and Asia, economically speaking Europeans were essentially middlemen, funneling American silver to Asia and competing with one another for a place in the rich markets of the East. The productivity of the Chinese economy was evident in Spanish America, where cheap and well-made Chinese goods easily outsold those of Spain. In 1594, the Spanish viceroy of Peru observed that "a man can clothe his wife in Chinese silks for [25 pesos], whereas he could not provide her with clothing of Spanish silks with 200 pesos."[12] Indian cotton textiles likewise outsold European woolen or linen textiles in the seventeenth century to such an extent that French laws in 1717 prohibited the wearing of Indian cotton or Chinese silk clothing as a means of protecting French industry.

The "World Hunt": Fur in Global Commerce[13]

In the early modern era, furs joined silver, textiles, and spices as major items of global commerce. Their production had an important environmental impact as well as serious implications for the human societies that generated and consumed them. Furs, of course, had long provided warmth and conveyed status in colder regions of the world, but the integration of North America and of northern Asia (Siberia) into a larger world economy vastly increased their significance in global trade.

■ **Change**
Describe the impact of the fur trade on North American native societies.

By 1500, European population growth and agricultural expansion had sharply diminished the supply of fur-bearing animals, such as beaver, rabbits, sable, marten, and deer. Furthermore, much of the early modern era witnessed a period of cooling temperatures and harsh winters, known as the Little Ice Age, which may well have increased the demand for furs. "The weather is bitterly cold and everyone is in furs although we are almost in July," observed a surprised visitor from Venice while in London in 1604.[14] These conditions pushed prices higher. The cost of a good-quality beaver pelt, for example, quadrupled in France between 1558 and 1611. This translated into strong economic incentives for European traders to tap the immense wealth of fur-bearing animals found in North America.

Like other aspects of imperial expansion, the fur trade was a highly competitive enterprise. The French were most prominent in the St. Lawrence valley, around the Great Lakes, and later along the Mississippi River; British traders pushed into the Hudson Bay region; and the Dutch focused their attention along the Hudson River in what is now New York. They were frequently rivals for the great prize of North American furs. In the southern colonies of British North America, deerskins by the hundreds of thousands found a ready market in England's leather industry (see Map 15.3).

Only a few Europeans directly engaged in commercial trapping or hunting. They usually waited for Indians to bring the furs or skins initially to their coastal settlements and later to their fortified trading posts in the interior of North America. European merchants paid for the furs with a variety of trade goods, including guns, blankets, metal tools, rum, and brandy, amid much ceremony, haggling over prices, and ritualized gift-giving. Native Americans represented a cheap labor force in this international commercial effort, but they were not a directly coerced labor force.

Over the three centuries of the early modern era, enormous quantities of furs and deerskins found their way to Europe, where they considerably enhanced the standard of living in those cold climates. The environmental price was paid in the

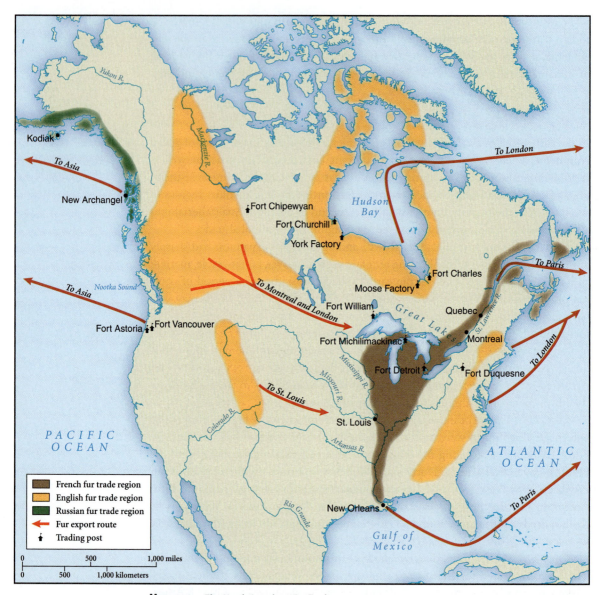

Map 15.3   The North American Fur Trade
North America, as well as Russian Siberia, funneled an apparently endless supply of furs into the circuits of global trade during the early modern era.

Americas, and it was high. A consistent demand for beaver hats led to the near extinction of that industrious animal in much of North America by the early nineteenth century. Many other fur-bearing species were seriously depleted as the trade moved inexorably westward. By the 1760s, hunters in southeastern British colonies took about 500,000 deer every year, seriously diminishing the deer population of the region.

For the Native American peoples who hunted, trapped, processed, and transported these products, the fur trade bore various benefits, particularly at the beginning. The Hurons, for example, who lived on the northern shores of Lakes Erie and Ontario in the early seventeenth century, annually exchanged some 20,000 to 30,000 pelts, mostly beaver, and in return received copper pots, metal axes, knives, cloth, firearms, and alcohol. Many of these items were of real value, which strengthened the Hurons in their relationship with neighboring peoples. These goods also enhanced the authority of Huron chiefs by providing them with gifts to distribute among their followers. At least initially, competition among Europeans ensured that Native American leaders could negotiate reasonable prices for their goods. Furthermore, their important role in the lucrative fur trade protected them for a time from the kind of extermination, enslavement, or displacement that was the fate of native peoples in Portuguese Brazil.

Nothing, however, protected them against the diseases carried by Europeans. In the 1630s and 1640s, to cite only one example of many, about half of the Hurons perished from influenza, smallpox, and other European-borne diseases. Furthermore, the fur trade generated warfare beyond anything previously known. Competition among Native American societies became more intense as the economic stakes grew higher. Catastrophic population declines owing to disease stimulated "mourning wars," designed to capture people who could be assimilated into much-diminished societies. A century of French-British rivalry for North America (1664–1763) forced Native American societies to take sides, to fight, and to die in these European imperial conflicts. Firearms, of course, made warfare far more deadly than before.

As many Native American peoples became enmeshed in commercial relationships with Europeans, they grew dependent on European trade goods. Among the Algonquians, for example, iron tools and cooking pots replaced those of stone, wood, or bone; gunpowder weapons took the place of bows and arrows; European textiles proved more attractive than traditional beaver and deerskin clothing; flint and steel were more effective for starting fires than wooden drills. A wide range of traditional crafts were thus lost, without the native peoples gaining a corresponding ability to manufacture the new items for themselves. Enthusiasm for these imported goods and continued European demands for furs and skins frequently eroded the customary restraint that characterized traditional hunting practices, resulting in the depletion of many species. One European observer wrote of the Creek Indians: "[They] wage eternal war against deer and bear... which is indeed carried to an unreasonable and perhaps criminal excess, since the white people have dazzled their senses with foreign superfluities."[15]

Beyond germs and guns, the most destructive of the imported goods was surely alcohol—rum and brandy, in particular. Whiskey, a locally produced grain-based alcohol, only added to the problem. With no prior experience of alcohol and little time to adjust to its easy availability, these drinks "hit Indian societies with explosive force."[16] Binge drinking, violence among young men, promiscuity, and addiction followed in many places. In 1753, Iroquois leaders complained bitterly to European authorities in Pennsylvania: "These wicked Whiskey Sellers, when they have once got the Indians in liquor, make them sell their very clothes from their backs.... If this practice be continued, we must be inevitably ruined."[17] In short, it was not so much the fur trade itself that decimated Native American societies, but all that accompanied it—disease, dependence, guns, alcohol, and the growing encroachment of European colonial empires.

■ **Comparison**

How did the North American and Siberian fur trades differ from each other? What did they have in common?

Much the same could be said about the other fur trade that was simultaneously taking shape within a rapidly expanding Russian Empire. As a new Russian state emerged from Mongol rule around the city of Moscow in the late fifteenth century, it became a major source of furs for both Western Europe and the Ottoman Empire. The profitability of that trade in furs was the chief incentive for Russia's rapid expansion during the sixteenth and seventeenth centuries across Siberia, where the "soft gold" of fur-bearing animals was abundant. With growing markets in both China and Europe, the fur trade greatly enriched the Russian state as well as many private merchants, trappers, and hunters. Here the silver trade and the fur trade intersected, as Europeans paid for Russian furs largely with American gold and silver.

The consequences for native Siberians were similar to those in North America as disease took its toll, as indigenous people became dependent on Russian goods, as the settler frontier encroached on native lands, and as many species of fur-bearing mammals were seriously depleted. In several ways, however, the Russian fur trade was unique. Whereas several European nations competed in North America and generally obtained their furs through commercial negotiations with Indian societies, no such competition accompanied Russian expansion across Siberia. Russian authorities imposed a tax or tribute, payable in furs, on every able-bodied Siberian male between eighteen and fifty years of age. To enforce the payment, they took hostages from Siberian societies, with death as a possible outcome if the required furs were not forthcoming. A further difference lay in the large-scale presence of private Russian hunters and trappers, who competed directly with their Siberian counterparts.

Fur and the Russians

This colored engraving shows a sixteenth-century Russian ambassador and his contingent arriving at the court of the Holy Roman Emperor and bearing gifts of animal pelts, the richest fruit of the expanding Russian Empire. (RIA Novosti)

Commerce in People: The Atlantic Slave Trade

Of all the commercial ties that linked the early modern world into a global network of exchange, none had more profound or enduring human consequences than the Atlantic slave trade. Between 1500 and 1866, this trade in humankind took an estimated 12.5 million people from African societies, shipped them across the Atlantic in the infamous Middle Passage, and deposited some 10.7 million of them in the Americas, where they lived out their often brief lives as slaves. About 1.8 million (14.4 percent) died during the transatlantic crossing, while countless millions more perished in the process of capture and transport to the African coast.[18] (See Map 15.4 and Documents: Voices of the Slave Trade, pp. 700–09, for various perspectives from the slave trade.)

Beyond the multitude of individual tragedies that it spawned—capture and sale, displacement from home cultures, forced labor, beatings and brandings, broken families—the Atlantic slave trade transformed the societies of all of its participants. Within Africa itself, some societies were thoroughly disrupted, others were strengthened, and many were corrupted. Elites were often enriched, while the slaves themselves, of course, were victimized beyond imagination.

Map 15.4   The Atlantic Slave Trade
Stimulated by the plantation complex of the Americas, the Atlantic slave trade represented an enormous extension of the ancient practice of people owning and selling other people.

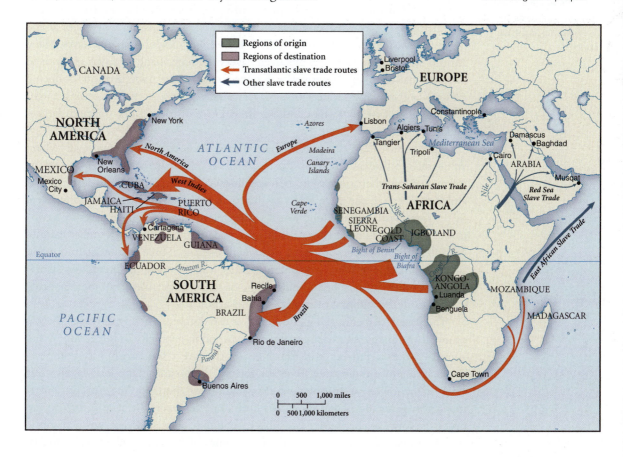

In the Americas, the slave trade added a substantial African presence to the mix of European and Native American peoples. This African diaspora (the transatlantic spread of African peoples) injected into these new societies issues of race that endure still in the twenty-first century. It also introduced elements of African culture, such as religious ideas, musical and artistic traditions, and cuisine, into the making of American cultures. The profits from the slave trade and the forced labor of African slaves certainly enriched European and Euro-American societies, even as the practice of slavery contributed much to the racial thinking of European peoples. Finally, slavery became a metaphor for many kinds of social oppression, quite different from plantation slavery, in the centuries that followed. Workers protested the slavery of wage labor, colonized people rejected the slavery of imperial domination, and feminists sometimes defined patriarchy as a form of slavery.

The Slave Trade in Context

■ **Comparison**

What was distinctive about the Atlantic slave trade? What did it share with other patterns of slave owning and slave trading?

The Atlantic slave trade and slavery in the Americas represented the most recent large-scale expression of an almost universal human practice—the owning and exchange of human beings. With origins in the earliest civilizations, slavery was widely accepted as a perfectly normal human enterprise and was closely linked to warfare and capture. Before 1500, the Mediterranean and Indian Ocean basins were the major arenas of the Old World slave trade, and southern Russia was a major source of slaves. Many African societies likewise both practiced slavery themselves and sold slaves into these international commercial networks. A trans-Saharan slave trade had long funneled African captives into Mediterranean slavery, and an East African slave trade brought Africans into the Middle East and the Indian Ocean basin. Both operated largely within the Islamic world.

Furthermore, slavery came in many forms. Although slaves were everywhere vulnerable "outsiders" to their masters' societies, in many places they could be assimilated into their owners' households, lineages, or communities. In some places, children inherited the slave status of their parents; elsewhere those children were free persons. Within the Islamic world, the preference was for female slaves by a two-to-one margin, while the later Atlantic slave trade favored males by a similar margin. Not all slaves, however, occupied degraded positions. Some in the Islamic world acquired prominent military or political status. Most slaves in the premodern world worked in their owners' households, farms, or shops, with smaller numbers laboring in large-scale agricultural or industrial enterprises.

The slavery that emerged in the Americas was distinctive in several ways. One was simply the immense size of the traffic in slaves and its centrality to the economies of colonial America. Furthermore, this New World slavery was largely based on plantation agriculture and treated slaves as a form of dehumanized property, lacking any rights in the society of their owners. Slave status throughout the Americas was inherited across generations, and there was little hope of eventual freedom for the vast majority. Nowhere else, with the possible exception of ancient Greece, was widespread slavery associated with societies affirming values of human freedom and equality.

Perhaps most distinctive was the racial dimension: Atlantic slavery came to be identified wholly with Africa and with "blackness." How did this exceptional form of slavery emerge?

The origins of Atlantic slavery clearly lie in the Mediterranean world and with that now common sweetener known as sugar. Until the Crusades, Europeans knew nothing of sugar and relied on honey and fruits to sweeten their bland diets. However, as they learned from the Arabs about sugarcane and the laborious techniques for producing usable sugar, Europeans established sugar-producing plantations within the Mediterranean and later on various islands off the coast of West Africa. It was a "modern" industry, perhaps the first one, in that it required huge capital investment, substantial technology, an almost factory-like discipline among workers, and a mass market of consumers. The immense difficulty and danger of the work, the limitations attached to serf labor, and the general absence of wage workers all pointed to slavery as a source of labor for sugar plantations.

Initially, Slavic-speaking peoples from the Black Sea region furnished the bulk of the slaves for Mediterranean plantations, so much so that "Slav" became the basis for the word "slave" in many European languages. In 1453, however, when the Ottoman Turks seized Constantinople, the supply of Slavic slaves was effectively cut off. At the same time, Portuguese mariners were exploring the coast of West Africa; they were looking primarily for gold, but they also found there an alternative source of slaves available for sale. Thus, when sugar, and later tobacco and cotton, plantations took hold in the Americas, Europeans had already established links to a West African source of supply.

Largely through a process of elimination, Africa became the primary source of slave labor for the plantation economies of the Americas. Slavic peoples were no longer available; Native Americans quickly perished from European diseases; marginal Europeans were Christians and therefore supposedly exempt from slavery; and European indentured servants were expensive and temporary. Africans, on the other hand, were skilled farmers; they had some immunity to both tropical and European diseases; they were not Christians; they were, relatively speaking, close at hand; and they were readily available in substantial numbers through African-operated commercial networks.

Moreover, Africans were black. The precise relationship between slavery and European

■ **Causation**
What explains the rise of the Atlantic slave trade?

The Middle Passage
This mid-nineteenth-century painting of slaves held below deck on a Spanish slave ship illustrates the horrendous conditions of the transatlantic voyage, a journey experienced by many millions of captured Africans. (The Art Archive)

racism has long been a much-debated subject. Historian David Brion Davis has suggested the controversial view that "racial stereotypes were transmitted, along with black slavery itself, from Muslims to Christians."[19] For many centuries, Muslims had drawn on sub-Saharan Africa as one source of slaves and in the process had developed a form of racism. The fourteenth-century Tunisian scholar Ibn Khaldun wrote that black people were "submissive to slavery, because Negroes have little that is essentially human and have attributes that are quite similar to those of dumb animals."[20]

Other scholars find the origins of racism within European culture itself. For the English, argues historian Audrey Smedley, the process of conquering Ireland had generated by the sixteenth century a view of the Irish as "rude, beastly, ignorant, cruel, and unruly infidels," perceptions that were then transferred to Africans enslaved on English sugar plantations of the West Indies.[21] Whether Europeans borrowed such images of Africans from their Muslim neighbors or developed them independently, slavery and racism soon went hand in hand. "Europeans were better able to tolerate their brutal exploitation of Africans," writes a prominent world historian, "by imagining that these Africans were an inferior race, or better still, not even human."[22]

The Slave Trade in Practice

■ Connection

What roles did Europeans and Africans play in the unfolding of the Atlantic slave trade?

The European demand for slaves was clearly the chief cause of this tragic commerce, and from the point of sale on the African coast to the massive use of slave labor on American plantations, the entire enterprise was in European hands. Within Africa itself, however, a different picture emerges, for over the four centuries of the Atlantic slave trade, European demand elicited an African supply. A few early efforts by the Portuguese at slave raiding along the West African coast convinced Europeans that such efforts were unnecessary and unwise, for African societies were quite capable of defending themselves against European intrusion, and many were willing to sell their slaves peacefully. Furthermore, Europeans died like flies when they entered the interior because they lacked immunities to common tropical diseases. Thus the slave trade quickly came to operate largely with Europeans waiting on the coast, either on their ships or in fortified settlements, to purchase slaves from African merchants and political elites. Certainly Europeans tried to exploit African rivalries to obtain slaves at the lowest possible cost, and the firearms they funneled into West Africa may well have increased the warfare from which so many slaves were derived. But from the point of initial capture to sale on the coast, the entire enterprise was normally in African hands. Almost nowhere did Europeans attempt outright military conquest; instead they generally dealt as equals with local African authorities.

An arrogant agent of the British Royal Africa Company in the 1680s learned the hard way who was in control when he spoke improperly to the king of Niumi, a small state in what is now Gambia. The company's records describe what happened next:

[O]ne of the grandees [of the king], by name Sambalama, taught him better manners by reaching him a box on the ears, which beat off his hat, and a few thumps

on the back, and seizing him, disarmed him together with the rest of his attendance, among which was Benedict Stafford, commander of the *Margaret*...(who
made his escape and ran like a lusty fellow to his ship) and several others, who
together with the agent were taken and put into the king's pound and stayed
there three or four days till their ransom was brought, value five hundred bars.[23]

In exchange for slaves, African sellers sought both European and Indian textiles,
cowrie shells (widely used as money in West Africa), European metal goods, firearms
and gunpowder, tobacco and alcohol, and various decorative items such as beads.
Europeans purchased some of these items—cowrie shells and Indian textiles, for
example—with silver mined in the Americas. Thus the slave trade connected with
commerce in silver and textiles as it became part of an emerging worldwide network
of exchange. Issues about the precise mix of goods African authorities desired, about
the number and quality of slaves to be purchased, and always about the price of everything were settled in endless negotiation (see Document 15.2, pp. 703–05). In most
places most of the time, a leading scholar concluded, the slave trade took place "not
unlike international trade anywhere in the world of the period."[24]

If African authorities and elite classes in many places controlled their side of
the slave trade, on occasion they were almost overwhelmed by it. Many small-scale
kinship-based societies, lacking the protection of a strong state, were thoroughly disrupted by raids from more powerful neighbors. Even some sizable states were desta-
bilized. In the early sixteenth century, the kingdom of Kongo, located mostly in
present-day Angola, was badly damaged by the commerce in slaves and the authority of its ruler severely undermined (see Document 15.3, pp. 705–07).

Whatever the relationship between European buyers and African sellers, for the
slaves themselves—who were seized in the interior, often sold several times on the har-
rowing journey to the coast, sometimes branded, and held in squalid slave dungeons
while awaiting transportation to the New World—it was anything but a normal commercial transaction (see Document 15.1, pp. 700–03). One European engaged in the
trade noted that "the negroes are so willful and loath to leave their own country, that
they have often leap'd out of the canoes, boat, and ship, into the sea, and kept under
water till they were drowned, to avoid being taken up and saved by our boats."[25]

Over the four centuries of the slave trade, millions of Africans underwent some
such experience, but their numbers varied considerably over time. During the sixteenth century, slave exports from Africa averaged under 3,000 annually. In those
years, the Portuguese were at least as much interested in African gold, spices, and
textiles. Furthermore, as in Asia, they became involved in transporting African
goods, including slaves, from one African port to another, thus becoming the "truck
drivers" of coastal West African commerce.[26] In the seventeenth century, the pace
picked up as the slave trade became highly competitive, with the British, Dutch, and
French contesting the earlier Portuguese monopoly. The century and a half between
1700 and 1850 marked the high point of the slave trade as the plantation economies
of the Americas boomed (see the Snapshot on p. 694).

$\mathcal{S}$napshot   **The Slave Trade in Numbers (1501–1866)[27]**

The Rise and Decline of the Slave Trade

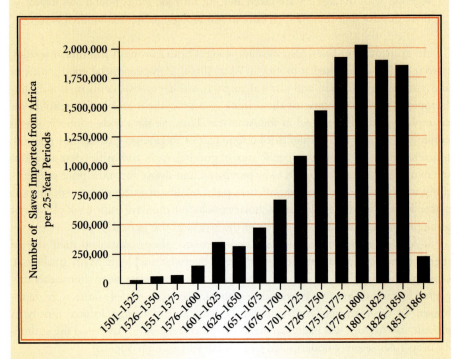

The Destinations of Slaves

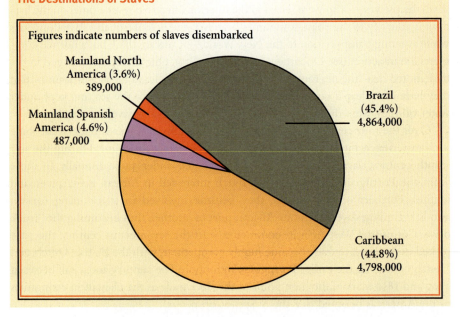

Where did these Africans come from, and where did they go? Geographically, the slave trade drew mainly on the societies of West Africa, from present-day Mauritania in the north to Angola in the south. Initially focused on the coastal regions, the slave trade progressively penetrated into the interior as the demand for slaves picked up. Socially, slaves were mostly drawn from various marginal groups in African societies—prisoners of war, criminals, debtors, people who had been "pawned" during times of difficulty. Thus Africans did not generally sell "their own people" into slavery. Divided into hundreds of separate, usually small-scale, and often rival communities—cities, kingdoms, microstates, clans, and villages—the various peoples of West Africa had no concept of an "African" identity. Those whom they captured and sold were normally outsiders, vulnerable people who lacked the protection of membership in an established community. When short-term economic or political advantage could be gained, such people were sold. In this respect, the Atlantic slave trade was little different from the experience of enslavement elsewhere in the world.

The destination of enslaved Africans, half a world away in the Americas, was very different. The vast majority wound up in Brazil or the Caribbean, where the labor demands of the plantation economy were most intense. Smaller numbers found themselves in North America, mainland Spanish America or in Europe itself. The journey across the Atlantic was horrendous almost beyond description, with the Middle Passage having an overall mortality rate of more than 14 percent (see Document 15.1, pp. 700–03). About 10 percent of the transatlantic voyages experienced a major rebellion by the desperate captives.

Comparing Consequences: The Impact of the Slave Trade in Africa

From the viewpoint of world history, the chief outcome of the slave trade lay in the new transregional linkages that it generated. Both commercially and demographically, Africa became a permanent part of an interacting Atlantic world. Millions of its people were now compelled to make their lives in the Americas. West African economies were increasingly connected to an emerging European-centered world economy. These vast processes set in motion a chain of consequences that have transformed the lives and societies of people on both sides of the Atlantic.

■ **Change**
In what different ways did the Atlantic slave trade transform African societies?

Although the slave trade did not result in the kind of population collapse that occurred in the Americas, it certainly slowed Africa's growth at a time when Europe, China, and other regions were expanding demographically. Scholars have estimated that sub-Saharan Africa represented about 18 percent of the world's population in 1600, but only 6 percent in 1900.[28] A portion of that difference reflects the slave trade's impact on Africa's population history.

That impact derived not only from the loss of millions of people over four centuries but also from the economic stagnation and political disruption that the slave trade generated. Economically, the slave trade stimulated little positive change in Africa because those Africans who benefited most from the traffic in people were not investing in the productive capacities of African societies. Although European imports generally did not displace traditional artisan manufacturing, no technological breakthroughs in agriculture or industry increased the wealth available to these societies. Maize and manioc (cassava), introduced from the Americas, added a new source of calories to African diets, but the international demand was for Africa's people, not its agricultural products.

Within particular African societies, the impact of the slave trade differed considerably from place to place and over time. Particularly in small-scale societies that were frequently subjected to slave raiding and that had little centralized authority, insecurity was pervasive. Oral traditions in southern Ghana, for example, reported that "there was no rest in the land," that people went about in groups rather than alone, and that mothers kept their children inside when European ships appeared.[29] Some larger kingdoms such as Kongo and Oyo slowly disintegrated as access to trading opportunities and firearms enabled outlying regions to establish their independence. However, African authorities also sought to take advantage of the new commercial opportunities and to manage the slave trade in their own interests, as the contrasting experience of the neighboring kingdoms of Benin and Dahomey illustrates.[30]

The kingdom of Benin, in the forest area of present-day Nigeria, was one of the oldest and most highly developed states in the coastal hinterland of West Africa, dating perhaps to the eleventh century C.E. Its capital was a large walled city with wide avenues, a lavish court, a wealthy elite, and a powerful monarch, or *oba*, who strictly controlled the country's trade. Benin's uniqueness lay in its relatively successful efforts to avoid a deep involvement in the slave trade and to diversify the exports with which it purchased European firearms and other goods. As early as 1516, the oba began to restrict the slave trade and soon forbade the export of male slaves altogether, a ban that lasted until the early eighteenth century. By then, the oba's authority over outlying areas had declined, and the country's major exports of pepper and cotton cloth had lost out to Asian and then European competition. In these circumstances, Benin felt compelled to resume limited participation in the slave trade. But even at the height of the trade, in the late eighteenth century, Benin exported fewer than 1,000 slaves a year.

Among the Aja-speaking peoples to the west of Benin, the situation was very different. There the slave trade had thoroughly disrupted a series of small and weak states along the coast. Some distance inland, the kingdom of Dahomey arose in the early eighteenth century, at least in part as an effort to contain the constant raiding and havoc occasioned by the coastal trade. It was a unique and highly authoritarian state in which commoners and chiefs alike were responsible directly to the king and in which the power of lineages and secret societies was considerably weakened. For a time, Dahomey tried to limit the external slave trade, to import European craftsmen, and to develop plantation agriculture within the kingdom, but all this failed. In view of hostile relations with the neighboring kingdom of Oyo and others, Dahomey instead turned to a vigorous involvement in the slave trade, under strict royal control.

The army conducted annual slave raids, and the government soon came to depend on the trade for its essential revenues. Unlike in Benin, the slave trade in Dahomey became the chief business of the state and remained so until well into the nineteenth century.

Reflections: Economic Globalization— Then and Now

The study of history reminds us of two quite contradictory truths. One is that our lives in the present bear remarkable similarities to those of people long ago. We are perhaps not so unique as we might think. The other is that our lives are very different from theirs and that things have changed substantially. This chapter about global commerce—long-distance trade in spices and textiles, silver and gold, beaver pelts and deerskins, slaves and sugar—provides both perspectives.

If we are accustomed to thinking about globalization as a product of the late twentieth century, early modern world history provides a corrective. Those three centuries reveal much that is familiar to people of the twenty-first century—the global circulation of goods; an international currency; production for a world market; the growing economic role of the West on the global stage; private enterprise, such as the British and Dutch East India companies, operating on a world scale; national governments eager to support their merchants in a highly competitive environment. By the eighteenth century, many Europeans dined from Chinese porcelain dishes called "china," wore Indian-made cotton textiles, and drank chocolate from Mexico, tea from China, and coffee from Yemen while sweetening these beverages with sugar from the Caribbean or Brazil. The millions who worked to produce these goods, whether slave or free, were operating in a world economy. Some industries were thoroughly international. New England rum producers, for example, depended on molasses imported from the Caribbean, while the West Indian sugar industry used African labor and European equipment to produce for a global market.

Nonetheless, early modern economic globalization was a far cry from that of the twentieth century. Most obvious perhaps were scale and speed. By 2000, immensely more goods circulated internationally and far more people produced for and depended on the world market than was the case even in 1750. Back-and-forth communications between England and India that took eighteen months in the eighteenth century could be accomplished in an hour by telegraph in the late nineteenth century and almost instantaneously via the Internet in the late twentieth century. Moreover, by 1900 globalization was firmly centered in the economies of Europe and North America. In the early modern era, by contrast, Asia in general and China in particular remained major engines of the world economy, despite the emerging presence of Europeans around the world. By the end of the twentieth century, the booming economies of India and China suggested at least a partial return to that earlier pattern.

Early modern globalization differed in still other ways from that of the contemporary world. Economic life then was primarily preindustrial, still powered by human and animal muscles, wind, and water and lacking the enormous productive capacity that accompanied the later technological breakthrough of the steam engine and the Industrial Revolution. Finally, the dawning of a genuinely global economy in the early modern era was tied unapologetically to empire building and to slavery, both of which had been discredited by the late twentieth century. Slavery lost its legitimacy during the nineteenth century, and formal territorial empires largely disappeared in the twentieth. Most people during the early modern era would have been surprised to learn that a global economy, as it turned out, could function effectively without either of these long-standing practices.

Second Thoughts

What's the Significance?

To assess your mastery of the material in this chapter, visit the **Student Center** at bedfordstmartins.com/strayer.

Indian Ocean commercial network
trading post empire
Philippines (Spanish)

British/Dutch East India companies
Tokugawa shogunate
"silver drain"

Potosí
"soft gold"
African diaspora
Benin/Dahomey

Big Picture Questions

1. In what specific ways did trade foster change in the world of the early modern era?
2. To what extent did Europeans transform earlier patterns of commerce, and in what ways did they assimilate into those older patterns?
3. Describe and account for the differing outcomes of European expansion in the Americas (see Chapter 14), Africa, and Asia.
4. How should we distribute the moral responsibility for the Atlantic slave trade? Is this a task appropriate for historians?
5. What lasting legacies of early modern globalization are evident in the early twenty-first century? Pay particular attention to the legacies of the slave trade.

Next Steps: For Further Study

For Web sites and additional documents related to this chapter, see **Make History** at bedfordstmartins.com/strayer.

Glenn J. Ames, *The Globe Encompassed: The Age of European Discovery, 1500–1700* (2007). An up-to-date survey of European expansion in the early modern era.

Andre Gunder Frank, *ReOrient: Global Economy in the Asian Age* (1998). An account of the early modern world economy that highlights the centrality of Asia.

Erik Gilbert and Jonathan Reynolds, *Trading Tastes: Commodity and Cultural Exchange to 1750* (2006). A world historical perspective on transcontinental and transoceanic commerce.

David Northrup, ed., *The Atlantic Slave Trade* (2002). A fine collection of essays about the origins, practice, impact, and abolition of Atlantic slavery.

John Richards, *The Endless Frontier* (2003). Explores the ecological consequences of early modern commerce.

John Thornton, *Africa and Africans in the Making of the Atlantic World* (1998). A well-regarded but somewhat controversial account of the slave trade, with an emphasis on African authorities as active and independent players in the process.

"Atlantic Slave Trade and Slave Life in the Americas: A Visual Record," http://hitchcock.itc.virginia .edu/Slavery/index.php. An immense collection of maps and images illustrating the slave trade and the life of slaves in the Americas.

Documents

Considering the Evidence: Voices from the Slave Trade

By any measure the Atlantic slave trade was an enormous enterprise and enormously significant in modern world history: its geographical scope encompassed four continents, it endured for over four centuries, its victims numbered in the many millions, its commercial operation was complex and highly competitive, and its consequences echo still in both public and private life (see pp. 689–97). The four documents that follow allow us to hear several individual voices from this vast historical process and to sample the evidence available to historians as they seek to understand this tragic chapter of the human story.

Document 15.1

The Journey to Slavery

We begin with the voice of an individual victim of the slave trade—Olaudah Equiano. Born in what is now the Igbo-speaking region of Nigeria around 1745, Equiano was seized from his home at the age of eleven and sold into the Atlantic slave trade at the high point of that infamous commerce (see Map 15.4, p. 689). In service to three different owners, his experience as a slave in the Americas was quite unusual. He learned to read and write, traveled extensively as a seaman aboard one of his masters' ships, and was allowed to buy his freedom in 1766. Settling in England, he became a prominent voice in the emerging abolitionist movement of the late eighteenth century and wrote a widely read account of his life, addressed largely to European Christians: "O, ye nominal Christians! Might not an African ask you, Learned you this from your God, who says unto you, Do unto all men as you would men should do unto you?" His book was published in 1789 as abolitionism was gaining wider acceptance.

Despite some controversy about his birthplace and birth date, most historians accept Equiano's autobiography as broadly accurate. Document 15.1 presents Equiano's account of his capture, his journey to the coast, his experience on a slave ship, and his arrival in the Americas. It was a journey forcibly undertaken by millions of others as well.

- How does Equiano describe the kind of slavery he knew in Africa itself? How does it compare with the plantation slavery of the Americas?

- What part did Africans play in the slave trade, according to this account?

- What aspects of the shipboard experience contributed to the slaves' despair?

OLAUDAH EQUIANO

The Interesting Narrative of the Life of Olaudah Equiano

1789

As we live in a country where nature is prodigal of her favours, our wants are few and easily supplied; of course we have few manufactures. They consist for the most part of calicoes, earthen ware, ornaments, and instruments of war and husbandry.... We have also markets, at which I have been frequently with my mother. These are sometimes visited by stout mahogany-coloured men from the south west of us:...They generally bring us fire-arms, gunpowder, hats, beads, and dried fish....They always carry slaves through our land;...Sometimes indeed we sold slaves to them, but they were only prisoners of war, or such among us as had been convicted of kidnapping or adultery, and some other crimes, which we esteemed heinous....

My father, besides many slaves, had a numerous family, of which seven lived to grow up, including myself and a sister, who was the only daughter....I was trained up from my earliest years in the art of war; my daily exercise was shooting and throwing javelins; and my mother adorned me with emblems, after the manner of our greatest warriors. In this way I grew up till I was turned the age of eleven, when an end was put to my happiness in the following manner....

Source: Olaudah Equiano, *The Interesting Narrative of the Life of Olaudah Equiano, or Gustavus Vassa, the African,* vol. 1 (London, 1789), chaps. 1, 2.

One day, when all our people were gone out to their works as usual, and only I and my dear sister were left to mind the house, two men and a woman got over our walls and in a moment seized us both, and, without giving us time to cry out, or make resistance, they stopped our mouths, and ran off with us into the nearest wood. Here they tied our hands, and continued to carry us as far as they could, till night came on....The next morning we left the house, and continued travelling all the day. For a long time we had kept the woods, but at last we came into a road which I believed I knew. I had now some hopes of being delivered; for we had advanced but a little way before I discovered some people at a distance, on which I began to cry out for their assistance: but my cries had no other effect than to make them tie me faster and stop my mouth, and then they put me into a large sack....

The next day proved a day of greater sorrow than I had yet experienced; for my sister and I were then separated, while we lay clasped in each other's arms. It was in vain that we besought them not to part us; she was torn from me, and immediately carried away....

At length, after many days traveling, during which I had often changed masters, I got into the hands of a chieftain, in a very pleasant country. This man had two wives and some children, and they all used me extremely well, and did all they could to comfort me; particularly the first wife, who was something like my mother. Although I was a great many days journey from my father's house, yet these people spoke exactly the same language with us....

[After about a month], I was again sold. I was now carried to the left of the sun's rising, through many different countries, and a number of large woods. The people I was sold to used to carry me very often, when I was tired, either on their shoulders or on their backs. I saw many convenient well-built sheds along the roads, at proper distances, to accommodate the merchants and travelers, who lay in those buildings along with their wives, who often accompany them; and they always go well armed.

I was again sold, and carried through a number of places, till, after traveling a considerable time, I came to a town called Tinmah, in the most beautiful country I had yet seen in Africa.... Their money consisted of little white shells, the size of the finger nail. I was sold here for one hundred and seventy-two of them by a merchant who lived and brought me there. I had been about two or three days at his house, when a wealthy widow, a neighbor of his, came there one evening, and brought with her an only son, a young gentleman about my own age and size. Here they saw me; and, having taken a fancy to me, I was bought of the merchant, and went home with them.... The next day I was washed and perfumed, and when meal-time came I was led into the presence of my mistress, and ate and drank before her with her son. This filled me with astonishment; and I could scarce help expressing my surprise that the young gentleman should suffer me, who was bound, to eat with him who was free; and not only so, but that he would not at any time either eat or drink till I had taken first, because I was the eldest, which was agreeable to our custom. Indeed everything here, and all their treatment of me, made me forget that I was a slave. The language of these people resembled ours so nearly, that we understood each other perfectly,... In this resemblance to my former happy state I passed about two months; and I now began to think I was to be adopted into the family, and was beginning to be reconciled to my situation, and to forget by degrees my misfortunes when all at once the delusion vanished; for, without the least

previous knowledge, one morning early, while my dear master and companion was still asleep, I was wakened out of my reverie to fresh sorrow, and hurried away....

Thus I continued to travel, sometimes by land, sometimes by water, through different countries and various nations, till, at the end of six or seven months after I had been kidnapped, I arrived at the sea coast.... The first object which saluted my eyes when I arrived on the coast was the sea, and a slave ship, which was then riding at anchor, and waiting for its cargo. These filled me with astonishment, which was soon converted into terror when I was carried on board. I was immediately handled and tossed up to see if I were sound by some of the crew; and I was now persuaded that I had gotten into a world of bad spirits, and that they were going to kill me. Their complexions too differing so much from ours, their long hair, and the language they spoke... united to confirm me in this belief.... When I looked round the ship too and saw a large furnace or copper boiling, and a multitude of black people of every description chained together, every one of their countenances expressing dejection and sorrow, I no longer doubted of my fate; and quite overpowered with horror and anguish, I fell motionless on the deck and fainted....

I was soon put down under the decks, and there I received such a salutation in my nostrils as I had never experienced in my life: so that, with the loathsomeness of the stench and crying together, I became so sick and low that I was not able to eat, nor had I the least desire to taste anything. I now wished for the last friend, death, to relieve me; but soon, to my grief, two of the white men offered me eatables; and on my refusing to eat, one of them held me fast by the hands, and laid me across I think the windlass and tied my feet, while the other flogged me severely....

I had never seen among any people such instances of brutal cruelty; and this not only shewn towards us blacks, but also to some of the whites themselves. One white man in particular I saw, when we were permitted to be on deck, flogged so unmercifully with a large rope near the foremast that he died in consequence of it; and they tossed him over the side as they would have done a brute....

The closeness of the place, and the heat of the climate, added to the number in the ship, which was so crowded that each had scarcely room to turn himself, almost suffocated us. This produced copious perspirations, so that the air soon became unfit for respiration, from a variety of loathsome smells, and brought on a sickness among the slaves, of which many died, thus falling victims to the improvident avarice, as I may call it, of their purchasers. This wretched situation was again aggravated by the galling of the chains, now become insupportable; and the filth of the necessary tubs, into which the children often fell, and were almost suffocated. The shrieks of the women, and the groans of the dying, rendered the whole a scene of horror almost inconceivable....

At last we came in sight of the island of Barbados, at which the whites on board gave a great shout, and made many signs of joy to us.... Many merchants and planters now came on board, though it was in the evening. They put us in separate parcels, and examined us attentively. They also made us jump, and pointed to the land, signifying we were to go there. We thought by this we should be eaten by those ugly men, as they appeared to us;... at last the white people got some old slaves from the land to pacify us. They told us we were not to be eaten, but to work, and were soon to go on land, where we should see many of our country people. This report eased us much; and sure enough, soon after we were landed, there came to us Africans of all languages. We were conducted immediately to the merchant's yard, where we were all pent up together like so many sheep in a fold, without regard to sex or age.

Document 15.2

The Business of the Slave Trade

For its African victims like Equiano, the slave trade was a horror beyond their imagination; for kings and merchants—both European and African—it was a business. Document 15.2 shows how that business was conducted. It comes from the journal of an English merchant, Thomas Phillips, who undertook a voyage to the kingdom of Whydah in what is now the West African country of Benin in 1693–1694.

- How would you describe the economic transactions described in the document? To what extent were they conducted between equal parties? Who, if anyone, held the upper hand in these dealings?

- What obstacles did European merchants confront in negotiating with African authorities?

- How might an African merchant have described the same transaction? How might Equiano describe it?

- Notice the outcomes of Phillips's voyage to Barbados in the last two paragraphs. What does this tell you about European preferences for slaves, about the Middle Passage, and about the profitability of the enterprise?

THOMAS PHILLIPS

A Journal of a Voyage Made in the Hannibal of London

1694

As soon as the king understood of our landing, he sent two of his cappasheirs, or noblemen, to compliment us at our factory, where we design'd to continue that night, and pay our [respects] to his majesty next day…whereupon he sent two more of his grandees to invite us there that night, saying he waited for us, and that all former captains used to attend him the first night: whereupon being unwilling to infringe the custom, or give his majesty any offence, we took our hamocks, and Mr. Peirson, myself, Capt. Clay, our surgeons, pursers, and about 12 men, arm'd for our guard, were carry'd to the king's town, which contains about 50 houses.…

We returned him thanks by his interpreter, and assur'd him how great affection our masters, the royal African company of England, bore to him, for his civility and fair and just dealings with their captains; and that notwithstanding there were many other places, more plenty of negro slaves that begg'd their custom, yet they had rejected all the advantageous offers made them out of their good will to him, and therefore had sent us to trade with him, to support his country with necessaries, and that we hop'd he would endeavour to continue their favour by his kind usage and fair dealing with us in our trade, that we may have our slaves with all expedition.… He answer'd that we should be fairly dealt with, and not impos'd upon; But he did not prove as good as his word…so after having examin'd us about our cargoe, what sort of goods we had, and what quantity of slaves we wanted, etc., we took our leaves and return'd to the factory.…

According to promise we attended his majesty with samples of our goods, and made our agreement about the prices, tho' not without much difficulty;… next day we paid our customs to the king and cappasheirs,… then the bell was order'd to go about to give notice to all people to bring their slaves to the trunk to sell us.…

Capt. Clay and I had agreed to go to the trunk to buy the slaves by turns, each his day, that we might have no distractions or disagreement in our trade, as often happens when there are here more ships than one, and…their disagreements create animosities, underminings, and out-bidding each other, whereby they enhance the prices to their general loss and detriment, the blacks well knowing how to make the best use of such opportunities, and as we found make it their business, and endeavour to create and foment misunderstandings and jealousies between commanders, it turning to their great account in the disposal of their slaves.

When we were at the trunk, the king's slaves, if he had any, were the first offer'd to sale,… and we must not refuse them, tho' as I observ'd they were generally the worst slaves in the trunk, and we paid more for them than any others, which we could not remedy, it being one of his majesty's perogatives: then the cappasheirs each brought out his slaves according to his degree and quality, the greatest first, etc. and our surgeon examin'd them well in all kinds, to see that they were sound wind and limb, making them jump, stretch out their arms swiftly, looking in their mouths to judge of their age; for the cappasheirs are so cunning, that they shave them all close before we see them, so that let them be never so old we can see no grey hairs in their heads or beards; and then having liquor'd them well and sleek with palm oil, 'tis no easy matter to know an old one from a middle-age one.…

When we had selected from the rest such as we liked, we agreed in what goods to pay for them, the prices being already stated before the king, how much of each sort of merchandize we were to give for a

Source: Thomas Phillips, "A Journal of a Voyage Made in the Hannibal of London in 1694," in *Documents Illustrative of the History of the Slave Trade to America*, edited by Elizabeth Donnan (Washington DC: Carnegie Institute, 1930), 399–405, 408, 410.

man, woman, and child, which gave us much ease, and saved abundance of disputes and wranglings.... [T]hen we mark'd the slaves we had bought in the breast, or shoulder, with a hot iron, having the letter of the ship's name on it, the place being before anointed with a little palm oil, which caus'd but little pain, the mark being usually well in four or five days, appearing very plain and white after....

After we are come to an agreement for the prices of our slaves,...we are oblig'd to pay our customs to the king and cappasheirs for leave to trade, protection and justice; which for every ship are as follow, *viz.*

To the king six slaves value in cowries, or what other goods we can perswade him to take, but cowries are most esteem'd and desir'd; all which are measur'd in his presence, and he would wrangle with us stoutly about heaping up the measure.

To the cappasheirs in all two slaves value, as above....

The best goods to purchase slaves here are cowries, the smaller the more esteem'd....

The next in demand are brass neptunes or basons, very large, thin, and flat; for after they have bought them they cut them in pieces to make...bracelets, and collars for their arms legs and necks....

[I]f they can discover that you have good store of cowries and brass aboard, then no other goods will serve their turn, till they have got as much as you have; and after, for the rest of the goods they will be indifferent, and make you come to their own terms, or else lie a long time for your slaves, so that those you have on board are dying while you are buying others ashore; therefore every man that comes here, ought to be very cautious in making his report to the king at first, of what sorts and quantities of goods he has, and be sure to say his cargo consists mostly in iron, coral, rangoes, chints, etc. so that he may dispose of those goods as soon as he can, and at last his cowries and brass will bring him slaves as fast as he can buy them; but this is to be understood of a single ship: or more, if the captains agree, which seldom happens; for where there are divers ships, and of separate interests, about buying the same commodity they commonly undermine, betray, and out-bid one the other; and the Guiney commanders words and promises are the least to be depended upon of any I know use the sea; for they would deceive their fathers in their trade if they could....

Having bought my compliment of 700 slaves, *viz.* 480 men and 220 women, and finish'd all my business at Whidaw, I took my leave of the old king, and his cappasheirs, and parted, with many affectionate expressions on both sides, being forced to promise him that I would return again the next year, with several things he desired me to bring him from England; and having sign'd bills of lading...for the negroes aboard, I set sail the 27th of July in the morning....

I deliver'd alive at Barbadoes to the company's factors 372, which being sold, came out at about nineteen pounds per head.

Document 15.3

The Slave Trade and the Kingdom of Kongo

While African elites often eagerly facilitated the traffic in slaves and benefited from doing so, in one well-known case, quite early in the slave trade era, an African ruler sought to curtail it. This occurred in the kingdom of Kongo, in what is now Angola (see Map 15.4, p. 689). That state had welcomed Portuguese traders as early as the 1480s, as its rulers imagined that an alliance with Portugal could strengthen their regime. The royal family converted to Christianity and encouraged the importation of European guns, cattle, and horses. Several Kongolese were sent to Portugal for education, while Portuguese priests, artisans, merchants, and soldiers found a place in the kingdom. None of this worked as planned, however, and by the early sixteenth century, Kongo was in disarray and the authority of its ruler greatly undermined. This was the context in which its monarch Nzinga Mbemba, whose Christian name was Affonso I, wrote a series of letters to King Jao of Portugal in 1526, two of which are presented here.

- According to King Affonso, how had the Portuguese connection in general and the slave trade in particular transformed his state?

- How did the operation of the slave trade in Kongo differ from that of Whydah as described in Document 15.2? How did the rulers of these two states differ in their relationship to Europeans?

- To what extent did Affonso seek the end of the slave trade? What was the basis for his opposition to it? Do you think he was opposed to slavery itself?

- What did Affonso seek from Portugal? What kind of relationship did he envisage with the Portuguese?

King Affonso I

Letters to King Jao of Portugal

1526

Sir, Your Highness [of Portugal] should know how our Kingdom is being lost in so many ways that it is convenient to provide for the necessary remedy, since this is caused by the excessive freedom given by your factors and officials to the men and merchants who are allowed to come to this Kingdom to set up shops with goods and many things which have been prohibited by us, and which they spread throughout our Kingdoms and Domains in such an abundance that many of our vassals, whom we had in obedience, do not comply because they have the things in greater abundance than we ourselves; and it was with these things that we had them content and subjected under our vassalage and jurisdiction, so it is doing a great harm not only to the service of God, but to the security and peace of our Kingdoms and State as well.

And we cannot reckon how great the damage is, since the mentioned merchants are taking every day our natives, sons of the land and the sons of our noblemen and vassals and our relatives, because the thieves and men of bad conscience grab them wishing to have the things and wares of this Kingdom which they are ambitious of; they grab them and get them to be sold; and so great, Sir, is the corruption and licentiousness that our country is being completely depopulated, and Your Highness should not agree with this nor accept it as in your service. And to avoid it we need from those [your] Kingdoms no more than some priests and a few people to teach in schools, and no other goods except wine and flour for the holy sacrament. That is why we beg of Your Highness to help and assist us in this matter, commanding your factors that they should not send here either merchants or wares, because it is *our will that in these Kingdoms there should not be any trade of slaves nor outlet for them.* Concerning what is referred

Source: Basil Davidson, *The African Past* (Boston: Little Brown, 1964), 191–94.

above, again we beg of Your Highness to agree with it, since otherwise we cannot remedy such an obvious damage. Pray Our Lord in His mercy to have Your Highness under His guard and let you do for ever the things of His service. I kiss your hands many times.

At our town of Congo, written on the sixth day of July.

João Teixeira did it in 1526.

The King. Dom Affonso.

[On the back of this letter the following can be read:

To the most powerful and excellent prince Dom João, King our Brother.]

Moreover, Sir, in our Kingdoms there is another great inconvenience which is of little service to God, and this is that many of our people, keenly desirous as they are of the wares and things of your Kingdoms, which are brought here by your people, and in order to satisfy their voracious appetite, seize many of our people, freed and exempt men; and very often it happens that they kidnap even noblemen and the sons of noblemen, and our relatives, and take them to be sold to the white men who are in our Kingdoms; and for this purpose thay have concealed them; and others are brought during the night so that they might not be recognized.

And as soon as they are taken by the white men they are immediately ironed and branded with fire, and when they are carried to be embarked, if they are caught by our guards' men the whites allege that they have bought them but they cannot say from whom, so that it is our duty to do justice and to restore to the freemen their freedom, but it cannot be done if your subjects feel offended, as they claim to be.

And to avoid such a great evil we passed a law so that any white man living in our Kingdoms and wanting to purchase goods in any way should first inform three of our noblemen and officials of our court whom we rely upon in this matter, and these are Dom Pedro Manipanza and Dom Manuel Manissaba, our chief usher, and Gonçalo Pires our chief freighter, who should investigate if the men-tioned goods are captives or free men, and if cleared by them there will be no further doubt nor embargo for them to be taken and embarked. But if the white men do not comply with it they will lose the aforementioned goods. And if we do them this favor and concession it is for the part Your Highness has in it, since we know that it is in your service too that these goods are taken from our Kingdom, otherwise we should not consent to this....

Sir, Your Highness has been kind enough to write to us saying that we should ask in our letters for anything we need, and that we shall be provided with everything, and as the peace and the health of our Kingdom depend on us, and as there are among us old folks and people who have lived for many days, it happens that we have continuously many and different diseases which put us very often in such a weakness that we reach almost the last extreme; and the same happens to our children, relatives, and natives owing to the lack in this country of physicians and surgeons who might know how to cure properly such diseases. And as we have got neither dispensaries nor drugs which might help us in this forlornness, many of those who had been already confirmed and instructed in the holy faith of Our Lord Jesus Christ perish and die; and the rest of the people in their majority cure themselves with herbs and breads and other ancient methods, so that they put all their faith in the mentioned herbs and ceremonies if they live, and believe that they are saved if they die; and this is not much in the service of God.

And to avoid such a great error and inconve-nience, since it is from God in the first place and then from your Kingdoms and from Your Highness that all the goods and drugs and medicines have come to save us, we beg of you to be agreeable and kind enough to send us two physicians and two apothecaries and one surgeon, so that they may come with their drug-stores and all the necessary things to stay in our king-doms, because we are in extreme need of them all and each of them. We shall do them all good and shall benefit them by all means, since they are sent by Your Highness, whom we thank for your work in their coming. We beg of Your Highness as a great favor to do this for us, because besides being good in itself it is in the service of God as we have said above.

Document 15.4

The Slave Trade and the Kingdom of Asante

Elsewhere in Africa, the slave trade did not have such politically destabilizing effects as it did in Kongo. In the region known as the Gold Coast (now the modern state of Ghana), the kingdom of Asante arose in the eighteenth century, occupying perhaps 100,000 square miles and incorporating some 3 million people (see Map 15.4, p. 689). It was a powerful conquest state, heavily invested in the slave trade, from which much of its wealth derived. Many slaves from its wars of expansion and from the tribute of its subject people were funneled into Atlantic commerce, while still others were used as labor in the gold mines and on the plantations within Asante itself. No wonder, then, that the ruler (or Asantehene) Osei Bonsu was dismayed in the early nineteenth century when, in reaction to the expanding abolitionist movement, the British stopped buying slaves. A conversation between Osei Bonsu and a British diplomat in 1820 highlights the role of the slave trade in Asante and in the thinking of its monarch.

- How did Osei Bonsu understand the slave trade and its significance for his kingdom?

- Some scholars have argued that the slave trade increased the incidence of warfare in West Africa as various states deliberately sought captives whom they could exchange for desired goods from Europe. How might Osei Bonsu respond to that idea? What was his understanding of the relationship between war and the slave trade?

- In what ways did Osei Bonsu compare Muslim traders from the north with European merchants from the sea?

OSEI BONSU

Conversation with Joseph Dupuis

1820

Now," said the king, after a pause, "I have another palaver, and you must help me to talk it. A long time ago the great king [of England] liked plenty of trade, more than now; then many ships came, and they bought ivory, gold, and slaves; but now he will not let the ships come as before, and the people buy gold and ivory only. This is what I have in my head, so now tell me truly, like a friend, why does the king do so?" "His majesty's question," I replied, "was connected with a great palaver, which my instructions did not authorise me to discuss. I had nothing to say regarding the slave trade." "I know that too," retorted the king; "because, if my master liked that trade, you would have told me so before. I only want to hear what you think as a friend: this is not like

Source: Osei Bonsu, *The Slave Trade and the Kingdom of Asante* (London: Henry Colburn, 1824), 162–64.

the other palavers." I was confessedly at a loss for an argument that might pass as a satisfactory reason, and the sequel proved that my doubts were not groundless. The king did not deem it plausible, that this obnoxious traffic should have been abolished from motives of humanity alone; neither would he admit that it lessened the number either of domestic or foreign wars.

Taking up one of my observations, he remarked, "[T]he white men who go to council with your master, and pray to the great God for him, do not understand my country, or they would not say the slave trade was bad. But if they think it bad now, why did they think it good before. Is not your law an old law, the same as the Crammo° law? Do you not both serve the same God, only you have different fashions and customs? Crammos are strong people in fetische,° and they say the law is good, because the great God made the book [Quran]; so they buy slaves, and teach them good things, which they knew not before. This makes every body love the Crammos, and they go every where up and down, and the people give them food when they want it. Then these men come all the way from the great water [Niger River], and from Manding, and Dagomba, and Killinga; they stop and trade for slaves, and then go home. If the great king would like to restore this trade, it would be good for the white men and for me too, because Ashantee is a country for war, and the people are strong; so if you talk that palaver for me properly, in the white country, if you go there, I will give you plenty of gold, and I will make you richer than all the white men."

°**Crammo:** Muslim.

°**fetische:** magical powers.

I urged the impossibility of the king's request, promising, however, to record his sentiments faithfully. "Well then," said the king, "you must put down in my master's book all I shall say, and then he will look to it, now he is my friend. And when he sees what is true, he will surely restore that trade. I cannot make war to catch slaves in the bush, like a thief. My ancestors never did so. But if I fight a king, and kill him when he is insolent, then certainly I must have his gold, and his slaves, and the people are mine too. Do not the white kings act like this? Because I hear the old men say, that before I conquered Fantee and killed the Braffoes and the kings, that white men came in great ships, and fought and killed many people; and then they took the gold and slaves to the white country: and sometimes they fought together. That is all the same as these black countries. The great God and the fetische made war for strong men every where, because then they can pay plenty of gold and proper sacrifice. When I fought Gaman, I did not make war for slaves, but because Dinkera (the king) sent me an arrogant message and killed my people, and refused to pay me gold as his father did. Then my fetische made me strong like my ancestors, and I killed Dinkera, and took his gold, and brought more than 20,000 slaves to Coomassy. Some of these people being bad men, I washed my stool in their blood for the fetische. But then some were good people, and these I sold or gave to my captains: many, moreover, died, because this country does not grow too much corn like Sarem, and what can I do? Unless I kill or sell them, they will grow strong and kill my people. Now you must tell my master that these slaves can work for him, and if he wants 10,000 he can have them. And if he wants fine handsome girls and women to give his captains, I can send him great numbers."

Using the Evidence:
Voices from the Slave Trade

1. **Highlighting differences:** What different experiences of the slave trade are reflected in these documents? How can you account for those differences?

2. **Noticing what's missing:** What perspectives are missing that might add other dimensions to our understanding of this commerce in people?

3. **Integrating documents and the text narrative:** In what ways do these documents support, illustrate, or contradict this chapter's narrative discussion of the slave trade?

4. **Assessing historical responsibility:** What light do these documents shed on the much-debated question about who should be held responsible for the tragedy of the Atlantic slave trade?

Visual Sources

Considering the Evidence: Exchange and Status in the Early Modern World

In many cultures across many centuries, the possession of scarce foreign goods has served not only to meet practical needs and desires but also to convey status. For centuries Chinese silk signified rank, position, or prestige across much of Eurasia. Pepper and other spices from South and Southeast Asia likewise appealed to elite Romans and Chinese, eager to demonstrate their elevated position in society. In the late twentieth century, American blue jeans were much in demand among Soviet young people who sought to display their independence from an oppressive communist regime, while Americans who could afford a German Porsche or an Italian Ferrari acquired an image of sophistication or glamour, setting them apart from others.

As global commerce expanded in the early modern era, so too did the exchange of foods, fashions, finery, and more. Already in 1500, according to a recent study, "it would be possible for a person in the Persian Gulf to wear cotton cloth from India while eating a bowl of rice also from India while sitting under a roof made of timber imported from East Africa. As he finished the rice he would see a Chinese character—the bowl itself came from China."[31] In the centuries that followed, growing numbers of people all across the world, particularly in elite social circles, had access to luxury goods from far away with which they could display, and perhaps enhance, their status. Some of these goods—sugar, pepper, tobacco, tea, and Indian cotton textiles, for example—gradually dropped in price, becoming more widely available. The images that follow illustrate this relationship between global trade and the display of status during the several centuries after 1500.

More than the peoples of other major civilizations, Europeans in the early modern era embraced the goods of the world. They had long been fascinated by and impressed with the wealth and splendor of Asia, which Marco Polo had described in the early fourteenth century after returning from his famous sojourn in China. Now in the early modern era, Western Europe was increasingly at the hub of a growing network of global commerce with access to products from around the world. Tea, porcelain, and silk from China; cotton textiles and spices from India and Southeast Asia; sugar, chocolate, and tobacco from the Americas; coffee from the Middle East—all of this and much more flooded into Europe. By the eighteenth century, a fascination for things Chinese had seized the elite classes of Europe—Chinese textiles, porcelains, tea, wall-paper, furniture, gardens, and artistic styles. The son of King George II of England built a "Mandarin yacht" resembling a Chinese pleasure boat to sail on a large artificial lake near London.

Visual Source 15.1, which shows a German painting from the early eighteenth century, illustrates the growing popularity of tea as a beverage of choice in Europe. Long popular in China and Japan, tea made its entry in Europe in the sixteenth century aboard Portuguese ships. Initially, it was extremely expensive and limited to the very wealthy, but the price dropped as the supply increased, and by the eighteenth century, it was widely consumed in Europe. Chinese teacups without handles also became popular and arrived via European merchant vessels packed in tea or rice. Like many other porcelains, these teacups had been created by Chinese artisans specifically for a European market. Those sitting on the table in front of the painting were manufactured in China between 1662 and 1722. Notice the practice of pouring the tea into the saucer to cool it.

- What foreign trade items can you identify in this painting?
- Note the European house on the teacup at the bottom left. What does this indicate about Chinese willingness to cater to the tastes of European customers?
- From what social class do you think the woman in the image comes?
- How might you explain the great European interest in Chinese products and styles during the eighteenth century? Why might their possession have suggested status?

Like tea from China and coffee from Ethiopia, chocolate from Mesoamerica also became an elite beverage and an indictor of high status in Europe during the early modern era. It was the Olmecs, the Maya, and the Aztecs who first discovered how to process the seeds of the cacao tree into a chocolate drink. After the Spanish conquest of the Aztec Empire, that drink was introduced into Spain, where it became highly fashionable in court and aristocratic circles. And from Spain it spread to much of the rest of Europe, also limited to the elite social classes, who could afford to purchase this expensive import. Not until the Industrial Revolution made it possible to produce solid chocolate candy for mass consumption did this Mesoamerican acquisition become more widely available. Unlike tobacco and coffee, however, chocolate did not take hold in the Islamic world or China until more recent times.

A part of the larger Columbian exchange, chocolate in Europe lost the religious or ritual associations with which the Aztecs had invested it, becoming a medicine, sometimes an aphrodisiac, and in general a recreational bever-

Visual Source 15.1 Tea and Porcelain in Europe (Erich Lessing/Art Resource, NY)

age. Cortés, the Spanish conqueror of the Aztecs, described chocolate as "the divine drink which builds up resistance and fights fatigue. A cup of this precious drink permits a man to walk for a whole day without food."[32] After some debate, the Church approved it as a nutritional substitute during times of fasting, when taking solid food was forbidden. Europeans also innovated with the beverage, adding sugar, cinnamon, and other spices, and later milk. With ingredients from the Americas and Asia, some of them produced by African slave labor, chocolate illustrated the process by which Europe was becoming the center of an emerging world economy.

Visual Source 15.2, a painted tile panel from the early eighteenth century, shows a *chocolatada*, or "chocolate party," in Valencia, Spain. Notice the saucer, or *mancerina*, also a European innovation for drinking chocolate without spilling it.

Visual Source 15.2 A Chocolate Party in Spain (Courtesy Museu de Cerámica, Barcelona. Photo: Guillem Fernandez-Huerta)

- ■ What marks this event as an upper-class occasion?
- ■ What steps in the preparation of the chocolate drink can you observe in the image?
- ■ Why do you think Europeans embraced a practice of people they regarded as uncivilized, bloodthirsty, and savage? What does this suggest about the process of cultural borrowing?

Europeans, of course, were not the only people to embrace foreign tastes newly available in the early modern era. Tobacco and coffee, like tea, soon found a growing range of consumers all across Eurasia. Originating in the Americas, tobacco smoking spread quickly to Europe and Asia. Well before 1700 it had become perhaps the first global recreation. In the Ottoman Empire, as elsewhere, it provoked strenuous opposition on the grounds that it was an intoxicant, like wine, and was associated with unwholesome and promiscuous behavior. It was also associated with coffee, which had entered the Ottoman

Empire in the sixteenth century from its place of origin in Ethiopia and Yemen. Coffee too encountered considerable opposition, partly because it was consumed in the new social arena of the coffeehouse. To moralists and other critics, the coffeehouse was a "refuge of Satan," which drew people away from the mosques even as it drew together all different classes. Authorities suspected that coffeehouses were places of political intrigue. None of this stopped the spread of either tobacco or coffee, and the coffeehouse, in the Ottoman Empire and in Europe, came to embody a new "public culture of fun" as it wore away at earlier religious restrictions on the enjoyment of life.[33]

Visual Source 15.3 is a sixteenth-century miniature painting depicting a Turkish coffeehouse in the Ottoman Empire.

■ What activities can you identify in the painting?

■ Would you read this painting as critical of the coffeehouse, as celebrating it, or as a neutral description? Notice that the musicians and those playing board games at the bottom were engaged in activities considered rather disreputable. How would you describe the general demeanor of the men in the coffeehouse?

■ Notice the cups that the patrons are using and those stacked in the upper right. Do they look similar to those shown in Visual Source 15.1? Certainly Ottoman elites by the sixteenth century preferred Chinese porcelain to that manufactured within their own empire.[34]

The emerging colonial societies of Spanish and Portuguese America gave rise to a wide variety of recognized mixed-race groups known as *castas*, or "castes," and defined in terms of the precise mixture of Native American, European, and African ancestry that an individual possessed. While this system slotted people into a hierarchical social order defined by race and heritage, it did allow for some social mobility. If individuals managed to acquire some education, land, or money, they might gain in social prestige and even pass as members of a more highly favored category (see pp. 636–37). Adopting the dress and lifestyle of higher-ranking groups could facilitate this process.

Visual Source 15.4 shows a woman of Indian ancestry and a man of African/ Indian descent as well as their child, who is categorized as a *loba*, or "wolf." It comes from a series of "casta paintings" created in eighteenth-century Mexico by the well-known Zapotec artist Miguel Cabrera to depict some eighteen or more mixed-race couples and their children, each with a distinct designation. The woman in this image is wearing a lovely *huipil*, a traditional Maya tunic or blouse, while the man is dressed in a European-style waistcoat, vest, and lace shirt as well as a black tricornered hat, widely popular in Europe during the seventeenth and eighteenth centuries. The popularity of such paintings reflected both a Spanish fascination with race and a more general European interest in classification, which was characteristic of eighteenth-century scientific thinking.

Visual Source 15.3 An Ottoman Coffeehouse (Chester Beatty Library, Dublin, Ms 439, folio 9)

De Chino cambujo y d India , Loba

Visual Source 15.4 Clothing and Status in Colonial Mexico (Oronoz)

- What indications of status ambition or upward mobility can you identify in this image? Keep in mind that status here is associated with race and gender as well as the possession of foreign products.

- Why do you think the woman is shown in more traditional costume, while the man is portrayed in European dress?

- Notice the porcelain items at the bottom right. Where might they have come from?

- In what cultural tradition do you think this couple raised their daughter? What problems might they have experienced in the process?

As West Africa became integrated into a European-centered Atlantic economy via the slave trade, its peoples gained access to a variety of goods and products from around the world: corn and tobacco from the Americas; metal goods, alcohol, textiles, decorative items, and gunpowder weapons from Europe; cowrie shells (used for money) and Indian cotton textiles from Asia. Many of these items were economically or militarily valuable, and some of them were also useful for purposes of display.

Visual Source 15.5 Procession and Display in the Kingdom of Dahomey (Private Collection/The Stapleton Collection/The Bridgeman Art Library)

Visual Source 15.5, an illustration entitled "Public Procession of the King's Women," is taken from a book by a British official stationed in West Africa during the late eighteenth century. It shows an elaborate ceremony in the kingdom of Dahomey, held in the presence of its powerful monarch. Several Europeans, perhaps slave merchants or officials, are depicted as guests of the king sitting behind the table in the bottom left. At the time, Dahomey was heavily involved in the slave trade, while keeping it under strict royal control (see pp. 695–97).

■ What material evidence of international trade can you find in this image?

■ What do you imagine was the purpose of this procession?

■ Why might the women be clad in European-style dresses?

Using the Evidence:
Exchange and Status in the Early Modern World

1. **Analyzing the display of status:** In what different ways did the possession of foreign objects convey status in the early modern world? Toward whom were these various claims of status directed? Notice the difference between the display of status in public and private settings.

2. **Noticing gender differences:** In what ways are men and women portrayed in these visual sources? Why might women be absent in Visual Sources 15.2 and 15.3?

3. **Exploring the functions of trade:** How might you use these visual sources to support the idea that "trade served more than economic needs"?

4. **Raising questions about cultural borrowing:** What issues about cross-cultural borrowing do these visual sources suggest?

5. **Evaluating images as evidence:** What are the strengths and limitations of visual sources as a means of understanding the relationship of trade and status in the early modern era? What other kinds of sources would be useful for pursuing this theme?

Religion and Science

1450–1750

Nigerian pastor Daniel Ajayi-Adeniran is a missionary...to the United States....with his mission field in the Bronx. The church he represents, the Redeemed Christian Church of God, began in Nigeria in 1952. It has acquired millions of members in Nigeria and boasts a missionary network with a presence in 100 countries. According to its leader, the church was "made in heaven, assembled in Nigeria, exported to the world." And the Redeemed Church of God is not alone. As secularism and materialism born of the Scientific Revolution and modern life have eroded religious faith in the West, many believers in Asia, Africa, and Latin America have felt called to reinvigorate Christianity in Europe and North America. In a remarkable reversal of an earlier pattern, they now seek to "reevangelize" the West, from which they originally received the faith. After all, more than 60 percent of the world's professing Christians now live outside Europe and North America, and, within the United States, one in six Catholic diocesan priests and one in three seminary students are foreign-born. For example, hundreds of Filipino priests, nuns, and lay workers now serve churches in the West. "We couldn't just throw up our hands and see these churches turned into nightclubs or mosques," declared Tokunboh Adeyemo, another Nigerian church leader seeking to minister to an "increasingly godless West."[1]

THE EARLY MODERN ERA OF WORLD HISTORY gave birth to two intersecting and perhaps contradictory trends that continue to play out in the twenty-first century. The first was the spread of

The Virgin of Guadalupe: According to Mexican tradition, a dark-skinned Virgin Mary appeared to an indigenous peasant named Juan Diego in 1531, an apparition reflected in this Mexican painting from 1720. Belief in the Virgin of Guadalupe represented the incorporation of Catholicism into the emerging culture and identity of Mexico. (National Palace Mexico City/Gianni Dagli Orti/The Art Archive)

Christianity to Asians, Africans, and Native Americans, some of whom now seem to be returning the favor. The second lay in the emergence of a modern scientific outlook, which sharply challenged Western Christianity even as it too acquired a global presence.

And so, alongside new empires and new patterns of commerce, the early modern centuries also witnessed novel cultural transformations that likewise connected distant peoples. Riding the currents of European empire building and commercial expansion, Christianity was established solidly in the Americas and the Philippines; far more modestly in Siberia, China, Japan, and India; and hardly at all within the vast and still growing domains of Islam. A cultural tradition largely limited to Europe now became a genuine world religion, spawning a multitude of cultural encounters. While this ancient faith was spreading, a new understanding of the universe and a new approach to knowledge were taking shape among European thinkers of the Scientific Revolution, giving rise to another kind of cultural encounter—that between science and religion. In some ways, science was a new and competing worldview, and for some it was almost a new religion. In time, it became a defining feature of global modernity, achieving a worldwide acceptance that exceeded that of Christianity or any other religious tradition.

Although Europeans were central players in the globalization of Christianity and the emergence of modern science, they did not act alone in the cultural transformations of the early modern era. Asian, African, and Native American peoples largely determined how Christianity would be accepted, rejected, or transformed as it entered new cultural environments. Science emerged within an international and not simply a European context, and it met varying receptions in different parts of the world. Islam continued a long pattern of religious expansion and renewal, even as Christianity began to compete with it as a world religion. Buddhism maintained its hold in much of East Asia, as did Hinduism in South Asia and numerous smaller-scale religious traditions in Africa. And Europeans themselves were certainly affected by the many "new worlds" that they now encountered. The cultural interactions of the early modern era, in short, did not take place on a one-way street.

The Globalization of Christianity

Despite its Middle Eastern origins, Christianity was largely limited to Europe at the beginning of the early modern era. In 1500, the world of Christendom stretched from Spain and England in the west to Russia in the east, with small and beleaguered communities of various kinds in Egypt, Ethiopia, southern India, and Central Asia. Internally, Christianity was seriously divided between the Roman Catholics of Western and Central Europe and the Eastern Orthodox of Eastern Europe and Russia. Externally, it was very much on the defensive against an expansive Islam. Muslims had ousted Christian Crusaders from their toeholds in the Holy Land by 1300, and with the Ottoman seizure of Constantinople in 1453, they had captured the prestigious capital of Eastern Orthodoxy. The Ottoman siege of Vienna in 1529 marked a

Muslim advance into the heart of Central Europe. Except in Spain, which had recently been reclaimed for Christendom after centuries of Muslim rule, the future, it must have seemed, lay with Islam rather than Christianity.

Western Christendom Fragmented: The Protestant Reformation

As if these were not troubles enough, in the early sixteenth century the Protestant Reformation shattered the unity of Roman Catholic Christianity, which for the previous 1,000 years had provided the cultural and organizational foundation of Western European civilization. The Reformation began in 1517 when a German priest, Martin Luther (1483–1546), publicly invited debate about various abuses within the Roman Catholic Church by issuing a document, known as the Ninety-five Theses, allegedly nailing it to the door of a church in Wittenberg. In itself, this was nothing new, for many people were critical of the luxurious life of the popes, the corruption and immorality of some clergy, the Church's selling of indulgences (said to remove the penalties for sin), and other aspects of church life and practice.

What made Luther's protest potentially revolutionary, however, was its theological basis. A troubled and brooding man who was anxious about his relationship with God, Luther recently had come to a new understanding of salvation, which held that it came through faith alone. Neither the good works of the sinner nor the sacraments of the Church had any bearing on the eternal destiny of the soul, for faith was a free gift of God, graciously granted to his needy and undeserving people. To Luther, the source of these beliefs, and of religious authority in general, was not the teaching of the Church, but the Bible alone, interpreted according to the individual's conscience. (See Document 16.1, pp. 749–51, for more of Luther's thinking.) All of this challenged the authority of the Church and called into question the special position of the clerical hierarchy and of the pope in particular. In sixteenth-century Europe, this was the stuff of revolution.

Contrary to Luther's original intentions, his ideas ultimately provoked a massive schism within the world of Catholic Christendom, for they came to express a variety of political, economic, and social tensions as well as religious differences. Some kings and princes, many of whom had long disputed the political authority of the pope, found in these ideas a justification for their own independence and an opportunity to gain the

■ **Change**
In what ways did the Protestant Reformation transform European society, culture, and politics?

The Protestant Reformation
This sixteenth-century painting by the well-known German artist Lucas Cranach the Elder shows Martin Luther and his supporters using a giant quill to write their demands for religious reform on a church door. It memorializes the posting of the Ninety-five Theses in 1517, which launched the Protestant Reformation. (Dr. Henning Schleifenbaum, Siegen, Germany/Visual Connection Archive)

Snapshot   Catholic/Protestant Differences in the Sixteenth Century

	Catholic	Protestant
Religious authority	Pope and church hierarchy	The Bible, as interpreted by individual Christians
Role of the pope	Ultimate authority in faith and doctrine	Denied the authority of the pope
Ordination of clergy	Apostolic succession: direct line between original apostles and all subsequently ordained clergy	Apostolic succession denied; ordination by individual congregations or denominations
Salvation	Importance of church sacraments as channels of God's grace	By faith alone; God's grace is freely and directly granted to believers
Status of Mary	Highly prominent, ranking just below Jesus; provides constant intercession for believers	Less prominent; denied Mary's intercession on behalf of the faithful
Prayer	To God, but often through or with Mary and saints	To God alone; no role for Mary and saints
Holy Communion	Transubstantiation: bread and wine become the actual body and blood of Christ	Denied transubstantiation; bread and wine have a spiritual or symbolic significance
Role of clergy	Generally celibate; sharp distinction between priests and laypeople; mediators between God and humankind	Ministers may marry; priesthood of all believers; clergy have different functions (to preach, administer sacraments) but no distinct spiritual status

lands and taxes previously held by the Church. In the Protestant idea that all vocations were of equal merit, middle-class urban dwellers found a new religious legitimacy for their growing role in society, since the Roman Catholic Church was associated in their eyes with the rural and feudal world of aristocratic privilege. For common people, who were offended by the corruption and luxurious living of some bishops, abbots, and popes, the new religious ideas served to express their opposition to the entire social order, particularly in a series of German peasant revolts in the 1520s. (See Visual Sources 16.1 and 16.2, pp. 762 and 763, for contrasting images of Protestant and Catholic churches.)

Although large numbers of women were attracted to Protestantism, Reformation teachings and practices did not offer them a substantially greater role in the church or society. In Protestant-dominated areas, the veneration of Mary and female saints ended, leaving the male Christ figure as the sole object of worship. Protestant opposition to celibacy and monastic life closed the convents, which had offered some women an alternative to marriage. Nor were Protestants (except the Quakers) any more willing than Catholics to offer women an official role within their churches. The importance that Protestants gave to reading the Bible for oneself stimulated education and literacy for women, but given the emphasis on women as wives and mothers subject to male supervision, they had little opportunity to use that education outside of the family.

Reformation thinking spread quickly both within and beyond Germany, thanks in large measure to the recent invention of the printing press. Luther's many pamphlets and his translation of the New Testament into German were soon widely available. "God has appointed the [printing] Press to preach, whose voice the pope is never able to stop," declared one Reformation leader.[2] As the movement spread to France, Switzerland, England, and elsewhere, it also splintered, amoeba-like, into a variety of competing Protestant churches—Lutheran, Calvinist, Anglican, Quaker, Anabaptist—many of which subsequently subdivided, producing a bewildering array of Protestant denominations. Each was distinctive, but none gave allegiance to Rome or the pope.

Thus to the divided societies and the fractured political system of Europe was now added the potent brew of religious difference, operating both within and between states (see Map 16.1). For more than thirty years (1562–1598), French society was torn by violence between Catholics and the Protestant minority known as Huguenots. On a single day, August 24, 1572, Catholic mobs in Paris massacred some 3,000 Huguenots, and thousands more perished in provincial towns in the weeks that followed. Finally, a war-weary monarch, Henry IV, issued the Edict of Nantes (1598), which granted a substantial measure of religious toleration to French Protestants, though with the intention that they would soon return to the Catholic Church. The culmination of European religious conflict took shape in the Thirty Years' War (1618–1648), a Catholic–Protestant struggle that began in the Holy Roman Empire but eventually engulfed most of Europe. It was a horrendously destructive war, during which, scholars estimate, between 15 and 30 percent of the German population perished from violence, famine, or disease. Finally, the Peace of Westphalia (1648) brought the conflict to an end, with some reshuffling of boundaries and an agreement that each state was sovereign, authorized to control religious affairs within its own territory. Whatever religious unity Catholic Europe had once enjoyed was now permanently broken.

The Protestant breakaway, combined with reformist tendencies within the Catholic Church itself, provoked a Catholic Counter-Reformation. In the Council of Trent (1545–1563), Catholics clarified and reaffirmed their unique doctrines and practices, such as the authority of the pope, priestly celibacy, the veneration of saints and relics, and the importance of church tradition and good works, all of which Protestants had rejected. Moreover, they set about correcting the abuses and corruption that had

Map 16.1   Reformation Europe in the Sixteenth Century

The rise of Protestantism added yet another set of religious divisions, both within and between states, to European Christendom, which was already sharply divided between the Roman Catholic Church and the Eastern Orthodox Church.

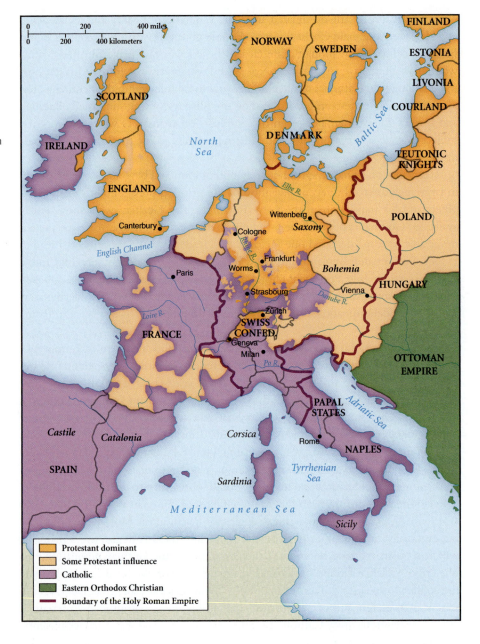

stimulated the Protestant movement by placing a new emphasis on the education of priests and their supervision by bishops. A crackdown on dissidents included the censorship of books, fines, exile, penitence, and occasionally the burning of heretics. Renewed attention was given to individual spirituality and personal piety. New religious orders, such as the Society of Jesus (Jesuits), provided a dedicated brotherhood of priests committed to the renewal of the Catholic Church and its extension abroad.

Although the Reformation was profoundly religious, it encouraged a skeptical attitude toward authority and tradition, for it had, after all, successfully challenged the immense prestige and power of the pope and the established Church. Protestant reformers fostered religious individualism as people were now encouraged to read and interpret the scriptures for themselves and to seek salvation without the mediation of the Church. In the centuries that followed, some people turned that skepticism and the habit of thinking independently against all revealed religion. Thus the Protestant Reformation opened some space for new directions in European intellectual life.

In short, it was a more highly fragmented but also a renewed and revitalized Christianity that established itself around the world in the several centuries after 1500.

Christianity Outward Bound

Christianity motivated European political and economic expansion and also benefited from it. The resolutely Catholic Spanish and Portuguese both viewed their movement overseas as a continuation of a long crusading tradition, which only recently had completed the liberation of their countries from Muslim control. When Vasco da Gama's small fleet landed in India in 1498, local authorities understandably asked, "What brought you hither?" The reply: they had come "in search of Christians and of spices."[3] Likewise, Columbus, upon arriving in the Americas, expressed the no doubt sincere hope that the people "might become Christians," even as he promised his Spanish patrons an abundant harvest of gold, spice, cotton, aloe wood, and slaves.[4] Neither man sensed any contradiction or hypocrisy in this blending of religious and material concerns.

■ **Connection**
How was European imperial expansion related to the spread of Christianity?

If religion drove and justified European ventures abroad, it is difficult to imagine the globalization of Christianity without the support of empire. Colonial settlers and traders, of course, brought their faith with them and sought to replicate it in their newly conquered homelands. New England Puritans, for example, planted a distinctive Protestant version of Christianity in North America, with an emphasis on education, moral purity, personal conversion, civic responsibility, and little tolerance for competing expressions of the faith. They did not show much interest in converting native peoples but sought rather to push them out of their ancestral territories. It was missionaries, mostly Catholic, who actively spread the Christian message beyond European communities. Organized in missionary orders such as the Dominicans, Franciscans, and Jesuits, Portuguese missionaries took the lead in Africa and Asia, while Spanish and French missionaries were most prominent in the Americas. Missionaries of the Russian Orthodox Church likewise accompanied the expansion of the Russian Empire across Siberia, where priests and monks ministered to Russian settlers and trappers, who often donated their first sable furs to a church or monastery.

Missionaries had their greatest success in Spanish America and in the Philippines, areas that shared two critical elements beyond their colonization by Spain. Most

Japanese Christian Martyrs
Christianity was beginning to take root in sixteenth-century Japan, but intensive persecution by Japanese authorities in the early seventeenth century largely ended that process. This monument was later erected in memory of twenty-six martyrs, Japanese and European alike, who were executed during this suppression of Christianity. (Photo Agency MH Martin Hladik, Photographer)

■ **Connection**
In what ways was European Christianity assimilated into the Native American cultures of Spanish America?

important, perhaps, was an overwhelming European presence, experienced variously as military conquest, colonial settlement, missionary activity, forced labor, social disruption, and disease. Surely it must have seemed as if the old gods had been bested and that any possible future lay with the powerful religion of the European invaders. A second common factor was the absence of a literate world religion in these two regions. Throughout the modern era, peoples solidly rooted in Confucian, Buddhist, Hindu, or Islamic traditions proved far more resistant to the Christian message than those who practiced more localized, small-scale, orally based polytheistic religions.

Conversion and Adaptation in Spanish America

Spanish America and China illustrate the difference between those societies in which Christianity became widely practiced and those that largely rejected it. Both cases, however, represent major cultural encounters of a kind that was becoming more frequent as European expansion brought the Christian faith to distant peoples with very different cultural traditions.

The decisive conquest of the Aztec and Inca empires and all that followed from it—disease, population collapse, loss of land to Europeans, forced labor, resettlement into more compact villages—created a setting in which the religion of the victors took hold in Spanish American colonies. Europeans saw their political and military success as a demonstration of the power of the Christian God. Native American peoples generally agreed, and by 1700 or earlier the vast majority had been baptized and saw themselves in some respects as Christians. After all, other conquerors such as the Aztecs and the Incas had always imposed their gods in some fashion on defeated peoples. It made sense, both practically and spiritually, to affiliate with the Europeans' God, saints, rites, and rituals. Many millions accepted baptism, contributed to the construction of village churches, attended services, and embraced images of Mary and other saints.

Earlier conquerors, however, had made no attempt to eradicate local deities and religious practices. The flexibility and inclusiveness of Mesoamerican and Andean religions had made it possible for subject people to accommodate the gods of their new rulers while maintaining their own traditions. But Europeans were different. They claimed an exclusive religious truth and sought the utter destruction of local gods and everything associated with them. Operating within a Spanish colonial regime that actively encouraged conversion, missionaries often proceeded by persuasion and patient teaching. At times, though, their frustration with the persistence of "idolatry, superstition, and error" boiled over into violent campaigns designed to uproot old religions once and for all. In 1535, the bishop of Mexico proudly claimed that he had destroyed 500 pagan shrines and 20,000 idols. During the seventeenth and early eighteenth centuries, church authorities in the Andean region periodically launched movements of "extirpation," designed to fatally undermine native religion. They destroyed religious images and ritual objects, publicly urinated on native "idols," desecrated the remains of ancestors, held religious trials and "processions of shame" aimed at humiliating offenders, and flogged "idolaters."[5]

Occasionally, overt resistance erupted. One such example was the religious revivalist movement in central Peru in the 1560s, known as Taki Onqoy (dancing sickness). Possessed by the spirits of local gods, or *huacas*, traveling dancers and teachers predicted that an alliance of Andean deities would soon overcome the Christian God, inflict the intruding Europeans with the same diseases that they had brought to the Americas, and restore the world of the Andes to an imagined earlier harmony. They called on native peoples to cut off all contact with the Spanish, to reject Christian worship, and to return to traditional practices. "The world has turned about," one member declared, "and this time God and the Spaniards [will be] defeated and all the Spaniards killed and their cities drowned; and the sea will rise and overwhelm them, so that there will remain no memory of them."[6]

More common than such frontal attacks on Christianity, which were quickly smashed by colonial authorities, were efforts at blending two religious traditions, reinterpreting Christian practices within an Andean framework, and incorporating local elements into an emerging Andean Christianity. Even female dancers in the Taki Onqoy movement sometimes took the names of Christian saints, seeking to appropriate for themselves the religious power of Christian figures. Within Andean Christian communities, people might offer the blood of a llama to strengthen a village church or make a cloth covering for the Virgin Mary and a shirt for an image of a huaca with the same material. Although the state cults of the Incas faded away, missionary attacks did not succeed in eliminating the influence of local huacas. Images and holy sites might be destroyed, but the souls of the huacas remained, and their representatives gained prestige. One resilient Andean resident inquired of a Jesuit missionary: "Father, are you tired of taking our idols from us? Take away that mountain if you can, since that is the God I worship."[7] (See Visual Source 16.3, p. 765, for an illustration of the blending of Andean religious symbols and the new Christian message.)

In Mexico as well, an immigrant Christianity was assimilated into patterns of local culture. Parishes were organized largely around precolonial towns or regions. Churches built on or near the sites of old temples became the focus of community identity. *Cofradias*, church-based associations of laypeople, organized community processions and festivals and made provision for a proper funeral and burial for their members. Central to an emerging Mexican Christianity were the saints who closely paralleled the functions of precolonial gods. Saints were imagined as parents of the local community and the true owners of its land, and their images were paraded through the streets on the occasion of great feasts and were collected by individual households. Although parish priests were almost always Spanish, the *fiscal*, or leader of the church staff, was a native Christian of great local prestige, who carried on the traditions and role of earlier religious specialists.

Throughout the colonial period and beyond, many Mexican Christians also took part in rituals derived from the past, with little sense that this was incompatible with Christian practice. Incantations to various gods for good fortune in hunting, farming, or healing; sacrifices of self-bleeding; offerings to the sun; divination; the use of hallucinogenic drugs—all of these rituals provided spiritual assistance in those areas of everyday life not directly addressed by Christian rites. Conversely, these practices also showed signs of Christian influence. Wax candles, normally used in Christian services, might now appear in front of a stone image of a precolonial god. The anger of a neglected saint, rather than that of a traditional god, might explain someone's illness and require offerings, celebration, or a new covering to regain his or her favor.[8] In such ways did Christianity take root in the new cultural environments of Spanish America, but it was a distinctly Andean or Mexican Christianity, not merely a copy of the Spanish version.

An Asian Comparison: China and the Jesuits

■ **Comparison**

Why were missionary efforts to spread Christianity so much less successful in China than in Spanish America?

The Chinese encounter with Christianity was very different from that of Native Americans in Spain's New World empire. The most obvious difference was the political context. The peoples of Spanish America had been defeated, their societies thoroughly disrupted, and their cultural confidence sorely shaken. China, on the other hand, encountered European Christianity between the sixteenth and eighteenth centuries during the powerful and prosperous Ming (1368–1644) and Qing (1644–1912) dynasties. Although the transition between these two dynasties occasioned several decades of internal conflict, at no point was China's political independence or cultural integrity threatened by the handful of European missionaries and traders working there.

The reality of a strong, independent, confident China required a different missionary strategy, for Europeans needed the permission of Chinese authorities to operate in the country. Whereas Spanish missionaries working in a colonial setting sought primarily to convert the masses, the leading missionary order in China, the Jesuits, took deliberate aim at the official Chinese elite. Following the lead of their most famous missionary, Matteo Ricci (in China 1582–1610), many Jesuits learned Chinese, became thoroughly acquainted with classical Confucian texts, and dressed like Chinese scholars. Initially, they downplayed their mission to convert and instead emphasized their interest in exchanging ideas and learning from China's ancient culture. As highly educated men, the Jesuits carried the recent secular knowledge of Europe—science, technology, geography, mapmaking—to an audience of curious Chinese scholars. In presenting Christian teachings, Jesuits were at pains to be respectful of Chinese culture, pointing out parallels between Confucianism and Christianity rather than portraying it as something new and foreign. They chose to define Chinese rituals honoring the emperor or venerating ancestors as secular or civil observances rather than as religious practices that had to be abandoned. Such efforts to accommodate Chinese culture contrast sharply with the frontal attacks on Native American religions in the Spanish Empire (see Visual Source 16.4, p. 767).

The religious and cultural outcomes of the missionary enterprise likewise differed greatly in the two regions. Nothing approaching the mass conversion to Christianity of Native American peoples took place in China. During the sixteenth and seventeenth centuries, a modest number of Chinese scholars and officials—who were attracted by the personal lives of the missionaries, by their interest in Western science, and by the moral certainty that Christianity offered—did become Christians. Jesuit missionaries found favor for a time at the Chinese imperial court, where their mathematical, astronomical, technological, and mapmaking skills rendered them useful. For more than a century, they were appointed to head the Chinese Bureau of Astronomy. Among ordinary people, Christianity spread very modestly amid tales of miracles attributed to the Christian God, while missionary teachings about "eternal life" sounded to some like Daoist prescriptions for immortality. At most, though, missionary efforts over the course of some 250 years (1550–1800) resulted in 200,000 to 300,000 converts, a minuscule number in a Chinese population approaching 300 million by 1800. What explains the very limited acceptance of Christianity in early modern China?

Fundamentally, the missionaries offered little that the Chinese really needed. Confucianism for the elites and Buddhism, Daoism, and a multitude of Chinese gods and spirits at the local level adequately supplied the spiritual needs of most Chinese. Furthermore, it became increasingly clear that Christianity was an all-or-nothing faith that required converts to abandon much of traditional Chinese culture. Christian monogamy, for example, seemed to require Chinese men to put away their concubines. What would happen to these deserted women?

Jesuits in China

In this seventeenth-century Dutch engraving, two Jesuit missionaries hold a map of China. Their mapmaking skills were among the reasons that the Jesuits were initially welcomed among the educated elite of that country. (Frontispiece to *China Illustrated* by Athanasius Kircher [1601–1680] 1667 [engraving], Dutch School, [17th century]/Private Collection, The Stapleton Collection/The Bridgeman Art Library)

By the early eighteenth century, the papacy and competing missionary orders came to oppose the Jesuit policy of accommodation. The pope claimed authority over Chinese Christians and declared that sacrifices to Confucius and the veneration of ancestors were "idolatry" and thus forbidden to Christians. The pope's pronouncements represented an unacceptable challenge to the authority of the emperor and an affront to Chinese culture. In 1715, an outraged Emperor Kangxi wrote:

> I ask myself how these uncultivated Westerners dare to speak of the great precepts of China.... [T]heir doctrine is of the same kind as the little heresies of the Buddhist and Taoist monks.... These are the greatest absurdities that have ever been seen. As from now I forbid the Westerners to spread their doctrine in China; that will spare us a lot of trouble.[9]

This represented a major turning point in the relationship of Christian missionaries and Chinese society. Many were subsequently expelled, and missionaries lost favor at court.

In other ways as well, missionaries played into the hands of their Chinese opponents. Their willingness to work under the Manchurian Qing dynasty, which came to power in 1644, discredited them with those Chinese scholars who viewed the Qing as uncivilized foreigners and their rule in China as disgraceful and illegitimate. Missionaries' reputation as miracle workers further damaged their standing as men of science and rationality, for elite Chinese often regarded miracles and supernatural religion as superstitions, fit only for the uneducated masses. Some viewed the Christian ritual of Holy Communion as a kind of cannibalism. Others came to see missionaries as potentially subversive, for various Christian groups met in secret, and such religious sects had often provided the basis for peasant rebellion. Nor did it escape Chinese notice that European Christians had taken over the Philippines and that their warships were active in the Indian Ocean. Perhaps the missionaries, with their great interest in maps, were spies for these aggressive foreigners. All of this contributed to the general failure of Christianity to secure a prominent presence in China.

Persistence and Change in Afro-Asian Cultural Traditions

Although Europeans were central players in the globalization of Christianity, theirs was not the only expanding or transformed culture of the early modern era. African religious ideas and practices, for example, accompanied slaves to the Americas. Common African forms of religious revelation—divination, dream interpretation, visions, spirit possession—found a place in the Africanized versions of Christianity that emerged in the New World. Europeans frequently perceived these practices as evidence of sorcery, witchcraft, or even devil worship and tried to suppress them. Nonetheless, syncretic (blended) religions such as Vodou in Haiti, Santeria in Cuba, and Candomble and Macumba in Brazil persisted. They derived from various West

African traditions and featured drumming, ritual dancing, animal sacrifice, and spirit possession. Over time, they incorporated Christian beliefs and practices such as church attendance, the search for salvation, and the use of candles and crucifixes and often identified their various spirits or deities with Catholic saints.

Expansion and Renewal in the Islamic World

The early modern era likewise witnessed the continuation of the "long march of Islam" across the Afro-Asian world. In sub-Saharan Africa, in the eastern and western wings of India, and in Central and Southeast Asia, the expansion of the Islamic frontier, a process already almost 1,000 years in the making, extended farther still. Conversion to Islam generally did not mean a sudden abandonment of old religious practices in favor of the new. Rather it was more often a matter of "assimilating Islamic rituals, cosmologies, and literatures into…local religious systems."[10]

■ **Explanation**
What accounts for the continued spread of Islam in the early modern era and for the emergence of reform or renewal movements within the Islamic world?

Continued Islamization usually was not the product of conquering armies and expanding empires. It depended instead on wandering Muslim holy men, Islamic scholars, and itinerant traders, none of whom posed a threat to local rulers. In fact, such people often were useful to those rulers and their village communities. They offered literacy in Arabic, established informal schools, provided protective charms containing passages from the Quran, served as advisers to local authorities and healers to the sick, often intermarried with local people, and generally did not insist that new converts give up their older practices. What they offered, in short, was connection to the wider, prestigious, prosperous world of Islam. Islamization extended modestly even to the Americas, where enslaved African Muslims planted their faith, particularly in Brazil. There Muslims led a number of slave revolts in the early nineteenth century.

To more orthodox Muslims, this religious syncretism, which accompanied Islamization almost everywhere, became increasingly offensive, even heretical. Such sentiments played an important role in movements of religious renewal and reform that emerged throughout the vast Islamic world of the eighteenth century. The leaders of such movements sharply criticized those practices that departed from earlier patterns established by Muhammad and from the authority of the Quran. For example, in India, which was governed by the Muslim Mughal Empire, religious resistance to official policies that accommodated Hindus found concrete expression during the reign of the emperor Aurangzeb (1658–1707) (see p. 646). A series of religious wars in West Africa during the eighteenth and early nineteenth centuries took aim at corrupt Islamic practices and the rulers, Muslim and non-Muslim alike, who permitted them. In Southeast and Central Asia, tension grew between practitioners of localized and blended versions of Islam and those who sought to purify such practices in the name of a more authentic and universal faith.

The most well-known and widely visible of these Islamic renewal movements took place during the mid-eighteenth century in Arabia itself, where the religion had been born more than 1,000 years earlier. It originated in the teachings of the

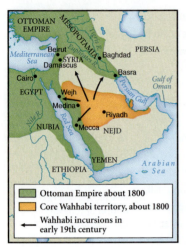

Ottoman Empire about 1800

Core Wahhabi territory, about 1800

← Wahhabi incursions in early 19th century

The Expansion of Wahhabi Islam

Islamic scholar Muhammad ibn Abd al-Wahhab (1703–1792). The growing difficulties of the Islamic world, such as the weakening of the Ottoman Empire, were directly related, he argued, to deviations from the pure faith of early Islam. Al-Wahhab was particularly upset by common religious practices in central Arabia that seemed to him idolatry—the widespread veneration of Sufi saints and their tombs, the adoration of natural sites, and even the respect paid to Muhammad's tomb at Mecca. All of this was a dilution of the absolute monotheism of authentic Islam.

The Wahhabi movement took a new turn in the 1740s when it received the political backing of Muhammad Ibn Saud, a local ruler who found al-Wahhab's ideas compelling. With Ibn Saud's support, the religious movement became an expansive state in central Arabia. Within that state, offending tombs were razed; "idols" were eliminated; books on logic were destroyed; the use of tobacco, hashish, and musical instruments was forbidden; and certain taxes not authorized by religious teaching were abolished. Likewise, male control of women was strengthened in strict accordance with the law, but al-Wahhab was also concerned about lack of attention to widows and orphans, about sexual immorality, and about women who had not received a proper share of their families' inheritance. By the early nineteenth century, this new reformist state encompassed much of central Arabia, with Mecca itself coming under Wahhabi control in 1803. Although an Egyptian army broke the power of the Wahhabis in 1818, the movement's influence continued to spread across the Islamic world. (See Document 16.4, pp. 756–57, for a statement of the Wahhabi outlook.)

Together with the ongoing expansion of the religion, these movements of reform and renewal signaled the continuing cultural vitality of the "abode of Islam," even as the European presence on the world stage assumed larger dimensions. In the nineteenth and twentieth centuries, such movements persisted and became associated with resistance to the political, military, and cultural intrusion of the European West into the affairs of the Islamic world.

China: New Directions in an Old Tradition

■ **Comparison**

In what ways did Asian cultural changes in the early modern era parallel those of Europe, and in what ways were they different?

Neither China nor India experienced cultural or religious change as dramatic as that of the Reformation in Europe, nor did Confucian or Hindu cultures during the early modern era spread widely, as did Christianity and Islam. Nonetheless, neither of these traditions remained static. As in Christian Europe, challenges to established orthodoxies in China and India emerged as commercial and urban life, as well as political change, fostered new thinking.

China during the Ming and Qing dynasties continued to operate broadly within a Confucian framework, enriched now by the insights of Buddhism and Daoism to generate a system of thought called Neo-Confucianism. Chinese Ming dynasty rulers, in their aversion to the despised Mongols, embraced and actively supported this native Confucian tradition, whereas the foreign Manchu or Qing rulers did so in order to woo Chinese intellectuals to support the new dynasty. Within this context, a considerable amount of controversy, debate, and new thinking emerged during the early modern era.

During late Ming times, for example, the influential thinker Wang Yangming (1472–1529) argued that truth and moral knowledge were innate to the human person. (See Document 16.3, pp. 754–55, for a selection from the writings of Wang Yangming.) Thus anyone could achieve a virtuous life by introspection and contemplation, without the extended education, study of the classical texts, and constant striving for improvement that traditional Confucianism prescribed for an elite class of "gentlemen." Such ideas figured prominently among Confucian scholars of the sixteenth century, although critics later contended that such thinking promoted an excessive individualism. They also argued that Wang Yangming's ideas had undermined the Ming dynasty and contributed to China's conquest by the foreign Manchus. Some Chinese Buddhists as well sought to make their religion more accessible to ordinary people, by suggesting that laypeople at home could undertake practices similar to those performed by monks in monasteries. Withdrawal from the world was not necessary for enlightenment. This kind of moral or religious individualism bore some similarity to the thinking of Martin Luther, who argued that individuals could seek salvation by "faith alone," without the assistance of a priestly hierarchy.

Another new direction in Chinese elite culture took shape in a movement known as *kaozheng*, or "research based on evidence." Intended to "seek truth from facts," kaozheng was critical of the unfounded speculation of conventional Confucian philosophy and instead emphasized the importance of verification, precision, accuracy, and rigorous analysis in all fields of inquiry. During the late Ming years, this emphasis generated works dealing with agriculture, medicine, pharmacology, botany, craft techniques, and more. In the Qing era, kaozheng was associated with a recovery and critical analysis of ancient historical documents, which sometimes led to sharp criticism of Neo-Confucian orthodoxy. It was a genuinely scientific approach to knowledge, but it was applied more to the study of the past than to the natural world of astronomy, physics, or anatomy, as in the West.

While such matters occupied the intellectual elite of China, in the cities a lively popular culture emerged among the less well educated. For city-dwellers, plays, paintings, short stories, and especially novels provided diversion and entertainment that were a step up from what could be found in teahouses and wine shops. Numerous "how-to" painting manuals allowed a larger public to participate in this favorite Chinese art form. Even though Confucian scholars disdained popular fiction, a vigorous printing industry responded to the growing demand for exciting novels. The most famous was Cao Xueqin's mid-eighteenth-century novel *The Dream of the Red Chamber*, a huge book that contained 120 chapters and some 400 characters, most of them women. It explored the social life of an eighteenth-century elite family with connections to the Chinese court.

India: Bridging the Hindu/Muslim Divide

Guru Nanak
In this early-eighteenth-century manuscript painting, Guru Nanak, the founder of Sikhism, and his constant companion Mardana (with a musical instrument) encounter a robber (the man with a sword) along the road. According to the story accompanying the painting, that experience persuaded the robber to abandon his wicked ways and become a follower of the Sikh path.
(© British Library Board)

In a largely Hindu India, ruled by the Muslim Mughal Empire, several significant cultural departures took shape in the early modern era that brought Hindus and Muslims together in new forms of religious expression. One was the flourishing of a devotional form of Hinduism known as *bhakti*. Through songs, prayers, dances, poetry, and rituals, devotees sought to achieve union with one or another of India's many deities. Appealing especially to women, the bhakti movement provided an avenue for social criticism. Its practitioners often set aside caste distinctions and disregarded the detailed rituals of the Brahmin priests in favor of direct contact with the divine. This emphasis had much in common with the mystical Sufi form of Islam and helped blur the distinction between these two traditions in India (see Document 16.5, pp. 758–59).

Among the most beloved of bhakti poets was Mirabai (1498–1547), a high-caste woman from northern India who abandoned her upper-class family and conventional Hindu practice. Upon her husband's death, tradition asserts, she declined to burn herself on his funeral pyre (a practice known as *sati*). She further offended caste restrictions by taking as her guru (religious teacher) an old untouchable shoemaker. To visit him, she apparently tied her saris together and climbed down the castle walls at night. Then she would wash his aged feet and drink the water from these ablutions. Much of her poetry deals with her yearning for union with Krishna, a Hindu deity she regarded as her husband, lover, and lord.

> What I paid was my social body, my town body, my family body, and all my inherited jewels.
> Mirabai says: The Dark One [Krishna] is my husband now.[11]

Yet another major cultural change that blended Islam and Hinduism emerged with the growth of Sikhism as a new and distinctive religious tradition in the Punjab region of northern India. Its founder, Guru Nanak (1469–1539), had been involved in the bhakti movement but came to believe that "there is no Hindu; there is no Muslim; only God." His teachings and those of subsequent gurus also generally ignored caste distinctions and untouchability and ended the seclusion of women, while proclaiming the "brotherhood of all mankind" as well as the essential equality of men and women. Drawing converts from Punjabi peasants and merchants, both Muslim and Hindu, the Sikhs gradually became a separate religious community. They developed their own sacred book, known as the Guru Granth (teacher book); created a central place of worship and pilgrimage in the Golden Temple of Amritsar; and prescribed certain dress requirements for men, including keeping hair and beards uncut, wearing a turban, and carrying a short sword. During the seventeenth century, Sikhs encountered hostility from both the Mughal Empire and some of their Hindu neighbors. In response, Sikhism evolved from a peaceful religious movement, blending Hindu and Muslim elements, into a militant community whose military skills were highly valued by the British when they took over India in the late eighteenth century.

A New Way of Thinking: The Birth of Modern Science

While some Europeans were actively attempting to spread the Christian faith to distant corners of the world, others were nurturing an understanding of the cosmos very much at odds with traditional Christian teaching. These were the makers of Europe's Scientific Revolution, a vast intellectual and cultural transformation that took place between the mid-sixteenth and early eighteenth centuries. These men of science would no longer rely on the external authority of the Bible, the Church, the speculations of ancient philosophers, or the received wisdom of cultural tradition. For them, knowledge would be acquired through a combination of careful observations, controlled experiments, and the formulation of general laws, expressed in mathematical terms. Those who created this revolution—Copernicus from Poland, Galileo from Italy, Descartes from France, Newton from England, and many others—saw themselves as departing radically from older ways of thinking. "The old rubbish must be thrown away," wrote a seventeenth-century English scientist. "These are the days that must lay a new Foundation of a more magnificent Philosophy."[12]

The long-term significance of the Scientific Revolution can hardly be overestimated. Within early modern Europe, it fundamentally altered ideas about the place of humankind within the cosmos and sharply challenged both the teachings and the authority of the Church. Over the past several centuries, it has substantially eroded religious belief and practice in the West, particularly among the well educated. When applied to the affairs of human society, scientific ways of thinking challenged ancient social hierarchies and political systems and played a role in the revolutionary upheavals of the modern era. But science also was used to legitimize racial and gender inequalities, by defining people of color and women as inferior by nature. When married to the technological innovations of the Industrial Revolution, science fostered both the marvels of modern production and the horrors of modern means of destruction. By the twentieth century, science had become so widespread that it largely lost its association with European culture and became the chief symbol of global modernity. Like Buddhism, Christianity, and Islam, modern science became a universal worldview, open to all who could accept its premises and its techniques.

The Question of Origins: Why Europe?

■ Comparison
Why did the Scientific
Revolution occur in
Europe rather than in
China or the Islamic
world?

Why did the breakthrough of the Scientific Revolution occur first in Europe and during the early modern era? The realm of Islam, after all, had generated the most advanced science in the world during the centuries between 800 and 1400. Arab scholars could boast of remarkable achievements in mathematics, astronomy, optics, and medicine, and their libraries far exceeded those of Europe.[13] And what of China? Its elite culture of Confucianism was both sophisticated and secular, less burdened by religious dogma than in the Christian or Islamic worlds; its technological accomplishments and economic growth were unmatched anywhere in the several centuries after 1000. In neither civilization, however, did these achievements lead to the kind of intellectual innovation that occurred in Europe.

Europe's historical development as a reinvigorated and fragmented civilization (see Chapter 10) arguably gave rise to conditions uniquely favorable to the scientific enterprise. By the twelfth and thirteenth centuries, Europeans had evolved a legal system that guaranteed a measure of independence for a variety of institutions— the Church, towns and cities, guilds, professional associations, and universities. This legal revolution was based on the idea of a "corporation," a collective group of people that was treated as a unit, a legal person, with certain rights to regulate and control its own members.

Most important for the development of science in the West was the autonomy of its emerging universities. By 1215, the University of Paris was recognized as a "corporation of masters and scholars," which could admit and expel students, establish courses of instruction, and grant a "license to teach" to its faculty. Such universities—for example, in Paris, Bologna, Oxford, Cambridge, and Salamanca—became "neutral zones of intellectual autonomy" in which scholars could pursue their studies in relative freedom from the dictates of church or state authorities. Within them, the study of the natural order began to slowly separate itself from philosophy and theology and to gain a distinct identity. Their curricula featured "a basically scientific core of readings and lectures" that drew heavily on the writings of the Greek thinker Aristotle, which had only recently become available to Western Europeans. Most of the major figures in the Scientific Revolution had been trained in and were affiliated with these universities.

In the Islamic world, by contrast, science was patronized by a variety of local authorities, but it occurred largely outside the formal system of higher education. Within colleges known as madrassas, Quranic studies and religious law held the central place, whereas philosophy and natural science were viewed with great suspicion. To religious scholars, the Quran held all wisdom, and scientific thinking might well challenge it. An earlier openness to free inquiry and religious toleration was increasingly replaced by a disdain for scientific and philosophical inquiry, for it seemed to lead only to uncertainty and confusion. "May God protect us from useless knowledge" was a saying that reflected this outlook. Nor did Chinese authorities permit independent institutions of higher learning in which scholars could conduct their studies in relative freedom. Instead Chinese education focused on preparing for a rigidly defined set of civil service examinations and emphasized the humanistic and moral texts of classical Confucianism. "The pursuit of scientific subjects," one recent historian concluded, "was thereby relegated to the margins of Chinese society."[14]

Beyond its distinctive institutional development, Western Europe was in a position to draw extensively upon the knowledge of other cultures, especially that of the Islamic world. Arab medical texts, astronomical research, and translations of Greek classics played a major role in the birth of European natural philosophy (as science was then called) between 1000 and 1500. In constructing his proofs for a sun-centered solar system, Copernicus in the sixteenth century likely drew upon astronomical work and mathematical formulations undertaken 200 to 300 years earlier in the Islamic world, particularly at the famous Muslim observatory of Maragha in present-day Iran.

In the sixteenth through the eighteenth centuries, Europeans found themselves at the center of a massive new exchange of information as they became aware of lands, peoples, plants, animals, societies, and religions from around the world. This tidal wave of new knowledge, uniquely available to Europeans, clearly shook up older ways of thinking and opened the way to new conceptions of the world. The sixteenth-century Italian doctor, mathematician, and writer Girolamo Cardano (1501–1576) clearly expressed this sense of wonderment: "The most unusual [circumstance of my life] is that I was born in this century in which the whole world became known; whereas the ancients were familiar with but a little more than a third part of it." He worried, however, that amid this explosion of knowledge, "certainties will be exchanged for uncertainties."[15] It was precisely those uncertainties—skepticism about established views—that provided such a fertile cultural ground for the emergence of modern science.

Muslim Astronomy and the Scientific Revolution
This diagram of the eclipses of the moon by the eleventh-century Muslim mathematician and astronomer al-Biruni is a reminder of Muslim scientific achievements, some of which stimulated European scientific thinking. (Roland and Sabrina Michaud/Rapho/Eyedea)

Science as Cultural Revolution

Before the Scientific Revolution, educated Europeans held a view of the world that derived from Aristotle, perhaps the greatest of the ancient Greek philosophers, and from Ptolemy, a Greco-Egyptian mathematician and astronomer who lived in Alexandria during the second century C.E. To medieval European thinkers, the earth

■ **Change**
What was revolutionary about the Scientific Revolution?

Snapshot   **Major Thinkers and Achievements of the Scientific Revolution**

Thinker/Scientist	Achievements
Nicolaus Copernicus (Polish; 1473–1543)	Posited that sun is at the center of solar system, earth rotates on its axis, and earth and planets revolve around the sun
Andreas Vesalius (Flemish; 1514–1564)	"Father of anatomy"; made detailed drawings of human body based on dissection
Francis Bacon (English; 1561–1626)	Emphasized observation and experimentation as the key to modern science
Galileo Galilei (Italian; 1564–1642)	Developed an improved telescope; discovered sunspots, mountains on the moon, and Jupiter's moons; performed experimental work on the velocity of falling objects
Johannes Kepler (German; 1571–1630)	Posited that planets follow elliptical, not circular, orbits; described laws of planetary motion
William Harvey (English; 1578–1657)	Described the circulation of the blood and the function of the heart
René Descartes (French; 1596–1650)	Emphasized the importance of mathematics and logical deduction in understanding the physical world; invented analytical geometry
Isaac Newton (English; 1642–1727)	Synthesized earlier findings around the concept of universal gravitation; invented calculus; formulated concept of inertia and laws of motion

was stationary and at the center of the universe, and around it revolved the sun, moon, and stars embedded in ten spheres of transparent crystal. This understanding coincided well with the religious outlook of the Catholic Church because the attention of the entire universe was centered on the earth and its human inhabitants, among whom God's plan for salvation unfolded. It was a universe of divine purpose, with angels guiding the hierarchically arranged heavenly bodies along their way while God watched over the whole from his realm beyond the spheres. The Scientific Revolution was revolutionary because it fundamentally challenged this understanding of the universe.

The initial breakthrough came from the Polish mathematician and astronomer Nicolaus Copernicus, whose famous book *On the Revolutions of the Heavenly Spheres* was published in the year of his death, 1543. Its essential argument was that "at the middle of all things lies the sun" and that the earth, like the other planets, revolved around it. Thus the earth was no longer unique or at the obvious center of God's attention.

Other European scientists built on Copernicus's central insight, and some even argued that other inhabited worlds and other kinds of humans existed. Less speculatively, in the early seventeenth century Johannes Kepler, a German mathematician, showed that the planets followed elliptical orbits, undermining the ancient belief that they moved in perfect circles. The Italian Galileo Galilei developed an improved telescope, with which he observed sunspots, or blemishes, moving across the face of the sun. This called into question the traditional notion that no change or imperfection marred the heavenly bodies. His discovery of the moons of Jupiter and many new stars suggested a cosmos far larger than the finite universe of traditional astronomy. Some thinkers began to discuss the notion of an unlimited universe in which humankind occupied a mere speck of dust in an unimaginable vastness. The French mathematician and philosopher Blaise Pascal (1623–1662) perhaps spoke for many when he wrote: "The eternal silence of infinite space frightens me."[16]

The culmination of the Scientific Revolution came in the work of Sir Isaac Newton, the Englishman who formulated the modern laws of motion and mechanics, which remained unchallenged until the twentieth century. At the core of Newton's thinking was the concept of universal gravitation. "All bodies whatsoever," Newton declared, "are endowed with a principle of mutual gravitation."[17] Here was the grand unifying idea of early modern science. The radical implication of this view was that the heavens and the earth, long regarded as separate and distinct spheres, were not so different after all, for the motion of a cannonball on earth or the falling of an apple from a tree obeyed the same natural laws that governed the orbiting planets.

By the time Newton died, a revolutionary new understanding of the physical universe had emerged among educated Europeans. That universe was no longer propelled by supernatural forces but functioned on its own according to scientific principles that could be described mathematically. In Kepler's view, "the machine of the universe is not similar to a divine animated being but similar to a clock."[18] Furthermore, it was a machine that regulated itself, requiring neither God nor angels to account for its normal operation. Knowledge of that universe could be obtained through human reason alone—by observation, deduction, and experimentation—without the aid of ancient authorities or divine revelation. The French philosopher René Descartes resolved "to seek no other knowledge than that which I might find within myself, or perhaps in the book of nature."[19]

Like the physical universe, the human body also lost some of its mystery. The careful dissections of cadavers and animals enabled doctors and scientists to describe the human body with much greater accuracy and to understand the circulation of the blood throughout the body. The heart was no longer the mysterious center of the body's heat and the seat of its passions; instead it was just another machine, a complex muscle that functioned as a pump.

Much of this thinking developed in the face of strenuous opposition from the Catholic Church, for both its teachings and its authority were under attack. The Italian philosopher Giordano Bruno, proclaiming an infinite universe and many worlds, was burned at the stake in 1600, and Galileo was compelled by the Church to publicly renounce his belief that the earth moved around an orbit and rotated on its axis.

But not all was conflict between the Church and an emerging science. None of the early scientists rejected Christianity. Galileo himself proclaimed the compatibility of science and faith when he wrote that "God is no less excellently revealed in Nature's actions than in the sacred statements of the Bible."[20] Newton was a serious biblical scholar and saw no necessary contradiction between his ideas and belief in God. "This most beautiful system of the sun, planets, and comets," he declared, "could only proceed from the counsel and dominion of an intelligent Being."[21] The Church gradually accommodated as well as resisted the new ideas, largely by compartmentalizing them. Science might prevail in its limited sphere of describing the physical universe, but religion was still the arbiter of truth about those ultimate questions concerning human salvation, righteous behavior, and the larger purposes of life.

Science and Enlightenment

■ Change
In what ways did the Enlightenment challenge older patterns of European thinking?

Initially limited to a small handful of scholars, the ideas of the Scientific Revolution spread to a wider European public during the eighteenth century. That process was aided by novel techniques of printing and book-making, by a popular press, and by a host of scientific societies. Moreover, the new approach to knowledge—rooted in human reason, skeptical of authority, expressed in natural laws—was now applied to human affairs, not just to the physical universe. The Scottish professor Adam Smith (1723–1790), for example, formulated laws that accounted for the operation of the economy and that, if followed, he believed, would generate inevitably favorable results for society. Growing numbers of people believed that the long-term outcome of scientific development would be "enlightenment," a term that has come to define the eighteenth century in European history. If human reason could discover the laws that governed the universe, surely it could uncover ways in which humankind might govern itself more effectively.

"What is Enlightenment?" asked the prominent German intellectual Immanuel Kant (1724–1804). "It is man's emergence from his self-imposed...inability to use one's own understanding without another's guidance....Dare to know! 'Have the courage to use your own understanding' is therefore the motto of the enlightenment."[22] Although they often disagreed sharply with one another, European Enlightenment thinkers shared this belief in the power of knowledge to transform human society. They also shared a satirical, critical style, a commitment to open-mindedness and inquiry, and in various degrees a hostility to established political and religious authority.

Many took aim at arbitrary governments, the "divine right of kings," and the aristocratic privileges of European society. The English philosopher John Locke (1632–1704) offered principles for constructing a constitutional government, a contract between rulers and ruled that was created by human ingenuity rather than divinely prescribed. Any number of writers, including many women, advocated education for women as a means of raising their status in society.

Much of Enlightenment thinking was directed against the superstition, ignorance, and corruption of established religion. In his *Treatise on Toleration*, the French writer Voltaire (1694–1778) reflected the outlook of the Scientific Revolution as he commented sarcastically on religious intolerance:

> This little globe, nothing more than a point, rolls in space like so many other globes; we are lost in its immensity. Man, some five feet tall, is surely a very small part of the universe. One of these imperceptible beings says to some of his neighbors in Arabia or Africa: "Listen to me, for the God of all these worlds has enlightened me; there are nine hundred million little ants like us on the earth, but only my anthill is beloved of God; He will hold all others in horror through all eternity; only mine will be blessed, the others will be eternally wretched."[23]

Voltaire's own faith, like many others among the "enlightened," was deism. Deists believed in a rather abstract and remote Deity, sometimes compared to a clockmaker, who had created the world, but not in a personal God who intervened in history or tampered with natural law. Others became *pantheists*, who believed that God and nature were identical. Here was a conception of religion shaped by the outlook of science. Sometimes called "natural religion," it was devoid of mystery, revelation, ritual, and spiritual practice, while proclaiming a God that could be "proven" by human rationality, logic, and the techniques of scientific inquiry. In this view, all else was superstition. Among the most radical of such thinkers were the several Dutchmen who wrote the *Treatise of Three Imposters*, which claimed that Moses, Jesus, and Muhammad were fraudulent imposters who based their teachings on "the ignorance of Peoples [and] resolved to keep them in it."[24]

Though solidly rooted in Europe, Enlightenment thought was influenced by the growing global awareness of its major thinkers. Voltaire, for example, idealized China as an empire governed by an elite of secular scholars selected for their talent, which stood in sharp contrast to continental Europe, where aristocratic birth and military prowess were far more important. The example of Confucianism—supposedly secular, moral, rational, and tolerant—encouraged Enlightenment thinkers to imagine a future for European civilization without the kind of supernatural religion that they found so offensive in the Christian West. (See Visual Source 15.1, p. 712, for European fascination with things Chinese.)

The central theme of the Enlightenment—and what made it potentially revolutionary—was the idea of progress. Human society was not fixed by tradition or divine command but could be changed, and improved, by human action guided by reason. No one expressed this soaring confidence in the unending perfectability of humankind more clearly than the French thinker the Marquis de Condorcet (1743–1794), whose views are excerpted in Document 16.2 on pages 752–54. Belief in

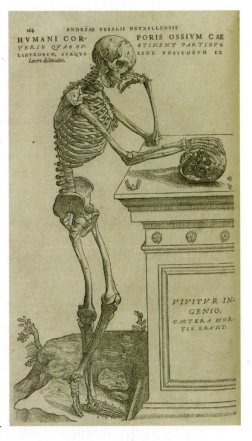

Uncovering the Human Skeleton
This drawing by the sixteenth-century Flemish anatomist Andreas Vesalius suggests a rational and philosophical approach to life, even as it presents the human skeleton with scientific precision. (Courtesy, National Library of Medicine)

progress was a sharp departure from much of premodern social thinking, and it inspired those who later made the American, French, Haitian, and Latin American revolutions. Born of the Scientific Revolution, that was the faith of the Enlightenment. For some, it was virtually a new religion.

The age of the Enlightenment, however, also witnessed a reaction against too much reliance on human reason. Jean-Jacques Rousseau (1712–1778) minimized the importance of book learning for the education of children and prescribed instead an immersion in nature, which taught self-reliance and generosity rather than the greed and envy fostered by "civilization." The Romantic movement in art and literature appealed to emotion, intuition, passion, and imagination rather than cold reason and scientific learning. Religious awakenings—complete with fiery sermons, public repentance, and intense personal experience of sin and redemption—shook Protestant Europe and North America. Science and the Enlightenment surely challenged religion, and for some they eroded religious belief and practice. Just as surely, though, religion persisted, adapted, and revived for many others.

Looking Ahead: Science in the Nineteenth Century

■ Change
How did nineteenth-century developments in the sciences challenge the faith of the Enlightenment?

The perspectives of the Enlightenment were challenged not only by romanticism and religious "enthusiasm" but also by the continued development of science itself. This remarkable phenomenon justifies a brief look ahead at several scientific developments in the nineteenth century.

Modern science was a cumulative and self-critical enterprise, which in the nineteenth century and after was applied to new domains of human inquiry in ways that undermined some of the assumptions of the Enlightenment. In the realm of biology, for example, Charles Darwin (1809–1882) laid out a complex argument that all of life was in flux, that an endless and competitive struggle for survival over millions of years constantly generated new species of plants and animals, while casting others into extinction. Human beings were not excluded from this vast process, for they too were the work of evolution operating through natural selection. Darwin's famous books *The Origin of Species* (1859) and *The Descent of Man* (1871) were as shattering to traditional religious views as Copernicus's ideas about a sun-centered universe had been several centuries earlier.

At the same time, Karl Marx (1818–1883) articulated a view of human history that likewise emphasized change and struggle. Conflicting social classes—slave owners and slaves, nobles and peasants, capitalists and workers—successively drove the process of historical transformation. Although he was describing the evolution of human civilization, Marx saw himself as a scientist. He based his theories on extensive historical research; like Newton and Darwin, he sought to formulate general laws that would explain events in a rational way. Nor did he believe in heavenly intervention, chance, or the divinely endowed powers of kings. The coming of socialism, in this view, was not simply a good idea; it was inscribed in the laws of historical development (see Document 18.1, pp. 856–59).

Like the intellectuals of the Enlightenment, Darwin and Marx believed strongly in progress, but in their thinking, conflict and struggle rather than reason and education were the motors of progress. The Enlightenment image of the thoughtful, rational, and independent individual was fading. Individuals—plant, animal, and human alike—were now viewed as enmeshed in vast systems of biological, economic, and social conflict.

The work of the Viennese doctor Sigmund Freud (1856–1939) applied scientific techniques to the operation of the human mind and emotions and in doing so cast further doubt on Enlightenment conceptions of human rationality. At the core of each person, Freud argued, lay primal impulses toward sexuality and aggression, which were only barely held in check by the thin veneer of social conscience derived from civilization. Our neuroses arose from the ceaseless struggle between our irrational drives and the claims of conscience. This too was a far cry from the Enlightenment conception of the human condition.

European Science beyond the West

In the long run, the achievements of the Scientific Revolution spread globally, becoming the most widely sought-after product of European culture and far more desired than Christianity, democracy, socialism, or Western literature. In the early modern era, however, the level of interest in European scientific thinking within major Asian societies was both modest and selective.

In China, for example, Qing dynasty emperors and scholars were most interested in European astronomy and mathematics, derived largely from Jesuit missionaries, because those disciplines proved useful in predicting eclipses, reforming the calendar, and making accurate maps of the empire. European medicine, however, held little interest for Chinese physicians before the nineteenth century. But the reputation of the Jesuits suffered when it became apparent in the 1760s that for two centuries the missionaries had withheld information about Copernican views of a sun-centered solar system because those ideas had been condemned by the Church. Nonetheless, European science had a substantial impact on a number of Chinese scholars as it interacted with the data-based kaozheng movement, described by one participant as "an ant-like accumulation of facts."[25] European mathematics was of particular interest to kaozheng researchers who were exploring the history of Chinese mathematics. To convince their skeptical colleagues that the barbarian Europeans had something to offer in this field, some Chinese scholars argued that European mathematics had in fact grown out of much earlier Chinese ideas and could therefore be adopted with comfort.[26] In such ways, early modern Chinese thinkers selectively assimilated Western science very much on their own terms.[27]

Although Japanese authorities largely closed their country off from the West in the early seventeenth century (see Chapter 15), one window remained open. Alone among Europeans, the Dutch were permitted to trade in Japan at a single location near Nagasaki, but not until 1720 did the Japanese lift the ban on importing Western

■ **Connection**

In what ways was European science received in the major civilizations of Asia in the early modern era?

books. Then a number of European texts in medicine, astronomy, geography, mathematics, and other disciplines were translated and studied by a small group of Japanese scholars. They were especially impressed with Western anatomical studies, for in Japan dissection was work fit only for outcasts. Returning from an autopsy conducted by Dutch physicians, several Japanese observers reflected on their experience: "We remarked to each other how amazing the autopsy had been, and how inexcusable it had been for us to be ignorant of the anatomical structure of the human body."[28] Nonetheless, this small center of "Dutch learning," as it was called, remained isolated amid a pervasive Confucian-based culture. Not until the mid-nineteenth century, when Japan was forcibly opened to Western penetration, would European science assume a prominent place in Japanese culture.

Like China and Japan, the Ottoman Empire in the sixteenth and seventeenth centuries was an independent, powerful, successful society whose intellectual elites saw no need for a wholesale embrace of things European. Ottoman scholars were conscious of the rich tradition of Muslim astronomy and chose not to translate the works of major European scientists such as Copernicus, Kepler, or Newton, although they were broadly aware of European scientific achievements by 1650. Insofar as they were interested in these developments, it was for their practical usefulness in making maps and calendars rather than for their larger philosophical implications. In any event, the notion of a sun-centered solar system did not cause the kind of upset that it did in Europe.[29]

More broadly, theoretical science of any kind—Muslim or European—faced an uphill struggle in the face of a conservative Islamic educational system. In 1580, for example, a highly sophisticated astronomical observatory was dismantled under pressure from conservative religious scholars and teachers, who interpreted an outbreak of the plague as God's disapproval with those who sought to understand his secrets. As in Japan, the systematic embrace of Western science would have to await the nineteenth century, when the Ottoman Empire was under far more intense European pressure and reform seemed more necessary.

Reflections: Cultural Borrowing and Its Hazards

Ideas are important in human history. They shape the mental or cultural worlds that people everywhere inhabit, and they often influence behavior as well. Many of the ideas developed or introduced during the early modern era have had enormous and continuing significance in the centuries that followed. The Western Hemisphere was solidly incorporated into Christendom. A Wahhabi version of Islam remains the official faith of Saudi Arabia into the twenty-first century and has influenced many contemporary Islamic revival movements, including al-Qaeda. Modern science and the associated notions of progress have become for many people something approaching a new religion.

Accompanying the development of these ideas has been a great deal of cultural borrowing. Filipinos, Siberians, and many Native American peoples borrowed elements of Christianity from Europeans. Numerous Asian and African peoples borrowed Islam from the Arabs. Northern Indian Sikhs drew upon both Hindu and Muslim teachings. Europeans borrowed scientific ideas from the Islamic world.

In virtually every case, though, that borrowing was selective rather than wholesale, even when it took place under conditions of foreign domination or colonial rule. Many peoples who appropriated Christianity or Islam certainly did not accept the rigid exclusivity and ardent monotheism of those faiths. Elite Chinese were far more interested in European astronomy and mathematics than in Western medicine, while Japanese scholars became fascinated with the anatomical work of the Dutch. Neither, however, adopted Christianity in a widespread manner.

Borrowing was frequently the occasion for serious conflict. Some objected to much borrowing at all, particularly when it occurred under conditions of foreign domination or foreign threat. Thus members of the Taki Onqoy movement in Peru sought to wipe out Spanish influence and control, while Chinese and Japanese authorities clamped down firmly on European missionaries, even as they maintained some interest in European technological and scientific skills. Another kind of conflict derived from the efforts to control the terms of cultural borrowing. For example, European missionaries and Muslim reformers alike sought to root out "idolatry" among native converts.

To ease the tensions of cultural borrowing, efforts to "domesticate" foreign ideas and practices proliferated. Thus the Jesuits in China tried to point out similarities between Christianity and Confucianism, and Native American converts identified Christian saints with their own gods and spirits. By the late seventeenth century, some local churches in central Mexico had come to associate Catholicism less with the Spanish than with ancient pre-Aztec communities and beliefs that were now, supposedly, restored to their rightful position.

The pace of global cultural borrowing and its associated tensions stepped up even more as Europe's modern transformation unfolded in the nineteenth century and as its imperial reach extended and deepened around the world.

Second Thoughts

What's the Significance?

Protestant Reformation	Wang Yangmin	Newton	To assess your mastery of the material in this chapter, visit the **Student Center** at bedfordstmartins.com/strayer.
Catholic Counter-Reformation	kaozheng	European Enlightenment	
Taki Onqoy	Mirabai	Voltaire	
Jesuits in China	Sikhism	Condorcet and the idea of	
Wahhabi Islam	Copernicus	progress	

Big Picture Questions

1. Why did Christianity take hold in some places more than in others?
2. In what ways was the missionary message of Christianity shaped by the cultures of Asian and American peoples?
3. Compare the processes by which Christianity and Islam became world religions.
4. In what ways did the spread of Christianity, Islam, and modern science give rise to culturally based conflicts?
5. Based on Chapters 13 through 16, how does the history of Islam in the early modern era challenge a Eurocentric understanding of those centuries?

Next Steps: For Further Study

For Web sites and additional documents related to this chapter, see **Make History** at bedfordstmartins.com/strayer.

Natana J. Delong-Bas, *Wahhabi Islam: From Revival and Reform to Global Jihad* (2004). A careful study of the origins of Wahhabi Islam and its subsequent development.

Patricia B. Ebrey et al., *East Asia: A Cultural, Social, and Political History* (2005). A broad survey by major scholars in the field.

Geoffrey C. Gunn, *First Globalization: The Eurasian Exchange, 1500–1800* (2003). Explores the two-way exchange of ideas between Europe and Asia in the early modern era.

Toby E. Huff, *The Rise of Early Modern Science* (2003). A fascinating and controversial explanation as to why modern science arose in the West rather than in China or the Islamic world.

Steven Shapin, *The Scientific Revolution* (1996). A brief, accessible, and scholarly account of the emergence of modern science.

Paul R. Spickard and Kevin M. Cragg, *A Global History of Christians* (1994). A broad-brush account of the global spread of Christianity and its various expressions in different cultures.

Internet Modern History Sourcebook, "The Scientific Revolution," http://www.fordham.edu/halsall/mod/modsbook09.html. A collection of primary-source documents dealing with the breakthrough to modern science in Europe.

Documents

Considering the Evidence:
Cultural Change in the Early Modern World

Cultural and religious traditions change over time in various ways and for various reasons. Some of those changes occur as a result of internal tensions or criticisms within those traditions or in response to social and economic transformations in the larger society. The Protestant Reformation, for example, grew out of deep disaffection with prevailing teachings and practices of the Roman Catholic Church and drew support from a growing middle class and a disaffected peasantry. At other times, cultural change occurred by incorporating or reacting against new ideas drawn from contact with outsiders. Chinese Confucianism took on a distinctive tone and flavor as it drew upon the insights of Buddhism, and a new South Asian religion called Sikhism sought to combine elements of Hindu and Muslim belief. Whatever the stimulus for cultural change, departures from accepted ways of thinking have sometimes been represented as a return to a purer and more authentic past, even if that past is largely imaginary. In other cases, however, change was presented as a necessary break from an outmoded past even if many elements from earlier times were retained.

All across the Eurasian world of the early modern era—in Western Europe, China, India, and the Middle East—important cultural changes were brewing. In each of the documents that follow, we are listening in on just one side of extended debates or controversies, focusing on those who sought some change from established ways of thinking. To what extent were these changes moving in the same direction? How did they differ? What were the sources of these changes and how were they expressed? How might those who opposed these changes respond?

Document 16.1

Luther's Protest

Europe was home to perhaps the most substantial cultural transformations of the early modern centuries. There the Protestant Reformation sharply challenged both the doctrines and the authority of the Roman Catholic Church, ending the religious monopoly that the Church had exercised in Western Europe for many centuries and introducing a bitter and often violent divide into the religious and political life of the region. Then the practitioners of the Scientific Revolution, and the Enlightenment that followed from it, introduced a revolutionary new understanding of both the physical world and human society and constructed novel means of obtaining knowledge.

The Protestant Reformation and the Scientific Revolution/Enlightenment shared a common hostility to established authority, and they both represented a clear departure from previous patterns of thought and behavior. But they differed sharply in how they represented the changes they sought. Reformation leaders looked to the past, seeking to restore or renew what they believed was an earlier and more genuine version of Christianity. Leaders of the Scientific Revolution and the Enlightenment, on the other hand, foresaw and embraced an altogether new world in the making. They were the "moderns" combating the "ancients."

The most prominent figure in the Protestant Reformation was Martin Luther (1483–1546), a German monk, priest, and theologian (see pp. 723–27). A prolific writer, Luther composed theological treatises, translations of the Bible into German, and many hymns. The excerpts in Document 16.1, however, come from conversations with his students, friends, and colleagues, which they carefully recorded. After Luther's death, these recollections of the reformer's thoughts were collected and published under the title *Table Talk*.

- Based on this document, what issues drove the Protestant Reformation?

- What theological questions are addressed in these excerpts? How does Luther understand the concepts of law, good works, grace, and faith?

- In what ways is Luther critical of the papacy, monks, and the monastic orders of the Catholic Church?

- Why might Catholic authorities challenge Luther's singular emphasis on the Bible? In what other ways might thoughtful Catholics respond to Luther's charges? (See pp. 725–27 on the Catholic Counter-Reformation.)

Martin Luther
Table Talk
Early Sixteenth Century

On the Bible

Let us not lose the Bible, but with diligence, in fear and invocation of God, read and preach it.

No greater mischief can happen to a Christian people, than to have God's Word taken from them, or falsified, so that they no longer have it pure and clear. The ungodly papists prefer the authority of the church far above God's Word; a blasphemy abominable and not to be endured; wherewith, void of all shame and piety, they spit in God's face.

Pope, cardinals, bishops, not a soul of them has read the Bible; 'tis a book unknown to them. They

Source: William Hazlitt, ed. and trans., *The Table Talk of Martin Luther* (London: H. G. Bohn, 1857).

are a pack of guzzling, stuffing wretches, rich, wallowing in wealth and laziness, resting secure in their power, and never, for a moment, thinking of accomplishing God's will.

On Salvation

He that goes from the gospel to the law, thinking to be saved by good works, falls as uneasily as he who falls from the true service of God to idolatry; for, without Christ, all is idolatry and fictitious imaginings of God, whether of the Turkish Koran, of the pope's decrees, or Moses' law.

The Gospel preaches nothing of the merit of works; he that says the Gospel requires works for salvation, I say, flat and plain, is a liar. Nothing that is properly good proceeds out of the works of the law, unless grace be present; for what we are forced to do, goes not from the heart, nor is acceptable.

But a true Christian says: I am justified and saved only by faith in Christ, without any works or merits of my own....

Prayer in popedom is mere tongue-threshing...; not prayer but a work of obedience.

On the Pope and the Church Hierarchy

The great prelates, the puffed-up saints, the rich usurers, the ox drovers that seek unconscionable gain, etc., these are not God's servants....

Our dealing and proceeding against the pope is altogether excommunication, which is simply the public declaration that a person is disobedient to Christ's Word. Now we affirm in public, that the pope and his retinue believe not; therefore we conclude that he shall not be saved, but be damned....

Antichrist is the pope and the Turk together; a beast full of life must have a body and soul; the spirit or soul of antichrist is the pope, his flesh or body the Turk.... Kings and princes coin money only out of metals, but the pope coins money out of every thing—indulgences, ceremonies, dispensations, pardons; 'tis all fish comes to his net....

The pope and his crew are mere worshippers of idols, and servants of the devil.... He pretends great holiness, under color of the outward service of God, for he has instituted orders with hoods, with shavings, fasting, eating of fish, saying mass, and such like.... [F]or his doctrine he gets money and wealth, honor and power, and is so great a monarch, that he can bring emperors under his girdle.

The chief cause that I fell out with the pope was this: the pope boasted that he was the head of the church, and condemned all that would not be under his power and authority....

If the pope were the head of the Christian church, then the church were a monster with two heads, seeing that St. Paul says that Christ is her head. The pope may well be, and is, the head of the false church.

The fasting of the friars is more easy to them than our eating to us. For one day of fasting there are three of feasting. Every friar for his supper has two quarts of beer, a quart of wine, and spice-cakes, or bread prepared with spice and salt, the better to relish their drink. Thus go on these poor fasting brethren; getting so pale and wan, they are like the fiery angels.

The state of celibacy is great hypocrisy and wickedness.... Christ with one sentence confutes all their arguments: God created them male and female.... Now eating, drinking, marrying, etc., are of God's making, therefore they are good.

[T]hey [the Catholic Church] must make full restitution of that which, with their lies and deceit, they have got and stolen from emperors, kings, princes, nobility, and other people.

A Christian's worshipping is not the external, hypocritical mask that our spiritual friars wear, when they chastise their bodies, torment and make themselves faint, with ostentatious fasting, watching, singing, wearing hair shirts, scourging themselves, etc. Such worshipping God desires not.

Document 16.2

Progress and Enlightenment

If the Protestant Reformation represented a major change within the framework of the Christian faith, the Scientific Revolution and the European Enlightenment (see pp. 737–44) came to be seen by many as a challenge to all Christian understandings of the world. After all, those two movements celebrated the powers of human reason to unlock the mysteries of the universe and proclaimed the possibility of a new human society shaped by human hands. Among the most prominent spokesmen for the Enlightenment was the Marquis de Condorcet (1743–1794), a French mathematician, philosopher, and active participant in the French Revolution. In his *Sketch of the Progress of the Human Mind*, Condorcet described ten stages of human development. Document 16.2 contains excerpts from "The Ninth Epoch," whose title refers to the era in which Cordorcet was living, and the "The Tenth Epoch," referring to the age to come. Condorcet's optimism about that future was not borne out in his own life, for he fell afoul of the radicalism of the French Revolution and died in prison in 1794.

- What is Condorcet's view of the relationship between the Scientific Revolution and the Enlightenment?

- How, precisely, does Condorcet imagine the future of humankind?

- How might Martin Luther respond to Condorcet's vision of the future? How do their understandings of human potential differ?

- To what extent have Condorcet's predictions come to fruition in the two centuries since his death?

Marquis de Condorcet

Sketch of the Progress of the Human Mind
1793–1794

The Ninth Epoch: From Descartes to the Formation of the French Republic

[T]he progress of philosophy...destroyed within the general mass of people the prejudices that have af-

Source: Marquis de Condorcet, *Sketch of the Progress of the Human Mind* (Paris: Firmin Didot Frères, 1847), Epoch IX and Epoch X.

flicted and corrupted the human race for so long a time.

Humanity was finally permitted to boldly proclaim the long ignored right to submit every opinion to reason, that is to utilize the only instrument given to us for grasping and recognizing the truth. Each human learned with a sort of pride that nature had never destined him to believe the word of others. The superstitions of antiquity and the abasement of reason before the madness of supernatural religion disappeared from society just as they had disappeared from philosophy....

If we were to limit ourselves to showing the benefits derived from the immediate applications of the sciences, or in their applications to man-made devices for the well-being of individuals and the prosperity of nations, we would be making known only a slim part of their benefits. The most important, perhaps, is having destroyed prejudices, and reestablished human intelligence, which until then had been forced to bend down to false instructions instilled in it by absurd beliefs passed on to the children of each generation by the terrors of superstition and the fear of tyranny....

The advances of scientific knowledge are all the more deadly to these errors because they destroy them without appearing to attack them, while lavishing on those who stubbornly defend them the degrading taunt of ignorance....

Finally this progress of scientific knowledge... results in a belief that not birth, professional status, or social standing gives anyone the right to judge something he does not understand. This unstoppable progress cannot be observed without having enlightened men search unceasingly for ways to make the other branches of learning follow the same path....

The Tenth Epoch: The Future Progress of the Human Mind

Our hopes for the future of the human species may be reduced to three important points: the destruction of inequality among nations; the progress of equality within nations themselves; and finally, the real improvement of humanity. Should not all the nations of the world approach one day the state of civilization reached by the most enlightened peoples such as the French and the Anglo-Americans? Will not the slavery of nations subjected to kings, the barbarity of African tribes, and the ignorance of savages gradually disappear?...

If we cast an eye at the existing state of the globe, we will see right away that in Europe the principles of the French constitution are already those of all enlightened men. We will see that they are too widely disseminated and too openly professed for the efforts

of tyrants and priests to prevent them from penetrating into the hovels of their slaves....

Can it be doubted that either wisdom or the senseless feuds of the European nations themselves, working with the slow but certain effects of progress in their colonies, will not soon produce the independence of the new world; and that then the European population, spreading rapidly across that immense land, must either civilize or make disappear the savage peoples that now inhabit these vast continents?...

Thus the day will come when the sun will shine only on free men born knowing no other master but their reason; where tyrants and their slaves, priests and their ignorant, hypocritical writings will exist only in the history books and theaters; where we will only be occupied with mourning their victims and their dupes; when we will maintain an active vigilance by remembering their horrors; when we will learn to recognize and stifle by the force of reason the first seeds of superstition and tyranny, if ever they dare to appear!...

If we consider the human creations based on scientific theories, we shall see that their progress can have no limits;... that new tools, machines, and looms will add every day to the capabilities and skill of humans; they will improve and perfect the precision of their products while decreasing the amount of time and labor needed to produce them....

A smaller piece of land will be able to produce commodities of greater usefulness and value than before; greater benefits will be obtained with less waste; the production of the same industrial product will result in less destruction of raw materials and greater durability.... [E]ach individual will work less but more productively and will be able to better satisfy his needs....

Among the advances of the human mind we should reckon as most important for the general welfare is the complete destruction of those prejudices that have established an inequality of rights between the sexes, and inequality damaging even to the party it favors....

The most enlightened people... will slowly come to perceive war as the deadliest plague and the most monstrous of crimes.... They will understand that they cannot become conquerors without losing their liberty; that perpetual alliances are the only way to preserve independence; and that they should seek their security, not power....

We may conclude then that the perfectibility of humanity is indefinite.

Finally, can we not also extend the same hopes to the intellectual and moral faculties?...Is it not also probable that education, while perfecting these qualities, will also influence, modify, and improve that bodily nature itself?...

Document 16.3

Debating Confucianism

Cultural change in early modern China was not as dramatic as in Europe. But Confucianism, which had long provided the framework for elite thinking and the basis for China's famous civil service examinations, was surely not a monolithic tradition. The version of Confucianism that prevailed in Ming dynasty China (1368–1644) emphasized strenuous educational efforts ("investigation of things") leading to moral self-improvement and appropriate action. In practice, this often amounted to the rote memorization of texts in order to pass the examinations, which in turn led to official positions and great social prestige for the elite few. Wang Yangming (1472–1529), a prominent Chinese philosopher, state official, and general, contested this kind of Confucianism. His was a more individualistic, inner-directed Confucianism, allowing ordinary people, not just the well-educated few, to achieve sagehood. Although he explicitly rejected both Buddhism and Daoism, he drew on the interior emphasis of both traditions. It is not surprising, therefore, that Wang Yangming's ideas stirred considerable controversy in elite circles (see p. 735). The selections that follow are presented as conversations between Wang Yangming and his followers.

- In what ways were Wang Yangming's ideas at odds with the prevailing Confucianism of his time?

- Why might his ideas have been subject to severe criticism by more established Confucian thinkers?

- What similarities might you find in the ideas of Martin Luther and Wang Yangming? What differences are apparent? Consider their views of human nature, the ability of individuals to achieve moral improvement, and their relationship to established authority.

WANG YANGMING

Conversations

Early Sixteenth Century

In 1520 I went to Qianzhou and saw Wang Yangming again. I told him that recently, although I was making a little headway in my studies, I was finding it hard to feel secure or happy. He responded, "The problem is that you go to your mind to seek Heavenly principles, a practice called obscuration by principle. There is a trick for what you want to do."

"Please tell me what it is."

"It is simply the extension of knowledge."

"How does one do it?" I asked.

"Take your intuitive moral knowledge as your personal standard. If you think about something, you will know it is right if it is right, wrong if it is wrong. You cannot conceal anything from your intuitive moral knowledge. Just don't try to deceive it. Honestly follow it in whatever you do. That way you will keep what is good and get rid of what is bad. . . ."

Once when Wang Yuzhong, Zou Shouyi, and I were attending him, Wang Yangming said, "Each person has a sage inside of him or her, which he or she suppresses because of lack of confidence." He then looked at Wang Yuzhong and said, "You have been a sage from the start." Yuzhong rose and politely demurred. The teacher added, "This is something everyone has. Why should you demur?"

"I do not deserve your praise."

"Everyone has this, so naturally you do. Why be so polite? Politeness is not appropriate here." Yuzhong then accepted with a smile.

Wang Yangming carried the discussion further. "Intuitive moral knowledge exists in people. No mat-

ter what they do, they cannot destroy it. Even robbers know that they should not rob. If you call them robbers they are embarrassed."

Wang Yuzhong said, "Material desires can obscure the intuitive moral knowledge in a person, but not make it disappear. It is like the clouds obscuring the sun. The sun is not lost."

Wang Yangming said, "You are so smart. No one else sees it."

A lower-ranking official, who had for a long time been listening to discussions of our teacher's doctrines, once said, "His doctrines are excellent, but because I am so busy keeping records and taking care of legal cases, I cannot study them further."

When Wang Yangming heard of his remark, he said to him, "When did I say you should abandon your records and legal cases to take up study? Since you have official duties, you should use them as a basis for your study. That is the true investigation of things. For instance, if you are questioning a plaintiff, you should not get angry because his answers are impolite or become pleased because he uses ingratiating language. You should not hate him for his efforts to go around you and purposely punish him. Nor should you bend your principles and forgive someone because he implores you. You should not dispose of a case quickly because your own affairs are too pressing, nor let other people's criticisms or praise or plots influence your decision. These ways of responding are all selfish. All you need to know is in yourself. Carefully check for any sign that you are biased, for that would confuse your recognition of right and wrong. This is how to investigate things and extend knowledge. Real learning is to be found in every aspect of record keeping and legal cases. What is empty is study that is detached from things."

Source: Patricia Buckley Ebrey, ed. and trans., *Chinese Civilization: A Sourcebook* (New York: Free Press, 1993), 257–58.

Document 16.4

The Wahhabi Perspective on Islam

Within the Islamic world, the major cultural movements of the early modern era were those of religious renewal. Such movements sought to eliminate the "deviations" that had crept into Islamic practice over the centuries and to return to a purer version of the faith that presumably had prevailed during the early years of the religion in the seventh century. The most influential of these movements was associated with Muhammad ibn Abd al-Wahhab (1703–1791), whose revivalist movement spread widely in Arabia during the second half of the eighteenth century (see pp. 733–34). Document 16.3, written by the grandson of al-Wahhab shortly after the capture of Mecca in 1803, provides a window into the outlook of Wahhabi Islam.

- What specific objections did the Wahhabis have to the prevailing practice of Islam in eighteenth-century Arabia?

- How did Wahhabis put their ideas into practice once they had seized control of Mecca?

- What similarities do you see between the outlook of the Wahhabis and that of Martin Luther? What differences can you identify?

- How might you compare eighteenth-century Wahhabi Islam with movements of Islamic renewal, or "fundamentalism," in the late twentieth and early twenty-first centuries? (See Chapter 24.)

ABDULLAH WAHHAB

History and Doctrines of the Wahhabis

1803

Now I was engaged in the holy war, carried on by those who truly believe in the Unity of God, when God, praised be He, graciously permitted us to enter Mecca.... Now, though we were more numerous, better armed and disciplined than the people of Mecca, yet we did not cut down their trees, neither did we hunt, nor shed any blood except the blood of victims, and of those four-footed beasts which the Lord has made lawful by his commands.

When our pilgrimage was over...our leader, whom the Lord saves, explained to the divines what we required of the people,...namely, a pure belief in the Unity of God Almighty. He pointed out to them that there was no dispute between us and them except on two points, and that one of these was a sincere belief in the Unity of God, and a knowledge of the different kinds of prayer....

They then acknowledged our belief, and there was not one among them who doubted.... And they swore a binding oath, although we had not asked them, that their hearts had been opened and their doubts removed, and that they were convinced who-

Source: J. O'Kinealy, "Translation of an Arabic Pamphlet on the History and Doctrines of the Wahhabis," *Journal of the Asiatic Society of Bengal* 43 (1874): 68–82.

ever said, "Oh prophet of God!" or "Oh Ibn 'Abbes!" or "Oh 'Abdul Qadir!" or called on any other created being, thus entreating him to turn away evil or grant what is good (where the power belongs to God alone), such as recovery from sickness, or victory over enemies, or protection from temptation, etc.; he is a *Mushrik*, guilty of the most heinous form of shirk,° his blood shall be shed and property confiscated.... Again, the tombs which had been erected over the remains of the pious, had become in these times as it were idols where the people went to pray for what they required; they humbled themselves before them, and called upon those lying in them, in their distress, just as did those who were in darkness before the coming of Muhammad....

We razed all the large tombs in the city which the people generally worshipped and believed in, and by which they hoped to obtain benefits or ward off evil, so that there did not remain an idol to be adored in that pure city, for which God be praised. Then the taxes and customs we abolished, all the different kinds of instruments for using tobacco we destroyed, and tobacco itself we proclaimed forbidden. Next we burned the dwellings of those selling *hashish*, and living in open wickedness, and issued a proclamation, directing the people to constantly exercise themselves in prayer. They were not to pray in separate groups..., but all were directed to arrange themselves at each time of prayer behind any Imam who is a follower of any of the four Imams.°... For in this way the Lord would be worshiped by as it were one voice, the faithful of all sects would become friendly disposed towards each other, and all dissensions would cease....

[W]e do not reject anyone who follows any of the four Imams, as do the Shias, the Zaidiyyahs, and the Imamiyyahs, &c. Nor do we admit them in any way to act openly according to their vicious creeds; on the contrary, we compelled them to follow one of the four Imams. We do not claim to exercise our reason in all matters of religion, and of our faith, save that we follow our judgment where a point is clearly demonstrated to us in either the Quran or the Sunnah.°... We do not command the destruction of any writings except such as tend to cast people into infidelity to injure their faith, such as those on Logic, which have been prohibited by all Divines. But we are not very exacting with regard to books or documents of this nature, if they appear to assist our opponents, we destroy them.... We do not consider it proper to make Arabs prisoners of war, nor have we done so, neither do we fight with other nations. Finally, we do not consider it lawful to kill women or children....

We consider pilgrimage is supported by legal custom, but it should not be undertaken except to a mosque, and for the purpose of praying in it. Therefore, whoever performs pilgrimage for this purpose, is not wrong, and doubtless those who spend the precious moments of their existence in invoking the Prophet, shall... obtain happiness in this world and the next.... We do not deny miraculous powers to the saints, but on the contrary allow them.... But whether alive or dead, they must not be made the object of any form of worship....

We prohibit those forms of Bidah° that affect religion or pious works. Thus drinking coffee, reciting poetry, praising kings, do not affect religion or pious works and are not prohibited....

All games are lawful. Our prophet allowed play in his mosque. So it is lawful to chide and punish persons in various ways; to train them in the use of different weapons; or to use anything which tends to encourage warriors in battle, such as a war-drum. But it must not be accompanied with musical instruments. These are forbidden, and indeed the difference between them and a war drum is clear.

_____

°**shirk:** unbelief.

°**the four Imams:** founders of the four major schools of Islamic law.

_____

°**Sunnah:** traditions of Muhammad's actions.

°**Bidah:** improper or erroneous behavior.

Document 16.5

The Poetry of Kabir

Early modern India was a place of much religious creativity and the interaction of various traditions. The majority of India's people practiced one or another of the many forms of Hinduism, while its Mughal rulers and perhaps 20 percent of the population were Muslims. And a new religion—Sikhism—took shape in the sixteenth century as well (see pp. 736–37). Certainly there was tension and sometimes conflict among these religious communities, but not all was hostility across religious boundaries. In the writings of Kabir (1440–1518), perhaps India's most beloved poet, the sectarian differences among these religions dissolved into a mystical and transcendent love of the divine in all of its many forms. Born into a family of Muslim weavers, Kabir as a young man became a student of a famous Hindu ascetic, Ramananda. Kabir's own poetry was and remains revered among Hindus, Muslims, and Sikhs alike. Document 16.5 contains selections from his poetry, translated by the famous Indian writer Rabindranath Tagore in the early twentieth century.

■ In what ways was Kabir critical of conventional religious practice—both Muslim and Hindu?

■ How would you describe Kabir's religious vision?

■ How might more orthodox Hindus and Muslims respond to Kabir? How would the Wahhabis in particular take issue with Kabir's religious outlook?

KABÎR

Poetry

ca. Late Fifteenth Century

O servant, where dost thou seek Me? Lo! I am beside thee.
I am neither in temple nor in mosque: I am neither in Kaaba° nor in Kailash:°
Neither am I in rites and ceremonies, nor in Yoga and renunciation.

If thou art a true seeker, thou shalt at once see Me:…
Kabir says, "O Sadhu!° God is the breath of all breath."

It is needless to ask of a saint the caste to which he belongs;
For the priest, the warrior, the tradesman, and all the thirty-six castes, alike are seeking for God.…

°**Kaaba:** the central shrine of Islam in Mecca.

°**Kailash:** a mountain sacred to Hindus.

Source: Rabindranath Tagore, trans., *The Songs of Kabir* (New York: The Macmillan Company, 1915).

°**Sadhu:** a Hindu spiritual seeker who has abandoned ordinary life.

The barber has sought God, the washerwoman, and the carpenter—
Even Raidas° was a seeker after God.
The Rishi Swapacha was a tanner by caste [an untouchable].
Hindus and Moslems alike have achieved that End, where remains no mark of distinction.

Within this earthen vessel° are bowers and groves, and within it is the Creator:
Within this vessel are the seven oceans and the unnumbered stars.
The touchstone and the jewel-appraiser are within;
And within this vessel the Eternal soundeth, and the spring wells up.
Kabir says: "Listen to me, my Friend! My beloved Lord is within."

Your Lord is near: yet you are climbing the palm-tree to seek Him.
The Brâhman priest goes from house to house and initiates people into faith:
Alas! the true fountain of life is beside you, and you have set up a stone to worship.
Kabir says: "I may never express how sweet my Lord is.

Yoga and the telling of beads, virtue and vice—these are naught to Him."

I do not ring the temple bell:
I do not set the idol on its throne:
I do not worship the image with flowers.
It is not the austerities that mortify the flesh which are pleasing to the Lord,
When you leave off your clothes and kill your senses, you do not please the Lord.
The man who is kind and who practices right-eousness, who remains passive amidst the affairs of the world, who considers all creatures on earth as his own self,
He attains the Immortal Being, the true God is ever with him.

There is nothing but water at the holy bathing places;
And I know that they are useless, for I have bathed in them.
The images are all lifeless, they cannot speak;
I know, for I have cried aloud to them.
The Purana° and the Koran are mere words; lifting up the curtain, I have seen.
Kabir gives utterance to the words of experience; and he knows very well that all other things are untrue.

_____

°**Raidas:** a Hindu poet from a low-ranking Sudra caste.

°**earthen vessel:** the human body.

_____

°**Purana:** Hindu religious texts.

Using the Evidence:
Cultural Change in the Early Modern World

1. **Identifying the object of protest:** Each of these documents is protesting or criticizing something. How might you compare the ideas, practices, or authorities against which they are reacting? What historical circumstances generated these protests?

2. **Comparing views of human potential:** In what different ways might each of these authors understand human potential? What do they believe is necessary to realize or fulfill that potential?

3. **Comparing religious reformers:** Consider the religious outlook of Luther, al-Wahhab, and Kabir. What similarities and differences can you identify? Do you think Wang Yangming should be included in this category of religious reformers?

4. **Imagining a conversation:** Construct an imaginary debate or conversation between Condorcet and one or more of the religious or spiritually inclined authors of these documents.

Visual Sources

Considering the Evidence:
Global Christianity in the Early Modern Era

During the early modern centuries, the world of Christendom, long divided between its Roman Catholic and Eastern Orthodox branches, underwent two major transformations. First, the Reformation sharply divided western Christendom into bitterly hostile Protestant and Catholic halves. And while that process was unfolding in Europe, missionaries—mostly Roman Catholic—rode the tide of European expansion to establish the faith in the Americas and parts of Asia. In those places, native converts sometimes imitated European patterns and at other times adapted the new religion to their own cultural traditions. Furthermore, smaller but ancient Christian communities persisted in Ethiopia, Armenia, Egypt, southern India, and elsewhere. Thus the Christian world of the early modern era was far more globalized and much more varied than ever before. That variety found expression in both art and architecture, as the visual sources that follow illustrate.

Some of the differences between Protestant and Catholic Christianity become apparent in the interiors of their churches. To Martin Luther, the founder of Protestant Christianity, elaborate church interiors, with their many sculptures and paintings, represented a spiritual danger, for he feared that the wealthy few who endowed such images would come to believe that they were buying their way into heaven rather than relying on God's grace. "It would be better," he wrote, "if we gave less to the churches and altars,... and more to the needy."[30] John Calvin, the prominent French-born Protestant theologian, went even further, declaring that "God forbade... the making of any images representing him."[31]

Behind such statements lay different understandings of the church building. While Roman Catholics generally saw a church as a temple or "house of God," sacred because it is where God dwells on earth, Protestants viewed churches more as meetinghouses, gathering places for a congregation. They were not sacred in themselves as places, but only on account of the worship that occurred within them.[32] Furthermore, to Protestants, images of the saints were an invitation to idolatry. Acting on such ideas, Protestants in various places stripped older churches of the offending images, decapitated statues, and sometimes ritually burned statues and paintings at the stake. The new churches they created were often quite different from their Catholic counterparts. Visual Source 16.1, a

Visual Source 16.1 Pieter Saenredam, *Interior of a Dutch Reformed Church* (Rijksmuseum Museum)

painting by Dutch artist Pieter Saenredam from about 1645, portrays the interior of a typical Dutch Reformed (Protestant) Church.

Roman Catholic response to the Reformation took shape in the Catholic Counter-Reformation (see pp. 725–27). That vigorous movement found expression in a style of church architecture known as Baroque, which emerged powerfully in Catholic Europe as well as in the Spanish and Portuguese colonies of Latin America during the seventeenth and eighteenth centuries. The interiors of such churches were ornately adorned with paintings, ceiling frescoes, and statues, depicting Jesus on the cross, the Virgin and child, numerous saints, and biblical stories. The exuberant art of these church interiors appealed to the senses, seeking to provoke an emotional response of mystery, awe, and grandeur while kindling the faith of the worshippers and binding them firmly to the Catholic Church in the face of Protestant competition. Visual Source 16.2 is a photograph of the interior of the Pilgrimage Church of Mariazell, located in present-day Austria. A church site since the twelfth century, the building was enlarged and refurbished in Baroque style in the seventeenth century.

■ What obvious differences do you notice between these two church interiors? What kind of emotional responses would each of them have evoked?

Visual Source 16.2 Catholic Baroque: Interior of Pilgrimage Church, Mariazell, Austria (Erich Lessing/Art Resource, NY)

- In what ways do these church interiors reflect differences between Protestant and Catholic theology? (See Snapshot, p. 724.) Why does the Protestant congregation face toward the pulpit, from which the minister presents his sermon, while the Catholic worshippers look toward the altar, where Holy Communion takes place? Pay attention as well to the kind of geometric shapes apparent in each church and to the role of preaching.

- How might Protestants and Catholics have reacted upon entering each other's churches?

- Keep in mind that Visual Source 16.1 is a painting. Why do you think the artist showed the people disproportionately small?

Throughout Latin America, Christianity was established in the context of conquest and colonial rule (see pp. 728–30). As the new faith took hold across the region, it incorporated much that was of European origin as the construction of many large and ornate Baroque churches illustrates. But local communities also sought to blend this European Catholic Christianity with religious symbols and concepts drawn from their own traditions in a process that historians call syncretism. In the Andes, for example, Inca religion featured a supreme creator god (Viracocha); a sun god (Inti), regarded as the creator of the Inca people; a moon goddess (Killa), who was the wife of Inti and was attended by an order of priestesses; and an earth mother goddess (Pachamama), associated with mountain peaks and fertility. Those religious figures found their way into Andean understanding of Christianity, as Visual Source 16.3 illustrates.

Painted around 1740 by an unknown artist, this striking image shows the Virgin Mary placed within the "rich mountain" of Potosí in Bolivia, from which the Spanish had extracted so much silver (see p. 683). A number of smaller figures within the mountain represent the native miners whose labor had enriched their colonial rulers. A somewhat larger figure at the bottom of the mountain is an Inca ruler dressed in royal garb receiving tribute from his people. At the bottom left are the pope and a cardinal, while on the right stands the Habsburg emperor Charles V and perhaps his wife.

- What is Mary's relationship to the heavenly beings standing above her as well as to the miners at work in the mountain? What is the significance of the crown above her head and her outstretched arms?

- The European figures at the bottom are shown in a posture of prayer or thanksgiving. What might the artist have been trying to convey? How would you interpret the relative size of the European and Andean figures?

- Why do you think the artist placed Mary actually inside the mountain rather than on it, while depicting her dress in a mountain-like form?

Visual Source 16.3 Cultural Blending in Andean Christianity (Nick Buxton, photographer)

- What marks this painting as an example of syncretism?

- Do you read this image as subversive of the colonial order or as supportive of it? Do you think the artist was a European or a Native American Christian?

In China, unlike Latin America, Christian missionaries operated in a setting wholly outside of European political control, bringing their faith to a powerful and proud civilization, long dominant in eastern Asia, where Confucianism, Daoism, and Buddhism had for many centuries mixed and mingled. The outcome of those missionary efforts was far more modest and much less successful than in the Americas (see pp. 730–32). Nonetheless, in China too the tendency toward syncretism was evident. Jesuit missionaries themselves sought to present the Christian message within a Chinese cultural context to the intellectual and political elites who were their primary target audience. And Chinese Christians often transposed the new religion into more familiar cultural concepts. European critics of the Jesuit approach, however, feared that syncretism watered down the Christian message and risked losing its distinctive character.

Visual Source 16.4 provides an example of Christianity becoming Chinese.[33] In the early seventeenth century, the Jesuits published several books in the Chinese language describing the life of Christ and illustrated them with a series of woodblock prints created by Chinese artists affiliated with the Jesuits. Although they were clearly modeled on European images, those prints cast Christian figures into an altogether Chinese setting. The woodblock print in Visual Source 16.4 portrays the familiar biblical story of the annunciation, when an angel informs Mary that she will be the mother of Christ. The house and furniture shown in the print suggest the dwelling of a wealthy Chinese scholar. The reading table in front of Mary was a common item in the homes of the literary elite of the time. The view from the window shows a seascape, mountains in the distance, a lone tree, and a "scholar's rock"—all of which were common features in Chinese landscape painting. The clouds that appear at the angel's feet and around the shaft of light shining on Mary are identical to those associated with sacred Buddhist and Daoist figures. To Chinese eyes, the angel might well appear as a Buddhist boddhisatva, while Mary may resemble a Ming dynasty noblewoman or perhaps Kuanyin, the Chinese Buddhist goddess of mercy and compassion.

- What specifically Chinese elements can you identify in this image?

- To whom might this image have been directed?

- How might educated Chinese have responded to this image?

- The European engraving on which this Chinese print was modeled included in the background the scene of Jesus' crucifixion. Why might the Chinese artist have chosen to omit that scene from his image?

Visual Source 16.4 Making Christianity Chinese (Courtesy, Archivum Romanum Societatis Iesu, Rome)

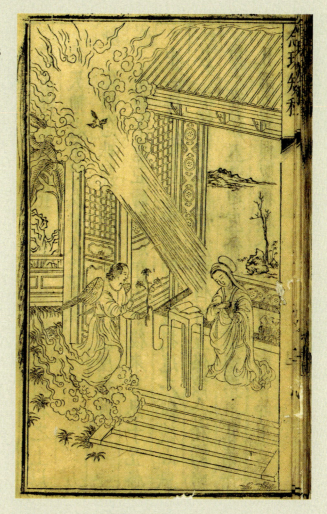

■ How would European critics of the Jesuits' approach to missionary work have reacted to this image? To what extent has the basic message of Catholic Christianity been retained or changed in this Chinese cultural setting?

As Chinese emperors welcomed Jesuit missionaries at court, so too did the rulers of Mughal India during the time of Akbar and Jahangir (1556–1627). But while Chinese elite circles received the Jesuits for their scientific skills, especially in astronomy, the Mughal court seemed more interested in the religious and artistic achievements of European civilization. Akbar invited the Jesuits to take part in cross-religious discussions that included Muslim, Hindu, Jain, and Zoroastrian scholars. Furthermore, the Mughal emperors eagerly embraced the art of late Renaissance Europe, which the Jesuits provided to them, much

Visual Source 16.5 Christian Art at the Mughal Court
(Rare Book Department, The Free Library of Philadelphia)

of it devotional and distinctly Christian. Mughal artists quickly learned to paint in the European style, and soon murals featuring Jesus, Mary, and Christian saints appeared on the walls of palaces, garden pavilions, and harems of the Mughal court, while miniature paintings adorned books, albums, and jewelry.

In religious terms, however, the Jesuit efforts were "a fantastic and extravagant failure,"[34] for these Muslim rulers of India were not in the least interested in abandoning Islam for the Christian faith, and few conversions of any kind occurred. Akbar and Jahangir, however, were cosmopolitan connoisseurs of art, which they collected, reproduced, and displayed. European religious art also had propaganda value in enhancing their status. Jesus and Mary, after all, had a prominent place within Islam. Jesus was seen both as an earlier prophet and as mystical figure, similar to the Sufi masters who were so important in Indian Islam. Mughal paintings, pairing the adult Jesus and Mary side by side, were placed above the imperial throne as well as on the emperor's jewelry and his official seal, suggesting an identification of Jesus and a semidivine emperor. That the mothers of both Akbar and Jahangir were named Mary only added to the appeal. Thus Akbar and Jahangir sought to incorporate European-style Christian art into their efforts to create a blended and tolerant religious culture for the elites of their vast and diverse realm. It was a culture that drew on Islam, Hinduism, Zoroastrianism, and Christianity.

But as Catholic devotional art was reworked by Mughal artists, it was also subtly changed. Visual Source 16.5 shows an early-seventeenth-century depiction of the Holy Family painted by an Indian artist.

- Why do you think that this Mughal painter portrayed Mary and Joseph as rather distinguished and educated persons rather than as the humble carpenter and his peasant wife, as in so many European images?

- Similarly, why might he have placed the family in rather palatial surroundings instead of a stable?

- How do you imagine European missionaries responded to this representation of the Holy Family?

- How might more orthodox Muslims have reacted to the larger project of creating a blended religion making use of elements from many traditions? Consider the possible reactions of the Wahhabis (Document 16.4, pp. 756–57) and Kabir (Document 16.5, pp. 758–59).

- What similarities can you identify between this Indian image and the Chinese print in Visual Source 16.4? Pay attention to the setting, the clothing, and the class status of the human figures, and the scenes outside the windows.

Using the Evidence:
Global Christianity in the Early Modern Era

1. **Making comparisons:** What common elements of Christianity can you identify in these visual sources? What differences in the expression of Christianity can you define?

2. **Considering Mary:** The Catholic Christian tradition as it developed in Latin America, China, and India as well as Europe provided a very important place for representations of the Virgin Mary. Why might this feature of the Christian message have been so widely appealing? But in what ways does the image of the Holy Mother differ in Visual Sources 16.3, 16.4, and 16.5? In what ways were those images adapted to the distinctive cultures in which they were created?

3. **Pondering syncretism:** From a missionary viewpoint, develop arguments for and against religious syncretism using these visual sources as points of reference.

4. **Considering visual sources as evidence:** What are the strengths and limitations of these visual sources, as opposed to texts, as historians seek to understand the globalization of Christianity in the early modern era? What other visual sources might be useful?

PART FIVE

The European Moment in World History

1750–1914

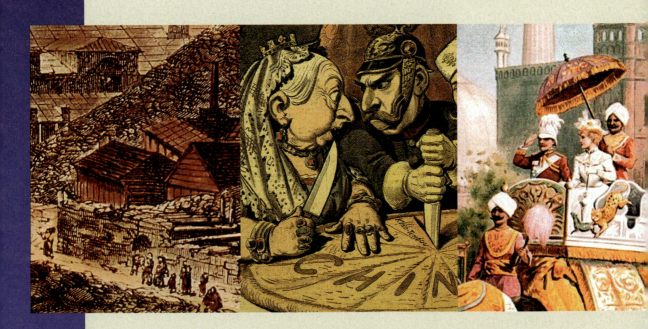

Contents

THE BIG PICTURE

European Centrality and the Problem of Eurocentrism

During the century and a half between 1750 and 1914, sometimes referred to as the "long nineteenth century," two new and related phenomena held center stage in the global history of humankind and represent the major themes of the four chapters that follow. The first of these, explored in Chapters 17 and 18, was the creation of a new kind of human society, commonly called "modern," which was the outgrowth of the Scientific, French, and Industrial revolutions, all of which took shape in Western Europe. Those societies generated many of the ideas that have guided human behavior over the past several centuries—notions of progress, constitutional government, political democracy, socialism, nationalism, feminism, and opposition to slavery.

The second theme of this long nineteenth century, which is addressed in Chapters 19 and 20, was the growing ability of these modern societies to exercise enormous power and influence over the rest of humankind. In some places, this occurred within growing European empires, such as those that governed India, Southeast Asia, and Africa. Elsewhere, it took place through less formal means—economic penetration, military intervention, diplomatic pressure, missionary activity—in states that remained officially independent, such as China, Japan, the Ottoman Empire, and various countries in Latin America.

Together, these two phenomena thrust Western Europe, and to a lesser extent North America, into a new and far more prominent role in world history than ever before. While various regions had experienced sprouts of modernity during the "early modern" centuries, it was in Western European societies that these novel ways of living emerged most fully. Those societies, and their North American offspring, also came to exercise a wholly unprecedented role in world affairs, as they achieved, collectively, something approaching global dominance by the early twentieth century.

Eurocentric Geography and History

That unprecedented power included the ability to rewrite geography and history in ways that centered the human story on Europe and to impose those views on other people. Thus maps placed Europe at the center of the world, while dividing Asia in half. Europe was granted continental status, even though it was more accurately only the western peninsula of Asia, much as India was its southern peninsula. Other regions of the world, such as the Far East or the Near (Middle) East, were defined in terms of their distance from Europe. The entire world came to measure

Conquest and Resistance in Colonial Africa (p. 927)

longitude from a line, known as the prime meridian, that passes through the Royal Astronomical Observatory in Greenwich, England.

History textbooks as well often reflected a Europe-centered outlook, sometimes blatantly. In 1874, the American author William O. Swinton wrote *An Outline of the World's History*, a book intended for use in high school and college classes, in which he flatly declared that "the race to which we belong, the Aryan, has always played the leading part in the great drama of the world's progress."[1] Other peoples and civilizations, by contrast, were long believed to be static and unchanging, thus largely lacking any real history. Most Europeans assumed that these "backward" peoples and regions must either imitate the Western model or face further decline and possible extinction. Until the mid-twentieth century, such ideas went largely unchallenged in the Western world. They implied that history was a race toward the finish line of modernity. That Europeans arrived there first seemed to suggest something unique, special, or superior about them or their culture, while everyone else struggled to overcome their inadequacy and catch up.

As the discipline of world history took shape in the decades after World War II, scholars and teachers actively sought to counteract such a Eurocentric understanding of the past, but they faced a special problem in dealing with recent centuries. How can we avoid an inappropriate Eurocentrism when dealing with a phase of world history in which Europeans were in fact central? The long nineteenth century, after all, was "the European moment," a time when Europeans were clearly the most powerful, most innovative, most prosperous, most expansive, and most widely imitated people on the planet.

Countering Eurocentrism

At least five answers to this dilemma are reflected in the chapters that follow. You may want to look for examples of them as you read. The first is simply to remind ourselves how recent and perhaps how brief the European moment in world history has been. Other peoples too had times of "cultural flowering" that granted them a period of primacy or influence—for example, the Greeks (500 B.C.E.–200 C.E.), Indians of South Asia (200–600 C.E.), Arabs (600–1000), Chinese (1000–1500), Mongols (1200–1350), Incas and Aztecs (fifteenth century)—but all of these were limited to particular regions of Afro-Eurasia or the Americas.[2] Even though the European moment operated on a genuinely global scale, Western peoples have enjoyed their worldwide primacy for at most two centuries. Some scholars have suggested that the events of the late twentieth and early twenty-first centuries—the end of colonial empires,

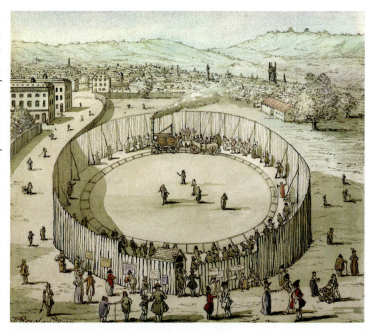

Railroads (p. 832)

the rise of India and especially China, and the assertion of Islam—mark the end, or at least the erosion, of the age of Europe.

Second, we need to remember that the rise of Europe occurred within an international context. It was the withdrawal of the Chinese naval fleet that allowed Europeans to dominate the Indian Ocean in the sixteenth century, while Native Americans' lack of immunity to European diseases and their own divisions and conflicts greatly assisted the European takeover. Europe's Scientific Revolution drew upon earlier Islamic science and was stimulated by the massive amounts of new information pouring in from around the world. The Industrial Revolution, explored in Chapter 18, likewise benefited from New World resources and markets and from the stimulus of superior Asian textile and pottery production. Chapters 19 and 20 make clear that European control of other regions everywhere depended on the cooperation of local elites. None of this diminishes the remarkable—indeed revolutionary—transformations of the European moment in world history. Rather it suggests that they did not derive wholly from some special European genius or long-term advantage but emerged from a unique intersection of European historical development with that of other peoples, regions, and cultures.

A third reminder is that the rise of Europe to a position of global dominance was not an easy or automatic process. Frequently it occurred in the face of ferocious resistance and rebellion, which often required Europeans to modify their policies and practices. The so-called Indian mutiny in mid-nineteenth-century South Asia, a massive uprising against British colonial rule, did not end British control, but it substantially transformed the character of the colonial experience. In

Africa, fear of offending Muslim sensibilities persuaded the British to keep European missionaries and mission schools out of northern Nigeria during the colonial era. Even when Europeans exercised political power, they could not do so precisely as they pleased. Empire, formal and informal alike, was always in some ways a negotiated arrangement.

Fourth, peoples the world over made active use of Europeans and European ideas for their own purposes, seeking to gain advantage over local rivals or to benefit themselves in light of new conditions. In Southeast Asia, for example, a number of highland minority groups, long oppressed by the dominant lowland Vietnamese, viewed the French invaders as liberators and assisted in their takeover of Vietnam. Hindus in India used the railroads, which had been introduced by the British, to go on pilgrimages to holy sites more easily, while the printing press made possible the more widespread distribution of their sacred texts. During the Haitian Revolution, examined in Chapter 17, enslaved Africans made use of radical French ideas about "the rights of man" in ways that most Europeans never intended. The leaders of a massive Chinese peasant upheaval in the mid-nineteenth century adopted a unique form of Christianity to legitimate their revolutionary assault on an ancient social order. Recognizing that Asian and African peoples remained active agents, pursuing their own interests even in oppressive conditions, is another way of countering residual Eurocentrism.

What was borrowed from Europe was always adapted to local circumstances. Thus Japanese or Russian industrial development did not wholly follow the pattern of England's Industrial Revolution. The Christianity that took root in the Americas or later in Africa evolved in culturally distinctive ways. Ideas of nationalism, born in Europe, were used to oppose European imperialism throughout Asia and Africa. Chinese socialism in the twentieth century departed in many ways from the vision of Karl Marx. The most interesting stories of modern world history are not simply those of European triumph or the imposition of Western ideas and practices but of encounters, though highly unequal, among culturally different peoples. It was from these encounters, not just from the intentions and actions of Europeans, that the dramatic global changes of the modern era arose.

A fifth and final antidote to Eurocentrism in an age of European centrality lies in the recognition that although Europeans gained an unprecedented prominence on the world stage, they were not the only game in town, nor were they the sole preoccupation of Asian, African, and Middle Eastern peoples. While China confronted Western aggression in the nineteenth century, it was also absorbing a huge population increase and experiencing massive peasant rebellions that grew out of distinctly Chinese conditions. The long relationship of Muslim and Hindu cultures in India continued to evolve under British colonial rule as it had for centuries under other political systems. West African societies in the nineteenth century experienced a wave of religious wars that created new states and extended and transformed the practice of Islam, and that faith continued its centuries-long spread on the continent even under European colonial rule. A further wave of wars and state formation in southern Africa transformed the political and ethnic landscape, even as European penetration picked up speed.

None of this diminishes the significance of the European moment in world history, but it sets that moment in a larger context of continuing patterns of historical development and of interaction and exchange with other peoples.

Landmarks of the European Moment in World History, 1750–1914

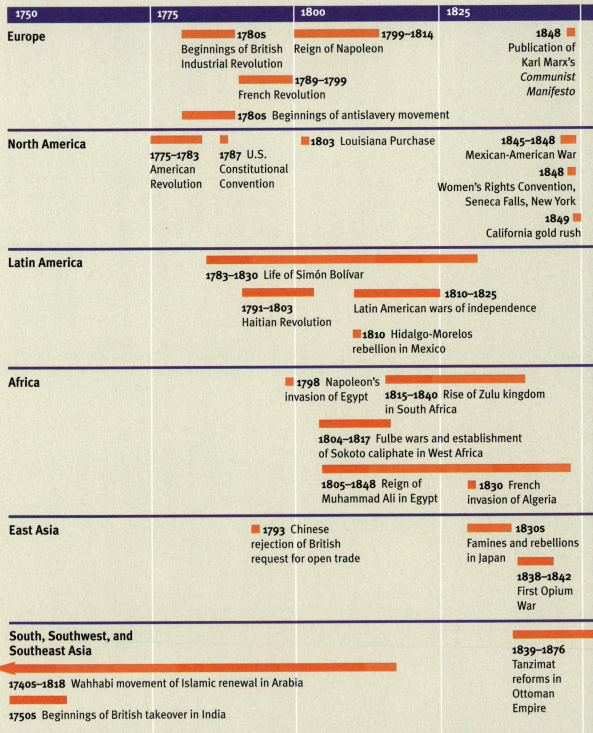

1750	1775	1800	1825

Europe

1780s Beginnings of British Industrial Revolution

1799–1814 Reign of Napoleon

1848 Publication of Karl Marx's *Communist Manifesto*

1789–1799 French Revolution

1780s Beginnings of antislavery movement

North America

1775–1783 American Revolution

1787 U.S. Constitutional Convention

1803 Louisiana Purchase

1845–1848 Mexican-American War

1848 Women's Rights Convention, Seneca Falls, New York

1849 California gold rush

Latin America

1783–1830 Life of Simón Bolívar

1791–1803 Haitian Revolution

1810–1825 Latin American wars of independence

1810 Hidalgo-Morelos rebellion in Mexico

Africa

1798 Napoleon's invasion of Egypt

1815–1840 Rise of Zulu kingdom in South Africa

1804–1817 Fulbe wars and establishment of Sokoto caliphate in West Africa

1805–1848 Reign of Muhammad Ali in Egypt

1830 French invasion of Algeria

East Asia

1793 Chinese rejection of British request for open trade

1830s Famines and rebellions in Japan

1838–1842 First Opium War

South, Southwest, and Southeast Asia

1839–1876 Tanzimat reforms in Ottoman Empire

1740s–1818 Wahhabi movement of Islamic renewal in Arabia

1750s Beginnings of British takeover in India

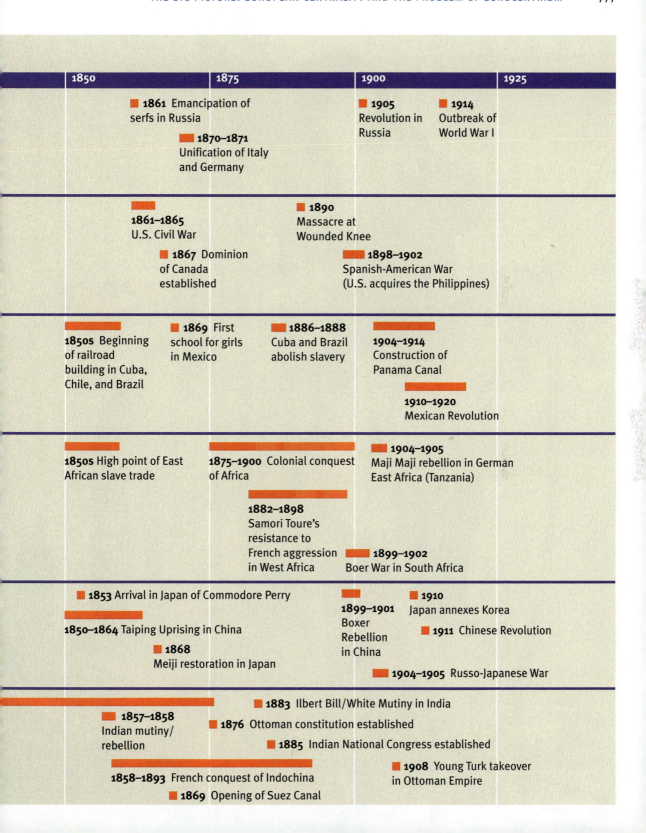

1850	1875	1900	1925

■ **1861** Emancipation of serfs in Russia

■ **1870–1871** Unification of Italy and Germany

■ **1905** Revolution in Russia

■ **1914** Outbreak of World War I

■ **1861–1865** U.S. Civil War

■ **1890** Massacre at Wounded Knee

■ **1867** Dominion of Canada established

■ **1898–1902** Spanish-American War (U.S. acquires the Philippines)

■ **1850s** Beginning of railroad building in Cuba, Chile, and Brazil

■ **1869** First school for girls in Mexico

■ **1886–1888** Cuba and Brazil abolish slavery

■ **1904–1914** Construction of Panama Canal

■ **1910–1920** Mexican Revolution

■ **1850s** High point of East African slave trade

■ **1875–1900** Colonial conquest of Africa

■ **1904–1905** Maji Maji rebellion in German East Africa (Tanzania)

■ **1882–1898** Samori Toure's resistance to French aggression in West Africa

■ **1899–1902** Boer War in South Africa

■ **1853** Arrival in Japan of Commodore Perry

■ **1850–1864** Taiping Uprising in China

■ **1899–1901** Boxer Rebellion in China

■ **1910** Japan annexes Korea

■ **1868** Meiji restoration in Japan

■ **1911** Chinese Revolution

■ **1904–1905** Russo-Japanese War

■ **1883** Ilbert Bill/White Mutiny in India

■ **1857–1858** Indian mutiny/rebellion

■ **1876** Ottoman constitution established

■ **1885** Indian National Congress established

■ **1858–1893** French conquest of Indochina

■ **1908** Young Turk takeover in Ottoman Empire

■ **1869** Opening of Suez Canal

CHAPTER SEVENTEEN

Atlantic Revolutions
and Their Echoes

1750–1914

On July 14, 1989, France celebrated the bicentennial of its famous revolution with a huge parade in Paris. At the head of that parade, strangely enough, were a number of Chinese students, pushing empty bicycles. Just a few weeks earlier, those students had been part of massive demonstrations in Beijing's Tiananmen Square, demanding from their communist government the kind of democratic political rights that the French Revolution had inspired two centuries before. In the process, they had created a thirty-foot-tall papier-mâché Goddess of Democracy, which resembled the U.S. Statue of Liberty. Chinese authorities had violently crushed those demonstrations, and now a few students who had escaped to France were paying tribute to the ideals that the French Revolution had unleashed. Their empty bicycles symbolized thousands of their colleagues who had been killed or jailed during the Chinese struggle for democracy. Thus the reverberations of the French Revolution of 1789 echoed still two centuries later and half a world away.

ESSENTIAL AS IT WAS TO THE HISTORY OF EUROPE, the French Revolution holds an even larger significance as the centerpiece of a more extensive revolutionary process that unfolded all around the Atlantic world in the century or so following 1775. The upheaval in France, of course, was preceded by the American Revolution, which gave birth to the United States. It was followed by the Haitian Revolution, the first successful slave revolt in history, and by the Latin American revolutions, in which Spanish and Portuguese colonial rule

The Three Estates of Old-Regime France: This satirical eighteenth-century illustration represents the three estates of prerevolutionary French society as women, with the peasant woman carrying a nun and an aristocratic lady on her back. Such social tensions contributed much to the making of the French Revolution. (Réunion des Musées Nationaux/Art Resource, NY)

was ended and the modern states of Latin America emerged. Further revolutionary outbreaks shook various European societies in 1830, 1848, and 1870.

These upheavals also had an impact well beyond the Atlantic world. The armies of revolutionary France, for example, invaded Egypt, Germany, Poland, and Russia, carrying seeds of change. The ideals that animated these Atlantic revolutions inspired efforts in many countries to abolish slavery, to extend the right to vote, and to secure greater equality for women. Nationalism, perhaps the most potent ideology of the modern era, was nurtured in the Atlantic revolutions and shaped much of nineteenth- and twentieth-century world history. The ideas of equality that were articulated in these revolutions later found expression in socialist and communist movements. And the Universal Declaration of Human Rights, adopted by the United Nations in 1948, echoed and amplified those principles while providing the basis for any number of subsequent protests against oppression, tyranny, and deprivation. The Atlantic revolutions had a long reach.

Comparing Atlantic Revolutions

■ **Causation**

In what ways did the ideas of the Enlightenment contribute to the Atlantic revolutions?

Writing to a friend in 1772, before any of the Atlantic revolutions had occurred, the French intellectual Voltaire asked, "My dear philosopher, doesn't this appear to you to be the century of revolutions?"[1] He was certainly on target: in the century that followed, revolutionary outbreaks punctuated the histories of three continents, with influences and echoes even farther afield. Nor were these various revolutions—in North America, France, Haiti, and Latin America—entirely separate and distinct events, for they clearly influenced one another. The American revolutionary leader Thomas Jefferson was the U.S. ambassador to France on the eve of the French Revolution, and while there he provided advice and encouragement to French reformers and revolutionaries. Simón Bolívar, a leading figure in Spanish American struggles for independence, twice visited Haiti, where he received military aid from the first black government in the Americas.

Beyond such direct connections, the various Atlantic revolutionaries shared a set of common ideas. The Atlantic basin had become a world of intellectual and cultural exchange as well as one of commercial and biological interaction. The ideas that animated the Atlantic revolutions derived from the European Enlightenment and were shared across the ocean in newspapers, books, and pamphlets. At the heart of these ideas was the radical notion that human political and social arrangements could be engineered, and improved, by human action. Thus conventional and long-established ways of living and thinking—the divine right of kings, state control of trade, aristocratic privilege, the authority of a single church—were no longer sacrosanct and came under repeated attack. New ideas of liberty, equality, free trade, religious tolerance, republicanism, and human rationality were in the air. Politically, the core notion was "popular sovereignty," which meant that the authority to govern derived from the people rather than from God or from established tradition. As the Englishman John Locke (1632–1704) had argued, the "social contract" between ruler and ruled

Snapshot   **Key Moments in the History of Atlantic Revolutions**

American Declaration of Independence	1776
British recognition of American independence	1783
U.S. Constitutional Convention	1787
Tupac Amaru revolt in Peru	1780s
Outbreak of French Revolution	1789
Haitian Revolution	1791–1804
French Terror, execution of Louis XVI	1793–1794
Napoleon's rise to power	1799
High point of Napoleon's empire	1810–1811
Hidalgo-Morelos rebellion in Mexico	1810–1813
Wars of Spanish American independence	1810–1825
Final defeat of Napoleon	1815
Independence of Brazil from Portugal	1822

should last only as long as it served the people well. In short, it was both possible and desirable to start over in the construction of human communities.

Such ideas generated endless controversy. Were liberty and equality compatible? What kind of government—unitary and centralized or federal and decentralized—best ensured freedom? And how far should liberty be extended? Except in Haiti, the chief beneficiaries of these revolutions were propertied white men of the "middling classes." Although women, slaves, Native Americans, and men without property did not gain much from these revolutions, the ideas that accompanied those upheavals gave them ammunition for the future. Because their overall thrust was to extend political rights further than ever before, these Atlantic movements have often been referred to as "democratic revolutions."

Beneath a common political vocabulary and a broadly democratic character, the Atlantic revolutions differed substantially from one another. They were triggered by different circumstances, expressed quite different social and political tensions, and varied considerably in their outcomes. Liberty, noted Simón Bolívar, "is a succulent morsel, but one difficult to digest."[2] "Digesting liberty" occurred in quite distinct ways in the various sites of the Atlantic revolutions.

The North American Revolution, 1775–1787

Every schoolchild in the United States learns early that the American Revolution was a struggle for independence from oppressive British rule. That struggle was

■ Change
What was revolutionary about the American Revolution, and what was not?

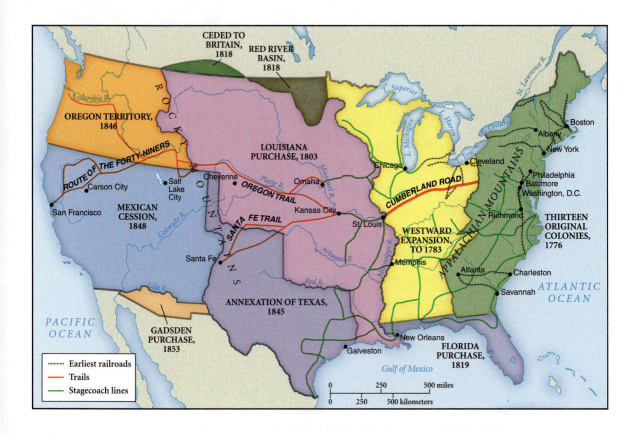

Map 17.1   The Expansion of the United States
The union of the thirteen British colonies in North America provided the foundation for the westward and transcontinental expansion of the United States during the nineteenth century, a process that turned the country into a global power by the early twentieth century.

launched with the Declaration of Independence in 1776, resulted in an unlikely military victory by 1781, and generated a federal constitution in 1787, joining thirteen formerly separate colonies into a new nation (see Map 17.1). It was the first in a series of upheavals that rocked the Atlantic world and beyond in the century that followed. But was it a genuine revolution? What, precisely, did it change?

In its break with Britain, the American Revolution marked a decisive political change, but in other ways it was, strangely enough, a conservative movement, because it originated in an effort to preserve the existing liberties of the colonies rather than to create new ones. For much of the seventeenth and eighteenth centuries, the British colonies in North America enjoyed a considerable degree of local autonomy as the British government was embroiled in its own internal conflicts and various European wars. Furthermore, Britain's West Indian colonies seemed more profitable and of greater significance than those of North America. In these circumstances, local elected assemblies in North America, dominated by the wealthier property-owning settlers, achieved something close to self-government. Colonists came to regard such autonomy as a birthright and part of their English heritage. Thus, until the mid-eighteenth century, almost no one in the colonies thought of breaking away from England because participation in the British Empire provided many advantages—protection in war, access to British markets, and confirmation of their continuing identity as "Englishmen"—and few drawbacks.

Within these colonies, English settlers had developed societies described by a leading historian as "the most radical in the contemporary Western world." Certainly class distinctions were real and visible, and a small class of wealthy "gentlemen"—the Adamses, Washingtons, Jeffersons, and Hancocks—wore powdered wigs, imitated the latest European styles, were prominent in political life, and were generally deferred to by ordinary people. But the ready availability of land following the elimination of Native Americans, the scarcity of people, and the absence of both a titled nobility and a single established church meant that social life was far more open than in Europe. No legal distinctions differentiated clergy, aristocracy, and commoners, as they did in France. All free men enjoyed the same status before the law, a situation that excluded black slaves and, in some ways, white women as well. These conditions made for less poverty, more economic opportunity, fewer social differences, and easier relationships among the classes than in Europe. The famous economist Adam Smith observed that British colonists were "republican in their manners . . . and their government" well before their independence from England.[3]

Thus the American Revolution did not grow out of social tensions within the colonies, but from a rather sudden and unexpected effort by the British government to tighten its control over the colonies and to extract more revenue from them. As Britain's global struggle with France drained its treasury and ran up its national debt, British authorities, beginning in the 1760s, looked to America to make good these losses. Abandoning its neglectful oversight of the colonies, Britain began to act like a genuine imperial power, imposing a variety of new taxes and tariffs on the colonies without their consent, for they were not represented in the British parliament. By challenging their economic interests, their established traditions of local autonomy, and their identity as true Englishmen, such measures infuriated many of the colonists. Armed with the ideas of the Enlightenment—popular sovereignty, natural rights, the consent of the governed—they went to war, and by 1781 they had prevailed, with considerable aid from the French.

What was revolutionary about the American experience was not so much the revolution itself but the kind of society that had already emerged within the colonies. Independence from Britain was not accompanied by any wholesale social transformation. Rather the revolution accelerated the established democratic tendencies of the colonial societies. Political authority remained largely in the hands of existing elites who had led the revolution, although property requirements for voting were lowered and more white men of modest means, such as small farmers and urban artisans, were elected to state legislatures.

This widening of political participation gradually eroded the power of traditional gentlemen, but no women or people of color shared in these gains. Land was not seized from its owners, except in the case of pro-British loyalists who had fled the country. Although slavery was gradually abolished in the northern states, where it counted for little, it remained firmly entrenched in the southern states, where it counted for much. Chief Justice John Marshall later gave voice to this conservative understanding of the American Revolution: "All contracts and rights, respecting property, remained unchanged by the Revolution."[4] In the century that followed independence, the United States did become the world's most democratic country, but it was less the direct product of the revolution and more the gradual working out in a reformist fashion of earlier practices and the principles of equality announced in the Declaration of Independence.

Nonetheless, many American patriots felt passionately that they were creating "a new order for the ages." James Madison in the *Federalist Papers* made the point clearly: "We pursued a new and more noble course... and accomplished a revolution that has no parallel in the annals of human society." Supporters abroad agreed. On the eve of the French Revolution, a Paris newspaper proclaimed that the United States was "the hope and model of the human race."[5] In both cases, they were referring primarily to the political ideas and practices of the new country. The American Revolution, after all, initiated the political dismantling of Europe's New World empires. The "right to revolution," proclaimed in the Declaration of Independence and made effective only in a great struggle, inspired revolutionaries and nationalists from Simón Bolívar in nineteenth-century Latin America to Ho Chi Minh in twentieth-century Vietnam. Moreover, the new U.S. Constitution—with its Bill of Rights, checks and balances, separation of church and state, and federalism—was one of the first sustained efforts to put the political ideas of the Enlightenment into practice. That document, and the ideas that it embraced, echoed repeatedly in the political upheavals of the century that followed.

The French Revolution, 1789–1815

■ Comparison

How did the French Revolution differ from the American Revolution?

Act Two in the drama of the Atlantic revolutions took place in France, beginning in 1789, although it was closely connected to Act One in North America. Thousands of French soldiers had provided assistance to the American colonists and now returned home full of republican enthusiasm. Thomas Jefferson, the U.S. ambassador in Paris, reported that France "has been awakened by our revolution."[6] More immediately, the French government, which had generously aided the Americans in an effort to undermine its British rivals, was teetering on the brink of bankruptcy and had long sought reforms that would modernize the tax system and make it more equitable. In a desperate effort to raise taxes against the opposition of the privileged classes, the French king, Louis XVI, had called into session an ancient representative body, the Estates General. It consisted of representatives of the three "estates," or legal orders, of prerevolutionary France: the clergy, the nobility, and the commoners. The first two estates comprised about 2 percent of the population, and the third estate included everyone else. When that body convened in 1789, representatives of the third estate soon organized themselves as the National Assembly, claiming the sole authority to make laws for the country. A few weeks later they drew up the Declaration of the Rights of Man and Citizen, which forthrightly declared that "men are born and remain free and equal in rights" (see Document 17.1, pp. 806–08). These actions, unprecedented and illegal in the *ancien régime* (the old regime), launched the French Revolution and radicalized many of the participants in the National Assembly.

That revolution was quite different from its North American predecessor. Whereas the American Revolution expressed the tensions of a colonial relationship with a distant imperial power, the French insurrection was driven by sharp conflicts within French society. Members of the titled nobility—privileged, prestigious, and wealthy—resented and resisted the monarchy's efforts to subject them to new taxes. Educated middle-class groups, such as doctors, lawyers, lower-level officials, and merchants, were growing in numbers and sometimes in wealth and were offended by the remaining privileges of the aristocracy, from which they were excluded. Ordinary urban residents, many of whose incomes had declined for a generation, were particularly hard-hit in the late 1780s by the rapidly rising price of bread and widespread unemployment. Peasants in the countryside, though largely free of serfdom, were subject to a variety of hated dues imposed by their landlords, taxes from the state, obligations to the Church, and the requirement to work without pay on public roads. As Enlightenment ideas penetrated French society, more and more people, mostly in the third estate but including some priests and nobles, found a language with which to articulate these grievances. The famous French writer Jean-Jacques Rousseau had told them that it was "manifestly contrary to the law of nature ... that a handful of people should gorge themselves with superfluities while the hungry multitude goes in want of necessities."[7]

These social conflicts gave the French Revolution, especially during its first five years, a much more violent, far-reaching, and radical character than its American counterpart. It was a profound social upheaval, more comparable to the revolutions of Russia and China in the twentieth century than to the earlier American Revolution. Initial efforts to establish a constitutional monarchy and promote harmony among the classes (see Visual Source 17.1, p. 818) gave way to more radical measures, as internal resistance and foreign opposition produced a fear that the revolution might be overturned. In the process, urban crowds organized insurrections. Some peasants attacked the castles of their lords, burning the documents that recorded their dues and payments. The National Assembly decreed the end of all legal privileges and ended what remained of feudalism in France. Even slavery was abolished, albeit briefly. Church lands were sold to raise revenue, and priests were put under government authority. (See Visual Sources 17.2 and 17.3, pp. 819 and 820, for images reflecting this more radical phase of the revolution.)

In 1793, King Louis XVI and his queen, Marie Antoinette, were executed, an act of regicide that shocked traditionalists all across Europe and marked a new stage in revolutionary violence (see Visual Source 17.4, p. 821). What followed was the Terror of 1793–1794. Under the leadership of Maximilien Robespierre and his Committee of Public Safety, tens of thousands deemed enemies of the revolution lost their lives on the guillotine. Shortly thereafter, Robespierre himself was arrested and guillotined, accused of leading France into tyranny and dictatorship. "The revolution," remarked one of its victims, "was devouring its own children."

Accompanying attacks on the old order were efforts to create a wholly new society, symbolized by a new calendar with the Year 1 in 1792, marking a fresh start

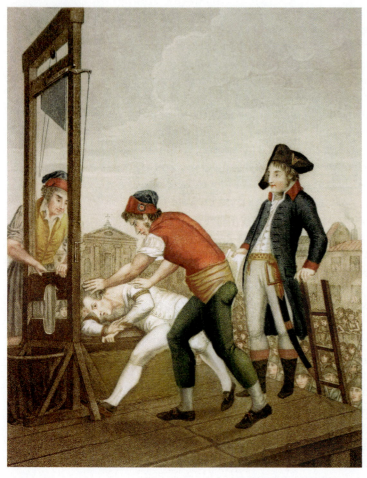

The Execution of Robespierre
The beheading of the radical leader Robespierre, who had himself brought thousands of others to the guillotine, marked a decisive turning point in the unfolding of the French Revolution and the end of its most violent phase. (Musée de la Revolution Française, Vizille, France/ Bridgeman Art Library)

for France. Unlike the Americans, who sought to restore or build upon earlier freedoms, French revolutionaries perceived themselves to be starting from scratch and looked to the future. For the first time in its history, the country became a republic and briefly passed universal male suffrage, although it was never implemented. The old administrative system was rationalized into eighty-three territorial departments, each with a new name. As revolutionary France prepared for war against its threatened and threatening neighbors, it created the world's largest army, with some 800,000 men, and all adult males were required to serve. Led by officers from the middle and even lower classes, this was an army of citizens representing the nation.

The impact of the revolution was felt in many ways. Streets got new names; monuments to the royal family were destroyed; titles vanished; people referred to one another as "citizen so-and-so." Real politics in the public sphere emerged for the first time as many people joined political clubs, took part in marches and demonstrations, served on local committees, and ran for public office. Common people, who had identified primarily with their local community, now began to think of themselves as belonging to a nation. The state replaced the Catholic Church as the place for registering births, marriages, and deaths, and revolutionary festivals substituted for church holidays.

More radical revolutionary leaders deliberately sought to convey a sense of new beginnings. A Festival of Unity held in 1793 to mark the first anniversary of the end of monarchy burned the crowns and scepters of the royal family in a huge bonfire while releasing a cloud of 3,000 white doves. The Cathedral of Notre Dame was temporarily turned into the Temple of Reason, while the "Hymn to Liberty" combined traditional church music with the explicit message of the Enlightenment:

Oh Liberty, sacred Liberty
Goddess of an enlightened people
Rule today within these walls.
Through you this temple is purified.
Liberty! Before you reason chases out deception,

Error flees, fanaticism is beaten down.
Our gospel is nature
And our cult is virtue.
To love one's country and one's brothers,
To serve the Sovereign People—
These are the sacred tenets
And pledge of a Republican.[8]

The French Revolution differed from the American Revolution also in the way its influence spread. At least until the United States became a world power at the end of the nineteenth century, what inspired others was primarily the example of its revolution and its constitution. French influence, by contrast, spread through conquest, largely under the leadership of Napoleon Bonaparte (ruled 1799–1814). A highly successful general who seized power in 1799, Napoleon is often credited with taming the revolution in the face of growing disenchantment with its more radical features and with the social conflicts it generated. He preserved many of its more moderate elements, such as civil equality, a secular law code, religious freedom, and promotion by merit, while reconciling with the Catholic Church and suppressing the revolution's more democratic elements in a military dictatorship. In short, Napoleon kept the revolution's emphasis on social equality but dispensed with liberty.

Like many of the revolution's ardent supporters, Napoleon was intent on spreading its benefits far and wide. In a series of brilliant military campaigns, his forces subdued most of Europe, thus creating the continent's largest empire since the days of the Romans (see Map 17.2). Within that empire, Napoleon imposed such revolutionary practices as ending feudalism, proclaiming equality of rights, insisting on religious toleration, codifying the laws, and rationalizing government administration. In many places, these reforms were welcomed, and seeds of further change were planted. But French domination was also resented and resisted, stimulating national consciousness throughout Europe. (See Visual Source 17.5, p. 822, for a German caricature of Napoleon.) That too was a seed that bore fruit in the century that followed. More immediately, national resistance, particularly from Russia and Britain, brought down Napoleon and his amazing empire by 1815 and marked an end to the era of the French Revolution, though not to the potency of its ideas.

The Haitian Revolution, 1791–1804

Nowhere did the example of the French Revolution echo more loudly than in the French Caribbean colony of Saint Domingue, later renamed Haiti (see Map 17.3, p. 791). Widely regarded as the richest colony in the world, Saint Domingue boasted 8,000 plantations, which in the late eighteenth century produced some 40 percent of the world's sugar and perhaps half of its coffee. A slave labor force of about 500,000 people made up the vast majority of the colony's population. Whites numbered about 40,000, sharply divided between very well-to-do plantation owners, merchants, and lawyers and those known as *petits blancs*, or poor whites. A third

■ **Comparison**

What was distinctive about the Haitian Revolution, both in world history generally and in the history of Atlantic revolutions?

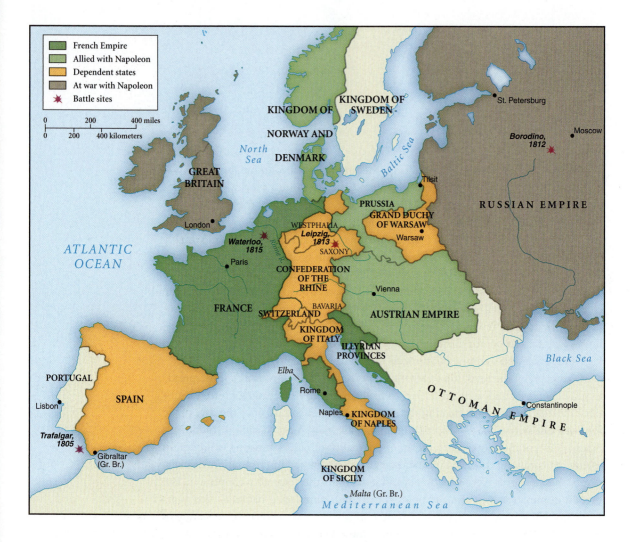

Map 17.2 Napoleon's European Empire
The French Revolution spawned a French empire, under Napoleon's leadership, that encompassed most of Europe and served to spread the principles of the revolution.

social group consisted of some 30,000 *gens de couleur libres* (free people of color), many of them of mixed-race background. Saint Domingue was a colonial society very different from the New England colonies or even the southern colonies of British North America. Given its enormous inequalities and its rampant exploitation, this Caribbean colony was primed for explosion.

In such a volatile setting, the ideas and example of the French Revolution lit several fuses and set in motion a spiral of violence that engulfed the colony for more than a decade. The principles of the revolution, however, meant different things to different people. To the *grands blancs*—the rich white landowners—it suggested greater autonomy for the colony and fewer economic restrictions on trade, but they resented the demands of the *petits blancs*, who sought equality of citizenship for all whites. Both white groups were adamantly opposed to the insistence of free people of color that the "rights of man" meant equal treatment for all free people regardless of race. To the slaves, the promise of the French Revolution was a personal freedom that threatened the entire slave labor system. In a massive revolt beginning in 1791, triggered by rumors that the French king had already declared an end to slavery, slaves burned 1,000 plantations and killed hundreds of whites as well as mixed-race people.

Soon warring factions of slaves, whites, and free people of color battled one another. Spanish and British forces, seeking to enlarge their own empires at the expense of the French, only added to the turmoil. Amid the confusion, brutality, and massacres of the 1790s, power gravitated toward the slaves, now led by the astute Toussaint Louverture, himself a former slave. He and his successor overcame internal resistance, outmaneuvered the foreign powers, and even defeated an attempt by Napoleon to reestablish French control.

When the dust settled in the early years of the nineteenth century, it was clear that something remarkable and unprecedented had taken place, a revolution unique in the Atlantic world and in world history. Socially, the last had become first. In the only completely successful slave revolt in recorded history, "the lowest order of the society—slaves— became equal, free, and independent citizens."[9] Politically, they had thrown off French colonial rule, becoming the second independent republic in the Americas and the first non-European state to emerge from Western colonialism. They renamed their country Haiti, a term meaning "mountainous" or "rugged" in the language of the original Taino people. It was a symbolic break with Europe and represented an effort to connect with the long-deceased native inhabitants of the land. Some, in fact, referred to themselves as "Incas." At the formal declaration of Haiti's independence on January 1, 1804, Jean-Jacques Dessalines, the new country's first head of state, declared: "I have given the French cannibals blood for blood; I have avenged America."[10] In defining all Haitians as "black," Haiti directly confronted an emerging racism, even as they declared all citizens legally equal regardless of race, color, or class. Economically, the country's plantation system, oriented wholly toward the export of sugar and coffee, had been largely destroyed. As whites fled or were killed, both private and state lands were redistributed among former slaves and free blacks, and Haiti became a nation of small-scale farmers producing mostly for their own needs, with a much smaller export sector.

The Haitian Revolution
This early-nineteenth-century engraving, entitled *Revenge Taken by the Black Army*, shows black Haitian soldiers hanging a large number of French soldiers, thus illustrating both the violence and the racial dimension of the upheaval in Haiti. (Schomburg Center, NY/Art Resource, NY)

The destructiveness of the Haitian Revolution, its bitter internal divisions of race and class, and continuing external opposition contributed much to Haiti's abiding poverty as well as to its authoritarian and unstable politics. In the early nineteenth century, however, it was a source of enormous hope and of great fear. Within weeks of the Haitian slave uprising in 1791, Jamaican slaves had composed songs in its honor, and it was not long before slave owners in the Caribbean and North America observed a new "insolence" in their slaves. Certainly its example inspired other slave rebellions, gave a boost to the dawning abolitionist movement, and has been a source of pride for people of African descent ever since.

To whites throughout the hemisphere, the cautionary saying "Remember Haiti" reflected a sense of horror at what had occurred there and a determination not to allow political change to reproduce that fearful outcome again. Particularly in Latin America, it injected a deep caution and social conservatism in the elites that led their countries to independence in the early nineteenth century. Ironically, though, the Haitian Revolution also led to a temporary expansion of slavery elsewhere. Cuban plantations and their slave workers considerably increased their production of sugar as that of Haiti declined. Moreover, Napoleon's defeat in Haiti persuaded him to sell to the United States the French territories known as the Louisiana Purchase, from which a number of "slave states" were carved out. In such contradictory ways did the echoes of the Haitian Revolution reverberate in the Atlantic world.

Spanish American Revolutions, 1810–1825

■ Connection
How were the Spanish American revolutions shaped by the American, French, and Haitian revolutions that happened earlier?

The final act in a half century of Atlantic revolutionary upheaval took place in the Spanish and Portuguese colonies of mainland Latin America (see Map 17.3). Their revolutions were shaped by preceding events in North America, France, and Haiti as well as by their own distinctive societies and historical experience. As in British North America, native-born elites in the Spanish colonies (known as *creoles*) were offended and insulted by the Spanish monarchy's efforts during the eighteenth century to exercise greater power over its colonies and to subject them to heavier taxes and tariffs. Creole intellectuals also had become familiar with ideas of popular sovereignty, republican government, and personal liberty derived from the European Enlightenment. But these conditions, similar to those in North America, led initially only to scattered and uncoordinated protests rather than to outrage, declarations of independence, war, and unity, as had occurred in the British colonies. Why did Spanish American struggles for independence occur decades later than those of British North America?

The settlers in the Spanish colonies had little tradition of local self-government such as had developed in North America, and their societies were far more authoritarian and divided by class. In addition, whites throughout Latin America were vastly outnumbered by Native Americans, people of African ancestry, and those of mixed race. All of this inhibited the growth of a movement for independence, despite the example of North America and similar provocations.

Despite their growing disenchantment with Spanish rule, creole elites did not so much generate a revolution as have one thrust upon them by events in Europe. In 1808, Napoleon invaded Spain and Portugal, deposing the Spanish king Ferdinand VII and forcing the Portuguese royal family into exile in Brazil. With legitimate royal authority now in disarray, Latin Americans were forced to take action. The outcome, ultimately, was independence for the various states of Latin America, established almost everywhere by 1826. But the way in which it occurred and the kind of societies it generated differed greatly from the experience of both North America and Haiti.

The process lasted more than twice as long as it did in North America, partly because Latin American societies were so conflicted and divided by class, race, and region. In North America, violence was directed almost entirely against the British and seldom spilled over into domestic disputes, except for

Map 17.3 Latin American Independence
With the exception of Haiti, Latin American revolutions brought independence to new states but offered little social change or political opportunity for the vast majority of people.

some bloody skirmishes with loyalists. Even then, little lasting hostility occurred, and some loyalists were able to reenter U.S. society after independence was achieved. In Mexico, by contrast, the move toward independence began in 1810 in a peasant insurrection, driven by hunger for land and by high food prices and led successively by two priests, Miguel Hidalgo and José Morelos. Alarmed by the social radicalism of the Hidalgo-Morelos rebellion, creole landowners, with the support of the Church, raised an army and crushed the insurgency. Later that alliance of clergy and creole elites brought Mexico to a more socially controlled independence in 1821. Such violent conflict among Latin Americans, along lines of race, class, and ideology, accompanied the struggle against Spain in many places.

The entire independence movement in Latin America took place under the shadow of a great fear—the dread of social rebellion from below—that had little counterpart in North America. The great violence of the French and Haitian revolutions was a lesson to Latin American elites that political change could easily get out of hand and was fraught with danger to themselves. An abortive rebellion of

Native Americans in Peru in the early 1780s, made in the name of the last Inca emperor, Tupac Amaru, as well as the Hidalgo-Morelos rebellion in Mexico, reminded whites that they sat atop a potentially explosive society, most of whose members were exploited and oppressed people of color.

And yet the creole sponsors of independence movements, both regional military leaders such as Simón Bolívar and José de San Martín and their civilian counterparts, required the support of "the people," or at least some of them, if they were to prevail against Spanish forces. The answer to this dilemma was found in nativism, which cast all of those born in the Americas—creoles, Indians, mixed-race people, free blacks—as *Americanos*, while the enemy was defined as those born in Spain or Portugal.[11] This was no easy task, because many creole whites and mestizos saw themselves as Spanish and because great differences of race, culture, and wealth separated the Americanos. Nonetheless, nationalist leaders made efforts to mobilize people of color into the struggle with promises of freedom, the end of legal restrictions, and social advancement. Many of these leaders were genuine liberals, who had been influenced by the ideals of the Enlightenment, the French Revolution and Spanish liberalism. In the long run, however, few of those promises were kept. Certainly the lower classes, Native Americans, and slaves benefited little from independence. "The imperial state was destroyed in Spanish America," concluded one historian, "but colonial society was preserved."[12]

A further difference in the Latin American situation lay in the apparent impossibility of uniting the various Spanish colonies, despite several failed efforts to do so. Thus no United States of Latin America emerged. Distances among the colonies and geographic obstacles to effective communication were certainly greater than in the eastern seaboard colonies of North America, and their longer colonial experience had given rise to distinct and deeply rooted regional identities. Shortly before his death in 1830, the "great liberator" Bolívar, who so admired George Washington and had so ardently hoped for greater unity, wrote in despair to a friend: "[Latin] America is ungovernable. Those who serve the revolution plough the sea."[13] (See Document 17.3, pp. 810–11, for Bolívar's views on the struggle for independence.)

Simón Bolívar
Among the heroic figures of Spanish American independence movements, none was more significant than Simón Bolívar (1783–1830), shown here in a moment of triumph entering his hometown of Caracas in present-day Venezuela. But Bolívar was immensely disappointed in the outcomes of independence as his dream of a unified South America perished amid the rivalries of separate countries. (akg-images)

The aftermath of independence in Latin America marked a reversal in the earlier relationship of the two American continents. The United States, which began its history as the leftover "dregs" of the New World, grew increasingly wealthy, industrialized, democratic, internationally influential, and generally stable, with the major exception of the Civil War. The Spanish colonies, which took shape in the wealthiest areas and among the most sophisticated cultures of the Americas, were widely regarded as the more promising region compared to the backwater reputation of England's North American territories. But in the nineteenth century, as newly independent countries in both regions launched a new phase of their histories, those in Latin America became relatively underdeveloped, impoverished, undemocratic, politically unstable, and dependent on foreign technology and investment (see pp. 846–48). Begun in broadly similar circumstances, the Latin American and North American revolutions occurred in very different societies and gave rise to very different historical trajectories.

Echoes of Revolution

The core values of the Atlantic revolutions continued to reverberate well after those upheavals had been concluded. Within Europe, which was generally dominated by conservative governments following Napoleon's final defeat, smaller revolutions erupted in 1830, more widely in 1848, and in Paris in 1870. They expressed ideas of republicanism, greater social equality, and national liberation from foreign rule. Such ideas and social pressures pushed the major states of Western Europe, the United States, and Argentina to enlarge their voting publics, generally granting universal male suffrage by 1914. An abortive attempt to establish a constitutional regime even broke out in autocratic Russia in 1825. It was led by military officers who had been influenced by ideals of the Enlightenment and the French Revolution while campaigning in Europe against Napoleon.

Beyond this limited extension of political democracy, three movements arose to challenge continuing patterns of oppression or exclusion. Abolitionists sought the end of slavery; nationalists hoped to do away with disunity and foreign rule; and feminists tried to end, or at least mitigate, male dominance. Each of these movements bore the marks of the Atlantic revolutions, and although they took root first in Europe, each came to have a global significance in the centuries that followed.

The Abolition of Slavery

In little more than a century, from roughly 1780 to 1890, a remarkable transformation occurred in human affairs as slavery, widely practiced and little condemned since the beginning of civilization, lost its legitimacy and was largely ended. In this amazing process, the ideas and practices of the Atlantic revolutions played an important role.

Enlightenment thinkers in eighteenth-century Europe had become increasingly critical of slavery as a violation of the natural rights of every person, and the public

■ **Change**
What accounts for the end of Atlantic slavery during the nineteenth century?

pronouncements of the American and French revolutions about liberty and equality likewise focused attention on this obvious breach of those principles. To this secular antislavery thinking was added an increasingly vociferous religious voice, expressed first by Quakers and then Protestant evangelicals in Britain and the United States. To them slavery was "repugnant to our religion" and a "crime in the sight of God."[14] What made these moral arguments more widely acceptable was the growing belief that, contrary to much earlier thinking, slavery was not essential for economic progress. After all, England and New England were among the most prosperous regions of the Western world in the early nineteenth century, and both were based on free labor. Slavery in this view was out of date, unnecessary in the new era of industrial technology and capitalism. Thus moral virtue and economic success were joined. It was an attractive argument. (See Document 17.4, pp. 811–13, for the views of the U.S. abolitionist Fredrick Douglass.)

The actions of slaves themselves likewise hastened the end of slavery. The dramatically successful Haitian Revolution was followed by three major rebellions in the British West Indies, all of which were harshly crushed, in the early nineteenth century. They demonstrated clearly that slaves were hardly "contented," and the brutality with which the revolts were suppressed appalled British public opinion. Growing numbers of the British public came to feel that slavery was "not only morally wrong and economically inefficient, but also politically unwise."[15]

These various strands of thinking—secular, religious, economic, and political— came together in abolitionist movements, most powerfully in Britain, which brought growing pressure on governments to close down the trade in slaves and then to ban slavery itself. In the late eighteenth century, such a movement gained wide support among middle- and working-class people in Britain. Its techniques included pamphlets with heartrending descriptions of slavery, numerous petitions to parliament, lawsuits, boycotts of slave-produced sugar, and frequent public meetings, some of which dramatically featured the testimony of Africans who had experienced the horrors of slavery firsthand. In 1807, Britain forbade the sale of slaves within its empire and in 1834 emancipated those who remained enslaved. Over the next half century, other nations followed suit, responding to growing international pressure, particularly from Britain, then the world's leading economic and military power. British naval vessels patrolled the Atlantic, intercepted illegal slave ships, and freed their human cargoes in a small West African settlement called Freetown, in present-day Sierra Leone. Following their independence, most Latin American countries abolished slavery by the 1850s. Brazil, in 1888, was the last to do so, bringing more than four centuries of Atlantic slavery to an end. A roughly similar set of conditions—fear of rebellion, economic inefficiency, and moral concerns—persuaded the Russian tsar to free the many serfs of that huge country in 1861, although there it occurred by fiat from above rather than from growing public pressure.

None of this happened easily. Slave economies continued to flourish well into the nineteenth century, and plantation owners vigorously resisted the onslaught of abolitionists. So did slave traders, both European and African, who together shipped

Abolitionism
This antislavery medallion was commissioned in the late eighteenth century by English Quakers, who were among the earliest participants in the abolitionist movement. Its famous motto, "Am I not a man and a brother," reflected both Enlightenment and Christian values of human equality. (The Art Archive)

millions of additional captives, mostly to Cuba and Brazil, long after the trade had been declared illegal. Osei Bonsu, the powerful king of the West African state of Asante, was puzzled as to why the British would no longer buy his slaves. "If they think it bad now," he asked a local British representative in 1820, "why did they think it good before?"[16] (See Document 15.4, pp. 708–09.) Nowhere was the persistence of slavery more evident and resistance to abolition more intense than in the southern states of the United States. It was the only slaveholding society in which the end of slavery occurred through such a bitter, prolonged, and highly destructive civil war (1861–1865).

The end of Atlantic slavery during the nineteenth century surely marked a major and quite rapid turn in the world's social history and in the moral thinking of humankind. Nonetheless, the outcomes of that process were often surprising and far from the expectations of abolitionists or the newly freed slaves. In most cases, the economic lives of the former slaves did not improve dramatically. Nowhere in the Atlantic world, except Haiti, did a redistribution of land follow the end of slavery. But freedmen everywhere desperately sought economic autonomy on their own land, and in parts of the Caribbean such as Jamaica, where unoccupied land was available, independent peasant agriculture proved possible for some. Elsewhere, as in the southern United States, various forms of legally free but highly dependent labor, such as sharecropping, emerged to replace slavery and to provide low-paid and often indebted workers for planters. The understandable reluctance of former slaves to continue working in plantation agriculture created labor shortages and set in motion a huge new wave of global migration. Large numbers of indentured servants from India and China were imported into the Caribbean, Peru, South Africa, Hawaii, Malaya, and elsewhere to work in mines, on sugar plantations, and in construction projects. There they often toiled in conditions not far removed from slavery itself.

■ **Change**
How did the end of slavery affect the lives of the former slaves?

Newly freed people did not achieve anything close to political equality, except in Haiti. White planters, farmers, and mine owners retained local authority in the Caribbean. In the southern United States, a brief period of "radical reconstruction," during which newly freed blacks did enjoy full political rights and some power, was followed by harsh segregation laws, denial of voting rights, a wave of lynching, and a virulent racism that lasted well into the twentieth century. For most former slaves, emancipation usually meant, in the words of a well-known historian, "nothing but freedom."[17]

Unlike the situation in the Americas, the end of serfdom in Russia transferred to the peasants a considerable portion of the nobles' land, but the need to pay for this land with "redemption dues" and the rapid growth of Russia's rural population ensured that most peasants remained impoverished and politically volatile. In both West and East Africa, the closing of the external slave trade decreased the price of slaves and increased their use within African societies to produce the export crops that the world economy now sought. Thus, as Europeans imposed colonial rule on Africa in the late nineteenth century, one of their justifications for doing so was the need to emancipate enslaved Africans. Europeans proclaiming the need to end slavery in a continent from which they had extracted slaves for more than four centuries was surely among the more ironic outcomes of the abolitionist process.

Nations and Nationalism

■ Explanation
What accounts for the growth of nationalism as a powerful political and personal identity in the nineteenth century?

In addition to contributing to the end of slavery, the Atlantic revolutions also gave new prominence to a relatively recent kind of human community—the nation. By the end of the twentieth century, the idea that humankind was divided into separate nations, each with a distinct culture and territory and deserving an independent political life, was so widespread as to seem natural and timeless. And yet for most of human experience, states did not usually coincide with the culture of a particular people, for all of the great empires and many smaller states governed culturally diverse societies. Few people considered rule by foreigners itself a terrible offense because the most important identities and loyalties were local, limited to clan, village, or region, with only modest connection to the larger state or empire that governed them. People might on occasion consider themselves part of larger religious communities (such as Christians or Muslims) or ethnolinguistic groupings such as Greek, Arab, or Mayan, but such identities rarely provided the basis for enduring states.

All of that began to change during the era of Atlantic revolutions. Independence movements in both North and South America were made in the name of new nations. The French Revolution declared that sovereignty lay with "the people," and its leaders mobilized this people to defend the "French nation" against its many external enemies. In 1793, the revolutionary government of France declared a mass conscription (*levée en masse*) with this stirring call to service:

> Henceforth, until the enemies have been driven from the territory of the Republic, all the French are in permanent requisition for army service. The young men shall go to battle; the married men shall forge arms and transport provisions; the women shall make tents and clothes, and shall serve in the hospitals; the children shall turn old linen into lint; the old men shall repair to the public places, to stimulate the courage of the warriors and preach the unity of the Republic and the hatred of kings.[18]

Moreover, Napoleon's conquests likewise stimulated national resistance in many parts of Europe. European states had long competed and fought with one another, but increasingly in the nineteenth century, those states were inhabited by people who felt themselves to be citizens of a nation, deeply bound to their fellows by ties of blood, culture, or common experience, not simply common subjects of a ruling dynasty. It was a novel form of political community.

Europe's modern transformation also facilitated nationalism, even as older identities and loyalties eroded. Science weakened the hold of religion on some. Migration to industrial cities or abroad diminished allegiance to local communities. At the same time, printing and the publishing industry standardized a variety of dialects

Snapshot   Key Moments in the Growth of Nationalism

Independence of colonies in the Americas	1776–1825
Mass conscription to defend the French Revolution	1793
Wars of resistance to Napoleonic empire	1800–1815
Greek independence from Ottoman Empire	1830
Polish insurrections against Russian rule	1830, 1863
Young Ireland movement begins	1842
First Ukrainian nationalist organization established	1846
Hungarian national uprising against Austrian Habsburg rule	1848
Unification of Italy and Germany	1870, 1871
Egyptian revolt against British and French imperialism	1880
Founding of Indian National Congress	1885
Political Zionism emerges, seeking a homeland in Palestine for Jews	1890s

into a smaller number of European languages, a process that allowed a growing reading public to think of themselves as members of a common linguistic group or nation. All of this encouraged political and cultural leaders to articulate an appealing idea of their particular nations and ensured a growing circle of people receptive to such ideas. Thus the idea of the "nation" was constructed or even invented, but it was often presented as a reawakening of older linguistic or cultural identities, and it certainly drew upon the songs, dances, folktales, historical experiences, and collective memories of earlier cultures (see Map 17.4).

Whatever its precise origins, nationalism proved to be an infinitely flexible and enormously powerful idea in the nineteenth-century Atlantic world and beyond. It inspired the political unification of both Germany and Italy, gathering their previously fragmented peoples into new states by 1871. It encouraged Greeks and Serbs to assert their independence from the Ottoman Empire; Czechs and Hungarians to demand more autonomy within the Austrian Empire; Poles and Ukrainians to become more aware of their oppression within the Russian Empire; and the Irish to seek "home rule" and separation from Great Britain. By the end of the nineteenth century, a small Zionist movement, seeking a homeland in Palestine, had emerged among Europe's frequently persecuted Jews. Popular nationalism made the normal rivalry among European states even more acute and fueled a highly competitive drive for colonies in Asia and Africa. The immensity of the suffering and sacrifice that nationalism generated in Europe was vividly disclosed during the horrors of World War I.

Map 17.4 The Nations and Empires of Europe, ca. 1880
By the end of the nineteenth century, the national principle had substantially reshaped the map of Europe, especially in the unification of Germany and Italy. However, several major empires (Russian, Austro-Hungarian, and Ottoman) remained, each with numerous subject peoples who likewise sought national independence.

Governments throughout the Western world claimed now to act on behalf of their nations and deliberately sought to instill national loyalties in their citizens through schools, public rituals, the mass media, and military service. Russian authorities, for example, imposed the use of the Russian language, even in parts of the country where it was not widely spoken. They succeeded, however, only in producing a greater awareness of Ukrainian, Polish, and Finnish nationalism.

As it became more prominent in the nineteenth century, nationalism took on a variety of political ideologies. Some supporters of liberal democracy and representative government, as in France or the United States, saw nationalism, with its emphasis on "the people," as an aid to their aspirations toward wider involvement in political life. Often called "civic nationalism," such a view identified the nation with a particular territory and maintained that people of various cultural backgrounds could assimilate into the dominant culture, as in the process of "becoming American." Other versions of nationalism, in Germany for example, sometimes defined the nation in racial terms, which excluded those who did not share a common ancestry, such as Jews. In the hands of conservatives, nationalism could be used to combat socialism and feminism, for those movements only divided the nation along class or gender lines. Thus nationalism generated endless controversy because it provided no clear answer to the questions of who belonged to the nation or who should speak for it.

Nor was nationalism limited to the Euro-American world in the nineteenth century. An "Egypt for the Egyptians" movement arose in the 1870s as British and French intervention in Egyptian affairs deepened. When Japan likewise confronted European aggression in the second half of the nineteenth century, its long sense of itself as a distinct culture was readily transformed into an assertive modern nationalism.

Nationalism in Poland
In the eighteenth century, Poland had been divided among Prussia, Austria, and Russia and disappeared as a separate and independent state. Polish nationalism found expression in the nineteenth century in a series of revolts, among which was a massive uprising in 1863, directed against Poland's Russian occupiers. This famous painting by Polish artist Jan Matejko shows a crowd of Polish prisoners awaiting transportation to imprisonment in Siberia, while Russian military officers supervise a blacksmith, who fastens fetters on a woman representing Poland. (Courtesy, Czartoryski Museum, Cracow)

Small groups of Western-educated men in British-ruled India began to think of their enormously diverse country as a single nation. The Indian National Congress, established in 1885, gave expression to this idea. The notion of the Ottoman Empire as a Turkish national state rather than a Muslim or dynastic empire took hold among a few people. By the end of the nineteenth century, some Chinese intellectuals began to think in terms of a Chinese nation beset both by a foreign ruling dynasty and by predatory Europeans. Along the West African coast, the idea of an "African nation" stirred among a handful of freed slaves and missionary-educated men. Although Egyptian and Japanese nationalism gained broad support, elsewhere in Asia and Africa such movements would have to wait until the twentieth century, when they exploded with enormous power on the stage of world history.

Feminist Beginnings

■ **Significance**
What were the achievements and limitations of nineteenth-century feminism?

A third echo of the Atlantic revolutions lay in the emergence of a feminist movement. Although scattered voices had earlier challenged patriarchy, never before had an organized and substantial group of women called into question this most fundamental and accepted feature of all preindustrial civilizations—the subordination of women to men. But in the century following the French Revolution, such a challenge took shape, especially in Europe and North America. Then, in the twentieth century, feminist thinking transformed "the way in which women and men work, play, think, dress, worship, vote, reproduce, make love and make war."[19] How did this extraordinary process get launched in the nineteenth century?

Thinkers of the European Enlightenment had challenged many ancient traditions, including on occasion that of women's intrinsic inferiority. The French writer Condorcet, for example, called for "the complete destruction of those prejudices that have established an inequality of rights between the sexes." The French Revolution then raised the possibility of re-creating human societies on new foundations. Many women participated in these events, and a few insisted, unsuccessfully, that the revolutionary ideals of liberty and equality must include women. In neighboring England, the French Revolution stimulated the writer Mary Wollstonecraft to pen her famous *Vindication of the Rights of Woman*, one of the earliest expressions of a feminist consciousness (see Document 17.2, pp. 808–09).

Within the growing middle classes of industrializing societies, more women found both educational opportunities and some freedom from household drudgery. Such women increasingly took part in temperance movements, charities, abolitionism, and missionary work, as well as socialist and pacifist organizations. Some of their working-class sisters became active trade unionists. On both sides of the Atlantic, small numbers of these women began to develop a feminist consciousness that viewed women as individuals with rights equal to those of men.[20] Others, particularly in France, based their claims less on abstract notions of equality and more on the distinctive role of women as mothers. "It is above all this holy function of motherhood...," wrote one advocate of "maternal feminism," "which requires that women watch over the futures of their children and gives women the right to intervene not only in all acts of civil life, but also in all acts of political life."[21] The first organized expression of this new feminism took place at a women's rights conference in Seneca Falls, New York, in 1848. At that meeting, Elizabeth Cady Stanton drafted a statement that began by paraphrasing the Declaration of Independence: "We hold these truths to be self-evident, that all men and women are created equal."

From the beginning, feminism was a transatlantic movement in which European and American women attended the same conferences, corresponded regularly, and read one another's work. Access to schools, universities, and the professions were among their major concerns as growing numbers of women sought these previously unavailable opportunities. The more radical among them refused to take their husbands' surname or wore trousers under their skirts. Elizabeth Cady Stanton published a Women's Bible, eliminating the parts she found offensive. As heirs to the French Revolution, feminists ardently believed in progress and insisted that it must now include a radical transformation of the position of women.

By the 1870s, feminist movements in the West were focusing primarily on the issue of suffrage and were gaining a growing constituency. Now many ordinary middle-class housewives and working-class mothers joined their better-educated sisters in the movement. By 1914, some 100,000 women took part in French feminist organizations, while the National American Woman Suffrage Association claimed 2 million members. Most operated through peaceful protest and persuasion, but the British Women's Social and Political Union organized a campaign of violence that included blowing up railroad stations, slashing works of art, and smashing department store windows. One British activist, Emily Davison, threw herself in front of the king's horse during a race in Britain in 1913 and was trampled to death. By the beginning of the twentieth century in the most highly industrialized countries of the West, the women's movement had become a mass movement.

That movement had some effect. By 1900, upper- and middle-class women had gained entrance to universities, though in small numbers, and women's literacy rates were growing steadily. In the United States, a number of states passed legislation allowing women to manage and control their own property and wages, separate from their husbands. Divorce laws were liberalized in some places. Professions such as medicine opened to a few, and teaching beckoned to many more. In Britain, Florence Nightingale professionalized nursing and attracted thousands of women into it, while Jane Addams in the United States virtually invented social work, which also became a female-dominated profession. Progress was slower in the political domain. In 1893, New Zealand became the first country to give the vote to all adult women; Finland followed in 1906. Elsewhere widespread voting rights for women in national elections were not achieved until after World War I and in France not until 1945.

Beyond these concrete accomplishments, the movement prompted an unprecedented discussion about the role of women in modern society. In Henrik Ibsen's play A Doll's House (1879), the heroine, Nora, finding herself in a loveless and oppressive marriage, leaves both her husband and her children. European audiences were

Women's Suffrage
What began as a few iso-
lated voices of feminist
protest in the early nineteenth century had become
by the end of the century a
mass movement in the
United States and Western
Europe. Here, in a photo-
graph of an American suf-
frage parade in 1912, is an
illustration of that movement in action. (The Granger
Collection, New York)

riveted, and many were outraged. Writers, doctors, and journalists addressed previously taboo sexual topics, including homosexuality and birth control. Socialists too
found themselves divided about women's issues. Did the women's movement distract
from the class solidarity that Marxism proclaimed, or did it provide added energy to
the workers' cause? Feminists themselves disagreed about the proper basis for women's
rights. Some took their stand on the modern idea of human equality: "Whatever is
right for a man is right for a woman." Others argued that women's traditional role as
mothers, the guardians of family life and social virtue, provided the stronger case for
women's rights.

Not surprisingly, feminism provoked bitter opposition. Some academic and medical experts argued that the strains of education and life in the world outside the
home would cause serious reproductive damage and as a consequence depopulate the
nation. Thus feminists were viewed as selfish, willing to sacrifice the family or even
the nation while pursuing their individual goals. Some saw suffragists, like Jews and
socialists, as "a foreign body in our national life." Never before in any society had such
a passionate and public debate about the position of women erupted. It was a novel
feature of Western historical experience in the aftermath of the Atlantic revolutions.

Like nationalism, a concern with women's rights spread beyond Western Europe
and the United States, though less widely. An overtly feminist newspaper was established in Brazil in 1852, and an independent school for girls was founded in Mexico

in 1869. A handful of Japanese women and men, including the empress Haruko, raised issues about marriage, family planning, and especially education as the country began its modernizing process after 1868, but the state soon cracked down firmly, forbidding women from joining political parties or even attending political meetings. In Russia, the most radical feminist activists operated within socialist or anarchist circles, targeting the oppressive tsarist regime. Within the Islamic world and in China, some modernists came to feel that education and a higher status for women strengthened the nation in its struggles for development and independence and therefore deserved support. (See Document 17.5, pp. 814–16, for an example from the Dutch East Indies.) Huda Sharawi, founder of the first feminist organization in Egypt, returned to Cairo in 1923 from an international conference in Italy and threw her veil into the sea. Many upper-class Egyptian women soon followed her example.

Nowhere did nineteenth-century feminism have thoroughly revolutionary consequences. But as an outgrowth of the French and Industrial revolutions, it raised issues that echoed repeatedly and more loudly in the century that followed.

Reflections: Revolutions Pro and Con

Not long before he died in 1976, the Chinese revolutionary and communist leader Zhou Enlai was asked what he thought about the French Revolution. His famous reply—"It's too early to say"—highlights the endless controversies that revolutions everywhere have spawned. Long after the dust had settled from these Atlantic upheavals, their legacies have continued to provoke controversy. Were these revolutions necessary? Did they really promote the freedoms that they advertised? Did their benefits outweigh their costs in blood and treasure?

To the people who made these revolutions, benefited from them, or subsequently supported them, they represented an opening to new worlds of human possibility, while sweeping away old worlds of oppression, exploitation, and privilege. Modern revolutionaries acted on the basis of Enlightenment ideas, believing that the structure of human societies was not forever ordained by God or tradition and that it was both possible and necessary to reconstruct those societies. They also saw themselves as correcting ancient and enduring injustices. To those who complained about the violence of revolutions, supporters pointed to the violence that maintained the status quo and the unwillingness of privileged classes to accommodate changes that threatened those privileges. It was persistent injustice that made revolution necessary and perhaps inevitable.

To their victims, critics, and opponents, revolutions appeared quite different. Conservatives generally viewed human societies, not as machines whose parts could be easily rearranged, but as organisms that evolved slowly. Efforts at radical and sudden change only invited disaster, as the unrestrained violence of the French Revolution at its height demonstrated. The brutality and bitterness of the Haitian Revolution arguably contributed much to the unhappy future of that country. Furthermore, critics charged that revolutions were largely unnecessary, since societies were in fact changing. France was becoming a modern society and feudalism was largely gone well before the revolution exploded. Slavery was ended peacefully in many places, and democratic reform proceeded gradually throughout the nineteenth century. Was this not a preferable alternative to that of revolutionary upheaval?

Historians too struggle with the passions of revolution—both pro and con— as they seek to understand the origins and consequences of these momentous events. Were revolutions the product of misery, injustice, and oppression? Or did they reflect the growing weakness of established authorities, the arrival of new ideas, or the presence of small groups of radical activists able to fan the little fires of ordinary discontent into revolutionary conflagrations? The outcomes of revolutions have been as contentious as their beginnings. Did the American Revolution enable the growth of the United States as an economic and political "great power"? Did the Haitian Revolution stimulate the later end of slavery elsewhere in the Atlantic world? Did the French Revolution and the threat of subsequent revolutions encourage the democratic reforms that followed in the nineteenth century? Such questions have been central to an understanding of eighteenth-century revolutions as well as to those that followed in Russia, China, and elsewhere in the twentieth century.

Second Thoughts

What's the Significance?

To assess your mastery of the material in this chapter, visit the **Student Center** at bedfordstmartins.com/strayer.

North American Revolution
French Revolution
Declaration of the Rights of
    Man and Citizen
Napoleon Bonaparte

Haitian Revolution
Spanish American
    revolutions
abolitionist movement
nationalism

*Vindication of the Rights of
    Woman*
maternal feminism
Elizabeth Cady Stanton

Big Picture Questions

1. Make a chart comparing the North American, French, Haitian, and Spanish American revolutions. What categories of comparison would be most appropriate to include?
2. Do revolutions originate in oppression and injustice, in the weakening of political authorities, in new ideas, or in the activities of small groups of determined activists?
3. "The influence of revolutions endured long after they ended." To what extent does this chapter support or undermine this idea?
4. In what ways did the Atlantic revolutions and their echoes give a new and distinctive shape to the emerging societies of nineteenth-century Europe and the Americas?

Next Steps: For Further Study

Benedict Anderson, *Imagined Communities: Reflections on the Origins and Spread of Nationalism* (1991). A now-classic though controversial examination of the process by which national identities were created.

Bonnie S. Anderson, *Joyous Greetings: The First International Women's Movement, 1830–1860* (2000). Describes the beginnings of transatlantic feminism.

Laurent Dubois and John Garrigus, *Slave Revolution in the Caribbean, 1789–1804* (2006). A brief and up-to-date summary of the Haitian Revolution, combined with a number of documents.

Susan Dunn, *Sister Revolutions* (1999). A stimulating comparative study of the American and French revolutions.

Eric Hobsbawm, *The Age of Revolution, 1789–1848* (1999). A highly respected survey by a well-known British historian.

Lynn Hunt, ed., *The French Revolution and Human Rights* (1996). A collection of documents, with a fine introduction by a prominent scholar.

"Liberty, Equality, Fraternity: Exploring the French Revolution," http://chnm.gmu.edu/revolution/browse/images/#. A collection of cartoons, paintings, and artifacts illustrating the French Revolution.

For Web sites and additional documents related to this chapter, see **Make History** at bedfordstmartins.com/strayer.

Documents

Considering the Evidence:
Claiming Rights

In the discourse of the age of revolution, no idea had a more enduring resonance than that of "rights"—natural rights, political and civic rights, and "the rights of man" or, in a more recent expression, "human rights." However those rights were defined, they were understood as both natural and universal. They were considered inherent in the human condition rather than granted by some authority, and they were envisioned as being the same for everyone rather than depending on a person's birth, rank, or status in society. Growing out of the European Enlightenment (see pp. 742–44), this understanding of "rights" was genuinely revolutionary, challenging almost all notions of government and society prior to the late eighteenth century. But even among supporters, the idea of human rights was highly controversial. What precisely were these rights? Did they support or contradict one another? Did they really apply equally to all persons? How should they be established and maintained? Such questions were central to this age of revolution and have informed much of the world's political history ever since.[22]

Document 17.1

The French Revolution and the "Rights of Man"

The most prominent example of the language of rights found expression during the French Revolution in the Declaration of the Rights of Man and Citizen. It was a document hammered out in the French National Assembly early in that revolutionary upheaval and adopted at the end of August 1789 (see pp. 784–87). Ever since, it has been viewed as the philosophical core of the French Revolution.

Clearly the French document bears similarities to the language of the U.S. Declaration of Independence, for both drew upon the ideas of the European Enlightenment. Furthermore, Thomas Jefferson, who largely wrote the U.S. Declaration, served as the ambassador to France at this time and was in close contact with Marquis de Lafayette, the principal author of the French

Declaration. And Lafayette in turn had earlier served with the American revolutionary forces seeking independence from England.

- What purposes did the writers of the Declaration expect it to fulfill?

- What specific rights are spelled out in this document? What rights does it omit?

- What was revolutionary about the Declaration? What grievances against the old regime did the declaration reflect?

- What grounds for debate or controversy can you indentify within the Declaration?

The Declaration of the Rights of Man and Citizen
1789

The representatives of the French people, constituted as a National Assembly, and considering that ignorance, neglect, or contempt of the rights of man are the sole causes of public misfortunes and governmental corruption, have resolved to set forth in a solemn declaration the natural, inalienable and sacred rights of man....

1. Men are born and remain free and equal in rights. Social distinctions may be based only on common utility.

2. The purpose of all political association is the preservation of the natural and imprescriptible rights of man. These rights are liberty, property, security, and resistance to oppression.

3. The principle of all sovereignty rests essentially in the nation. No body and no individual may exercise authority which does not emanate expressly from the nation.

4. Liberty consists in the ability to do whatever does not harm another; hence the exercise of the natural rights of each man has no other limits than those which assure to other members of society the enjoyment of the same rights. These limits can only be determined by the law.

5. The law only has the right to prohibit those actions which are injurious to society. No hindrance should be put in the way of anything not prohibited by the law, nor may any one be forced to do what the law does not require.

6. The law is the expression of the general will. All citizens have the right to take part, in person or by their representatives, in its formation. It must be the same for everyone whether it protects or penalizes. All citizens being equal in its eyes are equally admissible to all public dignities, offices, and employments, according to their ability, and with no other distinction than that of their virtues and talents.

7. No man may be indicted, arrested, or detained except in cases determined by the law and according to the forms which it has prescribed....

9. Every man being presumed innocent until judged guilty, if it is deemed indispensable to arrest him, all rigor unnecessary to securing his person should be severely repressed by the law.

10. No one should be disturbed for his opinions, even in religion, provided that their manifestation does not trouble public order as established by law.

11. The free communication of thoughts and opinions is one of the most precious of the rights of man. Every citizen may therefore speak, write, and print freely, if he accepts his own responsibility for any abuse of this liberty in the cases set by the law.

Source: Lynn Hunt, ed., *The French Revolution and Human Rights* (Boston: Bedford/St. Martin's, 1996), 77–79.

12. The safeguard of the rights of man and the citizen requires public powers. These powers are therefore instituted for the advantage of all, and not for the private benefit of those to whom they are entrusted.

13. For maintenance of public authority and for expenses of administration, common taxation is indispensable. It should be apportioned equally among all the citizens according to their capacity to pay....

17. Property being an inviolable and sacred right, no one may be deprived of it except when public necessity, certified by law, obviously requires it, and on the condition of a just compensation in advance.

Document 17.2

The Rights of Women

But did the "rights of man" include women? Although none of the legislative assemblies that arose during the French Revolution seriously considered granting women the right to vote or hold office, the question of women's rights was sharply debated. Just two years after the famous French Declaration, the French playwright and journalist Olympe de Gouges sought to apply those rights to women when she crafted her *Declaration of the Rights of Woman and the Female Citizen*. "Woman, wake up," she wrote, "the tocsin [warning bell] of reason is being heard throughout the whole universe; discover your rights."[23] Most men, however, even ardent revolutionaries, agreed with the French lawyer Jean-Denis Lanjuinais that "the physique of women, their goal in life [marriage and motherhood], and their position distance them from the exercise of a great number of political rights and duties."[24]

Debates about the "rights of women" were hardly limited to France. During the nineteenth century, they echoed loudly throughout Europe, North America, and beyond and gave rise to the world's first women's rights movement. Among the earliest expressions of that debate was a treatise titled *A Vindication of the Rights of Woman* (1792) by Mary Wollstonecraft, a British writer whose thinking about women's rights had been clearly stimulated by events in France. She wrote the book as a response to French diplomat Charles Talleyrand, who had recently advocated a very limited and domestic education for women.

- On what basis does Wollstonecraft argue for the rights of women? To what extent were her arguments based on the principles of the French Declaration?

- In what kind of rights does she seem most interested? What problems does the denial of those rights generate?

- Should Wollstonecraft be considered a feminist in the contemporary sense of insisting on the complete equality of women and men in every sphere of life? Keep in mind that the term "feminism" itself was not in use when she wrote in 1792.

MARY WOLLSTONECRAFT

A Vindication of the Rights of Woman

1792

Contending for the rights of woman, my main argument is built on this simple principle, that if she be not prepared by education to become the companion of man, she will stop the progress of knowledge and virtue; . . . but the education and situation of woman at present shuts her out from such investigations. . . .

Consider, sir, dispassionately these observations, for a glimpse of this truth seemed to open before you when you observed, "that to see one-half of the human race excluded by the other from all participation of government was a political phenomenon that, according to abstract principles, it was impossible to explain." If so, on what does your constitution rest? . . .

Consider—I address you as a legislator—whether, when men contend for their freedom, and to be allowed to judge for themselves respecting their own happiness, it be not inconsistent and unjust to subjugate women, even though you firmly believe that you are acting in the manner best calculated to promote their happiness? Who made man the exclusive judge, if woman partake with him of the gift of reason?

In this style argue tyrants of every denomination, from the weak king to the weak father of a family; they are all eager to crush reason, yet always assert that they usurp its throne only to be useful. Do you not act a similar part when you force all women, by denying them civil and political rights, to remain immured in their families groping in the dark? . . . They may be convenient slaves, but slavery will have its constant effect, degrading the master and the abject dependent. . . .

I have repeatedly asserted . . . that women cannot by force be confined to domestic concerns; for they will, however ignorant, intermeddle with more weighty affairs, neglecting private duties only to disturb, by cunning tricks, the orderly plans of reason which rise above their comprehension. . . .

Let there be then no coercion established in society, and the common law of gravity prevailing, the sexes will fall into their proper places. And now that more equitable laws are forming your citizens, marriage may become more sacred; your young men may choose wives from motives of affection, and your maidens allow love to root out vanity.

The father of a family will not then weaken his constitution and debase his sentiments by visiting the harlot, nor forget, in obeying the call of appetite, the purpose for which it was implanted. And the mother will not neglect her children to practise the arts of coquetry, when sense and modesty secure her the friendship of her husband.

But, till men become attentive to the duty of a father, it is vain to expect women to spend that time in their nursery which they, . . . choose to spend at their glass [mirror]; for this exertion of cunning is only an instinct of nature to enable them to obtain indirectly a little of that power of which they are unjustly denied a share; for, if women are not permitted to enjoy legitimate rights, they will render both men and themselves vicious to obtain illicit privileges.

I wish, sir, to set some investigations of this kind afloat in France; and should they lead to a confirmation of my principles when your constitution is revised, the Rights of Woman may be respected, if it be fully proved that reason calls for this respect, and loudly demands JUSTICE for one-half of the human race.

Source: Mary Wollstonecraft, *A Vindication of the Rights of Woman* (New York: W. W. Norton, 1967), Dedication.

Document 17.3

Rights and National Independence

The "rights of man" could be mobilized not only in the struggles of women but also on behalf of colonial subjects, as the American Declaration of Independence illustrated. Some thirty-five years after the outbreak of the North American revolution, Spain's American colonies were likewise in revolt. Among the most prominent political and military leaders of that struggle was Simón Bolívar, often regarded as the George Washington of Latin America. Born in Caracas, Venezuela, Bolívar hailed from an old, wealthy, and aristocratic family. Although his struggles were successful in ending Spanish colonial rule, they manifestly failed to achieve his lifelong dream of a federation, like that of North America, among the various newly independent republics of Latin America. In a well-known letter, written in 1815, Bolívar made the case for the independence of his continent.

- What understanding of "rights" informed Bolívar's demand for independence?

- What were his chief objections to Spanish rule?

- What difficulties did Bolívar foresee in achieving the kind of stable and unified independence that he so much desired?

- What might you infer from Bolívar's statements, or his silences, about his willingness to apply human rights thinking to people of Native American, African, or mixed-race ancestry?

SIMÓN BOLÍVAR

The Jamaica Letter

1815

Success will crown our efforts because the destiny of [Latin] America is irrevocably fixed; the tie that bound her to Spain is severed.... The hatred we feel for the Peninsula is greater than the sea separating us from it; it would be easier to bring the two continents together than to reconcile the spirits and the minds of the two countries. The habit of obedience, a commerce of shared interests, knowledge, and religion; mutual goodwill; a tender concern for the birthland and glory of our ancestors; in brief everything that constituted our hopes came to us from Spain.... Today the opposite is true: death, dishonor, everything harmful threatens us and makes us fearful. That wicked stepmother is the source of all our sufferings.... The chains have been broken, we've been liberated, and now our enemies want to make us slaves. That is why America fights with such defiance, and it would be rare should such desperate intensity not bring victory in its wake....

Source: David Bushnell, ed., *El Libertador: Writings of Simón Bolívar*, translated by Frederick H. Fornoff (Oxford: Oxford University Press, 2003), 13–14, 18–20, 27–28, 30.

[W]e are moreover neither Indians nor Europeans, but a race halfway between the legitimate owners of the land and the Spanish usurpers—in short, being Americans by birth and endowed with rights from Europe—find ourselves forced to defend these rights against the natives while maintaining our position in the land against the intrusion of the invaders. Thus we find ourselves in the most extraordinary and complicated situation....

The posture of those who dwell in the American hemisphere has been over the centuries purely passive. We are at a level even lower than servitude, and by that very reason hindered from elevating ourselves to the enjoyment of freedom.... From the beginning we were plagued by a practice that in addition to depriving us of the rights to which we were entitled left us in a kind of permanent infancy with respect to public affairs....

The Americans... occupy no other place in society than that of servants suited for work or, at best, that of simple consumers, and even this is limited by appalling restrictions: for instance the prohibition against the cultivation of European crops or the sale of products monopolized by the king, the restriction against the construction of factories that don't even exist on the peninsula, exclusive privileges for engaging in commerce even of items that are basic necessities, the barrier between American provinces, preventing them from establishing contact, or communicating, or doing business with one another. In short, would you like to know the extent of our destiny? Fields for the cultivation of indigo, grain, coffee, sugar cane, cacao, and cotton, empty prairies for raising cattle, wilderness for hunting ferocious beasts, the bowels of the earth for excavating gold that will never satisfy the lusts of that greedy nation.... Is this not an outrage and a violation of the rights of humanity?

We were... absent from the universe in all things relative to the science of government and the administration of the state. We were never viceroys, never governors, except in extraordinary circumstances; hardly ever bishops or archbishops; never diplomats; soldiers only in lower ranks; nobles, but without royal privileges. In short, we were never leaders, never financiers, hardly ever merchants....

From the foregoing, we can deduce certain consequences: The American provinces are involved in a struggle for emancipation, which will eventually succeed.... The idea of merging the entire New World into a single nation with a single unifying principle to provide coherence to the parts and to the whole is both grandiose and impractical. Because it has a common origin, a common language, similar customs, and one religion, we might conclude that it should be possible for a single government to oversee a federation of different states eventually to emerge. However, this is not possible, because America is divided by remote climates, diverse geographies, conflicting interests, and dissimilar characteristics.... Such a corporation might conceivably emerge at some felicitous moment in our regeneration....

When we are at last strong, under the auspices of a liberal nation that lends us its protection, then we will cultivate in harmony the virtues and talents that lead to glory; then we will follow the majestic path toward abundant prosperity marked out by destiny for South America; then the arts and sciences that were born in the Orient and that brought enlightenment to Europe will fly to a free Columbia, which will nourish and shelter them.

Document 17.4

Rights and Slavery

The language of "rights" resonated not only with women seeking equality and colonial subjects seeking independence but also with slaves demanding freedom. Clearly, the ideas and events of the French Revolution had sparked the massive slave uprising in Haiti in 1791 (see pp. 787–90). In the United States the language of the Declaration of Independence with its affirmation that "all men are created equal" stood in glaring contrast to the brutal realities of slavery. That great contradiction in the new American nation was forcefully highlighted in a famous speech by Frederick Douglass. Born a slave in 1818, Douglass had escaped from bondage to become a leading abolitionist, writer, newspaper publisher, and African American spokesperson. He was invited to address an antislavery meeting in Rochester, New York, on July 4, 1852.

- On what basis does Douglass demand the end of slavery? How do his arguments relate to the ideology of the American Revolution?

- How would you describe the rhetorical strategy of his speech?

- What does Douglass mean when he says "it is not light that is needed, but fire"?

- In what ways does he argue that slavery has poisoned American life?

- Why, in the end, can Douglass claim "I do not despair of this country"? How would you evaluate the following assertion in the last paragraph: "There are forces in operation, which must inevitably work the downfall of slavery"? What forces was he referring to?

FREDERICK DOUGLASS
What to the Slave Is the Fourth of July?
1852

Fellow-citizens, pardon me, allow me to ask, why am I called upon to speak here to-day? What have I, or those I represent, to do with your national independence? Are the great principles of political freedom and of natural justice, embodied in that Declaration of Independence, extended to us? and am I, therefore, called upon to bring our humble offering to the national altar, and to confess the benefits and express devout gratitude for the blessings resulting from your independence to us?

Would to God, both for your sakes and ours, that an affirmative answer could be truthfully returned to these questions!...

But, such is not the state of the case. I say it with a sad sense of the disparity between us. I am not included within the pale of this glorious anniversary! Your high independence only reveals the immeasurable distance between us....The sunlight that brought life and healing to you, has brought stripes and death to me. This Fourth [of] July is yours, not mine. You may rejoice, I must mourn. To drag a man in fetters into the grand illuminated temple of liberty, and call upon him to join you in joyous anthems, were inhuman mockery and sacrilegious irony. Do you mean, citizens, to mock me, by asking me to speak to-day?...

Fellow-citizens; above your national, tumultuous joy, I hear the mournful wail of millions!...I shall see, this day...from the slave's point of view....I do not hesitate to declare, with all my soul, that the character and conduct of this nation never looked blacker to me than on this 4th of July!...Standing with God and the crushed and bleeding slave on this occasion, I will...dare to call in question and to denounce, with all the emphasis I can command, everything

Source: Frederick Douglass, "What to the Slave Is the Fourth of July?" http://www.trinicenter.com/historicalviews/4thjuly.htm.

that serves to perpetuate slavery—the great sin and shame of America!

For the present, it is enough to affirm the equal manhood of the Negro race. Is it not astonishing that... while we are engaged in all manner of enterprises common to other men..., we are called upon to prove that we are men!

Would you have me argue that man is entitled to liberty? that he is the rightful owner of his own body? You have already declared it. Must I argue the wrongfulness of slavery? Is that a question for Republicans?...

At a time like this, scorching irony, not convincing argument, is needed.... For it is not light that is needed, but fire.... [T]he conscience of the nation must be roused;... the hypocrisy of the nation must be exposed; and its crimes against God and man must be proclaimed and denounced.

What, to the American slave, is your 4th of July? I answer: a day that reveals to him, more than all other days in the year, the gross injustice and cruelty to which he is the constant victim. To him, your celebration is a sham; your boasted liberty, an unholy license; your national greatness, swelling vanity; your sounds of rejoicing are empty and heartless; your denunciations of tyrants, brass-fronted impudence; your shouts of liberty and equality, hollow mockery; your prayers and hymns, your sermons and thanks-givings, with all your religious parade, and solemnity, are, to him, mere bombast, fraud, deception, impiety, and hypocrisy—a thin veil to cover up crimes which would disgrace a nation of savages. There is not a nation on the earth guilty of practices, more shocking and bloody, than are the people of these United States, at this very hour....

Fellow-citizens! I will not enlarge further on your national inconsistencies. The existence of slavery in this country brands your republicanism as a sham, your humanity as a base pretence, and your Christianity as a lie. It destroys your moral power abroad; it corrupts your politicians at home. It saps the foundation of religion; it makes your name a hiss-ing, and a byword to a mocking earth. It is the antagonistic force in your government, the only thing that seriously disturbs and endangers your Union. It fetters your progress; it is the enemy of improvement, the deadly foe of education; it fosters pride; it breeds insolence; it promotes vice; it shelters crime; it is a curse to the earth that supports it; and yet, you cling to it, as if it were the sheet anchor of all your hopes. Oh! be warned! be warned! a horrible reptile is coiled up in your nation's bosom; the venomous creature is nursing at the tender breast of your youthful republic; for the love of God, tear away, and fling from you the hideous monster, and let the weight of twenty millions crush and destroy it forever!...

Allow me to say, in conclusion..., I do not despair of this country. There are forces in operation, which must inevitably work the downfall of slavery.... While drawing encouragement from the Declaration of Independence, the great principles it contains, and the genius of American Institutions, my spirit is also cheered by the obvious tendencies of the age. Nations do not now stand in the same relation to each other that they did ages ago. No nation can now shut itself up from the surrounding world, and trot round in the same old path of its fathers without interference.... But a change has now come over the affairs of mankind. Walled cities and empires have become unfashionable. The arm of commerce has borne away the gates of the strong city. Intelligence is penetrating the darkest corners of the globe. It makes its pathway over and under the sea, as well as on the earth. Wind, steam, and lightning are its chartered agents. Oceans no longer divide, but link nations together. From Boston to London is now a holiday excursion. Space is comparatively annihilated. Thoughts expressed on one side of the Atlantic are distinctly heard on the other. The far off and almost fabulous Pacific rolls in grandeur at our feet. The Celestial Empire, the mystery of ages, is being solved. The fiat of the Almighty, "Let there be Light," has not yet spent its force.

Document 17.5

Rights in the Colonial World

The idea of rights did not long remain limited to the Atlantic world of Europe and the Americas. Much as that idea proved revolutionary in the colonial world of the Americas, so too did it have an impact in the new European colonial empires that took shape during the nineteenth century. As Western colonialism embraced much of Asia and Africa, such ideas gradually became familiar to at least a few people in those colonial societies. One example was Raden Adjeng Kartini, a young Javanese woman from an aristocratic family who had become fluent in Dutch, the language of the Netherlands, the colonial power that ruled her country. In 1899, at the age of twenty, she wrote a letter to a Dutch friend, describing the impact of European thinking on her own outlook and her own life.

- Although Kartini did not directly use the language of "rights," what evidence in the letter suggests that she might have been influenced by the idea of human rights?

- What elements of European thinking are most compelling to Kartini?

- In what ways does her encounter with European thinking generate conflict or dissatisfaction with her own society? What else provokes her desire for change?

- Some Indonesians have celebrated Kartini as a pioneer of both feminism and nationalism. To what extent does this letter support that view?

- How would you compare Kartini's thinking about women's emancipation with that of Wollstonecraft?

RADEN ADJENG KARTINI
Letter to a Friend
1899

I have longed to make the acquaintance of a "modern girl," that proud, independent girl who has all my sympathy!...I do not belong to the Indian world, but to that of my pale sisters who are struggling forward in the distant West.

If the laws of my land permitted it, there is nothing that I had rather do than give myself wholly to the working and striving of the new woman in Europe; but age-long traditions that cannot be broken hold us fast cloistered in their unyielding arms. Some day those arms will loosen and let us go, but that time lies as yet far from us, infinitely far. It will come, that I know; it may be three, four generations after us. Oh, you do not know what it is to love this young, this new age with heart and soul, and yet to

Source: Raden Adjeng Kartini, *Letters of a Javanese Princess*, translated by Agnes Louise Symmers (Oxford: Oxford University Press, 1976), 3–7.

be bound hand and foot, chained by all the laws, customs, and conventions of one's land. All our institutions are directly opposed to the progress for which I so long for the sake of our people. Day and night I wonder by what means our ancient traditions could be overcome. For myself, I could find a way to shake them off, to break them, were it not that another bond, stronger than any age-old tradition could ever be, binds me to my world; and that is the love which I bear for those to whom I owe my life, and whom I must thank for everything. Have I the right to break the hearts of those who have given me nothing but love and kindness my whole life long, and who have surrounded me with the tenderest care?

But it was not the voices alone which reached me from that distant, that bright, that new-born Europe, which made me long for a change in existing conditions. Even in my childhood, the word "emancipation" enchanted my ears; it had a significance that nothing else had, a meaning that was far beyond my comprehension, and awakened in me an evergrowing longing for freedom and independence—a longing to stand alone. Conditions both in my own surroundings and in those of others around me broke my heart, and made me long with a nameless sorrow for the awakening of my country.

Then the voices which penetrated from distant lands grew clearer and clearer, till they reached me, and to the satisfaction of some who loved me, but to the deep grief of others, brought seed which entered my heart, took root, and grew strong and vigorous.

And now I must tell you something of myself so that you can make my acquaintance.

I am the eldest of the three unmarried daughters of the Regent of Japara, and have six brothers and sisters. What a world, eh? My grandfather…was a great leader in the progressive movement of his day, and the first regent of middle Java to unlatch his door to that guest from over the sea—Western civilization. All of his children had European educations.…We girls, so far as education goes, fettered by our ancient traditions and conventions, have profited but little by these advantages. It was a great crime against the customs of our land that we should be taught at all, and especially that we should leave the house every day to go to school. For the customs of our country forbade girls in the strongest manner ever to go outside of the house. We were never allowed to go anywhere, however, save to the school, and the only place of instruction of which our city could boast, which was open to us, was a free grammar school for Europeans.

When I reached the age of twelve, I was kept at home—I must go into the "box." I was locked up, and cut off from all communication with the outside world, toward which I might never turn again save at the side of a bridegroom, a stranger, an unknown man whom my parents would choose for me, and to whom I should be betrothed without my own knowledge.…I went into my prison. Four long years I spent between thick walls, without once seeing the outside world.

How I passed through that time, I do not know.…But there was one great happiness left me: the reading of Dutch books and correspondence with Dutch friends was not forbidden. This—the only gleam of light in that empty, sombre time, was my all.…

At last in my sixteenth year, I saw the outside world again. Thank God! Thank God! I could leave my prison as a free human being and not chained to an unwelcome bridegroom.…

In the following year, at the time of the investiture of our young Princess [Queen Wilhelmina of the Netherlands], our parents presented us "officially" with our freedom. For the first time in our lives we were allowed to leave our native town, and to go to the city where the festivities were held in honour of the occasion. What a great and priceless victory it was! That young girls of our position should show themselves in public was here an unheard-of occurrence. The "world" stood aghast; tongues were set wagging at the unprecedented crime. Our European friends rejoiced, and as for ourselves, no queen was so rich as we. But I am far from satisfied. I would go still further, always further. I do not desire to go out to feasts, and little frivolous amusements. That has never been the cause of my longing for freedom. I long to be free, to be able to stand alone, to study, not to be subject to any one, and, above all, *never, never* to be obliged to marry.

But we *must* marry, must, must. Not to marry is the greatest sin which the [Muslim] woman can commit; it is the greatest disgrace which a native girl can bring to her family.

And marriage among us—Miserable is too feeble an expression for it. How can it be otherwise, when the laws have made everything for the man and nothing for the woman? When law and convention both are for the man; when everything is allowed to him?

Love! what do we know here of love? How can we love a man whom we have never known? And how could he love us? That in itself would not be possible. Young girls and men must be kept rigidly apart, and are never allowed to meet.

Using the Evidence:
Claiming Rights

1. **Making comparisons:** In what different ways does the idea of "rights" find expression in these five documents? Which documents speak more about individual rights and which focus attention on collective rights? What common understandings can you identify?

2. **Considering ideas and circumstances:** Historians frequently debate the relative importance of ideas in shaping historical events. What impact do you think the ideas about rights expressed in these documents had on the historical development of the Atlantic world and beyond? And what specific historical contexts or conditions shaped each writer's understanding of "rights"?

3. **Connecting past and present:** Read the Universal Declaration of Human Rights, adopted by the United Nations in 1948 (http://www.un .org/Overview/rights.html). To what extent does this document reflect the thinking about rights spelled out in the French declaration of 1789? What additional rights have been added to the more recent document? How might you account for the changes?

Visual Sources

Considering the Evidence:
Representing the French Revolution

The era of the French Revolution, generally reckoned to have lasted from 1789 to 1815, unfolded as a complex and varied process. Its first several years were relatively moderate, but by 1792 it had become far more radical and violent. After 1795 a reaction set in against the chaos and upheaval that it had generated, culminating in the seizure of power in 1799 by the successful general Napoleon Bonaparte. Nor was the revolution a purely French affair. Conservative opposition in the rest of Europe prompted prolonged warfare, and French efforts under Napoleon to spread the revolution led to a huge French empire in Europe and much resistance to it (see pp. 784–87).

All of this provoked enormous controversy, which found visual expression in paintings, cartoons, drawings, and portraits. The five visual sources that follow suggest something of the changing nature of the revolution and the varied reactions it elicited.

Like all major social upheavals, the French Revolution unleashed both enormous hopes and great fears, largely depending on an individual's position in French society. That society was divided into three legal orders, or estates—the clergy, the nobility, and the commoners. The first two of these estates, the most highly privileged groups of French society, together represented only about 2 percent of the population and were exempt from major forms of taxation in addition to holding much of the country's landed wealth. This generated considerable resentment among the commoners (the third estate) and was a critical motor of the revolution. Nonetheless, in the early stages of the revolution (1789–1791), many people hoped that France could become a constitutional monarchy with a far more limited role for the king and that the three estates could work together in harmony. The high point of this hope for social and national unity occurred during the Festival of the Federation, a massive military pageant featuring troops from all over the country. Watched by close to a million spectators, the festival took place on July 14, 1790, exactly one year after the storming of the Bastille, a large fortress, prison, and armory that had come to symbolize the oppressive old regime. Soldiers swore an oath of allegiance to the king and the National Assembly. Speakers gave public thanks for "this inseparable bond between all the French, regardless of sex, age, station in life or occupation."[25]

Revolutions of Industrialization

1750–1914

"Industrialization is, I am afraid, going to be a curse for mankind.... God forbid that India should ever take to industrialism after the manner of the West. The economic imperialism of a single tiny island kingdom (England) is today [1928] keeping the world in chains. If an entire nation of 300 millions took to similar economic exploitation, it would strip the world bare like locusts.... Industrialization on a mass scale will necessarily lead to passive or active exploitation of the villagers.... The machine produces much too fast."[1]

Such were the views of the famous Indian nationalist and spiritual leader Mahatma Gandhi, who subsequently led his country to independence from British colonial rule by 1947, only to be assassinated a few months later. However, few people anywhere have agreed with India's heroic figure. Since its beginning in Great Britain in the late eighteenth century, the idea of industrialization, if not always its reality, has been embraced in every kind of society, both for the wealth it generates and for the power it conveys. Even Gandhi's own country, once it achieved its independence, largely abandoned its founding father's vision of small-scale, village-based handicraft manufacturing in favor of modern industry. As the twenty-first century dawned, India was moving rapidly to develop a major high-technology industrial sector. At that time, across the river from the site in New Delhi where Gandhi was cremated in 1948 a large power plant belched black smoke.

FEW ELEMENTS OF EUROPE'S MODERN TRANSFORMATION HELD A GREATER SIGNIFICANCE for the history of humankind than the Industrial Revolution, which took place initially in the

Industrial Britain: The dirt, smoke, and pollution of early industrial societies are vividly conveyed in this nineteenth-century engraving of a copper foundry in Wales. (Bibliothèque des Arts Décoratifs Paris/Gianni Dagli Orti/The Art Archive)

century and a half between 1750 and 1900. It drew upon the Scientific Revolution and accompanied the unfolding legacy of the French Revolution to utterly transform European society and to propel Europe into a position of global dominance. Not since the breakthrough of the Agricultural Revolution some 12,000 years ago had human ways of life been so fundamentally altered. But the Industrial Revolution, unlike its agricultural predecessor, began independently in only one place, Western Europe, and more specifically Great Britain. From there, it spread far more rapidly than agriculture, though very unevenly, to achieve a worldwide presence in less than 250 years. Far more than Europe's Christian religion, its democratic political values, or its capitalist economic framework, the techniques of its Industrial Revolution have been intensely sought after virtually everywhere.

In any long-term reckoning, the history of industrialization is very much an unfinished story. It is hard to know whether we are at the beginning of a movement leading to worldwide industrialization, stuck in the middle of a world permanently divided into rich and poor countries, or approaching the end of an environmentally unsustainable industrial era. Whatever the future holds, this chapter focuses on the early stages of an immense transformation in the global condition of humankind.

Explaining the Industrial Revolution

The global context for this epochal economic transformation lies in a very substantial increase in human numbers from about 375 million people in 1400 to about 1 billion in the early nineteenth century. Accompanying this growth in population was an emerging energy crisis, most pronounced in Western Europe, China, and Japan, as wood and charcoal, the major industrial fuels, became more scarce and their prices rose. In short, "global energy demands began to push against the existing local and regional ecological limits."[2] In broad terms, the Industrial Revolution marks a human response to that dilemma as fossil fuels replaced the earlier reliance on wind, water, wood, and the muscle power of people and animals. All of those had derived from "recently captured solar energy," but now human ingenuity found the means to tap as well the anciently stored solar energy of coal, oil, and natural gas.[3] It was a breakthrough of unprecedented proportions that made available for human use immensely greater quantities of energy. It also wrought, of course, a mounting impact on the environment with which the world of the twenty-first century is increasingly occupied.

More immediately, however, that access to huge new sources of energy gave rise to an enormously increased output of goods and services. In Britain, where the Industrial Revolution began, industrial output increased some fiftyfold between 1750 and 1900. It was a wholly unprecedented and previously unimaginable jump in the capacity of human societies to produce wealth. Lying behind it was a great acceleration in the rate of technological innovation, not simply this or that invention—the spinning jenny, power loom, steam engine, or cotton gin—but a "culture of innovation," a widespread and almost obsessive belief that things could be endlessly improved.

Early signs of the technological creativity that spawned the Industrial Revolution appeared in eighteenth-century Britain, where a variety of innovations transformed cotton textile production. It was only in the nineteenth century, though, that Europeans in general and the British in particular more clearly forged ahead of the rest of the world. The great breakthrough was the coal-fired steam engine, which provided an inanimate and almost limitless source of power beyond that of wind, water, or muscle and could be used to drive any number of machines as well as locomotives and oceangoing ships. Soon the Industrial Revolution spread beyond the textile industry to iron and steel production, railroads and steamships, food processing, construction, chemicals, electricity, the telegraph and telephone, rubber, pottery, printing, and much more. Agriculture too was affected as mechanical reapers, chemical fertilizers, pesticides, and refrigeration transformed this most ancient of industries. Technical innovation occurred in more modest ways as well. Patents for horseshoes in the United States, for example, grew from fewer than five per year before 1840 to thirty to forty per year by the end of the century. Furthermore, industrialization spread beyond Britain to continental Western Europe and then in the second half of the century to the United States, Russia, and Japan.

In the twentieth century, the Industrial Revolution became global as a number of Asian, African, and Latin American countries developed substantial industrial sectors. Oil, natural gas, and nuclear reactions joined coal as widely available sources of energy, and new industries emerged in automobiles, airplanes, consumer durable goods, electronics, computers, and on and on. It was a cumulative process that, despite periodic ups and downs, accelerated over time. More than anything else, this continuous emergence of new techniques of production and the economic growth that they made possible mark the past 250 years as a distinct phase of human history.

Why Europe?

The Industrial Revolution has long been a source of great controversy among scholars. Why did it occur first in Europe? Within Europe, why did it occur first in Great Britain? And why did it take place in the late eighteenth and nineteenth centuries? Earlier explanations that sought the answer in some unique and deeply rooted feature of European society, history, or culture have been challenged by world historians because such views seemed to suggest that Europe alone was destined to lead the way to modern economic life. This approach not only was Eurocentric and deterministic but also flew in the face of much recent research.

■ **Change**
In what respects did the roots of the Industrial Revolution lie within Europe? In what ways did that transformation have global roots?

Historians now know that other areas of the world had experienced times of great technological and scientific flourishing. Between 750 and 1100 C.E., the Islamic world generated major advances in shipbuilding, the use of tides and falling water to generate power, papermaking, textile production, chemical technologies, water mills, clocks, and much more.[4] India had long been the world center of cotton textile production, the first place to turn sugarcane juice into crystallized sugar, and the source of many agricultural innovations and mathematical inventions. To the Arabs of the ninth century C.E., India was a "place of marvels."[5] More than either of these, China was clearly the world leader in technological innovation between 700 and 1400 C.E., prompting various scholars to suggest that China was on the edge of an industrial revolution by 1200 or so. For reasons much debated among historians, all of these flowerings of technological creativity had slowed down considerably or stagnated by the early modern era, when the pace of technological change in Europe began to pick up. But their earlier achievements certainly suggest that Europe was not alone in its capacity for technological innovation.

Nor did Europe enjoy any overall economic advantage as late as 1750. Over the past several decades, historians have carefully examined the economic conditions of various Eurasian societies in the eighteenth century and found them surprisingly alike. Economic indicators such as life expectancies, patterns of consumption and nutrition, wage levels, general living standards, widespread free markets, and prosperous merchant communities suggest broadly similar conditions across the major civilizations of Europe and Asia.[6] Thus Europe had no obvious economic lead, even on the eve of the Industrial Revolution. Rather, according to one leading scholar, "there existed something of a global economic parity between the most advanced regions in the world economy."[7]

A final reason for doubting any unique European capacity for industrial development lies in the relatively rapid spread of industrial techniques to many parts of the world over the past 250 years (a fairly short time by world history standards). Although the process has been highly uneven, industrialization has taken root, to one degree or another, in Japan, China, India, Brazil, Mexico, Indonesia, South Africa, Saudi Arabia, Thailand, South Korea, and elsewhere. Such a pattern weakens any suggestion that European culture or society was exceptionally compatible with industrial development.

Thus contemporary historians are inclined to see the Industrial Revolution erupting rather quickly and quite unexpectedly between 1750 and 1850 (see Map 18.1). Two intersecting factors help to explain why this process occurred in Europe rather than elsewhere. One lies in certain patterns of Europe's internal development that favored innovation. Its many small and highly competitive states, taking shape in the twelfth or thirteenth centuries, arguably provided an "insurance against economic and technological stagnation," which the larger Chinese, Ottoman, or Mughal empires perhaps lacked.[8] If so, then Western Europe's failure to re-create the earlier unity of the Roman Empire may have acted as a stimulus to innovation.

Furthermore, the relative newness of these European states and their monarchs' desperate need for revenue in the absence of an effective tax-collecting bureaucracy pushed European royals into an unusual alliance with their merchant classes. Small groups of merchant capitalists might be granted special privileges, monopolies, or even tax-collecting responsibilities in exchange for much-needed loans or payments to the state. It was therefore in the interest of governments to actively encourage commerce and innovation. Thus states granted charters and monopolies to private trading companies, and governments founded scientific societies and offered prizes to promote innovation. In this way, European merchants and other innovators from the fifteenth century onward gained an unusual degree of freedom from state control and in some

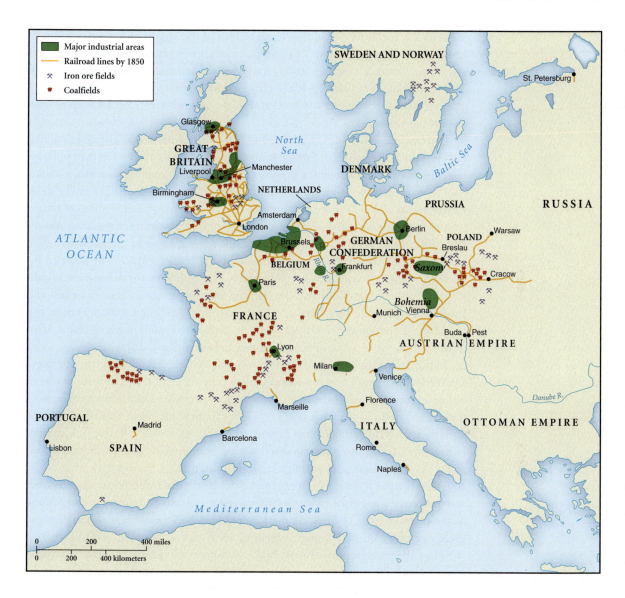

Map 18.1 The Early Phase of Europe's Industrial Revolution From its beginning in Great Britain, industrialization spread by 1850 across northwestern Europe to include parts of France, Germany, Belgium, Bohemia, and Italy.

places a higher social status than their counterparts in more established civilizations. In Venice and Holland, merchants actually controlled the state. By the eighteenth century major Western European societies were highly commercialized and governed by states generally supportive of private commerce. In short, they were well on their way toward capitalist economies—where buying and selling on the market was a widely established practice—before they experienced industrialization. Such internally competitive economies, coupled with a highly competitive system of rival states, arguably fostered innovation in the new civilization taking shape in Western Europe.

Europe's societies, of course, were not alone in developing market-based economies by the eighteenth century. Japan, India, and especially China were likewise highly commercialized or market driven. However, in the several centuries after 1500,

Western Europe alone "found itself at the hub of the largest and most varied network of exchange in history."[9] Widespread contact with culturally different peoples was yet another factor that historically has generated extensive change and innovation. This new global network, largely the creation of Europeans themselves, greatly energized European commerce and brought Europeans into direct contact with peoples around the world.

For example, Asia, home to the world's richest and most sophisticated societies, was the initial destination of European voyages of exploration. The German philosopher Gottfried Wilhelm Leibniz (1646–1716) encouraged Jesuit missionaries in China "not to worry so much about getting things European to the Chinese but rather about getting remarkable Chinese inventions to us."[10] Inexpensive and well-made Indian textiles began to flood into Europe, causing one English observer to note: "Almost everything that used to be made of wool or silk, relating either to dress of the women or the furniture of our houses, was supplied by the Indian trade."[11] The competitive stimulus of these Indian cotton textiles was certainly one factor driving innovation in the British textile industry. Likewise, the popularity of Chinese porcelain and Japanese lacquerware prompted imitation and innovation in England, France, and Holland.[12] Thus competition from desirable, high-quality, and newly available Asian goods played a role in stimulating Europe's Industrial Revolution.

In the Americas, Europeans found a windfall of silver that allowed them to operate in Asian markets. They also found timber, fish, maize, potatoes, and much else to sustain a growing population. Later, slave-produced cotton supplied an emerging textile industry with its key raw material at low prices, while sugar, similarly produced with slave labor, furnished cheap calories to European workers. "Europe's Industrial Revolution," concluded historian Peter Stearns, "stemmed in great part from Europe's ability to draw disproportionately on world resources."[13] The new societies of the Americas further offered a growing market for European machine-produced goods and generated substantial profits for European merchants and entrepreneurs. None of the other empires of the early modern era enriched their imperial heartlands so greatly or provided such a spur to technological and economic growth.

Thus the intersection of new, highly commercialized, competitive European societies with the novel global network of their own making provides a context for understanding Europe's Industrial Revolution. Commerce and cross-cultural exchange, acting in tandem, provided the seedbed for the impressive technological changes of the first industrial societies.

Why Britain?

■ **Comparison**

What was distinctive about Britain that may help to explain its status as the breakthrough point of the Industrial Revolution?

If the Industrial Revolution was a Western European phenomenon generally, it clearly began in Britain in particular. The world's first Industrial Revolution unfolded spontaneously in a country that concentrated some of the more general features of European society. It was both unplanned and unexpected.

Britain was the most highly commercialized of Europe's larger countries. Its landlords had long ago "enclosed" much agricultural land, pushing out the small farmers and producing for the market. A series of agricultural innovations—crop rotation, selective breeding of animals, lighter plows, higher-yielding seeds—increased agricultural output, kept food prices low, and freed up labor from the countryside. The guilds, which earlier had protected Britain's urban artisans, had largely disappeared by the eighteenth century, allowing employers to run their manufacturing enterprises as they saw fit. Coupled with a rapidly growing population, these processes ensured a ready supply of industrial workers who had few alternatives available to them. Furthermore, British aristocrats, unlike their counterparts in Europe, had long been interested in the world of business, and some took part in new mining and manufacturing enterprises. British commerce, moreover, extended around the world, its large merchant fleet protected by the Royal Navy. The wealth of empire and global commerce, however, were not themselves sufficient for spawning the Industrial Revolution, especially when we consider that Spain, the earliest beneficiary of American wealth, remained one of the more slowly industrializing European countries into the twentieth century.

British political life encouraged commercialization and economic innovation. Its policy of religious toleration, formally established in 1688, welcomed people with technical skills regardless of their faith, whereas France's persecution of its Protestant minority had chased out some of its most skilled workers. The British government favored men of business with tariffs to keep out cheap Indian textiles, with laws that made it easy to form companies and to forbid workers' unions, with roads and canals that helped create a unified internal market, and with patent laws that served to protect the interests of inventors. Checks on royal authority—trial by jury and the growing authority of parliament, for example—provided a freer arena for private enterprise than elsewhere in Europe.

Europe's Scientific Revolution also took a distinctive form in Great Britain in ways that fostered technological innovation.[14] Whereas science on the continent was largely based on logic, deduction, and mathematical reasoning, in Britain it was much more concerned with observation, experiment, precise measurements, mechanical devices, and practical commercial applications. Discoveries about atmospheric pressure and vacuums, for example, played an important role in the invention and improvement of the steam engine. Even though most inventors were artisans or craftsmen rather than scientists, in eighteenth-century Britain they were in close contact with scientists, makers of scientific instruments, and entrepreneurs, whereas in continental Europe these groups were largely separate. The British Royal Society, an association of "natural philosophers" (scientists) established in 1660, saw its role as one of promoting "useful knowledge." To this end, it established "mechanics' libraries," published broadsheets and pamphlets on recent scientific advances, and held frequent public lectures and demonstrations. The integration of science and technology became widespread and permanent after 1850, but for a century before, it was largely a British phenomenon.

Finally, several accidents of geography and history contributed something to Britain's Industrial Revolution. The country had a ready supply of coal and iron ore, often located close to each other and within easy reach of major industrial centers.

Although Britain took part in the wars against Napoleon, the country's island location protected it from the kind of invasions that so many continental European states experienced during the era of the French Revolution. Moreover, Britain's relatively fluid society allowed for adjustments in the face of social changes without widespread revolution. By the time the dust settled from the immense disturbance of the French Revolution, Britain was well on its way to becoming the world's first industrial society.

The First Industrial Society

Wherever it took hold, the Industrial Revolution generated, within a century or less, an economic miracle, at least in comparison with earlier technologies. The British textile industry, which used 52 million pounds of cotton in 1800, consumed 588 million pounds in 1850. Britain's output of coal soared from 5.23 million tons in 1750 to 68.4 million tons a century later.[15] Railroads crisscrossed Britain and much of Europe like a giant spider web (see Map 18.1, p. 829). Most of this dramatic increase in production occurred in mining, manufacturing, and services. Thus agriculture, for millennia the overwhelmingly dominant economic sector in every civilization, shrank in relative importance. In Britain, for example, agriculture generated only 8 percent of national income in 1891 and employed fewer than 8 percent of working Britons in 1914. Accompanying this vast economic change was an epic transformation of social life. "In two centuries," wrote one prominent historian, "daily life changed more than it had in the 7,000 years before."[16] Nowhere were the revolutionary dimensions of industrialization more apparent than in Great Britain, the world's first industrial society.

Railroads
The popularity of railroads, long a symbol of the Industrial Revolution, is illustrated in this early-nineteenth-century water-color, which shows a miniature train offered as a paid amusement for enthusiasts in London's Euston Square. (Science Museum, London, UK/The Bridgeman Art Library)

The social transformation of the Industrial Revolution both destroyed and created. Referring to the impact of the Industrial Revolution on British society, historian Eric Hobsbawm said: "[I]n its initial stages it destroyed their old ways of living and left them free to discover or make for themselves new ones, if they could and knew how. But it rarely told them how to set about it."[17] For many people, it was an enormously painful, even traumatic process, full of social conflict, insecurity, and false starts as well as new opportunities, an eventually higher standard of living, and greater participation in public life. Scholars, politicians, journalists, and ordinary people have endlessly debated the gains and losses associated with the

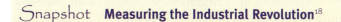

Snapshot   **Measuring the Industrial Revolution**[18]

Railroads are one useful measure of industrial development. This graph illustrates both Britain's head start and the beginning catch-up efforts of other countries.

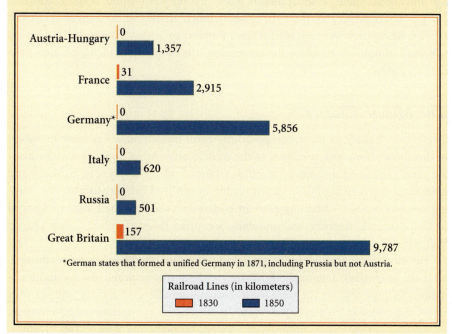

*German states that formed a unified Germany in 1871, including Prussia but not Austria.

Railroad Lines (in kilometers)	
▮ 1830	▮ 1850

Austria-Hungary: 0 / 1,357
France: 31 / 2,915
Germany*: 0 / 5,856
Italy: 0 / 620
Russia: 0 / 501
Great Britain: 157 / 9,787

Industrial Revolution. Amid the controversy, however, one thing is clear: not everyone was affected in the same way. (See Visual Sources: Art and the Industrial Revolution, pp. 867–74, for both celebratory and critical perspectives on industrialization.)

The British Aristocracy

Individual landowning aristocrats, long the dominant class in Britain, suffered little in material terms from the Industrial Revolution. In the mid-nineteenth century, a few thousand families still owned more than half of the cultivated land in Britain, most of it leased to tenant farmers, who in turn employed agricultural wage laborers to work it. Rapidly growing population and urbanization sustained a demand for food products grown on that land. For most of the nineteenth century, landowners continued to dominate the British parliament.

As a class, however, the British aristocracy, like large landowners in every industrial society, declined. As urban wealth became more important, landed aristocrats had to make way for the up-and-coming businessmen, manufacturers, and bankers who had been newly enriched by the Industrial Revolution. The aristocracy's declining political clout was demonstrated in the 1840s when high tariffs on foreign agricultural

■ Change
How did the Industrial Revolution transform British society?

imports, designed to protect the interests of British landlords, were finally abolished. By the end of the century, landownership had largely ceased to be the basis of great wealth, and businessmen, rather than aristocrats, led the major political parties. Even so, the titled nobility of dukes, earls, viscounts, and barons retained great social prestige and considerable personal wealth. Many among them found an outlet for their energies and opportunities for status and enrichment in the vast domains of the British Empire, where they went as colonial administrators or settlers. Famously described as a "system of outdoor relief for the aristocracy," the empire provided a cushion for a declining class.

The Middle Classes

■ **Change**

How did Britain's middle classes change during the nineteenth century?

Those who benefited most conspicuously from industrialization were members of that amorphous group known as the middle class. At its upper levels, the middle class contained extremely wealthy factory and mine owners, bankers, and merchants. Such rising businessmen readily assimilated into aristocratic life, buying country houses, obtaining seats in parliament, sending their sons to Oxford or Cambridge University, and gratefully accepting titles of nobility from Queen Victoria.

Far more numerous were the smaller businessmen, doctors, lawyers, engineers, teachers, journalists, scientists, and other professionals required in any industrial society. Such people set the tone for a distinctly middle-class society with its own values and outlooks. Politically they were liberals, favoring constitutional government, private property, free trade, and social reform within limits. Their agitation resulted in the Reform Bill of 1832, which broadened the right to vote to many men of the middle class, but not to middle-class women. Ideas of thrift and hard work, a rigid morality, and cleanliness characterized middle-class culture. The central value of that culture was "respectability," a term that combined notions of social status and virtuous behavior. Nowhere were these values more effectively displayed than in the Scotsman Samuel Smiles's famous book *Self-Help*, published in 1859. Individuals are responsible for their own destiny, Smiles argued. An hour a day devoted to self-improvement "would make an ignorant man wise in a few years." According to Smiles, this enterprising spirit was what distinguished the prosperous middle class from Britain's poor.

The Industrial Middle Class
This late-nineteenth-century painting shows a prosperous French middle-class family, attended by a servant. (Chateau de Versailles/SuperStock, Inc.)

The misery of the poorer classes was "voluntary and self-imposed—the results of idleness, thriftlessness, intemperance, and misconduct."[19]

Women in such middle-class families were increasingly cast as homemakers, wives, and mothers, charged with creating an emotional haven for their men and a refuge from a heartless and cutthroat capitalist world. They were also the moral center of family life and the educators of "respectability" as well as the managers of consumption as "shopping," a new concept in eighteenth-century Britain, became a central activity. An "ideology of domesticity" defined the home and charitable activities as the proper sphere for women, while paid employment and public life beckoned to men. The English poet Alfred, Lord Tennyson, aptly expressed this understanding in his poem "The Princess":

Man for the field and woman for the hearth:
Man for the sword and for the needle she:
Man with the head and woman with the heart:
Man to command and woman to obey.
All else confusion.

Middle-class women played a very different role from women in the peasant farm or the artisan's shop, where wives, though clearly subordinate, worked productively alongside their husbands. By the late nineteenth century, however, some middle-class women began to enter the teaching, clerical, and nursing professions.

As Britain's industrial economy matured, it also gave rise to a sizable lower middle class, which included people employed in the growing service sector as clerks, salespeople, bank tellers, hotel staff, secretaries, telephone operators, police officers, and the like. By the end of the nineteenth century, this growing class represented about 20 percent of Britain's population and provided new employment opportunities for women as well as men. In just twenty years (1881–1901), the number of female secretaries in Britain rose from 7,000 to 90,000. Almost all were single and expected to return to the home after marriage. For both men and women, such employment represented a claim on membership in the larger middle class and a means of distinguishing themselves clearly from a working class tainted by manual labor.

The Laboring Classes

The overwhelming majority of Britain's nineteenth-century population—some 70 percent or more—were, of course, neither aristocrats nor members of the middle classes. They were manual workers in the mines, ports, factories, construction sites, workshops, and farms of an industrializing Britain. Although their conditions varied considerably and changed over time, the laboring classes were the people who suffered most and benefited least from the epic transformations of the Industrial Revolution. Their efforts to accommodate, resist, protest, and change those conditions contributed much to the texture of the first industrial society.

DEATH'S DISPENSARY.

OPEN TO THE POOR, GRATIS, BY PERMISSION OF THE PARISH.

The Urban Poor of Industrial Britain
This 1866 political cartoon shows an impoverished urban family forced to draw its drinking water from a polluted public well, while a figure of Death operates the pump. (The Granger Collection, New York)

The lives of the laboring classes were shaped primarily by the new working conditions of the industrial era. Chief among those conditions was the rapid urbanization of British society. Liverpool's population alone grew from 77,000 to 400,000 in the first half of the nineteenth century. By 1851, a majority of Britain's population lived in towns and cities, an enormous change from the overwhelmingly rural life of almost all previous civilizations. By the end of the century, London was the world's largest city, with more than 6 million inhabitants.

These cities were vastly overcrowded and smoky, with wholly inadequate sanitation, periodic epidemics, endless row houses and warehouses, few public services or open spaces, and inadequate water supplies. This was the environment in which most urban workers lived in the first half of the nineteenth century. Nor was there much personal contact between the rich and the poor of industrial cities. Benjamin Disraeli's novel *Sybil*, published in 1845, described these two ends of the social spectrum as "two nations between whom there is no intercourse and no sympathy; who are ignorant of each other's habits, thoughts and feelings, as if they were dwellers in different zones or inhabitants of different planets."

The industrial factories to which growing numbers of desperate people looked for employment offered a work environment far different from the artisan's shop or the tenant's farm. Long hours, low wages, and child labor were nothing new for the poor, but the routine and monotony of work, dictated by the factory whistle and the needs of machines, imposed novel and highly unwelcome conditions of labor. Also objectionable were the direct and constant supervision and the rules and fines aimed at enforcing work discipline. The ups and downs of a capitalist economy made industrial work insecure as well as onerous. Unlike their middle-class sisters, many girls and young women of the laboring classes worked in mills or as domestic servants in order to supplement meager family incomes, but after marriage they too usually left outside paid employment because a man who could not support his wife was widely considered a failure. Within the home, however, many working-class women continued to earn money by taking in boarders, doing laundry, or sewing clothes.

Social Protest

For workers of the laboring classes, industrial life "was a stony desert, which they had to make habitable by their own efforts."[20] Such efforts took many forms. By 1815, about 1 million workers, mostly artisans, had created a variety of "friendly societies." With dues contributed by members, these working-class self-help groups provided insurance against sickness, a decent funeral, and an opportunity for social life in an otherwise bleak environment. Other skilled artisans, who had been displaced by machine-produced goods and forbidden to organize in legal unions, sometimes wrecked the offending machinery and burned the mills that had taken their jobs. The class consciousness of working people was such that one police informer reported that "most every creature of the lower order both in town and country are on their side."[21]

Others acted within the political arena by joining movements aimed at obtaining the vote for working-class men, a goal that was gradually achieved in the second half of the nineteenth century. When trade unions were legalized in 1824, growing numbers of factory workers joined these associations in their efforts to achieve better wages and working conditions. Initially their strikes, attempts at nationwide organization, and the threat of violence made them fearful indeed to the upper classes. One British newspaper in 1834 described unions as "the most dangerous institutions that were ever permitted to take root, under shelter of law, in any country,"[22] although they later became rather more "respectable" organizations.

Socialist ideas of various kinds gradually spread within the working class, challenging the assumptions of a capitalist society. Robert Owen (1771–1858), a wealthy British cotton textile manufacturer, urged the creation of small industrial communities where workers and their families would be well treated. He established one such community, with a ten-hour workday, spacious housing, decent wages, and education for children, at his mill in New Lanark in Scotland.

Of more lasting significance was the socialism of Karl Marx (1818–1883). German by birth, Marx spent much of his life in England, where he witnessed the brutal conditions of Britain's Industrial Revolution and wrote voluminously about history and economics. His probing analysis led him to the conclusion that industrial capitalism was an inherently unstable system, doomed to collapse in a revolutionary upheaval that would give birth to a classless socialist society, thus ending forever the ancient conflict between rich and poor. (See Document 18.1, pp. 856–59, for Marx's own understanding of industrial-era capitalism.)

In these ideas, the impact of Europe's industrial, political, and scientific revolutions found expression. Industrialization created both the social conditions against which Marx protested so bitterly and the enormous wealth he felt would make socialism possible. The French Revolution, still a living memory in Marx's youth, provided evidence that grand upheavals, giving rise to new societies, had in fact taken place and could do so again. Moreover, Marx regarded himself as a scientist, discovering the laws of social development in much the same fashion as Newton discovered the laws of

■ **Change**
How did Karl Marx understand the Industrial Revolution? In what ways did his ideas have an impact in the industrializing world of the nineteenth century?

motion. His was therefore a "scientific socialism," embedded in these laws of historical change; revolution was a certainty and the socialist future inevitable.

It was a grand, compelling, prophetic, utopian vision of human freedom and community—and it inspired socialist movements of workers and intellectuals amid the grim harshness of Europe's industrialization in the second half of the nineteenth century. Socialists established political parties in most European states and linked them together in international organizations as well. These parties recruited members, contested elections as they gained the right to vote, agitated for reforms, and in some cases plotted revolution. The so-called workers' hymn, the "Internationale," expressed the visionary possibilities of socialism and the threatening challenge it posed to the triumphant capitalism of industrial Europe (see Document 18.4, pp. 863–64).

In the later decades of the nineteenth century, such ideas echoed among more radical trade unionists and some middle-class intellectuals in Britain, and even more so in a rapidly industrializing Germany and elsewhere. By then, however, the British working-class movement was not overtly revolutionary. When a working-class political party, the Labour Party, was established in the 1890s, it advocated a reformist program and a peaceful democratic transition to socialism, largely rejecting the class struggle and revolutionary emphasis of classical Marxism. (See Document 18.2, pp. 859–61, for an argument favoring a democratic rather than a revolutionary path toward socialism.)

Improving material conditions during the second half of the nineteenth century helped to move the working-class movement in Britain and elsewhere away from a revolutionary posture. Marx had expected industrial capitalist societies to polarize into a small wealthy class and a huge and increasingly impoverished proletariat. However, standing between "the captains of industry" and the workers was a sizable middle and lower-middle class, constituting perhaps 30 percent of the population, most of whom were not really wealthy but were immensely proud that they were not manual laborers. Marx had not foreseen the development of this intermediate social group, nor had he imagined that workers could better their standard of living within a capitalist framework. But they did. Wages rose under pressure from unions; cheap imported food improved working-class diets; infant mortality rates fell; and shops and chain stores catering to working-class families multiplied. As English male workers gradually obtained the right to vote, politicians had an incentive to legislate in their favor, by abolishing child labor, regulating factory conditions, and even, in 1911, inaugurating a system of relief for the unemployed. Sanitary reform considerably cleaned up the "filth and stink" of early-nineteenth-century cities, and urban parks made a modest appearance. Contrary to Marx's expectations, capitalist societies demonstrated some capacity for reform.

Further eroding working-class radicalism was a growing sense of nationalism, which bound workers in particular countries to their middle-class employers and compatriots, offsetting to some extent the economic and social antagonism between them. When World War I broke out, the workers of the world, far from uniting against

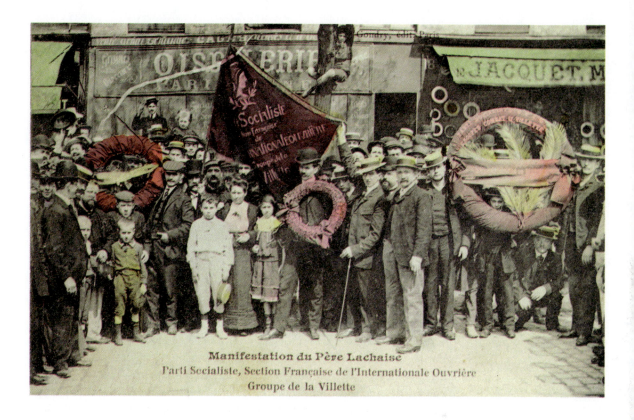

Manifestation du Père Lachaise
Parti Socialiste, Section Française de l'Internationale Ouvrière
Groupe de la Villette

their bourgeois enemies as Marx had urged them, instead set off to slaughter one another in enormous numbers on the battlefields of Europe. National loyalty had trumped class loyalty.

Nonetheless, as the twentieth century dawned, industrial Britain could hardly be described as a stable or contented society. Immense inequalities still separated the classes. Some 40 percent of the working class continued to live in conditions then described as "poverty." A mounting wave of strikes from 1910 to 1913 testified to the intensity of class conflict. The Labour Party was becoming a major force in parliament. Some socialists and some feminists were becoming radicalized. "Wisps of violence hung in the English air," wrote Eric Hobsbawm, "symptoms of a crisis in economy and society, which the [country's] self-confident opulence…could not quite conceal."[23] The world's first industrial society remained dissatisfied and conflicted.

It was also a society in economic decline relative to industrial newcomers such as Germany and the United States. Britain paid a price for its early lead, for its businessmen became committed to machinery that became obsolete as the century progressed. Latecomers invested in more modern equipment and in various ways had surpassed the British by the early twentieth century.

Socialist Protest

Socialism, a response to the injustices and inequalities of industrial capitalism, spread throughout Europe in the nineteenth and early twentieth centuries. Here a group of French socialists in 1908 are demonstrating in memory of an earlier uprising, the Paris commune of 1871. (Demonstration at Père-Lachaise for the commemoration of the Paris Commune, by Socialist party, French Section of the International Workingmen's Association, group of La Villette, 1st May 1908 [colored photo], Gondry, [19th–early 20th century]/ Private Collection/The Bridgeman Art Library)

Variations on a Theme: Comparing Industrialization in the United States and Russia

Not for long was the Industrial Revolution confined to Britain. It soon spread to continental Western Europe, and by the end of the nineteenth century, it was well under way in the United States, Russia, and Japan. The globalization of industrialization had begun. Everywhere it took hold, industrialization bore a range of outcomes broadly similar to those in Britain. New technologies and sources of energy generated vast increases in production and spawned an unprecedented urbanization as well. Class structures changed as aristocrats, artisans, and peasants declined as classes, while the middle classes and a factory working class grew in numbers and social prominence. Middle-class women generally withdrew from paid labor altogether, and their working-class counterparts sought to do so after marriage. Working women usually received lower wages than their male counterparts, had difficulty joining unions, and were subject to charges that they were taking jobs from men. Working-class frustration and anger gave rise to trade unions and socialist movements, injecting a new element of social conflict into industrial societies.

Nevertheless, different histories, cultures, and societies ensured that the Industrial Revolution unfolded variously in the diverse countries in which it became established. Differences in the pace and timing of industrialization, the size and shape of major industries, the role of the state, the political expression of social conflict, and many other factors have made this process rich in comparative possibilities. French industrialization, for example, occurred more slowly and perhaps less disruptively than did that of Britain. Germany focused initially on heavy industry—iron, steel, and coal—rather than on the textile industry with which Britain had begun. Moreover, German industrialization was far more highly concentrated in huge companies called cartels, and it generated a rather more militant and Marxist-oriented labor movement than in Britain.

Nowhere were the variations in the industrializing process more apparent than in those two vast countries that lay on the periphery of Europe. To the west across the Atlantic Ocean was the United States, a young, vigorous, democratic, expanding country, populated largely by people of European descent, along with a substantial number of slaves of African origin. To the east was Russia, with its Eastern Orthodox Christianity, an autocratic tsar, a huge population of serfs, and an empire stretching across all of northern Asia. In the early nineteenth century, the French observer Alexis de Tocqueville famously commented on these two emerging giants:

> The Anglo-American relies upon personal interest to accomplish his ends and gives free scope to the unguided strength and common sense of the people; the Russian centers all the authority of society in a single arm.... Their starting-point is different and their courses are not the same; yet each of them seems marked out by the will of Heaven to sway the destinies of half the globe.

By the early twentieth century, his prediction seemed to be coming true. Industrialization had turned the United States into a major global power and in Russia had spawned an enormous revolutionary upheaval that made that country the first outpost of global communism.

The United States: Industrialization without Socialism

American industrialization began in the textile industry of New England during the 1820s but grew explosively in the half century following the Civil War (1861–1865) (see Map 18.2). The country's huge size, the ready availability of natural resources, its growing domestic market, and its relative political stability combined to make the United States the world's leading industrial power by 1914. At that time, it produced 36 percent of the world's manufactured goods, compared to 16 percent for Germany, 14 percent for Great Britain, and 6 percent for France. Furthermore, U.S. industrialization was closely linked to that of Europe. About one-third of the capital investment

■ **Comparison**

What were the differences between industrialization in the United States and that in Russia?

Map 18.2 The Industrial United States in 1900
By the early twentieth century, manufacturing industries were largely in the Northeast and Midwest, whereas mining operations were more widely scattered across the country.

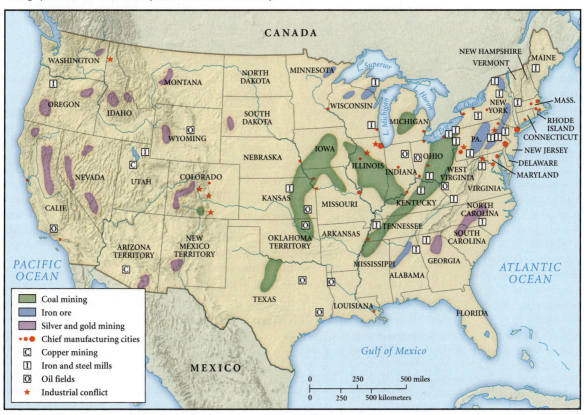

that financed its remarkable growth came from British, French, and German capitalists. But unlike Latin America, which also received much foreign investment, the United States was able to use those funds to generate an independent Industrial Revolution of its own.

As in other second-wave industrializing countries, the U.S. government played an important role, though less directly than in Germany or Japan. Tax breaks, huge grants of public land to the railroad companies, laws enabling the easy formation of corporations, and the absence of much overt regulation of industry all fostered the rise of very large business enterprises. The U.S. Steel Corporation, for example, by 1901 had an annual budget three times the size of the federal government. In this respect, the United States followed the pattern of Germany but differed from that of France and Britain, where family businesses still predominated.

The United States also pioneered techniques of mass production, using interchangeable parts, the assembly line, and "scientific management" to produce for a mass market. The nation's advertising agencies, Sears Roebuck's and Montgomery Ward's mail-order catalogs, and urban department stores generated a middle-class "culture of consumption." When the industrialist Henry Ford in the early twentieth century began producing the Model T at a price that many ordinary people could afford, he famously declared: "I am going to democratize the automobile." More so than in Europe, with its aristocratic traditions, self-made American industrialists of fabulous wealth such as Henry Ford, Andrew Carnegie, and John D. Rockefeller became cultural heroes, widely admired as models of what anyone could achieve with daring and hard work in a land of endless opportunity.

■ **Explanation**
Why did Marxist socialism not take root in the United States?

Nevertheless, well before the first Model T rolled off the assembly line, serious social divisions of a kind common to European industrial societies mounted. Pre-industrial America had boasted of a relative social equality, quite unlike that of Europe, but by the end of the nineteenth century, a widening gap separated the classes. In Carnegie's Homestead steel plant near Pittsburgh, employees worked every day except Christmas and the Fourth of July, often for twelve hours a day. In Manhattan, where millions of European immigrants disembarked, many lived in five- or six-story buildings with four families and two toilets on each floor. In every large city, such conditions prevailed close by the mansions of elite neighborhoods. To some, the contrast was a betrayal of American ideals, while others saw it as a natural outcome of competition and "the survival of the fittest."

As elsewhere, such conditions generated much labor protest, the formation of unions, and strikes, sometimes leading to violence. In 1877, when the eastern railroads announced a 10 percent wage cut for their workers, strikers disrupted rail service across the eastern half of the country, smashed equipment, and rioted. Both state militias and federal troops were called out to put down the movement. In 1892, the entire National Guard of Pennsylvania was sent to suppress a violent strike at the Homestead steel plant near Pittsburgh. Class consciousness and class conflict were intense in the industrial America of the late nineteenth and early twentieth centuries.

Unlike many European countries, however, no major political party emerged in the United States to represent the interests of the working class. Nor did the ideas of socialism, and especially Marxism, appeal to American workers nearly as much as they did in Europe. At its high point, the Socialist Party of America garnered just 6 percent of the vote for its presidential candidate in the 1912 election, whereas socialists at the time held more seats in Germany's parliament than any other party. Even in the depths of the Great Depression of the 1930s, no major socialist movement emerged to champion American workers. How might we explain this distinctive feature of American industrial development?

One answer lies in the relative conservatism of major American union organizations, especially the American Federation of Labor. Its focus on skilled workers excluded the more radical unskilled laborers, and its refusal to align with any party limited its influence in the political arena. Furthermore, the immense religious, ethnic, and racial divisions of American society contrasted sharply with the more homogeneous populations of many European countries. Catholics and Protestants; English, Irish, Germans, Slavs, Jews, and Italians; whites and blacks—such differences undermined the class solidarity of American workers, making it far more difficult to sustain class-oriented political parties and a socialist labor movement. Moreover, the country's remarkable economic growth generated on average a higher standard of living for American workers than their European counterparts experienced. Land was cheaper, and home ownership was more available. Workers with property generally found socialism less attractive than those without. By 1910, a particularly large group of white-collar workers in sales, services, and offices outnumbered factory laborers. Their middle-class aspirations further diluted impulses toward radicalism.

But political challenges to the abuses of capitalist industrialization did arise. Among small farmers in the U.S. South, West, and Midwest, "populists" railed against banks, industrialists, monopolies, the existing money system, and both major political parties, all of which they thought were dominated by the corporate interests of the eastern elites. More successful, especially in the early twentieth century, were the Progressives, who pushed for specific reforms, such as wages-and-hours legislation, better sanitation standards, antitrust laws, and greater governmental intervention in the economy. Socialism, however, came to be defined as fundamentally "un-American" in a country that so valued individualism and so feared "big government." It was a distinctive feature of the American response to industrialization.

Russia: Industrialization and Revolution

As a setting for the Industrial Revolution, it would be hard to imagine two more different environments than the United States and Russia. If the United States was the Western world's most exuberant democracy in the nineteenth century, Russia remained the sole outpost of absolute monarchy, in which the state exercised far greater control over individuals and society than anywhere in the Western world.

Russian Serfdom
This nineteenth-century cartoon by the French artist Gustave Doré shows Russian noblemen gambling with tied bundles of stiff serfs. Serfdom was not finally abolished in Russia until 1861. (The Granger Collection, New York)

At the beginning of the twentieth century, Russia still had no national parliament, no legal political parties, and no nationwide elections. The tsar, answerable to God alone, ruled unchecked. Furthermore, Russian society was dominated by a titled nobility of various ranks, whose upper levels included great landowners, who furnished the state with military officers and leading government officials. Until 1861, most Russians were peasant serfs, bound to the estates of their masters, subject to sale, greatly exploited, and largely at the mercy of their owners. In Russia at least, serfdom approximated slavery. A vast cultural gulf separated these two classes. Many nobles were highly Westernized, some speaking French better than Russian, whereas their serfs were steeped in a backwoods Orthodox Christianity that incorporated pre-Christian spirits, spells, curses, and magic.

A further difference between Russia and the United States lay in the source of social and economic change. In the United States, such change bubbled up from society as free farmers, workers, and businessmen sought new opportunities and operated in a political system that gave them varying degrees of expression. In autocratic Russia, change was far more often initiated by the state itself, in its continuing efforts to catch up with the more powerful and innovative states of Europe. This kind of "transformation from above" found an early expression in the reign of Peter the Great (reigned 1689–1725). His massive efforts included vast administrative changes, the enlargement and modernization of Russian military forces, a new educational system for the sons of noblemen, and dozens of manufacturing enterprises. Russian nobles were instructed to dress in European styles and to shave their sacred and much-revered beards. The newly created capital city of St. Petersburg was to be Russia's "window on the West." One of Peter's successors, Catherine the Great (reigned 1762–1796), followed up with further efforts to Europeanize Russian cultural and intellectual life, viewing herself as heir to the European Enlightenment.

Such state-directed change continued in the nineteenth century with the freeing of the serfs in 1861, an action stimulated by military defeat at the hands of British and French forces in the Crimean War (1854–1856). To many thoughtful Russians, serfdom seemed incompatible with modern civilization and held back the country's overall development, as did its economic and industrial backwardness. Thus, beginning in the 1860s, Russia began a program of industrial development, which was more heavily directed by the state than was the case in Western Europe or the United States.

By the 1890s, Russia's Industrial Revolution was launched and growing rapidly. It focused particularly on railroads and heavy industry and was fueled by a substantial amount of foreign investment. By 1900, Russia ranked fourth in the world in

■ **Change**
What factors contributed to the making of a revolutionary situation in Russia by the beginning of the twentieth century?

steel production and had major industries in coal, textiles, and oil. Its industrial enterprises, still modest in comparison to those of Europe, were concentrated in a few major cities—Moscow, St. Petersburg, and Kiev, for example—and took place in factories far larger than in most of Western Europe.

All of this contributed to the explosive social outcomes of Russian industrialization. A growing middle class of businessmen and professionals increasingly took shape. As modern and educated people, many in the middle class objected strongly to the deep conservatism of tsarist Russia and sought a greater role in political life, but they were also dependent on the state for contracts and jobs and for suppressing the growing radicalism of the workers, which they greatly feared. Although factory workers constituted only about 5 percent of Russia's total population, they quickly developed an unusually radical class consciousness, based on harsh conditions and the absence of any legal outlet for their grievances. Until 1897, a thirteen-hour working day was common. Ruthless discipline and overt disrespect from supervisors created resentment, while life in large and unsanitary barracks added to workers' sense of injustice. In the absence of legal unions or political parties, these grievances often erupted in the form of large-scale strikes.

In these conditions, a small but growing number of educated Russians found in Marxist socialism a way of understanding the changes they witnessed daily and hope for the future in a revolutionary upheaval of workers. In 1898, they created an illegal Russian Social-Democratic Labor Party and quickly became involved in workers' education, union organizing, and, eventually, revolutionary action. By the early twentieth century, the strains of rapid change and the state's continued intransigence had reached the bursting point, and in 1905, following its defeat in a naval war with Japan, Russia erupted in spontaneous insurrection. Workers in Moscow and St. Petersburg went on strike and created their own representative councils, called soviets. Peasant uprisings, student demonstrations, revolts of non-Russian nationalities, and mutinies in the military all contributed to the upheaval. Recently formed political parties, representing intellectuals of various persuasions, came out into the open.

The 1905 revolution, though brutally suppressed, forced the tsar's regime to make more substantial reforms than it had ever contemplated. It granted a constitution, legalized both trade unions and political parties, and permitted the election of a national assembly, called the Duma. Censorship was eased, and plans were under way for universal primary education. Industrial development likewise continued at a rapid rate, so that by 1914 Russia stood fifth in the world in terms of overall output. But in the first half of that year, some 1,250,000 workers, representing about 40 percent of the entire industrial workforce, went out on strike.

Thus the tsar's limited political reforms, which had been granted with great reluctance and were often reversed in practice, failed to tame working-class radicalism or to bring social stability to Russia. In 1906–1907, when a newly elected and radically inclined Duma refused to cooperate with the

The 1905 Revolution in Russia

Peasant unrest and land seizures

■ Workers' soviets

◆ Army mutinies

⚓ Naval mutinies

▲ Major strikes and armed workers' uprisings

tsar's new political system, Tsar Nicholas II twice dissolved that elected body and finally changed the electoral laws to favor the landed nobility. Consequently, in Russian political life, the people generally, and even the middle class, had only a limited voice. The representatives of even the privileged classes had become so alienated by the government's intransigence that many felt revolution was inevitable. Various revolutionary groups, many of them socialist, published pamphlets and newspapers, organized trade unions, and spread their messages among workers and peasants. Particularly in the cities, these revolutionary parties had an impact. They provided a language through which workers could express their grievances; they created links among workers from different factories; and they furnished leaders who were able to act when the revolutionary moment arrived.

World War I provided that moment. The enormous hardships of that war, coupled with the immense social tensions of industrialization within a still autocratic political system, sparked the Russian Revolution of 1917 (see Chapter 22). That massive upheaval quickly brought to power the most radical of the socialist groups operating in the country—the Bolsheviks, led by the charismatic Vladimir Ilyich Ulyanov, better known as Lenin. (See Document 18.5, pp. 864–65, for Lenin's view of revolution.) Only in Russia was industrialization associated with violent social revolution, and this was the most distinctive feature of Russia's modern historical development. And only in Russia was a socialist political party, inspired by the teachings of Karl Marx, able to seize power, thus launching the modern world's first socialist society, with enormous implications for the twentieth century.

The Industrial Revolution and Latin America in the Nineteenth Century

Beyond the world of Europe and North America, only Japan underwent a major industrial transformation during the nineteenth century, part of that country's overall response to the threat of European aggression. (See pp. 901–02 for a more detailed examination of Japan's industrialization.) Elsewhere—in colonial India, Egypt, the Ottoman Empire, China, and Latin America—very modest experiments in modern industry were undertaken, but nowhere did they drive the kind of major social transformation that had taken place in Britain, Europe, North America, and Japan. However, even in societies that did not experience their own Industrial Revolution, the profound impact of European and North American industrialization was hard to avoid. Such was the case in Latin America during the nineteenth century.

After Independence in Latin America

The struggle for independence in Latin America had lasted far longer and proved far more destructive than in North America. Decimated populations, diminished herds of livestock, flooded or closed silver mines, abandoned farms, shrinking international trade and investment capital, and empty national treasuries—these were

Snapshot   **The Industrial Revolution and the Global Divide**[24]

During the nineteenth century, the Industrial Revolution generated an enormous and unprecedented economic division in the world, as measured by the share of manufacturing output. What patterns can you see in this table?

SHARE OF TOTAL WORLD MANUFACTURING OUTPUT (PERCENT)

	1750	1800	1860	1880	1900
Europe as a Whole	23.2	28.1	53.2	61.3	62.0
UNITED KINGDOM	1.9	4.3	19.9	22.9	18.5
FRANCE	4.0	4.2	7.9	7.8	6.8
GERMANY	2.9	3.5	4.9	8.5	13.2
RUSSIA	5.0	5.6	7.0	7.6	8.8
United States	0.1	0.8	7.2	14.7	23.6
Japan	3.8	3.5	2.6	2.4	2.4
The Rest of the World	73.0	67.7	36.6	20.9	11.0
CHINA	32.8	33.3	19.7	12.5	6.2
SOUTH ASIA (INDIA/PAKISTAN)	24.5	19.7	8.6	2.8	1.7

among the conditions under which Latin American countries greeted independence. Furthermore, the four major administrative units (vice-royalties) of Spanish America ultimately dissolved into eighteen separate countries, and regional revolts wracked Brazil in the early decades of its independent life. A number of international wars in the postindependence century likewise shook these new nations. Peru and Bolivia briefly united and then broke apart in a bitter conflict (1836–1839); Mexico lost huge territories to the United States (1846–1848); and an alliance of Argentina, Brazil, and Uruguay went to war with Paraguay (1864–1870) in a conflict that devastated Paraguay's small population.

Within these new countries, political life was turbulent and unstable. Conservatives favored centralized authority and sought to maintain the social status quo of the colonial era in alliance with the Catholic Church, which at independence owned perhaps half of all productive land. Their often bitter opponents were liberals, who attacked the Church in the name of Enlightenment values, sought at least modest social reforms, and preferred federalism. In many countries, conflicts between these factions, often violent, enabled military strongmen known as *caudillos* to achieve power as defenders of order and property, although they too succeeded one another with great frequency. One of them, Antonio López de Santa Anna of Mexico, was president of his country at least nine separate times between 1833 and 1855. Constitutions too replaced one another with bewildering speed. Bolivia had ten constitutions during the nineteenth century, while Ecuador and Peru each had eight.

Social life did not change fundamentally in the aftermath of independence. Slavery, it is true, was abolished in most of Latin America by midcentury, although it persisted in both Brazil and Cuba until the late 1880s. Most of the legal distinctions among various racial categories also disappeared, and all free people were considered, at least officially, equal citizens. Nevertheless, productive economic resources such as businesses, ranches, and plantations remained overwhelmingly in the hands of creole whites, who were culturally oriented toward Europe. The military provided an avenue of mobility for a few skilled and ambitious mestizo men, some of whom subsequently became caudillos. Other mixed-race people found a place in a small middle class as teachers, shopkeepers, or artisans. The vast majority—blacks, Indians, and many mixed-race people—remained impoverished, working small subsistence farms or laboring in the mines or on the *haciendas* (plantations) of the well-to-do. Only rarely did the poor and dispossessed actively rebel against their social betters. One such case was the Caste War of Yucatán (1847–1901), a prolonged struggle of the Maya people of Mexico, aimed at cleansing their land of European and mestizo intruders.

Facing the World Economy

■ Connection
In what ways and with what impact was Latin America linked to the global economy of the nineteenth century?

During the second half of the nineteenth century, a measure of political consolidation took hold in Latin America, and countries such as Mexico, Peru, and Argentina entered periods of greater stability. At the same time, Latin America as a whole became more closely integrated into a world economy driven by the industrialization of Western Europe and North America. The new technology of the steamship cut the sailing time between Britain and Argentina almost in half, while the underwater telegraph instantly brought the latest news and fashions of Europe to Latin America.

The most significant economic outcome of this growing integration was a rapid growth of Latin American exports to the industrializing countries, which now needed the food products, raw materials, and markets of these new nations. Latin American landowners, businessmen, and governments proved eager to supply those needs, and in the sixty years or so after 1850, an export boom increased the value of Latin American goods sold abroad by a factor of ten.

Mexico continued to produce large amounts of silver, supplying more than half the world's new supply until 1860. Now added to the list of raw materials flowing out of Latin America were copper from Chile, a metal that the growing electrical industry required; tin from Bolivia, which met the mounting demand for tin cans; and nitrates from Chile and guano (bird droppings) from Peru, both of which were used for fertilizer. Wild rubber from the Amazon rain forest was in great demand for bicycle and automobile tires, as was sisal from Mexico, used to make binder twine for the proliferating mechanical harvesters of North America. Bananas from Central America, beef from Argentina, cacao from Ecuador, coffee from Brazil and Guatemala, and sugar from Cuba also found eager markets in the rapidly growing and increasingly prosperous world of industrializing countries. In return for these primary products, Latin Americans imported the textiles, machinery, tools, weapons, and luxury goods of Europe and the United States (see Map 18.3).

Accompanying this burgeoning commerce was large-scale investment of European capital in Latin America, $10 billion alone between 1870 and 1919. Most of this capital came from Great Britain, which invested more in Argentina in the late nineteenth century than in its colony of India, although France, Germany, Italy, and the United States also contributed to this substantial financial transfer. By 1910, U.S. business interests controlled 40 percent of Mexican property and produced half of its oil. Much of this capital was used to build railroads, largely to funnel Latin American exports to the coast, where they were shipped to overseas markets. Mexico had only 390 miles of railroad in 1876; it had 15,000 miles in 1910. By 1915, Argentina, with 22,000 miles of railroad, had more track per person than the United States.

Becoming like Europe?

To the economic elites of Latin America, intent on making their countries resemble Europe or the United States, all of this was progress. In some respects, they were surely right. Economies were growing and producing more than ever before. The population also was burgeoning; it increased from about 30 million in 1850 to more than 77 million in 1912 as public health measures (such as safe drinking water, inoculations, sewers, and campaigns to eliminate mosquitoes that carried yellow fever) brought down death rates.

■ **Comparison**
Did Latin America follow or diverge from the historical path of Europe during the nineteenth century?

Urbanization also proceeded rapidly. By the early twentieth century, wrote one scholar, "Latin American cities lost their colonial cobblestones, white-plastered walls, and red-tiled roofs. They became modern metropolises, comparable to urban giants anywhere. Streetcars swayed, telephones jangled, and silent movies flickered from Montevideo and Santiago to Mexico City and Havana."[25] Buenos Aires, Argentina's metropolitan center, boasted 750,000 people in 1900 and billed itself the "Paris of South America." There the educated elite, just like the English, drank tea in the afternoon, while discussing European literature, philosophy, and fashion, usually in French.

To become more like Europe, Latin America sought to attract more Europeans. Because civilization, progress, and modernity apparently derived from Europe, many Latin American countries actively sought to increase their European populations by deliberately recruiting impoverished people with the promise, mostly unfulfilled, of a new and prosperous life in the New World. Argentina received the largest wave of European immigrants (some 2.5 million between 1870 and 1915), mostly from Spain and Italy. Brazil and Uruguay likewise attracted substantial numbers of European newcomers.

Only a quite modest segment of Latin American society saw any great benefits from the export boom and all that followed from it. Upper-class landowners certainly gained as exports flourished and their property values soared. Middle-class urban dwellers—merchants, office workers, lawyers, and other professionals—also

U.S. Interventions

→ Puerto Rico, 1898–on
→ Panama, 1903
→ Cuba, 1898–1902, 1905–09, 1917–21
→ Haiti, 1915–34
→ Mexico, 1914, 1916–17
→ Nicaragua, 1909, 1912–25, 1927–32
→ Dominican Republic, 1916–24

MEXICO *$1329*

CUBA *$471*

$11 *$16* *$44*

$99 *$42*
$19 *$12*
$61 *$28*

VENEZUELA *$161*

COLOMBIA *$77*

ECUADOR *$41*

PERU *$197*

BRAZIL *$1913*

BOLIVIA *$59*

PARAGUAY *$27*

ARGENTINA *$4001*

CHILE *$668*

$475 URUGUAY

Bananas   Nitrate
Cacao   Oil
Cattle   Rubber
Coffee   Sheep
Copper and tin   Silver
Cotton   Sugar
Guano   Tobacco
Sisal   Wheat

$161   Foreign investment (in millions of U.S. dollars around 1914)

→ European immigration

Map 18.3   Latin America and the World, 1825–1935
During the nineteenth and early twentieth centuries, Latin American countries interacted with the industrializing world via investment, trade, immigration, and military intervention from the United States.

grew in numbers and prosperity as their skills proved valuable in a modernizing society. As a percentage of the total population, however, these were narrow elites. In Mexico in the mid-1890s, for example, the landowning upper class made up no more than 1 percent and the middle classes perhaps 8 percent of the population. Everyone else was lower-class, and most of them were impoverished.[26]

A new but quite small segment of this vast lower class emerged among urban workers who labored in the railroads, ports, mines, and a few factories. They organized themselves initially in a variety of mutual aid societies, but by the end of the nineteenth century, they were creating unions and engaging in strikes. To authoritarian governments interested in stability and progress, such activity was highly provocative and threatening, and they acted harshly to crush or repress unions and strikes. In 1906, the Mexican dictator Porfirio Díaz invited the Arizona Rangers to suppress a strike at Cananea near the U.S. border, an action that resulted in dozens of deaths. The following year in the Chilean city of Iquique, more than 1,000 men, women, and children were slaughtered by police when nitrate miners protested their wages and working conditions.

The vast majority of the lower class lived in rural areas, where they suffered the most and benefited the least from the export boom. Government attacks on communal landholding and peasant indebtedness to wealthy landowners combined to push many farmers off their land or into remote and poor areas where they could barely make a living. Many wound up as dependent laborers or peons on the haciendas of the wealthy, where their wages were often too meager to support a family. Thus women and children, who had earlier remained at home to tend the family plot, were required to join their menfolk as field laborers. Many immigrant Italian farmworkers in Argentina and Brazil were unable to acquire their own farms, as they had expected, and so drifted into the growing cities or returned to Italy.

Although local protests and violence were frequent, only in Mexico did these vast inequalities erupt into a nationwide revolution. There, in the early twentieth century, middle-class reformers joined with workers and peasants to overthrow the long dictatorship of Porfirio Díaz (1876–1911). What followed was a decade of bloody conflict (1910–1920) that cost Mexico some 1 million lives, or roughly 10 percent of the population. Huge peasant armies under charismatic leaders such as Pancho Villa and Emiliano Zapata helped oust Díaz. Intent on seizing land and redistributing it to the peasants, they then went on to attack many of Mexico's large haciendas. But unlike the later Russian and Chinese revolutions, in which the most radical elements seized state power, Villa and Zapata proved unable to do so, in part because they were hobbled by factionalism and focused on local or regional issues. Despite this limitation and its own internal conflicts, the Mexican Revolution transformed the country. When the dust settled, Mexico had a new constitution (1917) that proclaimed universal suffrage; provided for the redistribution of land; stripped the Catholic Church of any role in public education and forbade it to own land; announced unheard-of rights for workers, such as a minimum wage and an eight-hour workday;

The Mexican Revolution
Women were active participants in the Mexican
Revolution. They prepared
food, nursed the wounded,
washed clothes, and at
times served as soldiers on
the battlefield, as illustrated
in this cover image from a
French magazine in 1913.
(© Archivo Iconografico,
S.A./Corbis)

and placed restrictions on foreign ownership of property. Much of Mexico's history
in the twentieth century involved working
out the implications of these nationalist and
reformist changes. The revolution's direct
influence, however, was largely limited to
Mexico itself, without the wider international impact of the Russian and Chinese
upheavals.

Perhaps the most significant outcome of
the export boom lay in what did *not* happen, for nowhere in Latin America did it
jump-start a thorough Industrial Revolution, despite a few factories that processed
foods or manufactured textiles, clothing,
and building materials. The reasons are
many. A social structure that relegated some
90 percent of its population to an impoverished lower class generated only a very small
market for manufactured goods. Moreover,
economically powerful groups such as
landowners and cattlemen benefited greatly
from exporting agricultural products and
had little incentive to invest in manufacturing. Domestic manufacturing enterprises
could only have competed with cheaper and higher-quality foreign goods if they
had been protected for a time by high tariffs. But Latin American political leaders had
thoroughly embraced the popular European doctrine of prosperity through free
trade, and many governments depended on taxing imports to fill their treasuries.

Instead of its own Industrial Revolution, Latin Americans developed a form of
economic growth that was largely financed by capital from abroad and dependent on
European and North American prosperity and decisions. Brazil experienced this kind
of dependence when its booming rubber industry suddenly collapsed in 1910–1911,
after seeds from the wild rubber tree had been illegally exported to Britain and were
used to start competing and cheaper rubber plantations in Malaysia.

Later critics saw this "dependent development" as a new form of colonialism,
expressed in the power exercised by foreign investors. The influence of the U.S.-
owned United Fruit Company in Central America was a case in point. Allied with
large landowners and compliant politicians, the company pressured the governments of these "banana republics" to maintain conditions favorable to U.S. business.
This indirect or behind-the-scenes imperialism was supplemented by repeated U.S.
military intervention in support of American corporate interests in Cuba, Haiti, the
Dominican Republic, Nicaragua, and Mexico. The United States also controlled

the Panama Canal and acquired Puerto Rico as a territory in the aftermath of the Spanish-American War (see Map 18.3, p. 850).

Thus, despite its domination by people of European descent and its close ties to the industrializing countries of the Atlantic world, Latin America's historical trajectory in the nineteenth century diverged considerably from that of Europe and North America.

Reflections: History and Horse Races

Historians and students of history seem endlessly fascinated by "firsts"—the first breakthrough to agriculture, the first civilization, the first domestication of horses, the first use of gunpowder, the first printing press, and so on. Each of these firsts presents a problem of explanation: why did it occur in some particular time and place rather than somewhere else or at some other time? Such questions have assumed historical significance both because "first achievements" represent something new in the human journey and because many of them conveyed unusual power, wealth, status, or influence on their creators.

Nonetheless, the focus on firsts can be misleading as well. Those who accomplished something first may see themselves as generally superior to those who embraced that innovation later. Historians too can sometimes adopt a winners-and-losers mentality, inviting a view of history as a horse race toward some finish line of accomplishment. Most first achievements in history, however, were not the result of intentional efforts but rather were the unexpected outcome of converging circumstances.

The Industrial Revolution is a case in point. Understanding the European beginnings of this immense breakthrough is certainly justified by its pervasive global consequences and its global spread over the past several centuries. In terms of our ability to dominate the natural environment and to extract wealth from it, the Industrial Revolution marks a decisive turning point in human history. But Europeans' attempts to explain their Industrial Revolution have at times stated or implied their own unique genius. In the nineteenth century, many Europeans saw their technological mastery as a sure sign of their cultural and racial superiority as they came to use "machines as the measure of men."[27] In attempting to answer the "why Europe?" question, historians too have sometimes sought the answer in some distinct or even superior feature of European civilization.

In emphasizing the unexpectedness of the first Industrial Revolution, and the global context within which it occurred, world historians have attempted to avoid a "history as horse race" syndrome. Clearly the first industrial breakthrough in Britain was not a self-conscious effort to win a race; it was the surprising outcome of countless decisions by many people to further their own interests. Subsequently, however, other societies and their governments quite deliberately tried to catch up, seeking the wealth and power that the Industrial Revolution promised.

The rapid spread of industrialization across the planet, though highly uneven, promises to diminish the importance of the "why Europe?" issue. Just as no one views agriculture as a Middle Eastern phenomenon, even though it occurred first in that region, it seems likely that industrialization will be seen increasingly as a global process rather than one uniquely associated with Europe. If industrial society proves to be a sustainable future for humankind—and this is presently an open question— historians of the future may well be more interested in the pattern of its global spread and in efforts to cope with its social and environmental consequences than with its origins in Western Europe.

Second Thoughts

What's the Significance?

To assess your mastery of the material in this chapter, visit the **Student Center** at bedfordstmartins.com/strayer.

steam engine	Karl Marx	Russian Revolution of 1905
Indian cotton textiles	Labour Party	*caudillos*
British Royal Society	proletariat	Latin American export boom
middle-class values	socialism in the United States	Mexican Revolution
lower middle class	Progressives	dependent development

Big Picture Questions

1. What was revolutionary about the Industrial Revolution?
2. What was common to the process of industrialization everywhere, and in what ways did that process vary from place to place?
3. What did humankind gain from the Industrial Revolution, and what did it lose?
4. In what ways might the Industrial Revolution be understood as a global rather than simply a European phenomenon?

Next Steps: For Further Study

For Web sites and additional documents related to this chapter, see **Make History** at bedfordstmartins.com/strayer.

John Charles Chasteen, *Born in Blood and Fire* (2006). A lively and well-written account of Latin America's turbulent history since the sixteenth century.

Jack Gladstone, *Why Europe? The Rise of the West in World History, 1500–1850* (2009). An original synthesis of recent research provided by a leading world historian.

David S. Landes, *The Wealth and Poverty of Nations* (1998). An argument that culture largely shapes the possibilities for industrialization and economic growth.

Robert B. Marks, *The Origins of the Modern World* (2007). An effective summary of new thinking about the origins of European industrialization.

Peter Stearns, *The Industrial Revolution in World History* (1998). A global and comparative perspective on the Industrial Revolution.

Peter Waldron, *The End of Imperial Russia, 1855–1917* (1997). A brief account of Russian history during its early industrialization.

Bridging World History, Units 18 and 19, http://www.learner.org/channel/courses/worldhistory. An innovative world history Web site that provides pictures, video, and text dealing with "Rethinking the Rise of the West" and "Global Industrialization."

Documents

Considering the Evidence:
Varieties of European Marxism

A mong the ideologies and social movements that grew out of Europe's Industrial Revolution, none was more important than socialism. When it emerged in the nineteenth century, the word "socialism" referred to public or state ownership and control of the means of production and distribution (land, railroads, and factories, for example). Adherents hoped to achieve far greater equality and cooperation than was possible under the competitive and cutthroat capitalism of an industrializing Europe. Clearly the most important socialist ideas derived from the writings of Karl Marx. Known widely as Marxism, those ideas spawned a variety of interpretations, applications, and debates. For many people, they also served as a way of understanding the world perhaps akin to an alternative religion, or an alternative to religion.

The historical significance of Marxist socialism was immense. First, it offered a devastating critique of the industrializing process as it unfolded during the nineteenth century—its inequalities, its instability, its materialism, its exploitation of workers. For followers of Marx, however, that critique was thoroughly modern, embracing the new science, technology, and means of production that the Industrial Revolution had generated, while deploring the social outcomes of that process and the capitalist economic system in which it took place. Second, socialists offered an alternative model for industrializing societies, imagining a future that would more fully realize the promise of modern industry and more equally distribute its benefits. Third, Marxist thinking gave a sharp edge to the social conflicts that characterized industrializing Europe. Those conflicts featured two classes, both of which grew substantially during the nineteenth century (see pp. 833–36). One was the wealthy industrial business class, the bourgeoisie, those who owned and managed the mines, factories, and docks of an industrializing Europe. The other involved the proletariat, the workers in those enterprises—often impoverished, exploited, and living in squalid conditions. Finally, nineteenth-century Marxism provided the foundation for twentieth-century world communism as it took shape in Russia, China, Vietnam, Cuba, and elsewhere.

By the end of the nineteenth century, socialism had become a major element of European political and intellectual life, and it enjoyed a modest presence in the United States and Japan and among a handful of intellectuals elsewhere. Its spread to the rest of the world would have to await developments in the twentieth century. The documents that follow illustrate some of the ways that Marxist socialism was expressed and contested within a nineteenth-century European context.

Document 18.1

Socialism According to Marx

The early currents of socialist thinking took shape during the first quarter of the nineteenth century in the minds of various thinkers—the Englishman Robert Owen and the Frenchman Charles Fourier, for example, both of whom were appalled by the social divisions that industrial society generated. As an alternative they proposed small-scale, voluntary, and cooperative communities, and their followers actually established a number of such experimental groups in Europe and the United States. But the most significant expression of modern socialism took shape in the fertile mind of the brilliant German intellectual Karl Marx (1818–1883). His life coincided with perhaps the harshest phase of capitalist industrialization in Europe. At that time an encompassing market economy was rudely shattering older institutions and traditions, but the benefits of this new and highly productive system were not yet widely shared (see pp. 835–36). But in this brutal process, Marx discerned the inevitable approach of a new world. Document 18.1 presents excerpts from the most famous of Marx's writings, the *Communist Manifesto*, first published in 1848. In this effort and throughout much of his life, Marx was assisted by another German thinker, Friedrich Engels (1820–1895), the son of a successful textile manufacturer. Engels became radicalized as he witnessed the devastating social results of capitalist industrialization.

Marx and Engels's *Manifesto* begins with a summary description of the historical process. Much of the document then analyzes what the authors call the "bourgeoisie" or the "bourgeois epoch," terms that refer to the age of industrial capitalism.

- How do Marx and Engels understand the motor of change in human history? How do they view the role of class?

- What are Marx and Engels's criticisms of the existing social system? What do they see as its major achievements?

- Why do Marx and Engels believe that the capitalist system is doomed?

- How does the industrial proletariat differ from the lower class of the preindustrial era? What role do Marx and Engels foresee for the proletariat?

- Which of Marx and Engels's descriptions and predictions ring true even now? In what respects was their analysis disproved by later developments?

■ How do Marx and Engels describe the socialist society that will follow the collapse of the capitalist system? Why do they believe that only a revolution, "the forcible overthrow of all existing social conditions," will enable the creation of a socialist society?

KARL MARX AND FRIEDRICH ENGELS
The Communist Manifesto
1848

The history of all hitherto existing society is the history of class struggles. Freeman and slave, patrician and plebeian, lord and serf, guild-master and journeyman, in a word, oppressor and oppressed, stood in constant opposition to one another, carried on an uninterrupted, now hidden, now open fight, a fight that each time ended, either in a revolutionary reconstitution of society at large, or in the common ruin of the contending classes....

Our epoch, the epoch of the bourgeoisie, possesses, however, this distinct feature: it has simplified class antagonisms. Society as a whole is more and more splitting up into two great hostile camps, into two great classes directly facing each other—bourgeoisie and proletariat....

Modern industry has established the world market, for which the discovery of America paved the way. This market has given an immense development to commerce, to navigation, to communication by land....

[T]he bourgeoisie has at last, since the establishment of Modern Industry and of the world market, conquered for itself, in the modern representative state, exclusive political sway. The executive of the modern state is but a committee for managing the common affairs of the whole bourgeoisie.

The bourgeoisie, historically, has played a most revolutionary part.

The bourgeoisie, wherever it has got the upper hand, has put an end to all feudal, patriarchal, idyllic relations. It has pitilessly torn asunder the motley feudal ties that bound man to his "natural superiors," and has left no other nexus between people than naked self-interest, than callous "cash payment." It has drowned out the most heavenly ecstasies of religious fervor, of chivalrous enthusiasm, of philistine sentimentalism, in the icy water of egotistical calculation. It has resolved personal worth into exchange value, and in place of the numberless indefeasible chartered freedoms, has set up that single, unconscionable freedom—Free Trade. In one word, for exploitation, veiled by religious and political illusions, it has substituted naked, shameless, direct, brutal exploitation.

The bourgeoisie has stripped of its halo every occupation hitherto honored and looked up to with reverent awe. It has converted the physician, the lawyer, the priest, the poet, the man of science, into its paid wage laborers.

The bourgeoisie has torn away from the family its sentimental veil, and has reduced the family relation into a mere money relation....

It has been the first to show what man's activity can bring about. It has accomplished wonders far surpassing Egyptian pyramids, Roman aqueducts, and Gothic cathedrals....

The need of a constantly expanding market for its products chases the bourgeoisie over the entire surface of the globe. It must nestle everywhere, settle everywhere, establish connections everywhere....

All old-established national industries have been destroyed or are daily being destroyed. They are dislodged by new industries, whose introduction becomes a life and death question for all civilized nations, by industries that no longer work up indigenous raw material, but raw material drawn from the

Source: John E. Toews, ed., *The Communist Manifesto by Karl Marx and Frederick Engels with Related Documents* (Boston: Bedford/St. Martin's, 1999), 63–96.

remotest zones; industries whose products are consumed, not only at home, but in every quarter of the globe. In place of the old wants, satisfied by the production of the country, we find new wants, requiring for their satisfaction the products of distant lands and climes. In place of the old local and national seclusion and self-sufficiency, we have intercourse in every direction, universal interdependence of nations....

The bourgeoisie, by the rapid improvement of all instruments of production, by the immensely facilitated means of communication, draws all, even the most barbarian, nations into civilization. The cheap prices of commodities are the heavy artillery with which it forces the barbarians' intensely obstinate hatred of foreigners to capitulate. It compels all nations, on pain of extinction, to adopt the bourgeois mode of production; it compels them to introduce what it calls civilization into their midst, i.e., to become bourgeois themselves. In one word, it creates a world after its own image.

The bourgeoisie has subjected the country to the rule of the towns. It has created enormous cities, has greatly increased the urban population as compared with the rural, and has thus rescued a considerable part of the population from the idiocy of rural life. Just as it has made the country dependent on the towns, so it has made barbarian and semi-barbarian countries dependent on the civilized ones, nations of peasants on nations of bourgeois, the East on the West....

The bourgeoisie, during its rule of scarce one hundred years, has created more massive and more colossal productive forces than have all preceding generations together. Subjection of nature's forces to man, machinery, application of chemistry to industry and agriculture, steam navigation, railways, electric telegraphs, clearing of whole continents for cultivation, canalization or rivers, whole populations conjured out of the ground—what earlier century had even a presentiment that such productive forces slumbered in the lap of social labor?...

It is enough to mention the commercial crises that, by their periodical return, put the existence of the entire bourgeois society on its trial, each time more threateningly.... In these crises, there breaks out an epidemic that, in all earlier epochs, would have seemed an absurdity—the epidemic of overproduction....

But not only has the bourgeoisie forged the weapons that bring death to itself; it has also called into existence the men who are to wield those weapons—the modern working class—the proletarians....

These laborers, who must sell themselves piecemeal, are a commodity, like every other article of commerce, and are consequently exposed to all the vicissitudes of competition, to all the fluctuations of the market.

Owing to the extensive use of machinery, and to the division of labor, the work of the proletarians has lost all individual character, and, consequently, all charm for the workman. He becomes an appendage of the machine, and it is only the most simple, most monotonous, and most easily acquired knack, that is required of him....

Masses of laborers, crowded into the factory, are organized like soldiers. As privates of the industrial army, they are placed under the command of a perfect hierarchy of officers and sergeants. Not only are they slaves of the bourgeois class, and of the bourgeois state; they are daily and hourly enslaved by the machine, by the overlooker, and, above all, by the individual bourgeois manufacturer himself....

The lower strata of the middle class—the small tradespeople, shopkeepers, and retired tradesmen generally, the handicraftsmen and peasants—all these sink gradually into the proletariat....Thus, the proletariat is recruited from all classes of the population....

This organization of the proletarians into a class, and, consequently, into a political party, is continually being upset again by the competition between the workers themselves. But it ever rises up again, stronger, firmer, mightier....

Finally, in times when the class struggle nears the decisive hour, ... a small section of the ruling class cuts itself adrift, and joins the revolutionary class, the class that holds the future in its hands....What the bourgeoisie therefore produces, above all, are its own grave-diggers. Its fall and the victory of the proletariat are equally inevitable....

We have seen above that the first step in the revolution by the working class is to raise the proletariat to the position of ruling class, to win the battle of democracy.

The proletariat will use its political supremacy to wrest, by degree, all capital from the bourgeoisie, to centralize all instruments of production in the hands of the state, i.e., of the proletariat organized as the ruling class; and to increase the total productive forces as rapidly as possible.

Of course, in the beginning, this cannot be effected except by means of despotic inroads on the rights of property.…

These measures will, of course, be different in different countries.

Nevertheless, in most advanced countries, the following will be pretty generally applicable.

1. Abolition of property in land and application of all rents of land to public purposes.
2. A heavy progressive or graduated income tax.
3. Abolition of all rights of inheritance.
4. Confiscation of the property of all emigrants and rebels.
5. Centralization of credit in the banks of the state, by means of a national bank with state capital and an exclusive monopoly.
6. Centralization of the means of communication and transport in the hands of the state.
7. Extension of factories and instruments of production owned by the state; the bringing into cultivation of waste lands, and the improvement of the soil generally in accordance with a common plan.
8. Equal obligation of all to work. Establishment of industrial armies, especially for agriculture.
9. Combination of agriculture with manufacturing industries; gradual abolition of all the distinction between town and country by a more equable distribution of the populace over the country.
10. Free education for all children in public schools. Abolition of children's factory labor in its present form. Combination of education with industrial production, etc.

When, in the course of development, class distinctions have disappeared, and all production has been concentrated in the hands of a vast association of the whole nation, the public power will lose its political character. Political power, properly so called, is merely the organized power of one class for oppressing another. If the proletariat during its contest with the bourgeoisie is compelled, by the force of circumstances, to organize itself as a class; if, by means of a revolution, it makes itself the ruling class, and, as such, sweeps away by force the old conditions of production, then it will, along with these conditions, have swept away the conditions for the existence of class antagonisms and of classes generally, and will thereby have abolished its own supremacy as a class.

In place of the old bourgeois society, with its classes and class antagonisms, we shall have an association in which the free development of each is the condition for the free development of all.…

The Communists disdain to conceal their views and aims. They openly declare that their ends can be attained only by the forcible overthrow of all existing social conditions. Let the ruling classes tremble at a communist revolution. The proletarians have nothing to lose but their chains. They have a world to win.

Document 18.2

Socialism without Revolution

Karl Marx and Friedrich Engels provided the set of ideas that informed much of the European socialist movement during the second half of the nineteenth century. Organized in various national parties and joined together in international organizations as well, socialists usually referred to themselves as social democrats, for they were seeking to extend the principles of democracy from the political arena (voting rights, for example) into the realm of the economy and society. By the 1890s, however, some of them had begun to question at least part of Marx's teachings, especially the need for violent revolution. The chief spokesperson for this group of socialists, known as "revisionists," was Eduard Bernstein (1850–1932), a prominent member of the German Social Democratic Party. His ideas provoked a storm of controversy within European socialist circles. Document 18.2 is drawn from the preface of Bernstein's 1899 book, *Evolutionary Socialism*.

■   In what ways and for what reasons was Bernstein critical of Marx and Engels's analysis of capitalism?

■   Why do you think he refers so often to Engels?

■   What strategy does Bernstein recommend for the German Social Democratic Party?

■   What does he mean by saying that "the movement means everything to me and…'the final aim of socialism' is nothing"?

■   Why would some of Marx's followers have considered Bernstein a virtual traitor to the socialist cause?

EDUARD BERNSTEIN
Evolutionary Socialism
1899

It has been maintained in a certain quarter that the practical deductions from my treatises would be the abandonment of the conquest of political power by the proletariat organized politically and economically. That [idea]…I altogether deny.

I set myself against the notion that we have to expect shortly a collapse of the bourgeois economy….

The adherents of this theory of a catastrophe, base it especially on the conclusions of the *Communist Manifesto*. This is a mistake….

Social conditions have not developed to such an acute opposition of things and classes as is depicted in the *Manifesto*. It is not only useless, it is the greatest folly to attempt to conceal this from ourselves. The number of members of the possessing classes is today not smaller but larger. The enormous increase of social wealth is not accompanied by a decreasing number of large capitalists but by an increasing number of capitalists of all degrees. The middle classes change their character but they do not disappear from the social scale.

The concentration in productive industry is not being accomplished even today in all its departments with equal thoroughness and at an equal rate…. Trade statistics show an extraordinarily elaborated graduation of enterprises in regard to size….

In all advanced countries we see the privileges of the capitalist bourgeoisie yielding step by step to democratic organizations. Under the influence of this, and driven by the movement of the working classes which is daily becoming stronger, a social reaction has set in against the exploiting tendencies of capital…. Factory legislation, the democratizing of local government, and the extension of its area of work, the freeing of trade unions and systems of co-operative trading from legal restrictions, the consid-

Source: Eduard Bernstein, *Evolutionary Socialism*, translated by Edith C. Harvey (New York: Schocken Books, 1961), xxiv–xxx.

eration of standard conditions of labor in the work undertaken by public authorities—all these characterize this phase of the evolution.

But the more the political organizations of modern nations are democratized, the more the needs and opportunities of great political catastrophes are diminished....

[Engels] points out in conformity with this opinion that the next task of the party should be "to work for an uninterrupted increase of its votes" or to carry on a slow *propaganda of parliamentary activity*....

Shall we be told that he [Engels] abandoned the conquest of political power by the working classes...?

[F]or a long time yet the task of social democracy is, instead of speculating on a great economic crash, "to organize the working classes politically and develop them as a democracy and to fight for all reforms in the State which are adapted to raise the working classes and transform the State in the direction of democracy."...

[T]he movement means everything for me and that what is *usually* called "the final aim of socialism" is nothing....

The conquest of political power by the working classes, the expropriation of capitalists, are not ends themselves but only means for the accomplishment of certain aims and endeavors.... But the conquest of political power necessitates the possession of political *rights*; German social democracy [must] devise the best ways for the extension of the political and economic rights of the German working classes.

Document 18.3

Socialism and Women

Marxist socialism focused largely on issues of class, but that movement coincided with the emergence of feminism, giving rise to what many socialists called "the woman question." The main theoretical issue was the source of female subjugation. Did it derive from private property and the class structure of capitalist society, or was it the product of deeply rooted cultural attitudes independent of class? While middle-class feminists generally assumed the second view, orthodox Marxist thinking aligned with the first one, believing that the lack of economic independence was the root cause of women's subordination. Their liberation would follow, more or less automatically, after the creation of socialist societies. On a more practical level, the question was whether socialist parties should seek to enroll women by actively supporting their unique concerns—suffrage, equal pay, education, maternity insurance. Or did such efforts divide the working class and weaken the socialist movement? Should socialists treat women as members of an oppressed class or as members of an oppressed sex?

Among the leading figures addressing such issues was Clara Zetkin (1857–1933), a prominent German socialist and feminist. In Document 18.3 Zetkin outlines the efforts of the German Social Democratic Party to reach out to women and describes the party's posture toward middle-class feminism.

- How would you describe Zetkin's view of the relationship between socialism and feminism? Which one has priority in her thinking?

- Why is she so insistent that the Social Democratic Party of Germany address the concerns of women? How precisely did it do so?

- Why does she believe that women's issues will be better served within a socialist framework than in a bourgeois women's rights movement?

- How might critics—both feminist and socialist—argue with Zetkin?

CLARA ZETKIN
The German Socialist Women's Movement
1909

In 1907 the Social-Democratic Party of Germany [SDP] embraced 29,458 women members, in 1908 they numbered 62,257.... One hundred and fifty lecture and study circles for women have been established.... Socialist propaganda amongst the workers' wives and women wage-earners has been carried on by many hundred public meetings, in which women comrades addressed more particularly working-class women....

The women's office works now in conjunction with the Party's Executive....They are to make a vigorous propaganda that the wage-earning women shall in large numbers exercise the franchise to the administrative bodies of the State Sick-Insurance, the only kind of franchise women possess in Germany. The women comrades were further engaged to form local committees for the protection of children.... Besides this, Socialist women were reminded to found and improve protective committees for women-workers, and collect their grievances on illegal and pernicious conditions of labor, forwarding them to the factory inspector.

Besides their activity in that line, the Socialist women have continued their propaganda in favor of the full political emancipation of their sex. The struggle for universal suffrage...was a struggle for adult suffrage for both sexes, vindicated in meetings and leaflets. Public and factory meetings in great number; and an indefatigable activity in other different forms, have served the trade union organizations of the women workers....The work of our trade unions to enlighten, train, and organize wage-earning women is not smaller nor less important than what the S.D.P. has done to induce women to join in political struggles of the working class....

The most prominent feature of the Socialist women's movement in Germany is its clearness and revolutionary spirit as to Socialist theories and principles. The women who head it are fully conscious that the social fate of their sex is indissolubly connected with the general evolution of society, the most powerful moving force of which is the evolution of labor, of economic life. The integral human emancipation of all women depends in consequence on the social emancipation of labor; that can only be realized by the class-war of the exploited majority. Therefore, our Socialist women oppose strongly the bourgeois women righters' credo that the women of all classes must gather into an unpolitical, neutral movement striving exclusively for women's rights. In theory and practice they maintain the conviction that the class antagonisms are much more powerful, effective, and decisive than the social antagonisms between the sexes.... [T]hus the working-class women will [only] win their full emancipation...in the class-war of all the exploited, without difference of sex, against all who exploit, without difference of sex. That does not mean at all that they undervalue the importance of the political emancipation of the female sex. On the contrary, they employ much more energy than the German women-righters to conquer the suffrage. But the vote is, according to their views, not the last word and term of their aspirations, but only a weapon—a means in struggle for a revolutionary aim—the Socialistic order.

Source: Clara Zetkin, *The German Socialist Women's Movement*, Marxists Internet Archive, www.marxists.org.

The Socialist women's movement in Germany... strives to help change the world by awakening the consciousness and the will of working-class women to join in performing the most Titanic deed that history will know: the emancipation of labor by the laboring class themselves.

Document 18.4

Socialism in Song

While European socialists argued theory, debated strategy, and organized workers, they also sang. The hymn of the socialist movement was "The Internationale," composed in 1871 by Eugene Pottier, a French working-class activist, poet, and songwriter. Document 18.4 offers an English translation made in 1900 by Charles Kerr, an American publisher of radical books. The song gave expression to both the oppression and the hopes of ordinary people as they worked for a socialist future.

- What evidence of class consciousness is apparent in the song? What particular grievances are expressed in it?

- How does "The Internationale" portray the struggle and the future?

- What evidence of Marxist thinking can you find in its lyrics?

- How does this song, intended for a mass audience, differ from the more political and intellectual documents above?

EUGENE POTTIER (TRANS. CHARLES KERR)

The Internationale

1871

Arise, ye prisoners of starvation!
Arise, ye wretched of the earth!
For justice thunders condemnation,
A better world's in birth!
No more tradition's chains shall bind us,
Arise ye slaves, no more in thrall!
The earth shall rise on new foundations,
We have been nought, we shall be all.

(Chorus)
'Tis the final conflict,
Let each stand in his place.

The international working class
Shall be the human race.

We want no condescending saviors
To rule us from a judgment hall;
We workers ask not for their favors;
Let us consult for all.
To make the thief disgorge his booty
To free the spirit from its cell,
We must ourselves decide our duty,
We must decide, and do it well.
(Chorus)

The law oppresses us and tricks us,
wage slav'ry drains the workers' blood;

Source: "The Internationale," http://en.wikisource.org/wiki/The_Internationale_(Kerr).

The rich are free from obligations,
The laws the poor delude.
Too long we've languished in subjection,
Equality has other laws;
"No rights," says she, "without their duties,
No claims on equals without cause."
(Chorus)

Behold them seated in their glory
The kings of mine and rail and soil!
What have you read in all their story,
But how they plundered toil?
Fruits of the workers' toil are buried
In the strong coffers of a few;

In working for their restitution
The men will only ask their due.
(Chorus)

Toilers from shops and fields united,
The union we of all who work;
The earth belongs to us, the workers,
No room here for the shirk.
How many on our flesh have fattened;
But if the noisome birds of prey
Shall vanish from the sky some morning,
The blessed sunlight still will stay.
(Chorus)

Document 18.5

Lenin and Russian Socialism

By the late nineteenth century, most West European socialist parties were operating in a more or less democratic environment in which they could organize
legally, contest elections, and serve in parliament. Some of them, following
Eduard Bernstein, had largely abandoned any thoughts of revolution in favor of
a peaceful and democratic path to socialism. For others, this amounted to a
betrayal of the Marxist vision. This was particularly the case for Vladimir Ilyich
Ulyanov, better known as Lenin, then a prominent figure in the small Russian
Social Democratic Labor Party, established in 1898. Lenin was particularly
hostile to what he called "economism" or "trade-unionism," which focused on
immediate reforms such as higher wages, shorter hours, and better working
conditions. He was operating in a still autocratic Russian state, where neither
political parties nor trade unions were legal and where no national parliament
or elections allowed for the expression of popular grievances.

In a famous pamphlet titled *What Is to Be Done?* (1902), Lenin addressed
many of these issues, well before he became the leader of the world's first successful socialist revolution in 1917.

- What were Lenin's objections to economism?

- What kind of party organization did he favor?

- Why did Lenin believe that workers were unlikely to come to a revolutionary consciousness on their own? What was necessary to move them
  in that direction?

- Was Lenin more faithful to the views of Marx himself than the revisionists
  and economists were?

- In what ways did Lenin's views reflect the specific conditions of Russia?

V. I. LENIN

What Is to Be Done?

1902

The history of all countries shows that the working class, exclusively by its own effort, is able to develop only trade union consciousness, *i.e.*, it may itself realize the necessity for combining in unions, for fighting against the employers, and for striving to compel the government to pass necessary labor legislation, etc. The theory of socialism, however, grew out of the philosophic, historical, and economic theories that were elaborated by the educated representatives of the propertied classes, the intellectuals.... [I]n Russia... it arose as a natural and inevitable outcome of the development of ideas among the revolutionary socialist intelligentsia.

It is only natural that a Social Democrat, who conceives the political struggle as being identical with the "economic struggle against the employers and the government," should conceive of an "organization of revolutionaries" as being more or less identical with an "organization of workers."...

[O]n questions of organization and politics, the Economists are forever lapsing from Social Democracy into trade unionism. The political struggle carried on by the Social Democrats is far more extensive and complex than the economic struggle the workers carry on against the employers and the government. Similarly... the organization of a revolutionary Social Democratic Party must inevitably *differ* from the organizations of the workers designed for the latter struggle. A workers' organization... must be as wide as possible; and... it must be as public as conditions will allow.... On the other hand, the organizations of revolutionaries must consist first and foremost of people whose profession is that of a revolutionary.... Such an organization must of necessity be not too extensive and as secret as possible....

I assert:

1. that no movement can be durable without a stable organization of leaders to maintain continuity;
2. that the more widely the masses are spontaneously drawn into the struggle and form the basis of the movement and participate in it, the more necessary is it to have such an organization....
3. that the organization must consist chiefly of persons engaged in revolutionary activities as a profession;
4. that in a country with an autocratic government, the more we restrict the membership of this organization to persons who are engaged in revolutionary activities as a profession and who have been professionally trained in the art of combating the political police, the more difficult will it be to catch the organization....

The centralization of the more secret functions in an organization of revolutionaries will not diminish, but rather increase the extent and the quality of the activity of a large number of other organizations intended for wide membership.... [I]n order to "serve" the mass movement we must have people who will devote themselves exclusively to Social Democratic activities, and that such people must *train* themselves patiently and steadfastly to be professional revolutionaries....

Let no active worker take offense at these frank remarks, for as far as insufficient training is concerned, I apply them first and foremost to myself. I used to work in a circle that set itself great and all-embracing tasks; and every member of that circle suffered to the point of torture from the realization that we were proving ourselves to be amateurs at a moment in history when we might have been able to say, paraphrasing a well-known epigram: "Give us an organization of revolutionaries, and we shall overturn the whole of Russia!"

Source: V. I. Lenin, *What Is to Be Done?* Pamphlet, 1902. Marxist Internet Archives, www.marxists.org.

Using the Evidence:
Varieties of European Marxism

1. **Comparing socialisms:** While the various strands of Marxist socialism in nineteenth-century Europe shared some common views and values, it was also a sharply divided movement. How would you describe those commonalities as well as the divisions and controversies?

2. **Connecting human rights and socialism:** To what extent did socialist thinking reflect the human rights concerns expressed in the documents of Chapter 17? In what ways might socialists have taken issue with human rights advocates?

3. **Understanding class:** In what ways do these documents help you understand the experience of "class" during the first century of the industrial era?

4. **Considering responses to socialism:** With which of the variant forms of socialism might Marx himself been most and least sympathetic? Which of them do you think would have had most appeal in the United States? How might a manager or owner of a modern industrial enterprise respond to these ideas?

Visual Sources

Considering the Evidence:
Art and the Industrial Revolution

The immense economic and social transformations of the Industrial Revolution left almost no one untouched in those societies that experienced it most fully. But its impact varied greatly across social classes; among men, women, and children; and over time. Those variations registered not only in politics but also in the work of artists. Through their eyes and in their images we can find the full range of perceptions and reactions—from celebratory to devastatingly critical—which this epic upheaval generated. From the endless visual representations of the Industrial Revolution that are available to historians, we present six, drawn mostly from Great Britain, where it all began. The first three visual sources highlight positive perceptions of industrialization, while the final three illustrate the enormous cost of that process.

By the mid-nineteenth century, the Industrial Revolution and a growing global empire had generated for many people in Great Britain feelings of enormous pride, achievement, and superiority. Nowhere did that sensibility register more clearly than in the Crystal Palace Exhibition of 1851. Held in London, the exhibition was housed in a huge modernistic structure made of cast iron and glass and constructed in only nine months. It attracted more than 6 million visitors and contained some 14,000 exhibits from all around the world, allowing Britain to contrast its own achievements with those of "lesser" peoples. Visual Source 18.1, an engraving from the exhibition's "machinery department" first published in a London newspaper, illustrates the growing tendency of Europeans to view "technology as the main measure of human achievement."[28]

- What overall impression of Britain's industrial technology was this engraving intended to convey? Notice the building itself as well as the machinery.

- How are the visitors to this exhibit portrayed? What segment of British society do you think they represent? What does their inclusion suggest about the beneficiaries of the Industrial Revolution?

The most prominent symbol of the Industrial Revolution was the railroad (see the photo on p. 832). To industrial-age enthusiasts, it was a thing of wonder, power, and speed. Samuel Smiles, a nineteenth-century British writer and

Visual Source 18.1 The Machinery Department of the Crystal Palace (Mary Evans Picture Library/The Image Works)

advocate of self-help and individualism, wrote rhapsodically of the railroad's beneficent effects:

> The iron rail proved a magicians' road. The locomotive gave a new celerity to time. It virtually reduced England to a sixth of its size. It brought the country nearer to the town and the town to the country.... It energized punctuality, discipline, and attention; and proved a moral teacher by the influence of example.[29]

Visual Source 18.2, dating from the 1870s, shows a family in a railroad compartment, returning home from a vacation.

- What attitude toward the railroad in particular and the industrial age in general does this image suggest?

- Notice the view out the window. What do the telegraph lines and St. Paul's Cathedral, a famous feature of the London landscape, contribute to the artist's message?

- What marks this family as middle class? How would you compare this image with the painting of middle class life on page 834? Do the two families derive from the same segments of the middle class? Do you think they could mix socially?

■ What does the poem at the top of the image suggest about the place of "home" in industrial Britain? How does the image itself present the railway car as a home away from home?

And Papa and Mamma took them home the same day,—
They were glad to go home, and yet wanted to stay;
But the train went quite fast, and it seemed a nice change
To be back in their own home, where nothing was strange:

And always they reckon'd that seeing these sights
Was a thing to remember—a week of delights;
And, though they may see them all many times more,
They'll never enjoy them so much, I am sure.

Visual Source 18.2 The Railroad as a Symbol of the Industrial Era (Mary Evans Picture Library/The Image Works)

Visual Source 18.3 Outside the Factory: Eyre Crowe, *The Dinner Hour, Wigan* (© Manchester Art Gallery, UK/The Bridgeman Art Library)

The Industrial Revolution was more than invention and technological innovation, for it also involved a new organization of work, symbolized by the modern factory. The human impact of factory labor was a central feature in the debate about this massive transformation of economic life. Visual Source 18.3, an 1874 painting by English artist Eyre Crowe, shows a number of young women factory workers during their dinner hour outside the cotton textile mill in the industrial town of Wigan. Art critics at the time commented variously on the painting. One wrote, "We think it was a pity Mr. Crowe wasted his time on such unattractive materials." Another suggested, "Crowe has apparently set himself to record the unpictorial lives of the working classes of the manufacturing districts in a prosaic but entirely honest manner." Yet a third declared, "The picture is not a mere romantic invention: it is a veracious [truthful] statement."[30]

- How would you respond to these comments on Crowe's painting? In particular, do you think it was an "entirely honest" portrayal of factory life for women? What was missing?

- Why do you think Crowe set this scene outside the factory rather than within it?

- Notice the details of the painting—the young women's relationship to one another, the hairnets on their heads, their clothing, their activities during this break from work. What marks them as working-class women? What impression of factory life did Crowe seek to convey? Was he trying to highlight or minimize the class differences of industrial Britain?

- Notice the small male figure in a dark coat and carrying a cane. At least one observer of this painting has suggested that he may well be the mill owner, the "figure around which their [the women's] life depends."[31] If so, how would you imagine his relationship to the young women?

Turning to more negative and critical perspectives on industrialization, we begin with a sharply contrasting image of factory life, this time a colorized photograph of women and children at work in a vegetable cannery in Baltimore in 1912 (Visual Source 18.4). It was taken by Lewis W. Hine (1874–1940), a prominent American photographer who spent much of his professional life documenting child labor and factory working life. Often Hine briefly interviewed the children he photographed. When he asked one young girl her age, she replied: "I don't remember. I'm not old enough to work, but do just the same." A twelve-year-old illiterate boy told Hine: "Yes I want to learn, but can't when I work all the time."[32] Hine's photographs played a role in the passage of child labor laws in the United States.

- What impressions of factory life does Hine seek to convey in this photograph?

- How do the women and children in this image compare with those in Visual Source 18.3?

- How would you imagine a conversation between Hine and Crowe discussing these two images?

- Notice the male figure smoking a pipe. What do you think his role in the factory might be?

- Is a photograph necessarily a more truthful image than a painting? Consider the advantages and disadvantages of each as a source of information for historians.

Prominent among the criticisms of the industrialization process was its impact on the environment. The massive extraction of nonrenewable raw

Visual Source 18.4 Inside the Factory: Lewis Hine, *Child Labor, 1912* (Oil over photograph, 1912, by Lewis W. Hine. The Granger Collection, New York)

materials to feed and to fuel industrial machinery—coal, iron ore, petroleum, and much more—altered the landscape in many places. Sewers and industrial waste emptied into rivers, turning them into poisonous cesspools. In 1858, the Thames River running through London smelled so bad that the British House of Commons had to suspend its session. Smoke from coal-fired industries and domestic use polluted the air in urban areas and sharply increased the incidence of respiratory illness. (See the chapter opening image on p. 824.) Against these conditions a number of individuals and small groups raised their voices. Romantic poets such as William Blake and William Wordsworth inveighed against the "dark satanic mills" of industrial England and nostalgically urged a return to the "green and pleasant land" of an earlier time.

Nowhere in Britain were the environmental changes of the early industrial era more visible than in Coalbrookdale, a major center of the iron industry. A visitor wrote of the place in 1768:

Coalbrookdale is a very romantic spot, it is a winding glen between two immense hills..., all thickly covered with wood....Indeed too

Visual Source 18.5 Philip James de Louterbourg, *Coalbrookdale by Night* (Science Museum/Science & Society Picture Library)

beautiful to be much in unison with that variety of horrors art spread at the bottom: the noises of the forges, mills, etc., with all their vast machinery, the flames bursting from the furnaces with the burning of coal and the smoke of the lime kilns.[33]

In 1801, Philip James de Louterbourg, an English artist born in France, painted *Coalbrookdale by Night* (Visual Source 18.5), an image that became for many people emblematic of the early Industrial Revolution in Britain.

■ To what extent does that image reflect the description of Coalbrookdale above? Why do you think the artist set the image at night?

■ How would you interpret the flames issuing from the iron foundry? What is conveyed by the industrial debris in the foreground of the image?

■ How are human figures portrayed?

■ What overall impression of the industrial age does this painting suggest? Does the painting strike you as beautiful, horrific, or both?

CAPITAL AND LABOUR.

Visual Source 18.6 John Leech, *Capital and Labour* (The Granger Collection, New York)

In critiques of the industrial era, social issues loomed far larger than environmental concerns. Visual Source 18.6, an image by British artist John Leech, was published in 1843 in *Punch*, a magazine of humor and social satire. It reflects a common theme in the artistic and literary representations of industrial Britain.

- How precisely would you define that theme?

- How are the sharp class differences of industrial Britain represented in this visual source?

- How does this visual source connect the Industrial Revolution with Britain's colonial empire? Notice the figure in the upper right reclining in exotic splendor, perhaps in India.

- To what extent does the image correspond with Karl Marx and Frederick Engels's description of industrial society in Document 18.1 (pp. 856–59)?

- How might you understand the figure of the woman and small angel behind a door at the left?

Using the Evidence:
Art and the Industrial Revolution

1. **Deciphering class:** In what different ways is social class treated in these visual sources?

2. **Celebrating industrialization:** Based on these visual sources, the documents on socialism (pp. 855–66), and the text of Chapter 18, construct an argument in celebration of the Industrial Revolution.

3. **Criticizing industrialization:** Construct another argument based on the evidence in the chapter criticizing the Industrial Revolution.

4. **Considering images as evidence:** What are the strengths and limitations of visual sources such as these in helping historians understand the Industrial Revolution?

5. **Distinguishing capitalism and industrialization:** To what extent are the visual sources in this section actually dealing with the Industrial Revolution itself and in what ways are they addressing the economic system known as capitalism? How useful is this distinction for understanding reactions to the industrial age?

CHAPTER NINETEEN

Internal Troubles, External Threats

China, the Ottoman Empire, and Japan

1800–1914

In the early twenty-first century, Japanese history textbooks became a serious issue in the relationship between Japan and its Chinese neighbor. From a Chinese point of view, those textbooks had minimized or whitewashed Japanese atrocities committed against China during World War II. In particular, many Chinese were outraged at the treatment of the so-called Rape of Nanjing, which witnessed the killing of perhaps 200,000 people, most of them civilians, and the rape of countless women. "Nanjing city was soaked with bloodshed and piles of bodies were everywhere," declared one survivor of those events. "Japanese rightist groups distort history and attempt to cover the truth of Nanjing Massacre. This makes me extremely angry."[1] Another issue was the Japanese use of Chinese "comfort women," perhaps 200,000 of them, sexual slaves forced to service Japanese troops. Japan, they argued, had not sufficiently acknowledged this outrage in their history textbooks, nor had the Japanese government adequately apologized for it.

To an observer from, say, the fifteenth century or even the eighteenth century, all of this—Japanese aggression during World War II, its enormous economic success after the war, and the continuing fear and resentment of Japan reflected in the textbook controversy—would have seemed strange indeed. For many centuries, after all, Japan had lived in the shadow of its giant Chinese neighbor, borrowing many elements of Chinese culture. Certainly it was never a threat to China. Beginning in the mid-nineteenth century, however, a remarkable reversal of roles occurred in East Asia when both China and Japan experienced a series of internal crises and, at the

Carving Up the Pie of China: In this French cartoon from the late 1890s, the Great Powers of the day (from left to right: Great Britain's Queen Victoria, Germany's Kaiser Wilhelm, Russia's Tsar Nicholas II, a female figure representing France, and the Meiji emperor of Japan) participate in dividing China, while a Chinese figure behind them tries helplessly to stop the partition of his country. (Gianni Dagli Orti/The Art Archive)

same time, had to confront the novel reality of an industrialized, newly powerful, intrusive Western world. It was their very different responses to these internal crises and external challenges that led to their changed relationship in the century or more that followed and to the continuing suspicions and tensions that still characterize their relationship.

CHINA AND JAPAN WERE NOT ALONE IN FACING THE EXPANSIVE FORCES OF EUROPE AND THE UNITED STATES. During the nineteenth century, and in some places earlier, most of the peoples of Asia, the Middle East, and Africa, as well as those living in the newly independent states of Latin America, were required to deal with European or American imperialism of one kind or another. Whatever their other differences, this was a common thread that gave these diverse peoples something of a shared history.

But—and this can hardly be emphasized too strongly—dealing with Europe was not the only item on their agendas. Many African peoples were occupied with Islamic revival movements and the rise and fall of their own states; population growth and peasant rebellion wracked China; the great empires of the Islamic world shrank or disappeared; Hindus and Muslims persisted in their sometimes competitive and sometimes cooperative relationship in India; and rivalry among competing elites troubled Latin American societies. Encounters with an expansive Europe were conditioned everywhere by particular local circumstances. Those encounters provided a mirror in which the peoples of Asia and Africa viewed themselves, as they alternately celebrated, criticized, and sought to transform their own cultures.

This chapter examines the experience of societies that confronted these crises while retaining their formal independence, with China, the Ottoman Empire, and Japan as primary examples. The following chapter turns the spotlight on the colonial experience of those peoples who fell under the official control of one or another of the European powers. In both cases, they were dealing with a new thrust of European expansion, one that drew its energy from the Industrial Revolution.

Four dimensions of an expansive Europe confronted these societies. First, they faced the immense military might and political ambitions of rival European states. Second, they became enmeshed in networks of trade, investment, and sometimes migration that radiated out from an industrializing and capitalist Europe to generate a new world economy. Third, they were touched by various aspects of traditional European culture, as some among them learned the French, English, or German language; converted to Christianity; or studied European literature and philosophy. Finally, Asians and Africans engaged with the culture of modernity—its scientific rationalism; its technological achievements; its belief in a better future; and its ideas of nationalism, socialism, feminism, and individualism. In those epic encounters, they sometimes resisted, at other times accommodated, and almost always adapted what came from the West. They were active participants in the global drama of nineteenth-century world history, not simply its passive victims or beneficiaries.

The External Challenge: European Industry and Empire

More than at any other time, the nineteenth century was Europe's age of global expansion. During that century, Europe became the center of the world economy, with ties of trade and investment in every corner of the globe. Between 1812 and 1914, millions of Europeans migrated to new homes outside Europe. Missionaries and explorers penetrated the distant interiors of Asia and Africa. European states incorporated India, Africa, Southeast Asia, and the islands of the Pacific into their overseas colonial empires and seriously diminished the sovereignty and independence of the once proud domains of China, the Ottoman Empire, and Persia. Many newly independent states in Latin America became economically dependent on Europe and the United States (see pp. 846–48). How can we explain such dramatic changes in the scope, character, and intensity of European expansion?

New Motives, New Means

Behind much of Europe's nineteenth-century expansion lay the massive fact of its Industrial Revolution. That process gave rise to new economic needs, many of which found solutions abroad. The enormous productivity of industrial technology and Europe's growing affluence now created the need for extensive raw materials and agricultural products: wheat from the American Midwest and southern Russia, meat from Argentina, bananas from Central America, rubber from Brazil, cocoa and palm oil from West Africa, tea from Ceylon, gold and diamonds from South Africa. This demand radically changed patterns of economic and social life in the countries of their origin.

■ Change
In what ways did the Industrial Revolution shape the character of nineteenth-century European imperialism?

Furthermore, Europe needed to sell its own products. One of the peculiarities of industrial capitalism was that it periodically produced more manufactured goods than its own people could afford to buy. By 1840, for example, Britain was exporting 60 percent of its cotton-cloth production, annually sending 200 million yards to Europe, 300 million yards to Latin America, and 145 million yards to India. This last figure is particularly significant because for centuries Europe had offered little that Asian societies were willing to buy. Part of European and American fascination with China during the nineteenth and twentieth centuries lay in the enormous potential market represented by its huge population.

Much the same could be said for capital, for European investors often found it more profitable to invest their money abroad than at home. Between 1910 and 1913, Britain was sending about half of its savings abroad as foreign investment. In 1914, it had about 3.7 billion pounds sterling invested abroad, about equally divided between Europe, North America, and Australia on the one hand and Asia, Africa, and Latin America on the other hand.

Wealthy Europeans also saw social benefits to foreign markets, which served to keep Europe's factories humming and its workers employed. The English imperialist Cecil Rhodes confided his fears to a friend:

Yesterday I attended a meeting of the unemployed in London and having listened to the wild speeches which were nothing more than a scream for bread, I returned home convinced more than ever of the importance of imperialism.... In order to save the 40 million inhabitants of the United Kingdom from a murderous civil war, the colonial politicians must open up new areas to absorb the excess population and create new markets for the products of the mines and factories.... The British Empire is a matter of bread and butter. If you wish to avoid civil war, then you must become an imperialist.[2]

Thus imperialism promised to solve the class conflicts of an industrializing society while avoiding revolution or the serious redistribution of wealth.

But what made imperialism so broadly popular in Europe, especially in the last quarter of the nineteenth century, was the growth of mass nationalism. By 1871, the unification of Italy and Germany made Europe's always competitive political system even more so, and much of this rivalry spilled over into the struggle for colonies or economic concessions in Asia and Africa. Colonies and spheres of influence abroad became a symbol of national "Great Power" status, and their acquisition was a matter of urgency, even if they possessed little immediate economic value. After 1875, it seemed to matter, even to ordinary people, whether some remote corner of Africa or some obscure Pacific island was in British, French, or German hands. Imperialism, in short, appealed on economic and social grounds to the wealthy or ambitious, seemed politically and strategically necessary in the game of international power politics, and was emotionally satisfying to almost everyone. It was a potent mix.

If the industrial era made overseas expansion more desirable or even urgent, it also provided new means for achieving those goals. Steam-driven ships, moving through the new Suez Canal, allowed Europeans to reach distant Asian and African ports more quickly and predictably and to penetrate interior rivers as well. The underwater telegraph made possible almost instant communication with far-flung outposts of empire. The discovery of quinine to prevent malaria greatly reduced European death rates in the tropics. Breech-loading rifles and machine guns vastly widened the military gap between Europeans and everyone else.

The Gatling Gun
The Gatling gun, which was designed by the American Richard Gatling during the Civil War, was one of the earliest machine guns. By the late nineteenth century, this weapon, together with breech-loading rifles, gave European powers and the United States an enormous military advantage. (Courtesy, Royal Artillery Historical Trust)

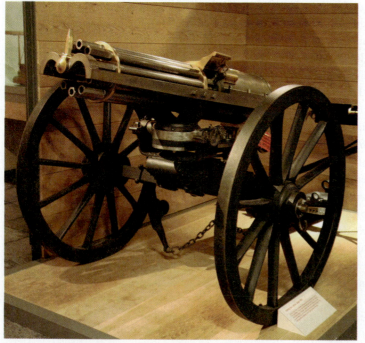

New Perceptions of the "Other"

Industrialization also occasioned a marked change in the way Europeans perceived themselves and others. In earlier centuries, Europeans had defined others largely in religious terms. "They" were heathen; "we" were Christian. Even as they held on to this sense of religious superiority, Europeans nonetheless adopted many of the ideas and techniques of more advanced societies. They held many aspects of Chinese and Indian civilization in high regard; they freely mixed and mingled with Asian and African elites and often married their women; some even saw the more technologically simple peoples of Africa and America as "noble savages."

■ **Change**
What contributed to changing European views of Asians and Africans in the nineteenth century?

With the advent of the industrial age, however, Europeans developed a secular arrogance that fused with or in some cases replaced their notions of religious superiority. They had, after all, unlocked the secrets of nature, created a society of unprecedented wealth, and used both to produce unsurpassed military power. These became the criteria by which Europeans judged both themselves and the rest of the world.

By such standards, it is not surprising that their opinions of other cultures dropped sharply. The Chinese, who had been highly praised in the eighteenth century, were reduced in the nineteenth century to the image of "John Chinaman," weak, cunning, obstinately conservative, and, in large numbers, a distinct threat, the "yellow peril" of late-nineteenth-century European fears. African societies, which had been regarded even in the slave-trade era as nations and their leaders as kings, were demoted in nineteenth-century European eyes to the status of tribes led by chiefs as a means of emphasizing their "primitive" qualities.

Increasingly, Europeans viewed the culture and achievements of Asian and African peoples through the prism of a new kind of racism, expressed now in terms of modern science. Although physical differences had often been a basis of fear or dislike, in the nineteenth century Europeans increasingly used the prestige and apparatus of science to support their racial preferences and prejudices. Phrenologists, craniologists, and sometimes physicians used allegedly scientific methods and numerous instruments to classify the size and shape of human skulls and concluded, not surprisingly, that those of whites were larger and therefore more advanced. Nineteenth-century biologists, who classified the varieties of plants and animals, applied these notions of rank to varieties of human beings as well. The result was a hierarchy of races, with the whites, naturally, on top and the less developed "child races" beneath them. Race, in this view, determined human intelligence, moral development, and destiny. "Race is everything," declared the British anatomist Robert Knox in 1850; "civilization depends on it."[3] Furthermore, as the germ theory of disease took hold in nineteenth-century Europe, it was accompanied by fears that contact with "inferior" peoples threatened the health and even the biological future of more advanced or "superior" peoples.

These ideas influenced how Europeans viewed their own global expansion. Almost everyone saw it as inevitable, a natural outgrowth of a superior civilization.

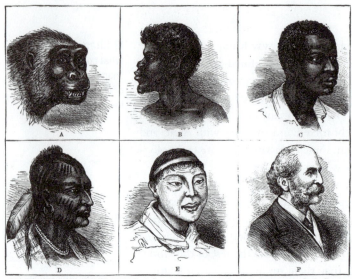

PROGRESSIVE DEVELOPMENT OF MAN.—(2) EVOLUTION ILLUSTRATED WITH THE SIX CORRESPONDING LIVING FORMS.

European Racial Images
This nineteenth-century chart, depicting the "Progressive Development of Man" from apes to modern Europeans, reflected the racial categories that were so prominent at the time. It also highlights the influence of Darwin's evolutionary ideas as they were applied to varieties of human beings. (The Granger Collection, New York)

For many, though, this viewpoint was tempered with a genuine, if condescending, sense of responsibility to the "weaker races" that Europe was fated to dominate. "Superior races have a right, because they have a duty," declared the French politician Jules Ferry in 1883. "They have the duty to civilize the inferior races."[4] That "civilizing mission," as Europeans regarded it, included bringing Christianity to the heathen, good government to disordered lands, work discipline and production for the market to "lazy natives," a measure of education to the ignorant and illiterate, clothing to the naked, and health care to the sick, while suppressing "native customs" that ran counter to Western ways of living. All of this was defined as "progress" and "civilization."

Another, harsher side to the ideology of imperialism derived from an effort to apply, or perhaps misapply, the evolutionary thinking of Charles Darwin to an understanding of human history. The key concept of this "social Darwinism," though not necessarily shared by Darwin himself, was "the survival of the fittest," suggesting that European dominance inevitably involved the displacement or destruction of backward peoples or "unfit" races. Referring to native peoples of Australia, a European bishop declared:

> Everyone who knows a little about aboriginal races is aware that those races which are of a low type mentally and who are at the same time weak in constitution rapidly die out when their country comes to be occupied by a different race much more rigorous, robust, and pushing than themselves.[5]

Such views made imperialism, war, and aggression seem both natural and progressive, for they were predicated on the notion that weeding out "weaker" peoples of the world would allow the "stronger" to flourish. These were some of the ideas with which industrializing and increasingly powerful Europeans confronted the peoples of Asia and Africa in the nineteenth century. Among those confrontations, none was more important than Europe's encounter with China.

Reversal of Fortune: China's Century of Crisis

In 1793 in a famous letter to King George III, the Chinese emperor Qianlong sharply rebuffed British requests for a less restricted trading relationship with his country. "Our Celestial Empire possesses all things in prolific abundance...," he declared. "There was therefore no need to import the manufactures of outside barbarians" (see

Document 19.1, pp. 905–07). Qianlong's snub simply continued the pattern of the previous several centuries, during which Chinese authorities had strictly controlled and limited the activities of European missionaries and merchants. By 1912, little more than a century later, China's long-established imperial state had collapsed, and the country had been transformed from a central presence in the Afro-Eurasian world to a weak and dependent participant in a European-dominated world system. It was a stunning reversal of fortune for a country that in Chinese eyes was the civilized center of the entire world—in their terms, the Middle Kingdom.

The Crisis Within

In many ways, China was the victim of its own earlier success. Its robust economy and American food crops had enabled massive population growth, from about 100 million people in 1685 to some 430 million in 1853. Unlike Europe, though, where a similar population spurt took place, no Industrial Revolution accompanied this vast increase in the number of people, nor was agricultural production able to keep up. The result was growing pressure on the land, smaller farms for China's huge peasant population, and, in all too many cases, unemployment, impoverishment, misery, and starvation.

■ **Causation**
What accounts for the massive peasant rebellions of nineteenth-century China?

Furthermore, China's famed centralized and bureaucratic state did not enlarge itself to keep pace with the growing population. In 1400, the lowest administrative unit, a county, encompassed perhaps 50,000 people and was governed by a magistrate and a small staff. By 1800, that same magistrate had to deal with 200,000 people, with no increase in his staff. Thus the state was increasingly unable to effectively perform its many functions, such as tax collection, flood control, social welfare, and public security. Gradually the central state lost power to provincial officials and local gentry. Among such officials, corruption was endemic, and harsh treatment of peasants was common. According to an official report issued in 1852, "[D]ay and night soldiers are sent out to harass taxpayers. Sometimes corporal punishments are imposed upon tax delinquents; some of them are so badly beaten to exact the last penny that blood and flesh fly in all directions."[6]

This combination of circumstances, traditionally associated with a declining dynasty, gave rise to growing numbers of bandit gangs roaming the countryside and, even more dangerous, to outright peasant rebellion. Beginning in the late eighteenth century, such rebellions drew upon a variety of peasant grievances and found leadership in charismatic figures proclaiming a millenarian religious message. Increasingly they also expressed opposition to the Qing dynasty on account of its foreign Manchu origins. "We wait only for the northern region to be returned to a Han emperor," declared one rebel group in the early nineteenth century.[7]

The culmination of China's internal crisis lay in the Taiping Uprising, which set much of the country aflame between 1850 and 1864. This was a different kind of peasant upheaval. Its leaders largely rejected Confucianism, Daoism, and Buddhism alike, finding their primary ideology in a unique form of Christianity. Its leading figure, Hong Xiuquan (1814–1864), proclaimed himself the younger brother of Jesus, sent to cleanse the world of demons and to establish a "heavenly kingdom of great peace." Nor were these leaders content to restore an idealized Chinese society; instead they insisted on genuinely revolutionary change. They called for the abolition of private property; a radical redistribution of land; the equality of men and women; the end of foot binding, prostitution, and opium smoking; and the organization of society into sexually segregated military camps of men and women. Hong fiercely denounced the Qing dynasty as foreigners who had "poisoned China" and "defiled the emperor's throne." His cousin, Hong Rengan, developed plans for transforming China into an industrial nation, complete with railroads, health insurance for all, newspapers, and widespread public education.

With a rapidly swelling number of followers, Taiping forces swept out of southern China and established their capital in Nanjing in 1853. For a time, the days of the Qing dynasty appeared to be over. But divisions and indecisiveness within the Taiping leadership and their inability to link up with several other rebel groups also operating separately in China provided an opening for Qing dynasty loyalists to rally and by 1864 to crush this most unusual of peasant rebellions. Western military support for pro-Qing forces likewise contributed to their victory. It was not, however, the imperial military forces of the central government that defeated the rebels. Instead provincial gentry landowners, fearing the radicalism of the Taiping program, mobilized their own armies, which in the end crushed the rebel forces.

Thus the Qing dynasty was saved, but it was also weakened as the provincial gentry consolidated their power at the expense of the central state. The intense conservatism of both imperial authorities and their gentry supporters postponed any resolution of China's peasant problem, delayed any real change for China's women, and deferred vigorous efforts at modernization until the communists came to power in the mid-twentieth century. More immediately, the devastation and destruction occasioned by this massive civil war seriously disrupted and weakened China's economy. Estimates of the number of lives lost range from 20 to 30 million. In human terms, it was the most costly conflict in the world of the nineteenth century, and it took China more than a decade to recover from that devastation. China's internal crisis in general and the Taiping Uprising in particular also provided a highly unfavorable setting for the country's encounter with a Europe newly invigorated by the Industrial Revolution.

Western Pressures

■ Connection

How did Western pressures stimulate change in China during the nineteenth century?

Nowhere was the shifting balance of global power in the nineteenth century more evident than in China's changing relationship with Europe, a transformation that registered most dramatically in the famous Opium Wars. Derived from Arab traders in the eighth century or earlier, opium had long been used on a small scale as a drinkable medicine, regarded as a magical cure for dysentery and described by one poet as "fit for Buddha."[8] It did not become a serious problem until the late eighteenth century,

Snapshot   **Chinese/British Trade at Canton, 1835–1836**[9]

What do these figures suggest about the role of opium in British trade with China? Calculate opium exports as a percentage of British exports to China, Britain's trade deficit without opium, and its trade surplus with opium. What did this pattern mean for China?

	Item	Value (in Spanish dollars)
British Exports to Canton	Opium	17,904,248
	Cotton	8,357,394
	All other items (sandlewood, lead, iron, tin, cotton yarn and piece goods, tin plates, watches, clocks)	6,164,981
	Total	32,426,623
British Imports from Canton	Tea (black and green)	13,412,243
	Raw silk	3,764,115
	Vermilion	705,000
	All other goods (sugar products, camphor, silver, gold, copper, musk)	5,971,541
	Total	23,852,899

when the British began to use opium, grown and processed in India, to cover their persistent trade imbalance with China. By the 1830s, British, American, and other Western merchants had found an enormous, growing, and very profitable market for this highly addictive drug. From 1,000 chests (each weighing roughly 150 pounds) in 1773, China's opium imports exploded to more than 23,000 chests in 1832.

By then, Chinese authorities recognized a mounting problem on many levels. Because opium importation was illegal, it had to be smuggled into China, thus flouting Chinese law. Bribed to turn a blind eye to the illegal trade, many officials were corrupted. Furthermore, a massive outflow of silver to pay for the opium reversed China's centuries-long ability to attract much of the world's silver supply, and this imbalance caused serious economic problems. Finally, China found itself with many millions of addicts—men and women, court officials, students preparing for exams, soldiers going into combat, and common laborers seeking to overcome the pain and drudgery of their work. Following an extended debate at court in 1836—whether to legalize the drug or to crack down on its use—the emperor decided on suppression (see Documents 19.2 and 19.3, pp. 907–10). An upright official, Commissioner

Addiction to Opium
Throughout the nineteenth century, opium imports created a massive addiction problem in China, as this photograph of an opium den from around 1900 suggests. Not until the early twentieth century did the British prove willing to curtail the opium trade from their Indian colony. (Hulton-Deutsch Collection/Corbis)

Lin Zexu, led the campaign against opium use as a kind of "drug czar." His measures included seizing and destroying, without compensation, more than 3 million pounds of opium from Western traders and expelling them from the country.

The British, offended by this violation of property rights and emboldened by their new military power, sent a large naval expedition to China, determined to end the restrictive conditions under which they had long traded with that country. In the process, they would teach the Chinese a lesson about the virtues of free trade and the "proper" way to conduct relations among countries. Thus began the first Opium War, in which Britain's industrialized military might proved decisive. (See Documents: Voices from the Opium War, pp. 905–13, for more on the origins of that conflict.) The Treaty of Nanjing, which ended the war in 1842, largely on British terms, imposed numerous restrictions on Chinese sovereignty and opened five ports to European traders. Its provisions reflected the changed balance of global power that had emerged with Britain's Industrial Revolution. To the Chinese, that agreement represented the first of the "unequal treaties" that seriously eroded China's independence by the end of the century.

But it was not the last of those treaties. Britain's victory in a second Opium War (1856–1858) was accompanied by the brutal vandalizing of the emperor's exquisite Summer Palace outside Beijing and resulted in further humiliations. Still more ports were opened to foreign traders. Now those foreigners were allowed to travel freely and buy land in China, to preach Christianity under the protection of Chinese authorities, and to patrol some of China's rivers. Furthermore, the Chinese were forbidden to use the character for "barbarians" to refer to the British in official documents. Following military defeats at the hands of the French (1885) and Japanese (1895), China lost control of Vietnam, Korea, and Taiwan. By the end of the century, the Western nations plus Japan and Russia all had carved out spheres of influence within China, granting themselves special privileges to establish military bases, extract raw materials, and build railroads. Many Chinese believed that their country was being "carved up like a melon" (see Map 19.1 and the photo on p. 876).

Coupled with its internal crisis, China's encounter with European imperialism had reduced the proud Middle Kingdom to dependency on the Western powers as it became part of a European-based "informal empire." China was no longer the center of civilization to which barbarians paid homage and tribute, but just one nation

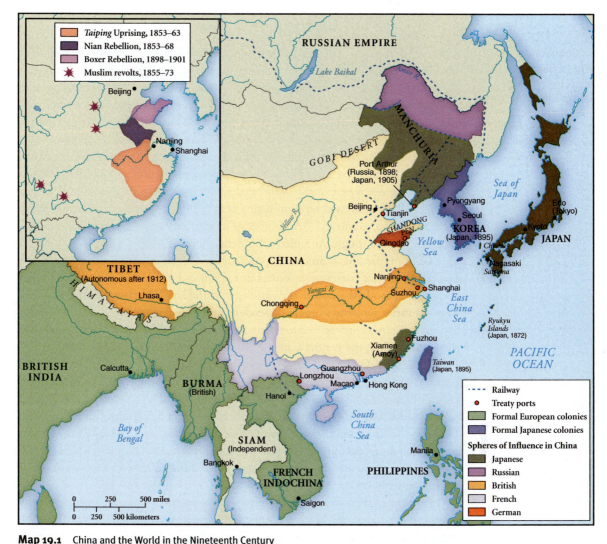

Map 19.1   China and the World in the Nineteenth Century
As China was reeling from massive internal upheavals during the nineteenth century, it also faced external assaults from Russia, Japan, and various European powers. By the end of the century, large parts of China were divided into spheres of influence, each affiliated with one of the major industrial powers of the day.

among many others, and a weak dependent nation at that. The Qing dynasty remained in power, but in a weakened condition, which served European interests well and Chinese interests poorly. Restrictions imposed by the unequal treaties clearly inhibited China's industrialization, as foreign goods and foreign investment flooded the country largely unrestricted. Chinese businessmen mostly served foreign firms, rather than developing as an independent capitalist class capable of leading China's own Industrial Revolution.

The Failure of Conservative Modernization

■ Connection
What strategies did China adopt to confront its various problems? In what ways did these strategies reflect China's own history and culture as well as the new global order?

Chinese authorities were not passive in the face of their country's mounting crises, both internal and external. Known as "self-strengthening," their policies during the 1860s and 1870s sought to reinvigorate a traditional China while borrowing cautiously from the West. An overhauled examination system, designed to recruit qualified candidates for official positions, sought the "good men" who could cope with the massive reconstruction that China faced in the wake of the Taiping rebellion. Support for landlords and the repair of dikes and irrigation helped restore rural social and economic order. A few industrial factories producing textiles and steel were established, coal mines were expanded, and a telegraph system was initiated. One Chinese general in 1863 confessed his humiliation that "Chinese weapons are far inferior to those of foreign countries."[10] A number of modern arsenals, shipyards, and foreign-language schools sought to remedy this deficiency.

Self-strengthening as an overall program for China's modernization was inhibited by the fears of conservative leaders that urban, industrial, or commercial development would erode the power and privileges of the landlord class. Furthermore, the new industries remained largely dependent on foreigners for machinery, materials, and expertise. And they served to strengthen local authorities who largely controlled them, rather than the central Chinese state.

The general failure of "self-strengthening" became apparent at the end of the century, when an antiforeign movement known as the Boxer uprising (1898–1901) erupted in northern China. Led by militia organizations calling themselves the Society of Righteous and Harmonious Fists, the "Boxers" killed numerous Europeans and Chinese Christians and laid siege to the foreign embassies in Beijing. When Western powers and Japan occupied Beijing to crush the rebellion and imposed a huge payment on China as a punishment, it was clear that China remained a dependent country, substantially under foreign control.

No wonder, then, that growing numbers of educated Chinese, including many in official elite positions, became highly disillusioned with the Qing dynasty, which was both foreign and ineffective in protecting China. By the late 1890s, such people were organizing a variety of clubs, study groups, and newspapers to examine China's desperate situation and to explore alternative paths. The names of these organizations reflect their outlook—the National Rejuvenation Study Society, Society to Protect the Nation, and Understand the National Shame Society. They admired not only Western science and technology but also Western political practices that limited the authority of the ruler and permitted wider circles of people to take part in public life. They believed that only a truly unified nation in which rulers and ruled were closely related could save China from dismemberment at the hands of foreign imperialists. Thus was born the immensely powerful force of Chinese nationalism, directed against both the foreign imperialists and the foreign Qing dynasty, which many held responsible for China's nineteenth-century disasters.

The Qing dynasty response to these new pressures proved inadequate. More extensive reform in the early twentieth century, including the end of the old examination system and the promise of a national parliament, was a classic case of too little too late. In 1911, the ancient imperial order that had governed China for two millennia collapsed, with only a modest nudge from organized revolutionaries. It was the end of a long era in China and the beginning of an immense struggle over the country's future.

The Ottoman Empire and the West in the Nineteenth Century

Like China, the Islamic world represented a highly successful civilization that felt little need to learn from the "infidels" or "barbarians" of the West until it collided with an expanding and aggressive Europe in the nineteenth century. Unlike China, though, Islamic civilization had been a near neighbor to Europe for 1,000 years. Its most prominent state, the Ottoman Empire, had long governed substantial parts of the Balkans and posed a clear military and religious threat to Europe in the sixteenth and seventeenth centuries. But if its encounter with the West was less abrupt than that of China, it was no less consequential. Neither the Ottoman Empire nor China fell under direct colonial rule, but both were much diminished as the changing balance of global power took hold; both launched efforts at "defensive modernization" aimed at strengthening their states and preserving their independence; and in both societies, some people held tightly to old identities and values, even as others embraced new loyalties associated with nationalism and modernity.

"The Sick Man of Europe"

In 1750, the Ottoman Empire was still the central political fixture of a widespread Islamic world. From its Turkish heartland of Anatolia, it ruled over much of the Arab world, from which Islam had come. It protected pilgrims on their way to Mecca, governed Egypt and coastal North Africa, and incorporated millions of Christians in the Balkans. Its ruler, the sultan, claimed the role of caliph, successor to the Prophet Muhammad, and was widely viewed as the leader, defender, and primary representative of the Islamic world. But by the middle, and certainly by the end, of the nineteenth century, the Ottoman Empire was no longer able to deal with Europe from a position of equality, let alone superiority. Among the Great Powers of the West, it was now known as "the sick man of Europe." Within the Muslim world, the Ottoman Empire, once viewed as "the strong sword of Islam," was unable to prevent region after region—India, Indonesia, West Africa, Central Asia—from falling under the control of Christian powers.

The Ottoman Empire's own domains shrank considerably at the hands of Russian, British, Austrian, and French aggression (see Map 19.2). In 1798, Napoleon's invasion

■ Change
What lay behind the decline of the Ottoman Empire in the nineteenth century?

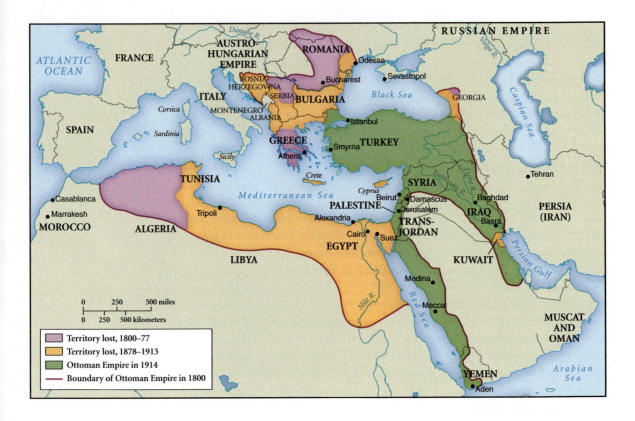

Map 19.2 The Contraction of the Ottoman Empire Foreign aggression and nationalist movements substantially diminished the Ottoman Empire during the nineteenth century, but they also stimulated a variety of efforts to revive and reform Ottoman society.

of Egypt, which had long been a province of the Ottoman Empire, was a particularly stunning blow. A contemporary observer, Abd al-Rahman al-Jabarti, described the French entry into Cairo:

> [T]he French entered the city like a torrent rushing through the alleys and streets without anything to stop them, like demons of the Devil's army.... And the French trod in the Mosque of al-Azhar with their shoes, carrying swords and rifles.... They plundered whatever they found in the mosque.... They treated the books and Quranic volumes as trash.... Furthermore, they soiled the mosque, blowing their spit in it, pissing and defecating in it. They guzzled wine and smashed bottles in the central court.[11]

When the French left, a virtually independent Egypt pursued a modernizing and empire-building program of its own and on one occasion came close to toppling the Ottoman Empire itself.

Beyond territorial losses to stronger European powers, other parts of the empire, such as Greece, Serbia, Bulgaria, and Romania, achieved independence based on their own surging nationalism and support from the British or the Russians. The continued independence of the core region of the Ottoman Empire owed much to the inability of Europe's Great Powers to agree on how to divide it up among themselves.

Behind the contraction of the Ottoman Empire lay other problems. As in China, the central Ottoman state had weakened, particularly in its ability to raise necessary revenue, as provincial authorities and local warlords gained greater power. Moreover, the Janissaries, once the effective and innovative elite infantry units of the Ottoman Empire, lost their military edge, becoming a highly conservative force within the empire. The technological and military gap with the West was clearly growing.

Economically, the earlier centrality of the Ottoman and Arab lands in Afro-Eurasian commerce diminished as Europeans achieved direct oceanic access to the treasures of Asia. Competition from cheap European manufactured goods hit Ottoman artisans hard and led to urban riots protesting foreign imports. Furthermore, a series of agreements, known as capitulations, between European countries and the Ottoman Empire granted Westerners various exemptions from Ottoman law and taxation. Like the unequal treaties in China, these agreements facilitated European penetration of the Ottoman economy and became widely resented. Such measures eroded Ottoman sovereignty and reflected the changing position of that empire relative to Europe. So too did the growing indebtedness of the Ottoman Empire, which came to rely on foreign loans to finance its efforts at economic development. By 1882, its inability to pay the interest on those debts led to foreign control of much of its revenue-generating system and the outright occupation of Egypt by the British. Like China, the Ottoman Empire had fallen into a position of considerable dependency on Europe.

Reform and Its Opponents

The leadership of the Ottoman Empire recognized many of its "illnesses" and during the nineteenth century mounted increasingly ambitious programs of "defensive modernization" that were earlier, more sustained, and far more vigorous than the timid and half-hearted measures of self-strengthening in China. One reason perhaps lay in the absence of any internal upheaval, such as the Taiping uprising in China, which threatened the very existence of the ruling dynasty. Nationalist revolts on the empire's periphery, rather than Chinese-style peasant rebellion at the center, represented the primary internal crisis of nineteenth-century Ottoman history. Nor did the Middle East in general experience the explosive population growth that contributed so much to China's nineteenth-century crisis. Furthermore, the long-established Ottoman leadership was Turkic and Muslim, culturally similar to its core population, whereas China's Qing dynasty rulers were widely regarded as foreigners from Manchuria.

Ottoman reforms began in the late eighteenth century when Sultan Selim III sought to reorganize and update the army and to draw on European advisers and techniques. Even these modest innovations stirred the hostility of powerful factions among both the *ulama* (religious scholars) and the elite military corps of Janissaries, who saw them in conflict with both Islam and their own institutional interests. Opposition to his measures was so strong that Selim was overthrown in 1807 and then murdered.

■ **Change**

In what different ways did the Ottoman state respond to its various problems?

Subsequent sultans, however, crushed the Janissaries and brought the ulama more thoroughly under state control than elsewhere in the Islamic world.

Then, in the several decades after 1839, more far-reaching reformist measures, known as Tanzimat (reorganization), took shape as the Ottoman leadership sought to provide the economic, social, and legal underpinnings for a strong and newly recentralized state. Factories producing cloth, paper, and armaments; modern mining operations; reclamation and resettlement of agricultural land; telegraphs, steamships, railroads, and a modern postal service; Western-style law codes and courts; new elementary and secondary schools—all of these new departures began a long process of modernization and Westernization in the Ottoman Empire.

Even more revolutionary, at least in principle, were changes in the legal status of the empire's diverse communities, which now gave non-Muslims equal rights under the law. An imperial proclamation of 1839 declared:

> Every distinction or designation tending to make any class whatever of the subjects of my Empire inferior to another class, on account of their religion, language or race shall be forever effaced.... No subject of my Empire shall be hindered in the exercise of the religion that he professes.... All the subjects of my Empire, without distinction of nationality, shall be admissible to public employment.

This declaration represented a dramatic change that challenged the fundamentally Islamic character of the state. Mixed tribunals with representatives from various religious groups were established to hear cases involving non-Muslims. More Christians were appointed to high office. A mounting tide of secular legislation and secular

The Ottoman Empire and the West

The intense interaction of the Ottoman Empire and the world of European powers is illustrated in this nineteenth-century Austrian painting, which depicts an elaborate gathering of Ottoman officials with members of the Austrian royal family around 1850. (Miramare Palace Trieste/Alfredo Dagli Orti/The Art Archive)

schools, drawing heavily on European models, now competed with traditional Islamic institutions.

The reform process raised profound and highly contested questions. What was the Ottoman Empire, and who were its people? To those who supported the reforms, the Ottoman Empire was a secular state whose people were loyal to the dynasty that ruled it, rather than a primarily Muslim state based on religious principles. This was the outlook of a new class spawned by the reform process itself—lower-level officials, military officers, writers, poets, and journalists, many of whom had a modern Western-style education. Dubbed the Young Ottomans, they were active during the middle decades of the nineteenth century, as they sought major changes in the Ottoman political system itself. They favored a more European-style democratic, constitutional regime that could curtail the absolute power of the emperor. Only such a political system, they felt, could mobilize the energies of the country to overcome backwardness and preserve the state against European aggression. Known as Islamic modernism, such ideas found expression in many parts of the Muslim world in the second half of the century. Muslim societies, they argued, needed to embrace Western technical and scientific knowledge, while rejecting its materialism. Islam in their view could accommodate a full modernity without sacrificing its essential religious character. After all, the Islamic world had earlier hosted impressive scientific achievements and had incorporated elements of Greek philosophical thinking.

In 1876, the Young Ottomans experienced a short-lived victory when the Sultan Abd al-Hamid (1876–1909) accepted a constitution and an elected parliament, but not for long. Under the pressure of war with Russia, the Sultan soon suspended the reforms and reverted to an older style of despotic rule for the next thirty years, even renewing the claim that he was the caliph, successor to the Prophet and the protector of Muslims everywhere.

Opposition to this revived despotism soon surfaced among both military and civilian elites known as the Young Turks. Largely abandoning any reference to Islam, they advocated a militantly secular public life, were committed to thoroughgoing modernization along European lines, and increasingly thought about the Ottoman Empire as a Turkish national state. "There is only one civilization, and that is European civilization," declared Abdullah Cevdet, a prominent figure in the Young Turk movement. "Therefore we must borrow western civilization with both its rose and its thorn."[12]

A military coup in 1908 finally allowed the Young Turks to exercise real power. They pushed for a radical secularization of schools, courts, and law codes; permitted elections and competing parties; established a single Law of Family Rights for all regardless of religion; and encouraged Turkish as the official language of the empire. They also opened up modern schools for women, allowed them to wear Western clothing, restricted polygamy, and permitted women to obtain divorces in some situations. But the nationalist conception of Ottoman identity antagonized non-Turkic peoples and helped stimulate Arab and other nationalisms in response. For some, a secular nationality was becoming the most important public loyalty, with Islam relegated to private life. Such nationalist sentiments contributed to the complete disintegration

■ **Comparison**

In what different ways did various groups define the Ottoman Empire during the nineteenth century?

of the Ottoman Empire following World War I, but the secularizing and Western-izing principles of the Young Turks informed the policies of the Turkish republic that replaced it.

Outcomes: Comparing China and the Ottoman Empire

By the beginning of the twentieth century, both China and the Ottoman Empire, recently centers of proud and vibrant civilizations, had experienced the consequences of a rapidly shifting balance of global power. Now they were "semicolonies" within the "informal empires" of Europe, although they retained sufficient independence for their governments to launch catch-up efforts of defensive modernization. But nei-ther was able to create the industrial economies or strong states required to fend off European intrusion and restore their former status in the world. Despite their dimin-ished power, however, both China and the Ottoman Empire gave rise to new nation-alist conceptions of society, which were initially small and limited in appeal but of great significance for the future.

In the early twentieth century, that future witnessed the end of both the Chinese and Ottoman empires. In China, the collapse of the imperial system in 1911 was fol-lowed by a vast revolutionary upheaval that by 1949 led to a communist regime within largely the same territorial space as the old empire. By contrast, the collapse of the Ottoman Empire following World War I led to the creation of a new but much smaller nation-state in the Turkish heartland of the old empire, having lost its vast Arab and European provinces.

China's twentieth-century revolutionaries rejected traditional Confucian culture far more thoroughly than the secularizing leaders of modern Turkey rejected Islam. Almost everywhere in the Islamic world, traditional religion retained its hold on the private loyalties of most people and later in the twentieth century became a basis for social renewal in many places. Islamic civilization, unlike its Chinese counterpart, had many independent centers and was never so closely associated with a single state. Fur-thermore, it was embedded in a deeply religious tradition that was personally mean-ingful to millions of adherents, in contrast to the more elitist and secular outlook of Confucianism. Many rural Chinese, however, retained traditional Confucian values such as filial piety, and Confucianism has made something of a comeback in China over the past several decades. Nonetheless, Islam retained a hold on its civilization in the twentieth century rather more firmly than Confucianism did in China.

The Japanese Difference: The Rise of a New East Asian Power

Like China and the Ottoman Empire, the island country of Japan confronted the aggressive power of the West during the nineteenth century, most notably in the form of U.S. commodore Matthew Perry's "black ships," which steamed into Tokyo Bay in 1853 and forcefully demanded that this reclusive nation open up to more "normal" relations with the world. However, the outcome of that encounter differed sharply from the others. In the second half of the nineteenth century, Japan undertook a radical transformation of its society—a "revolution from above," according to some historians—turning it into a powerful, modern, united, industrialized nation. It was an achievement that neither China nor the Ottoman Empire was able to duplicate. Far from succumbing to Western domination, Japan joined the club of imperialist countries by creating its own East Asian empire, largely at the expense of China. In building a society that was both modern and distinctly Japanese, Japan demonstrated that modernity was not a uniquely European phenomenon. This "Japanese miracle," as some have called it, was both promising and ominous for the rest of Asia. How had it occurred?

The Tokugawa Background

For 250 years prior to Perry's arrival, Japan had been governed by a *shogun* (a military ruler) from the Tokugawa family who acted in the name of a revered but powerless emperor, who lived in Kyoto, 300 miles away from the seat of power in Edo (Tokyo). The chief task of this Tokugawa shogunate was to prevent the return of civil war among some 260 rival feudal lords, known as *daimyo*, each of whom had a cadre of armed retainers, the famed samurai warriors of Japanese tradition.

■ **Comparison**
How did Japan's historical development differ from that of China and the Ottoman Empire during the nineteenth century?

Based on their own military power and political skills, successive shoguns gave Japan more than two centuries of internal peace (1600–1850). To control the restive daimyo, they required these local authorities to create second homes in Edo, the country's capital, where they had to live during alternate years. When they left for their rural residences, families stayed behind, almost as hostages. Nonetheless, the daimyo, especially the more powerful ones, retained substantial autonomy in their own domains and behaved in some ways like independent states with separate military forces, law codes, tax systems, and currencies. With no national army, no uniform currency, and little central authority at the local level, Tokugawa Japan was "pacified...but not really unified."[13] To further stabilize the country, the Tokugawa regime issued highly detailed rules governing occupation, residence, dress, hairstyles, and behavior of the four hierarchically ranked status groups into which Japanese society was divided—samurai at the top, then peasants, artisans, and, at the bottom, merchants.

Much was changing within Japan during these 250 years of peace in ways that belied the control and orderliness of Tokugawa regulations. For one thing, the samurai, in the absence of wars to fight, evolved into a salaried bureaucratic or administrative class amounting to 5 to 6 percent of the total population, but they were still fiercely devoted to their daimyo lords and to their warrior code of loyalty, honor, and self-sacrifice.

■ **Change**
In what ways was Japan changing during the Tokugawa era?

More generally, centuries of peace contributed to a remarkable burst of economic growth, commercialization, and urban development. Entrepreneurial peasants, using fertilizers and other agricultural innovations, grew more rice than ever before and engaged in a variety of rural manufacturing enterprises as well. By 1750, Japan had become perhaps the world's most urbanized country, with about 10 percent of its population living in sizable towns or cities. Edo, with a million residents, was the world's largest city. Well-functioning markets linked urban and rural areas, marking Japan as an emerging capitalist economy. The influence of Confucianism encouraged education and generated a remarkably literate population, with about 40 percent of men and 15 percent of women able to read and write. Although no one was aware of it at the time, these changes during the Tokugawa era provided a solid foundation for Japan's remarkable industrial growth in the late nineteenth century.

These changes also undermined the shogunate's efforts to freeze Japanese society in the interests of stability. Some samurai found the lowly but profitable path of commerce too much to resist. "No more shall we have to live by the sword," declared one of them in 1616 while renouncing his samurai status. "I have seen that great profit can be made honorably. I shall brew *sake* and soy sauce, and we shall prosper."[14] Many merchants, though hailing from the lowest-ranking status group, prospered in the new commercial environment and supported a vibrant urban culture, while not a few daimyo found it necessary, if humiliating, to seek loans from these social inferiors. Thus merchants had money, but little status, whereas samurai enjoyed high status but were often indebted to inferior merchants. Both resented their position.

Despite prohibitions to the contrary, many peasants moved to the cities, becoming artisans or merchants and imitating the ways of their social betters. A decree of 1788 noted that peasants "have become accustomed to luxury and forgetful of their status." They wore inappropriate clothing, used umbrellas rather than straw hats in the rain, and even left the villages for the city. "Henceforth," declared the shogun, "all luxuries should be avoided by the peasants. They are to live simply and devote themselves to farming."[15] This decree, like many others before it, was widely ignored.

More than social change undermined the Tokugawa regime. Corruption was widespread, to the disgust of many. The shogunate's failure to deal successfully with a severe famine in the 1830s eroded confidence in its effectiveness. At the same time, a mounting wave of local peasant uprisings and urban riots expressed the many grievances of the poor. The most striking of these outbursts left the city of Osaka in flames in 1837. Its leader, Oshio Heihachiro, no doubt spoke for many ordinary people when he wrote:

> We must first punish the officials who torment the people so cruelly; then we must execute the haughty and rich Osaka merchants. Then we must distribute the gold, silver, and copper stored in their cellars, and bands of rice hidden in their storehouses.[16]

From the 1830s on, one scholar concluded, "there was a growing feeling that the *shogunate* was losing control."[17]

American Intrusion and the Meiji Restoration

It was foreign intervention that brought matters to a head. Since the expulsion of European missionaries and the harsh suppression of Christianity in the early seventeenth century (see p. 681), Japan had deliberately limited its contact with the West to a single port, where only the Dutch were allowed to trade. By the early nineteenth century, however, various European countries and the United States were knocking at the door. All were turned away, and even shipwrecked sailors or whalers were expelled, jailed, or executed. As it happened, it was the United States that forced the issue, sending Commodore Perry in 1853 to demand humane treatment for castaways, the right of American vessels to refuel and buy provisions, and the opening of ports for trade. Authorized to use force

The "Opening" of Japan This nineteenth-century Japanese woodblock print depicts Commodore Perry's meeting with a Japanese official in 1853. It was this encounter that launched Japan on a series of dramatic changes that resulted in the country's modernization and its emergence as one of the world's major industrialized powers by the early twentieth century. (Bettmann/Corbis)

if necessary, Perry presented his reluctant hosts, among other gifts, with a white flag for surrender should hostilities follow. (For a Japanese perception of Perry and his ships, see Visual Sources 19.1 and 19.2, pp. 916 and 917.)

In the end, war was avoided. Aware of what had happened to China in resisting European demands, Japan agreed to a series of unequal treaties with various Western powers. That humiliating capitulation to the demands of the "foreign devils" further eroded support for the shogunate, triggered a brief civil war, and by 1868 led to a political takeover by a group of young samurai from southern Japan. This decisive turning point in Japan's history was known as the Meiji restoration, for the country's new rulers claimed that they were restoring to power the young emperor, then a fifteen-year-old boy whose throne name was Meiji, or Enlightened Rule. But despite his youth, he was regarded as the most recent link in a chain of descent that traced the origins of the imperial family back to the sun goddess Amaterasu. Having eliminated the shogunate, the patriotic young men who led the takeover soon made their goals clear — to save Japan from foreign domination, not by futile resistance, but by a thorough transformation of Japanese society, drawing upon all that the modern West had to offer. "Knowledge shall be sought throughout the world," they declared, "so as to strengthen the foundations of imperial rule."

Japan now had a government committed to a decisive break with the past, and it had acquired that government without massive violence or destruction. By contrast, the defeat of the Taiping Uprising had deprived China of any such opportunity for a fresh start, while saddling it with enormous devastation and massive loss of life. Furthermore, Japan was of less interest to Western powers than either China, with its huge potential market and reputation for riches, or the Ottoman Empire, with its strategic location at the crossroads of Asia, Africa, and Europe. The American Civil War and its aftermath likewise deflected U.S. ambitions in the Pacific for a time, further reducing the Western pressure on Japan.

Modernization Japanese Style

■ Change
In what respects was
Japan's nineteenth-
century transformation
revolutionary?

These circumstances gave Japan some breathing space, and its new rulers moved quickly to take advantage of that unique window of opportunity by directing a cascading wave of dramatic changes that rolled over the country in the last three decades of the nineteenth century. Those reforms, which were revolutionary in their cumulative effect, transformed Japan far more thoroughly than even the most radical of the Ottoman efforts, let alone the modest self-strengthening policies of the Chinese.

The first task was genuine national unity, which required an attack on the power and privileges of both the daimyo and the samurai. In a major break with the past, the new regime soon ended the semi-independent domains of the daimyo, replacing them with governors appointed by and responsible to the emerging national government. The central state, not the local authorities, now collected the nation's taxes and raised a national army based on conscription from all social classes.

Thus the samurai relinquished their ancient role as the country's warrior class and with it their cherished right to carry swords. The old Confucian-based social order with its special privileges for various classes was largely dismantled, and almost all Japanese became legally equal as commoners and as subjects of the emperor. Limitations on travel and trade likewise fell as a nationwide economy came to parallel the centralized state. Although there was some opposition to these measures, including a brief rebellion of resentful samurai in 1877, it was on the whole a remarkably peaceful process in which a segment of the old ruling class abolished its own privileges. Many, but not all, of these displaced elites found a soft landing in the army, bureaucracy, or business enterprises of the new regime, thus easing a painful transition.

Accompanying these social and political changes was a widespread and eager fascination with almost everything Western (see Visual Source 19.3, p. 918). Knowledge about the West—its science and technology; its various political and constitutional arrangements; its legal and educational systems; its dances, clothing, and hairstyles—was enthusiastically sought out by official missions to Europe and the United States, by hundreds of students sent to study abroad, and by many ordinary Japanese at home. Western writers were translated into Japanese; for example, Samuel Smiles's *Self-Help*, which focused on "achieving success and rising in the world," sold a million copies. "Civilization and Enlightenment" was the slogan of the time, and both were to be found in the West. The most prominent popularizer of Western knowledge, Fukuzawa Yukichi, summed up the chief lesson of his studies in the mid-1870s—Japan was backward and needed to learn from the West: "If we compare the knowledge of the Japanese and Westerners, in letters, in technique, in commerce, or in industry, from the largest to the smallest matter, there is not one thing in which we excel.... In Japan's present condition there is nothing in which we may take pride vis-à-vis the West."[18]

After this initial wave of uncritical enthusiasm for everything Western receded, Japan proceeded to borrow more selectively and to combine foreign and Japanese

Snapshot   **Key Moments in the Rise of Japan in the Nineteenth Century and Beyond**

Famines, urban and rural rebellions	1830s
Commodore Perry arrives in Japan	1853
Meiji restoration	1868
Government-run enterprises in railroad construction, manufacturing, and mining	1870s
Western dress prescribed for court and official ceremonies	1872
Samurai rebellion crushed	1877
Government sells state industries to private investors	1880s
Ito Hirobumi travels to Europe to study political systems	1882
Peak of peasant protest against high taxes and prices	1883–1884
Women banned from political parties and meetings	1887
Japan's modern constitution announced	1889
Sino-Japanese War	1894–1895
Japan's labor movement crushed	by 1901
Anglo-Japanese alliance marks Japan's acceptance as Great Power	1902
Russo-Japanese War	1904–1905
Universal primary education	1905
Japanese annexation of Korea	1910
Meiji emperor dies	1912

elements in distinctive ways (see Visual Source 19.4, p. 919). For example, the constitution of 1889, drawing heavily on German experience, introduced an elected parliament, political parties, and democratic ideals, but that constitution was presented as a gift from a sacred emperor descended from the Sun Goddess. The parliament could advise, but ultimate power, and particularly control of the military, lay theoretically with the emperor and in practice with an oligarchy of prominent reformers acting in his name. Likewise, a modern educational system, which achieved universal primary schooling by the early twentieth century, was also laced with Confucian-based moral instruction and exhortations of loyalty to the emperor. Neither Western-style feminism nor Christianity made much headway in Meiji Japan, but Shinto, an ancient religious tradition featuring ancestors and nature spirits, was elevated to the status of an official state cult. Japan's earlier experience in borrowing massively but selectively from Chinese culture perhaps served it better in these new circumstances than either the Chinese disdain for foreign cultures or the reluctance of many Muslims to see much of value in the infidel West.

At the core of Japan's effort at defensive modernization lay its state-guided industrialization program. More than in Europe or the United States, the government itself established a number of enterprises, later selling many of them to private investors. It also acted to create a modern infrastructure by building railroads, creating a postal system, and establishing a national currency and banking system. By the early twentieth century, Japan's industrialization, organized around a number of large firms called *zaibatsu*, was well under way. The country became a major exporter of textiles and was able to produce its own munitions and industrial goods as well. Its major cities enjoyed mass-circulation newspapers, movie theaters, and electric lights. All of this was accomplished through its own resources and without the massive foreign debt that so afflicted Egypt and the Ottoman Empire. No other country outside of Europe and North America had been able to launch its own Industrial Revolution in the nineteenth century. It was a distinctive feature of Japan's modern transformation.

Less distinctive, however, were the social results of that process. Taxed heavily to pay for Japan's ambitious modernization program, many peasant families slid into poverty. Their sometimes violent protests peaked in 1883–1884 with attacks on government offices and moneylenders' homes that were aimed at destroying records of debt. Despite substantial private relief efforts, the Japanese countryside witnessed infanticide, the sale of daughters, and starvation.

As elsewhere during the early stages of industrial growth, urban workers were treated badly. The majority of Japan's textile workers were young women from poor

Japan's Modernization
In Japan, as in Europe, railroads quickly became a popular symbol of the country's modernization, as this woodblock print from the 1870s illustrates. (Visual Arts Library [London]/Alamy)

families in the countryside. Their pay was low and their working conditions terrible. Anarchist and socialist ideas circulated among intellectuals. Efforts to create unions and organize strikes, both illegal in Japan at the time, were met with harsh repression even as corporate and state authorities sought to depict the company as a family unit to which workers should give their loyalty, all under the beneficent gaze of the divine emperor.

Japan and the World

Japan's modern transformation soon registered internationally. By the early twentieth century, its economic growth, openness to trade, and embrace of "civilization and enlightenment" from the West persuaded the Western powers to revise the unequal treaties in Japan's favor. This had long been a primary goal of the Meiji regime, and the Anglo-Japanese Treaty of 1902 now acknowledged Japan as an equal player among the Great Powers of the world.

■ **Connection**
How did Japan's relationship to the larger world change during its modernization process?

Not only did Japan escape from its semicolonial entanglements with the West, but it also launched its own empire-building enterprise, even as European powers and the United States were carving up much of Asia and Africa into colonies or spheres of influence. It was what industrializing Great Powers did in the late nineteenth century, and Japan followed suit. Successful wars against China (1894–1895) and Russia (1904–1905) established Japan as a formidable military competitor in East Asia and the first Asian state to defeat a major European power. Through those victories, Japan also gained colonial control of Taiwan and Korea and a territorial foothold in Manchuria. (See Visual Source 19.5, p. 920, for an image of Japan's new relationship with China and the West.)

Japan's entry onto the broader global stage was felt in many places (see Map 19.3). It added yet one more imperialist power to those already burdening a beleaguered China. Defeat at the hands of Japanese upstarts shocked Russia and triggered the 1905 revolution in that country. To Europeans and Americans, Japan was now an economic, political, and military competitor in Asia.

In the world of subject peoples, the rise of Japan and its defeat of Russia generated widespread admiration among those who saw Japan as a model for their own modern development and perhaps as an ally in the struggle against imperialism. Some Poles, Finns, and Jews viewed the Russian defeat in 1905 as an opening for their own liberation from the Russian Empire and were grateful to Japan for the opportunity. Despite Japan's aggression against their country, many Chinese reformers and nationalists found in the Japanese experience valuable lessons for themselves. Thousands flocked to Japan to study its achievements. Newspapers throughout the Islamic world celebrated Japan's victory over Russia as an "awakening of the East," which might herald Muslims' own liberation. Some Turkish women gave their children Japanese names. Indonesian Muslims from Aceh wrote to the Meiji emperor asking for help in their struggle against the Dutch, and Muslim poets wrote odes in his honor. The Egyptian nationalist Mustafa Kamil spoke for many when he declared:

Map 19.3 The Rise of Japan

As Japan modernized after the Meiji restoration, it launched an empire-building program that provided a foundation for further expansion in the 1930s and during World War II.

"We are amazed by Japan because it is the first Eastern government to utilize Western civilization to resist the shield of European imperialism in Asia."[19]

Those who directly experienced Japanese imperialism in Taiwan or Korea no doubt had a less positive view, for its colonial policies matched or exceeded the brutality of European practices. In the twentieth century, China and much of Southeast Asia suffered bitterly under Japanese imperial aggression. Nonetheless, both the idea of Japan as a liberator of Asia from the European yoke and the reality of Japan as an oppressive imperial power in its own right derived from the country's remarkable modern transformation and its unique response to the provocation of Western intrusion.

Reflections: Success and Failure in History

Beyond describing what happened in the past and explaining why, historians often find themselves evaluating the events they study. When they make judgments about the past, notions of success and failure frequently come into play. Should Europe's Industrial Revolution and its rise to global power be regarded as a success? If so, does that imply that others were failures? Should we consider Japan more successful than China or the Ottoman Empire during the nineteenth century? Three considerations suggest that we should be very careful in applying these ideas to the complexities of the historical record.

First, and most obviously, is the question of criteria. If the measure of success is national wealth and power, then the Industrial Revolution surely counts as a great accomplishment. But if preservation of the environment, spiritual growth, and the face-to-face relationships of village life are more highly valued, then industrialization, according to some, might be more reasonably considered as a disaster.

Second, there is the issue of "success for whom?" British artisans who lost their livelihood to industrial machines as well as those Japanese women textile workers who suffered through the early stages of industrialization might be forgiven for not appreciating the "success" of their countries' transformation, even if their middle-class counterparts and subsequent generations benefited. In cases such as this, issues of both social and generational justice complicate any easy assessment of the past.

Finally, success is frequently associated with good judgment and wise choices, yet actors in the historical drama are never completely free in making their decisions, and none, of course, have the benefit of hindsight, which historians enjoy. Did the leaders of China and the Ottoman Empire fail to push industrial development more strongly, or were they not in a position to do so? Were Japanese leaders wiser and more astute than their counterparts elsewhere, or did their knowledge of China's earlier experience and their unique national history simply provide them with circumstances more conducive to modern development? Such questions regarding the possibilities and limitations of human action have no clear-cut answers, but they might caution us about any easy use of notions of success and failure.

Second Thoughts

What's the Significance?

social Darwinism	China, 1911	informal empires
Taiping Uprising	"the sick man of Europe"	Tokugawa Japan
Opium Wars	Tanzimat	Meiji restoration
unequal treaties	Young Ottomans	Russo-Japanese War,
self-strengthening movement	Sultan Abd al-Hamid II	1904–1905
Boxer uprising	Young Turks	

To assess your mastery of the material in this chapter, visit the **Student Center** at bedfordstmartins.com/strayer.

Big Picture Questions

1. How did European expansion in the nineteenth century differ from that of the early modern era (see Chapters 14–16)?
2. What differences can you identify in how China, the Ottoman Empire, and Japan experienced Western imperialism and confronted it? How might you account for those differences?
3. "The response of each society to European imperialism grew out of its larger historical development and its internal problems." What evidence might support this statement?
4. What kinds of debates, controversies, and conflicts were generated by European intrusion within each of the societies examined in this chapter?

Next Steps: For Further Study

For Web sites and additional documents related to this chapter, see **Make History** at bedfordstmartins.com/strayer.

William Bowman et al., *Imperialism in the Modern World* (2007). A collection of short readings illustrating the various forms and faces of European expansion over the past several centuries.

Carter V. Finley, *The Turks in World History* (2004). A study placing the role of Turkish-speaking peoples in general and the Ottoman Empire in particular in a global context.

Maurice Jansen, *The Making of Modern Japan* (2000). A well-regarded account of Japan since 1600 by a leading scholar.

Jonathan Spence, *The Search for Modern China* (1999). Probably the best single-volume account of Chinese history from about 1600 through the twentieth century.

E. Patricia Tsurumi, *Factory Girls: Women in the Thread Mills of Meiji Japan* (1990). An examination of the lives of women in Japan's nineteenth-century textile factories.

Arthur Waley, *The Opium War through Chinese Eyes* (1968). An older classic that views the Opium War from various Chinese points of view.

Justin Jesty, "Japanese History from 1868 to the Present," http://ceas.uchicago.edu/outreach/1868%20to%20Present.pdf. A guide to modern Japanese history, with many links to pictures, documents, and further information.

Documents

Considering the Evidence:
Voices from the Opium War

The Opium War of 1839–1842 marked a dramatic turn in China's long history and in its relationship with the wider world. It was also indicative of the new kinds of cross-cultural encounters that were increasingly taking place as Europe's global power mounted. The five documents in this section of the chapter allow us to follow the unfolding of that encounter, largely from a Chinese point of view.

By the early nineteenth century, China had long enjoyed a position of unrivaled dominance in East Asia. Furthermore, its wealth and technological innovations had given it a major role in the world economy of the early modern era, reflected in the flow of much of the world's silver into China. At the same time, the island nation of Great Britain was emerging as a major global economic and military power, thanks to its position as the first site of the Industrial Revolution and its increasingly dominant role in India.

At the heart of the emerging conflict between these two countries was trade rather than territory. From the British point of view, the problem lay in the sharp restrictions that the Chinese had long imposed on commerce between the two nations. The British were permitted to trade only in a single city, Canton, and even there had to deal with an officially approved group of Chinese merchants. This so-called Canton system meant that Europeans had no direct access to the Chinese market. Thus in the early 1790s, the British government sent a major diplomatic mission to China, headed by Lord George Macartney, to seek greater access to the Chinese market.

Document 19.1

A Chinese Response to Lord Macartney

Despite a polite reception at the Chinese court, Macartney's mission was an almost total failure from the British point of view. At its conclusion the Chinese emperor Qianlong sent a message to the British monarch George III replying to Macartney's requests.

■ What reasons does Emperor Qianlong give for rejecting British requests?

- What does this document reveal about the Chinese view of trade in general?

- What does it show about China's relations with foreign "barbarians," and about China's understanding of its place in the world?

- In what historical context does the Chinese emperor understand Macartney's mission?

EMPEROR QIANLONG
Message to King George III
1793

You, O King, from afar have yearned after the blessings of our civilization, and in your eagerness to come into touch with our converting influence have sent an Embassy across the sea bearing a memorial. I have already taken note of your respectful spirit of submission, have treated your mission with extreme favor and loaded it with gifts, besides issuing a mandate to you, O King, and honoring you with the bestowal of valuable presents. Thus has my indulgence been manifested.

Yesterday your Ambassador petitioned my Ministers to memorialize me regarding your trade with China, but his proposal is not consistent with our dynastic usage and cannot be entertained. Hitherto, all European nations, including your own country's barbarian merchants, have carried on their trade with our Celestial Empire at Canton. Such has been the procedure for many years, although our Celestial Empire possesses all things in prolific abundance and lacks no product within its own borders. There was therefore no need to import the manufactures of outside barbarians in exchange for our own produce. But as the tea, silk, and porcelain which the Celestial Empire produces are absolute necessities to European nations and to yourselves, we have permitted, as a signal mark of favor, that foreign *hongs*°

should be established at Canton, so that your wants might be supplied and your country thus participate in our beneficence. But your Ambassador has now put forward new requests which completely fail to recognize the Throne's principle to "treat strangers from afar with indulgence," and to exercise a pacifying control over barbarian tribes, the world over. Moreover, our dynasty, swaying the myriad races of the globe, extends the same benevolence toward all. Your England is not the only nation trading at Canton. If other nations, following your bad example, wrongfully importune my ear with further impossible requests, how will it be possible for me to treat them with easy indulgence? Nevertheless, I do not forget the lonely remoteness of your island, cut off from the world by intervening wastes of sea, nor do I overlook your excusable ignorance of the usages of our Celestial Empire. I have consequently commanded my Ministers to enlighten your Ambassador on the subject, and have ordered the departure of the mission....

Your request for a small island near Chusan, where your merchants may reside and goods be warehoused, arises from your desire to develop trade. As there are neither foreign *hongs* nor interpreters in or near Chusan, where none of your ships have ever called, such an island would be utterly useless for your purposes. Every inch of the territory of our Empire is marked on the map and the strictest vigilance is exercised over it all: even tiny islets and far-lying sand-banks are clearly defined as part of the provinces to which they belong. Consider, more-

°*hongs*: approved Chinese trading firms.

Source: "Edict on Trade with Great Britain," in J. O. P. Brand, *Annals and Memoirs of the Court of Peking* (Boston: Houghton Mifflin, 1914), 325–31.

over, that England is not the only barbarian land which wishes to establish relations with our civilization and trade with our Empire: supposing that other nations were all to imitate your evil example and beseech me to present them each and all with a site for trading purposes, how could I possibly comply? This also is a flagrant infringement of the usage of my Empire and cannot possibly be entertained....

Regarding your nation's worship of the Lord of Heaven, it is the same religion as that of other European nations. Ever since the beginning of history, sage Emperors and wise rulers have bestowed on China a moral system and inculcated a code, which from time immemorial has been religiously observed by the myriads of my subjects [Confucianism]. There has been no hankering after heterodox doctrines. Even the European officials [missionaries] in my capital are forbidden to hold intercourse with Chinese subjects; they are restricted within the limits of their appointed residences, and may not go about propagating their religion. The distinction between Chinese and barbarian is most strict, and your Ambassador's request that barbarians shall be given full liberty to disseminate their religion is utterly unreasonable....

[Perhaps] you yourself are ignorant of our dynastic regulations and had no intention of transgressing them when you expressed these wild ideas and hopes.... If, after the receipt of this explicit decree, you lightly give ear to the representations of your subordinates and allow your barbarian merchants to proceed to Zhejiang and Tianjin, with the object of landing and trading there, the ordinances of my Celestial Empire are strict in the extreme, and the local officials, both civil and military, are bound reverently to obey the law of the land. Should your vessels touch the shore, your merchants will assuredly never be permitted to land or to reside there, but will be subject to instant expulsion. In that event your barbarian merchants will have had a long journey for nothing. Do not say that you were not warned in due time! Tremblingly obey and show no negligence! A special mandate!

Documents 19.2 and 19.3

Debating the Opium Problem

With Europe engulfed in the Napoleonic wars, Great Britain made no immediate response to China's 1793 rebuff. But in the several decades following Napoleon's 1815 defeat, the issue reemerged. This time the question was not just trade in general but opium in particular. By the early nineteenth century, that addictive drug was providing a solution to another of Great Britain's problems in its trade relations with China—the difficulty of finding Western goods that the Chinese were willing to buy. This had long meant that the British had to pay for much-desired Chinese products with major exports of silver. Now, however, opium grown in British India proved increasingly attractive in China, and imports soared.

But this solution to a British problem had by the mid-1830s provoked a growing and many-sided crisis for China. The country's legal prohibition on the importing of opium was widely ignored, silver was flowing out of the country to pay for the drug, and addiction was increasing, even among the elite. This dire situation prompted the Chinese emperor Daoguang to seek advice from his senior officials. The two documents that follow illustrate the sharp division within Chinese official circles, one side advocating legalization and the other counseling suppression.

- What arguments are made for each position? On what issues did they disagree?

- How might each respond to the arguments of the other?

- What similarities and differences do you see between this debate within the Chinese court of the 1830s and contemporary discussion about the legalization of marijuana in the United States?

XU NAIJI

An Argument for Legalization

1836

Xu Naiji, Vice-President of the Sacrificial Court, presents the following memorial in regard to opium, to show that the more severe the interdicts against it are made, the more widely do the evils arising therefrom spread....

In Keenlung's reign, as well as previously, opium was inserted in the tariff of Canton as a medicine, subject to a duty.... After this, it was prohibited.... Yet the smokers of the drug have increased in number, and the practice has spread almost throughout the whole empire....

Formerly, the barbarian merchants brought foreign money to China; which being paid in exchange for goods, was a source of pecuniary advantage to the people of all the sea-board provinces. But latterly, the barbarian merchants have clandestinely sold opium for money, which has rendered it unnecessary for them to import foreign silver. Thus foreign money has been going out of the country, while none comes into it.

It is proposed entirely to cut off the foreign trade, thus to remove the root, to dam up the source of the evil. The Celestial Dynasty would not, indeed, hesitate to relinquish the few millions of duties arising therefrom. But all the nations of the West have had a general market open to their ships for upward of a thousand years, while the dealers in opium are the English alone; it would be wrong, for the sake of cut-

ting off the English trade, to cut off that of all the other nations. Besides, the hundreds of thousands of people living on the sea-coast depend wholly on trade for their livelihood, and how are they to be disposed of? Moreover, the barbarian ships, being on the high seas, can repair to any island that may be selected as an entrepôt, and the native sea-going vessels can meet them there; it is then impossible to cut off the trade....Thus it appears that, though the commerce of Canton should be cut off, yet it will not be possible to prevent the clandestine introduction of merchandise.

It will be found, on examination, that the smokers of opium are idle, lazy vagrants, having no useful purpose before them, and are unworthy of regard or even of contempt. And though there are smokers to be found who have overstepped the threshold of age, yet they do not attain to the long life of other men. But new births are daily increasing the population of the empire; and there is no cause to apprehend a diminution therein; while, on the other hand, we cannot adopt too great, or too early, precautions against the annual waste which is taking place in the resources, the very substance of China.

Since then, it will not answer to close our ports against [all trades], and since the laws issued against opium are quite inoperative, the only method left is to revert to the former system, to permit the barbarian merchants to import opium paying duty thereon as a medicine, and to require that, after having passed the Custom-House, it shall be delivered to the Hong merchants only in exchange for merchandise, and

Source: "Memorial from Heu-Naetse," in *Blue Book— Correspondence Relating to China* (London, 1840), 56–59.

that no money be paid for it. The barbarians finding that the amount of dues to be paid on it, is less than what is now spent in bribes, will also gladly comply therein. Foreign money should be placed on the same footing with sycee silver, and the exportation of it should be equally prohibited. Offenders, when caught, should be punished by the entire destruction of the opium they may have, and the confiscation of the money that may be found with them....

It becomes my duty, then, to request that it be enacted, that any officer, scholar, or soldier, found guilty of secretly smoking opium, shall be immedi-

ately dismissed from public employ, without being made liable to any other penalty....

Lastly, that no regard be paid to the purchase and use of opium on the part of the people generally....

Besides, the removal of the prohibitions refers only to the vulgar and common people, those who have no official duties to perform. So long as the officers of the Government, the scholars, and the military are not included, I see no detriment to the dignity of the Government. And by allowing the proposed importation and exchange of the drug for other commodities, more than ten millions of money will annually be prevented from flowing out of the Central land.

YUAN YULIN

An Argument for Suppression

1836

I, your minister, believe that the success or failure in government and the prosperity or decay of administration depend largely upon our capacity to distinguish between right and wrong, between what is safe and what is dangerous.... The prevailing evil of to-day is the excuse that things are hard to get done, and the foremost example of such hypocrisy is the proposal to legalize opium....

In my humble opinion, the proposal for legalization has overlooked the distinction between right and wrong.... Further, it fails to appreciate what is safe and what is dangerous....

The prohibition of opium is most solemnly recorded on the statute books.... The proposal to change the established law is thus a violation of an inherited institution and of the imperial edicts.

Uniformity is the most important element in the decrees of the Court. Now it has been proposed that the prohibition of opium-smoking would reach the officers of the Government, the scholars, and the military, but not the common people. But it is forgotten that the common people of to-day will be

the officers, scholars, and the military of the future. Should they be allowed to smoke at first and then be prohibited from it in the future? Moreover, the officers, scholars, and the military of to-day may be degraded to the rank of the common people. In that case, are they to be freed from the prohibition once imposed on them? Prohibition was proclaimed because opium is pernicious. It follows then that the ban should not be abolished until it ceases to be an evil. A partial prohibition or partial legalization is a confusion of rules by the government itself; consequently good faith in its observance can hardly be expected. When the law was all for prohibition, decrees had not been followed. How can the people respect the restrictions or punishments should the law be in confusion? The logical consequence will be the ruin of government and demoralization of our culture....

Even if the duties be raised to twofold, it would be only a little over 200,000 taels. Further doubled, the figure will stand at only 500,000 taels.... Hence, if our Government should seek its revenue from the duties on opium, it is to make an enormous sacrifice for a scanty profit....

The drain of silver, to be sure, arouses apprehension. But the point is whether inspection is faithfully

Source: "Memorial from Yuan Yu-lin," in P. C. Kuo, *A Critical Study of the First Anglo-Chinese War* (Shanghai: Commercial Press, 1935), 211–13.

enforced or not. Should the inspection be faithful, opium prohibition will be effective; so also will be the ban on the silver export. If it be not faithful, opium prohibition will come to naught, and so will the ban on silver export. It must not be supposed that inspection will be facilitated by relaxing opium prohibition or that it will be difficult if the prohibition is severe....

It has been argued that since the imported opium costs an enormous sum of money, the cultivation of the poppy should be allowed in the interior of the country.... [But], the farm lands of our country are fixed in number.... The valuable acres yielding crops may easily be turned into a vast field of opium. This means to destroy agriculture and ruin the very foundation of the lives of the people.

If the habit of smoking secretly spreads over the country under the present prohibition, its legalization will mean greater disasters: fathers would no longer be able to teach their sons; husbands would no longer be able to admonish their wives; masters would no longer be able to restrain their servants; and teachers would no longer be able to train their pupils. The habitual smokers would continue it as a regular practice, while others would strive for imitation. The perpetration of evils will be fathomless. It would mean the end of the life of the people and the destruction of the soul of the nation.

As a result of the smoking of opium, the soldiers of Kwangtung were enfeebled. Your Majesty admonished them on that account during the late rebellion of the mountaineers in the said province. Now should the proposal be adhered to that soldiers, but not the people, be prohibited from smoking opium, then at the future recruitment of the army it would be found that old soldiers had already been spoiled by secret smoking, while fresh recruits would be habitual smokers!... The very trick of the cunning barbarians is to weaken our nation with poison. If they now actually succeed in fooling our people, it means the disintegration of our national defense and the opening up of the same to their penetration....

[W]hat arouses our gravest apprehension is the perpetration of an evil which might completely go out of control. Once opium is legalized, the people will flock to it. When the evil becomes alarming and when we come to repent the wrong of legalization... we will readily find that the country is so heavily saddled with its bad results that recovery is well-nigh impossible....

Document 19.4

A Moral Appeal to Queen Victoria

The Chinese emperor soon decided this debate in favor of suppression and sent a prominent official, Commissioner Lin Zexu, to enforce it. Lin did so vigorously, seizing and destroying millions of pounds of the drug, flushing it out to the sea with a prayer to the local spirit: "[You] who wash away all stains and cleanse all impurities."[20] At the same time (1839), Lin wrote a letter to the British monarch, Queen Victoria, appealing for her assistance in ending this noxious trade.

- On what basis does Commissioner Lin appeal to Queen Victoria?

- How might you compare this letter with that of Document 19.1? What similarities and differences can you notice?

- What assumptions about the West does this letter reveal? Which were accurate and which represented misunderstandings?

- Although there is no evidence of a response to the letter, how might you imagine British reaction to it?

COMMISSIONER LIN ZEXU
Letter to Queen Victoria
1839

A communication: magnificently our great Emperor soothes and pacifies China and the foreign countries, regarding all with the same kindness. If there is profit, then he shares it with the people of the world; if there is harm, then he removes it on behalf of the world....

We find that your country is sixty or seventy thousand *li*° from China. Yet there are barbarian ships that strive to come here for trade for the purpose of making a great profit. The wealth of China is used to profit the barbarians.... By what right do they... use this poisonous drug to injure the Chinese people?...

Let us ask, where is your conscience? I have heard that the smoking of opium is very strictly forbidden by your country; that is because the harm caused by opium is clearly understood. Since it is not permitted to do harm to your country, then even less should you let it be passed on to the harm of other countries—how much less to China! Of all that China exports to foreign countries, there is not a single thing which is not beneficial to people: they are of benefit when eaten, or of benefit when used, or of benefit when resold: all are beneficial. Is there a single article from China which has done any harm to foreign countries? Take tea and rhubarb,° for example; the foreign countries cannot get along for a single day without them. If China cuts off these benefits with no sympathy for those who are to suffer, then what can the barbarians rely upon to keep themselves alive?...On the other hand, articles coming from the outside to China can only be used as toys. We can take them or get along without them.... Nevertheless our Celestial Court lets tea, silk, and other goods be shipped without limit and circulated everywhere without begrudging it in the slightest. This is for no other reason but to share the benefit with the people of the whole world....

We have heard heretofore that your honorable ruler is kind and benevolent. Naturally you would not wish to give unto others what you yourself do not want....

Suppose a man of another country comes to England to trade, he still has to obey the English laws; how much more should he obey in China the laws of the Celestial Dynasty?...

Therefore in the new regulations, in regard to those barbarians who bring opium to China, the penalty is fixed at decapitation or strangulation. This is what is called getting rid of a harmful thing on behalf of mankind....

After receiving this dispatch will you immediately give us a prompt reply regarding the details and circumstances of your cutting off the opium traffic? Be sure not to put this off.

°*li*: approximately one-third of a mile.

°**rhubarb:** used as a medicine.

Source: Dun J. Li, ed., *China in Transition, 1517–1911* (London: Wadsworth, 1969), 64–67.

Document 19.5

War and Defeat

While Queen Victoria and British authorities apparently never received Commissioner Lin's letter and certainly did not respond to it, they did react to the commissioner's actions. Citing the importance of free trade and the violation of British property rights, they launched a major military expedition in which their steamships and heavy guns reflected the impact of the Industrial Revolution on the exercise of British power. This was the first Opium War, and the Chinese lost it badly. One prominent scholar has described it as "the most decisive reversal the Manchus [Qing dynasty] had ever received."[21] The Treaty of Nanjing, which ended that conflict in 1842, was largely imposed by the British. It was the first of many "unequal treaties" that China was required to sign with various European powers and the United States in the decades that followed. While Chinese authorities tried to think about the treaty as a means of "subduing and conciliating" the British, as they had done with other barbarian intruders, it represented in fact a new, much diminished, and dependent position for China on the world stage.

- What were the major provisions of the treaty? Why do you think that opium, ostensibly the cause of the conflict, was rarely mentioned in the treaty?

- In what respects did the treaty signal an unequal relationship between China and Great Britain? What aspects of Chinese independence were lost or compromised by the treaty?

- What provisions of the treaty most clearly challenged traditional Chinese understandings of their place in the world?

The Treaty of Nanjing
1842

I.

There shall henceforward be peace and friendship between Her Majesty the Queen of the United Kingdom of Great Britain and Ireland and His Majesty the Emperor of China, and between their respective subjects, who shall enjoy full security and protection for their persons and property within the dominions of the other.

II.

His Majesty the Emperor of China agrees, that British subjects, with their families and establishments, shall be allowed to reside, for the purposes of carrying on their mercantile pursuits, without molestation or restraint, at the cities and towns of Canton, Amoy, Foochowfoo, Ningpo, and Shanghai....

III.

It being obviously necessary and desirable that British subjects should have some port whereat they may [maintain] and refit their ships when required, and keep stores for that purpose, His Majesty the Emperor of China cedes to Her Majesty the Queen of Great Britain, &c., the Island of Hong-Kong....

IV.

The Emperor of China agrees to pay the sum of 6,000,000 of dollars, as the value of the opium which was delivered up at Canton in the month of March,

Source: Treaty of Nanjing, in *Treaties, Conventions, etc., between China and Foreign States* (London: Statistical Department of the Inspectorate General of Customs, 1917), 1:351–56.

1839, as a ransom for the lives of Her Britannic Majesty's Superintendent and subjects, who had been imprisoned and threatened with death by the Chinese High Officers....

V.

The Government of China having compelled the British merchants trading at Canton to deal exclusively with certain Chinese merchants, called Hong merchants (or Co-Hong)...the Emperor of China agrees to abolish that practice in future at all ports where British merchants may reside, and to permit them to carry on their mercantile transactions with whatever persons they please; and His Imperial Majesty further agrees to pay to the British Government the sum of 3,000,000 of dollars, on account of debts due to British subjects by some of the said Hong merchants, who have become insolvent, and who owe very large sums of money to subjects of Her Britannic Majesty.

VI.

The Government of Her Britannic Majesty having been obliged to send out an expedition to demand and obtain redress for the violent and unjust proceedings of the Chinese High Authorities towards Her Britannic Majesty's officer and subjects, the Emperor of China agrees to pay the sum of 12,000,000 of dollars, on account of the expenses incurred....

VIII.

The Emperor of China agrees to release, unconditionally, all subjects of Her Britannic Majesty (whether natives of Europe or India), who may be in confinement at this moment in any part of the Chinese empire.

X.

...[T]he Emperor further engages, that when British merchandise shall have once paid at any of the said ports the regulated customs and dues,...such merchandise may be conveyed by Chinese merchants to any province or city in the interior of the Empire of China....

XI.

It is agreed that Her Britannic Majesty's Chief High Officer in China shall correspond with the Chinese High Officers, both at the capital and in the provinces,...on a footing of perfect equality....

XII.

On the assent of the Emperor of China to this Treaty being received, and the discharge of the first instalment of money, Her Britannic Majesty's forces will retire from Nanking and the Grand Canal, and will no longer molest or stop the trade of China. The military post at Chinhai will also be withdrawn, but the Islands of Koolangsoo, and that of Chusan, will continue to be held by Her Majesty's forces until the money payments, and the arrangements for opening the ports to British merchants, be completed.

Using the Evidence:
Voices from the Opium War

1. **Defining the issues in the Opium War:** The Opium War was about more than opium. How would you support or challenge this statement?

2. **Characterizing the Opium War:** In what ways might the Opium War be regarded as a clash of cultures? In what respects might it be seen as a clash of interests? Was it an inevitable conflict or were there missed opportunities for avoiding it? (Note: You may want to consider the data in the Snapshot on p. 885 as well as Documents 19.1–19.5, pp. 905–13.)

3. **Interpreting the Treaty of Nanjing:** In the context of British and Chinese views of the world, how do you understand the Treaty of Nanjing? Which country's view of the world is more clearly reflected in that treaty?

4. **Exploring Chinese views of the British:** Based on these documents, how well or how poorly did the Chinese understand the British? How might you account for their misunderstandings?

Visual Sources

Considering the Evidence:
Japanese Perceptions of the West

The second half of the nineteenth century witnessed a profound transformation of Japanese life. (See pp. 894–902) The Tokugawa shogunate, which had governed the country for over two centuries, came to an inglorious end in the Meiji restoration of 1868, and the country then embarked on a massive process of modernization and industrialization. Accompanying these upheavals, Japan's political and military relationship to the West changed dramatically, as its government and its people found themselves required to confront both Western power and Western culture, a common feature of nineteenth-century world history in many places. Accordingly, Japanese understanding of the West, and what they had to fear or gain from it, also changed. Those evolving perceptions of the West found artistic expression, especially in Japanese woodblock printing, an art form that reached its high point in the late nineteenth century. Those images provide for historians a window into Japanese thinking about their own society and the larger world impinging upon them during this critical half-century.

The initial occasion for serious Japanese reflection on the West occurred in 1853–1854, in the context of American commodore Matthew Perry's efforts to "open" Japan to regular commercial relationships with the United States. His nine coal-fired steamships, belching black smoke and carrying a crew of some 1,800 men and more than 100 mounted cannons, became known in Japan as the "black ships." Visual Source 19.1, created around 1854, represents perhaps the best known of many such Japanese depictions of the American warships.

- What general impression of the American intrusion did the artist seek to convey?

- What specific features of the image help the artist make his case?

- Why might the artist have chosen to depict the gunfire coming from the American ship as streams of light?

Beyond portraying the American warships, Japanese artists sought to depict their inhabitants, especially Commodore Perry and his top aides. Some Japanese men rowed their small boats out to the black ships, hoping to catch a glimpse of Perry himself. But the commodore remained largely inaccessible, and the

Visual Source 19.1 The Black Ships (Courtesy, Ryosenji Treasure Museum)

Japanese called his secluded on-board cabin "The Abode of His High and Mighty Mysteriousness." Visual Source 19.2 represents one of many portrayals of Perry (on the right), together with his second-in-command, Commander Henry A. Adams.

- What overall impression of the Americans was the artist seeking to communicate?

- What features of this image seem intended to show the Americans as "other" or different from the Japanese?

- The Japanese had long portrayed a particular kind of goblin, known as *tengu*, with long noses and viewed them as dangerous, demonic, and warlike. What aspects of this depiction of the Americans suggest that the artist sought to associate them with *tengu*?

- But not all portrayals of the Americans displayed such gross and negative features. Compare this image with the woodblock print on page 897. How would you describe the difference between the two portrayals of the Americans? How might you account for the difference?

Visual Source 19.2 Depicting the Americans (Courtesy, Ryosenji Treasure Museum)

By the 1880s, Japan was in the midst of an amazing transformation, in part the outcome of Perry's forced "opening" of the country. By then Japan had a new government committed to the country's rapid modernization. Dozens of official missions and thousands of students had been sent abroad to learn from the West. Particularly among the young, there was an acute awareness of the need to create a new culture that could support a revived Japan. "We have no history," declared one of these students; "our history begins today."[22] In this context, much that was Western was enthusiastically embraced. The technological side of this borrowing was illustrated in woodblock print on page 900. But it extended as well to more purely cultural matters. Eating beef became popular, despite Buddhist objections. Many men adopted Western hairstyles and grew beards, even though the facial hair of Westerners had earlier been portrayed as ugly. In 1872, Western dress was ordered for all official ceremonies. Women in elite circles likewise adopted Western ways, as illustrated in Visual Source 19.3, an 1887 woodblock print titled *Illustration of Singing by the Plum Garden*. At the same time, the dress of the woman in the middle seems to reflect

Visual Source 19.3 Women and Westernization (Museum of Fine Arts, Boston, Gift of L. Aaron Lebowich. RES.53.82-4. Photograph © 2010 Museum of Fine Arts, Boston)

earlier Japanese court traditions that encouraged women to wear many layers of kimonos.

- What elements of Western culture can you identify in this visual source?

- In what ways does this print reflect the continuing appeal of Japanese culture? Pay attention to the scenery, the tree, and the flowers.

- Why were so many Japanese so enamored of Western culture during this time? And why did the Japanese government so actively encourage their interest?

Not everyone in Japan was so enthusiastic about the adoption of Western culture, and by the late 1870s and into the next decade numerous essays and images satirized the apparently indiscriminate fascination with all things European. Visual Source 19.4, drawn by Japanese cartoonist Kobayashi Kiyochika in 1879, represents one of those images. Its full English-language caption read as follows: "Mr. Morse [an American zoologist who introduced Darwin's theory of evolution to Japan in 1877] explains that all human beings were monkeys in the beginning. In the beginning—but even now aren't we still monkeys? When it comes to Western things we think the red beards are the most skillful at everything."[23]

- What specific aspects of Japan's efforts at Westernization is the artist mocking?

- Why might the artist have used a Western scientific theory (Darwinian evolution) to criticize excessive Westernization in Japan?

■ Why do you think a reaction set in against the cultural imitation of Europe?

Behind Japan's modernization and Westernization was the recognition that Western imperialism was surging in Asia, and that China was a prime example of what happened to countries unable to defend themselves against it. Accordingly, achieving political and military equality with the Great Powers of Europe and the United States became a central aim of Japan's modernization program.

Strengthening Japan against Western aggression increasingly meant "throwing off Asia," a phrase that implied rejecting many of Japan's own cultural traditions as well as creating an Asian empire of its own. Fukuzawa Yukichi, a popular advocate of Western knowledge, declared:

> We must not wait for neighboring countries to become civilized so that we can together promote Asia's revival. Rather we should leave their ranks and join forces with the civilized countries of the West. We don't have to give China and Korea any special treatment just because they are neighboring countries. We should deal with them as Western people do. Those who have bad friends cannot avoid having a bad reputation. I reject the idea that we must continue to associate with bad friends in East Asia.[24]

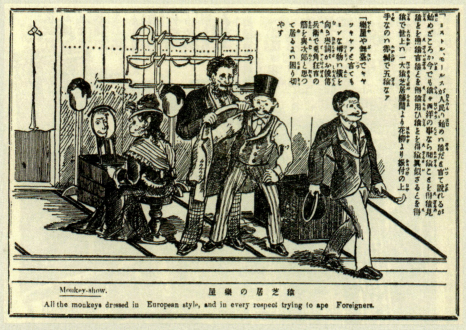

Monkey-show.   屋蔡の居芝猿

All the monkeys dressed in European style, and in every respect trying to ape Foreigners.

Visual Source 19.4 Kobayashi Kiyochika's Critique of Wholesale Westernization (Library of Congress)

Visual Source 19.5 Japan, China, and Europe: A Reversal of Roles (Museum of Fine Arts, Boston, Leonard A. Lauder Collection of Japanese Postcards. 2002.3504. Photograph © 2010 Museum of Fine Arts, Boston)

Historically the Japanese had borrowed a great deal from China—Buddhism, Confucianism, court rituals, city-planning ideas, administrative traditions, and elements of the Chinese script. But Japan's victory in a war with China in 1894–1895 showed clearly that it had thrown off the country in whose cultural shadow it had lived for centuries. Furthermore, Japan had begun to acquire an East Asian empire in Korea and Taiwan. And its triumph over Russia in another war ten years later illustrated its ability to stand up to a major European power. The significance of these twin victories is expressed in Visual Source 19.5, a Japanese image created during the Russo-Japanese War and titled *The Japanese Navy Uses China as Bait to Trap the Greedy Russian*.

■ What overall message did the artist seek to convey in this print?

■ What is the significance of the Chinese figure with a chicken in hand, lying as "bait" at the bottom of the image?

■ How is the Russia character portrayed?

■ What had changed in Japanese thinking about China and Europe during the nineteenth century?

Using the Evidence:
Changing Japanese Perceptions of the West

1. **Explaining change:** How and why had Japanese perceptions of themselves and their relationship to the West changed in the half century since the Meiji restoration? What elements of continuity in Japanese traditions are evident in these visual sources?

2. **Making comparisons:** Based on these visual sources and the documents about the Opium War, how might you compare Japanese and Chinese perceptions of the West during the nineteenth century? What accounts for both the similarities and differences?

3. **Distinguishing modernization and westernization:** Based on a careful reading of Chapter 19, including the documents and images, do you think that technological borrowing (modernization) requires cultural borrowing (westernization) as well? Is it possible to modernize while avoiding the incorporation of western culture at the same time? What do the examples of China, the Ottoman Empire, and Japan in the nineteenth century suggest about this issue?

Colonial Encounters

1750–1914

In mid-1967, I was on summer break from a teaching assignment with the Peace Corps in Ethiopia and was traveling with some friends in neighboring Kenya, just four years after that country had gained its independence from British colonial rule. The bus we were riding on broke down, and I found myself hitchhiking across Kenya, heading for Uganda. Soon I was picked up by a friendly Englishman, one of Kenya's many European settlers who had stayed on after independence. At one point, he pulled off the road to show me a lovely view of Kenya's famous Rift Valley, and we were approached by a group of boys selling baskets and other tourist items. They spoke to us in good English, but my British companion replied to them in Swahili. He later explained that Europeans generally did not speak English with the "natives." I was puzzled, but reluctant to inquire further.

Several years later, while conducting research about British missionaries in Kenya in the early twentieth century, I found a clue about the origins of this man's reluctance to speak his own language with Kenyans. It came in a letter from a missionary in which the writer argued against the teaching of English to Africans. Among his reasons were "the danger in which such a course would place our white women and girls" and "the danger of organizing against the government and Europeans."[1] Here, clearly displayed, was the European colonial insistence on maintaining distance and distinction between whites and blacks, for both sexual and political reasons. Such monitoring of racial boundaries was a central feature of many nineteenth- and early-twentieth-century colonial societies and, in the case of my new British acquaintance, a practice that persisted even after the colonial era had ended.

The Imperial Durbar of 1903: To mark the coronation of British monarch Edward VII and his installation as the Emperor of India, colonial authorities in India mounted an elaborate assembly, or *durbar*. The durbar was intended to showcase the splendor of the British Empire, and its pageantry included sporting events; a state ball; a huge display of Indian arts, crafts, and jewels; and an enormous parade in which a long line of British officials and Indian princes passed by on bejeweled elephants. (Topham/The Image Works)

FOR MANY MILLIONS OF AFRICANS AND ASIANS, colonial rule—by the British, French, Germans, Italians, Belgians, Portuguese, Russians, or Americans—was the major new element in their historical experience during the nineteenth century. Between roughly 1750 and 1950, much of the Afro-Asian-Pacific world was enveloped within this new wave of European empire building. The encounter with European power in these colonized societies was more immediate, and often more intense, than in those regions that were buffered by their own independent governments, such as Latin America, China, Persia, and the Ottoman Empire. Of course, no single colonial experience characterized these two centuries across this vast region. Much depended on the cultures and prior history of various colonized people. Policies of the colonial powers sometimes differed sharply and changed over time. Men and women experienced the colonial era differently, as did traditional elites, Western-educated classes, urban artisans, peasant farmers, and migrant laborers. Furthermore, the varied actions and reactions of such people, despite their oppression and exploitation, shaped the colonial experience, perhaps as much as the policies, practices, and intentions of their temporary European rulers. All of them—colonizers and colonized alike—were caught up in the flood of change that accompanied the Industrial Revolution and a new burst of European imperialism.

A Second Wave of European Conquests

■ Comparison

In what different ways did the colonial takeover of Asia and Africa occur?

If the sixteenth- and seventeenth-century takeover of the Americas represented the first phase of European colonial conquests, the century and a half between 1750 and 1900 was a second and quite distinct round of that larger process. Now it was focused in Asia and Africa rather than in the Western Hemisphere. It featured a number of new players—Germany, Italy, Belgium, the United States, Japan—who were not at all involved in the earlier phase, while the Spanish and Portuguese now had only minor roles. In mainland Asia and Africa, nineteenth-century European conquests nowhere had the devastating demographic consequences that had so sharply reduced the Native American populations. Furthermore, this second wave of European colonial conquests, at least by the mid-nineteenth century, was conditioned by Europe's Industrial Revolution. In both their formal colonies and their "informal empires" (Latin America, China, the Ottoman Empire, and for a time Japan), European motives and activities were shaped by the military capacity and economic power that the Industrial Revolution conveyed. In general, Europeans preferred informal control, for it was cheaper and less likely to provoke wars. But where rivalry with other European states made it impossible or where local governments were unable or unwilling to cooperate, Europeans proved more than willing to undertake the expense and risk of conquest and outright colonial rule.

The construction of these second-wave European empires in the Afro-Asian world, like empires everywhere, involved military force or the threat of using it. Initially, the European military advantage lay in organization, drill and practice, and command structure. Increasingly in the nineteenth century, the Europeans also pos-

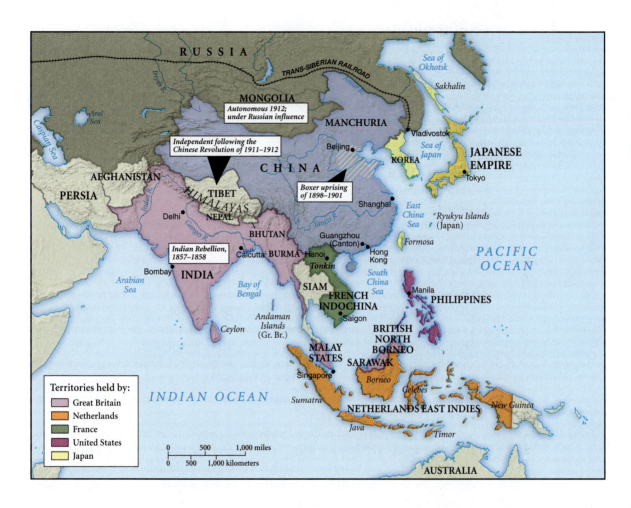

Map 20.1 Colonial Asia in the Early Twentieth Century By the early 1900s, several of the great population centers of Asia had come under the colonial control of Britain, the Netherlands, France, the United States, or Japan.

sessed overwhelming advantages in firepower, deriving from the recently invented repeating rifles and machine guns. A much-quoted jingle by the English writer Hilaire Belloc summed up the situation:

> Whatever happens we have got
> The Maxim gun [an automatic machine gun] and they have not.

Nonetheless, Europeans had to fight, often long and hard, to create their new empires, as countless wars of conquest attest. In the end, though, they prevailed almost everywhere, largely against adversaries who did not have Maxim guns or in some cases any guns at all. Thus were African and Asian peoples of all kinds incorporated within one or another of the European empires. Gathering and hunting bands in Australia, agricultural village societies or chiefdoms on Pacific islands and in Africa, pastoralists of the Sahara and Central Asia, residents of states large and small, and virtually everyone in the large and complex civilizations of India and Southeast Asia—all of them alike lost the political sovereignty and freedom of action they had previously exercised.

For some, such as Hindus governed by the Muslim Mughal Empire, it was an exchange of one set of foreign rulers for another. But now all were subjects of a European colonial state.

The passage to colonial status occurred in various ways. For the peoples of India and Indonesia, colonial conquest grew out of earlier interaction with European trading firms. Particularly in India, the British East India Company, rather than the British government directly, played the leading role in the colonial takeover of South Asia. The fragmentation of the Mughal Empire and the absence of any overall sense of cultural or political unity both invited and facilitated European penetration. A similar situation of many small and rival states assisted the Dutch acquisition of Indonesia. However, neither the British nor the Dutch had a clear-cut plan for conquest. Rather it evolved slowly as local authorities and European traders made and unmade a variety of alliances over roughly a century in India (1750–1850). In Indonesia, a few areas held out until the early twentieth century (see Map 20.1).

For most of Africa, mainland Southeast Asia, and the Pacific islands, colonial conquest came later, in the second half of the nineteenth century, and rather more abruptly and deliberately than in India or Indonesia. The "scramble for Africa," for example, pitted half a dozen European powers against one another as they partitioned the entire continent among themselves in only about twenty-five years (1875–1900). (See Visual Sources: The Scramble for Africa, pp. 960–67, for various perspectives on the "scramble.") European leaders themselves were surprised by the intensity of their rivalries and the speed with which they acquired huge territories, about which they knew very little (see Map 20.2).

That process involved endless but peaceful negotiations among the competing Great Powers about "who got what" and extensive and bloody military action, sometimes lasting decades, to make their control effective on the ground. Among the most difficult to subdue were those decentralized societies without a formal state structure. In such cases, Europeans confronted no central authority with which they could negotiate or that they might decisively defeat. It was a matter of village-by-village conquest against extended resistance. As late as 1925, one British official commented on the process as it operated in central Nigeria: "I shall of course go on walloping them until they surrender. It's a rather piteous sight watching a village being knocked to pieces and I wish there was some other way, but unfortunately there isn't."[2]

The South Pacific territories of Australia and New Zealand, both of which were taken over by the British during the nineteenth century, were more similar to the earlier colonization of North America than to contemporary patterns of Asian and African conquest. In both places, conquest was accompanied by massive European settlement and diseases that reduced native numbers by 75 percent or more by 1900. Like Canada and the United States, these became settler colonies, "neo-European" societies in the Pacific. Aboriginal Australians constituted only about 2.4 percent of their country's population in the early twenty-first century, and the indigenous Maori were a minority of about 15 percent in New Zealand. With the exception of Hawaii, nowhere else in the nineteenth-century colonial world were existing

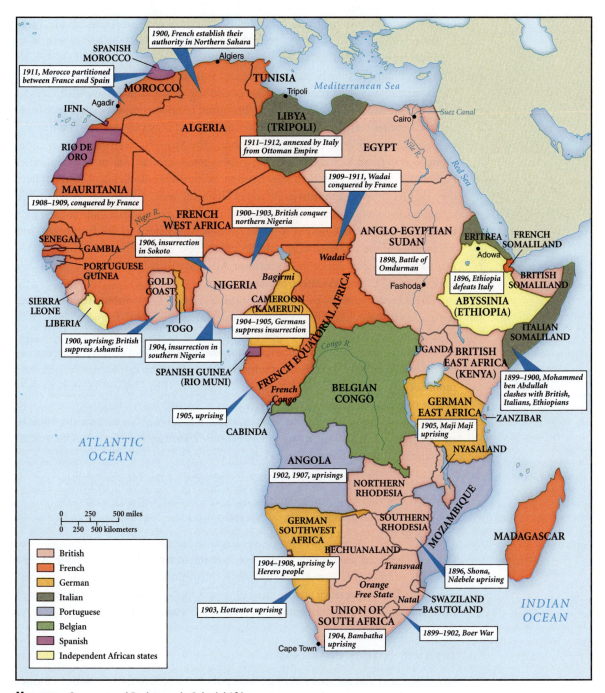

Map 20.2 Conquest and Resistance in Colonial Africa

By the early twentieth century, the map of Africa reflected the outcome of the "scramble for Africa," a conquest that was heavily resisted in many places. The boundaries established during that process still provide the political framework for Africa's independent states.

Text within the map image:

1900, French establish their authority in Northern Sahara

1911, Morocco partitioned between France and Spain

1911–1912, annexed by Italy from Ottoman Empire

1909–1911, Wadai conquered by France

1908–1909, conquered by France

1900–1903, British conquer northern Nigeria

1906, insurrection in Sokoto

1898, Battle of Omdurman

1896, Ethiopia defeats Italy

1904–1905, Germans suppress insurrection

1900, uprising; British suppress Ashantis

1904, insurrection in southern Nigeria

1899–1900, Mohammed ben Abdullah clashes with British, Italians, Ethiopians

1905, uprising

1905, Maji Maji uprising

1902, 1907, uprisings

1904–1908, uprising by Herero people

1896, Shona, Ndebele uprising

1903, Hottentot uprising

1904, Bambatha uprising

1899–1902, Boer War

Legend:
- British
- French
- German
- Italian
- Portuguese
- Belgian
- Spanish
- Independent African states

Place labels: SPANISH MOROCCO, MOROCCO, IFNI, RIO DE ORO, MAURITANIA, SENEGAL, GAMBIA, PORTUGUESE GUINEA, SIERRA LEONE, LIBERIA, GOLD COAST, TOGO, SPANISH GUINEA (RIO MUNI), ALGERIA, TUNISIA, LIBYA (TRIPOLI), FRENCH WEST AFRICA, NIGERIA, CAMEROON (KAMERUN), FRENCH EQUATORIAL AFRICA, CABINDA, French Congo, EGYPT, ANGLO-EGYPTIAN SUDAN, ERITREA, FRENCH SOMALILAND, BRITISH SOMALILAND, ABYSSINIA (ETHIOPIA), ITALIAN SOMALILAND, UGANDA, BRITISH EAST AFRICA (KENYA), GERMAN EAST AFRICA, ZANZIBAR, BELGIAN CONGO, ANGOLA, NORTHERN RHODESIA, NYASALAND, GERMAN SOUTHWEST AFRICA, BECHUANALAND, SOUTHERN RHODESIA, MOZAMBIQUE, MADAGASCAR, Transvaal, Orange Free State, Natal, SWAZILAND, BASUTOLAND, UNION OF SOUTH AFRICA, Cape Town, Mediterranean Sea, Suez Canal, Red Sea, Nile R., Niger R., Congo R., ATLANTIC OCEAN, INDIAN OCEAN, Algiers, Tripoli, Cairo, Agadir, Adowa, Fashoda, Wadai, Bagirmi

Scale: 0 250 500 miles / 0 250 500 kilometers

populations so decimated and overwhelmed as they were in Australia and New Zealand.

Elsewhere other variations on the theme of imperial conquest unfolded. Japan's takeover of Taiwan and Korea bore marked similarities to European actions. The westward expansion of the United States and the Russian penetration of Central Asia brought additional millions under European control as these two states continued their earlier territorial growth. Filipinos acquired new colonial rulers when the United States took over from Spain following the Spanish-American War of 1898. Some 13,000 freed U.S. slaves, seeking greater freedom than was possible at home, migrated to West Africa, where they became, ironically, a colonizing elite in the land they named Liberia. Ethiopia and Siam (Thailand) were notable for avoiding the colonization to which their neighbors succumbed. Those countries' military and diplomatic skills, their willingness to make modest concessions to the Europeans, and the rivalries of the imperialists all contributed to these exceptions to the rule of colonial takeover in East Africa and Southeast Asia. (See Visual Source 20.5, p. 966, for an account of Ethiopia's defeat of Italian forces.)

These broad patterns of colonial conquest dissolved into thousands of separate encounters as Asian and African societies were confronted with decisions about how to respond to encroaching European power in the context of their local circumstances. Many initially sought to enlist Europeans in their own internal struggles for power or in their external rivalries with neighboring states or peoples. As pressures mounted and European demands escalated, some tried to play off imperial powers against one another. Many societies were sharply divided between those who wanted to fight and those who believed that resistance was futile. After extended resistance against French aggression, the nineteenth-century Vietnamese emperor Tu Duc argued with those who wanted the struggle to go on:

> Do you really wish to confront such a power with a pack of [our] cowardly soldiers? It would be like mounting an elephant's head or caressing a tiger's tail.... With what you presently have, do you really expect to dissolve the enemy's rifles into air or chase his battleships into hell?[3]

Others negotiated, attempting to preserve as much independence and power as possible. The rulers of the East African kingdom of Buganda, for example, saw opportunity in the British presence and negotiated an arrangement that substantially enlarged their state and personally benefited the kingdom's elite class.

Under European Rule

In many places and for many people, incorporation into European colonial empires was a traumatic experience. Especially for small-scale societies, the loss of life, homes, cattle, crops, and land was devastating. In 1902, a British soldier in East Africa described what happened in a single village: "Every soul was either shot or bayoneted.... We burned all the huts and razed the banana plantations to the ground."[4]

For the Vietnamese elite, schooled for centuries in Chinese-style Confucian thinking, conquest meant that the natural harmonies of life had been badly disrupted; it was a time when "water flowed uphill." Nguyen Khuyen (1835–1909), a senior Vietnamese official, retired to his ancestral village to farm and write poetry after the French conquest. In his poems he expressed his anguish at the passing of the world he had known:

> Fine wine but no good friends,
> So I buy none though I have the money.
> A poem comes to mind, but I choose not to write it down.
> If it were written, to whom would I give it?
> The spare bed hangs upon the wall in cold indifference.
> I pluck the lute, but it just doesn't sound right.[5]

Many others also withdrew into private life, feigning illness when asked to serve in public office under the French.

Cooperation and Rebellion

Although violence was a prominent feature of colonial life both during conquest and after, various groups and many individuals willingly cooperated with colonial authorities to their own advantage. Many men found employment, status, and security in European-led armed forces. The shortage and expense of European administrators and the difficulties of communicating across cultural boundaries made it necessary for colonial rulers to rely heavily on a range of local intermediaries. Thus Indian princes, Muslim emirs, and African rulers, often from elite or governing families, found it possible to retain much of their earlier status and privileges while gaining considerable wealth by exercising authority, both legally and otherwise, at the local level. For example, in French West Africa, an area eight times the size of France itself and with a population of about 15 million in the late 1930s, the colonial state consisted of just 385 French administrators and more than 50,000 African "chiefs." Thus colonial rule rested upon and reinforced the most conservative segments of Asian and African societies.

Both colonial governments and private missionary organizations had an interest in promoting a measure of European education. From this process arose a small Western-educated class, whose members served the colonial state, European businesses, and Christian missions as teachers, clerks, translators, and lower-level administrators. A few received higher education abroad and returned home as lawyers, doctors, engineers, or journalists. As colonial governments and business enterprises became more sophisticated, Europeans increasingly depended on the Western-educated class at the expense of the more traditional elites.

If colonial rule enlisted the willing cooperation of some, it provoked the bitter opposition of many others. Thus periodic rebellions, both large and small, punctuated the history of colonial regimes everywhere. The most famous among them was

■ **Explanation**
Why might subject people choose to cooperate with the colonial regime? What might prompt them to rebel or resist?

THE DEVILFISH IN EGYPTIAN WATERS.

An American View of British Imperialism
In this American cartoon dating to 1882, the British Empire is portrayed as an octopus whose tentacles are already attached to many countries, while one tentacle is about to grasp still another one, Egypt. (The Granger Collection, New York)

the Indian Rebellion of 1857–1858, which was triggered by the introduction into the colony's military forces of a new cartridge smeared with animal fat from cows and pigs. Because Hindus venerated cows and Muslims regarded pigs as unclean, both groups viewed the innovation as a plot to render them defiled and to convert them to Christianity. Behind this incident were many groups of people with a whole series of grievances generated by the British colonial presence: local rulers who had lost power; landlords deprived of their estates or their rent; peasants overtaxed and exploited by urban moneylenders and landlords alike; unemployed weavers displaced by machine-manufactured textiles; and religious leaders exposed to missionary preaching. A mutiny among Indian troops in Bengal triggered the rebellion, which soon spread to other regions of the colony and other social groups. Soon much of India was aflame. Some rebel leaders presented their cause as an effort to revive an almost-vanished Mughal Empire and thereby attracted support from those with strong resentments against the British (see Document 20.3, pp. 953–55). Although it was crushed in 1858, the rebellion greatly widened the racial divide in colonial India and eroded British tolerance for those they viewed as "nigger natives" who had betrayed their trust. It made the British more conservative and cautious about deliberately trying to change Indian society for fear of provoking another rebellion. Moreover, it convinced the British government to assume direct control over India, ending the era of British East India Company rule in the subcontinent.

Colonial Empires with a Difference

■ **Comparison**

What was distinctive about European colonial empires of the nineteenth century?

At one level, European colonial empires were but the latest in a very long line of imperial creations, all of which had enlisted cooperation and experienced resistance from their subject peoples, but the nineteenth-century European version of empire differed from the others in several remarkable ways. One was the prominence of race in distinguishing rulers and ruled, as the high tide of "scientific racism" in Europe coincided with the acquisition of Asian and African colonies (see pp. 881–82). In East Africa, for example, white men were referred to as *bwana* (Swahili for "master"), whereas Europeans regularly called African men "boy." Education for colonial subjects was both limited and skewed toward practical subjects rather than scientific and literary studies, which were widely regarded as inappropriate for the "primitive mind" of "natives." Particularly affected by European racism were those whose Western education and aspirations most clearly threatened the racial divide. Europeans were exceedingly reluctant to allow even the most highly educated Asians and Africans to enter the higher ranks of the colonial civil service. A proposal in 1883 to allow Indian judges to hear cases involving whites provoked outrage and massive demonstrations among European inhabitants of India.

In those colonies that had a large European settler population, the pattern of racial separation was much more pronounced than in places such as Nigeria, which had few permanently settled whites. The most extreme case was South Africa, where a large European population and the widespread use of African labor in mines and industries brought blacks and whites into closer and more prolonged contact than elsewhere. The racial fears that were aroused resulted in extraordinary efforts to establish race as a legal, not just a customary, feature of South African society. This racial system provided for separate "homelands," educational systems, residential areas, public facilities, and much more. In what was eventually known as apartheid, South African whites attempted the impossible task of creating an industrializing economy based on cheap African labor, while limiting African social and political integration in every conceivable fashion.

A further distinctive feature of nineteenth-century European empires lay in the extent to which colonial states were able to penetrate the societies they governed. Centralized tax-collecting bureaucracies, new means of communication and transportation, imposed changes in landholding patterns, integration of colonial economies into a global network of exchange, public health and sanitation measures, and the activities of missionaries all touched the daily lives of many people far more deeply than in earlier empires. Not only were Europeans foreign rulers, but they also bore the seeds of a very different way of life, which grew out of their own modern transformation.

Nineteenth-century European colonizers were extraordinary as well in their penchant for counting and classifying their subject people. With the assistance of anthropologists and missionaries, colonial governments collected a vast amount of information, sought to organize it "scientifically," and used it to manage the unfamiliar, complex, varied, and fluctuating societies that they governed. In India, the British found in classical texts and Brahmin ideology an idealized description of the caste system, based on the notion of four ranked and unchanging varnas, which made it possible to bring order out of the immense complexity and variety of caste as it actually operated. Thus the British invented or appropriated a Brahmin version of "traditional India" that they favored and sought to preserve, while scorning as "non-Indian" the new elite educated in European schools and enthusiastic about Western ways of life (see Document 20.2, pp. 951–53). This view of India reflected the great influence of Brahmins on British thinking and clearly served the interests of this Indian upper class.

Likewise within African colonies, Europeans identified, and sometimes invented, distinct tribes, each with its own clearly defined territory, language, customs, and

chief. The notion of a "tribal Africa" expressed the Western view that African societies were primitive or backward, representing an earlier stage of human development.
It was also a convenient idea, for it reduced the enormous complexity and fluidity of
African societies to a more manageable state and thus made colonial administration
easier.

Finally, European colonial policies contradicted their own core values and their
practices at home to an unusual degree. While nineteenth-century Britain and France
were becoming more democratic, their colonies were essentially dictatorships, offering perhaps order and stability, but certainly not democratic government, because
few colonial subjects were participating citizens. Empire of course was wholly at
odds with European notions of national independence, and ranked racial classifica-
tions went against the grain of both Christian and Enlightenment ideas of human
equality. Furthermore, many Europeans were distinctly reluctant to encourage within
their colonies the kind of modernization—urban growth, industrialization, individual values, religious skepticism—that was sweeping their own societies. They
feared that this kind of social change, often vilified as "detribalization," would encourage unrest and challenge colonial rule. As a model for social development, they
much preferred "traditional" rural society, with its established authorities and social
hierarchies, though shorn of abuses such as slavery and *sati* (widow-burning). Such
contradictions between what Europeans preached at home and what they practiced
in the colonies became increasingly apparent to many Asians and Africans and
played a major role in undermining the foundations of colonial rule in the twentieth century.

Ways of Working: Comparing Colonial Economies

Colonial rule affected the lives of its subject people in many ways, but the most pronounced change was in their ways of working. The colonial state—with its power to
tax, to seize land for European enterprises, to compel labor, and to build railroads,
ports, and roads—played an important role in these transformations. Even more powerful was the growing integration of Asian and African societies into a world economy
that increasingly demanded their gold, diamonds, copper, tin, rubber, coffee, cotton,
sugar, cocoa, and many other products. But the economic transformations born of
these twin pressures were far from uniform. Various groups—migrant workers and
cash-crop farmers, plantation laborers and domestic servants, urban elites and day
laborers, men and women—experienced the colonial era differently as their daily
working lives underwent profound changes.

To various degrees, old ways of working were eroded almost everywhere in the
colonial world. Subsistence farming, in which peasant families produced largely for
their own needs, diminished as growing numbers directed at least some of their energies to working for wages or selling what they produced for a cash income. That
money was both necessary to pay their taxes and school fees and useful for buying
the various products—such as machine-produced textiles, bicycles, and kerosene—
that the industrial economies of Europe sent their way. As in Europe, artisans suffered

greatly when cheaper machine-manufactured merchandise displaced their own hand-made goods. A flood of inexpensive textiles from Britain's new factories ruined the livelihood of tens of thousands of India's handloom weavers. Iron smelting largely disappeared in Africa, and occupations such as blacksmithing and tanning lost ground. Furthermore, Asian and African merchants, who had earlier handled the trade between their countries and the wider world, were squeezed out by well-financed European commercial firms.

Economies of Coercion: Forced Labor and the Power of the State

Many of the new ways of working that emerged during the colonial era derived directly from the demands of the colonial state. The most obvious was required and unpaid labor on public projects, such as building railroads, constructing government buildings, and transporting goods. In French Africa, all "natives" were legally obligated for "statute labor" of ten to twelve days a year, a practice that lasted through 1946. It was much resented. A resident of British West Africa, interviewed in 1996, bitterly recalled this feature of colonial life: "They [British officials] were rude, and they made us work for them a lot. They came to the village and just rounded us up and made us go off and clear the road or carry loads on our heads."[6]

■ **Connection**
How did the power of colonial states transform the economic lives of colonial subjects?

The most infamous cruelties of forced labor occurred during the early twentieth century in the Congo Free State, then governed personally by Leopold II of Belgium. Private companies in the Congo, operating under the authority of the state, forced villagers to collect rubber, which was much in demand for bicycle and automobile tires, with a reign of terror and abuse that cost millions of lives. One refugee from these horrors described the process:

> We were always in the forest to find the rubber vines, to go without food, and our women had to give up cultivating the fields and gardens. Then we starved. . . . We begged the white man to leave us alone, saying we could get no more rubber, but the white men and their soldiers said "Go. You are only beasts yourselves. . . . " When we failed and our rubber was short, the soldiers came to our towns and killed us. Many were shot, some had their ears cut off; others were tied up with ropes round their necks and taken away.[7]

Eventually such outrages were widely publicized in Europe, where they created a scandal, forcing the Belgian government to take control of the Congo in 1908 and ending Leopold's reign of terror.

A variation on the theme of forced labor took shape in the so-called cultivation system of the Netherlands East Indies (Indonesia) during the nineteenth century. Peasants were required to cultivate 20 percent or more of their land in cash crops such as sugar or coffee to meet their tax obligation to the state. Sold to government contractors at fixed and low prices, those crops, when resold on the world market, proved highly profitable for Dutch traders and shippers as well as for the Dutch state and its citizens. According to one scholar, the cultivation system "performed a

Colonial Violence in the Congo
These young boys with severed hands were among the victims of a brutal regime of forced labor undertaken in the Congo during the late nineteenth and early twentieth centuries. Such mutilation was punishment for their villages' inability to supply the required amount of wild rubber. (Courtesy, Anti-Slavery Organization, London)

miracle for the Dutch economy," enabling it to avoid taxing its own people and providing capital for its Industrial Revolution.[8] It also enriched and strengthened the position of those "traditional authorities" who enforced the system, often by using lashings and various tortures, on behalf of the Dutch. For the peasants of Java, however, it meant a double burden of obligations to the colonial state as well as to local lords. Many became indebted to moneylenders when they could not meet those obligations. Those demands, coupled with the loss of land and labor now excluded from food production, contributed to a wave of famines during the mid-nineteenth century in which hundreds of thousands perished.

The forced cultivation of cash crops was widely and successfully resisted in many places. In German East Africa, for example, colonial authorities in the late nineteenth century imposed the cultivation of cotton, which seriously interfered with production of local food crops. Here is how one man remembered the experience:

> The cultivation of cotton was done by turns. Every village was allotted days on which to cultivate.... After arriving you all suffered very greatly. Your back and your buttocks were whipped and there was no rising up once you stooped to dig.... And yet he [the German] wanted us to pay him tax. Were we not human beings?[9]

Such conditions prompted a massive rebellion in 1905 and persuaded the Germans to end the forced growing of cotton. In Mozambique, where the Portuguese likewise brutally enforced cotton cultivation, a combination of peasant sabotage, the planting of unauthorized crops, and the smuggling of cotton across the border to more profitable markets ensured that Portugal never achieved its goal of becoming self-sufficient in cotton production. In such ways did the actions of colonized peoples alter or frustrate the plans of the colonizers.

Economies of Cash-Crop Agriculture: The Pull of the Market

■ **Change**

How did cash-crop agriculture transform the lives of colonized peoples?

Many Asian and African peoples had produced quite willingly for an international market long before they were enclosed within colonial societies. They offered for trade items such as peanuts and palm oil in West Africa, cotton in Egypt, spices in Indonesia, and pepper and textiles in India. In some places, colonial rule created conditions that facilitated and increased cash-crop production to the advantage of local farmers. British authorities in Burma, for example, acted to encourage rice production among small farmers by ending an earlier prohibition on rice exports, providing irrigation and transportation facilities, and enacting land tenure laws that facilitated private ownership of small farms. Under these conditions, the population of the Irrawaddy Delta boomed, migrants from Upper Burma and India poured into the region, and rice exports soared. Local small farmers benefited considerably because they were now able to own their own land, build substantial houses, and buy imported goods. For several decades in the late nineteenth century, standards of living improved sharply, and huge increases in rice production fed millions of people in other parts of Asia and elsewhere. It was a very different situation from that of peasants forced to grow crops that seriously interfered with their food production.

But that kind of colonial development, practiced also in the Mekong River delta of French-ruled Vietnam, had important environmental consequences. It involved the destruction of mangrove forests and swamplands along with the fish and shellfish that supplemented local diets. New dikes and irrigation channels inhibited the depositing of silt from upstream and thus depleted soils in the deltas of these major river systems. And, unknown to anyone at the time, this kind of agriculture generates large amounts of methane gas, a major contributor to global warming.[10]

Profitable cash-crop farming also developed in the southern Gold Coast (present-day Ghana), a British territory in West Africa. Unlike Burma, it was African farmers themselves who took the initiative to develop export agriculture. Planting cacao trees in huge quantities, they became the world's leading supplier of cocoa, used to make chocolate, by 1911. Cacao was an attractive crop because, unlike cotton, it was compatible with the continued production of foods and did not require so much labor time. In the early twentieth century, it brought a new prosperity to many local farmers. "A hybrid society was taking shape," wrote one scholar, "partly peasant, in that most members farmed their own land with family labor . . . and partly capitalist, in that a minority employed wage laborers, produced chiefly for the market, and reinvested profits."[11]

That success brought new problems in its wake. A shortage of labor fostered the employment of former slaves as dependent and exploited workers and also generated tensions between the sexes when some men married women for their labor power but refused to support them adequately. Moreover, the labor shortage brought a huge influx of migrants from the drier interior parts of West Africa, generating ethnic and class tensions. Furthermore, many colonies came to specialize in one or two cash crops, creating an unhealthy dependence when world market prices dropped. Thus African and Asian farmers were increasingly subject to the uncertain rhythms of the international marketplace as well as to those of the seasons and the weather.

Economies of Wage Labor: Working for Europeans

Yet another new way of working in colonial societies involved wage labor in some European enterprise. Driven by the need for money, by the loss of land adequate to support their families, or sometimes by the orders of colonial authorities, millions of colonial subjects across Asia and Africa sought employment in European-owned

■ Change
What kinds of wage labor were available in the colonies? Why might people take part in it? How did doing so change their lives?

Thus, after more than half a century of colonial rule, British authorities themselves acknowledged that normal family life in the colony's major urban center proved out of reach for the vast majority. It was quite an admission.

Women and the Colonial Economy: An African Case Study

■ Change
How were the lives of African women altered by colonial economies?

If economic life in European empires varied greatly from place to place, even within the same colony, it also offered a different combination of opportunities and hardships to women than it did to men, as the experience of colonial Africa shows.[13] In precolonial times, African women were almost everywhere active farmers, with responsibility for planting, weeding, and harvesting in addition to food preparation and child care. Men cleared the land, built houses, herded the cattle, and in some cases assisted with field work. Within this division of labor, women were expected to feed their own families and were usually allocated their own fields for that purpose. Many also were involved in local trading activity. Though clearly subordinate to men, African women nevertheless had a measure of economic autonomy.

As the demands of the colonial economy grew, women's lives diverged more and more from those of men. In colonies where cash-crop agriculture was dominant, men often withdrew from subsistence production in favor of more lucrative export crops. Among the Ewe people of southern Ghana, men almost completely dominated the highly profitable cacao farming, whereas women assumed near total responsibility for domestic food production. In neighboring Ivory Coast, women had traditionally grown cotton for their families' clothing; but when that crop acquired a cash value, men insisted that cotton grown for export be produced on their own personal fields. Thus men acted to control the most profitable aspects of cash-crop agriculture and in doing so greatly increased the subsistence workload of women. One study from Cameroon estimated that women's working hours increased from forty-six per week in precolonial times to more than seventy by 1934.

Women in Colonial Africa
The movement of many African men into wage labor thrust even more of the domestic responsibilities onto women. Here in a photograph from colonial Kenya in 1936 a woman carries on the ancient craft of making clay pots. (Elspeth Huxley/ Huxley Collection/Images of Empire, British Empire & Commonwealth Museum)

Further increasing women's workload and differentiating their lives from those of men was labor migration. As more and more men sought employment in the cities, on settler farms, or in the mines, their wives were left to manage the domestic economy almost alone. In many cases, women also had to supply food to men in the cities to compensate for very low urban wages. They often took over such traditionally male tasks as breaking the ground for planting, milking the cows, and supervising the herds, in addition to their normal responsibilities. In South Africa, where the demands of the European economy were particularly heavy, some 40 to 50 percent of able-bodied adult men were absent from the rural areas, and women headed 60 percent of households. In Botswana, which supplied much male labor to South Africa, married couples by the 1930s rarely lived together for more than two months at a time. In such situations, the lives and cultures of men and women increasingly diverged, with one focused on the cities and working for wages and the other on village life and subsistence agriculture.

Women coped with these difficult circumstances in a number of ways. Many sought closer relations with their families of birth rather than with their absent husbands' families, as would otherwise have been expected. Among the Luo of Kenya, women introduced laborsaving crops, adopted new farm implements, and earned some money as traders. In the cities, they established a variety of self-help associations, including those for prostitutes and for brewers of beer.

The colonial economy sometimes provided a measure of opportunity for enterprising women, particularly in small-scale trade and marketing. In some parts of West Africa, women came to dominate this sector of the economy by selling foodstuffs, cloth, and inexpensive imported goods, while men or foreign firms controlled the more profitable wholesale and import-export trade. Such opportunities sometimes gave women considerable economic autonomy. By the 1930s, for example, Nupe women in northern Nigeria had gained sufficient wealth as itinerant traders that they were contributing more to the family income than their husbands and frequently lent money to them. Among some Igbo groups in southern Nigeria, men were responsible for growing the prestigious yams, but women's crops—especially cassava—came to have a cash value during the colonial era, and women were entitled to keep the profits from selling it. "What is man? I have my own money" expressed the growing economic independence of such women.[14]

At the other end of the social scale, women of impoverished rural families, by necessity, often became virtually independent heads of household in the absence of their husbands. Others took advantage of new opportunities in mission schools, towns, and mines to flee the restrictions of rural patriarchy. Such challenges to patriarchal values elicited various responses from men, including increased accusations of witchcraft against women and fears of impotence. Among the Shona in Southern Rhodesia, and no doubt elsewhere, senior African men repeatedly petitioned the colonial authorities for laws and regulations that would criminalize adultery and restrict women's ability to leave their rural villages.[15] The control of women's sexuality and mobility was a common interest of European and African men.

Assessing Colonial Development

Beyond the many and varied changes that transformed the working lives of millions in the colonial world lies the difficult and highly controversial question of the overall economic impact of colonial rule on Asian and African societies. Defenders, both then and now, praise it for jump-starting modern growth, but numerous critics cite a record of exploitation and highlight the limitations and unevenness of that

■ Change
Did colonial rule bring "economic progress" in its wake?

growth. Amid the continuing debates, three things seem reasonably clear. First, colonial rule served, for better or worse, to further the integration of Asian and African economies into a global network of exchange, now centered in Europe. In many places, that process was well under way before conquest imposed foreign rule, and elsewhere it occurred without formal colonial control. Nonetheless, it is apparent that within the colonial world far more land and labor were devoted to production for the global market at the end of the colonial era than at its beginning.

Second, Europeans could hardly avoid conveying to the colonies some elements of their own modernizing process. It was in their interests to do so, and many felt duty bound to "improve" the societies they briefly governed. Modern administrative and bureaucratic structures facilitated colonial control; communication and transportation infrastructure (railroads, motorways, ports, telegraphs, postal services) moved products to the world market; schools trained the army of intermediaries on which colonial rule depended; and modest health care provisions fulfilled some of the "civilizing mission" to which many Europeans felt committed. These elements of modernization made an appearance, however inadequately, during the colonial era.

Third, nowhere in the colonial world did a breakthrough to modern industrial society of Japanese dimensions occur. When India became independent after two centuries of colonial rule by the world's first industrial society, it was still one of the poorest of the world's developing countries. The British may not have created Indian poverty, but neither did they overcome it to any substantial degree. Scholars continue to debate the reasons for that failure: was it the result of deliberate British policies, or was it due to the conditions of Indian society? The nationalist movements that surged across Asia and Africa in the twentieth century had their own answer. To their many millions of participants, colonial rule, whatever its earlier promise, had become an economic dead end, whereas independence represented a grand opening to new and more hopeful possibilities. Paraphrasing a famous teaching of Jesus, Kwame Nkrumah, the first prime minister of an independent Ghana, declared, "Seek ye first the political kingdom, and all these other things [schools, factories, hospitals, for example] will be added unto you."

Snapshot Long-Distance Migration in an Age of Empire, 1846–1940[16]

The age of empire was also an age of global migration. Beyond the long-distance migration shown here, shorter migrations within particular regions or colonies set millions more into motion.

Origins	Destination	Numbers
Europe	Americas	55–58 million
India, southern China	Southeast Asia, Indian Ocean rim, South Pacific	48–52 million
Northeast Asia, Russia	Manchuria, Siberia, Central Asia, Japan	46–51 million

Believing and Belonging: Identity and Cultural Change in the Colonial Era

The experience of colonial rule—its racism, its exposure to European culture, its social and economic upheavals—contributed much to cultural change within Asian and African societies. Coping with these enormous disruptions induced many colonized peoples to alter the ways they thought about themselves and their communities. Cultural identities, of course, are never static, but the transformations of the colonial era catalyzed substantial and quite rapid changes in what people believed and in how they defined the societies to which they belonged. Those transformed identities continued to echo long after European rule had ended.

Education

For an important minority, it was the acquisition of Western education, obtained through missionary or government schools, that generated a new identity. To previously illiterate people, the knowledge of reading and writing of any kind often suggested an almost magical power. Within the colonial setting, it could mean an escape from some of the most onerous obligations of living under European control, such as forced labor. More positively, it meant access to better-paying positions in government bureaucracies, mission organizations, or business firms and to the exciting imported goods that their salaries could buy. Moreover, education often provided social mobility and elite status within their own communities and an opportunity to achieve, or at least approach, equality with whites in racially defined societies. An African man from colonial Kenya described an encounter he had as a boy in 1938 with a relative who was a teacher in a mission school:

■ **Change**
What impact did Western education have on colonial societies?

> Aged about 25, he seems to me like a young god with his smart clothes and shoes, his watch, and a beautiful bicycle. I worshipped in particular his bicycle that day and decided that I must somehow get myself one. As he talked with us, it seemed to me that the secret of his riches came from his education, his knowledge of reading and writing, and that it was essential for me to obtain this power.[17]

Many such people ardently embraced European culture, dressing in European clothes, speaking French or English, building European-style houses, getting married in long white dresses, and otherwise emulating European ways (see Document 20.1, pp. 950–51). Some of the early Western-educated Bengalis from northeastern India boasted about dreaming in English and deliberately ate beef, to the consternation of their elders. In a well-known poem entitled "A Prayer for Peace," Léopold Senghor, a highly educated West African writer and political leader, enumerated the many crimes of colonialism and yet confessed, "I have a great weakness for France." Asian and African colonial societies now had a new cultural divide: between the small number who had mastered to varying degrees the ways of their rulers and the vast majority who had not. Literate Christians in the East African kingdom of Buganda referred with contempt to their "pagan" neighbors as "they who do not read."

The Educated Elite

Throughout the Afro-Asian world of the nineteenth century, the European presence generated a small group of people who enthusiastically embraced the culture and lifestyle of Europe. Here King Chulalongkorn of Siam poses with the crown prince and other young students, all of them garbed impeccably in European clothing. (Hulton-Deutsch Collection/Corbis)

Many among the Western-educated elite saw themselves as a modernizing vanguard, leading the regeneration of their societies in association with colonial authorities. For them, at least initially, the colonial enterprise was full of promise for a better future. The Vietnamese teacher and nationalist Nguyen Thai Hoc, while awaiting execution in 1930 by the French for his revolutionary activities, wrote about his earlier hopes: "At the beginning, I had thought to cooperate with the French in Indochina in order to serve my compatriots, my country, and my people, particularly in the areas of cultural and economic development."[18] Senghor too wrote wistfully about an earlier time when "we could have lived in harmony [with Europeans]."

In nineteenth-century India, Western-educated people organized a variety of reform societies, which sought a renewed Indian culture that was free of idolatry, child marriages, caste, and discrimination against women, while drawing inspiration from the classic texts of Hinduism. For a time, some of these Indian reformers saw themselves working in tandem with British colonial authorities. One of them, Keshub Chunder Sen (1838–1884), spoke to his fellow Indians in 1877: "You are bound to be loyal to the British government that came to your rescue, as God's ambassador, when your country was sunk in ignorance and superstition. . . . India in her present fallen condition seems destined to sit at the feet of England for many long years, to learn western art and science."[19] (See Document 20.2, pp. 951–53, for another such view.)

Such fond hopes for the modernization of Asian and African societies within a colonial framework would be bitterly disappointed. Europeans generally declined to treat their Asian and African subjects—even those with a Western education—as equal partners in the enterprise of renewal. The frequent denigration of their cultures as primitive, backward, uncivilized, or savage certainly rankled, particularly among the well-educated. "My people of Africa," wrote the West African intellectual James Aggrey in the 1920s, "we were created in the image of God, but men have made us think that we are chickens, and we still think we are; but we are eagles. Stretch forth your wings and fly."[20] In the long run, the educated classes in colonial societies everywhere found European rule far more of an obstacle to their countries' development than a means of achieving it. Turning decisively against a now-despised foreign imperialism, they led the many struggles for independence that came to fruition in the second half of the twentieth century.

Religion

Religion too provided the basis for new or transformed identities during the colonial era. Most dramatic were those places where widespread conversion to Christianity took place, such as New Zealand, the Pacific islands, and especially non-Muslim Africa. Some 10,000 missionaries had descended on Africa by 1910; by the 1960s, about 50 million Africans, roughly half of the non-Muslim population, claimed a Christian identity. The attractions of the new faith were many. As in the Americas centuries earlier, military defeat shook confidence in the old gods and local practices, fostering openness to new sources of supernatural power that could operate in the wider world now impinging on their societies. Furthermore, Christianity was widely associated with modern education, and, especially in Africa, mission schools were the primary providers of Western education. The young, the poor, and many women—all of them oppressed groups in many African societies—found new opportunities and greater freedom in some association with missions. Moreover, the spread of the Christian message was less the work of European missionaries than of those many thousands of African teachers, catechists, and pastors who brought the new faith to remote

■ Change
What were the attractions of Christianity within some colonial societies?

The Missionary Factor

Among the major change agents of the colonial era were the thousands of Christian missionaries who brought not only a new religion but also elements of European medicine, education, gender roles, and culture. Here is an assembly at a mission school for girls in New Guinea in the early twentieth century. (Rue des Archives/The Granger Collection, New York)

villages as well as the local communities that begged for a teacher and supplied the labor and materials to build a small church or school.

As elsewhere, Christianity in Africa soon became Africanized. Within mission-based churches, many converts continued using protective charms and medicines and consulting local medicine men, all of which caused their missionary mentors to speak frequently of "backsliding." Other converts continued to believe in their old gods and spirits but now deemed them evil and sought their destruction. Furthermore, thousands of separatist movements established a wide array of independent churches, which were thoroughly Christian but under African rather than missionary control and which in many cases incorporated African cultural practices and modes of worship. It was a twentieth-century "African Reformation."

In India, where Christianity made only very modest inroads, leading intellectuals and reformers began to define their region's endlessly varied beliefs, practices, sects, rituals, and schools of philosophy as a more distinct, unified, and separate religion that we now know as Hinduism. It was in part an effort to provide for India a religion wholly equivalent to Christianity, "an accessible tradition and a feeling of historical worth when faced with the humiliation of colonial rule."[21] To Swami Vivekananda (1863–1902), one of nineteenth-century India's most influential religious figures, a revived Hinduism, shorn of its distortions, offered a means of uplifting the country's village communities, which were the heart of Indian civilization. Moreover, it could offer spiritual support to a Western world mired in materialism and militarism, a message that he took to the First World Parliament of Religions held in 1893 in Chicago. Here was India speaking back to Europe:

> Let the foreigners come and flood the land with their armies, never mind. Up, India and conquer the world with your spirituality.... The whole of the Western world is a volcano which may burst tomorrow, go to pieces tomorrow.... Now is the time to work so that India's spiritual ideas may penetrate deep into the West.[22]

This new notion of Hinduism provided a cultural foundation for emerging ideas of India as a nation, but it also contributed to a clearer sense of Muslims as a distinct community in India. Before the British takeover, little sense of commonality united the many diverse communities who practiced Islam—urban and rural dwellers; nomads and farmers; artisans, merchants, and state officials.

■ **Change**
How and why did Hinduism emerge as a distinct religious tradition during the colonial era in India?

Hinduism in the West
The cultural interactions of the colonial era brought Asian traditions such as Hinduism to the attention of small groups in Europe and the United States. The visit of India's Swami Vivekananda to the First World Parliament of Religions in Chicago in 1893 was part of that process, illustrated here by a famous poster that circulated at that event. (Courtesy, Goes Lithographics, Chicago, after photo by Frank Parlato Jr. Image provided by www.vivekananda.net)

But the British had created separate inheritance laws for all Muslims and others for all Hindus; in their census taking, they counted the numbers of people within these now sharply distinguished groups; and they allotted seats in local councils according to these artificial categories. As some anti-British patriots began to cast India in Hindu terms, the idea of Muslims as a separate community, which was perhaps threatened by the much larger number of Hindus, began to make sense to some who practiced Islam. In the early twentieth century, a young Hindu Bengali schoolboy noticed that "our Muslim school-fellows were beginning to air the fact of their being Muslims rather more consciously than before and with a touch of assertiveness."[23] Here were the beginnings of what became in the twentieth century a profound religious and political division within the South Asian peninsula.

"Race" and "Tribe"

In Africa as well, intellectuals and ordinary people alike forged new ways of belonging as they confronted the upheavals of colonial life. Central to these new identities were notions of race and ethnicity. By the end of the nineteenth century, a number of African thinkers, familiar with Western culture, began to define the idea of an "African identity." Previously, few if any people on the continent had regarded themselves as Africans. Rather they were members of particular local communities, usually defined by language; some were also Muslims; and still others inhabited some state or empire. Now, however, influenced by the common experience of colonial oppression and by a highly derogatory European racism, well-educated Africans began to think in broader terms, similar to Indian reformers who were developing the notion of Hinduism. It was an effort to revive the cultural self-confidence of their people by articulating a larger, common, and respected "African tradition," equivalent to that of Western culture.

> ■ **Change**
>
> In what way were "race" and "tribe" new identities in colonial Africa?

This effort took various shapes. One line of argument held that African culture and history in fact possessed the very characteristics that Europeans exalted. Knowing that Europeans valued large empires and complex political systems, African intellectuals pointed with pride to the ancient kingdoms of Ethiopia, Mali, Songhay, and others. C. A. Diop, a French-educated scholar from Senegal, insisted that Egyptian civilization was in fact the work of black Africans. Reversing European assumptions, Diop argued that Western civilization owed much to Egyptian influence and was therefore derived from Africa. Black people, in short, had a history of achievement fully comparable to that of Europe and therefore deserved just as much respect and admiration.

An alternative approach to defining an African identity lay in praising the differences between African and European cultures. The most influential proponent of such views was Edward Blyden (1832–1912), a West African born in the West Indies and educated in the United States who later became a prominent scholar and political official in Liberia. Blyden accepted the assumption that the world's various races were different but argued that each had its own distinctive contribution to make to world civilization. The uniqueness of African culture, Blyden wrote, lay in its communal, cooperative, and egalitarian societies, which contrasted sharply with Europe's highly individualistic, competitive, and class-ridden societies; in its harmonious relationship with nature as opposed to Europe's efforts to dominate and exploit the natural order; and particularly in its profound religious sensibility, which Europeans had lost in centuries of attention to material gain. Like Vivekananda in India, Blyden argued that Africa had a global mission "to be the spiritual conservatory of the world."[24]

In the twentieth century, such ideas resonated with a broader public. Hundreds of thousands of Africans took part in World War I, during which they encountered other Africans as well as Europeans. Some were able to travel widely. Contact with American black leaders such as Booker T. Washington, W. E. B. DuBois, Marcus Garvey, and various West Indian intellectuals further stimulated among a few a sense of belonging to an even larger pan-African world. Such notions underlay the growing nationalist movements that contested colonial rule as the twentieth century unfolded.

For the vast majority, however, the most important new sense of belonging that evolved from the colonial experience was not the notion of "Africa"; rather, it was the idea of "tribe" or, in the language of contemporary scholars, that of ethnic identity. African peoples, of course, had long recognized differences among themselves based on language, kinship, clan, village, or state, but these were seldom sharp or clearly defined. Boundaries fluctuated and were hazy; local communities often incorporated a variety of culturally different peoples. The idea of an Africa sharply divided into separate and distinct "tribes" was in fact a European notion that facilitated colonial administration and reflected Europeans' belief in African primitiveness. When the British, for example, began to govern the peoples living along the northern side of Lake Tanganyika, in present-day Tanzania, they found a series of communities that were similar to one another in language and customs but that governed themselves separately and certainly had not regarded themselves as a tribe. It was British attempts to rule them as a single people, first through a "paramount chief" and later through a council of chiefs and elders, that resulted in their being called, collectively, the Nyakyusa. A tribe had been born. By requiring people to identify their tribe on applications for jobs, schools, and identity cards, colonial governments spread the idea of tribe widely within their colonies.

New ethnic identities were not simply imposed by Europeans; Africans increasingly found ethnic or tribal labels useful. This was especially true in rapidly growing urban areas. Surrounded by a bewildering variety of people and in a setting where competition for jobs, housing, and education was very intense, migrants to the city found it helpful to categorize themselves and others in larger ethnic terms. Thus, in many colonial cities, people who spoke similar languages, shared a common culture, or came from the same general part of the country began to think of themselves as a single people—a new tribe. They organized a rich variety of ethnic or tribal associations to provide mutual assistance while in the cities and to send money back home to build schools or clinics. Migrant workers, far from home and concerned to protect their rights to land and to their wives and families, found a sense of security in being part of a recognized tribe, with its chiefs, courts, and established authority.

The Igbo people of southeastern Nigeria represent a case in point. Prior to the twentieth century, they were organized in a series of independently governed village groups. Although they spoke related languages, they had no unifying political system and no myth of common ancestry. Occupying a region of unusually dense population, many of these people eagerly seized on Western education and moved in large numbers to the cities and towns of colonial Nigeria. There they gradually discovered what they had in common and how they differed from the other peoples of Nigeria. By the 1940s, they were organizing on a national level and calling on Igbos everywhere to "sink all differences" in order to achieve "tribal unity, cooperation, and progress of all the Igbos." Fifty years earlier, however, no one had regarded himself or herself as an Igbo. One historian summed up the process of creating African ethnic identities in this way: "Europeans believed Africans belonged to tribes; Africans built tribes to belong to."[25]

Reflections: Who Makes History?

Winners may write history, but they do not make history, at least not alone. Dominant groups everywhere—slave owners, upper classes, men generally, and certainly colonial rulers—have found their actions constrained and their choices limited by the sheer presence of subordinated people and the ability of those people to act. Europeans who sought to make their countries self-sufficient in cotton by requiring colonized Africans to grow it generally found themselves unable to achieve that goal. Missionaries who tried to impose their own understanding of Christianity in the colonies found their converts often unwilling to accept missionary authority or the cultural framework in which the new religion was presented. In the twentieth century, colonial rulers all across Asia and Africa found that their most highly educated subjects became the leaders of those movements seeking to end colonial rule. Clearly this was not what they had intended.

In recent decades, historians have been at pains to uncover the ways in which subordinated people—slaves, workers, peasants, women, the colonized—have been able to act in their own interests, even within the most oppressive conditions. This kind of "history from below" found expression in a famous book about American slavery that was subtitled *The World the Slaves Made*. Historians of women's lives have sought to show women not only as victims of patriarchy but also as historical actors in their own right. Likewise, colonized people in any number of ways actively shaped the history of the colonial era. On occasion, they resisted and rebelled; in various times and places, they embraced, rejected, and transformed a transplanted Christianity; many eagerly sought Western education but later turned it against the colonizers; women both suffered from and creatively coped with the difficulties of colonial life; and everywhere people created new ways of belonging. None of this diminishes the hardships, the enormous inequalities of power, or the exploitation and oppression of the colonial experience. Rather it suggests that history is often made through the struggle of unequal groups and that the outcome corresponds to no one's intentions.

Perhaps we might let Karl Marx have the last word on this endlessly fascinating topic: "Men make their own history," he wrote, "but they do not make it as they please nor under conditions of their own choosing." In the colonial experience of the nineteenth and early twentieth centuries, both the colonizers and the colonized "made history," but neither was able to do so as they pleased.

Second Thoughts

What's the Significance?

To assess your mastery of the material in this chapter, visit the **Student Center** at bedfordstmartins.com/strayer.

scramble for Africa	cash-crop agriculture	European racism
Indian Rebellion, 1857–1858	Western-educated elite	Edward Blyden
Congo Free State/Leopold II	Africanization of Christianity	colonial tribalism
cultivation system	Swami Vivekananda	

Big Picture Questions

1. Why were Asian and African societies incorporated into European colonial empires later than those of the Americas? How would you compare their colonial experiences?
2. In what ways did colonial rule rest upon violence and coercion, and in what ways did it elicit voluntary cooperation or generate benefits for some people?
3. In what respects were colonized people more than victims of colonial conquest and rule? To what extent could they act in their own interests within the colonial situation?
4. Was colonial rule a transforming, even a revolutionary, experience, or did it serve to freeze or preserve existing social and economic patterns? What evidence can you find to support both sides of this argument?

Next Steps: For Further Study

For Web sites and additional documents related to this chapter, see **Make History** at bedfordstmartins.com/strayer.

A. Adu Boahen, *African Perspectives on Colonialism* (1987). An examination of the colonial experience by a prominent African scholar.

Alice Conklin and Ian Fletcher, *European Imperialism, 1830–1930* (1999). A collection of both classical reflections on empire and examples of modern scholarship.

Scott B. Cook, *Colonial Encounters in the Age of High Imperialism* (1996). Seven case studies of the late-nineteenth-century colonial experience.

Adam Hochschild, *King Leopold's Ghost* (1999). A journalist's evocative account of the horrors of early colonial rule in the Congo.

Douglas Peers, *India under Colonial Rule* (2006). A concise and up-to-date exploration of colonial India.

Bonnie Smith, ed., *Imperialism* (2000). A fine collection of documents, pictures, and commentary on nineteenth- and twentieth-century empires.

Margaret Strobel, *Gender, Sex, and Empire* (1994). A brief account of recent historical thinking about colonial life and gender.

"History of Imperialism," http://members.aol.com/TeacherNet/World.html. A Web site with dozens of links to documents, essays, maps, cartoons, and pictures dealing with modern empires.

Documents

Considering the Evidence:
Indian Responses to Empire

The European empires of the nineteenth and early twentieth centuries elicited a variety of responses from their colonial subjects—acceptance and even gratitude, disappointment with unfulfilled promises, active resistance, and sharp criticism. The documents that follow present a range of Indian commentary on British rule from the late eighteenth to the early twentieth centuries.

During that roughly 150 years, India was Britain's "jewel in the crown," the centerpiece of its expanding empire in Asia and Africa (see Map 20.1, p. 926). Until the late 1850s, Britain's growing involvement with South Asia was organized and led by the British East India Company, a private trading firm that had acquired a charter from the Crown allowing it to exercise military, political, and administrative functions in India as well as its own commercial operations (see pp. 679–80). As the Mughal Empire decayed, the company assumed a governing role for increasingly large parts of the subcontinent. But after the explosive upheaval of the Indian Rebellion of 1857–1858, the British government itself assumed control of the region. Throughout the colonial era, the British relied heavily on an alliance with traditional elite groups in Indian society—landowners; the "princes" who governed large parts of the region; and the Brahmins, the highest-ranking segment of India's caste-based society.

Document 20.1

The Wonders of British Calcutta

Originally a small village in Bengal, Calcutta grew into a major trading settlement under the British East India Company, becoming the capital of British India in 1772. In the late eighteenth century, a widely traveled Indian Muslim scholar named Nawab Muhabbat Khan described in poetry his impressions of this British city.

- ■ What features of Calcutta most surprised Muhabbat Khan?

- ■ What were his attitudes toward the British themselves?

■ What might you infer about his posture toward an emerging British political presence in India?

Nawab Muhabbat Khan

On Calcutta

Late Eighteenth Century

Calcutta is a wonderful city, in the country of
    Bang.°
It is a specimen of both China and Farang.°
Its buildings are heart-attracting and delightful....
From the beauty of the works of the European
    artists
The senses of the spectator are overpowered.
The hat-wearing Englishmen who dwell in them
All speak the truth and have good dispositions....
As a multitude of persons like the planets roam in
    every direction,
The streets take the resemblance of the Milky Way.

°**Bang:** Bengal.

°**Farang:** the West.

Source: Sir H. M. Elliot, *The History of India as Told by Its Own Historians* (London: Trubner and Co., 1877), 8:382–83.

You will see, if you go to the bazaar, all the excellent
    things of the world.
All things which are produced in any part of the
    inhabited world
Are found in its bazaar without difficulty.
If I attempt to write in praise of the marvels of
    the city,
The pen will refuse its office.
But it is well known to all of every degree
That it combines the beauties of China and
    Farang.
The ground is as level as the face of the sky,
And the roads in it are as straight as the line of
    the equator.
People go out to walk on them,
And there they meet together like the planets.
Such a city as this in the country of the
    Bengalis
Nobody has seen or heard of in the world.

Document 20.2

Seeking Western Education

Ram Mohan Roy (1772–1833), born and highly educated within a Brahmin Hindu family, subsequently studied both Arabic and Persian, learned English, came into contact with British Christian missionaries, and found employment with the British East India Company. He emerged in the early nineteenth century as a leading advocate for religious and social reform within India, with a particular interest in ending *sati*, the practice in which widows burned themselves on their husbands' funeral pyres. In 1823, he learned about a British plan to establish a school in Calcutta that was to focus on Sanskrit texts and traditional Hindu learning. Document 20.2 records his response to that school, and to British colonial rule, in a letter to the British governor-general of India.

PART SIX

The Most Recent Century

1914–2010

Contents

The Twentieth Century: A New Period in World History?

Dividing up time into coherent segments—periods, eras, ages—is the way historians mark major changes in the lives of individuals, local communities, social groups, nations, and civilizations and also in the larger story of humankind as a whole. Because all such divisions are artificial, imposed by scholars on a continuously flowing stream of events, they are endlessly controversial and never more so than in the case of the twentieth century. To many historians, that century, and a new era in the human journey, began in 1914 with the outbreak of World War I. That terrible conflict, after all, represented a fratricidal civil war within Western civilization, triggered the Russian Revolution and the beginning of world communism, and stimulated many in the colonial world to work for their own independence. The way it ended set the stage for an even more terrible struggle in World War II.

But do the almost 100 years since 1914 represent a separate phase of world history? Granting them that status has become conventional in many world history textbooks, including this one, but there are reasons to wonder whether future generations will agree. One problem, of course, lies in the brevity of this period—less than 100 years, compared to the many centuries or millennia that comprise earlier eras. Furthermore, an immense overload of information about these decades makes it difficult to distinguish what will prove of lasting significance and what will later seem of only passing importance. Furthermore, because we are so close to the events we study and obviously ignorant of the future, we cannot know if or when this most recent period of world history will end. Or, as some have argued, has it ended already, perhaps with the collapse of the Soviet Union in 1991, with the attacks of September 11, 2001, or with the global economic crisis beginning in 2008? If so, are we now in yet another phase of historical development?

Old and New in the Twentieth Century

Like all other historical periods, this most recent century both carried on from the past and developed distinctive characteristics as well. Whether that combination of the old and new merits the designation of a separate era in world history will likely be debated for a long time to come. For our purposes, it will be enough to highlight both its continuities with the past and the sharp changes that the last 100 years have witnessed.

Consider, for example, the world wars that played such an important role in the first half of the century. They grew out of Europeans' persistent inability to embody their civilization within a single state or empire, as China had long done. They also represent a further stage of European rivalries around the globe that had been going on for four centuries. Nonetheless, the world wars of the twentieth century were also new in the extent to which whole populations were mobilized to fight them and in the enormity of the destruction that they caused. During World War II, for example, Hitler's attempted extermination of the Jews in the Holocaust and the United States' dropping of atomic bombs on Japanese cities marked something new in the history of human conflict.

The communist phenomenon provides another illustration of the blending of old and new. The Russian (1917) and Chinese (1949) revolutions, both of which were enormous social upheavals, brought to power regimes committed to remaking their societies from top to bottom along socialist lines. They were the first large-scale attempts in modern world history to undertake such a gigantic task, and in doing so they broke sharply with the capitalist democratic model of the West. They also created a new and global division of humankind, expressed most dramatically in the cold war between the communist East and the capitalist West. On the other hand, the communist experience also drew much from the past. The great revolutions of the twentieth century derived from long-standing conflicts within Russian and Chinese societies, particularly between impoverished and exploited peasants and dominant landlord classes. The ideology of those communist governments came from the thinking of the nineteenth-century German intellectual Karl Marx. Their intention, like that of their capitalist enemies, was modernization and industrialization. They simply claimed to do it better—more rapidly and more justly.

Another distinguishing feature of the twentieth century lay in the disintegration of its great empires—the Austro-Hungarian, Ottoman, Russian, British, French, Japanese, Soviet, and more—and in their wake the emergence of dozens of new nation-states. At one level, this is simply the latest turn of the wheel in the endless rise and fall of empires, dating back to the ancient Assyrians. But something new occurred this time, for the very idea of empire was rendered illegitimate in the twentieth century, much as slavery lost its international acceptance in the nineteenth century. The superpowers of the second half of the twentieth century—the Soviet Union and the United States—both claimed an anticolonial ideology, even as both of them constructed their own "empires" of a different kind. By the beginning of the twenty-first century, some 200 nation-states, each claiming sovereignty and legal equality with all the others, provided a distinctly new political order for the planet.

The less visible underlying processes of the twentieth century, just like the more dramatic wars, revolutions, and political upheavals, also had roots in the past as well as new expressions in the new century. Perhaps the most fundamental process was explosive population growth, as human numbers more than quadrupled since 1900, leaving the planet with about 6.8 billion people by mid-2009. This was an absolutely unprecedented rate of growth that conditioned practically every other feature of

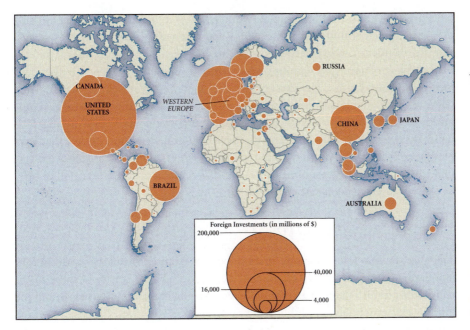

Foreign Investments (in millions of $)
200,000
40,000
16,000
4,000

RUSSIA

CANADA
UNITED
STATES
WESTERN
EUROPE
CHINA   JAPAN
BRAZIL
AUSTRALIA

Globalization in Action:
Trade and Investment in the
Early Twenty-first Century
(p. 1136)

the century's history. Still, this new element of twentieth-century world history built upon earlier achievements, most notably the increased food supply deriving from the global spread of American crops such as corn and potatoes. Improvements in medicine and sanitation, which grew out of the earlier Scientific and Industrial revolutions, likewise drove down death rates and thus spurred population growth.

While global population increased fourfold in the twentieth century, industrial output grew fortyfold. This unprecedented economic growth, despite large variations over time and place, was associated with a cascading rate of scientific and technological innovation as well as with the extension of industrial production to many regions of the world. This too was a wholly novel feature of twentieth-century world history and, combined with population growth, resulted in an extraordinary and mounting human impact on the environment. Historian J. R. McNeill wrote that "this is the first time in human history that we have altered ecosystems with such intensity, on such a scale, and with such speed.... The human race, without intending anything of the sort, has undertaken a gigantic uncontrolled experiment on the earth."[1] From a longer-term perspective, of course, these developments represent a continued unfolding of the Scientific and Industrial revolutions. Both began in Europe, but in the twentieth century they largely lost their unique association with the West as they took hold in many cultures. Furthermore, the human impact on the earth itself and other living creatures has a history dating back to the extinction of some large mammals at the hands of Paleolithic hunters.

Much the same might be said about that other grand process of twentieth-century world history—globalization. It too has a genealogy reaching deep into the past, reflected in the Silk Road trading network; Indian Ocean and trans-Saharan commerce; the spread of Buddhism, Christianity, and Islam; and the Columbian exchange. But the twentieth century deepened and extended the connections among the distinct peoples, nations, and regions of the world in ways unparalleled in earlier centuries. A few strokes on a keyboard can send money racing around the planet; radio, television, and the Internet link the world in an unprecedented network of communication; the warming of the lower atmosphere due to the accumulation of greenhouse gases portends radical changes for the whole planet; far more people than ever before produce for and depend on the world market; and global inequalities increasingly surface as sources of international conflict. For good or ill, we live—all of us— in a new phase of an ancient process.

Three Regions—One World

The chapters that follow explore these themes of twentieth-century world history in a particular way. Chapters 21, 22, and 23 tell the separate stories of three major regions or groups of countries—the Western world; the communist world; and the third world, sometimes called the world of developing countries. Chapter 21, which focuses on the Western world of capitalist countries, highlights the dramatic changes that occurred at the center of the global network. The European heartland of the world system collapsed in war and economic depression during the first half of the century but recovered in the second half as leadership of the West passed to the United States.

Accompanying those changes was the emergence of world communism. Chapter 22 addresses four highly significant features of the communist phenomenon: the revolutionary origins of communism, especially in Russia and China; the efforts of those two communist giants to build new and socialist societies; the global conflict of the cold war, which arose from the expansion of communism; and the amazing abandonment of communism as the century ended.

Chapter 23 turns the historical spotlight on the colonial world of Asia and Africa. Two major themes serve to structure the twentieth-century history of this vast region. The first focuses attention on the struggles for independence, the end of colonial empires, and the emergence of dozens of new nations. The second describes the increasingly important role on the global stage that these new states have played in the second half of the century. The assertion of African, Asian, and Middle Eastern peoples, joined by those of Latin America, made the world of the early twenty-first century a very different place from that of a hundred years earlier.

These histories of the Western world, the communist world, and the third world during the past century not only paralleled each other but also frequently intersected and overlapped, as Chapters 21, 22, and 23 repeatedly indicate. However, they were also part of an even larger story, known everywhere now as globalization. The post–World War II acceleration of this much older process is the "big picture" theme of Chapter 24, which examines both its economic and cultural dimensions. Thus it focuses attention on the development of the world economy as well as on the global expressions of feminism, religious fundamentalism, and environmentalism.

Perhaps there is enough that is new about the century following 1914 to treat it, tentatively, as a distinct era in human history, but only what happens next will determine how this period will be understood by later generations. Will it be regarded as the beginning of the end of the modern age, as human demands upon the earth prove unsustainable? Or will it be seen as the midpoint of an ongoing process that extends a full modernity to the entire planet? Like all of our ancestors, every one of them, we too live in a fog when contemplating our futures and see more clearly only in retrospect. In this strange way, our future will shape the telling of the past, even as the past shapes the living of the future.

Landmarks of the Most Recent Century, 1914–2010

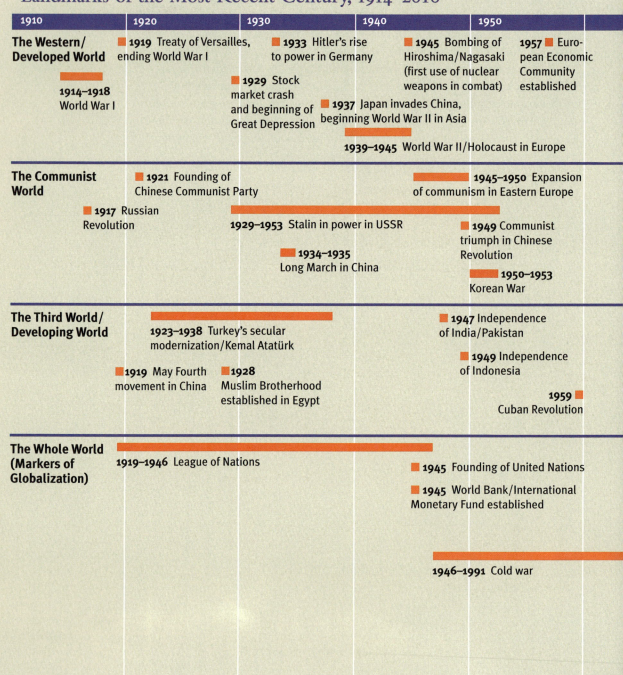

	1910	1920	1930	1940	1950

The Western/ Developed World

1919 Treaty of Versailles, ending World War I

1933 Hitler's rise to power in Germany

1945 Bombing of Hiroshima/Nagasaki (first use of nuclear weapons in combat)

1957 European Economic Community established

1914–1918 World War I

1929 Stock market crash and beginning of Great Depression

1937 Japan invades China, beginning World War II in Asia

1939–1945 World War II/Holocaust in Europe

The Communist World

1921 Founding of Chinese Communist Party

1945–1950 Expansion of communism in Eastern Europe

1917 Russian Revolution

1929–1953 Stalin in power in USSR

1949 Communist triumph in Chinese Revolution

1934–1935 Long March in China

1950–1953 Korean War

The Third World/ Developing World

1923–1938 Turkey's secular modernization/Kemal Atatürk

1947 Independence of India/Pakistan

1919 May Fourth movement in China

1928 Muslim Brotherhood established in Egypt

1949 Independence of Indonesia

1959 Cuban Revolution

The Whole World (Markers of Globalization)

1919–1946 League of Nations

1945 Founding of United Nations

1945 World Bank/International Monetary Fund established

1946–1991 Cold war

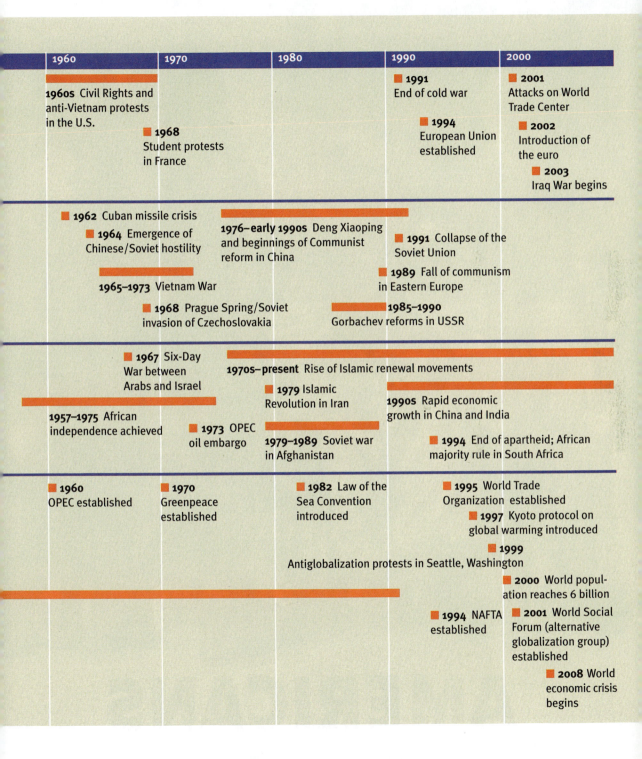

1960	1970	1980	1990	2000

1960s Civil Rights and anti-Vietnam protests in the U.S.

1968 Student protests in France

1991 End of cold war

1994 European Union established

2001 Attacks on World Trade Center

2002 Introduction of the euro

2003 Iraq War begins

1962 Cuban missile crisis

1964 Emergence of Chinese/Soviet hostility

1976–early 1990s Deng Xiaoping and beginnings of Communist reform in China

1991 Collapse of the Soviet Union

1965–1973 Vietnam War

1989 Fall of communism in Eastern Europe

1968 Prague Spring/Soviet invasion of Czechoslovakia

1985–1990 Gorbachev reforms in USSR

1967 Six-Day War between Arabs and Israel

1970s–present Rise of Islamic renewal movements

1979 Islamic Revolution in Iran

1990s Rapid economic growth in China and India

1957–1975 African independence achieved

1973 OPEC oil embargo

1979–1989 Soviet war in Afghanistan

1994 End of apartheid; African majority rule in South Africa

1960 OPEC established

1970 Greenpeace established

1982 Law of the Sea Convention introduced

1995 World Trade Organization established

1997 Kyoto protocol on global warming introduced

1999 Antiglobalization protests in Seattle, Washington

2000 World population reaches 6 billion

1994 NAFTA established

2001 World Social Forum (alternative globalization group) established

2008 World economic crisis begins

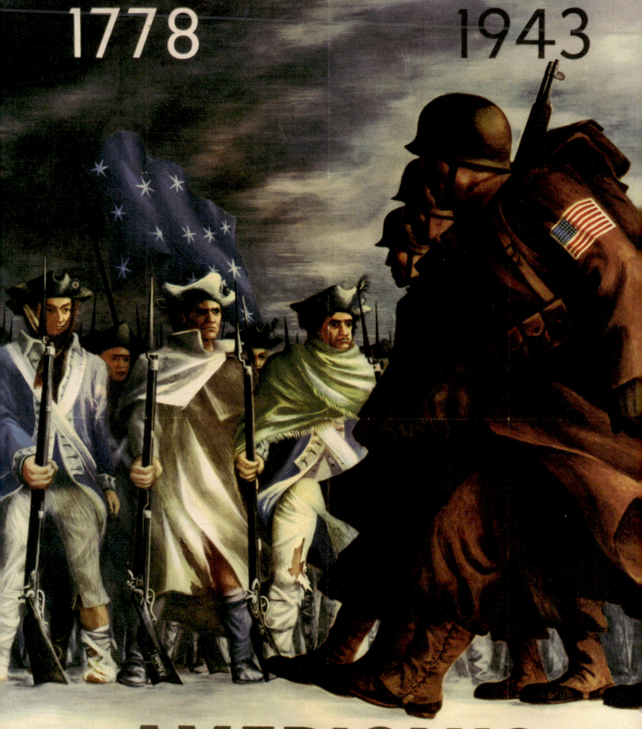

1778

1943

AMERICANS
will <u>always</u> fight for liberty

The Collapse and Recovery of Europe

1914–1970s

"I was told that I was fighting a war that would end all wars, but that wasn't the case." Spoken a few years before his death, these were the thoughts of Alfred Anderson, a World War I veteran who died in Scotland in November 2005, at the age of 109. He was apparently the last survivor of the famous Christmas truce of 1914, when British and German soldiers, enemies on the battlefield of that war, briefly mingled, exchanged gifts, and played football in the no-man's land that lay between their entrenchments in Belgium. He had been especially dismayed when in 2003 his own unit, the famous Black Watch regiment, was ordered into Iraq along with other British forces.[1] Despite his disappointment at the many conflicts that followed World War I, Anderson's own lifetime had witnessed the fulfillment of the promise of the Christmas truce. By the time he died, the major European nations had put aside their centuries-long hostilities, and war between Britain and Germany, which had erupted twice in the twentieth century, seemed unthinkable. What happened to Europe, and to the larger civilization of which it was a part, during the life of this one man is the focus of this chapter.

THE "GREAT WAR," WHICH CAME TO BE CALLED THE FIRST WORLD WAR (1914–1918), effectively launched the twentieth century, considered as a new phase of world history. That bitter conflict—essentially a European civil war with a global reach—was followed by the economic meltdown of the Great Depression, by the rise of Nazi Germany and the horror of the Holocaust, and by

The United States and World War II: The Second World War and its aftermath marked the decisive emergence of the United States as a global superpower. In this official 1943 poster, U.S. soldiers march forward to "fight for liberty" against fascism while casting a sideways glance for inspiration at the ragged colonial militiamen of their Revolutionary War. (Library of Congress, LC-USZC4-2119)

an even bloodier and more destructive World War II. During those three decades, Western Europe, for more than a century the dominant and dominating center of the modern "world system," largely self-destructed, in a process with profound and long-term implications far beyond Europe itself. By 1945, an outside observer might well have thought that Western civilization, which for several centuries was in the ascendancy on the global stage, had damaged itself beyond repair.

In the second half of the century, however, that civilization proved quite resilient. Its Western European heartland recovered remarkably from the devastation of war, rebuilt its industrial economy, and set aside its war-prone nationalist passions in a loose European Union. But as Europe revived after 1945, it lost both its overseas colonial possessions and its position as the political, economic, and military core of Western civilization. That role now passed across the Atlantic to the United States, marking a major change in the historical development of the West. The offspring now overshadowed its parent.

Map 21.1   The World in 1914
A map of the world in 1914 shows an unprecedented situation in which one people—Europeans or those of European descent—exercised enormous control and influence over virtually the entire planet.

The First World War: European Civilization in Crisis, 1914–1918

Since 1500, Europe had assumed an increasingly prominent position on the global stage, driven by its growing military capacity and the marvels of its Scientific and Industrial revolutions. By 1900, Europeans, or people with a European ancestry, largely controlled the world's other peoples through their formal empires, their informal influence, or the weight of their numbers (see Map 21.1). That unique situation pro-

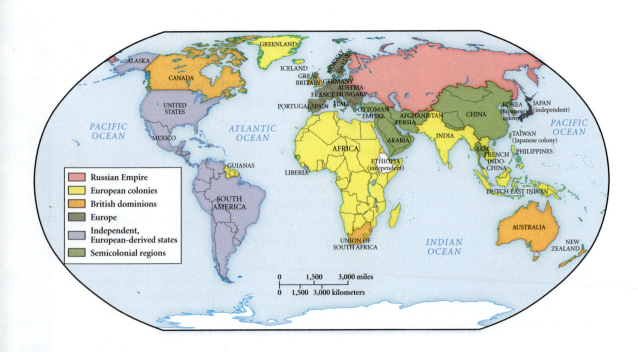

vided the foundation for Europeans' pride, self-confidence, and sense of superiority. Few could have imagined that this "proud tower" of European dominance would lie shattered less than a half century later. The starting point in that unraveling was the First World War.

An Accident Waiting to Happen

Europe's modern transformation and its global ascendancy were certainly not accompanied by a growing unity or stability among its own peoples—quite the opposite. The most obvious division was among its competing states, a long-standing feature of European political life. Those historical rivalries further sharpened as both Italy and Germany joined their fragmented territories into two major new powers around 1870. German unification had occurred in the context of a short war with France (the Franco-Prussian War of 1870–1871), which embittered relations between these two large countries for the next half century. More generally, the arrival on the international scene of a powerful and rapidly industrializing Germany, seeking its "place in the sun" as Kaiser Wilhelm put it, was a disruptive new element in European political life, especially for the more established powers, such as Britain, France, and Russia. Since the defeat of Napoleon in 1815, a fragile and fluctuating balance of power had generally maintained the peace among Europe's major countries. By the early twentieth century, that balance of power was expressed in two rival alliances, the Triple Alliance of Germany, Austria, and Italy and the Triple Entente of Russia, France, and Britain. It was those commitments, undertaken in the interests of national security, that transformed a minor incident in the Balkans into a conflagration that consumed all of Europe.

That incident occurred on June 28, 1914, when a Serbian nationalist assassinated the heir to the Austrian throne, Archduke Franz Ferdinand. To the rulers of Austria, the surging nationalism of Serbian Slavs was a mortal threat to the cohesion of their fragile multinational empire, which included other Slavic peoples as well, and they determined to crush it. But behind Austria lay its far more powerful ally, Germany; and behind tiny Serbia lay Russia, with its self-proclaimed mission of protecting other Slavic peoples; and allied to Russia were the French and the British. Thus a system of alliances intended to keep the peace created obligations that drew the Great Powers of Europe into a general war by early August 1914 (see Map 21.2).

The outbreak of that war was an accident, in that none of the major states planned or predicted the archduke's assassination or deliberately sought a prolonged conflict, but the system of rigid alliances made Europe prone to that kind of accident. Moreover, behind those alliances lay other factors that contributed to the eruption of war and shaped its character. One of them was a mounting popular nationalism (see pp. 796–800). Slavic nationalism and Austrian opposition to it certainly lay at the heart of the war's beginning. More important, the rulers of the major countries of Europe saw the world as an arena of conflict and competition among rival nation-states. The Great Powers of Europe competed intensely for colonies, spheres

■ **Explanation**
What aspects of Europe's nineteenth-century history contributed to the First World War?

Map 21.2   Europe on the Eve of World War I
Despite many elements of common culture, Europe in 1914 was a powder keg, with its major states armed to the teeth and divided into two rival alliances. In the early stages of the war, Italy changed sides to join the French, British, and Russians.

of influence, and superiority in armaments. Schools, mass media, and military service had convinced millions of ordinary Europeans that their national identities were profoundly and personally meaningful. The public pressure of these competing nationalisms allowed statesmen little room for compromise and ensured widespread popular support, at least initially, for the decision to go to war. Men rushed to recruiting offices, fearing that the war might end before they could enlist. Celebratory parades sent them off to the front. For conservative governments, the prospect of war was a welcome occasion for national unity in the face of the mounting class- and gender-based conflicts of European society.

Also contributing to the war was an industrialized militarism. Europe's armed rivalries had long ensured that military men enjoyed great social prestige, and most heads of state wore uniforms in public. All of the Great Powers had substantial standing armies and, except for Britain, relied on conscription (compulsory military service) to staff them. One expression of the quickening rivalry among these states was a mounting arms race in naval warships, particularly between Germany and Britain. Furthermore, each of the major states had developed elaborate "war plans" spelling out in great detail the movement of men and materials that should occur immediately upon the outbreak of war. Such plans created a hair-trigger mentality, since each country had an incentive to strike first so that its particular strategy could be implemented on schedule and without interruption or surprise. The rapid industrialization of warfare had generated an array of novel weapons, including submarines, tanks, airplanes, poison gas, machines guns, and barbed wire. This new military technology contributed to the staggering casualties of the war, including some 10 million deaths; perhaps twice that number wounded, crippled, or disfigured; and countless women for whom there would be no husbands or children.

Europe's imperial reach around the world likewise shaped the scope and conduct of the war. It funneled colonial troops and laborers by the hundreds of thousands into the war effort, with men from Africa, India, China, Southeast Asia, Australia, New Zealand, Canada, and South Africa taking part in the conflict (see Visual Source 21.3, p. 1023). Battles raged in Africa and the South Pacific as British and French forces sought to seize German colonies abroad. Japan, allied with Britain, took various German possessions in China and the Pacific and made heavy demands on China itself. The Ottoman Empire, which entered the conflict on the side of Germany, became the site of intense military actions and witnessed an Arab revolt against Ottoman control. Finally, the United States, after initially seeking to avoid involvement in European quarrels, joined the war in 1917 when German submarines threatened American shipping. Some 2 million Americans took part in the first U.S. military action on European soil and helped turn the tide in favor of the British and French. Thus the war, though centered in Europe, had global dimensions and certainly merited its familiar title as a "world war."

Legacies of the Great War

The Great War was a conflict that shattered almost every expectation. Most Europeans believed in the late summer of 1914 that "the boys will be home by Christmas," but instead the war ground relentlessly on for more than four years before ending in a German defeat in November 1918. (See Visual Sources: Propaganda and Critique in World War I, pp. 1019–27, for various representations of the war.) At

■ **Change**
In what ways did World War I mark new departures in the history of the twentieth century?

THESE WOMEN ARE DOING THEIR BIT

LEARN TO MAKE MUNITIONS

Women and the Great War
World War I temporarily brought a halt to the women's suffrage movement as well as to women's activities on behalf of international peace. Most women on both sides actively supported their countries' war efforts, as suggested by this British wartime poster, inviting women to work in the munitions industry. (Eileen Tweedy/The Art Archive)

the beginning, most military experts expected a war of movement and attack, but it soon bogged down on the western front into a war of attrition, in which trench warfare resulted in enormous casualties while gaining or losing only a few yards of muddy, blood-soaked ground (see Visual Source 21.4, p. 1025). Extended battles lasting months—such as those at Verdun and the Somme—generated casualties of a million or more each, as the destructive potential of industrialized warfare made itself tragically felt. Moreover, everywhere it became a "total war," requiring the mobilization of each country's entire population. Thus the authority of governments expanded greatly. The German state, for example, assumed such control over the economy that its policies became known as "war socialism." Vast propaganda campaigns sought to arouse citizens by depicting a cruel and inhuman enemy who killed innocent children and violated women. In factories, women replaced the men who had left for the battlefront, while labor unions agreed to suspend strikes and accept sacrifices for the common good.

No less surprising were the outcomes of the war. In the European cockpit of that conflict, unprecedented casualties, particularly among elite and well-educated groups, and physical destruction, especially in France, led to a widespread disillusionment among intellectuals with their own civilization (see Visual Source 21.5, p. 1026). The war seemed to mock the Enlightenment values of progress, tolerance, and rationality. Who could believe any longer that the West was superior or that its vaunted science and technology were unquestionably good things? In the most famous novel to emerge from the war, the German veteran Erich Remarque's *All Quiet on the Western Front*, one soldier expressed what many no doubt felt: "It must all be lies and of no account when the culture of a thousand years could not prevent this stream of blood being poured out."

Furthermore, from the collapse of the German, Russian, and Austrian empires emerged a new map of Central Europe with an independent Poland, Czechoslovakia, Yugoslavia, and other nations (see Map 21.3). Such new states were based on the principle of "national self-determination," a concept championed by the U.S. president Woodrow Wilson, but each of them also contained dissatisfied ethnic minorities, who claimed the same principle. In Russia, the strains of war triggered a vast revolutionary upheaval that brought the radical Bolsheviks to power in 1917 and took Russia out of the war. Thus was launched world communism, which was to play such a prominent role in the history of the twentieth century (see Chapter 22).

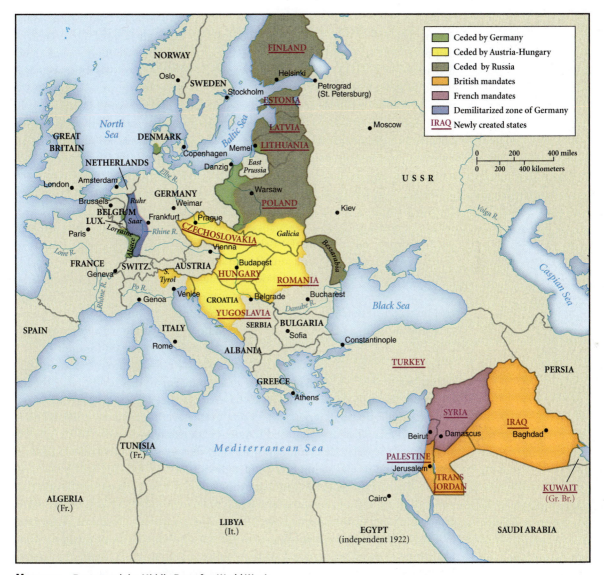

Map 21.3   Europe and the Middle East after World War I
The Great War brought into existence a number of new states that were carved out of the old German, Austro-Hungarian, Russian, and Ottoman empires. Turkey and the new states in Europe were independent, but those in the Middle East—Syria, Palestine, Iraq, and Transjordan—were administered by Britain or France as mandates of the League of Nations.

The Treaty of Versailles, which formally concluded the war in 1919, proved in retrospect to have established conditions that generated a second world war only twenty years later. In that treaty, Germany lost its colonial empire and 15 percent of its European territory, was required to pay heavy reparations to the winners, had its military forces severely restricted, and had to accept sole responsibility for the outbreak of the war. All of this created immense resentment in Germany. One of the country's many demobilized and disillusioned soldiers declared in 1922: "It cannot be that two million Germans should have fallen in vain. . . . No, we do not pardon, we demand—vengeance."[2] His name was Adolf Hitler, and within two decades he had begun to exact that vengeance.

The Great War generated profound changes in the world beyond Europe as well. During the war itself, Ottoman authorities, suspecting that some of their Armenian population were collaborating with the Russian enemy, massacred or deported an estimated 1 million Armenians. Although the term had not yet been invented, those atrocities merit the label of "genocide" and established a precedent on which the Nazis later built. The war also brought a final end to a declining Ottoman Empire, creating the modern map of the Middle East, with the new states of Turkey, Syria, Iraq, Jordan, and Palestine. Thus Arabs emerged from Turkish rule, but many of them were governed for a time by the British or French, as "mandates" of the League of Nations (see Map 21.3). Conflicting British promises to both Arabs and Jews regarding Palestine set the stage for an enduring struggle over that ancient and holy land.

In the world of European colonies, the war echoed loudly. Millions of Asian and African men had watched Europeans butcher one another without mercy, had gained new military skills and political awareness, and returned home with less respect for their rulers and with expectations for better treatment as a reward for their service. To gain Indian support for the war, the British had publicly promised to put that colony on the road to self-government, an announcement that set the stage for the independence struggle that followed. In East Asia, Japan emerged strengthened from the war, with European support for its claim to take over German territory and privileges in China. That news enraged Chinese nationalists and among a few sparked an interest in Soviet-style communism, for only the new communist rulers of Russia seemed willing to end the imperialist penetration of China.

Finally, the First World War brought the United States to center stage as a global power. Its manpower had contributed much to the defeat of Germany, and its financial resources turned the United States from a debtor nation into Europe's creditor. When the American president Woodrow Wilson arrived in Paris for the peace conference in 1919, he was greeted with an almost religious enthusiasm. His famous Fourteen Points seemed to herald a new kind of international life, one based on moral principles rather than secret deals and imperialist machinations. Particularly appealing to many was his idea for the League of Nations, a new international peacekeeping organization based on the principle of "collective security" and intended to avoid any repetition of the horrors that had just ended. Wilson's idealistic vision largely failed, however. Germany was treated more harshly than he had wished. And in his own country, the U.S. Senate refused to join the League, on which he had pinned his hopes for a lasting peace. Its opponents feared that Americans would be forced to bow to "the will of other nations." That refusal seriously weakened the League of Nations as a vehicle for a new international order.

Capitalism Unraveling: The Great Depression

The aftermath of war brought substantial social and cultural changes to the European and American victors in that conflict. Integrating millions of returning veterans into ordinary civilian life was no easy task, for they had experienced horrors almost beyond imagination. Governments sought to accommodate them—for example, with housing programs called "homes for heroes" and with an emphasis on traditional family values. French authorities proclaimed Mother's Day as a new holiday designed to encourage childbearing and thus replace the millions lost in the war.

Nonetheless, the war had loosened the hold of tradition in many ways. Enormous casualties promoted social mobility, allowing commoners to move into positions previously dominated by aristocrats. Women increasingly gained the right to vote. Young middle-class women, sometimes known as "flappers," began to flout convention by appearing at nightclubs, smoking, dancing, drinking hard liquor, cutting their hair short, wearing revealing clothing, and generally expressing a more open sexuality. A new consumerism encouraged those who could to acquire cars, washing machines, vacuum cleaners, electric irons, gas ovens, and other newly available products. Radio and the movies now became vehicles of popular culture, transmitting American jazz to Europe and turning Hollywood stars into international celebrities.

Far and away the most influential change of the postwar decades lay in the Great Depression. If World War I represented the political collapse of Europe, this catastrophic downturn suggested that its economic system was likewise failing. During the nineteenth century, European industrial capitalism had spurred the most substantial economic growth in world history and had raised the living standards of millions, but to many people it was a troubling system. Its very success generated an individualistic materialism that seemed to conflict with older values of community and spiritual life. To socialists and many others, its immense social inequalities were unacceptable. Furthermore, its evident instability—with cycles of boom and bust, expansion and recession—generated profound anxiety and threatened the livelihood of both industrial workers and those who had gained a modest toehold in the middle class.

■ **Connection**

In what ways was the Great Depression a global phenomenon?

Never had the flaws of capitalism been so evident or so devastating as during the decade that followed the outbreak of the Great Depression in 1929. All across the Euro-American heartland of the capitalist world, this vaunted economic system seemed to unravel. For the rich, it meant contracting stock prices that wiped out paper fortunes almost overnight. On the day that the American stock market initially crashed (October 24, 1929), eleven Wall Street financiers committed suicide, some by jumping out of skyscrapers. Banks closed, and many people lost their life savings. Investment dried up, world trade dropped by 62 percent within a few years, and businesses contracted when they were unable to sell their products. For ordinary people, the worst feature of the Great Depression was the loss of work. Unemployment soared everywhere, and in both Germany and the United States it

The Great Depression
This famous photograph of an impoverished American mother of three children, which was taken in 1936, came to symbolize the agonies of the Depression and the apparent breakdown of capitalism in the United States. (Library of Congress)

reached 30 percent or more by 1932 (see the Snapshot on p. 987). Vacant factories, soup kitchens, bread lines, shantytowns, and beggars came to symbolize the human reality of this economic disaster.

Explaining its onset, its spread from America to Europe and beyond, and its continuation for a decade has been a complicated task for historians. Part of the story lies in the United States' booming economy during the 1920s. In a country physically untouched by the war, wartime demand had greatly stimulated agricultural and industrial capacity. By the end of the 1920s, its farms and factories were producing more goods than could be sold because a highly unequal distribution of income meant that many people could not afford to buy the products that American factories were churning out. Nor were major European countries able to purchase those goods. Germany and Austria had to make huge reparation payments and were able to do so only with extensive U.S. loans. Britain and France, which were much indebted to the United States, depended on those reparations to repay their loans. Furthermore, Europeans generally had recovered enough to begin producing some of their own goods, and their expanding production further reduced the demand for American products. Meanwhile, a speculative stock market frenzy had driven up stock prices to an unsustainable level. When that bubble burst in late 1929, this intricately connected and fragile economic network across the Atlantic collapsed like a house of cards.

Much as Europe's worldwide empires had globalized the war, so too its economic linkages globalized the Great Depression. Countries or colonies tied to exporting one or two products were especially hard-hit. Chile, which was dependent on copper mining, found the value of its exports cut by 80 percent. In an effort to maintain the price of coffee, Brazil destroyed enough of its coffee crop to have supplied the world for a year. Colonial Southeast Asia, the world's major rubber-producing region, saw the demand for its primary export drop dramatically as automobile sales in Europe and the United States were cut in half. In Britain's West African colony of the Gold Coast (present-day Ghana), farmers who had staked their economic lives on producing cocoa for the world market were badly hurt by the collapse of commodity prices. Depending on a single crop or product rendered these societies extraordinarily vulnerable to changes in the world market.

The Great Depression sharply challenged the governments of capitalist countries, which generally had believed that the economy would regulate itself through the market. The market's apparent failure to self-correct led many people to look twice at the Soviet Union, a communist state whose more equal distribution of income and state-controlled economy had generated an impressive growth with no unemployment in the 1930s, even as the capitalist world was reeling. No Western country opted for the dictatorial and draconian socialism of the USSR, but in Britain, France, and Scandinavia, the Depression energized a "democratic socialism" that sought greater regulation of the economy and a more equal distribution of wealth through peaceful means and electoral politics.

The United States' response to the Great Depression came in the form of President Franklin Roosevelt's New Deal (1933–1942), an experimental combination of reforms seeking to restart economic growth and to prevent similar calamities in the future. These measures reflected the thinking of John Maynard Keynes, a prominent British economist who argued that government actions and spending programs could moderate the recessions and depressions to which capitalist economies were prone. Although this represented a departure from standard economic thinking, none of it was really "socialist," even if some of the New Deal's opponents labeled it as such.

Nonetheless, Roosevelt's efforts permanently altered the relationship among government, the private economy, and individual citizens. Through immediate programs

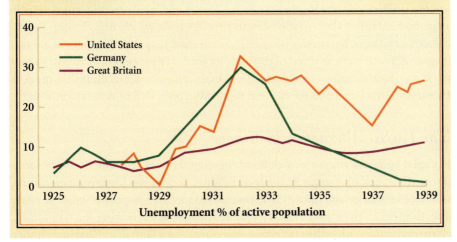

Snapshot   **Comparing the Impact of the Depression**[3]

As industrial production dropped during the Depression, unemployment soared. Yet the larger Western capitalist countries differed considerably in the duration and extent of this unemployment. Note especially the differences between Germany and the United States. How might you account for this difference?

Unemployment % of active population

of public spending (for dams, highways, bridges, and parks), the New Deal sought to prime the pump of the economy and thus reduce unemployment. The New Deal's longer-term reforms, such as the Social Security system, the minimum wage, and various relief and welfare programs, attempted to create a modest economic safety net to sustain the poor, the unemployed, and the elderly. By supporting labor unions, the New Deal strengthened workers in their struggles with business owners or managers. Subsidies for farmers gave rise to a permanent agribusiness that encouraged continued production even as prices fell. Finally, a mounting number of government agencies marked a new degree of federal regulation and supervision of the economy.

Ultimately, none of the New Deal's programs worked very well to end the Great Depression. Not until the massive government spending required by World War II kicked in did that economic disaster abate in the United States. The most successful efforts to cope with the Depression came from unlikely places—Nazi Germany and an increasingly militaristic Japan.

Democracy Denied: Comparing Italy, Germany, and Japan

Despite the victory of the democratic powers in World War I—Britain, France, and the United States—their democratic political ideals and their cultural values celebrating individual freedom came under sharp attack in the aftermath of that bloody conflict. One challenge derived from communism, which was initiated in the Russian Revolution of 1917 and expressed most fully in the cold war during the second half of the twentieth century (see Chapter 22). In the 1920s and 1930s, however, the more immediate challenge to the victors in the Great War came from highly authoritarian, intensely nationalistic, territorially aggressive, and ferociously anticommunist regimes, particularly those that took shape in Italy, Germany, and Japan. (See Documents: Ideologies of the Axis Powers, pp. 1010–18, for the ideas underlying these regimes.) The common features of these three countries drew them together by 1936–1937 in a political alliance directed against the Soviet Union and international communism. In 1940, they solidified their relationship in a formal military alliance, creating the so-called Axis powers. Within this alliance, Germany and Japan clearly stand out, though in quite different ways, in terms of their impact on the larger patterns of world history, for it was their efforts to "establish and maintain a new order of things," as the Axis Pact put it, that generated the Second World War both in East Asia and in Europe.

The Fascist Alternative in Europe

■ Change
In what ways did fascism challenge the ideas and practices of European liberalism and democracy?

Between 1919 and 1945, a new political ideology, known as fascism, found expression across much of Europe. At the level of ideas, fascism was intensely nationalistic, seeking to revitalize and purify the nation and to mobilize its people for some grand task. Its spokesmen praised violence against enemies as a renewing force in society, celebrated action rather than reflection, and placed their faith in a charismatic leader.

Fascists also bitterly condemned individualism, liberalism, feminism, parliamentary democracy, and communism, all of which, they argued, divided and weakened the nation. In their determination to overthrow existing regimes, they were revolutionary; in their embrace of traditional values and their opposition to much of modern life, however, they were conservative or reactionary.

Such ideas appealed to aggrieved people all across the social spectrum. In the devastation that followed the First World War, the numbers of such people grew substantially. In the aftermath of the Russian Revolution of 1917, some among the middle and upper classes saw the rise of socialism and communism as a dire threat; small-scale merchants, artisans, and farmers feared the loss of their independence to either big business or socialist revolution; demobilized soldiers had few prospects and nursed many resentments; and intellectuals were appalled by the materialism and artificiality of modern life. Such people had lost faith in the capacity of liberal democracy and capitalism to create a good society and to protect their interests. Some among them proved a receptive audience for the message of fascism.

Small fascist movements appeared in many Western European countries, including France, Great Britain, and the Netherlands, but they had little political impact. More substantial movements took shape in Austria, Hungary, and Romania. In Spain, the rise of a fascist movement led to a bitter civil war (1936–1939) and a dictatorial regime that lasted into the 1970s. But in Italy and Germany, such movements achieved prolonged power in major states, with devastating consequences for Europe and the world.

The fascist alternative took shape first in Italy. That nation had become a unified state only in 1870 and had not yet developed a modern democratic culture. In the early twentieth century, conservative landlords still dominated much of the countryside. Northern Italy, however, had begun to industrialize in the late nineteenth century, generating the characteristic tension between a factory working class and a substantial middle class. The First World War gave rise to resentful veterans, many of them unemployed, and to patriots who believed that Italy had not gained the territory it deserved from the Treaty of Versailles. During the serious economic downturn after World War I, trade unions, peasant movements, and various communist and socialist parties threatened the established social order with a wave of strikes and land seizures.

Into this setting stepped a charismatic orator and a former journalist with a socialist background, Benito Mussolini (1883–1945). With the help of a private army of disillusioned veterans and jobless men known as the Black Shirts, Mussolini swept to power in 1922, promising an alternative to both communism and ineffective democratic rule. Considerable violence accompanied Mussolini's rise to power as bands of Black Shirts destroyed the offices of socialist newspapers and attacked striking workers. Fearful of communism, big business threw its support to Mussolini, who promised order in the streets, an end to bickering party-based politics, and the maintenance of the traditional social order. That Mussolini's government allegedly made the trains run on time became evidence that these promises might be fulfilled. The symbol of this

The Faces of European Fascism
Benito Mussolini (left) and Adolf Hitler came to symbolize fascism in Europe in the several decades between the two world wars. In this photograph from September 1937, they are reviewing German troops in Munich during Mussolini's visit to Germany, a trip that deepened the growing relationship between their two countries.
(Luce/Keystone/Getty Images)

■ **Comparison**

What was distinctive about the German expression of fascism? What was the basis of popular support for the Nazis?

movement was the *fasces*, a bundle of birch rods bound together around an axe, which represented power and strength in unity and derived from ancient Rome. Thus fascism was born. (See Document 22.1, pp. 1010–12, for Mussolini's understanding of fascism.)

Mussolini promised his mass following major social reforms, though in practice he concentrated instead on consolidating the power of the central state. Democracy in Italy was suspended, and opponents were imprisoned, deported, or sometimes executed. Independent labor unions and peasant groups were disbanded, as were all political parties except the Fascist Party. In economic life, a "corporate state" took shape, at least in theory, in which workers, employers, and various professional groups were organized into "corporations" that were supposed to settle their disagreements and determine economic policy under the supervision of the state.

Culturally, fascists invoked various aspects of traditional Italian life. Mussolini, though personally an atheist, embraced the Catholic culture of Italy in a series of agreements with the Church (the Lateran Accords of 1929) that made the Vatican a sovereign state and Catholicism Italy's national religion. In fascist propaganda, women were portrayed in highly traditional terms as domestic creatures, particularly as mothers creating new citizens for the fascist state, with no hint of equality or liberation. Nationalists were delighted when Italy invaded Ethiopia in 1935, avenging the embarrassing defeat that Italians suffered at the hands of Ethiopians in 1896. In the eyes of Mussolini and fascist believers, all of this was the beginning of a "new Roman Empire" that would revitalize Italian society and give it a global mission.

Hitler and the Nazis

Far more important in the long run was the German expression of European fascism, which took shape as the Nazi Party under the leadership of Adolf Hitler (1889–1945). In many respects, it was similar to its Italian counterpart. Both espoused an extreme nationalism, openly advocated the use of violence as a political tool, generated a single-party dictatorship, were led by charismatic figures, despised parliamentary democracy, hated communism, and viewed war as a positive and ennobling experience.[4] The circumstances that gave rise to the Nazi movement were likewise broadly similar to those of Italian fascism, although the Nazis did not achieve national power until 1933.

The end of World War I witnessed the collapse of the German imperial government, itself less than a half century old. It was left to the democratic politicians of a new government—known as the Weimar Republic—to negotiate a peace settlement with the victorious allies. Traditional elites, who had withdrawn from public life in disgrace, never explicitly took responsibility for Germany's defeat; instead they attacked the democratic politicians who had the unenviable task of signing the Treaty of Versailles and enforcing it. In this setting, some began to argue that German military forces had not really lost the war but that civilian socialists, communists, and Jews had betrayed the nation, "stabbing it in the back."

As in postwar Italy, liberal or democratic political leaders during the 1920s faced considerable hostility. Paramilitary groups of veterans known as the Freikorps assassinated hundreds of supporters of the Weimar regime. Gradually, some among the middle classes as well as conservative landowners joined in opposition to the Weimar regime, both groups threatened by the ruinous inflation of 1923 and then the Great Depression. The German economy largely ground to a halt in the early 1930s amid massive unemployment among workers and the middle class alike. Everyone demanded decisive action from the state. Many industrial workers looked to socialists and communists for solutions; others turned to fascism. Large numbers of middle-class people deserted moderate political parties in favor of conservative and radical right-wing movements.

This was the context in which Adolf Hitler's National Socialist, or Nazi, Party gained growing public support. Founded shortly after the end of World War I, the Nazi Party under Hitler's leadership proclaimed a message of intense German nationalism cast in terms of racial superiority, bitter hatred for Jews as an alien presence, passionate opposition to communism, a determination to rescue Germany from the humiliating requirements of the Treaty of Versailles, and a willingness to decisively tackle the country's economic problems. Throughout the 1920s, the Nazis were a minor presence in German politics, gaining only 2.6 percent of the vote in the national elections of 1928. Just four years later, however, in the wake of the Depression's terrible impact and the Weimar government's inability to respond effectively, the Nazis attracted 37 percent of the vote. In 1933, Hitler was legally installed as the chancellor of the German government. Thus did the Weimar Republic, a democratic regime that never gained broad support, give way to the Third Reich.

Once in power, Hitler moved quickly to consolidate Nazi control of Germany. All other political parties were outlawed; independent labor unions were ended; thousands of opponents were arrested; and the press and radio came under state control. Far more thoroughly than Mussolini in Italy, Hitler and the Nazis established their control over German society.[5]

By the late 1930s, Hitler apparently had the support of a considerable majority of the population, in large measure because his policies successfully brought Germany out of the Depression. The government invested heavily in projects such as superhighways, bridges, canals, and public buildings and, after 1935, in rebuilding and rearming the country's diminished military forces. These policies drove down the number of unemployed Germans from 6.2 million in 1932 to fewer than 500,000 in 1937. Two years later Germany had a labor shortage. Erna Kranz, a teenager in the 1930s, later remembered the early years of Nazi rule as "a glimmer of hope...not just for the unemployed but for everybody because we all knew that we were downtrodden.... It was a good time...there was order and discipline."[6] Millions agreed with her.

Other factors as well contributed to Nazi popularity. Like Italian fascists, Hitler too appealed to rural and traditional values that many Germans feared losing as their country modernized. In Hitler's thinking and in Nazi propaganda, Jews became the symbol of the urban, capitalist, and foreign influences that were undermining traditional German culture. Thus the Nazis reflected and reinforced a broader and long-established current of anti-Semitism that had deep roots in much of Europe. In his book *Mein Kampf* (*My Struggle*), Hitler outlined his case against the Jews and his call for the racial purification of Germany in vitriolic terms. (See Document 21.2, pp. 1012–15, for a statement of Hitler's thinking.)

Far more than elsewhere, this insistence on a racial revolution was a central feature of the Nazi program and differed from the racial attitudes in Italy, where Jews were a tiny minority of the population and deeply assimilated into Italian culture. Early on, Mussolini had ridiculed Nazi racism, but as Germany and Italy drew closer together, Italy too began a program of overt anti-Semitism, though nothing approaching the extremes that characterized Nazi Germany.

Upon coming to power, Hitler implemented policies that increasingly restricted Jewish life. Soon Jews were excluded from universities, professional organizations, and civil employment. In 1935, the Nuremberg Laws ended German citizenship for Jews and forbade marriage or sexual relations between Jews and Germans. On the night of November 9, 1938, known as Kristallnacht, persecution gave way to terror, when Nazis smashed and looted Jewish shops. Such actions made clear the Nazis' determination to rid Germany of its Jewish population, thus putting into effect the most radical element of Hitler's program. Still, it was not yet apparent that this "racial revolution" would mean the mass killing of Europe's Jews. That horrendous development emerged only in the context of World War II.

Also sustaining Nazi rule were massive torchlight ceremonies celebrating the superiority of the

Nazi Hatred of the Jews
This picture served as the cover of a highly anti-Semitic book of photographs entitled *The Eternal Jew*, published by the Nazis in 1937. It effectively summed up many of the themes of the Nazi case against the Jews, showing them as ugly and subhuman, as the instigators of communism (the hammer and sickle on a map of Russia), as greedy capitalists (coins in one hand), and as seeking to dominate the world (the whip). (akg-images)

German race and its folk culture. In these settings, Hitler was the mystical leader, the Führer, a mesmerizing orator who would lead Germany to national greatness and individual Germans to personal fulfillment.

If World War I and the Great Depression brought about the political and economic collapse of Europe, the Nazi phenomenon represented a moral collapse within the West, deriving from a highly selective incorporation of earlier strands of European culture. On the one hand, the Nazis actively rejected some of the values—rationalism, tolerance, democracy, human equality—that for many people had defined the core of Western civilization since the Enlightenment. On the other hand, they claimed the legacy of modern science, particularly in their concern to classify and rank various human groups. Thus they drew heavily on the "scientific racism" of the nineteenth century and its expression in phrenology, which linked the size and shape of the skull to human behavior and personality. Moreover, in their effort to purify German society, the Nazis reflected the Enlightenment confidence in the perfectibility of humankind and in the social engineering necessary to achieve it.

Japanese Authoritarianism

In various ways, the modern history of Japan paralleled that of Italy and Germany. All three were newcomers to great power status, with Japan joining the club of industrializing and empire-building states only in the late nineteenth century as its sole Asian member (see pp. 898–901). Like Italy and Germany, Japan had a rather limited experience with democratic politics, for its elected parliament was constrained by a very small electorate (only 1.5 million men in 1917) and by the exalted position of a semidivine emperor and his small coterie of elite advisers. During the 1930s, Japan too moved toward authoritarian government and a denial of democracy at home, even as it launched an aggressive program of territorial expansion in East Asia.

■ Comparison

How did Japan's experience during the 1920s and 1930s resemble that of Germany, and how did it differ?

Despite these broad similarities, Japan's history in the first half of the twentieth century was clearly distinctive. In sharp contrast to Italy and Germany, Japan's participation in World War I was minimal, and its economy grew considerably as other industrialized countries were engaged in the European war. At the peace conference ending that war, Japan was seated as an equal participant, allied with the winning side of democratic countries such as Britain, France, and the United States.

During the 1920s, Japan seemed to be moving toward a more democratic politics and Western cultural values. Universal male suffrage was achieved in 1925; cabinets led by leaders of the major parties, rather than bureaucrats or imperial favorites, governed the country; and a two-party system began to emerge. Supporters of these developments generally embraced the dignity of the individual, free expression of ideas, and greater gender equality. Education expanded; an urban consumer society developed; middle-class women entered new professions; young women known as *moga* (modern girls) sported short hair and short skirts, while dancing with *mobo* (modern boys) at jazz clubs and cabarets. To such people, the Japanese were becoming world citizens and their country was becoming "a province of the world" as they participated increasingly in a cosmopolitan and international culture.

In this environment, the accumulated tensions of Japan's modernizing and industrializing processes found expression. "Rice riots" in 1918 brought more than a million people into the streets of urban Japan to protest the rising price of that essential staple. Union membership tripled in the 1920s as some factory workers began to think in terms of entitlements and workers' rights rather than the benevolence of their employers. In rural areas, tenant unions multiplied, and disputes with landowners increased amid demands for a reduction in rents. A mounting women's movement advocated a variety of feminist issues, including suffrage and the end of legalized prostitution. "All the sleeping women are now awake and moving," declared Yosano Akiko, a well-known poet, feminist, and social critic. Within the political arena, a number of "proletarian parties"—the Labor-Farmer Party, the Socialist People's Party, and a small Japan Communist Party—promised in various ways to "bring about the political, economic and social emancipation of the proletarian class."[7]

To many people in established elite circles—bureaucrats, landowners, industrialists, military officials—all of this was alarming, even appalling, and suggested echoes of the Russian Revolution of 1917. A number of political activists were arrested, and a few were killed. A Peace Preservation Law, enacted in 1925, promised long prison sentences, or even the death penalty, to anyone who organized against the existing imperial system of government or private property.

As in Germany, however, it was the impact of the Great Depression that paved the way for harsher and more authoritarian action. That worldwide economic catastrophe hit Japan hard. Shrinking world demand for silk impoverished millions of rural dwellers who raised silkworms. Japan's exports fell by half between 1929 and 1931, leaving a million or more urban workers unemployed. Many young workers returned to their rural villages only to find food scarce, families forced to sell their daughters to urban brothels, and neighbors unable to offer the customary money for the funerals of their friends. In these desperate circumstances, many began to doubt the ability of parliamentary democracy and capitalism to address Japan's "national emergency." Politicians and business leaders alike were widely regarded as privileged, self-centered, and heedless of the larger interests of the nation.

Such conditions energized a growing movement in Japanese political life known as Radical Nationalism or the Revolutionary Right. Expressed in dozens of small groups, it was especially appealing to younger army officers. The movement's many separate organizations shared an extreme nationalism, hostility to parliamentary democracy, a commitment to elite leadership focused around an exalted emperor, and dedication to foreign expansion. The manifesto of one of those organizations, the Cherry Blossom Society, expressed these sentiments clearly in 1930:

> As we observe recent social trends, top leaders engage in immoral conduct, political parties are corrupt, capitalists and aristocrats have no understanding of the masses, farming villages are devastated, unemployment and depression are serious.... The rulers neglect the long term interests of the nation, strive to win only the pleasure of foreign powers and possess no enthusiasm for external expansion.... The people are with us in craving the appearance of a vigorous

and clean government that is truly based upon the masses, and is genuinely centered around the Emperor.[8]

Members of such organizations managed to assassinate a number of public officials and prominent individuals, in the hope of provoking a return to direct rule by
the emperor, and in 1936 a group of junior officers attempted a military takeover of
the government, which was quickly suppressed. In sharp contrast to developments
in Italy and Germany, however, no right-wing party gained wide popular support,
nor was any such party able to seize power in Japan. Although individuals and small
groups sometimes espoused ideas similar to those of European fascists, no major fascist party emerged. Nor did Japan produce any charismatic leader on the order of
Mussolini or Hitler. People arrested for political offenses were neither criminalized
nor exterminated, as in Germany, but instead were subjected to a process of "reso-
cialization" that brought the vast majority of them to renounce their "errors" and
return to the "Japanese way." Japan's established institutions of government were sufficiently strong, and traditional notions of the nation as a family headed by the emperor were sufficiently intact, to prevent the development of a widespread fascist
movement able to take control of the country.[9]

In the 1930s, though, Japanese public life clearly changed in ways that reflected
the growth of right-wing nationalist thinking. Parties and the parliament continued
to operate, and elections were held, but major cabinet positions now went to prominent bureaucratic or military figures rather than to party leaders. The military in
particular came to exercise a more dominant role in Japanese political life, although
military men had to negotiate with business and bureaucratic elites as well as party
leaders. Censorship limited the possibilities of free expression, and a single news agency
was granted the right to distribute all national and most international news to the
country's newspapers and radio stations. An Industrial Patriotic Federation replaced
independent trade unions with factory-based "discussion councils" to resolve local
disputes between workers and managers.

Established authorities also adopted many of the ideological themes of the Radical Right. In 1937, the Ministry of Education issued a new textbook, *The Cardinal
Principles of Our National Polity*, for use in all Japanese schools (see Document 21.3,
pp. 1015–17). That document proclaimed the Japanese to be "intrinsically quite different from the so-called citizens of Occidental [Western] countries." Those nations
were "conglomerations of separate individuals" with "no deep foundation between
ruler and citizen to unite them." In Japan, by contrast, an emperor of divine origin
related to his subjects as a father to his children. It was a natural, not a contractual,
relationship, expressed most fully in the "sacrifice of the life of a subject for the
Emperor." In addition to studying this text, students were now required to engage
in more physical training, in which Japanese martial arts replaced baseball in the
physical education curriculum.

The erosion of democracy and the rise of the military in Japanese political life
reflected long-standing Japanese respect for the military values of its ancient samurai
warrior class as well as the relatively independent position of the military in Japan's

Meiji constitution. The state's success in quickly bringing the country out of the Depression likewise fostered popular support. As in Nazi Germany, state-financed credit, large-scale spending on armaments, and public works projects enabled Japan to emerge from the Depression more rapidly and more fully than major Western countries. "By the end of 1937," noted one Japanese laborer, "everybody in the country was working."[10] By the mid-1930s, the government increasingly assumed a supervisory or managerial role in economic affairs that included subsidies to strategic industries; profit ceilings on major corporations; caps on wages, prices, and rents; and a measure of central planning. Private property, however, was retained, and the huge industrial enterprises called *zaibatsu* continued to dominate the economic landscape.

Although Japan during the 1930s shared some common features with fascist Italy and Nazi Germany, it remained, at least internally, a less repressive and more pluralistic society than either of those European states. Japanese intellectuals and writers had to contend with government censorship, but they retained some influence in the country. Generals and admirals exercised great political authority as the role of an elected parliament declined, but they did not govern alone. Political prisoners were few and were not subjected to execution or deportation as in European fascist states. Japanese conceptions of their racial purity and uniqueness were directed largely against foreigners rather than an internal minority. Nevertheless, like Germany and Italy, Japan developed extensive imperial ambitions. Those projects of conquest and empire building collided with the interests of established world powers such as the United States and Britain, launching a second, and even more terrible, global war.

A Second World War

World War II, even more than the Great War, was a genuinely global conflict with independent origins in both Asia and Europe. Their common feature lay in dissatisfied states in both continents that sought to fundamentally alter the international arrangements that had emerged from World War I. Many Japanese, like their counterparts in Italy and Germany, felt stymied by Britain and the United States as they sought empires that they regarded as essential for their national greatness and economic well-being.

The Road to War in Asia

■ Comparison
In what ways were the origins of World War II in Asia and in Europe similar to each other? How were they different?

World War II began in Asia before it occurred in Europe. In the late 1920s and the 1930s, Japanese imperial ambitions mounted as the military became more powerful in Japan's political life and as an earlier cultural cosmopolitanism gave way to more nationalist sentiments. An initial problem was the rise of Chinese nationalism, which seemed to threaten Japan's sphere of influence in Manchuria, acquired after the Russo-Japanese War of 1904–1905. Acting independently of civilian authorities in Tokyo, units of the Japanese military seized control of Manchuria in 1931 and established a puppet state called Manchukuo. This action infuriated Western powers, prompting Japan to withdraw from the League of Nations, to break politically with its Western allies, and in 1936 to align more closely with Germany and Italy. By that time, relations with an increasingly nationalist China had deteriorated further, leading to a full-scale attack on heartland China in 1937 and escalating a bitter conflict that would last another eight years. World War II in Asia had begun (see Map 21.4).

As the war with China unfolded, the view of the world held by Japanese authorities and many ordinary people hardened. Increasingly, they felt isolated, surrounded, and threatened. A series of international agreements in the early 1920s that had granted Japan a less robust naval force than Britain or the United States as well as anti-Japanese immigration policies in the United States convinced some Japanese that European racism prevented the West from acknowledging Japan as an equal power. Furthermore, Japan was quite dependent on foreign and especially American sources of strategic goods. By the late 1930s, some 73 percent of Japan's scrap iron, 60 percent of its imported machine tools, 80 percent of its oil, and about half of its copper came from the United States, which was becoming increasingly hostile to Japanese ambitions in Asia. Moreover, Western imperialist powers—the British, French, and Dutch—controlled resource-rich colonies in Southeast Asia. Finally, the Soviet Union, proclaiming an alien communist ideology, loomed large in northern Asia. To growing numbers of Japanese, their national survival was at stake.

Thus in 1940–1941, Japan extended its military operations to the French, British, Dutch, and American colonies of Indochina, Malaya, Burma, Indonesia, and the Philippines in an effort to acquire those resources that would free it from dependence on the West. In carving out this Pacific empire, the Japanese presented themselves as liberators and modernizers, creating an "Asia for Asians" and freeing their continent from European dominance. Experience soon showed that Japan's concern was far more for Asia's resources than for its liberation and that Japanese rule exceeded in brutality even that of the Europeans.

A decisive step in the development of World War II in Asia lay in the Japanese attack on the United States at Pearl Harbor in Hawaii in December 1941. Japanese authorities undertook that attack with reluctance and only after negotiations to end American hostility to Japan's empire-building enterprise proved fruitless and an American oil embargo was imposed on Japan in July 1941. American opinion in the 1930s increasingly saw Japan as aggressive, oppressive, and a threat to U.S. economic interests in Asia. In the face of this hostility, Japan's leaders felt that the alternatives for their country boiled down to either an acceptance of American terms, which they feared would reduce Japan to a second- or third-rank power, or a war with an uncertain outcome. Given those choices, the decision for war was made more with foreboding than with enthusiasm. A leading Japanese admiral made the case for war in this way in late 1941: "The government has decided that if there were no war the fate of the nation is sealed. Even if there is a war, the country may be ruined. Nevertheless a nation that does not fight in this plight has lost its spirit and is doomed."[11]

Map 21.4 World War II in Asia
Japanese aggression temporarily dislodged the British, French, Dutch, and Americans from their colonial possessions in Asia, while inflicting vast devastation on China.

As a consequence of the attack on Pearl Harbor, the United States entered the war in the Pacific, beginning a long and bloody struggle that ended only with the use of atomic bombs against Hiroshima and Nagasaki in 1945. The Pearl Harbor action also joined the Asian theater of the war and the ongoing conflict in Europe into a single global struggle that pitted Germany, Italy, and Japan (the Axis powers) against the United States, Britain, and the Soviet Union (the Allies).

The Road to War in Europe

If Japan was the dissatisfied power in Asia, Nazi Germany occupied that role in Europe even more sharply. As a consequence of its defeat in World War I and the harsh terms of the Treaty of Versailles, many Germans harbored deep resentments about their country's position in the international arena. Taking advantage of those resentments, the Nazis pledged to rectify the treaty's perceived injustices. Thus, to most historians, the origins of World War II in Europe lie squarely in German aggression, although with many twists and turns and encouraged by the initial unwillingness of Britain, France, and the Soviet Union to confront that aggression forcefully and collectively. If World War I was accidental and unintended, World War II was more deliberate and planned, perhaps even desired by the German leadership and by Hitler in particular.

War was central to the Nazi phenomenon in several ways. Nazism was born out of World War I, the hated treaty that ended it, and the disillusioned ex-soldiers who emerged from it. Furthermore, the celebration of war as a means of ennobling humanity and enabling the rise of superior peoples was at the core of Nazi ideology. "Whoever would live must fight," Hitler declared. "Only in force lies the right of possession." He consistently stressed the importance for Germany of gaining *lebensraum* (living space) in the east, in the lands of Slavic Poland and Russia. Inevitably, this required war (see Document 21.2, pp. 1012–15).

Slowly at first and then more aggressively, Hitler prepared the country for war and pursued territorial expansion. A major rearmament program began in 1935. The next year, German forces entered the Rhineland, which the Treaty of Versailles had declared demilitarized. In 1938, Germany annexed Austria and the German-speaking parts of Czechoslovakia. At a famous conference in Munich in that year, the British and the French gave these actions their reluctant blessing, hoping that this "appeasement" of Hitler could satisfy his demands and avoid all-out war. But it did not. In the following year, 1939, Germany unleashed a devastating attack on Poland, an action that triggered the Second World War in Europe, as Britain and France declared war on Germany. Quickly defeating France, the Germans launched a destructive air war against Britain and in 1941 turned their war machine loose on the Soviet Union. By then, most of Europe was under Nazi control (see Map 21.5).

Although Germany was central to both world wars, the second one was quite different from the first. It was not welcomed with the kind of mass enthusiasm that

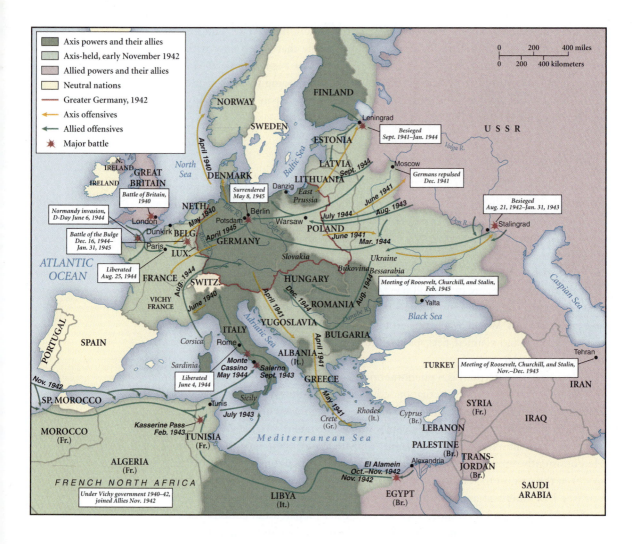

Legend:
- Axis powers and their allies
- Axis-held, early November 1942
- Allied powers and their allies
- Neutral nations
- Greater Germany, 1942
- Axis offensives
- Allied offensives
- ★ Major battle

Leningrad — Besieged Sept. 1941–Jan. 1944

Moscow — Germans repulsed Dec. 1941

Stalingrad — Besieged Aug. 21, 1942–Jan. 31, 1943

Surrendered May 8, 1945

Battle of Britain, 1940

Normandy invasion, D-Day June 6, 1944

Battle of the Bulge Dec. 16, 1944–Jan. 31, 1945

Liberated Aug. 25, 1944

Meeting of Roosevelt, Churchill, and Stalin, Feb. 1945

Meeting of Roosevelt, Churchill, and Stalin, Nov.–Dec. 1943

Liberated June 4, 1944

Kasserine Pass, Feb. 1943

El Alamein Oct.–Nov. 1942

Under Vichy government 1940–42, joined Allies Nov. 1942

Map 21.5 World War II in Europe

For a brief moment during World War II, Nazi Germany came close to bringing all of Europe and much of the Mediterranean basin under its rule.

had accompanied the opening of World War I in 1914. The bitter experience of the Great War suggested to most people that only suffering lay ahead. The conduct of the two wars likewise differed. The first war had quickly bogged down in trench warfare that emphasized defense, whereas in the second war the German tactic of *blitzkrieg* (lightning war) coordinated the rapid movement of infantry, tanks, and airpower over very large areas.

Such military tactics were initially successful and allowed German forces, aided by their Italian allies, to sweep over Europe, the western Soviet Union, and North Africa. The tide began to turn in 1942 when the Soviet Union absorbed the German onslaught and then began to counterattack, slowly and painfully moving westward toward the German heartland. The United States, with its enormous material and human resources, fully joined the struggle against Germany in 1942. Three more years of bitter fighting ensued before the German defeat in May 1945.

The Outcomes of Global Conflict

The Second World War was the most destructive conflict in world history, with total deaths estimated at around 60 million, some six times the deaths in World War I. More than half of those casualties were civilians. Partly responsible for this horrendous toll were the new technologies of warfare—heavy bombers, jet fighters, missiles, and atomic weapons. Equally significant, though, was the almost complete blurring of the traditional line between civilian and military targets, as entire cities and whole populations came to be defined as the enemy.

Nowhere was that blurring more complete than in the Soviet Union, which accounted for more than 40 percent of the total deaths in the war—probably around 25 million, with an equal number made homeless and thousands of towns, villages, and industrial enterprises destroyed. German actions fulfilled Hitler's instructions to his leading generals: "The war against Russia will be such that it cannot be conducted in a knightly fashion; the struggle is one of ideologies and racial differences and will

■ **Comparison**

How did World War II differ from World War I?

Snapshot   **Key Moments in the History of World War II**

Japanese invasion of Manchuria	1931
Hitler's rise to power	1933
Italian invasion of Ethiopia	1935
Anti-Comintern Pact (alliance of Germany, Japan, and Italy)	1936–1937
Japanese invasion of China/Rape of Nanjing	1937–1938
German takeover of Austria and Sudetenland in Czechoslovakia	1938
German invasion of Poland (beginning of World War II in Europe)	1939
The fall of France and German air war on Britain	1940
Japanese seizure of French, British, Dutch, and U.S. colonies in Asia	1940–1942
German invasion of USSR; Japanese attack on Pearl Harbor, Hawaii	1941
The Holocaust	1941–1945
U.S. victory in Battle of Midway (turning point in the Pacific war)	1942
Soviet victory in Battle of Stalingrad (turning point in the European war)	1943
D-day: Allied forces invade France	1944
Yalta Conference (Britain, United States, Soviet Union) to determine fate of postwar Europe	1945
Soviets capture Berlin; atomic bombing of Hiroshima and Nagasaki; Germany and Japan surrender	1945

have to be conducted with unprecedented, unmerciful, and unrelenting harshness.... German soldiers guilty of breaking international law... will be excused."[12]

In China as well, perhaps 15 million deaths and uncounted refugees grew out of prolonged Chinese resistance and the shattering Japanese response, including the killing of every person and every animal in many villages. During the infamous Rape of Nanjing in 1937–1938, some 200,000 to 300,000 Chinese civilians were killed and often mutilated within a few months, and countless women were sexually assaulted. Indiscriminate German bombing of British cities and the Allied firebombing of Japanese and German cities likewise reflected the new morality of total war, as did the dropping of atomic bombs on Hiroshima and Nagasaki, which in a single instant vaporized tens of thousands of people. This was total war with a scale, intensity, and indiscriminate brutality that exceeded even the horrors of World War I.

A further dimension of total war lay in governments' efforts to mobilize their economies, their people, and their propaganda machines even more extensively than before. Colonial resources were harnessed once again. The British in particular made extensive use of colonial troops and laborers from India and Africa. Japan compelled several hundred thousand women from Korea, China, and elsewhere to serve the sexual needs of Japanese troops as "comfort women," who often accommodated twenty to thirty men a day.

Everywhere, the needs of the war drew large numbers of women into both industry and the military, although in Britain and the United States this was regarded as

Hiroshima

The dropping of atomic bombs on Hiroshima (August 6, 1945) and a few days later on Nagasaki marked the end of World War II in the Pacific and the opening of a nuclear arms race that cast an enormous shadow on the world ever since. In this photograph from an utterly devastated Hiroshima, a group of survivors waits for help in the southern part of the city a few hours after the bomb was dropped. (AP Images/ Wide World Photos)

a temporary necessity. In the United States, "Rosie the Riveter" represented those women who now took on heavy industrial jobs, which previously had been reserved for men. In the USSR, women constituted more than half of the workforce by 1945. A much smaller percentage of Japanese women were mobilized for factory work, but a Greater Japan Women's Society enrolled some 19 million members, who did volunteer work and promised to lay aside their gold jewelry and abandon extravagant weddings. As always, war heightened the prestige of masculinity, and given the immense sacrifices that men had made, few women were inclined to directly challenge the practices of patriarchy immediately following the war.

Among the most haunting outcomes of the war was the Holocaust. The outbreak of that war closed off certain possibilities, such as forced emigration, for implementing the Nazi dream of ridding Germany of its Jewish population. It also brought millions of additional Jews in Poland and Russia under German control and triggered among Hitler's enthusiastic subordinates various schemes for a "final solution" to the Jewish question. From this emerged the death camps that included Auschwitz, Dachau, and Bergen-Belsen. Altogether, some 6 million Jews perished in a technologically sophisticated form of mass murder that set a new standard for human depravity. Millions more whom the Nazis deemed inferior, undesirable, or dangerous—Russians, Poles, and other Slavs; Gypsies, or the Roma; mentally or physically handicapped people; homosexuals; communists; and Jehovah's Witnesses— likewise perished in Germany's efforts at racial purification.

Although the Holocaust was concentrated in Germany, its significance in twentieth-century world history has been huge. It has haunted postwar Germany in particular and the Western world in general. How could such a thing have occurred in a Europe bearing the legacy of both Christianity and the Enlightenment? More specifically, it sent many of Europe's remaining Jews fleeing to Israel and gave urgency to the establishment of a modern Jewish nation in the ancient Jewish homeland. That action outraged many Arabs, some of whom were displaced by the arrival of the Jews, and has fostered an enduring conflict in the Middle East. Furthermore, the Holocaust defined a new category of crimes against humanity—genocide, the attempted elimination of entire peoples. Universal condemnation of the Holocaust, however, did not end the practice, as cases of mass slaughter in Cambodia, Rwanda, Bosnia, and the Sudan have demonstrated.

On an even larger scale than World War I, this second global conflict rearranged the architecture of world politics. As the war ended, Europe was impoverished, its industrial infrastructure shattered, many of its great cities in ruins, and millions of its people homeless or displaced. Within a few years, this much-weakened Europe was effectively divided, with its western half operating under an American umbrella and the eastern half subject to Soviet control. It was clear that Europe's dominance in world affairs was finished.

Over the next two decades, Europe's greatly diminished role in the world registered internationally as its Asian and African colonies achieved independence. Not only had the war weakened both the will and the ability of European powers to hold onto their colonies, but it had also emboldened nationalist and anticolonial movements everywhere (see Chapter 23). Japanese victories in Southeast Asia had certainly damaged European prestige, for British, Dutch, and American military forces fell to Japanese conquerors, sometimes in a matter of weeks. Japanese authorities staged long and brutal marches of Western prisoners of war, partly to drive home to local people that the era of Western domination was over. Furthermore, tens of thousands of Africans had fought for the British or the French, had seen white people die, had enjoyed the company of white women, and had returned home with very different ideas about white superiority and the permanence of colonial rule. Colonial subjects everywhere were very much aware that U.S. president Franklin Roosevelt and British prime minister Winston Churchill had solemnly declared in 1941 that "we respect the right of all peoples to choose the form of government under which they will live." Many asked whether those principles should not apply to people in the colonial world as well as to Europeans.

A further outcome of World War II lay in the consolidation and extension of the communist world. The Soviet victory over the Nazis, though bought at an unimaginable cost in blood and treasure, gave immense credibility to that communist regime and to its leader, Joseph Stalin. In the decades that followed, Soviet authorities nurtured a virtual cult of the war: memorials were everywhere; wedding parties made pilgrimages to them, and brides left their bouquets behind; May 9, Victory Day, saw elaborately orchestrated celebrations; veterans were honored and granted modest privileges. Furthermore, communist parties, largely dominated by the Soviet Union and supported by its armed forces, took power all across Eastern Europe, pushing the communist frontier deep into the European heartland. Even more important was a communist takeover in China in 1949. The Second World War allowed the Chinese Communist Party to gain support and credibility by leading the struggle against Japan. By 1950, the communist world seemed to many in the West very much on the offensive (see Chapter 22).

The horrors of two world wars within a single generation prompted a renewed interest in international efforts to maintain the peace in a world of competing and sovereign states. The chief outcome was the United Nations (UN), established in 1945 as a successor to the moribund League of Nations. As a political body dependent on agreement among its most powerful members, the UN proved more effective as a forum for international opinion than as a means of resolving the major conflicts of the postwar world, particularly the Soviet/American hostility during the cold war decades. Further evidence for a growing internationalism lay in the creation in late 1945 of the World Bank and International Monetary Fund, whose purpose was to regulate the global economy, prevent another depression, and stimulate economic growth, especially in the poorer nations.

What these initiatives shared was the dominant presence of the United States. Unlike the aftermath of World War I, when an isolationist United States substantially withdrew from world affairs, the half century following the end of World War II witnessed the emergence of the United States as a global superpower. This was one of the major outcomes of the Second World War and a chief reason for the remarkable recovery of a badly damaged and discredited Western civilization.

The Recovery of Europe

The tragedies that afflicted Europe in the first half of the twentieth century— fratricidal war, economic collapse, the Holocaust—were wholly self-inflicted, and yet despite the sorry and desperate state of heartland Europe in 1945, that civilization had not permanently collapsed. In the twentieth century's second half, Europeans rebuilt their industrial economies and revived their democratic political systems, while the United States, a European offshoot, assumed a dominant and often dominating role both within Western civilization and in the world at large.

■ **Change**
How was Europe able to recover from the devastation of war?

Three factors help to explain this astonishing recovery. One is the apparent resiliency of an industrial society, once it has been established. The knowledge, skills, and habits of mind that enabled industrial societies to operate effectively remained intact, even if the physical infrastructure had been largely destroyed. Thus even the most terribly damaged countries—Germany, the Soviet Union, and Japan—had substantially recovered, both economically and demographically, within a quarter of a century. A second factor lay in the ability of the major Western European countries to integrate their recovering economies. After centuries of military conflict climaxed by the horrors of the two world wars, the major Western European powers were at last willing to put aside some of their prickly nationalism in return for enduring peace and common prosperity.

Perhaps most important, Europe had long ago spawned an overseas extension of its own civilization in what became the United States. In the twentieth century, that country served as a reservoir of military manpower, economic resources, and political leadership for the West as a whole. By 1945, the center of gravity within Western civilization had shifted decisively, relocated now across the Atlantic. With Europe diminished, divided, and on the defensive against the communist threat, leadership of the Western world passed, almost by default, to the United States. It was the only major country physically untouched by the war. Its economy had demonstrated enormous productivity during that struggle and by 1945 was generating fully 50 percent of total world production. Its overall military strength was unmatched, and it was in sole possession of the atomic bomb, the most powerful weapon ever constructed. Thus the United States became the new heartland of the West as well as a global superpower. In 1941, the publisher Henry Luce had proclaimed the twentieth century as "the American century." As the Second World War ended, that prediction seemed to be coming true.

An early indication of the United States' intention to exercise global leadership took shape in its efforts to rebuild and reshape shattered European economies. Known as the Marshall Plan, that effort funneled into Europe some $12 billion, at the time a very large amount, together with numerous advisers and technicians. It was motivated by some combination of genuine humanitarian concern, a desire to prevent a new depression by creating overseas customers for American industrial goods, and an interest in undermining the growing appeal of European communist parties. This economic recovery plan was successful beyond anyone's expectations. Between 1948 and the early 1970s, Western European economies grew rapidly, generating a widespread prosperity and improving living standards; at the same time, Western Europe became both a major customer for American goods and a major competitor in global markets.

The Marshall Plan also required its European recipients to cooperate with one another. After decades of conflict and destruction almost beyond description, many Europeans were eager to do so. That process began in 1951 when Italy, France, West Germany, Belgium, the Netherlands, and Luxembourg created the European Coal and Steel Community to jointly manage the production of these critical items. In 1957, these six countries deepened their level of cooperation by establishing the European Economic Community (EEC), more widely known as the Common Market, whose members reduced their tariffs and developed common trade policies. Over the next half century, the EEC expanded its membership to include almost all of Europe, including many former communist states. In 1994, the EEC was renamed the European Union, and in 2002 twelve of its members adopted a common currency, the euro (see Map 21.6). All of this sustained Europe's remarkable economic recovery and expressed a larger European identity, although it certainly did not erase deeply rooted national loyalties. Nor did it lead, as some had hoped, to a political union, a United States of Europe.

Beyond economic assistance, the American commitment to Europe soon came to include political and military security against the distant possibility of renewed German aggression and the more immediate communist threat from the Soviet Union. Without that security, economic recovery was unlikely to continue. Thus was born the military and political alliance known as the North Atlantic Treaty Organization (NATO) in 1949. It committed the United States and its nuclear arsenal to the defense of Europe against the Soviet Union, and it firmly anchored West Germany within the Western alliance. Thus, as Western Europe revived economically, it did so under the umbrella of U.S. political and military leadership, which Europeans generally welcomed. It was perhaps an imperial relationship, but to historian John Gaddis, it was "an empire by invitation" rather than by imposition.[13]

A parallel process in Japan, which was under American occupation between 1945 and 1952, likewise revived that country's devastated but already industrialized economy. In the two decades following the occupation, Japan's economy grew at the remarkable rate of 10 percent a year, and the nation became an economic giant on the world stage. This "economic miracle" received a substantial boost from some $2 billion in American aid during the occupation and even more from U.S. military purchases in Japan during the Korean War (1950–1953). Furthermore, the democratic

Map 21.6   The Growth of European Integration Gradually during the second half of the twentieth century, Europeans put aside their bitter rivalries and entered into various forms of economic cooperation with one another, although these efforts fell short of complete political union. This map illustrates the growth of what is now called the European Union (EU). Notice the eastward expansion of the EU following the collapse of communism in Eastern Europe and the Soviet Union.

Map legend:
- Original members of EU
- New members, 1973–1986
- New members, 1990–2007
- Candidates for membership, 2007

constitution imposed on Japan by American occupation authorities required that "land, sea, and air forces, as well as other war potential, will never be maintained." This meant that Japan, even more so than Europe, depended on the United States for its military security. Because it spent only about 1 percent of its gross national product on defense, more was available for productive investment.

The Western world had changed dramatically during the twentieth century. It began that century with its European heartland clearly the dominant imperial center of a global network. That civilization substantially self-destructed in the first half of the century, but it revived during the second half in a changed form—without its Afro-Asian colonies and with a new and powerful core in the United States. Accompanying this process and intersecting with it was another major theme of twentieth-century world history—the rise and fall of world communism, which is the focus of the next chapter.

Reflections: War and Remembrance: Learning from History

When asked about the value of studying history, most students respond with some version of the Spanish-born philosopher George Santayana's famous dictum: "Those who cannot remember the past are condemned to repeat it." At one level, this notion of learning from the "lessons of history" has much to recommend it, for there is, after all, little else except the past on which we can base our actions in the present. And yet historians in general are notably cautious about drawing particular lessons from the past and applying them to present circumstances.

For one thing, the historical record, like the Bible or any other sacred text, is sufficiently rich and complex to allow many people to draw quite different lessons from it. The world wars of the twentieth century represent a case in point, as writer Adam Gopnik has pointed out:

> The First World War teaches that territorial compromise is better than full-scale war, that an "honor-bound" allegiance of the great powers to small nations is a recipe for mass killing, and that it is crazy to let the blind mechanism of armies and alliances trump common sense. The Second teaches that searching for an accommodation with tyranny by selling out small nations only encourages the tyrant, that refusing to fight now leads to a worse fight later on.... The First teaches us never to rush into a fight, the Second never to back down from a bully. [14]

Did the lessons of the First World War lead Americans to ignore the rise of fascism until the country was directly threatened by Japanese attack? Did the lessons of World War II contribute to unnecessary wars in Vietnam and more recently in Iraq? There are no easy answers to such questions, for the lessons of history are many, varied, and changing.

Behind any such lesson is the common assumption that history repeats itself. This too is a notion to which historians bring considerable skepticism. They are generally more impressed with the complexity and particularity of major events such as wars rather than with their common features. Here is a further basis for caution in easily drawing lessons from the past.

But the wars of the past century perhaps share one broad similarity: all of them led to unexpected consequences. Few people expected the duration and carnage of World War I. The Holocaust was literally unimaginable when Hitler took power in 1933 or even at the outbreak of the Second World War in 1939. Who would have expected an American defeat at the hands of the Vietnamese? And the invasion of Iraq in 2003 generated a long list of surprises for the United States, including the absence of weapons of mass destruction and a prolonged insurgency. History repeats itself most certainly only in its unexpectedness.

Second Thoughts

What's the Significance?

World War I

Treaty of Versailles

Woodrow Wilson/Fourteen
  Points

Great Depression

New Deal

fascism

Mussolini

Nazi Germany/Hitler

Revolutionary Right (Japan)

World War II in Asia

World War II in Europe

total war

Holocaust

Marshall Plan

European Economic
  Community

NATO

To assess your mastery of the material in this chapter, visit the **Student Center** at bedfordstmartins.com/strayer.

Big Picture Questions

1. What explains the disasters that befell Europe in the first half of the twentieth century?

2. In what ways were the world wars a motor for change in the history of the twentieth century?

3. To what extent were the two world wars distinct and different conflicts, and in what ways were they related to each other? In particular, how did the First World War and its aftermath lay the foundations for World War II?

4. In what ways did Europe's internal conflicts between 1914 and 1945 have global implications?

Next Steps: For Further Study

Michael Burleigh, *The Third Reich: A New History* (2001). A fresh and thorough look at the Nazi era in Germany's history.

John Keegan, *The Second World War* (2005). A comprehensive account by a well-known scholar.

Bernd Martin, *Japan and Germany in the Modern World* (1995). A comparative study of these two countries' modern history and the relationship between them.

Mark Mazower, *Dark Continent* (2000). A history of Europe in the twentieth century that views the era as a struggle among liberal democracy, fascism, and communism.

Michael S. Nieberg, *Fighting the Great War: A Global History* (2006). An exploration of the origins and conduct of World War I.

Dietman Rothermund, *The Global Impact of the Great Depression, 1929–1939* (1996). An examination of the origins of the Depression in America and Europe and its impact in Asia, Africa, and Latin America.

First World War.com, http://www.firstworldwar.com. A Web site rich with articles, documents, photos, diaries, and more that illustrate the history of World War I.

"Nazi Rule," http://www.ushmm.org/outreach/nrule.htm. A great Web site, sponsored by the U.S. Holocaust Memorial Museum, for exploring various aspects of the Nazi experience.

For Web sites, images, and additional documents related to this chapter, see **Make History** at bedfordstmartins.com/strayer.

Documents

Considering the Evidence:
Ideologies of the Axis Powers

Even more than the Great War of 1914–1918, the Second World War was a conflict of ideas and ideologies as well as a struggle of nations and armies. Much of the world was immensely grateful that the defeat of Italy, Germany, and Japan discredited the ideas that underlay those regimes. Yet students of history need to examine these ideas, however repellant they may be, to understand the circumstances in which they arose and to assess their consequences. Described variously as fascist, authoritarian, right-wing, or radically nationalist, the ideologies of the Axis powers differed in tone and emphasis. But they shared a repudiation of mainstream Western liberalism, born of the Enlightenment, as well as an intense hatred of Marxist communism. The three documents that follow provide an opportunity to define their common features and to distinguish among them.

Document 21.1

Mussolini on Fascism

In 1932, after ten years in power, the Italian fascist leader Benito Mussolini wrote a short article for an Italian encyclopedia outlining the political and social ideas that informed the regime that he headed. It was an effort to provide some philosophical coherence for the various measures and policies that had characterized the first decade of his rule. (See pp. 988–90 for background on Italian fascism.)

- To what ideas and historical circumstances is Mussolini reacting in this document?

- What is his criticism of pacifism, socialism, democracy, and liberalism?

- How does Mussolini understand the state? What is its relationship to individual citizens?

- Why might these ideas have been attractive to many in Italy in the 1920s and 1930s?

BENITO MUSSOLINI
The Political and Social Doctrine of Fascism
1933

Above all, Fascism...believes neither in the possibility nor the utility of perpetual peace. It thus repudiates the doctrine of Pacifism—born of a renunciation of the struggle and an act of cowardice in the face of sacrifice. War alone brings up to its highest tension all human energy and puts the stamp of nobility upon the peoples who have the courage to meet it....This anti-Pacifist spirit is carried by Fascism even into the life of the individual;...it is the education to combat, the acceptation of the risks which combat implies, and a new way of life for Italy. Thus the Fascist...conceives of life as duty and struggle and conquest, life which should be high and full, lived for oneself, but above all for others—those who are at hand and those who are far distant, contemporaries, and those who will come after....

Fascism repudiates any universal embrace, and in order to live worthily in the community of civilized peoples watches its contemporaries with vigilant eyes....

Such a conception of Life makes Fascism the complete opposite of...Marxian Socialism, the materialist conception of history; according to which the history of human civilization can be explained simply through the conflict of interests among the various social groups and by the change and development in the means and instruments of production.... Fascism, now and always, believes in holiness and in heroism; that is to say, in actions influenced by no economic motive, direct or indirect.... It follows that the existence of an unchangeable and unchanging class war is also denied.... And above all Fascism denies that class-war can be the preponderant force in the transformation of society.... Fascism repudiates the conception of "economic" happiness, to be realized by Socialism.... Fascism denies the validity of the equation, well-being = happiness, which would reduce men to the level of animals, caring for one thing only—to be fat and well-fed and would thus degrade humanity to a purely physical existence.

After Socialism, Fascism combats the whole complex system of democratic ideology, and repudiates it.... Fascism denies that the majority, by the simple fact that it is a majority, can direct human society; it denies that numbers alone can govern by means of a periodical consultation, and it affirms the immutable, beneficial, and fruitful inequality of mankind, which can never be permanently leveled through the mere operation of a mechanical process such as universal suffrage. The democratic regime may be defined as from time to time giving the people the illusion of sovereignty, while the real effective sovereignty lies in the hands of other concealed and irresponsible forces....

The foundation of Fascism is the conception of the State, its character, its duty, and its aim. Fascism conceives of the State as an absolute, in comparison with which all individuals or groups are relative, only to be conceived of in their relation to the State.... [T]he Fascist State is itself conscious, and has itself a will and a personality.... For us Fascists, the State is not merely a guardian, preoccupied solely with the duty of assuring the personal safety of the citizens; nor is it an organization with purely material aims, such as to guarantee a certain level of well-being and peaceful conditions of life....The State, as conceived of and as created by Fascism, is a spiritual and moral fact in itself....The State is the guarantor of security, both internal and external, but it is also the custodian and transmitter of the spirit of the people, as it has grown up through the centuries in language, in customs and in faith.... [I]t represents the immanent spirit of the nation.... It is the State which educates its citizens in civic virtue, gives them a consciousness of their mission, and welds them into unity.... It leads men from primitive tribal life to that highest expression of human power which is Empire.

Source: Benito Mussolini, *The Political and Social Doctrine of Fascism*, translated by Jane Soames (London: Leonard and Virginia Woolf at the Hogarth Press, 1933).

[T]he Fascist State... is not reactionary, but revolutionary, in that it anticipates the solution of the universal political problems which elsewhere have to be settled in the political field by the rivalry of parties, the excessive power of the Parliamentary regime and the irresponsibility of political assemblies; while it meets the problems of the economic field by a system of syndicalism°... and in the moral field enforces order, discipline, and obedience to that which is the determined moral code of the country. Fascism desires the State to be a strong and organic body, at the same time reposing upon broad and popular support....The Fascist State organizes the nation, but leaves a sufficient margin of liberty to the individual; the latter is deprived of all useless and possibly harmful freedom, but retains what is essential; the deciding power in this question cannot be the individual, but the State alone. The Fascist State is not indifferent to the fact of religion in general, or to that particular

and positive faith which is Italian Catholicism. The State professes no theology, but a morality, and in the Fascist State religion is considered as one of the deepest manifestations of the spirit of man, thus it is not only respected but defended and protected.

For Fascism the growth of Empire, that is to say the expansion of the nation, is an essential manifestation of vitality, and its opposite a sign of decadence. Peoples which are rising, or rising again after a period of decadence, are always imperialist; any renunciation is a sign of decay and of death. Fascism is the doctrine best adapted to represent the tendencies and the aspirations of a people, like the people of Italy, who are rising again after many centuries of abasement and foreign servitude. But Empire demands discipline, the coordination of all forces and a deeply felt sense of duty and sacrifice: this fact explains... the necessarily severe measures which must be taken against those who would oppose this spontaneous and inevitable movement of Italy in the twentieth century... for never before has the nation stood more in need of authority, of direction, and of order.

_____

°**syndicalism:** federations of trade unions under state direction.

Document 21.2

Hitler on Nazism

Unlike Mussolini, Adolph Hitler published his political views well before he came to power. Born in Austria, Hitler absorbed a radical form of German nationalism, which he retained as a profoundly disillusioned veteran of World War I. In 1919, he joined a very small extremist group called the German Workers Party, where he rose quickly to a dominant role based on his powerful oratorical abilities. Inspired by Mussolini's recent victory in Italy, Hitler launched in 1923 an unsuccessful armed uprising in Munich for which he was arrested and imprisoned. During his brief stay in prison (less than a year), he wrote *Mein Kampf (My Struggle)*, part autobiography and part an exposition of his political and social philosophy. Armed with these ideas, Hitler assumed the leadership of Germany in 1933 (see pp. 990–93).

■   What larger patterns in European thinking does Hitler's book reflect and what elements of European thought does he reject? Consider in particular his use of social Darwinism, then an idea with wide popularity in Europe.

- How does Hitler distinguish between Aryans and Jews? How does he understand the role of race in human affairs?

- What kind of political system does Hitler advocate?

- What goals for Germany—both domestic and foreign—did Hitler set forth in *Mein Kampf*?

- What aspects of Hitler's thinking might have had wide appeal in Germany during the 1930s?

- How do you think Mussolini and Hitler might have responded to each other's ideas?

ADOLPH HITLER

Mein Kampf (My Struggle)
1925–1926

Nation and Race

There are some truths which are so obvious that for this very reason they are not seen or at least not recognized by ordinary people.... Every animal mates only with a member of the same species.... Any crossing of two beings not at exactly the same level produces a medium between the level of the two parents.... Such mating is contrary to the will of Nature for a higher breeding of all life.... The stronger must dominate and not blend with the weaker, thus sacrificing his own greatness. Only the born weakling can view this as cruel..., for if this law did not prevail, any conceivable higher development of organic living beings would be unthinkable.

In the struggle for daily bread all those who are weak and sickly or less determined succumb, while the struggle of the males for the female grants the right or opportunity to propagate only to the healthiest.... No more than Nature desires the mating of weaker with stronger individuals, even less does she desire the blending of a higher with a lower race, since, if she did, her whole work of higher breeding, over perhaps hundreds of thousands of years, might be ruined with one blow.... All great cultures of the past perished only because the originally creative race died out from blood poisoning.

Those who want to live, let them fight, and those who do not want to fight in this world of eternal struggle do not deserve to live....

All the human culture, all the results of art, science, and technology that we see before us today, are almost exclusively the creative product of the Aryan.... [H]e alone was the founder of all higher humanity, therefore representing the prototype of all that we understand by the word "man." He is the Prometheus of mankind from whose bright forehead the divine spark of genius has sprung at all times.... Exclude him, and perhaps after a few thousand years darkness will again descend on the earth, human culture will pass, and the world turn to a desert.

All who are not of good race in this world are chaff.

The mightiest counterpart to the Aryan is represented by the Jew.... Since the Jew...was never in possession of a culture of his own, the foundations of his intellectual work were always provided by others. His intellect at all times developed through the cultural world surrounding him....

He lacks completely the most essential requirement for a cultured people, the idealistic attitude. In the Jewish people the will to self-sacrifice does not go beyond the individual's naked instinct of

Source: Adolph Hitler, *Mein Kampf* (originally published 1925–26).

self-preservation. Their apparently great sense of solidarity is based on the very primitive herd instinct that is seen in many other living creatures in this world.... [T]he Jew is led by nothing but the naked egoism of the individual.

With satanic joy in his face, the black-haired Jewish youth lurks in wait for the unsuspecting girl whom he defiles with his blood, thus stealing her from her people. With every means he tries to destroy the racial foundations of the people he has set out to subjugate.... And so he tries systematically to lower the racial level by a continuous poisoning of individuals. And in politics he begins to replace the idea of democracy by the dictatorship of the proletariat. In the organized mass of Marxism he has found the weapon which lets him ... subjugate and govern the peoples with a dictatorial and brutal fist.

In economics he undermines the states until the social enterprises which have become unprofitable are taken from the state and subjected to his financial control.

In the political field he refuses the state the means for its self-preservation, destroys the foundations of all national self-maintenance and defense, destroys faith in the leadership, scoffs at its history and past, and drags everything that is truly great into the gutter.

Culturally he contaminates art, literature, the theater, makes a mockery of natural feeling, overthrows all concepts of beauty and sublimity, of the noble and the good, and instead drags men down into the sphere of his own base nature. Religion is ridiculed, ethics and morality represented as outmoded, until the last props of a nation in its struggle for existence in this world have fallen.

If we pass all the causes of the German collapse [defeat in World War I] in review, the ultimate and most decisive remains the failure to recognize the racial problem and especially the Jewish menace.... The lost purity of the blood alone destroys inner happiness forever, plunges man into the abyss for all time, and the consequences can never more be eliminated from body and spirit.... All really significant symptoms of decay of the pre–War period can in the last analysis be reduced to racial causes.

The State

The State is only a means to an end.... Above all, it must preserve the existence of the race.... We, as Aryans, can consider the State only as the living organism of a people, an organism which does not merely maintain the existence of a people, but functions in such a way as to lead its people to a position of supreme liberty by the progressive development of the intellectual and cultural faculties.

We National Socialists know that in holding these views we take up a revolutionary stand in the world of today and that we are branded as revolutionaries....

As a State the German Reich shall include all Germans. Its task is not only to gather in and foster the most valuable sections of our people but to lead them slowly and surely to a dominant position in the world.... It will be the task of the People's State to make the race the centre of the life of the community. It must make sure that the purity of the racial strain will be preserved.... Those who are physically and mentally unhealthy and unfit must not perpetuate their own suffering in the bodies of their children....

One thing is certain: our world is facing a great revolution. The only question is whether the outcome will be propitious for the Aryan portion of mankind or whether the everlasting Jew will profit by it. By educating the young generation along the right lines, the People's State will have to see to it that a generation of mankind is formed which will be adequate to this supreme combat that will decide the destinies of the world....

[T]he People's State must mercilessly expurgate ... the parliamentarian principle, according to which decisive power through the majority vote is invested in the multitude. Personal responsibility must be substituted in its stead.... The best constitution and the best form of government is that which makes it quite natural for the best brains to reach a position of dominant importance and influence in the community.... Genius of an extraordinary stamp is not to be judged by normal standards whereby we judge other men.

There are no decisions made by the majority vote, but only by responsible persons. And the word "council" is once more restored to its original meaning. Every man in a position of responsibility will have councilors at his side, but the decision is made by that individual person alone. . . .

[T]he principle of parliamentarian democracy, whereby decisions are enacted through the majority vote, has not always ruled the world. On the contrary, we find it prevalent only during short periods of history, and those have always been periods of decline in nations and States. . . .

Eastern Orientation or Eastern Policy

[W]e National Socialists must hold unflinchingly to our aim in foreign policy, namely, to secure for the German people the land and soil to which they are entitled on this earth. . . . If we speak of soil in Europe today, we can primarily have in mind only Russia and her vassal border states. . . .

The National Socialist movement must strive to eliminate the disproportion between our population and our area—viewing this latter as a source of food as well as a basis for power politics—between our historical past and the hopelessness of our present impotence. And in this it must remain aware that we, as guardians of the highest humanity on this earth, are bound by the highest obligation, and the more it strives to bring the German people to racial awareness . . . , the more it will be able to meet this obligation. . . .

State boundaries are made by man and changed by man. . . . And in this case, right lies in this strength alone. . . . Just as our ancestors did not receive the soil on which we live today as a gift from Heaven, but had to fight for it at the risk of their lives, in the future no folkish grace will win soil for us . . . but only the might of a victorious sword. . . .

Never forget that the most sacred right on this earth is a man's right to have earth to till with his own hands, and the most sacred sacrifice the blood that a man sheds for this earth.

Document 21.3

The Japanese Way

In the Japanese language the word *kokutai* is an evocative term that refers to the national essence or the fundamental character of the Japanese nation and people. Drawing both on long-established understandings and on recently developed nationalist ideas, the Ministry of Education in 1937 published a small volume, widely distributed in schools and homes throughout the country, entitled the *Kokutai No Hongi* (*Cardinal Principles of the National Entity of Japan*). That text, excerpted in Document 21.3, defined the uniqueness of Japan and articulated the philosophical foundation of its authoritarian regime. (See pp. 993–96 for the background to this document.) When the Americans occupied a defeated and devastated Japan in 1945, they forbade the further distribution of the book.

- According to *Cardinal Principles*, what was *kokutai*? How did the document define the national essence of Japan? How did its authors compare Japan to the West?

- What was the ideal role of the individual in Japanese society?

- What were the major tasks confronting Japan in the 1930s, according to the document?

- How might this document have been used to justify Japan's military and territorial expansion?

- Why do you think the American occupation authorities banned the document?

- What aspects of this document might Hitler have viewed with sympathy, and what parts of it might he have found distasteful or offensive?

Cardinal Principles of the National Entity of Japan
1937

The various ideological and social evils of present-day Japan are the result of ignoring the fundamental and running after the trivial, of lack of judgment, and a failure to digest things thoroughly; and this is due to the fact that since the days of *Meiji* so many aspects of European and American culture, systems, and learning, have been imported, and that, too rapidly. As a matter of fact, the foreign ideologies imported into our country are in the main ideologies of the [European] Enlightenment that have come down from the eighteenth century, or extensions of them. The views of the world and of life that form the basis of these ideologies ... lay the highest value on, and assert the liberty and equality of, individuals....

We have already witnessed the boundless Imperial virtues. Wherever this Imperial virtue of compassion radiates, the Way for the subjects naturally becomes clear. The Way of the subjects exists where the entire nation serves the Emperor united in mind.... That is, we by nature serve the Emperor and walk the Way of the Empire....

We subjects are intrinsically quite different from the so-called citizens of the Occidental countries....

When citizens who are conglomerations of separate individuals independent of each other give support to a ruler, ... there exists no deep foundation between ruler and citizen to unite them. However, the relationship between the Emperor and his sub-

jects arises from the same fountainhead, and has prospered ever since the founding of the nation as one in essence....

Our country is established with the Emperor.... For this reason, to serve the Emperor and to receive the Emperor's great august Will as one's own is the rationale of making our historical "life" live in the present....

Loyalty means to reverence the Emperor as [our] pivot and to follow him implicitly.... Hence, offering our lives for the sake of the Emperor does not mean so-called self-sacrifice, but the casting aside of our little selves to live under his august grace and the enhancing of the genuine life of the people of a State.... An individual is an existence belonging to the State and her history, which forms the basis of his origin, and is fundamentally one body with it....

We must sweep aside the corruption of the spirit and the clouding of knowledge that arises from setting up one's "self" and from being taken up with one's "self" and return to a pure and clear state of mind that belongs intrinsically to us as subjects, and thereby fathom the great principle loyalty....

Indeed, loyalty is our fundamental Way as subject, and is the basis of our national morality. Through loyalty are we become Japanese subjects; in loyalty do we obtain life and herein do we find the source of all morality....

In our country filial piety is a Way of the highest importance. Filial piety originates with one's family as its basis, and in its larger sense has the nation for its foundation....

Our country is a great family nation, and the Imperial Household is the head family of the sub-

Source: J. O. Gauntlett, trans., and R. K. Hall, ed., *Kokutai No Hongi* (*Cardinal Principles of the National Entity of Japan*) (Cambridge: Harvard University Press, 1949), 53–183.

jects and the nucleus of national life. The subjects revere the Imperial Household, which is the head family, with the tender esteem they have for their ancestors; and the Emperor loves his subjects as his very own....

When we trace the marks of the facts of the founding of our country and the progress of our history, what we always find there is the spirit of harmony....The spirit of harmony is built upon the concord of all things. When people determinedly count themselves as masters and assert their egos, there is nothing but contradictions and the setting of one against the other; and harmony is not begotten....That is, a society of individualism is one of the clashes between [masses of] people... and all history may be looked upon as one of class wars....

And this, this harmony is clearly seen in our nation's martial spirit. Our nation is one that holds bushido° in high regard, and there are shrines deifying warlike spirits....Bushido may be cited as showing an outstanding characteristic of our national morality....That is to say, though a sense of obligation binds master and servant, this has developed in a spirit of self-effacement and meeting death with a perfect calmness. In this, it was not that death was made light of so much as that many tempered himself to death and in a true sense regarded it with esteem. In effect, man tried to fulfill true life by the way of death....

°**bushido:** the way of the warrior.

To put it in a nutshell, while the strong points of Occidental learning and concepts lie in their analytical and intellectual qualities, the characteristics of Oriental learning and concepts lie in their intuitive and aesthetic qualities. These are natural tendencies that arise through racial and historical differences; and when we compare them with our national spirits, concepts, or mode of living, we cannot help recognizing further great and fundamental differences. Our nation has in the past imported, assimilated, and sublimated Chinese and Indian ideologies, and has therewith supported the Imperial Way, making possible the establishment of an original culture based on her national polity....

Since the *Meiji* restoration our nation has adapted the good elements of the advanced education seen among European and American nations, and has exerted efforts to set up an educational system and materials for teaching. The nation has also assimilated on a wide scale the scholarship of the West, not only in the fields of natural science, but of the mental sciences, and has thus striven to see progress made in our scholastic pursuits and to make education more popular....

However, at the same time, through the infiltration of individualistic concepts, both scholastic pursuits and education have tended to be taken up with a world in which the intellect alone mattered....

In order to correct these tendencies, the only course open to us is to clarify the true nature of our national polity, which is at the very source of our education, and to strive to clear up individualistic and abstract ideas.

Using the Evidence:
Ideologies of the Axis Powers

1. **Making comparisons:** What similar emphases can you find in these three documents? What differences can you identify? Consider especially the relationship of individuals and the state.

2. **Criticizing the West:** In what ways did Mussolini, Hitler, and the authors of *Cardinal Principles* find fault with mainstream Western societies and their political and social values?

3. **Considering ideas and circumstances:** From what concrete conditions did the ideas expressed in these documents arise? Why did they achieve such widespread popularity? You might even consider using these documents to make the case in favor of fascist or authoritarian government from the viewpoint of the 1930s.

4. **Considering ideas and action:** To what extent did the ideas articulated in these documents find expression in particular actions or policies of political authorities?

5. **Noticing continuity and change:** To what extent were the ideas in these documents new and revolutionary? In what respects did they draw on long-standing traditions in their societies? In what ways did they embrace modern life and what aspects of it did they reject? Have these ideas been completely discredited or do they retain some resonance in contemporary political discourse?

Visual Sources

Considering the Evidence:
Propaganda and Critique in World War I

More than any other conflict before it, World War I was represented visually and publically in many ways. Newspapers competed to print the most sensational pictures, many taken by soldiers themselves using handheld cameras. The war also offered a highly popular theme for the new technology of cinema and the emerging motion picture industry. One of the most pervasive uses of art and artists involved the prolific creation, under government auspices, of posters designed to generate public support for the war. Independent artists, many of whom participated in the war, tried to depict its horror and devastation, both during the conflict and after it finally ended. The first three visual sources illustrate the official propaganda dimension of the war's representation, while the final two provide examples of how that enormous conflict and its outcomes were subjected to artistic scrutiny.

The "total" character of World War I ensured that women would be mobilized for the struggle in many ways. In Russia, after the revolution of early 1917, a number of all-female combat units were created to shame or inspire the war-weary male soldiers into greater action. Some British women even presented men not in uniform with a white feather, symbolizing cowardice, to encourage them to enlist. More widely, women were recruited into war-related industries to replace the men who were away fighting, as the British poster on page 982 indicates. American women were strongly encouraged to save food, especially wheat, to support the war effort. Posters also gave the great struggle a feminine face. Visual Source 21.1 is a 1917 U.S. poster meant to encourage people to buy Liberty Bonds, which raised money for the war effort and demonstrated the buyer's patriotism.

- How would you describe the posture of the woman in this poster? What image of a woman does it seek to convey?

- What message does the backdrop of the poster communicate? Notice the church and city in flames.

- In appealing for sacrifice or public support in time of war, why might a feminine image be more effective than a masculine image?

- Compare this poster with the British one shown on page 982 in this chapter. What different message about the role of women does this image convey? To what kind of audience did each of these posters appeal?

Visual Source 21.1 Women and the War (Library of Congress, LC-USZCA-9462)

Among the chief uses of wartime propaganda posters was to portray the enemy in the most despicable terms. German posters, for example, often depicted the country's enemies as animals or misbehaving children, suggesting that they were something less than fully human. They usually showed Russians as alcoholics. Visual Source 21.2 is a French poster from around 1915.

It pictures Germany as Thor, an ancient pagan Germanic god of thunder, who had been turned into a demonic figure as Christianity took hold in Europe. The caption at the top of the image reads: "The god Thor—the most barbaric of the barbarian divinities of old Germany."

- What does the poster convey by presenting Germany as Thor?

- Note the Prussian imperial eagle standing on a bomb. What impression of German goals does that convey?

- How do you understand the religious imagery of this French print? Notice Thor preparing to destroy a church with his hammer as well as the broken cross between his feet at the bottom.

- To whom do you think such images were directed and for what purpose?

A distinctive feature of World War I was the extensive use of troops drawn from the colonies of the contending powers. Many thousands of African and Asian men took part in that struggle, both in their homelands and in Europe. The French, for example, were initially reluctant to employ colonial troops, fearing to arm black men and perhaps uncertain of their loyalty. But the desperate need for manpower finally overcame these reservations, and France recruited large numbers of men from its North and West African colonies as well as from Southeast Asia. Some 71,000 French colonial soldiers died in the war. Visual Source 21.3 shows a French wartime poster; the French translates as "Day of the African Army and Colonial Troops."

- What image of African soldiers does the poster suggest? How might this image be at variance with that of earlier European stereotypes of their African subjects?

- What is conveyed by the juxtaposition of an African soldier and his French counterpart fighting together?

- Why might the French have set aside a special day to honor colonial troops?

- How might the experience of fighting in Europe have affected the outlook of a West African soldier?

The destructiveness of the Great War was almost beyond the imagination of contemporary Europeans. Among its most notable and horrific features was the long period of trench warfare, in which lines of entrenched men, often not far apart, periodically went "over the top," only to gain a few yards of bloody ground before being thrown back with enormous causalities. Visual Source 21.4 shows a particular instance of this process by the British painter John Nash (1893–1977), who was an official war artist. Nash was also part of an eighty-man British unit that was sent over the top in late 1917 and one of only twelve

Visual Source 21.2 Defining the Enemy (The Art Archive)

JOURNÉE DE L'ARMÉE D'AFRIQUE ET DES TROUPES COLONIALES

DEVAMBEZ . PARIS

Visual Source 21.3 War and the Colonies (Private collection/Barbara Singer/The Bridgeman Art Library

survivors of that attack. Three months later he painted this haunting picture from his memory of that experience.

- What posture toward the war does this image convey? Do you think Nash's military superiors were pleased by the painting?

- How does the painting portray the attitude of the soldiers?

- What does war do to human beings? What answer to this question does this image suggest?

- How might you imagine the response of those who created the first three images to John Nash and this portrayal of trench warfare?

Among the many outcomes of the Great War was the presence in every European country of disillusioned, maimed, and disfigured veterans, many of them literally "men without faces." For some intellectuals and artists, they represented the fundamentally flawed civilization that had given rise to such carnage. Often neglected or overlooked, such men were reminders of a terrible past that others wanted to forget. The German artist Otto Dix (1891–1969), who served in his country's military forces throughout the war and was seriously wounded, portrayed this situation in a 1920 painting called *Prague Street* (Visual Source 21.5). In 1924, he joined with other artists to mount an exhibition entitled No More War. His antiwar activism later earned Dix the enmity of the Hitler regime, which fired him from his academic position and destroyed some of his paintings. Artistically, Dix worked in a style known as the "new objectivity," which focused heavily on the horrendous outcomes of the war. It deliberately included subject matter that was upsetting and even ugly, and it made little attempt to create a unified image, preferring to present disconnected "particles of experience."

- How does the painting describe the situation of the veterans?

- On the left, the arm of a wealthy man drops a coin into the outstretched hand of a maimed veteran, while on the right, a well-dressed woman in a pink dress and high heels walks by with her dog. What do these features add to the portrayal of the plight of the veterans?

- Notice the leaflet on the skateboard of the legless cripple at the bottom. It reads *"Juden raus"* (Jews out)." What does this suggest about the political views of these veterans? Keep in mind that Hitler, although not maimed, was a disillusioned veteran of World War I, as were many of his early followers.

- What do the images in the store windows suggest?

- What commentary does this painting make on German society after the country's defeat in World War I? How does it foreshadow what was to come?

Visual Source 21.4 The Battlefield (Imperial War Museum, London/The Bridgeman Art Library)

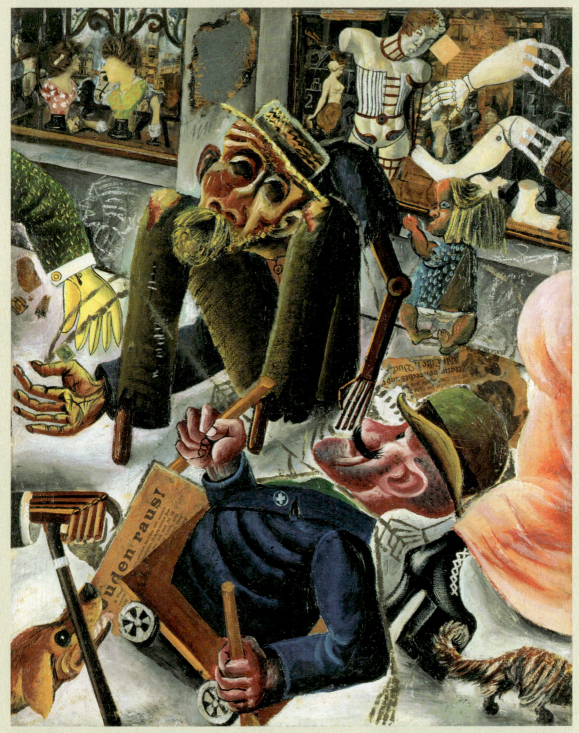

Visual Source 21.5 The Aftermath of War (Kunstmuseum-Stuttgart © 2010 Artist's Rights Society (ARS), New York/VG Bildkunst, Bonn)

Using the Evidence:
Propaganda and Critique in World War I

1. **Describing the war:** Based on these visual sources, how would you define the novel or distinctive features of World War I compared to earlier European conflicts?

2. **Considering war and progress:** How do you think Otto Dix and John Nash might have responded to the ideas of Condorcet contained in Document 16.2, pages 752–54?

3. **Images as propaganda and criticism:** This selection of visual sources contains a mix of those that express essentially government-sponsored messages and those that convey the outlook of individual artists. What ideas about the war did governments seek to inculcate in their citizens? How do the paintings of John Nash and Otto Dix respond to those ideas?

4. **Seeking further evidence:** What other kinds of visual sources would be useful in constructing a visual history of World War I?

ЛЕНИН –
ЖИЛ,
ЛЕНИН –
ЖИВ,
ЛЕНИН –
БУДЕТ ЖИТ

ВЛ. МАЯКОВСКИЙ.

The Rise and Fall of World Communism

1917—PRESENT

"I was living in Germany on the day the wall came down and well remember talking to my German neighbour. With tears streaming down his face he kept saying in English and German: 'I never thought I would live to see this.'

"For anyone who didn't experience the Wall, it will be hard to imagine what an overwhelming feeling of relief, of joy, of unreality filled one that this monster was dead, and people had conquered it."[1]

Both of these eyewitness comments referred to that remarkable day, November 9, 1989, when the infamous Berlin Wall in Germany was breached. Built in 1961 to prevent the residents of communist East Berlin from escaping to the West, that concrete barrier had become a potent symbol of communist tyranny. Its fall, amid the overthrow of communist governments all across Eastern Europe, was part of a larger process that marked the collapse or the abandonment of communism as the twentieth century entered its final decade. In the midst of that euphoria, it was hard to remember that earlier in the century communism had been greeted with enthusiasm by many people—in Russia, China, Cuba, Vietnam, and elsewhere—as a promise of liberation from inequality, oppression, exploitation, and backwardness.

COMMUNISM WAS A PHENOMENON OF ENORMOUS SIGNIFICANCE IN THE WORLD OF THE TWENTIETH CENTURY. Communist regimes came to power almost everywhere in the tumultuous wake of war, revolution, or both. Once established, those regimes set about a thorough and revolutionary transformation of their societies—"building socialism," as they so often put it. Internationally, world communism

Lenin: Vladimir Ulyanov, better known as Lenin, was the Bolshevik leader of the Russian Revolution. He became the iconic symbol of world communism and in his own country was the focus of a semireligious cult. This widely distributed Soviet propaganda poster reads "Lenin lived; Lenin lives; Lenin will live." (David King Collection)

posed a profound military and political/ideological threat to the Western world of capitalism and democracy, particularly during the decades of the cold war (1946–1991). That struggle divided continents, countries, and cities into communist and non-communist halves. It also prompted a global rivalry between the United States and the Soviet Union (USSR) for influence in the third world. Most hauntingly, it spawned an arms race in horrendously destructive nuclear weapons that sent school-children scrambling under their desks during air raid drills, while sober scientists speculated about the possible extinction of human life, and perhaps all life, in the event of a major war.

Then, to the amazement of everyone, it was over, more with a whimper than a bang. The last two decades of the twentieth century witnessed the collapse of communist regimes or the abandonment of communist principles practically everywhere. The great global struggle of capitalism and communism, embodied in the United States and the Soviet Union, was resolved in favor of the former far more quickly and much more peacefully than anyone had imagined possible.

Global Communism

■ **Description**
When and where did communism exercise influence during the twentieth century?

Modern communism found its political and philosophical roots in nineteenth-century European socialism, inspired by the teachings of Karl Marx. (See p. 837 and Chapter 18's Documents: Varieties of European Marxism, pp. 855–66.) Although most European socialists came to believe that they could achieve their goals peacefully and through the democratic process, those who defined themselves as communists in the twentieth century disdained such reformism and advocated uncompromising revolution as the only possible route to a socialist future. Russia was the first country to experience such a revolution. Other movements that later identified or allied with the Soviet Union, as the Russian Empire was renamed after its 1917 revolution, likewise defined themselves as communist. In Marxist theory, communism also referred to a final stage of historical development when social equality and collective living would be most fully developed, wholly without private property. Socialism was an intermediate stage along the way to that final goal.

By the 1970s, almost one-third of the world's population lived in societies governed by communist regimes. By far the most significant were the Soviet Union, the world's largest country in size, and China, the world's largest country in population. This chapter focuses primarily on a comparison of these two large-scale experiments in communism and their global impact.

Beyond the Soviet Union and China, communism also came to Eastern Europe in the wake of World War II and the extension of the Soviet military presence there. In Asia, following Japan's defeat in that war, its Korean colony was partitioned, with the northern half coming under Soviet and therefore communist control. In Vietnam, a much more locally based communist movement, under the leadership of Ho Chi Minh, embodied both a socialist vision and Vietnamese nationalism as it battled Japanese, French, and later American invaders and established communist control first in the northern half of the country and after 1975 throughout the whole country. The victory of the Vietnamese communists spilled over into neighboring Laos and Cambodia, where communist parties took power in the mid-1970s. In Latin America, Fidel Castro led a revolutionary nationalist movement against a repressive and American-backed government in Cuba. On coming to power in 1959, he moved toward communism and an alliance with the Soviet Union. Finally, a shaky communist regime took power in Afghanistan in 1979, propped up briefly only by massive Soviet military support. None of these countries had achieved the kind of advanced industrial capitalism that Karl Marx had viewed as a prerequisite for revolution and socialism. In one of history's strange twists, the great revolutions of the twentieth century took place instead in largely agrarian societies.

In addition to those countries where communist governments exercised state power, communist parties took root in still other places, where they exercised various degrees of influence. In the aftermath of World War II, such parties played important political roles in Greece, France, and Italy. In the 1950s, a small communist party in the United States became the focus of an intense wave of fear and political repression known as McCarthyism. Revolutionary communist movements threatened established governments in the Philippines, Malaya, Indonesia, Bolivia, Peru, and elsewhere, sometimes provoking brutal crackdowns by those governments. A number of African states in the 1970s proclaimed themselves Marxist for a time and aligned with the Soviet Union in international affairs. All of this was likewise part of global communism.

These differing expressions of communism were linked to one another in various ways. They shared a common ideology derived from European Marxism, although it was substantially modified in many places. That ideology minimized the claims of national loyalty and looked forward to an international revolutionary movement of the lower classes and a worldwide socialist federation. The Russian Revolution of 1917 served as an inspiration and an example to aspiring revolutionaries elsewhere, and the new Soviet Communist Party and government provided them aid and advice. Through an organization called Comintern (Communist International), Soviet authorities also sought to control their policies and actions.

During the cold war decades, the Warsaw Pact brought the Soviet Union and Eastern European communist states together in a military alliance designed to counter the threat from the Western capitalist countries of the NATO alliance. A parallel organization called the Council on Mutual Economic Assistance tied Eastern European economies tightly to the economy of the Soviet Union. A Treaty of Friendship between the Soviet Union and China in 1950 joined the two communist giants in an alliance that caused many in the West to view communism as a unified international movement aimed at their destruction. Nevertheless, rivalry, outright hostility, and on occasion military conflict marked the communist world as much or more than solidarity and cooperation. Eastern European resentment of their Soviet overlords was expressed in periodic rebellions, even as the Soviet Union and China came close to war in the late 1960s.

Although the globalization of communism found expression primarily in the second half of the twentieth century, that process began with two quite distinct and different revolutionary upheavals—one in Russia and the other in China—in the first half of that century.

Comparing Revolutions as a Path to Communism

■ Comparison

Identify the major differences between the Russian and Chinese revolutions.

Communist movements of the twentieth century quite self-consciously drew on the mystique of the earlier French Revolution, which suggested that new and better worlds could be constructed by human actions. Like their French predecessors, communist revolutionaries ousted old ruling classes and dispossessed landed aristocracies. Those twentieth-century upheavals also involved vast peasant upheavals in the countryside and an educated leadership with roots in the cities. All three revolutions—French, Russian, and Chinese—found their vision of the good society in a modernizing future, not in some nostalgic vision of the past. Communists also worried lest their revolutions end up in a military dictatorship like that of Napoleon following the French Revolution.

But the communist revolutions were distinctive as well. They were made by highly organized parties guided by a Marxist ideology, were committed to an industrial future, pursued economic as well as political equality, and sought the abolition of private property. In doing so, they mobilized, celebrated, and claimed to act on behalf of society's lower classes—exploited urban workers and impoverished rural peasants. The middle classes, who were the chief beneficiaries of the French Revolution, numbered among the many victims of the communist upheavals. The Russian and Chinese revolutions shared these features, but in other respects they differed sharply from each other.

Russia: Revolution in a Single Year

In Russia, communists came to power on the back of a revolutionary upheaval that took place within a single year, 1917. The immense pressures of World War I, which was going very badly for the Russians, represented the catalyst for that revolution as the accumulated tensions of Russian society exploded (see pp. 843–46). Much exploited and suffering from wartime shortages, workers, men and women alike, took to the streets to express their outrage at the incompetence and privileges of their social betters. Activists from various parties, many of them socialist, recruited members, organized demonstrations, published newspapers, and plotted revolution. By February 1917, Tsar Nicholas II had lost almost all support and was forced to abdicate the throne, thus ending the Romanov dynasty, which had ruled Russia for more than three centuries.

That historic event opened the door to a massive social upheaval. Ordinary soldiers, seeking an end to a terrible war and despising their upper-class officers, deserted in substantial numbers. In major industrial centers such as St. Petersburg

Map 22.1   Russia in 1917
During the First World War, the world's largest state, bridging both Europe and Asia, exploded in revolution in 1917. The Russian Revolution brought to power the twentieth century's first communist government and launched an international communist movement that eventually incorporated about one-third of the world's people.

and Moscow, new trade unions arose to defend workers' interests, and some workers seized control of their factories. Grassroots organizations of workers and soldiers, known as soviets, emerged to speak for ordinary people. Peasants, many of whom had been serfs only a generation or two ago, seized landlords' estates, burned their manor houses, and redistributed the land among themselves. Non-Russian nationalists in Ukraine, Poland, Muslim Central Asia, and the Baltic region demanded greater autonomy or even independence (see Map 22.1).

This was social revolution, and it quickly demonstrated the inadequacy of the Provisional Government, which had come to power after the tsar abdicated. Consisting of middle-class politicians and some socialist leaders, that government was divided and ineffectual, unable or unwilling to meet the demands of Russia's revolutionary masses. Nor was it willing to take Russia out of the war, as many were now demanding. Impatience and outrage against the Provisional Government provided an opening for more radical groups. The most effective were the Bolsheviks, a small socialist party with a determined and charismatic leader, Vladimir Ilyich Ulyanov, more commonly known as Lenin. He had long believed that Russia, despite its industrial backwardness, was nonetheless ready for a socialist revolution that would, he expected, spark further revolutions in the more developed countries of Europe (see

■ **Change**
Why were the Bolsheviks able to ride the Russian Revolution to power?

Document 18.5, pp. 864–65). Thus backward Russia would be a catalyst for a more general socialist breakthrough. It was a striking revision of Marxist thinking to accommodate the conditions of a largely agrarian Russian society.

In the desperate circumstances of 1917, his party's message—an end to the war, land for the peasants, workers' control of factories, self-determination for non-Russian nationalities—resonated with an increasingly rebellious public mood, particularly in the major cities. Lenin and the Bolsheviks also called for the dissolution of the Provisional Government and a transfer of state power to the new soviets. On the basis of this program, the Bolsheviks—claiming to act on behalf of the highly popular soviets, in which they had a major presence—seized power in late October during an overnight coup in the capital city of St. Petersburg. Members of the discredited Provisional Government fled or were arrested, even as the Bolsheviks also seized power elsewhere in the country.

Taking or claiming power was one thing; holding on to it was another. A three-year civil war followed in which the Bolsheviks, now officially calling their party "communist," battled an assortment of enemies—tsarist officials, landlords, disaffected socialists, and regional nationalist forces, as well as troops from the United States, Britain, France, and Japan, all of which were eager to crush the fledgling communist regime. Remarkably, the Bolsheviks held on and by 1921 had staggered to victory over their divided and uncoordinated opponents. That remarkable victory was assisted by the Bolsheviks' willingness to sign a separate peace treaty with Germany, thus taking Russia out of World War I in early 1918, but at a great, though temporary, loss of Russian territory.

During the civil war (1918–1921), the Bolsheviks had harshly regimented the economy, seized grain from angry peasants, suppressed nationalist rebellions, and perpetrated bloody atrocities, as did their enemies as well. But they also had integrated many lower-class men into the Red Army, as Bolshevik military forces were known, and into new local governments, providing them an avenue of social mobility not previously available. By battling foreign troops from the United States, Britain, France, and Japan, the Bolsheviks claimed to be defending Russia from imperialists and protecting the downtrodden masses from their exploiters. The civil war exaggerated even further the Bolsheviks' authoritarian tendencies and their inclination to use force. Shortly after that war ended, they renamed their country the Union of Soviet Socialist Republics and set about its transformation.

For the next twenty-five years, the Soviet Union remained a communist island in a capitalist sea. The next major extension of communist control occurred in Eastern Europe in the aftermath of World War II, but it took place quite differently than in Russia. The war had ended with Soviet military forces occupying much of Eastern Europe. Furthermore, Stalin, the USSR's longtime leader, had determined that Soviet security required "friendly" governments in the region so as to permanently end the threat of invasion from the West. When the Marshall Plan seemed to suggest American plans to incorporate Eastern Europe into a Western economic network,

Stalin acted to install fully communist governments, loyal to himself, in Poland, East Germany, Czechoslovakia, Hungary, Romania, and Bulgaria. Backed by the pressure and presence of the Soviet army, communism was largely imposed on Eastern Europe from outside rather than growing out of a domestic revolution, as had happened in Russia itself.

Local communist parties, however, had some domestic support, deriving from their role in the resistance against the Nazis and their policies of land reform. In Hungary and Poland, for example, communist pressures led to the redistribution of much land to poor or landless peasants, and in free elections in Czechoslovakia in 1946, communists received 38 percent of the vote. Furthermore, in Yugoslavia, a genuinely popular communist movement had played a leading role in the struggle against Nazi occupation and came to power on its own with little Soviet help. Its leader, Josef Broz, known as Tito, openly defied Soviet efforts to control it, claiming that "our goal is that everyone should be master in his own house."[2]

China: A Prolonged Revolutionary Struggle

Communism triumphed in the ancient land of China in 1949, about thirty years after the Russian Revolution, likewise on the heels of war and domestic upheaval. But that revolution, which was a struggle of decades rather than a single year, was far different from its earlier Russian counterpart. The Chinese imperial system had collapsed in 1911, under the pressure of foreign imperialism, its own inadequacies, and mounting internal opposition (see pp. 888–89). Unlike Russia, where intellectuals had been discussing socialism for half a century or more before the revolution, the ideas of Karl Marx were barely known in China in the early twentieth century. Not until 1921 was a small Chinese Communist Party (CCP) founded, aiming its efforts initially at organizing the country's minuscule urban working class.

Over the next twenty-eight years, that small party, with an initial membership of only sixty people, grew enormously, transformed its strategy, found a charismatic leader in Mao Zedong, engaged in an epic struggle with its opponents, fought the Japanese heroically, and in 1949 emerged victorious as the rulers

■ **Change**
What was the appeal of communism in China before 1949?

Mao Zedong and the Long March
An early member of China's then minuscule Communist Party, Mao rose to a position of dominant leadership during the Long March of 1934–1935, when beleaguered communists from southeastern China trekked to a new base area in the north. This photograph shows Mao on his horse during that epic journey of some 6,000 miles. (Collection J.A. Fox/Magnum Photos)

of China. The victory was all the more surprising because the CCP faced a far more formidable foe than the weak Provisional Government over which the Bolsheviks had triumphed in Russia. That opponent was the Guomindang (Nationalist Party), which governed China after 1928. Led by a military officer, Chiang Kai-shek, that party promoted a measure of modern development (railroads, light industry, banking, airline services) in the decade that followed. However, the impact of these achievements was limited largely to the cities, leaving the rural areas, where most people lived, still impoverished. The Guomindang's base of support was also narrow, deriving from urban elites, rural landlords, and Western powers.

Chased out of China's cities in a wave of Guomindang-inspired anticommunist terror in 1927, the CCP groped its way toward a new revolutionary strategy, quite at odds with both classical Marxism and Russian practice. Whereas the Bolsheviks had found their primary audience among workers in Russia's major cities, Chinese communists increasingly looked to the country's peasant villages for support. Thus European Marxism was adapted once again, this time to fit the situation in a mostly peasant China. Still, it was no easy sell. Chinese peasants did not rise up spontaneously against their landlords, as Russian peasants had. However, years of guerrilla warfare, experiments with land reform in areas under communist control, efforts to empower women, and the creation of a communist military force to protect liberated areas from Guomindang attack and landlord reprisals—all of this slowly gained for the CCP a growing measure of respect and support among China's peasants. In the process, Mao Zedong, the son of a prosperous Chinese peasant family and a professional revolutionary since the early 1920s, emerged as the party's leader.

It was Japan's brutal invasion of China that gave the CCP a decisive opening, for that attack destroyed Guomindang control over much of the country and forced it to retreat to the interior, where it became even more dependent on conservative landlords. The CCP, by contrast, grew from just 40,000 members in 1937 to more than 1.2 million in 1945, while the communist-led People's Liberation Army mushroomed to 900,000 men, supported by an additional 2 million militia troops (see Map 22.2). Much of this growing support derived from the vigor with which the CCP waged war against the Japanese invaders. Using guerrilla warfare techniques learned in the struggle against the Guomindang, communist forces established themselves behind enemy lines and, despite periodic setbacks, offered a measure of security to many Chinese faced with Japanese atrocities. The Guomindang, by contrast, sometimes seemed to be more interested in eliminating the communists than in actively fighting the Japanese. Furthermore, in the areas it controlled, the CCP reduced rents, taxes, and interest payments for peasants; taught literacy to adults; and mobilized women for the struggle. As the war drew to a close, more radical action followed. Teams of activists, called cadres, encouraged poor peasants to "speak bitterness" in public meetings, to "struggle" with landlords, and to "settle accounts" with them.

Thus the CCP frontally addressed both of China's major problems—foreign imperialism and peasant exploitation. It expressed Chinese nationalism as well as a demand for radical social change. It gained a reputation for honesty that contrasted

Map 22.2 The Rise of Communism in China Communism arose in China at the same time as the country was engaged in a terrible war with Japan and in the context of a civil war with Guomindang forces.

sharply with the massive corruption of Guomindang officials. It put down deep roots among the peasantry in a way that the Bolsheviks never did. And whereas the Bolsheviks gained support by urging Russian withdrawal from the highly unpopular First World War, the CCP won support by aggressively pursuing the struggle against Japanese invaders during World War II. In 1949, four years after the war's end, the Chinese communists swept to victory over the Guomindang, many of whose followers fled to Taiwan. Mao Zedong announced triumphantly in Beijing's Tiananmen Square that "the Chinese people have stood up."

Building Socialism in Two Countries

Once they came to power, the communist parties of the Soviet Union and China set about the construction of socialist societies. In the Soviet Union, this massive undertaking occurred under the leadership of Joseph Stalin in the 1920s and 1930s. The corresponding Chinese effort took place during the 1950s and 1960s with Mao Zedong at the helm.

To communist regimes, building socialism meant first of all the modernization and industrialization of their backward societies. In this respect, they embraced many of the material values of Western capitalist societies and were similar to the new nations of the twentieth century, all of which were seeking development. The communists, however, sought a distinctly socialist modernity. This involved a frontal attack on long-standing inequalities of class and gender, an effort to prevent the making of new inequalities as the process of modern development unfolded, and the promotion of cultural values of selflessness and collectivism that could support a socialist society.

Those imperatives generated a political system thoroughly dominated by the Communist Party. Top-ranking party members enjoyed various privileges but were expected to be exemplars of socialism in the making by being disciplined, selfless, and utterly loyal to their country's Marxist ideology. The party itself penetrated society in ways that Western scholars called "totalitarian," for other parties were forbidden, the state controlled almost the entire economy, and political authorities ensured that the arts, education, and the media conformed to approved ways of thinking. Mass organizations for women, workers, students, and various professional groups operated under party control, with none of the independence that characterized civil society in the West.

In undertaking these tasks, the Soviet Union and China started from different places, most notably their international positions. In 1917 Russian Bolsheviks faced a hostile capitalist world alone, while Chinese communists, coming to power over thirty years later, had an established Soviet Union as a friendly northern neighbor and ally. Furthermore, Chinese revolutionaries had actually governed parts of their huge country for decades, gaining experience that the new Soviet rulers had altogether lacked, since they had come to power so quickly. And the Chinese communists were firmly rooted in the rural areas and among the country's vast peasant population, while their Russian counterparts had found their support mainly in the cities.

If these comparisons generally favored China in its efforts to "build socialism," in economic terms, that country faced even more daunting prospects than did the Soviet Union. Its population was far greater, its industrial base far smaller, and the availability of new agricultural land far more limited than in the Soviet Union. China's literacy and modern education as well as its transportation network were likewise much less developed. Even more than the Soviets, Chinese communists had to build a modern society from the ground up.

Communist Feminism

Among the earliest and most revolutionary actions of these new communist regimes were efforts at liberating and mobilizing their women. Communist countries in fact pioneered forms of women's liberation that only later were adopted in the West. This communist feminism was largely state-directed, with the initiative coming from the top rather than bubbling up from grassroots movements as in the West. In the Soviet Union, where a small women's movement had taken shape in pre–World War I Russia, the new communist government almost immediately issued a series of laws and decrees regarding women. These measures declared full legal and political equality for women; marriage became a civil procedure among freely consenting adults; divorce was legalized and made easier, as was abortion; illegitimacy was abolished; women no longer had to take their husbands' surnames; pregnancy leave for employed women was mandated; and women were actively mobilized as workers in the country's drive to industrialization.

In 1919, the party set up a special organization called Zhenotdel (Women's Department), whose radical leaders, all women, pushed a decidedly feminist agenda in the 1920s. They organized numerous conferences for women, trained women to run day-care centers and medical clinics, published newspapers and magazines aimed at a female audience, provided literacy and prenatal classes, and encouraged Muslim women to take off their veils. Much of this encountered opposition from male communist officials and from ordinary people as well, and Stalin abolished Zhenotdel in 1930. While it lasted, though, it was a remarkable experiment in women's liberation by means of state action, animated by an almost utopian sense of new possibilities set loose by the revolution.

Similar policies took shape in communist China. The Marriage Law of 1950 was a direct attack on patriarchal and Confucian traditions. It decreed free choice in marriage, relatively easy divorce, the end of concubinage and child marriage, permission for widows to remarry, and equal property rights for women. A short but intense campaign by the CCP in the early 1950s sought to implement these changes, often against strenuous opposition. The party also launched a Women's Federation, a mass organization that enrolled millions of women. Its leadership, however, was far less radical than that of the Bolshevik feminists who led Zhenotdel in the 1920s. In China,

■ **Change**

What changes did communist regimes bring to the lives of women?

Mobilizing Women for Communism
As the Soviet Union mobilized for rapid economic development in the 1930s, women entered the workforce in great numbers. Here two young women are mastering the skills of driving a tractor on one of the large collective farms that replaced the country's private agriculture. (Sovfoto/Eastfoto)

there was little talk of "free love" or the "withering away of the family," as there had been in the USSR. Nevertheless, like their Soviet counterparts, Chinese women became much more actively involved in production outside the home. By 1978, 50 percent of agricultural workers and 38 percent of nonagricultural laborers were female. "Women can do anything" became a famous party slogan in the 1960s (see Visual Source 22.3, p. 1075).

Still, communist-style women's liberation had definite limits. Fearing that the women's question would detract from his emphasis on industrial production, Stalin declared it "solved" in 1930. Little direct discussion of women's issues was permitted in the several decades that followed. In neither the Soviet Union nor China did the Communist Party undertake a direct attack on male domination within the family. Thus the double burden of housework and child care plus paid employment continued to afflict most women. Moreover, women appeared only very rarely in the top political leadership of either country.

Socialism in the Countryside

■ **Comparison**

How did the collectivization of agriculture differ between the USSR and China?

In their efforts to build socialism, both the Soviet Union and China first expropriated landlords' estates and redistributed that land on a much more equitable basis to the peasantry. Such actions, although clearly revolutionary, were not socialist, for peasants initially received their land as private property. In Russia, the peasants had spontaneously redistributed the land among themselves, and the victorious Bolsheviks merely ratified their actions. In China after 1949, it was a more prolonged and difficult process. Hastily trained land reform teams were dispatched to the newly liberated areas, where they mobilized the poorer peasants in thousands of separate villages to confront and humiliate the landlords or the more wealthy peasants and seized their land, animals, tools, houses, and money for redistribution to the poorer members of the village. In the villages, the land reform teams encountered the age-old deference that peasants traditionally had rendered to their social superiors. One young woman activist described the confrontational meetings intended to break this ancient pattern:

> "Speak bitterness meetings," as they were called, would help [the peasants] to understand how things really had been in the old days, to realize that their lives were not blindly ordained by fate, that poor peasants had a community of interests, having suffered similar disasters and misery in the past—and that far from owing anything to the feudal landlords, it was the feudal landlords who owed them a debt of suffering beyond all reckoning.[3]

It was, as Mao Zedong put it, "not a dinner party." Approximately 1 to 2 million landlords were killed in the process, which was largely over by 1952.

A second and more distinctly socialist stage of rural reform sought to end private property in land by collectivizing agriculture. In China, despite brief resistance from richer peasants, collectivization during the 1950s was a generally peaceful process, owing much to the close relationship between the Chinese Communist Party and the peasantry, which had been established during three decades of struggle. This contrasted markedly with the experience of the Soviet Union from 1928 to 1933, when peasants were forced into collective farms and violence was extensive. Russian peasants slaughtered and consumed hundreds of thousands of animals rather than surrender them to the collectives. Stalin singled out the richer peasants, known as *kulaks*, for exclusion from the new collective farms. Some were killed, and many others were deported to remote areas of the country. With little support or experience in the countryside, Soviet communists, who came mostly from the cities, were viewed as intrusive outsiders in Russian peasant villages. A terrible famine ensued, with some 5 million deaths from starvation or malnutrition. (See Document 22.2, pp. 1062–64, for a firsthand account of the collectivization process.)

China pushed collectivization even further than the Soviet Union did, particularly in huge "people's communes" during the Great Leap Forward in the late 1950s. It was an effort to mobilize China's enormous population for rapid development and at the same time to move toward a more fully communist society with an even greater degree of social equality and collective living. (See Visual Source 22.2, p. 1073, for more on communes.) Administrative chaos, disruption of marketing networks, and bad weather combined to produce a massive famine that killed an amazing 20 million people or more between 1959 and 1962, dwarfing even the earlier Soviet famine.

Communism and Industrial Development

Both the Soviet Union and China defined industrialization as a fundamental task of their regimes. That process was necessary to end humiliating backwardness and poverty, to provide the economic basis for socialism, and to create the military strength that would enable their revolutions to survive in a hostile world. Though strongly anticapitalist, communists everywhere were ardent modernizers.

■ **Change**
What were the achievements of communist efforts at industrialization? What problems did these achievements generate?

When the Chinese communists began their active industrialization efforts in the early 1950s, they largely followed the model pioneered by the Soviet Union in the late 1920s and the 1930s. That model involved state ownership of property, centralized planning embodied in successive five-year plans, priority to heavy industry, massive mobilization of the nation's human and material resources, and intrusive Communist Party control of the entire process. (See Document 22.1, pp. 1060–62, and Document 22.3, pp. 1064–67, for more on Soviet industrialization.) Both countries experienced major—indeed unprecedented—economic growth. The Soviet Union constructed the foundations of an industrial society in the 1930s that proved itself in the victory over Nazi Germany in World War II and which by the 1960s and 1970s generated substantially improved standards of living. China too quickly expanded its output (see the Snapshot on p. 1042). In addition, both countries achieved massive improvements in their literacy rates and educational opportunities, allowing far greater social mobility for millions of people than ever before. In both countries, industrialization fostered a similar set of social outcomes: rapid urbanization, exploitation of the countryside to provide resources for modern industry in the cities, and

Snapshot   **China under Mao, 1949–1976**

The following table reveals some of the achievements, limitations, and tragedies of China's communist experience during the era of Mao Zedong.[4]

Steel production	from 1.3 million to 23 million tons
Coal production	from 66 million to 448 million tons
Electric power generation	from 7 million to 133 billion kilowatt-hours
Fertilizer production	from 0.2 million to 28 million tons
Cement production	from 3 million to 49 million tons
Industrial workers	from 3 million to 50 million
Scientists and technicians	from 50,000 to 5 million
"Barefoot doctors" posted to countryside	1 million
Annual growth rate of industrial output	11 percent
Annual growth rate of agricultural output	2.3 percent
Total population	from 542 million to 1 billion
Average population growth rate per year	2 percent
Per capita consumption of rural dwellers	from 62 to 124 yuan annually
Per capita consumption of urban dwellers	from 148 to 324 yuan
Overall life expectancy	from 35 to 65 years
Counterrevolutionaries killed (1949–1952)	between 1 million and 3 million
People labeled "rightists" in 1957	550,000
Deaths from famine during Great Leap Forward	20 million or more
Deaths during Cultural Revolution	500,000
Officials sent down to rural labor camps during Cultural Revolution	3 million or more
Urban youth sent down to countryside (1967–1976)	17 million

the growth of a privileged bureaucratic and technological elite intent on pursuing their own careers and passing on their new status to their children.

Perhaps the chief difference in the industrial histories of the Soviet Union and China lies in the leadership's response to these social outcomes. In the Soviet Union under Stalin and his successors, they were largely accepted. Industrialization was centered in large urban areas, which pulled from the countryside the most ambitious and talented people. A highly privileged group of state and party leaders emerged in the

Stalin era and largely remained the unchallenged ruling class of the country until the 1980s. Even in the 1930s, the outlines of a conservative society, which had discarded much of its revolutionary legacy, were apparent. Stalin himself endorsed Russian patriotism, traditional family values, individual competition, and substantial differences in wages to stimulate production, even as an earlier commitment to egalitarianism was substantially abandoned. Increasingly the invocation of revolutionary values was devoid of real content, and by the 1970s the perception of official hypocrisy was widespread.

The unique feature of Chinese history under Mao Zedong's leadership was a recurrent effort to combat these perhaps inevitable tendencies of any industrializing process and to revive and preserve the revolutionary spirit, which had animated the Communist Party during its long struggle for power. By the mid-1950s, Mao and some of his followers had become persuaded that the Soviet model of industrialization was leading China away from socialism and toward new forms of inequality, toward individualistic and careerist values, and toward an urban bias that privileged the cities at the expense of the countryside. The Great Leap Forward of 1958–1960 marked Mao's first response to these distortions of Chinese socialism. It promoted small-scale industrialization in the rural areas rather than focusing wholly on large enterprises in the cities; it tried to foster widespread and practical technological education for all rather than relying on a small elite of highly trained technical experts; and it envisaged an immediate transition to full communism in the "people's communes" rather than waiting for industrial development to provide the material basis for that transition. The disruptions and resentments occasioned by this Great Leap Forward, coupled with a series of droughts, floods, and typhoons, threw China into a severe crisis, including a massive famine that brought death and malnutrition to some 20 million people between 1959 and 1962.

In the mid-1960s, Mao launched yet another campaign—the Great Proletarian Cultural Revolution—to combat the capitalist tendencies that he believed had penetrated even the highest ranks of the Communist Party itself. The Cultural Revolution also involved new policies to bring health care and education to the countryside and to reinvigorate earlier efforts at rural industrialization under local rather than central control. In these ways, Mao struggled, though without great success, to

Substituting Manpower for Machinery
Lacking sophisticated equipment, Chinese communist leaders pursued a labor-intensive form of development, mobilizing the country's huge population in constructing the economic infrastructure for its industrial development. Here thousands of workers using ancient techniques participate in the building of a modern dam during China's Great Leap Forward in 1958. (Henry Cartier-Bresson/Magnum Photos)

overcome the inequalities associated with China's modern development and to create a model of socialist modernity quite distinct from that of the Soviet Union.

The Search for Enemies

■ **Explanation**

Why did communist regimes generate terror and violence on such a massive scale?

Despite their totalitarian tendencies, the communist societies of the Soviet Union and China were laced with conflict. Under both Stalin and Mao, those conflicts erupted in a search for enemies that disfigured both societies. An elastic concept of "enemy" came to include not only surviving remnants from the prerevolutionary elites but also, and more surprisingly, high-ranking members and longtime supporters of the Communist Party who allegedly had been corrupted by bourgeois ideas. Refracted through the lens of Marxist thinking, these people became class enemies who had betrayed the revolution and were engaged in a vast conspiracy, often linked to foreign imperialists, to subvert the socialist enterprise and restore capitalism. In the rhetoric of the leadership, the class struggle continued and in fact intensified as the triumph of socialism drew closer.

In the Soviet Union, that process culminated in the Terror, or the Great Purges, of the late 1930s, which enveloped tens of thousands of prominent communists, including virtually all of Lenin's top associates, and millions of more ordinary people. (See Document 22.4, pp. 1067–69, for personal experiences of the Terror.) Based on suspicious associations in the past, denunciations by colleagues, connections to foreign countries, or simply bad luck, such people were arrested, usually in the dead of night, and then tried and sentenced either to death or to long years in harsh and remote labor camps known as the gulag. Many of the accused were linked, almost always falsely, to the Nazis, who were then a real and growing external threat to the Soviet Union. A series of show trials publicized the menace that these "enemies of the people" allegedly posed to the country and its revolution. Close to 1 million people were executed between 1936 and 1941. Perhaps an additional 4 or 5 million were sent to the gulag, where they were forced to work in horrendous conditions and died in appalling numbers. Victimizers too were numerous: the Terror consumed the energies of a huge corps of officials, investigators, interrogators, informers, guards, and executioners, many of whom themselves were arrested, exiled, or executed in the course of the purges.

In the Soviet Union, the search for enemies occurred under the clear control of the state. In China, however, it became a much more public process, escaping the control of the leadership, particularly during the Cultural Revolution of 1966–1969. Mao had become convinced that many within the Communist Party had been seduced by capitalist values of self-seeking and materialism and were no longer animated by the idealistic revolutionary vision of earlier times. Therefore, he called for rebellion, against the Communist Party itself. Millions of young people responded, and, organized as Red Guards, they set out to rid China of those who were "taking the capitalist road." Following gigantic and ecstatic rallies in Beijing, they fanned out across the country and attacked local party and government officials, teachers, intellectuals, factory managers, and others they defined as enemies. (See Visual Sources 22.1 and 22.4, pp. 1072 and 1077). Rival revolutionary groups soon began fighting with one another, violence erupted throughout the country, and civil war threatened China. Mao found himself forced to call in the military to restore order and Communist Party control. Both the Soviet Terror and the Chinese Cultural Revolution badly discredited the very idea of socialism and contributed to the ultimate collapse of the communist experiment at the end of the century.

East versus West: A Global Divide and a Cold War

Not only did communist regimes bring revolutionary changes to the societies they governed, but they also launched a global conflict that restructured international life and touched the lives of almost everyone, particularly in the twentieth century's second half. That rift began soon after the Russian Revolution when the new communist government became the source of fear and loathing to many in the Western capitalist world. The common threat of Nazi Germany temporarily made unlikely allies of the Soviet Union, Britain, and the United States, but a few years after World War II ended, that division erupted again in what became known as the cold war. Underlying that conflict were the geopolitical and ideological realities of the postwar world. The Soviet Union and the United States were now the major political/military powers, replacing the shattered and diminished states of Western Europe, but they represented sharply opposed views of history, society, politics, and international relations. Conflict, in retrospect, seemed almost inevitable.

Military Conflict and the Cold War

The initial arena of the cold war was Europe, where Soviet insistence on security and control in Eastern Europe clashed with American and British desires for open and democratic societies with ties to the capitalist world economy. What resulted were rival military alliances (NATO and the Warsaw Pact), a largely voluntary American sphere of influence in Western Europe, and an imposed Soviet sphere in Eastern Europe. The heavily fortified border between Eastern and Western Europe came to be known as the Iron Curtain. Thus Europe was bitterly divided. But although tensions flared across this dividing line, particularly in Berlin, no shooting war occurred between the two sides (see Map 22.3).

■ **Connection**
In what different ways was the cold war expressed?

By contrast, the extension of communism into Asia—China, Korea, and Vietnam—globalized the cold war and led to its most destructive and prolonged "hot wars." A North Korean invasion of South Korea in 1950 led to both Chinese and American involvement in a bitter three-year war (1950–1953), which ended in an essential standoff that left the Korean peninsula still divided in the early twenty-first century. Likewise in Vietnam, military efforts by South Vietnamese communists and the already communist North Vietnamese government to unify their country prompted massive American intervention in the 1960s, peaking at some 550,000 U.S. troops. To American authorities, a communist victory opened the door to further communist expansion in Asia and beyond. Armed and supported by the Soviets and Chinese and willing to endure enormous losses, the Vietnamese communists bested

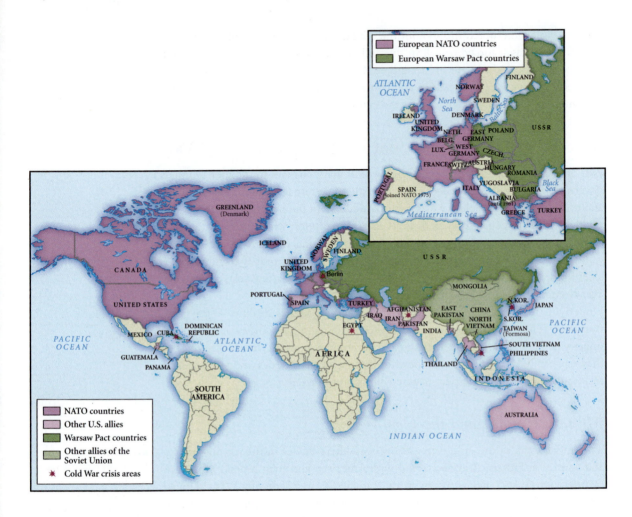

Map 22.3   The Global Cold War

The cold war sharply divided the world as a whole as well the continent of Europe; the countries of Korea, Vietnam, and Germany; and the city of Berlin. In many places, it also sparked crises that brought the nuclear-armed superpowers of the United States and the USSR to the brink of war, although in every case they managed to avoid direct military conflict between themselves.

the Americans, who were hobbled by growing protest at home. The Vietnamese united their country under communist control by 1975.

A third major military conflict of the cold war era occurred in Afghanistan, where a Marxist party had taken power in 1978. Soviet leaders were delighted at this extension of communism on their southern border, but radical land reforms and efforts to liberate Afghan women soon alienated much of this conservative Muslim country and led to a mounting opposition movement. Fearing the overthrow of a new communist state and its replacement by Islamic radicals, Soviet forces intervened militarily and were soon bogged down in a war they could not win. For a full decade (1979–1989), that war was a "bleeding wound," sustained in part by U.S. aid to Afghan guerrillas. Under widespread international pressure, Soviet forces finally withdrew in 1989, and the Afghan communist regime soon collapsed. In Vietnam and Afghanistan, both superpowers painfully experienced the limits of their power.

The most haunting battle of the cold war era was one that never happened. The setting was Cuba. When the revolutionary Fidel Castro came to power in 1959, his nationalization of American assets provoked great U.S. hostility and efforts to overthrow his regime. Such pressure only pushed this revolutionary nationalist closer to the Soviet Union, and gradually he began to think of himself and his revolution as Marxist. Soviet authorities were elated. "You Americans must realize what Cuba means to us old Bolsheviks," declared one high-ranking Soviet official. "We have been waiting all our lives for a country to go communist without the Red Army. It has happened in Cuba, and it makes us feel like boys again."[5] Fearing the loss of their newfound Caribbean ally to American aggression, the Soviet leader Nikita Khrushchev, who had risen to power after Stalin's death in 1953, secretly deployed nuclear-tipped Soviet missiles to Cuba, believing that this would deter further U.S. action against Castro. When the missiles were discovered in October 1962, the world held its breath for thirteen days as American forces blockaded the island and prepared for an invasion. A nuclear exchange between the superpowers seemed imminent, but that catastrophe was averted by a compromise between Khrushchev and U.S. president John F. Kennedy. Under its terms, the Soviets removed their missiles from Cuba in return for an American promise not to invade the island.

Nuclear Standoff and Third World Rivalry

The Cuban missile crisis gave concrete expression to the most novel and dangerous dimension of the cold war—the arms race in nuclear weapons. An American monopoly on those weapons when World War II ended prompted the Soviet Union to redouble its efforts to acquire them, and in 1949 it succeeded. Over the next forty years, the world moved from a mere handful of nuclear weapons to a global arsenal of close to 60,000 warheads. Delivery systems included bomber aircraft and missiles that could rapidly propel numerous warheads across whole continents and oceans with accuracies measured in hundreds of feet. During those decades, the world's many peoples lived in the shadow of weapons whose destructive power is scarcely within the bounds of human imagination. A single bomb in a single instant could have obliterated any major city in the world. The detonation of even a small fraction of the weapons then in the arsenals of the Soviet Union and the United States could have reduced the target countries to radioactive rubble and social chaos. Responsible scientists seriously discussed the possible extinction of the human species under such conditions.

Awareness of this possibility is surely the primary reason that no shooting war of any kind occurred between the two superpowers. During the two world wars, the participants had been greatly surprised by the destructiveness of modern

The Hydrogen Bomb
During the 1950s and early 1960s, tests in the atmosphere of ever larger and more sophisticated hydrogen bombs made images of enormous fireballs and mushroom-shaped clouds the universal symbol of these weapons, which were immensely more powerful than the atomic bombs dropped on Japan. The American test pictured here took place in 1957. (Image courtesy The Nuclear Weapon Archive)

weapons. During the cold war, however, the leaders of the two superpowers knew beyond any doubt that a nuclear war would produce only losers and utter catastrophe. Already in 1949, Stalin had observed that "atomic weapons can hardly be used without spelling the end of the world."[6] Furthermore, the deployment of reconnaissance satellites made it possible to know with some clarity the extent of the other side's arsenals. Particularly after the frightening Cuban missile crisis of 1962, both sides carefully avoided further nuclear provocation, even while continuing the buildup of their respective arsenals. Moreover, because they feared that a conventional war would escalate to the nuclear level, they implicitly agreed to sidestep any direct military confrontation at all.

Still, opportunities for conflict abounded as the U.S.-Soviet rivalry spanned the globe. Using military and economic aid, educational opportunities, political pressure, and covert action, both sides courted countries just emerging from colonial rule. (These became known as "third-world" countries—distinct from the "first world" of the developed West and the "second world" of communist countries.) Cold war fears of communist penetration prompted U.S. intervention, sometimes openly and often secretly, in Iran, the Philippines, Guatemala, El Salvador, Chile, the Congo, and elsewhere. In the process the United States frequently supported anticommunist but corrupt and authoritarian regimes. However, neither superpower was able to completely dominate its supposed third-world allies, many of whom resisted the role of pawns in superpower rivalries. Some countries, such as India, took a posture of nonalignment in the cold war, while others tried to play off the superpowers against each other. Indonesia received large amounts of Soviet and Eastern European aid, but that did not prevent it from destroying the Indonesian Communist Party in 1965, butchering half a million suspected communists in the process. When the Americans refused to assist Egypt in building the Aswan Dam in the mid-1950s, that country developed a close relationship with the Soviet Union. Later, in 1972, Egypt expelled 21,000 Soviet advisers and again aligned more clearly with the United States.

The United States: Superpower of the West, 1945–1975

■ Connection

In what ways did the United States play a global role after World War II?

World War II and the cold war provided the context for the emergence of the United States as a global superpower, playing a role that has often been compared to that of Great Britain in the nineteenth century. Much of that effort was driven by the perceived demands of the cold war, during which the United States spearheaded the Western effort to contain a worldwide communist movement that seemed to be advancing. A series of global alliances and military bases sought to create a barrier against further communist expansion and to provide launching pads for military action should it become necessary. By 1970, one writer observed, "the United States had more than 1,000,000 soldiers in 30 countries, was a member of four regional defense alliances and an active participant in a fifth, had mutual defense treaties with 42 nations, was a member of 53 international organizations, and was furnishing military or economic aid to nearly 100 nations across the face of the globe."[7]

The need for quick and often secret decision making gave rise in the United States to a strong or "imperial" presidency and a "national security state," in which defense and intelligence agencies acquired great power within the government and were often unaccountable to Congress. With power so focused in the executive branch, critics charged that democracy itself was undermined. Fear of internal sub-version produced an intense anticommunism in the 1950s and in general narrowed the range of political debate in the country as both parties competed to appear tough on communism. All of this served to strengthen the influence of what U.S. president Dwight Eisenhower (1953–1961) called the "military-industrial complex," a coalition of the armed services, military research laboratories, and private defense industries that both stimulated and benefited from increased military spending and cold war tensions.

Sustaining this immense military effort was a flourishing U.S. economy and an increasingly middle-class society. The United States, of course, was the only major industrial society to escape the physical devastation of war on its own soil. As World War II ended with Europe, the Soviet Union, and Japan in ruins, the United States was clearly the world's most productive economy. "The whole world is hungry for American goods," wrote one American economist in 1945. "Everyone would like to have the opportunity of riding in American automobiles, of drinking American fruit juices, and of possessing electric refrigerators and other conveniences of life."[8] Americans were a "people of plenty," ready and willing "to show to other countries the path that may lead them to plenty like our own."[9] Beyond their goods, Amer-icans sent their capital abroad in growing amounts—from $19 billion in 1950 to $81 billion in 1965. Huge American firms such as General Motors, Ford, Mobil, Sears, General Electric, and Westinghouse established factories, offices, and subsidi-aries in many countries and sold their goods locally. The U.S. dollar replaced the British pound as the most trusted international currency.

Accompanying the United States' political and economic penetration of the world was its popular culture. In musical terms, first jazz, then rock-and-roll, and most recently rap have found receptive audiences abroad, particularly among the young. Blacks in South Africa took up American "Negro spirituals." In the Soviet Union, American rock-and-roll became the music of dissent and a way of challenging the values of communist culture. Muslim immigrants to France as well as young Japanese have developed local traditions of rap. By the 1990s, American movies took about 70 percent of the market in Europe, and some 20,000 McDonald's restaurants in 100 countries served 30 million customers every day. Various American brand names—Kleenex, Coca-Cola, Jeep, Spam, Nike, Kodak—became common points of reference around the world. English became a global language, while American slang terms—"groovy," "crazy," "cool"—were integrated into many of the world's languages.

The Communist World, 1950s–1970s

On the communist side, the cold war was accompanied by considerable turmoil both within and among the various communist states. Joseph Stalin, Soviet dictator and

■ **Description**
What were the strengths and weaknesses of the communist world by the 1970s?

acknowledged leader of the communist world in general, died in 1953 as that global conflict was mounting. His successor, Nikita Khrushchev, stunned his country and communists everywhere with a lengthy speech delivered to a party congress in 1956 in which he presented a devastating account of Stalin's crimes, particularly those against party members. "Everywhere and in everything, he [Stalin] saw 'enemies,' 'two-facers,' and 'spies,'" declared Khrushchev. "Possessing unlimited power, he indulged in great willfulness and choked a person morally and physically."[10] These revelations shocked many of the party faithful, for Stalin had been viewed as the "genius of all time." Now he was presented as a criminal.

In the Soviet Union, the superpower of the communist world, the cold war justified a continuing emphasis on military and defense industries after World War II and gave rise to a Soviet version of the military-industrial complex. Sometimes called a "metal-eater's alliance," this complex joined the armed forces with certain heavy industries to press for a weapons buildup that benefited both. Soviet citizens, even more than Americans, were subject to incessant government propaganda that glorified the Soviet system and vilified that of their American opponents.

As the communist world expanded, so too did divisions and conflicts among its various countries. Many in the West had initially viewed world communism as a monolithic force whose disciplined members meekly followed Soviet dictates in cold war solidarity against the West. And Marxists everywhere contended that revolutionary socialism would erode national loyalties as the "workers of the world" united in common opposition to global capitalism. Nonetheless, the communist world experienced far more bitter and divisive conflict than did the Western alliance, which was composed of supposedly warlike, greedy, and highly competitive nations.

In Eastern Europe, Yugoslav leaders early on had rejected Soviet domination of their internal affairs and charted their own independent road to socialism. Fearing that reform might lead to contagious defections from the communist bloc, Soviet forces actually invaded their supposed allies in Hungary (1956–1957) and Czechoslovakia (1968) to crush such movements. In the early 1980s, Poland was seriously threatened with a similar action. The brutal suppression of these reform movements gave credibility to Western perceptions of the cold war as a struggle between tyranny and freedom and badly tarnished the image of Soviet communism as a reasonable alternative to capitalism.

Even more startling, the two communist giants, the Soviet Union and China, found themselves sharply opposed, owing to territorial disputes, ideological dif-

Czechoslovakia, 1968
In August 1968, Soviet forces invaded Czechoslovakia, where a popular reform movement proclaiming "socialism with a human face" threatened to erode established communist control. The Soviet troops that crushed this so-called Prague Spring were greeted by thousands of peaceful street demonstrators begging them to go home. (Bettmann/Corbis)

ferences, and rivalry for communist leadership. The Chinese bitterly criticized Khrushchev for backing down in the Cuban missile crisis, while to the Soviet leadership, Mao was insanely indifferent to the possible consequences of a nuclear war. In 1960, the Soviet Union backed away from an earlier promise to provide China with the prototype of an atomic bomb and abruptly withdrew all Soviet advisers and technicians, who had been assisting Chinese development. By the late 1960s, China on its own had developed a modest nuclear capability, and the two countries were at the brink of war, with the Soviet Union hinting at a possible nuclear strike on Chinese military targets. Their enmity certainly benefited the United States, which in the 1970s was able to pursue a "triangular diplomacy," easing tensions and simultaneously signing arms control agreements with the USSR and opening a formal relationship with China. Beyond this central conflict, a communist China in fact went to war against a communist Vietnam in 1979, while Vietnam invaded a communist Cambodia in the late 1970s. Nationalism, in short, proved more powerful than communist solidarity, even in the face of cold war hostilities with the West.

Despite its many internal conflicts, world communism remained a powerful global presence during the 1970s, achieving its greatest territorial reach. China was emerging from the chaos of the Cultural Revolution. The Soviet Union had matched U.S. military might; in response, the Americans launched a major buildup of their own military forces in the early 1980s. Despite American hostility, Cuba remained a communist outpost in the Western Hemisphere, with impressive achievements in education and health care for its people. Communism triumphed in Vietnam, dealing a major setback to the United States. A number of African countries affirmed their commitment to Marxism. Few people anywhere expected that within two decades most of the twentieth century's experiment with communism would be gone.

Comparing Paths to the End of Communism

More rapidly than its beginning, and far more peacefully, the communist era came to an end during the last two decades of the twentieth century. It was a drama in three acts. Act One began in China during the late 1970s, following the death of its towering revolutionary leader Mao Zedong in 1976. Over the next several decades, the CCP gradually abandoned almost everything that had been associated with Maoist communism, even as the party retained its political control of the country. Act Two took place in Eastern Europe in the "miracle year" of 1989, when popular movements toppled despised communist governments one after another all across the region. The climactic act in this "end of communism" drama occurred in 1991 in the Soviet Union, where the entire "play" had opened seventy-four years earlier. There the reformist leader Mikhail Gorbachev had come to power in 1985 intending to revive and save Soviet socialism from its accumulated dysfunctions. Those efforts, however, only exacerbated the country's many difficulties and led to the political disintegration of the Soviet Union on Christmas Day of 1991. The curtain had fallen on the communist era and on the cold war as well.

■ Change
What explains the rapid end of the communist era?

Behind these separate stories lay two general failures of the communist exper-iment, measured both by their own standards and by those of the larger world. The first was economic. Despite their early successes, communist economies by the late 1970s showed no signs of catching up to the more advanced capitalist countries. The highly regimented Soviet economy in particular was largely stagnant; its citizens were forced to stand in long lines for consumer goods and complained endlessly about their poor quality and declining availability. This was enormously embarrassing, for it had been the proud boast of communist leaders everywhere that they had found a better route to modern prosperity than their capitalist rivals. Furthermore, these com-parisons were increasingly well known, thanks to the global information revolution. They had security implications as well, for economic growth, even more than military capacity, was the measure of state power as the twentieth century approached its end.

The second failure was moral. The horrors of Stalin's Terror and the gulag, of Mao's Cultural Revolution, of something approaching genocide in communist Cambodia—all of this wore away at communist claims to moral superiority over capitalism. More-over, this erosion occurred as global political culture more widely embraced democracy and human rights as the universal legacy of humankind, rather than the exclusive pos-session of the capitalist West. In both economic and moral terms, the communist path to the modern world was increasingly seen as a road to nowhere.

Communist leaders were not ignorant of these problems, and particularly in China and the Soviet Union, they moved aggressively to address them. But their approach to doing so varied greatly, as did the outcomes of those efforts. Thus, much as the Russian and Chinese revolutions differed and their approaches to building socialism diverged, so too did these communist giants chart distinct paths during the final years of the communist experiment.

China: Abandoning Communism and Maintaining the Party

As the dust settled from the political shakeout following Mao's death in 1976, Deng Xiaoping emerged as China's "paramount leader," committed to ending the periodic upheavals of the Maoist era while fostering political stability and economic growth. Soon previously banned plays, operas, films, and translations of Western classics reap-peared, and a "literature of the wounded" exposed the sufferings of the Cultural Rev-olution. Some 100,000 political prisoners, many of them high-ranking communists, were released and restored to important positions. A party evaluation of Mao severely criticized his mistakes during the Great Leap Forward and the Cultural Revolution, while praising his role as a revolutionary leader.

Even more dramatic were Deng's economic reforms. In the rural areas, these reforms included a rapid dismantling of the country's system of collectivized farm-ing and a return to something close to small-scale private agriculture. Impoverished Chinese peasants eagerly embraced these new opportunities and pushed them even further than the government had intended. Industrial reform proceeded more gradually. Managers of state enterprises were given greater authority and encouraged to act like private owners, making many of their own decisions and seeking profits. China opened itself to the world economy and welcomed foreign investment in special enterprise zones along the coast, where foreign capitalists received tax breaks and other inducements. Local governments and private entrepreneurs joined forces in thousands of flourishing "township and village enterprises" that produced food, clothing, building materials, and much more.

The outcome of these reforms was stunning economic growth, the most rapid and sustained in world history, and a new prosperity for millions. Better diets, lower mortality rates, declining poverty, massive urban construction, and surging exports accompanied China's rejoining of the world economy, contributed to a much-improved material life for many of its citizens, and prompted much commentary about China as the economic giant of the twenty-first century. On the other hand, the country's burgeoning economy also generated massive corruption among Chinese officials, sharp inequalities between the coast and the interior, a huge problem of urban overcrowding, terrible pollution in major cities, and periodic inflation as the state loosened its controls over the economy. Urban vices such as street crime, prostitution, gambling, drug addiction, and a criminal underworld, which had been largely eliminated after 1949, surfaced again in China's booming cities. Nonetheless, something remarkable had occurred in China: an essentially capitalist economy had been restored, and by none other than the Communist Party itself. Mao's worst fears had been realized, as China "took the capitalist road." (See Visual Source 22.5, p. 1078, and Visual Source 24.2, p. 1183.)

Although the party was willing to largely abandon communist economic policies, it was adamantly unwilling to relinquish its political monopoly or to promote democracy at the national level. "Talk about democracy in the abstract," Deng Xiaoping declared, "will inevitably lead to the unchecked spread of ultra-democracy and anarchism, to the complete disruption of political stability, and to the total failure of our modernization program.... China will once again be plunged into chaos, division, retrogression, and darkness."[11] Such attitudes associated democracy with the chaos and uncontrolled mass action of the Cultural Revolution. Thus, when a democracy movement spearheaded by university and secondary school students surfaced in the late 1980s, Deng ordered the brutal crushing of its brazen demonstration in Beijing's Tiananmen Square before the television cameras of the world.

After Communism in China Although the Communist Party still governed China in the early twenty-first century, communist values of selflessness, community, and simplicity had been substantially replaced for many by Western-style consumerism. Here a group of young people in Shanghai are eating at a Kentucky Fried Chicken restaurant, drinking Pepsi, wearing clothing common to modern youth everywhere, and using their ubiquitous cell phones. (Mike Kemp/Corbis)

China entered the new millennium as a rapidly growing economic power with an essentially capitalist economy presided over by an intact and powerful Communist Party. Culturally, some combination of nationalism, consumerism, and a renewed respect for ancient traditions had replaced the collectivist and socialist values of the Maoist era. It was a strange and troubled hybrid.

The Soviet Union: The Collapse of Communism and Country

■ **Comparison**

How did the end of communism in the Soviet Union differ from communism's demise in China?

By the mid-1980s, the reformist wing of the Soviet Communist Party, long squelched by an aging conservative establishment, had won the top position in the party as Mikhail Gorbachev assumed the role of general secretary. Like Deng Xiaoping in China, Gorbachev was committed to aggressively tackling the country's many problems—economic stagnation, a flourishing black market, public apathy, and cynicism about the party. His economic program, launched in 1987 and known as *perestroika* (restructuring), paralleled aspects of the Chinese approach by freeing state enterprises from the heavy hand of government regulation, permitting small-scale private businesses called cooperatives, offering opportunities for private farming, and cautiously welcoming foreign investment in joint enterprises.

Heavy resistance to these modest efforts from entrenched party and state bureaucracies persuaded Gorbachev to seek allies outside of official circles. The vehicle was *glasnost* (openness), a policy of permitting a much wider range of cultural and intellectual freedoms in Soviet life. He hoped that glasnost would overcome the pervasive, long-standing distrust between society and the state and would energize Soviet society for the tasks of economic reform. "We need *glasnost*," Gorbachev declared, "like we need the air."[12]

In the late 1980s, glasnost hit the Soviet Union like a bomb. Newspapers and TV exposed social pathologies—crime, prostitution, child abuse, suicide, corruption, and homelessness—that previously had been presented solely as the product of capitalism. Films broke the ban on nudity and explicit sex. TV reporters climbed the wall of a secluded villa to film the luxurious homes of the party elite. Soviet history was also reexamined as revelations of Stalin's crimes poured out of the media. The Bible and the Quran became more widely available, atheistic propaganda largely ceased, and thousands of churches and mosques were returned to believers and opened for worship. Plays, poems, films, and novels that had long been buried "in the drawer" were now released to a public that virtually devoured them. "Like an excited boy reads a note from his girl," wrote one poet, "that's how we read the papers today."[13]

Beyond glasnost lay democratization and a new parliament with real powers, chosen in competitive elections. When those elections occurred in 1989, dozens of leading communists were rejected at the polls. And when the new parliament met and actually debated controversial issues, its televised sessions were broadcast to a transfixed audience of 100 million or more. In foreign affairs, Gorbachev moved to end the cold war by making unilateral cuts in Soviet military forces, engaging in arms control negotiations with the United States, and refusing to intervene as communist governments in Eastern Europe were overthrown. Thus the Soviet reform program was far more broadly based than that of China, for it embraced dramatic cultural and political changes, which Chinese authorities refused to consider.

Despite his good intentions, almost nothing worked out as Gorbachev had antic-ipated. Far from strengthening socialism and reviving a stagnant Soviet Union, the reforms led to its further weakening and collapse. In a dramatic contrast with China's booming economy, that of the Soviet Union spun into a sharp decline as its planned economy was dismantled before a functioning market-based system could emerge. Inflation mounted; consumer goods were in short supply, and ration coupons reap-peared; many feared the loss of their jobs. Unlike Chinese peasants, few Soviet farm-ers were willing to risk the jump into private farming, and few foreign investors found the Soviet Union a tempting place to do business.

Furthermore, the new freedoms provoked demands that went far beyond what Gorbachev had intended. A democracy movement of unofficial groups and parties now sprang to life, many of them seeking a full multiparty democracy and a market-based economy. They were joined by independent labor unions, which actually went on strike, something unheard of in the "workers' state." Most corrosively, a multitude of nationalist movements used the new freedoms to insist on greater autonomy, or even independence, from the Soviet Union. In the Baltic republics of Latvia, Lithuania, and Estonia, nationalists organized a human chain some 370 miles long, sending the word "freedom" along the line of a million people. Even in Russia, growing num-bers came to feel that they too might be better off without the Soviet Union. In the face of these mounting demands, Gorbachev resolutely refused to use force to crush the protesters, another sharp contrast with the Chinese experience.

Events in Eastern Europe now intersected with those in the Soviet Union. Gorbachev's reforms had lit a fuse in these Soviet satellites, where communism had been imposed and maintained from outside. If the USSR could practice glasnost and hold competitive elections, why not Eastern Europe as well? This was the back-ground for the "miracle year" of 1989. Massive demonstrations, last-minute efforts at reforms, the breaching of the Berlin Wall, the surfacing of new political groups—all of this and more quickly overwhelmed the highly unpopular communist regimes of Poland, Hungary, East Germany, Bulgaria, Czechoslovakia, and Romania, which were quickly swept away. This success then emboldened nationalists and democrats in the Soviet Union. If communism had been overthrown in Eastern Europe, perhaps it could be overthrown in the USSR as well. Soviet conservatives and patriots, how-ever, were outraged. To them, Gorbachev had stood idly by while the political gains of World War II, for which the Soviet Union had paid in rivers of blood, vanished before their eyes. It was nothing less than treason.

A brief and unsuccessful attempt to restore the old order through a military coup in August 1991 triggered the end of the Soviet Union and its communist regime.

From the wreckage there emerged fifteen new and independent states, following the internal political divisions of the USSR (see Map 22.4). Within Russia itself, the Communist Party was actually banned for a time in the place of its origin.

The Soviet collapse represented a unique phenomenon in the world of the late twentieth century. Simultaneously, the world's largest state and its last territorial empire vanished; the first Communist Party disintegrated; a powerful command economy broke down; an official socialist ideology was repudiated; and a forty-five-year global struggle between the East and the West ended. In Europe, Germany was reunited, and a number of former communist states joined NATO and the European Union, ending the division of that continent. At least for the moment, capitalism and democracy seemed to triumph over socialism and authoritarian governments. In many places, the end of communism allowed simmering ethnic tensions to explode into open conflict. Beyond the disintegration of the Soviet Union, both Yugoslavia and Czechoslovakia fragmented, the former amid terrible violence and the latter peacefully. Chechens in Russia, Abkhazians in Georgia, Russians in the Baltic states and Ukraine, Tibetans and Uighurs in China—all of these minorities found themselves in opposition to the states in which they lived.

As the twenty-first century dawned, the communist world had shrunk considerably from its high point just three decades earlier. In the Soviet Union and East-

Map 22.4   The Collapse of the Soviet Empire
Soviet control over its Eastern European dependencies vanished as those countries threw off their communist governments in 1989. Then, in 1991, the Soviet Union itself disintegrated into fifteen separate states, none of them governed by communist parties.

ern Europe, communism had disappeared entirely as the governing authority and dominant ideology, although communist parties continued to play a role in some countries. China had largely abandoned its communist economic policies as a market economy took shape. Like China, Vietnam and Laos remained officially communist, even while they pursued Chinese-style reforms, though more cautiously. Even Cuba, which was beset by economic crisis in the 1990s after massive Soviet subsidies ended, allowed small businesses, private food markets, and tourism to grow, while harshly repressing opposition political groups. An impoverished North Korea remained the most unreformed and repressive of the remaining communist countries.

International tensions born of communism remained only in East Asia and the Caribbean. North Korea's threat to develop nuclear weapons posed a serious international issue. Continuing tension between China and Taiwan as well as between the United States and Cuba were hangovers from the cold war era. But either as a primary source of international conflict or as a compelling path to modernity and social justice, communism was effectively dead. The communist era in world history had ended.

Reflections: To Judge or Not to Judge

Should historians or students of history make moral judgments about the people and events they study? On the one hand, some would argue, scholars do well to act as detached and objective observers of the human experience, at least as much as possible. The task is to describe what happened and to explain why things turned out as they did. Whether we approve or condemn the outcomes of the historical process is, in this view, beside the point. On the other hand, all of us, scholars and students alike, stand somewhere. We are members of particular cultures; we have values and outlooks on the world that inevitably affect the way we write or think about the past. Perhaps it is better to recognize and acknowledge these limitations than to pretend some unattainable objectivity that places us above it all. Furthermore, making judgments is a way of connecting with the past, of affirming our continuing relationship with those who have gone before us. It shows that we care.

The question of making judgments arises strongly in any examination of the communist phenomenon. In a United States without a strong socialist tradition, sometimes saying anything positive about communism or even noting its appeal to millions of people has brought charges of whitewashing its crimes. Within the communist world, even modest criticism was usually regarded as counterrevolutionary and was largely forbidden and harshly punished. Certainly few observers were neutral in their assessment of the communist experiment.

Were the Russian and Chinese revolutions a blow for human freedom and a cry for justice on the part of oppressed people, or did they simply replace one tyranny with another? Was Stalinism a successful effort to industrialize a backward country or a ferocious assault on its moral and social fabric? Did Chinese reforms of the late twentieth century represent a return to sensible policies of modernization, a continued denial of basic democratic rights, or an opening to capitalist inequalities, corruption, and acquisitiveness? Passionate debate continues on all of these questions.

Communism, like many human projects, has been an ambiguous enterprise. On the one hand, communism brought hope to millions by addressing the manifest injustices of the past; by providing new opportunities for women, workers, and peasants; by promoting rapid industrial development; and by ending Western domination. On the other hand, communism was responsible for mountains of crimes—millions killed and wrongly imprisoned; massive famines partly caused by radical policies; human rights violated on an enormous scale; lives uprooted and distorted by efforts to achieve the impossible.

Studying communism challenges our inclination to want definitive answers and clear moral judgments. Can we hold contradictory elements in some kind of tension? Can we affirm our own values while acknowledging the ambiguities of life, both past and present? Doing so is arguably among the essential tasks of growing up and achieving a measure of intellectual maturity. That is the gift, both painful and enormously enriching, that the study of history offers to us all.

Second Thoughts

What's the Significance?

To assess your mastery of the material in this chapter, visit the **Student Center** at bedfordstmartins.com/strayer.

Russian Revolution (1917)	Stalin	Nikita Khrushchev
Bolsheviks/Lenin	Zhenotdel	Mikhail Gorbachev
Guomindang	collectivization	Deng Xiaoping
Chinese Revolution	Cultural Revolution	perestroika/glasnost
Mao Zedong	Great Purges/Terror	
building socialism	Cuban missile crisis	

Big Picture Questions

1. What was the appeal of communism, in terms of both its promise and its achievements? To what extent did it fulfill that promise?
2. Why did the communist experiment, which was committed to equality and a humane socialism, generate such oppressive, brutal, and totalitarian regimes?
3. What is distinctive about twentieth-century communist industrialization and modernization compared to the same processes in the West a century earlier?
4. What was the global significance of the cold war?
5. "The end of communism was as revolutionary as its beginning." Do you agree with this statement?
6. In what different ways did the Soviet Union and China experience communism during the twentieth century?

Next Steps: For Further Study

Archie Brown, *The Gorbachev Factor* (1996). A careful examination of Gorbachev's role in the collapse of the Soviet Union.

Jung Chang, *Wild Swans* (2004). A compelling view of twentieth-century Chinese history through the eyes of three generations of women in a single family.

Timothy Check, *Mao Zedong and China's Revolutions* (2002). A collection of documents about the Chinese Revolution and a fine introduction to the life of Mao.

John L. Gaddis, *The Cold War: A New History* (2005). An overview by one of the most highly regarded historians of the cold war.

Peter Kenez, *A History of the Soviet Union from the Beginning to the End* (1999). A thoughtful overview of the entire Soviet experience.

Maurice Meisner, *Mao's China and After* (1999). A provocative history of Mao's China and what followed.

Robert Strayer, *The Communist Experiment: Revolution, Socialism, and Global Conflict in the Twentieth Century* (2007). A comparative study of Soviet and Chinese communism.

"Mao Zedong Reference Archive," http://www.marxists.org/reference/archive/mao. A Web site offering the translated writings of Mao, including poetry and some images.

"Soviet Archives Exhibit," http://www.ibiblio.org/expo/soviet.exhibit/entrance.html. A rich Web site from the Library of Congress, focusing on the operation of the Soviet system and relations with the United States.

For Web sites and additional documents related to this chapter, see **Make History** at bedfordstmartins.com/strayer.

Documents

Considering the Evidence:
Experiencing Stalinism

For the Soviet Union, the formative period in establishing communism encompassed the years of Joseph Stalin's rule (1929–1953). Born in Georgia in 1878 rather than in Russia itself, the young Stalin grew up with a brutal and abusive father, trained for the priesthood as a young man, but slowly gravitated toward the emerging revolutionary movement of the time. He subsequently joined the Bolsheviks, led by Lenin, though he played only a modest role in the Russian Revolution of 1917. After Lenin's death in 1924, Stalin rose to the dominant position in the Communist Party amid a long and bitter struggle among the Bolsheviks. By 1929 he had consolidated his authority and exercised enormous personal power until his death in 1953.

To Stalin and the Soviet leadership, the 1930s was a time of "building socialism," that is, creating the modern, abundant, and just society that would replace an outdated, corrupt, and exploitative capitalism. Undertaking that gigantic task meant social upheaval on an enormous scale, offering undreamed-of opportunities for some and disruption and trauma beyond imagination for others. The documents that follow allow us to see something of the Stalinist vision for the country as well as to gain some insight into the lives of ordinary people—peasants, workers, women, ethnic minorities, the young, and the upwardly mobile—as they experienced what scholars have come to call simply "Stalinism."

Document 22.1

Stalin on Stalinism

In January 1933, Stalin appeared before a group of high-ranking party officials to give a report on the achievements of the country's first five-year plan for overall development. The years encompassed by that plan, roughly 1928–1932, coincided with Stalin's rise to the position of supreme leader within the governing Communist Party of the Soviet Union.

■ What larger goals for the country underlay Stalin's report? Why did he feel those goals had to be achieved so rapidly?

- To what indications of success did Stalin point? Which of these claims do you find most/least credible?

- What criticisms of Stalin's policies can you infer from the document?

- What do you think Stalin meant when he referred to the "world-wide historic significance" of the Soviet Union's achievement? Keep in mind what was happening in the capitalist world at the time.

JOSEPH STALIN

The Results of the First Five-Year Plan

1933

The fundamental task of the five-year plan was to convert the U.S.S.R. from an agrarian and weak country, dependent upon the caprices of the capitalist countries, into an industrial and powerful country, fully self-reliant and independent of the caprices of world capitalism, ... to completely oust the capitalist elements, to widen the front of socialist forms of economy, and to create the economic basis for the abolition of classes in the U.S.S.R., for the building of a socialist society....

The fundamental task of the five-year plan was to transfer small and scattered agriculture on to the lines of large-scale collective farming, so as to ensure the economic basis of socialism in the countryside....

[O]nly a modern large-scale industry...can serve as a real and reliable foundation for the Soviet regime....

Let us pass now to the results of the fulfillment of the five-year plan....

We did not have an iron and steel industry, the basis for the industrialization of the country. Now we have one.

[Stalin follows with a long list of new industries developed during the first five-year plan: tractors, automobiles, machine tools, chemicals, agricultural machinery, electric power, oil and coal, metals.]

And we have not only created these new great industries, but have created them on a scale and in dimensions that eclipse...European industry.

And as a result of all this the capitalist elements have been completely and irrevocably ousted from industry, and socialist industry has become the sole form of industry in the U.S.S.R....

Finally, as a result of all this the Soviet Union has been converted from a weak country, unprepared for defense, into a country mighty in defense..., a country capable of producing on a mass scale all modern means of defense and of equipping its army with them in the event of an attack from abroad.

We are told: This is all very well; many new factories have been built, and the foundations for industrialization have been laid; but it would have been far better...to produce more cotton fabrics, shoes, clothing, and other goods for mass consumption.... Then we would now have more cotton fabrics, shoes, and clothing. But we would not have a tractor industry or an automobile industry; we would not have anything like a big iron and steel industry; we would not have metal for the manufacture of machinery—and we would remain unarmed while encircled by capitalist countries armed with modern technique....

It was necessary to urge forward a country which was a hundred years behindhand and which was faced with mortal danger because of its backwardness....

The five-year plan in the sphere of agriculture was a five-year plan of collectivization.... [I]t was

Source: Joseph Stalin, "The Results of the First Five-Year Plan," *Pravda*, January 10, 1933.

necessary in addition to industrialization, to pass from small, individual peasant farming to...large collective farms, equipped with all the modern implements of highly developed agriculture, and to cover unoccupied land with model state farms....

The Party has succeeded in routing the kulaks° as a class, although they have not yet been dealt the final blow; the laboring peasants have been emancipated from kulak bondage and exploitation, and the Soviet regime has been given a firm economic basis in the countryside, the basis of collective farming.

In our country, the workers have long forgotten unemployment.... Look at the capitalist countries: what horrors result there from unemployment! There

---

°**kulaks:** relatively rich peasants.

are now no less than 30–40 million unemployed in those countries....

The same thing must be said of the peasants.... It has brought them into the collective farms and placed them in a secure position. It has thus eliminated the possibility of the differentiation of the peasantry into exploiters — kulaks — and exploited — poor peasants — and abolished destitution in the countryside.... Now the peasant is in a position of security, a member of a collective farm which has at its disposal tractors, agricultural machinery, seed funds, reserve funds....

[W]e have achieved such important successes as to evoke admiration among the working class all over the world; we have achieved a victory that is truly of world-wide historic significance.

Document 22.2

Living through Collectivization

For Russian peasants, and those of other nationalities as well, the chief experience of Stalinism was that of collectivization — the enforced bringing together of many small-scale family farms into much larger collective farms called *kolhozy*. Thus private ownership of land was largely ended, except for some small plots, which peasants could till individually. That process generally began with the arrival of outside "agitators" or Community Party officials who sought to persuade, or if necessary to force, the villagers to enter the *kolhoz*. They divided peasants (*muzhiks*) into class categories: rich peasants (*kulaks*) were to be excluded from the collective farms as incipient capitalists; poor (*bedniak*) and middle (*seredniak*) peasants were expected to join.

One witness to this process was Maurice Hindus, a Russian-born American writer who returned to his country of origin in 1929, when Soviet collectivization was beginning in earnest. There he roamed on foot around the countryside, recording conversations with those he met. The extract that follows begins with a letter he received from "Nadya," a young activist who was among many sent to the rural areas to encourage, or enforce, collectivization. Then Hindus records a discussion between peasants objecting to collectivization and an "agitator," like Nadya, seeking to convince them of its benefits.

■   How do Nadya and the agitator understand collectivization and their role in this process? Why do they believe that it was so critical to building socialism?

■ How do village peasants view collectivization? On what grounds do they object to it? How might they view the role of the agitators?

■ How did the peasants understand themselves and their village community? How did they respond to the communists' insistence on defining them in rigid class terms? Why do you think they finally entered the collective farms?

■ Why were Stalin and the Communist Party so insistent on destroying the *kulaks*?

MAURICE HINDUS

Red Bread

1931

Nadya Speaks

I am off in villages with a group of other brigadiers organizing *kolhozy*. It is a tremendous job, but we are making amazing progress. It would do you worlds of good to be with us and watch us draw the stubborn peasant into collectivization. Contrary to all your affirmations and prophecies, our *muzhik* is yielding to persuasion. He is joining the *kolhozy*, and I am confident that in time not a peasant will remain on his own land. We shall yet smash the last vestiges of capitalism and forever rid ourselves of exploitation. Come, join us; see with your own eyes what is happening, how we are rebuilding the Russian villages. The very air here is afire with a new spirit and a new energy.

Nadya

The Peasants Speak

"There was a time,"... began Lukyan, who had been a blacksmith,..."when we were just neighbors in this village. We quarreled, we fooled, sometimes we cheated one another. But we were neighbors. Now we are *bedniaks, seredniaks, koolacks*.° I am a *seredniak*,

°**koolacks:** variant spelling of "kulaks."

Source: Maurice Hindus, *Red Bread: Collectivization in a Russian Village* (Bloomington: Indiana University Press, 1988), 1, 22–34.

Boris here is a *bedniak*, and Nisko is a *koolack*, and we are supposed to have a class war—pull each other's hair or tickle each other on the toes, eh? One against the other, you understand?...

"But it is other things that worry us," continued the flat-faced *muzhik*..., "it is the *kolhoz*. That, citizen, is a serious matter—the most serious we have ever encountered. Who ever heard of such a thing—to give up our land and our cows and our horses and our tools and our farm buildings, to work all the time and divide everything with others? Nowadays members of the same family get in each other's way and quarrel and fight, and here we, strangers, are supposed to be like one family. Can we—dark, beastly *muzhiks*—make a go of it without scratching each other's faces, pulling each other's hair or hurling stones at one another?"...

"We won't even be sure," someone else continued the lament, "of having enough bread to eat. Now, however poor we may be, we have our own rye and our own potatoes and our own cucumbers and our own milk. We know we won't starve. But in the *kolhoz*, no more potatoes of our own, no more anything of our own. Everything will be rationed out by orders; we shall be like mere *batraks*° on the landlord's estates in the old days. Serfdom—that is what it is—and who wants to be a serf?"...

°**batraks:** hired help.

"Dark-minded beasts we may be," wailed another *muzhik*.…"We are not learned; we are not wise. But a little self-respect we have, and we like the feeling of independence. Today we feel like working, and we work; tomorrow we feel like lying down, and we lie down; the next day we feel like going to town, and we go to town. We do as we please. But in the *kolhoz*, brother, it is do-as-you-are-told, like a horse—go this way and that, and don't dare turn off the road or you get it hard, a stroke or two of the whip on bare flesh.…We'll just wither away on the socialist farm, like grass torn out by the roots.".…

The Communist Party Official Speaks

At this point a new visitor arrived, a tall youth, in boots, in a black blouse and with a shaved head.… A stranger in the village, he was the organizer of the *kolhoz*, therefore a person of stern importance.…

"Everything is possible, grandfather, if we all pool our resources and our powers together," replied the visitor.

More laughter and more derisive comment.…

"Tell me, you wretched people, what hope is there for you if you remain on individual pieces of land? Think, and don't interrupt.… From year to year as you increase in population you divide and subdivide your strips of land. You cannot even use machinery on your land because no machine man ever made could stand the rough ridges that the strip system creates. You will have to work in your own old way and stew in your old misery. Don't you see that under your present system there is nothing ahead of you but ruin and starvation?…You do not think of a future, of ten, twenty, a hundred years from now, and we do. That's the difference between you and us. The coming generations mean nothing to you. Else you would see a real deliverance in the *kolhoz*, where you will work with machinery in a modern organized way, with the best seeds obtainable and under the direction of experts.… Isn't it about time you stopped thinking each one for himself, for his own piggish hide? You *koolacks* of course will never become reconciled to a new order. You love to fatten on other people's blood. But we know how to deal with you. We'll wipe you off the face of the earth, even as we have the capitalists in the city. Make no mistake about our intentions and our powers. We shan't allow you to profit from the weakness of the *bedniak*. And we shan't allow you to poison his mind, either! Enough. But the others here—you *bedniaks* and you *seredniaks*—what have you gained from this stiff-necked individualism of yours? What? Look at yourselves, at your homes—mud, squalor, fleas, bedbugs, cockroaches, *lapti*.° Are you sorry to let these go? Oh, we know you *muzhiks*—too well.…You can whine eloquently and pitifully.… But we know you—you cannot fool us. We have grown hardened to your wails. Remember that. Cry all you want to, curse all you want to. You won't hurt us, and I warn you that we shan't desist. We shall continue our campaign for the *kolhozy* until we have won our goal and made you free citizens in a free land."

————————————
°**lapti:** cheap wooden shoes.

Document 22.3

Living through Industrialization

A second major feature of the Stalinist era was rapid state-controlled industrialization. "We are fifty to a hundred years behind the advanced countries," declared Stalin. "We must make good this distance in ten years. Either we shall do it or we shall go under." During the 1930s, that enormous process brought huge numbers of peasants from the countryside to the cities, sent many of them to new and distant industrial sites such as Magnitogorsk—a huge new iron and steel enterprise—and thrust millions into recently established technical institutes where they learned new skills and nurtured new ambitions. The brief excerpts in Document 22.3 disclose the voices of some of these workers as they celebrated the new possibilities and lamented the disappointments and injustices of Stalinist industrialization. These sources come from letters written to newspapers or to high government officials, from private letters and diaries, or from reports filed by party officials based on what they had heard in the factories.

■ In what respects might Soviet workers have benefited from Stalinist industrialization?

■ What criticisms were voiced in these extracts? Do they represent fundamental opposition to the idea of socialism or disappointments in how it was implemented?

■ Which of these selections do you find most credible?

■ Through its control of education and the media, the Stalinist regime sought to instill a single view of the world in its citizens. Based on these selections, to what extent had they succeeded or failed?

Personal Accounts of Soviet Industrialization

1930s

Letter in a Newspaper from a Tatar Electrician

I am a Tatar.° Before October, in old tsarist Russia, we weren't even considered people. We couldn't even dream about education, or getting a job in a state enterprise. And now I'm a citizen of the USSR. Like all citizens, I have the right to a job, to education, to leisure. I can elect and be elected to the soviet [legislative council]. Is this not an indication of the supreme achievements of our country?...

Two years ago I worked as the chairman of a village soviet in the Tatar republic. I was the first

°**Tatar:** a Turkic ethnic group.

Source: First and second selections: Stephen Kotkin, *Magnetic Mountain* (Berkeley: University of California Press, 1995), 221–22, 349–50; third through seventh selections: Sarah Davies, *Popular Opinion in Stalin's Russia* (New York: Cambridge University Press, 1997), 39, 72, 134–35, 139, 173–74.

person there to enter the kolhoz and then I led the collectivization campaign. Collective farming is flourishing with each year in the Tatar republic.

In 1931 I came to Magnitogorsk. From a common laborer I have turned into a skilled worker. I was elected a member of the city soviet. As a deputy, every day I receive workers who have questions or need help. I listen to each one like to my own brother, and try to do what is necessary to make each one satisfied.

I live in a country where one feels like living and learning. And if the enemy should attack this country, I will sacrifice my life in order to destroy the enemy and save my country.

Newspaper Commentary by an Engineer, 1938

Soon it will be seven years that I'm working in Magnitogorsk [a huge new iron and steel enterprise]. With my own eyes I've seen the pulsating, creative life of the builders of the Magnitogorsk giant. I myself have taken an active part in this construction with great enthusiasm. Our joy was great when we obtained the first Magnitogorsk steel from the wonderful open-hearth ovens. At the time there was no greater happiness for me than working in the open-hearth shop.... Here I enriched my theoretical knowledge and picked up practical habits... of work. Here as well I grew politically, acquired good experience in public-political work. I came to Magnitogorsk nonparty. The party organization... accepted me into a group of sympathizers. Not long ago I entered the ranks of the Leninist-Stalinist [communist] party.... I love my hometown Magnitka with all my heart. I consider my work at the Magnitogorsk factory to be a special honor and high trust shown to me, a Soviet engineer, by the country.

Letter to a Soviet Official from a Worker, 1938

In fact, there's been twenty years of our [Soviet] power. Fifteen to sixteen of these have been peaceful construction.... The people struggled with zeal, overcame difficulties. Socialism has been built in the main. As we embark on the third five-year plan we shout at meetings, congresses, and in newspapers "Hurray, we have reached a happy, joyful life!" However, incidentally, if one is to be honest, those shouts are mechanical, made from habit, pumped by social organizations. The ordinary person makes such speeches like a street newspaper-seller. In fact, in his heart, when he comes home, this bawler, eulogist, will agree with his family, his wife who reproaches him that today she has been torturing herself in queues and did not get anything—there are no suits, no coats, no meat, no butter.

Letter from a Student to His Teacher, No Date

I worked at a factory for five years. Now I'll have to leave my studies at the institute. Who will study? Very talented Lomonosovs° and the sons of Soviet rulers,

_____

°**Lomonosovs:** i.e., brilliant students (Mikhal Lomonosov, 1711–1765, was a Russian scientist and writer).

since they have the highest posts and are the best paid. In this way education will be available only to the highest strata (a sort of nobility), while for the lowest strata, the laboring people, the doors will be closed.

Two Comments from Factory Workers Found in Soviet Archives, 1930s

What is there to say about the successes of Soviet power? It's lies. The newspapers cover up the real state of things. I am a worker, wear torn clothes, my four children go to school half-starving, in rags. I, an honest worker, am a visible example of what Soviet power has given the workers in the last twenty years.

How can we liquidate classes, if new classes have developed here, with the only difference being that they are not called classes? Now there are the same parasites who live at the expense of others. The worker produces and at the same time works for many people who live off him. From the example of our factory it is clear that there is a huge apparat of factory administrators, where idlers sit. There are many administrative workers who travel about in cars and get three to four times more than the worker. These people live in the best conditions and live at the expense of the labor of the working class.

Entry from a Worker's Diary, 1936

[T]he portraits of party leaders are now displayed the same way icons used to be: a round portrait framed and attached to a pole. Very convenient, hoist it onto your shoulder and you're on your way. And all these preparations are just like what people used to do before church holidays.... They had their own activists then, we have ours now. Different paths, the same old folderol.

Comment from an Anonymous Communist in Soviet Archives, 1938

Do you not think that comrade Stalin's name has begun to be very much abused? For example:

Stalin's people's commissar…
Stalin's canal…
Stalin's harvest…
Stalin's five-year plan…
Stalin's constitution…
Stalin's Komsomol°…

°**Komsomol:** youth organization.

I could give a hundred other examples, even of little meaning. Everything is Stalin, Stalin, Stalin. You only have to listen to a radio program about our achievements, and every fifth or tenth word will be the name of comrade Stalin. In the end this sacred and beloved name—Stalin—may make so much noise in people's heads that it is very possible that it will have the opposite effect.

Document 22.4

Living through the Terror

More than anything else, it was the Terror—sometimes called the Great Purges—that came to define Stalinism as a distinctive phenomenon in the history of Soviet communism (see p. 1038). Millions of people were caught up in this vast process of identifying and eliminating so-called "enemies of the people," many of them loyal communist citizens. The three selections that follow, all from women, provide a small taste of what it meant to experience arrest and interrogation, life in the camps of the Gulag, and the agony of those left behind waiting for loved ones who had vanished into the Terror.

- ■ What might you infer from these selections about purposes of the Terror, the means by which it was implemented, and its likely outcomes, whether intended or not?

- ■ Many innocent people who were arrested believed that others were guilty as charged, while in their own case a mistake had been made. How might you account for this widespread response to the Terror?

- ■ In what different ways did people experience the Stalinist Terror? What do you think motivated each of these women who wrote about it?

- ■ The extent of the Terror did not become widely known until well after Stalin's death in 1953. How do you imagine that knowledge was used by critics of communism? What impact might it have had on those who had ardently believed in the possibilities of a socialist future?

- ■ How might you compare the Soviet terror and the Nazi Holocaust?

Personal Accounts of the Terror

1930s

[The first excerpt is from the memoirs of Irina Kakhovskaya, an ardent revolutionary, though not a party member, who was arrested in 1937 and spent seventeen years either in prison or in a labor camp. Here she describes her arrest and interrogation.]

Early on the morning of February 8, 1937, a large group of men appeared at the door of our quiet apartment in Ufa. We were shown a search warrant and warrants for our arrest. The search was carried out in violent, pogrom-like fashion and lasted all day. Books went pouring down from the shelves; letters and papers, out of boxes. They tapped the walls and, when they encountered hollow spots, removed the bricks. Everything was covered with dust and pieces of brick....

At the prison everything was aimed at breaking prisoners' spirits immediately, intimidating and stupefying them, making them feel that they were no longer human, but "enemies of the people," against whom everything was permitted. All elementary human needs were disregarded (light, air, food, rest, medical care, warmth, toilet facilities)....

In the tiny, damp, cold, half-lit cell were a bunk and a half bunk. The bunk was for the prisoner under investigation and on the half bunk, their legs drawn up, the voluntary victims, the informers from among the common criminals, huddled together. Their duty was never to let their neighbor out of their sight, never to let the politicals communicate with one another... and above all to prevent the politicals from committing suicide.... The air was fouled by the huge wooden latrine bucket....

The interrogation began on the very first night.... Using threats, endearments, promises and enigmatic hints, they tried to confuse, wear down, frighten, and break the will of each individual, who was kept totally isolated from his or her comrades.... Later stools were removed and the victim had to simply stand for hours on end....

At first it seemed that the whole thing was a tremendous and terrible misunderstanding, that it was our duty to clear it up.... But it soon became apparent that what was involved was deliberate ill will and the most cynical possible approach to the truth....

In the interrogation sessions, I now had several investigators in a row, and the "conveyor belt" questioning would go on for six days and nights on end.... Exhaustion reached the ultimate limit. The brain, inadequately supplied with blood, began to misfunction.... "Sign! We won't bother you anymore. We'll give you a quiet cell and a pillow and you can sleep...." That was how the investigator would try to bribe a person who was completely debilitated and stupefied from lack of sleep.

Each of us fought alone to keep an honest name and save the honor of our friends, although it would have been far easier to die than to endure this hell month after month. Nevertheless the accused remained strong in spirit and, apart from the unfortunate Mayorov, not one real revolutionary did they manage to break.

[The second selection comes from the memoirs of Eugenia Ginsberg, a woman who survived many years in perhaps the most notorious of the gulag camps—Kolyma in the frigid northeastern corner of the Soviet Union. In this selection, Ginsberg recounts an ordinary day in camps.]

The work to which I was assigned...went by the imposing name of "land improvement." We set out before dawn and marched in ranks of five for about three miles, to the accompaniment of shouts from the guards and bad language from the common criminals who were included in our party as a punish-

Source: First selection: Irina Kakhovskaya, "Our Fate" in *An End to Silence*, translated by George Saunders and edited by Stephen Cohen (New York: Norton, 1982), 81–90; second selection: Eugenia Semyonovna Ginzburg, *Journey into the Whirlwind* (New York: Harcourt, Brace Jovanovich, 1967), 366–67; third selection: Anna Akhnatova, *Poems*, selected and translated by Lyn Coffin (New York: Norton, 1983), 82, 85.

ment for some misdeed or other. In time we reached a bleak, open field where our leader, another common criminal called Senka—a disgusting type who preyed on the other prisoners and made no bones about offering a pair of warm breeches in return for an hour's "fun and games"—handed out picks and iron spades with which we attacked the frozen soil of Kolyma until one in the afternoon. I cannot remember, and perhaps I never knew, the rational purpose this "improvement" was supposed to serve. I only remember the ferocious wind, the forty-degree frost, the appalling weight of the pick, and the wild, irregular thumping of one's heart. At one o'clock we were marched back for dinner. More stumbling in and out of snowdrifts, more shouts and threats from the guards whenever we fell out of line. Back in the camp we received our longed-for piece of bread and soup and were allowed half an hour in which to huddle around the stove in the hope of absorbing enough warmth to last us halfway back to the field. After we had toiled again with our picks and spades till late in the evening, Senka would come and survey what we had done and abuse us for not doing more. How could the assignment ever be completed if we spoiled women fulfilled only thirty percent of the norm?... Finally a night's rest, full of nightmares, and the dreaded banging of a hammer on an iron rail which was the signal for a new day to begin.

[The third selection is from the poetry of Anna Akhmatova, probably Russia's most famous modern poet. In this poem, "Requiem," Akhmatova writes passionately about endlessly standing in line, either seeking information about her imprisoned son or trying to send him parcels, an experience that paralleled that of countless other mothers and wives during the Terror.]

In the awful years of Yezhovian horror,° I spent seventeen months standing in line in front of various prisons in Leningrad. One day someone "recognized" me. Then a woman with blue lips, who was standing behind me, and who, of course, had never heard my name, came out of the stupor which typified all of us, and whispered into my ear (everyone there spoke only in whispers):

—Can you describe this?

And I said:

—I can.

Then something like a fleeting smile passed over what once had been her face.

For months I've filled the air with pleas,
Trying to call you back.
I've thrown myself at the hangman's knees,
You are my son and my rack....
I've seen how a face can fall like a leaf,
How, from under the lids, terror peeks,
I've seen how suffering and grief
Etches hieroglyphs on cheeks,
How ash-blonde hair, from roots to tips,
Turns black and silver overnight.
How smiles wither on submissive lips,
And in a half-smile quivers fright.
Not only for myself do I pray,
But for those who stood in front and behind me,
In the bitter cold, on a hot July day
Under the red wall that stared blindly.

———————————

°**Yezhovian horror:** i.e., the Terror (Nikolay Yezhov, 1895–1939, a communist official, administered the most severe stage of the purges).

Using the Evidence:
Experiencing Stalinism

1. **Defending Stalinism:** Develop an argument that the fundamental goals of Stalinism (building socialism) were largely achieved during the 1930s.

2. **Criticizing Stalinism:** Develop an argument that genuine socialism was essentially betrayed or perverted by the developments of the Stalin era.

3. **Assessing change:** In what ways did the Stalin era represent a revolutionary transformation of Soviet society? In what ways did it continue older patterns of Russian history?

4. **Considering moral judgments:** Why do you think that historians have found it so difficult to write about the Stalin era without passing judgment on it? Does this represent a serious problem for scholars? Should students of the past seek to avoid moral judgments or is it an inevitable, perhaps even useful, part of the historian's craft?

Visual Sources

Considering the Evidence: Poster Art in Mao's China

"I wanted to be the girl in the poster when I was growing up. Every day I dressed up like that girl in a white cotton shirt with a red scarf around my neck, and I braided my hair in the same way. I liked the fact that she was surrounded by revolutionary martyrs whom I was taught to worship since kindergarten."[14] As things turned out, this young girl, Anchee Min, did become the subject of one of the many thousands of propaganda posters with which the Chinese communist government flooded the country during the thirty years or so following the Chinese Revolution of 1949.

In China, as in other communist countries, art served the state and the Communist Party. Nowhere was this more apparent than in these propaganda posters, which were found in homes, schools, workplaces, railway stations, and elsewhere. The artists who created these images were under the strict control of Communist Party officials and were expected to use their skills to depict the party's leaders and achievements favorably, even grandly. They were among the "engineers of the human soul" who were reshaping the consciousness of individuals and remaking their entire society. One young man, born in 1951, testified to the effectiveness of these posters: "They...were my signposts through life. They made sure we did not make mistakes.... [M]y life is reflected in them."[15]

The posters that follow illustrate the kind of society and people that the communist leadership sought to create during the years that Mao Zedong ruled the country (1949–1976). The realities behind these images, of course, were often far different.

Coming to power in 1949, Chinese Communist Party leaders recognized that their enemies were by no means totally defeated. A persistent theme throughout the years of Mao's rule was an effort to eliminate those enemies or convert them to the communist cause. Spies, imperialist sympathizers, those infected with "bourgeois values" such as materialism and individualism, landowners or capitalists yearning for the old life—all of these had to be identified and confronted. So too were many "enemies" within the Communist Party itself, people who were suspected of opposition to the radical policies of Mao. Some of these alleged enemies were killed, others imprisoned, and still others— millions of them—were subjected to endless self-criticism sessions or sent down to remote rural areas to "learn from the peasants." This need to demolish the

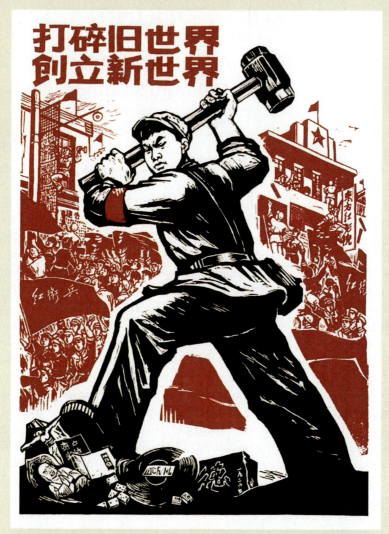

Visual Source 22.1 Smashing the Old Society (Courtesy, Centre for the Study of Democracy, University of Westminster, London, Chinese Poster Collection)

old society and old values is reflected in Visual Source 22.1, a poster from 1967, the height of the Cultural Revolution (see pp. 1043–44). Its caption reads: "Destroy the Old World; Establish the New World."

- Notice the various items beneath this young revolutionary's feet. What do they represent to the ardent revolutionaries seeking to "destroy the old world"? What groups of people were most likely to be affected by such efforts?

- What elements of a new order are being constructed in this image?

■ How does the artist distinguish visually between the old and the new? Note the use of colors and the size of various figures and objects in the poster.

The centerpiece of Mao's plans for the vast Chinese countryside lay in the "people's communes." Established during the so-called Great Leap Forward in the late 1950s, these were huge political and economic units intended to work the land more efficiently and collectively, to undertake large-scale projects such as building dams and irrigation systems, to create small-scale industries in the rural areas, and to promote local self-reliance. They also sought to move China more rapidly toward genuine communism by eliminating virtually every form of private property and emphasizing social equality and shared living. Commune members ate together in large dining halls, and children were cared for during the day in collective nurseries rather than by their own families. Visual Source 22.2, a poster created in 1958 under the title "The People's Communes Are Good," shows a highly idealized image of one such commune.

■ What appealing features of commune life and a communist future are illustrated in this poster? Notice the communal facilities for eating and washing clothes as well as the drill practice of a "people's militia" unit at the bottom of the picture.

■ One of Mao's chief goals was to overcome the sharp division between industrial cities and the agricultural countryside. How is this effort illustrated in the poster?

The actual outcomes of the commune movement departed radically from their idealistic goals. Economic disruption occasioned by the creation of communes contributed a great deal to the enormous famines of the late 1950s, in which many millions perished. Furthermore, efforts to involve the peasants in iron and steel production through the creation of much-heralded "backyard furnaces," illustrated in this image, proved a failure. Most of the metal produced in these primitive facilities was of poor quality and essentially unusable. Such efforts further impoverished the rural areas as peasants were encouraged to contribute their pots, pans, and anything made of iron to the smelting furnaces.

Among the core values of Maoist communism were human mastery over the natural order, rapid industrialization, and the liberation of women from ancient limitations and oppressions in order to mobilize them for the task of building socialism. Visual Source 22.3, a 1975 poster, illustrates these values. Its caption reads: "Women Can Hold Up Half the Sky; Surely the Face of Nature Can Be Transformed."

Visual Source 22.2 Building the New Society: The People's Commune (Shanghai Educational Publishing House/Coll. SL (Stefan Landsberger)/IISH)

- In what ways does this poster reflect Maoist communism's core values?

- How is the young woman in this image portrayed? What does the expression on her face convey? Notice her clothing and the shape of her forearms, and the general absence of a feminine figure. Why do you think she is portrayed in this largely sexless fashion? What does this suggest about the communist attitude toward sexuality?

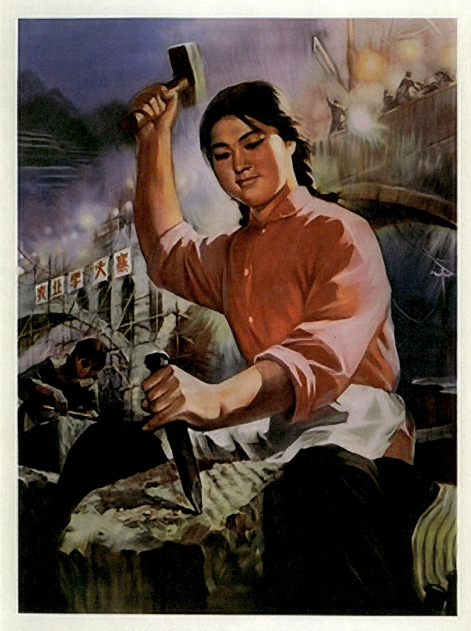

Visual Source 22.3 Women, Nature, and Industrialization (Courtesy, Centre for the Study of Democracy, University of Westminster, London, Chinese Poster Collection)

■ What does this image suggest about how the party sought to realize gender equality? What is the significance of the work the young woman is doing?

■ Notice the lights that illuminate a nighttime work scene. What does this suggest about attitudes toward work and production?

A central feature of Chinese communism, especially during the Cultural Revolution of 1966–1976, was the growing veneration, even adoration, of Chairman Mao. Portraits, statues, busts, and Mao badges proliferated. Everyone was expected to read repeatedly the "Red Treasured Book," which offered a selection of quotations from Mao's writings and which was widely believed to facilitate solutions to almost all problems, both public and private. Many families erected "tablets of loyalty" to Mao, much like those previously devoted to ancestors. People made pilgrimages to "sacred shrines" associated with key events in his life. Schoolchildren began the day by chanting, "May Chairman Mao live ten thousand times ten thousand years."

And Mao was the centerpiece of endless posters. Visual Source 22.4, a poster created in 1968, portrays a familiar scene from the Cultural Revolution. Millions of young people, organized as Red Guards and committed to revolutionary action, flocked to Beijing, where enormous and ecstatic rallies allowed them to catch a glimpse of their beloved leader and to unite with him in the grand task of creating communism in China. The poster's caption reads: "The reddest, reddest, red sun in our heart, Chairman Mao, and us together."

■ What relationship between Mao and his young followers does the poster suggest? Why might some scholars have seen a quasi-religious dimension to that relationship?

■ How do you understand the significance of the "Red Treasured Book" of quotations from Mao, which the young people are waving?

■ How might you account for the unbridled enthusiasm expressed by the Red Guards? In this case, the poster portrays the realities of these rallies with considerable accuracy. Can you think of other comparable cases of such mass enthusiasm?

After Mao's death in 1976, the Communist Party backed away from the disruptive radicalism of the Cultural Revolution and initiated the market-based reforms that have generated such spectacular economic growth in China in recent decades (see pp. 1052–54). In this new era, the poster tradition of the Maoist years faded, and party control over the arts loosened. Visual Source 22.5 reflects the new values of the post-Mao era. Dating from 1993, it is a New Year's "good luck" print featuring the traditional gods of wealth, happiness, and longevity. Its caption reads: "The Gods of wealth enter the home from everywhere; wealth, treasures, and peace beckon." Another poster reflecting the post-Mao era in China can be found in Visual Source 24.2 on page 1183.

我们心中最红最红的红太阳毛主席和我们在一起

Visual Source 22.4 The Cult of Mao (Zhejiang People's Art Publishing House/Coll. SL (Stefan Landsberger)/IISH)

CHAPTER TWENTY-THREE

Independence and Development in the Global South

1914—PRESENT

"During my lifetime I have dedicated myself to this struggle of the African people. I have fought against white domination, and I have fought against black domination. I have cherished the ideal of a democratic and free society in which all persons live together in harmony and with equal opportunity. It is an ideal which I hope to live for and to achieve. But, if need be, it is an ideal for which I am prepared to die."[1]

Nelson Mandela, South Africa's nationalist leader, first uttered these words in 1964 at his trial for treason, sabotage, and conspiracy to overthrow the apartheid government of his country. Convicted of those charges, he spent the next twenty-seven years in prison, sometimes working at hard labor in a stone quarry. Often the floor was his bed, and a bucket was his toilet. For many years, he was allowed one visitor a year for thirty minutes and permitted to write and receive one letter every six months. When he was finally released from prison in 1990 under growing domestic and international pressure, he concluded his first speech as a free person with the words originally spoken at his trial. Four years later in 1994, South Africa held its first election in which blacks and whites alike were able to vote. The outcome of that election made Mandela the country's first black African president, and it linked South Africa to dozens of other countries all across Africa and Asia that had thrown off European rule or the control of white settlers during the second half of the twentieth century.

VARIOUSLY CALLED THE STRUGGLE FOR INDEPENDENCE OR DECOLONIZATION, that process carried an immense significance

Nelson Mandela: In April 1994, the long struggle against apartheid and white domination in South Africa came to an end in the country's first democratic and nonracial election. The symbol of that triumph was Nelson Mandela, long a political prisoner, head of the African National Congress, and the country's first black African president. He is shown here voting in that historic election. (Peter Turnley/Corbis)

for the history of the twentieth century. It marked a dramatic change in the world's political architecture, as nation-states triumphed over the empires that had structured much of African and Asian life in the nineteenth and early twentieth centuries. It mobilized millions of people, thrusting them into political activity and sometimes into violence and warfare. Decolonization signaled the declining legitimacy of both empire and race as credible bases for political or social life. It promised not only national freedom but also personal dignity, abundance, and opportunity.

What followed in the decades after independence was equally significant. Political, economic, and cultural experiments proliferated across these newly independent nations, which during the cold war were labeled as the third world and now are often referred to as developing countries or the Global South. Their peoples, who represented the vast majority of the world's population, faced enormous challenges: the legacies of empire; their own deep divisions of language, ethnicity, religion, and class; their rapidly growing numbers; the competing demands of the capitalist West and the communist East; the difficult tasks of simultaneously building modern economies, stable politics, and coherent nations; and all of this in a world still shaped by the powerful economies and armies of the wealthy, already industrialized nations. The emergence of the developing countries onto the world stage as independent and assertive actors has been a distinguishing feature of world history in this most recent century.

Toward Freedom: Struggles for Independence

In 1900, European colonial empires in Africa and Asia appeared as permanent features of the world's political landscape. Well before the end of the twentieth century, they were gone. The first major breakthroughs occurred in Asia and the Middle East in the late 1940s, when the Philippines, India, Pakistan, Burma, Indonesia, Syria, Iraq, Jordan, and Israel achieved independence. The period from the mid-1950s through the mid-1970s was the age of African independence as colony after colony, more than fifty in total, emerged into what was then seen as the bright light of freedom.

The End of Empire in World History

■ **Comparison**
What was distinctive about the end of Europe's African and Asian empires compared to other cases of imperial disintegration?

At one level, this vast process was but the latest case of imperial dissolution, a fate that had overtaken earlier empires, including those of the Assyrians, Romans, Arabs, and Mongols. But never before had the end of empire been so associated with the mobilization of the masses around a nationalist ideology; nor had these earlier cases generated a plethora of nation-states, each claiming an equal place in a world of nation-states. More comparable perhaps was that first decolonization, in which the European colonies in the Americas threw off British, French, Spanish, or Portuguese rule during the late eighteenth and early nineteenth centuries (see Chapter 17). Like their twentieth-century counterparts, these new nations claimed an international status equivalent to that of their former rulers. In the Americas, however, many of the colonized people were themselves of European origin, sharing much of their culture with their colonial rulers. In that respect, the African and Asian struggles of the twentieth century were very different, for they not only asserted political independence but also affirmed the vitality of their cultures, which had been submerged and denigrated during the colonial era.

The twentieth century witnessed the demise of many empires. The Austrian and Ottoman empires collapsed following World War I, giving rise to a number of new states in Europe and the Middle East. The Russian Empire also unraveled, although it was soon reassembled under the auspices of the Soviet Union. World War II ended the German and Japanese empires. African and Asian movements for independence shared with these other end-of-empire stories the ideal of national self-determination. This novel idea—that humankind was naturally divided into distinct peoples or nations, each of which deserved an independent state of its own—was loudly proclaimed by the winning side of both world wars. The belief in national self-determination gained a global following in the twentieth century and rendered empire illegitimate in the eyes of growing numbers of people.

Empires without territory, such as the powerful influence that the United States exercised in Latin America and elsewhere, likewise came under attack from highly nationalist governments. An intrusive U.S. presence was certainly one factor stimulating the Mexican Revolution, which began in 1910. One of the outcomes of that upheaval was the nationalization in 1937 of Mexico's oil industry, much of which was owned by American and British investors. Similar actions accompanied Cuba's revolution of 1959–1960 and also occurred in other places throughout Latin America and elsewhere. National self-determination likewise lay behind the disintegration of the Soviet Union in 1991, when the last of the major territorial empires of the twentieth century came to an inglorious end with the birth of fifteen new states. Although the winning of political independence for Europe's African and Asian colonies was perhaps the most spectacular challenge to empire in the twentieth century, that achievement was part of a larger pattern in modern world history (see Map 23.1).

Explaining African and Asian Independence

As the twentieth century closed, the end of European empires seemed an almost "natural" phenomenon, for colonial rule had lost any credibility as a form of political order. What could be more natural than for people to seek to rule themselves? Yet at the beginning of the century, few observers were predicting the collapse of these empires, and the idea that "the only legitimate government is self-government" was not nearly so widespread as it subsequently became. This situation has presented historians with a problem of explanation—how to account for the fall of European colonial empires and the emergence of dozens of new nation-states.

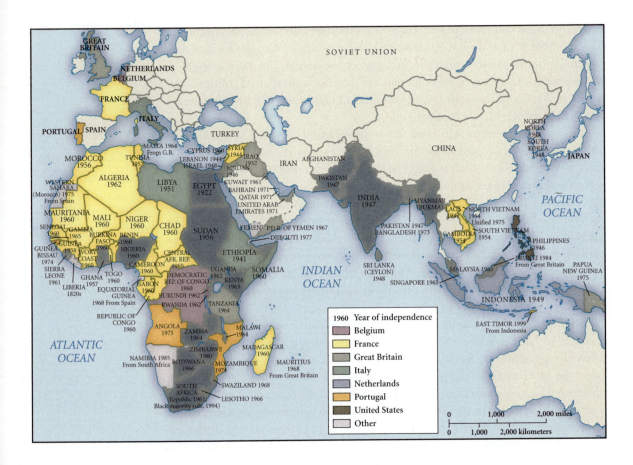

The following place names and labels appear on the map:

GREAT BRITAIN · NETHERLANDS · BELGIUM · FRANCE · ITALY · PORTUGAL · SPAIN · SOVIET UNION · TURKEY · CHINA · NORTH KOREA 1948 · SOUTH KOREA 1948 · JAPAN · PACIFIC OCEAN

MALTA 1964 From G.B. · CYPRUS 1960 · SYRIA 1944 · LEBANON 1944 · ISRAEL 1948 · IRAQ 1932 · JORDAN 1946 · IRAN · AFGHANISTAN

MOROCCO 1956 · TUNISIA 1956 · ALGERIA 1962 · LIBYA 1951 · EGYPT 1922 · KUWAIT 1961 · BAHRAIN 1971 · QATAR 1971 · UNITED ARAB EMIRATES 1971 · PAKISTAN 1947 · INDIA 1947 · MYANMAR (BURMA) · LAOS 1954 · NORTH VIETNAM Unified 1975

WESTERN SAHARA (Morocco) 1975 From Spain · MAURITANIA 1960 · MALI 1960 · NIGER 1960 · CHAD 1960 · SUDAN 1956 · YEMEN · P.D.R. OF YEMEN 1967 · DJIBOUTI 1977 · PAKISTAN 1947 · BANGLADESH 1973 · CAMBODIA 1954 · SOUTH VIETNAM 1954

SENEGAL 1960 · GAMBIA 1965 · GUINEA 1958 · GUINEA BISSAU 1974 · SIERRA LEONE 1961 · LIBERIA 1820s · BURKINA FASO 1960 · BENIN 1960 · IVORY COAST 1960 · GHANA 1957 · TOGO 1960 · NIGERIA 1960 · CENTRAL AFR. REP. 1960 · CAMEROON 1960 · EQUATORIAL GUINEA 1968 From Spain · GABON 1960 · ETHIOPIA 1941 · UGANDA 1962 · SOMALIA 1960 · KENYA 1963 · DEMOCRATIC REP. OF CONGO 1960 · BURUNDI 1962 · RWANDA 1962 · TANZANIA 1964 · SRI LANKA (CEYLON) 1948 · SINGAPORE 1965 · MALAYSIA 1963 · BRUNEI 1984 From Great Britain · PHILIPPINES 1946 · PAPUA NEW GUINEA 1975

INDIAN OCEAN · REPUBLIC OF CONGO 1960 · ANGOLA 1975 · ZAMBIA 1964 · MALAWI 1964 · MADAGASCAR 1960 · MAURITIUS 1968 From Great Britain · INDONESIA 1949 · EAST TIMOR 1999 From Indonesia

ATLANTIC OCEAN · NAMIBIA 1985 From South Africa · BOTSWANA 1966 · ZIMBABWE 1980 · MOZAMBIQUE 1974 · SWAZILAND 1968 · SOUTH AFRICA (Republic 1961; Black majority rule, 1994) · LESOTHO 1966

1960 Year of independence

- Belgium
- France
- Great Britain
- Italy
- Netherlands
- Portugal
- United States
- Other

0   1,000   2,000 miles
0   1,000   2,000 kilometers

Map 23.1   **The End of European Empires**
In the second half of the twentieth century, under pressure from nationalist movements, Europe's Asian and African empires dissolved into dozens of new independent states.

■ Change
What international circumstances and social changes contributed to the end of colonial empires?

One approach to explaining the end of colonial empires focuses attention on fundamental contradictions in the entire colonial enterprise that arguably rendered its demise more or less inevitable. The rhetoric of both Christianity and material progress sat awkwardly with the realities of colonial racism, exploitation, and poverty. The increasingly democratic values of European states ran counter to the essential dictatorship of colonial rule. The ideal of national self-determination was profoundly at odds with the possession of colonies that were denied any opportunity to express their own national character. The enormously powerful force of nationalism, having earlier driven the process of European empire building, now played a major role in its disintegration. Colonial rule, in this argument, dug its own grave.

But why did this "fatal flaw" of European colonial rule lead to independence in the post–World War II era rather than earlier or later? In explaining the timing of the end of empire, historians frequently use the notion of "conjuncture," the coming together of several separate developments at a particular time. At the international level, the world wars had weakened Europe, while discrediting any sense of European moral superiority. Both the United States and the Soviet Union, the new global superpowers, generally opposed the older European colonial empires. Meanwhile, the

United Nations provided a prestigious platform from which to conduct anticolonial agitation. All of this contributed to the global illegitimacy of empire, a transformation of social values that was enormously encouraging to Africans and Asians seeking political independence.

At the same time, social and economic circumstances within the colonies themselves generated the human raw material for anticolonial movements. By the early twentieth century in Asia and the mid-twentieth century in Africa, a second or third generation of Western-educated elites, largely male, had arisen throughout the colonial world. These young men were thoroughly familiar with European culture, were deeply aware of the gap between its values and its practices, no longer viewed colonial rule as a vehicle for their peoples' progress as their fathers had, and increasingly insisted on independence now. Moreover, growing numbers of ordinary people also were receptive to this message. Veterans of the world wars; young people with some education but no jobs commensurate with their expectations; a small class of urban workers who were increasingly aware of their exploitation; small-scale traders resentful of European privileges; rural dwellers who had lost land or suffered from forced labor; impoverished and insecure newcomers to the cities—all of these groups had reason to believe that independence held great promise.

A third approach to explaining the end of colonial empires puts the spotlight squarely on particular groups or individuals whose deliberate actions brought down the colonial system. Here the emphasis is on the "agency"—the deliberate initiatives—of historical actors rather than on impersonal contradictions or conjunctures. But which set of actors were most important in this end-of-empire drama?

Particularly in places such as West Africa or India, where independence occurred peacefully and through a negotiated settlement, the actions of colonial rulers have received considerable attention from historians. As the twentieth century wore on, these rulers were increasingly on the defensive and were actively planning for a new political relationship with their Asian and African colonies. With the colonies integrated into a global economic network and with local elites now modernized and committed to maintaining those links, outright colonial rule seemed less necessary to many Europeans. It was now possible to imagine retaining profitable economic interests in Asia and Africa without the expense and bother of formal colonial government. Deliberate planning for decolonization included gradual political reforms; investments in railroads, ports, and telegraph lines; the holding of elections; and the writing of constitutions. To some observers, it seemed as if independence was granted by colonial rulers rather than gained or seized by nationalist movements.

But these reforms and, ultimately, independence itself occurred only under considerable pressure from mounting nationalist movements. Creating such movements was no easy task. Political leaders, drawn from the ranks of the educated few, organized political parties, recruited members, plotted strategy, developed an ideology, and negotiated with one another and with the colonial state. The most prominent among them became the "fathers" of their new countries as independence dawned— Mahatma Gandhi and Jawaharlal Nehru in India, Sukarno in Indonesia, Ho Chi

■ Description
What obstacles confronted the leaders of movements for independence?

Minh in Vietnam, Kwame Nkrumah in Ghana, and Nelson Mandela in South Africa. In places where colonial rule was particularly intransigent—settler-dominated colonies and Portuguese territories, for example—leaders also directed military operations and administered liberated areas.

Agency within nationalist movements was not limited to leaders and the educated few. Millions of ordinary people decided to join Gandhi's nonviolent campaigns; tens of thousands of freedom fighters waged guerrilla warfare in Algeria, Kenya, Mozambique, and Zimbabwe; workers went on strike; market women in West Africa joined political parties, as did students, farmers, and the unemployed. In short, the struggle for independence did not happen automatically. It was deliberately made by the conscious personal choices of innumerable individuals across Asia and Africa.

In some places, that struggle, once begun, produced independence within a few years, four in the case of the Belgian Congo. Elsewhere it was measured in decades. But everywhere it was a contested process. Those efforts were rarely if ever cohesive movements of uniformly oppressed people. More often they were fragile alliances of conflicting groups and parties representing different classes, ethnic groups, religions, or regions. Beneath the common goal of independence, they struggled with one another over questions of leadership, power, strategy, ideology, and the distribution of material benefits, even as they fought and negotiated with their colonial rulers. The very notion of "national self-government" posed obvious but often contentious questions: What group of people constituted the "nation" that deserved to rule itself? And who should speak for it?

Comparing Freedom Struggles

Two of the most extended freedom struggles—in India and South Africa—illustrate both the variations and the complexity of this process, which was so central to twentieth-century world history. India was among the first colonies to achieve independence and provided both a model and an inspiration to others, whereas South Africa, though not formally a colony, was among the last to throw off political domination by whites.

The Case of India: Ending British Rule

■ Change

How did India's nationalist movement change over time?

Surrounded by the Himalayas and the Indian Ocean, the South Asian peninsula, commonly known as India, enjoyed a certain geographic unity. But before the twentieth century few of its people thought of themselves as "Indians." Cultural identities were primarily local and infinitely varied, rooted in differences of family, caste, village, language, region, tribe, and religious practice. In earlier centuries—during the Mauryan, Gupta, and Mughal empires, for example—large areas of the subcontinent had been temporarily enclosed within a single political system, but always these were imperial overlays, constructed on top of enormously diverse Indian societies.

So too was British colonial rule, but the British differed from earlier invaders in ways that promoted a growing sense of Indian identity. Unlike previous foreign rulers, the British never assimilated into Indian society because their acute sense of racial and cultural distinctiveness kept them apart. This served to intensify Indians' awareness of their collective difference from their alien rulers. Furthermore, British railroads, telegraph lines, postal services, administrative networks, newspapers, and schools as well as the English language bound India's many regions and peoples together more firmly than ever before and facilitated communication among its educated elite. Early-nineteenth-century cultural nationalists, seeking to renew and reform Hinduism, registered this sense of India as a cultural unit.

The most important political expression of an all-Indian identity took shape in the Indian National Congress (INC), which was established in 1885. This was an association of English-educated Indians—lawyers, journalists, teachers, businessmen—drawn overwhelmingly from regionally prominent high-caste Hindu families. Its founding represented the beginning of a new kind of political protest, quite different from the rebellions, banditry, and refusal to pay taxes that had periodically erupted in the rural areas of colonial India. The INC was largely an urban phenomenon and quite moderate in its demands. Initially, its well-educated members did not seek to overthrow British rule; rather they hoped to gain greater inclusion within the political, military, and business life of British India. From such positions of influence, they argued, they could better protect the interests of India than could their foreign-born rulers. The British mocked their claim to speak for ordinary Indians, referring to them as "babus," a derogatory term that implied a semiliterate "native" with only a thin veneer of modern education.

Even in the first two decades of the twentieth century, the INC remained largely an elite organization; as such, it had difficulty gaining a mass following among India's vast peasant population. That began to change in the aftermath of World War I. To attract Indian support for the war effort, the British in 1917 had promised "the gradual development of self-governing institutions," a commitment that energized nationalist politicians to demand more rapid political change. Furthermore, British attacks on the Islamic Ottoman Empire antagonized India's Muslims. The end of the war was followed by a massive influenza epidemic, which cost the lives of millions of Indians. Finally, a series of repressive actions antagonized many, particularly the killing of some 400 people who had defied a ban on public

Mahatma Gandhi
The most widely recognized and admired figure in the global struggle against colonial rule was India's Mahatma Gandhi. In this famous photograph, he is sitting cross-legged on the floor, clothed in a traditional Indian garment called a *dhoti*, while nearby stands a spinning wheel, symbolizing the independent and nonindustrial India that Gandhi sought. (Margaret Bourke-White/Time Life Pictures/Getty Images)

meetings to celebrate a Hindu festival in the city of Amritsar. This was the context in which Mohandas Gandhi (1869–1948) arrived on the Indian political scene and soon transformed it.

■ Change
What was the role of Gandhi in India's struggle for independence?

Gandhi was born in the province of Gujarat in western India to a pious Hindu family of the Vaisya, or business, caste. He was married at the age of thirteen, had only a mediocre record as a student, and eagerly embraced an opportunity to study law in England when he was eighteen. He returned as a shy and not very successful lawyer, and in 1893 he accepted a job with an Indian firm in South Africa, where a substantial number of Indians had migrated as indentured laborers during the nineteenth century. While in South Africa, Gandhi personally experienced overt racism for the first time and as a result soon became involved in organizing Indians, mostly Muslims, to protest that country's policies of racial segregation. He also developed a concept of India that included Hindus and Muslims alike and pioneered strategies of resistance that he would later apply in India itself. His emerging political philosophy, known as *satyagraha* (truth force), was a confrontational, though nonviolent, approach to political action. As Gandhi argued,

> Non-violence means conscious suffering. It does not mean meek submission to the will of the evil-doer, but it means the pitting of one's whole soul against the will of the tyrant.... [I]t is possible for a single individual to defy the whole might of an unjust empire to save his honour, his religion, his soul.[2]

Returning to India in 1914, Gandhi quickly rose within the leadership ranks of the INC. During the 1920s and 1930s, he applied his approach in periodic mass campaigns that drew support from an extraordinarily wide spectrum of Indians—peasants and the urban poor, intellectuals and artisans, capitalists and socialists, Hindus and Muslims. The British responded with periodic repression as well as concessions that allowed a greater Indian role in political life. Gandhi's conduct and actions—his simple and unpretentious lifestyle, his support of Muslims, his frequent reference to Hindu religious themes—appealed widely in India and transformed the INC into a mass organization. To many ordinary people, Gandhi possessed magical powers and produced miraculous events. He was the Mahatma, the Great Soul.

His was a radicalism of a different kind. He did not call for social revolution but sought the moral transformation of individuals. He worked to raise the status of India's untouchables (the lowest and most ritually polluting groups within the caste hierarchy), although he launched no attack on caste in general and accepted support from businessmen and their socialist critics alike. His critique of India's situation went far beyond colonial rule. "India is being ground down," he argued, "not under the English heel, but under that of modern civilization"—its competitiveness, its materialism, its warlike tendencies, its abandonment of religion.[3] Almost alone among nationalist leaders in India or elsewhere, Gandhi opposed a modern industrial future for his country, seeking instead a society of harmonious self-sufficient villages drawing on ancient Indian principles of duty and morality. (See Document 20.5, pp. 957–59, for a more extended statement of Gandhi's thinking.)

Gandhi and the INC or Congress Party leadership had to contend with a wide range of movements, parties, and approaches, whose very diversity tore at the national unity that they so ardently sought. Whereas Gandhi rejected modern industrialization, his own chief lieutenant, Jawaharlal Nehru, thoroughly embraced science, technology, and industry as essential to India's future. Nor did everyone accept Gandhi's nonviolence or his inclusive definition of India. A militant Hindu organization preached hatred of Muslims and viewed India as an essentially Hindu nation. To some in the Congress Party, movements to improve the position of women or untouchables seemed a distraction from the chief task of gaining independence from Britain. Whether to participate in British-sponsored legislative bodies without complete independence also became a divisive issue. Furthermore, a number of smaller parties advocated on behalf of particular regions or castes. India's nationalist movement, in short, was beset by division and controversy. (For an image that illustrates these divisions, see Visual Source 23.1, p. 1124.)

By far the most serious threat to a unified movement derived from the growing divide between the country's Hindu and Muslim populations. As early as 1906, the formation of an All-India Muslim League contradicted the Congress Party's claim to speak for all Indians. As the British allowed more elected Indian representatives on local councils, the League demanded separate electorates, with a fixed number of seats on local councils for Muslims. As a distinct minority within India, some Muslims feared that their voice could be swamped by a numerically dominant Hindu population, despite Gandhi's inclusive philosophy. Some Hindu politicians confirmed those fears when they cast the nationalist struggle in Hindu religious terms, hailing their country, for example, as a goddess, Bande Mataram (Mother India). When elections in 1937 gave the Congress Party control of many provincial governments, some of those governments began to enforce the teaching of Hindi in schools and to protect cows from slaughter, both of which antagonized Muslims.

As the movement for independence gained ground, the Muslim League and its leader, Muhammad Ali Jinnah, increasingly argued that those parts of India that had a Muslim majority should have a separate political status. They called it Pakistan, the land of the pure. In this view, India was not a single nation, as Gandhi had long argued. Jinnah put his case succinctly:

> The Muslims and Hindus belong to two different religious philosophies, social customs, and literatures. They neither intermarry nor interdine [eat] together and, indeed, they belong to two different civilizations.[4]

With great reluctance and amid mounting violence, Gandhi and the Congress Party finally agreed to partition as the British declared their intention to leave India after World War II.

Thus colonial India became independent in 1947 as two countries—a Muslim Pakistan, itself divided into two wings 1,000

■ **Description**

What conflicts and differences divided India's nationalist movement?

The Independence of British South Asia

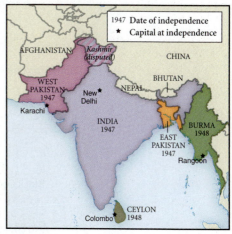

miles apart, and a mostly Hindu India governed by a secular state. Dividing colonial India in this fashion was horrendously painful. A million people or more died in the communal violence that accompanied partition, and some 12 million refugees moved from one country to the other to join their religious compatriots. Gandhi himself, desperately trying to stem the mounting tide of violence in India's villages, refused to attend the independence celebrations. He was assassinated in 1948 by a Hindu extremist. The great triumph of independence, secured from the powerful British Empire, was shadowed by an equally great tragedy in the violence of partition.

The Case of South Africa: Ending Apartheid

■ Comparison

Why was African majority rule in South Africa delayed until 1994, whereas the overthrow of European colonialism had occurred much earlier in the rest of Africa and Asia?

The setting for South Africa's freedom struggle was very different from the situation in India. In the twentieth century, that struggle was not waged against an occupying European colonial power, for South Africa had in fact been independent of Great Britain since 1910. That independence, however, had been granted to a government wholly controlled by a white settler minority, which represented less than 20 percent of the total population. The country's black African majority had no political

Snapshot   Key Moments in South African History

Earliest humans in South Africa	by 50,000 years ago
Arrival of iron-using, Bantu-speaking agricultural peoples	by 500 C.E.
First Dutch settlement	1652
Shaka and creation of a Zulu state	early 19th century
British takeover of South Africa	1806
Great Trek: Afrikaner migration to the interior to escape more liberal British rule	1830s
European conquest of interior African societies	mid- to late 19th century
Gold and diamond mining begins	late 19th century
Great Britain defeats Afrikaners in Boer War	1899–1902
South Africa independent under white minority government	1910
African National Congress established	1912
National Party comes to power; apartheid formally established	1948
Sharpville massacre	1960
ANC launches armed struggle	1961
Black Consciousness movement; urban insurrection	1970s
Nelson Mandela released from prison	1990
ANC comes to power following first all-race elections	1994

rights whatsoever within the central state. Black South Africans' struggle therefore was against this internal opponent rather than against a distant colonial authority, as in India. Economically, the most prominent whites were of British descent. They or their forebears had come to South Africa during the nineteenth century, when Great Britain was the ruling colonial power. But the politically dominant section of the white community, known as Boers or Afrikaners, was descended from the early Dutch settlers, who had arrived in the mid-seventeenth century. The term "Afrikaner" reflected their image of themselves as "white Africans," permanent residents of the continent rather than colonial intruders. They had unsuccessfully sought independence from a British-ruled South Africa in a bitter struggle (the Boer War, 1899–1902), and a sense of difference and antagonism lingered. Despite a certain hostility between white South Africans of British and Afrikaner background, both felt that their way of life and standard of living were jeopardized by any move toward black African majority rule. The intransigence of this sizable and threatened settler community helps explain why African rule was delayed until 1994, while India, lacking any such community, had achieved independence almost a half century earlier.

Unlike a predominantly agrarian India, South Africa by the early twentieth century had developed a mature industrial economy, based initially in gold and diamond mining, but by midcentury including secondary industries such as steel, chemicals, automobile manufacturing, rubber processing, and heavy engineering. Particularly since the 1960s, the economy benefited from extensive foreign investment and loans. Almost all black Africans were involved in this complex modern economy, working in urban industries or mines, providing labor for white-owned farms, or receiving payments from relatives who did. The extreme dependence of most Africans on the white-controlled economy rendered individuals highly vulnerable to repressive action, but collectively the threat to withdraw their essential labor also gave them a powerful weapon.

A third unique feature of the South African situation was the overwhelming prominence of race, expressed most clearly in the policy of apartheid, which attempted to separate blacks from whites in every conceivable way while retaining Africans' labor power in the white-controlled economy. An enormous apparatus of repression enforced that system. Rigid "pass laws" monitored and tried to control the movement of Africans into the cities, where they were subjected to extreme forms of social segregation. In the rural areas, a series of impoverished and overcrowded "native reserves," or Bantustans, served as ethnic homelands that kept Africans divided along tribal lines. Even though racism was present in colonial India, nothing of this magnitude developed there.

As in India, various forms of opposition—resistance to conquest, rural rebellions, urban strikes, and independent churches—arose to contest the manifest injustices of South African life. There too an elite-led political party provided an organizational umbrella for many of the South African resistance efforts in the twentieth century. Established in 1912, the African National Congress (ANC), like its Indian predecessor, was led by educated, professional, and middle-class Africans who sought not to overthrow the existing order, but to be accepted as "civilized men" within it. They

■ Change
How did South Africa's struggle against white domination change over time?

appealed to the liberal, humane, and Christian values that white society claimed. For four decades, its leaders pursued peaceful and moderate protest—petitions, multiracial conferences, delegations appealing to the authorities—even as racially based segregationist policies were implemented one after another. By 1948, when the Afrikaner-led National Party came to power on a platform of apartheid, it was clear that such "constitutional" protest had produced nothing.

During the 1950s, a new and younger generation of the ANC leadership, which now included Nelson Mandela, broadened its base of support and launched nonviolent civil disobedience—boycotts, strikes, demonstrations, and the burning of the hated passes that all Africans were required to carry. All of these actions were similar to and inspired by the tactics that Gandhi had used in India twenty to thirty years earlier. The government of South Africa responded with tremendous repression, including the shooting of sixty-nine unarmed demonstrators at Sharpville in 1960, the banning of the ANC, and the imprisonment of its leadership. This was the context in which Mandela was arrested and sentenced to his long prison term.

At this point, the freedom struggle in South Africa took a different direction than it had in India. Its major political parties were now illegal. Underground nationalist leaders turned to armed struggle, authorizing selected acts of sabotage and assassination, while preparing for guerrilla warfare in camps outside the country. Active opposition within South Africa was now primarily expressed by student groups that were part of the Black Consciousness movement, an effort to foster pride, unity, and political awareness among the country's African majority. Such young people were at the center of an explosion of protest in 1976 in a sprawling, segregated, impoverished black neighborhood called Soweto, outside Johannesburg, in which hundreds were killed. The initial trigger for the uprising was the government's decision to enforce education for Africans in the hated language of the white Afrikaners rather than English. However, the momentum of the Soweto rebellion persisted, and by the mid-1980s, spreading urban violence and the radicalization of urban young people had forced the government to declare a state of emergency. Furthermore, South Africa's black labor movement, legalized only in 1979, became increasingly active and political. In June 1986, to commemorate the tenth anniversary of the Soweto uprising, the Congress of South African Trade Unions orchestrated a general strike involving some 2 million workers.

Independence in Kenya, East Africa
Almost everywhere in the colonial world, the struggle for independence climaxed in a formal and joyful ceremony in which power was transferred from the colonial authority to the leader of the new nation. Here a jubilant Jomo Kenyatta takes the oath of office in 1964 as Kenya's first president, while a dour and bewigged British official looks on. (Bettmann/Corbis)

Beyond this growing internal pressure, South Africa faced mounting international demands to end apartheid as well. Exclusion from most international sporting events, including the Olympics; the refusal of many artists and entertainers to perform in South Africa; economic boycotts; the withdrawal of private investment funds—all of this isolated South Africa from a Western world in which its white rulers claimed membership. This was another feature of the South African freedom movement that had no parallel in India.

The combination of these internal and external pressures persuaded many white South Africans by the late 1980s that discussion with African nationalist leaders was the only alternative to a massive, bloody, and futile struggle to preserve white privileges. The outcome was the abandonment of key apartheid policies, the release of Nelson Mandela from prison, the legalization of the ANC, and a prolonged process of negotiations that in 1994 resulted in national elections, which brought the ANC to power. To the surprise of almost everyone, the long nightmare of South African apartheid came to an end without a racial bloodbath (see Map 23.2).

Map 23.2   South Africa after Apartheid
Under apartheid, all black Africans were officially designated as residents of small, scattered, impoverished Bantustans, shown on the inset map. Many of these people, of course, actually lived in white South Africa, where they worked. The main map shows the new internal organization of the country as it emerged after 1994, with the Bantustans abolished and the country divided into nine provinces. Lesotho and Swaziland had been British protectorates during the colonial era and subsequently became separate independent countries, although surrounded by South African territory.

As in India, the South African nationalist movement that finally won freedom was divided and conflicted. Unlike India, though, these divisions did not occur along religious lines. Rather it was race, ethnicity, and ideology that generated dissension and sometimes violence. Whereas the ANC generally favored a broad alliance of everyone opposed to apartheid (black Africans, Indians, "coloreds" or mixed-race people, and sympathetic whites), a smaller group known as the Pan Africanist Congress rejected cooperation with other racial groups and limited its membership to black Africans. During the urban uprisings of the 1970s and 1980s, young people supporting the Black Consciousness movements and those following Mandela and the ANC waged war against each other in the townships of South African cities. Perhaps most threatening to the unity of the nationalist struggle were the separatist tendencies of the Zulu-based Inkatha Freedom Party. Its leader, Gatsha Buthelezi, had cooperated with the apartheid state and even received funding from it. As negotiations for a transition to African rule unfolded in the early 1990s, considerable violence between Inkatha followers, mostly Zulu migrant workers, and ANC supporters broke out in a number of cities. None of this, however, approached the massive killing of Hindus and Muslims that accompanied the partition of India. South Africa, unlike India, acquired its political freedom as an intact and unified state.

Experiments with Freedom

Africa's first modern nationalist hero, Kwame Nkrumah of Ghana, paraphrased a biblical quotation when he urged his followers, "Seek ye first the political kingdom and all these other things will be added unto you." However, would winning the political kingdom of independence or freedom from European rule really produce "all these other things"—opportunity for political participation, industrial growth, economic development, reasonably unified nations, and a better life for all? That was the central question confronting the new nations emerging from colonial rule. They were joined in that quest by already independent but nonindustrialized countries and regions such as China, Thailand, Ethiopia, Iran, Turkey, and Central and South America. Together they formed the bloc of nations known variously as the third world, the developing countries, or the Global South (see Map 23.3). In the second half of the twentieth century, these countries represented perhaps 75 percent of the world's population. They accounted for almost all of the fourfold increase in human numbers that the world experienced during the twentieth century. That immense surge in global population, at one level a great triumph for the human species, also underlay many of the difficulties these nations faced as they conducted their various experiments with freedom.

Almost everywhere, the moment of independence generated something close to euphoria. Having emerged from the long night of colonial rule, free peoples had the opportunity to build anew. The developing countries would be laboratories for fresh approaches to creating modern states, nations, cultures, and economies. In the decades that followed, experiments with freedom multiplied, but the early optimism was soon tempered by the difficulties and disappointments of those tasks.

Experiments in Political Order: Comparing African Nations and India

All across the developing world, efforts to create political order had to contend with a set of common conditions. Populations were exploding. Expectations for independence ran very high, often exceeding the available resources. Most developing countries were culturally diverse, with little loyalty new to the central state. Nonetheless, public employment mushroomed as the state assumed greater responsibility for economic development. In conditions of widespread poverty and weak private economies, groups and individuals sought to capture the state, or parts of it, both for the salaries and status it offered and for the opportunities for private enrichment that political office provided.

This was the formidable setting in which developing countries had to hammer out their political systems. The range of that effort was immense: Communist Party control in China, Vietnam, and Cuba; multiparty democracy in India and South Africa; one-party democracy in Tanzania and Senegal; military regimes for a time in much of Latin America and Africa; personal dictatorships in Uganda and the Philippines. In many places, one kind of political system followed another in kaleidoscopic succession. The political evolution of postindependence Africa illustrates the complexity and the difficulty of creating a stable political order in developing countries.

Map 23.3 The "Worlds" of the Cold War
During the cold war, the term "third world" referred to those countries not solidly in either the Western or the Communist bloc of nations. Gradually it came to designate developing countries, those less wealthy and less industrialized societies seeking to catch up to the more developed countries of Europe, North America, and Japan. China, Vietnam, and Cuba, although governed by communist regimes, have been widely regarded as part of the developing world as well.

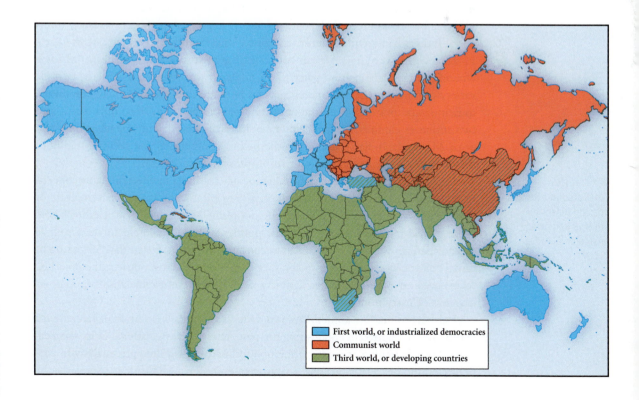

First world, or industrialized democracies
Communist world
Third world, or developing countries

Although colonial rule had been highly authoritarian and bureaucratic with little interest in African participation, during the 1950s the British, the French, and the Belgians attempted, rather belatedly, to transplant democratic institutions to their colonies. They established legislatures, permitted elections, allowed political parties to operate, and in general anticipated the development of constitutional, parliamentary, multiparty democracies similar to their own. It was with such institutions that most African states greeted independence.

By the early 1970s, however, few such regimes were left among the new states of Africa. Many of the apparently popular political parties that had led the struggle for independence lost mass support and were swept away by military coups. When the army took power in Ghana in 1966, no one lifted a finger to defend the party that had led the country to independence only nine years earlier. Other states evolved into one-party systems, sometimes highly authoritarian and bureaucratic and sometimes more open and democratic. Still others degenerated into personal tyrannies or dictatorships. Freedom from colonial rule certainly did not automatically generate the internal political freedoms associated with democracy.

■ **Comparison**

Why was Africa's experience with political democracy so different from that of India?

The contrast between Africa's political evolution and that of India has been particularly striking. In India, Western-style democracy, including regular elections, multiple parties, civil liberties, and peaceful changes in government, has been practiced almost continuously since independence. The struggle for independence in India had been a far more prolonged affair, thus providing time for an Indian political leadership to sort itself out. Furthermore, the British began to hand over power in a gradual way well before complete independence was granted in 1947. Thus a far larger number of Indians had useful administrative or technical skills than was the case in Africa. In sharp contrast to most African countries, the nationalist movement in India was embodied in a single national party (the Congress Party), which encompassed a wide variety of other parties and interest groups. Its leadership was genuinely committed to democratic practice. Even the tragic and painful partition of colonial India into two countries eliminated a major source of internal discord as independent India was born. Moreover, Indian statehood could be built on cultural and political traditions that were far more deeply rooted than in most African states.

■ **Change**

What accounts for the ups and downs of political democracy in postcolonial Africa?

Explaining the initial rejection of democracy in Africa has been a major concern of politicians and scholars alike. Some have argued, on the basis of paternalistic or even racist assumptions, that Africans were not ready for democracy or that they lacked some crucial ingredient for democratic politics—an educated electorate, a middle class, or perhaps a thoroughly capitalist economy. Others suggested that Africa's traditional culture, based on communal rather than individualistic values and concerned to achieve consensus rather than majority rule, was not compatible with the competitiveness of party politics.

Furthermore, some argued, Western-style democracy was simply inadequate for the tasks of development confronting the new states. Creating national unity was certainly more difficult when competing political parties identified primarily with particular ethnic or "tribal" groups, as was frequently the case in Africa. Similarly, the immense problems that inevitably accompany the early stages of modern economic development were compounded by the heavy demands of a political system based on universal suffrage. Certainly Europe did not begin its modernizing process with such a system. Why, many Africans asked, should they be expected to do so?

Beyond these general considerations, more immediate conditions likewise undermined the popular support of many postindependence governments in Africa and discredited their initial democracies. One was widespread economic disappointment. By almost any measure, African economic performance since independence has been the poorest in the developing world. This has translated into students denied the white-collar careers they expected, urban migrants with little opportunity for work, farmers paid low prices for their cash crops, consumers resentful about shortages and inflation, and millions of impoverished and malnourished peasants pushed to the brink of starvation. These were people for whom independence was unable to fulfill even the most minimal of expectations, let alone the grandiose visions of a better life that so many had embraced in the early 1960s. Since modern governments everywhere staked their popularity on economic performance, it is little wonder that many Africans became disaffected and withdrew their support from governments they had enthusiastically endorsed only a few years earlier.

Nevertheless, economic disappointment did not affect everyone to the same extent, and for some, independence offered great opportunities for acquiring status, position, and wealth. Unlike the situation in Latin America and parts of Asia, those who benefited most from independence were not large landowners, for most African societies simply did not have an established class whose wealth was based in landed estates. Rather they were members of the relatively well-educated elite who had found high-paying jobs in the growing bureaucracies of the newly independent states. The privileges of this dominant class were widely resented. Government ministers in many countries earned the title "Mr. Ten Percent," a reference to the bribes or "gifts" they received from private contractors working for the state. This kind of resentment broke out in Zaire between 1964 and 1968 in the form of a widespread peasant rebellion calling for a "second independence" against the "new whites" of the elite class.

Frequently, however, the resentments born of inequality and of competition for jobs, housing, educational opportunities, development projects, and political position found expression in ethnic conflict, as Africa's immense cultural diversity became intensely politicized. In many places, a judicious balancing of appointments and budgetary allocations among major ethnic groups contained conflict within a peaceful political process. Elsewhere it led to violence. An ethnically based civil war in Nigeria during the late 1960s cost the lives of millions, while in the mid-1990s ethnic hatred led Rwanda into the realm of genocide.

Thus economic disappointment, class resentments, and ethnic conflict eroded support for the transplanted democracies of the early independence era. The most common alternative involved government by soldiers, a familiar pattern in Latin America as well. By the early 1980s, the military had intervened in at least thirty of Africa's forty-six independent states and actively governed more than half of them.

Usually, the military took power in a crisis, after the civilian government had lost most of its popular support. The soldiers often claimed that the nation was in grave danger, that corrupt civilian politicians had led the country to the brink of chaos, and that only the military had the discipline and strength to put things right. And so they swept aside the old political parties and constitutions and vowed to begin anew, while promising to return power to civilians and restore democracy at some point in the future.

Since the early 1980s, a remarkable resurgence of Western-style democracy has brought popular movements, multiparty elections, and new constitutions to a number of African states, including Ghana, Kenya, Mali, Senegal, and Zambia. It was part of a late-twentieth-century democratic revival of global dimensions that included Southern and Eastern Europe, most of Latin America, and parts of Asia and the Middle East. How can we explain this rather sudden, though still fragile, resumption of democracy in Africa? Perhaps the most important internal factor was the evident failure of authoritarian governments to remedy the disastrous economic situation. Disaffected students, religious organizations, urban workers, and women's groups joined in a variety of grassroots movements to demand democratic change as a means to a better life. This pressure from below for political change reflected the growing strength of civil society in many African countries as organizations independent of the state provided a social foundation for the renewal of democracy.

Such movements found encouragement in the demands for democracy that accompanied the South African struggle against apartheid and the collapse of Soviet and Eastern European communism. The end of the cold war reduced the willingness of the major industrial powers to underwrite their authoritarian client states. For many Africans, democracy increasingly was viewed as a universal political principle to which they could also aspire rather than an alien and imposed system deriving from the West. None of this provided an immediate solution for the economic difficulties, ethnic conflicts, and endemic corruption of African societies, but it did suggest a willingness to continue the political experiments that had begun with independence.

Experiments in Economic Development: Changing Priorities, Varying Outcomes

■ **Change**

What obstacles impeded the economic development of third-world countries?

At the top of the agenda everywhere in the Global South was economic development, a process that meant growth or increasing production as well as distributing the fruits of that growth to raise living standards. This quest for development, now operating all across the planet, represented the universal acceptance of beliefs unheard of not many centuries earlier—that poverty was no longer inevitable and that it was possible to deliberately improve the material conditions of life for everyone. Economic development was a central promise of all independence struggles, and it was increasingly the standard by which people measured and granted legitimacy to their governments.

Achieving economic development, however, proved immensely difficult. It took place in societies sharply divided by class, religion, ethnic group, and gender and in the face of explosive population growth. In many places, colonial rule had provided only the most slender foundations for modern development to these newly independent nations, which had low rates of literacy, few people with managerial experience, a weak private economy, and transportation systems oriented to export rather than national integration. Furthermore, the entire effort occurred in a world split by rival superpowers and economically dominated by the powerful capitalist economies of the West. Despite their political independence, most developing countries had little leverage in negotiations with the wealthy nations of the Global North and their immense transnational corporations. It was hardly an auspicious environment in which to seek a fundamental economic transformation.

Beyond these structural difficulties, it was hard for leaders of developing countries to know what strategies to pursue. The academic field of "development economics" was new; its experts disagreed and often changed their minds; and conflicting political pressures, both internal and international, only added to the confusion. All of this resulted in considerable controversy, changing policies, and much experimentation. (See Documents: Debating Development in Africa, pp. 1110–21, for various African views about development.)

One fundamental issue lay in the role of the state. All across the developing world and particularly in newly independent nations, most people expected that state authorities would take major responsibility for spurring the economic development of their countries. After all, the private economy was weakly developed; few entrepreneurs had substantial funds to invest; the example of rapid Soviet industrialization under state direction was hopeful; and state control held the promise of protecting vulnerable economies from the ravages of international capitalism. Some state-directed economies had real successes. China launched a major industrialization effort and massive land reform under the leadership of the Communist Party. A communist Cuba, even while remaining dependent on its sugar production, wiped out illiteracy and provided basic health care to its entire population, raising life expectancy to seventy-six years by 1992, equivalent to that of the United States. Elsewhere as well—in Turkey, India, South Korea, and much of Africa—the state provided tariffs, licenses, loans, subsidies, and overall planning, while most productive property was owned privately.

Yet in the last several decades of the twentieth century, an earlier consensus in favor of state direction largely collapsed, replaced by a growing dependence on the market to generate economic development. This was most apparent in the abandonment of much communist planning in China and the return to private farming (see pp. 1052–54). India and many Latin American and African states privatized their state-run industries and substantially reduced the role of the state in economic affairs. In part, this sharp change in economic policies reflected the failure, mismanagement, and corruption of many state-run enterprises, but it also was influenced by the collapse in the Soviet Union of the world's first state-dominated economy. Western pressures, exercised through international organizations such as the World Bank, likewise pushed developing countries in a capitalist direction. In China and India, the new approach generated rapid economic growth, but also growing inequalities and social conflict. As the new millennium dawned, a number of Latin American countries—Venezuela,

■ **Change**

In what ways did thinking about the role of the state in the economic life of developing countries change? Why did it change?

Snapshot   **Economic Development in the Global South by the Early Twenty-first Century**[5]

This table samples the economic performance of fourteen developing countries and five major regions of the Global South by the early twenty-first century. Similar data for the United States, Japan, and Russia are included for comparative purposes. Which indicators of development do you find most revealing? What aspects

Regions/Countries	Population Growth Rate Average Annual 2000–2007 (%)	Gross National Income per Capita, 2007 (U.S. $)	Purchasing Power per Capita, 2007 (U.S. $)
East Asia	0.8	2,180	4,937
China	0.6	2,360	5,370
Philippines	2.0	1,620	3,370
Latin America	1.3	5,540	9,321
Mexico	1.0	8,340	12,580
Brazil	1.4	5,910	9,370
Guatemala	2.5	2,440	4,520
Middle East and North Africa	1.8	2,794	7,385
Egypt	1.8	1,580	5,400
Turkey	1.3	8,020	12,090
Iran	1.5	3,470	10,800
Saudi Arabia	2.3	15,440	22,910
South Asia	1.6	880	2,537
India	1.4	950	2,470
Indonesia	1.3	1,650	3,580
Sub-Saharan Africa	2.5	952	1,870
Nigeria	2.4	930	1,770
Congo	3.0	140	290
Tanzania	2.5	400	1,200
For comparison			
High-income countries	0.7	37,566	36,100
United States	0.9	46,040	45,850
Japan	0.1	37,670	34,600
Russia	−0.5	7,560	14,400

of development does each of them measure? Based on these data, which countries or regions would you consider the most and the least successful? Does your judgment about "success" vary depending on which measure you use?

Life Expectancy in years, 2003–2006		Adult Literacy (%) 2005	Infant Mortality (Deaths under Age 5 per 1,000)		CO$_2$ Emission per Capita, 2004 (Metric Tons)
MALE	FEMALE		1990	2006	
69	73	91	56	29	3.3
70	74	91	45	24	3.9
69	74	93	62	32	1.0
70	76	90	55	20	2.7
72	77	92	53	35	4.3
69	76	89	57	20	1.8
66	74	69	82	41	1.0
68	72	73	78	42	4.2
69	73	71	91	35	2.2
69	74	87	82	26	3.2
69	72	82	72	34	6.4
71	75	83	44	25	13.7
63	66	58	123	83	1.1
63	66	61	115	76	1.2
66	70	90	91	34	1.7
49	52	59	184	157	0.9
46	47	69	230	191	0.8
45	47	67	205	205	0.0
51	53	69	161	118	0.1
76	82	99	12	7	13.1
75	81	99	11	8	20.6
79	86	99	6	4	9.8
59	73	99	27	16	10.6

Microloans

Bangladesh's Grameen Bank pioneered an innovative approach to economic development by offering modest loans to poor people, enabling them to start small businesses. Here a group of women who received such loans meet in early 2004 to make an installment payment to an officer of the bank. (Rafiqur Rahman/Reuters/Corbis)

Brazil, and Bolivia, for example—once again asserted a more prominent role for the state in their quests for economic development and social justice.

Other issues as well inspired debate. In many places, an early emphasis on city-based industrial development, stirred by visions of a rapid transition to modernity, led to a neglect or exploitation of rural areas and agriculture. This "urban bias" subsequently came in for much criticism and some adjustment in spending priorities. A growing recognition of the role of women in agriculture led to charges of "male bias" in development planning and to mounting efforts to assist women farmers directly (see Document 23.4). Women also were central to many governments' increased interest in curtailing population growth. Women's access to birth control, education, and employment, it turned out, provided powerful incentives to limit family size. Another debate pitted the advocates of capital- and technology-driven projects (dams and factories, for example) against those who favored investment in "human capital," such as education, technical training, health care, and nutrition. The benefits and drawbacks of foreign aid, investment, and trade have likewise been contentious issues. Should developing countries seek to shield themselves from the influences of international capitalism, or are they better off vigorously engaging with the global economy?

Economic development was never simply a matter of technical expertise or deciding among competing theories. Every decision was political, involving winners and losers in terms of power, advantage, and wealth. Where to locate schools, roads, factories, and clinics, for example, provoked endless controversies, some of them expressed in terms of regional or ethnic rivalries. It was an experimental process, and the stakes were high.

The results of those experiments have varied considerably, as the Snapshot on pages 1100–01 indicates. East Asian countries in general have had the strongest record of economic growth. South Korea, Taiwan, Singapore, and Hong Kong were dubbed "newly industrialized countries," and China boasted the most rapid economic growth in the world by the end of the twentieth century, replacing Japan as the world's second-largest economy. In the 1990s, Asia's other giant, India, opened itself more fully to the world market and launched rapid economic growth with a powerful high-tech sector and an expanding middle class. Oil-producing countries reaped a bonanza when they were able to demand much higher prices for that essential commodity in the 1970s and after. Several Latin American states (Chile and Brazil, for example) entered the world market vigorously and successfully with growing industrial sectors. Limited principally to Europe, North America, and Japan in the nineteenth century, industrialization had become a global phenomenon in the twentieth century.

Elsewhere, the story was very different. In most of Africa, much of the Arab world, and parts of Asia—regions representing about one-third of the world's population—there was little sign of catching up and frequent examples of declining standards of living since the end of the 1960s. Between 1980 and 2000, the average income in forty-three of Africa's poorest countries dropped by 25 percent, pushing living standards for many below what they had been at independence.

Scholars and politicians alike argue about the reasons for such sharp differences. Variables such as geography and natural resources, differing colonial experiences, variations in regional cultures, the degree of political stability and social equality, state economic policies, population growth rates, and varying forms of involvement with the world economy have been invoked to explain the widely diverging trajectories among developing countries.

Experiments with Culture: The Role of Islam in Turkey and Iran

The quest for economic development represented the embrace of an emerging global culture of modernity—with its scientific outlook, its technological achievements, and its focus on material values. It also exposed developing countries to the changing culture of the West, including feminism, rock and rap, sexual permissiveness, consumerism, and democracy. But the peoples of the Global South also had inherited cultural patterns from the more distant past—Hindu, Confucian, or Islamic, for example. A common issue all across the developing world involved the uneasy relationship between these older traditions and the more recent outlooks associated with modernity and the West. This tension provided the raw material for a series of cultural experiments in the twentieth century, and nowhere were they more consequential than in the Islamic world. No single answer emerged to the question of how Islam and modernity should relate to each other, but the experience of Turkey and Iran illustrate two quite different approaches to this fundamental issue.

In the aftermath of World War I, modern Turkey emerged from the ashes of the Ottoman Empire, led by an energetic general, Mustafa Kemal Atatürk (1881–1938), who fought off British, French, Italian, and Greek efforts to dismember what was left of the old empire. Often compared to Peter the Great in Russia (see p. 844), Atatürk then sought to transform his country into a modern, secular, and national state. Such ambitions were not entirely new, for they built upon the efforts of nineteenth-century

■ **Comparison**

In what ways did cultural revolutions in Turkey and Iran reflect different understandings of the role of Islam in modern societies?

Iran, Turkey, and the Middle East

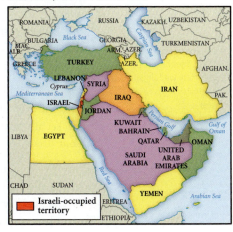

Westernization in Turkey
Mustafa Kemal Atatürk, the founder of modern Turkey, often appeared in public in elegant European dress, symbolizing for his people a sharp break with traditional Islamic ways of living. Here he is dancing with his adopted daughter at her high-society wedding in 1929. (Hulton Archive/Getty Images)

Ottoman reformers, who, like Atatürk, greatly admired European Enlightenment thinking and sought to bring its benefits to their country.

To Atatürk and his followers, to become modern meant "to enter European civilization completely." They believed that this required the total removal of Islam from public life, relegating it to the personal and private realm. In doing so, Atatürk argued that "Islam will be elevated, if it will cease to be a political instrument." In fact, he sought to broaden access to the religion by translating the Quran into Turkish and issuing the call to prayer in Turkish rather than Arabic.

Ataturk largely ended, however, the direct political role of Islam. The old sultan or ruler of the Ottoman Empire, whose position had long been sanctified by Islamic tradition, was deposed as Turkey became a republic. Furthermore the caliphate, by which Ottoman sultans had claimed leadership of the entire Islamic world, was abolished. Various Sufi organizations, sacred tombs, and religious schools were closed and a number of religious titles abolished. Islamic courts were likewise dissolved, while secular law codes, modeled on those of Europe, replaced the *sharia*. In history textbooks, pre-Islamic Turkish culture was celebrated as the foundation for all ancient civilizations. The Arabic script in which the Turkish language had long been written was exchanged for a new Western-style alphabet that made literacy much easier but rendered centuries of Ottoman culture inaccessible to these newly literate people. (See Document 24.1, pp. 1167–68, for an example of Atatürk's thinking.)

The most visible symbols of Atatürk's revolutionary program occurred in the realm of dress. Turkish men were ordered to abandon the traditional headdress known as the *fez* and to wear brimmed hats. According to Atatürk,

> A civilized, international dress is worthy and appropriate for our nation, and we will wear it. Boots or shoes on our feet, trousers on our legs, shirt and tie, jacket and waistcoat—and of course, to complete these, a cover with a brim on our heads.[6]

Although women were not forbidden to wear the veil, many elite women abandoned it and set the tone for feminine fashion in Turkey.

In Atatürk's view, the emancipation of women was a cornerstone of the new Turkey. In a much-quoted speech, he declared:

> If henceforward the women do not share in the social life of the nation, we shall never attain to our full development. We shall remain irremediably backward, incapable of treating on equal terms with the civilizations of the West.[7]

Thus polygamy was abolished; women were granted equal rights in divorce, inheritance, and child custody; and in 1934 Turkish women gained the right to vote and hold public office, a full decade before French women gained that right. Public beaches were now opened to women as well.

These reforms represented a "cultural revolution" unique in the Islamic world of the time, and they were imposed against considerable opposition. After Atatürk's death in 1938, some of them were diluted or rescinded. The call to prayer returned to the traditional Arabic in 1950, and various political groups urged a greater role for Islam in the public arena. In 1996, a moderate Islamic political party came to power, and in early 2008 the Turkish parliament voted to end the earlier prohibition on women wearing headscarves in universities. Nevertheless, the essential secularism of the Turkish state, backed by a powerful military establishment, remained an enduring legacy of the Atatürk revolution. But elsewhere in the Islamic world, other solutions to the question of Islam and modernity took shape.

A very different answer emerged in Iran in the final quarter of the twentieth century. By that time all across the Islamic world, disappointments abounded with the social and economic results of political independence and secular development, while hostility to continuing Western cultural, military, and political intrusion grew apace. These conditions gave rise to numerous movements of Islamic revival or renewal that cast the religion as a guide to public as well as private life. If Western models of a good society had failed, it seemed reasonable to many people to turn their attention to distinctly Islamic solutions.

Iran seemed an unlikely place for an Islamic revolution. Under the government of Shah Mohammad Reza Pahlavi (ruled 1941–1979), Iran had undertaken what many saw as a quite successful modernization effort. The country had great wealth in oil, a powerful military, a well-educated elite, and a solid alliance with the United States. Furthermore, the shah's so-called White Revolution, intended to promote the country's modernization, had redistributed land to many of the Iran's impoverished peasantry, granted women the right to vote, invested substantially in rural health care and education, initiated a number of industrial projects, and offered workers a share in the profits of those industries. But beneath the surface of apparent success, discontent and resentment were brewing. Traditional merchants, known as *bazaaris*, felt threatened by an explosion of imported Western goods and by competition from large-scale businesses. Religious leaders, the *ulama*, were offended by secular education programs that bypassed Islamic schools and by state control of religious institutions. Educated professionals found Iran's reliance on the West disturbing. Rural migrants to the country's growing cities, especially Tehran, faced rising costs and uncertain employment.

A repressive and often brutal government allowed little outlet for such grievances. Thus, opposition to the shah's regime came to center on the country's many

mosques, where Iran's Shi'ite religious leaders invoked memories of earlier persecution and martyrdom as they mobilized that opposition and called for the shah's
removal. The emerging leader of that movement was the high-ranking Shia cleric
Ayatollah Ruholla Khomeini (1902–1989), who in 1979 returned from long exile in
Paris to great acclaim. By then, massive urban demonstrations, strikes, and defections
from the military had eroded support for the shah, who abdicated the throne and left
the country.

What followed was also a cultural revolution, but one that moved in precisely the
opposite direction from that of Atatürk's Turkey—toward, rather than away from,
the Islamization of public life. The new government defined itself as an Islamic republic, with an elected parliament and a constitution, but in practice it represented the
rule of Islamic clerics, in which conservative ulama, headed by Khomeini, exercised
dominant power. The Council of Guardians, composed of leading legal scholars,
was empowered to interpret the constitution, to supervise elections, and to review
legislation—all designed to ensure compatibility with a particular vision of Islam.
Opposition to the new regime was harshly crushed, with some 1,800 executions in
1981 alone for those regarded as "waging war against God."[8]

Khomeini, whose ideas are illustrated more fully in Document 24.3 on pages
1171–73, believed that the purpose of government was to apply the law of Allah
as expressed in the sharia. Thus all judges now had to be competent in Islamic law,
and those lacking that qualification were dismissed. The secular law codes under
which the shah's government had operated were discarded in favor of those based
solely on Islamic precedents. Islamization likewise profoundly affected the domain
of education and culture. In June 1980 the new government closed some 200 universities and colleges for two years while textbooks, curricula, and faculty were
"purified" of un-Islamic influences. Elementary and secondary schools, largely secular under the shah, now gave priority to religious instruction and the teaching of
Arabic, even as about 40,000 teachers lost their jobs for lack of sufficient Islamic
piety. Pre-Islamic Persian literature and history were now out of favor, while the
history of Islam and Iran's revolution predominated in schools and the mass media.
Western loan words were purged from the Farsi language, replaced by their Arabic
equivalents.

As in Turkey, the role of women became a touchstone of this Islamic cultural
revolution. By 1983, all women were required to wear the modest head-to-toe covering known as *hijab*, a regulation enforced by roving groups of militants or "revolutionary guards." Those found with "bad hijab" were subject to harassment and
sometimes lashings or imprisonment. Sexual segregation was imposed in schools,
parks, beaches, and public transportation. The legal age of marriage for girls, set at
eighteen under the shah, was reduced to nine with parental consent and thirteen,
later raised to fifteen, without it. Married women could no longer file for divorce or
attend school. Yet, despite such restrictions, many women supported the revolution
and over the next several decades found far greater opportunities for employment

and higher education than before. By the early twenty-first century, almost 60 percent of university students were women. And women's right to vote was left intact.

While Atatürk's cultural revolution of Westernization and secularism was largely an internal affair that freed Turkey from the wider responsibilities of the caliphate, Khomeini clearly sought to export Iran's Islamic revolution. He openly called for the replacement of insufficiently Islamic regimes in the Middle East and offered training and support for their opponents. In Lebanon, Syria, Bahrain, Saudi Arabia, Iraq, and elsewhere, Khomeini appealed to Shi'ite minorities and other disaffected people, and Iran became a model to which many Islamic radicals looked. An eight-year war with Saddam Hussein's highly secularized Iraq (1980–1988) was one of the outcomes and generated enormous casualties. That conflict reflected the differences between Arabs and Persians, between Sunni and Shia versions of Islam, and between a secular Iraqi regime and Khomeini's revolutionary Islamic government.

After Khomeini's death in 1989, some elements of this revolution eased a bit. For a time enforcement of women's dress code was not so stringent, and a more moderate government came to power in 1997, raising hopes for a loosening of strict Islamic regulations. By 2005, however, more conservative elements were back in control and a new crackdown on women's clothing soon surfaced. A heavily disputed election

Women and the Iranian Revolution
One of the goals of Iran's Islamic Revolution was to enforce a more modest and traditional dress code for the country's women. In this photo from 2004, a woman clad in hijab and talking on her cell phone walks past a poster of the Ayatollah Khomeini, who led that revolution in 1979. (AP Images)

in 2009 revealed substantial opposition to the country's rigid Islamic regime. Iran's ongoing Islamic revolution, however, did not mean the abandonment of economic modernity. The country's oil revenues continued to fund its development, and by the early twenty-first century, Iran was actively pursuing nuclear power and perhaps nuclear weapons, in defiance of Western opposition to these policies.

Reflections: History in the Middle of the Stream

Historians are usually more at ease telling stories that have clear endings, such as those that describe ancient Egyptian civilization, Chinese maritime voyages, the collapse of the Aztec Empire, or the French Revolution. There is a finality to these stories and a distance from them that makes it easier for historians to assume the posture of detached observer, even if their understandings of those events change over time. Finality, distance, and detachment are harder to come by when historians are describing the events of the past century, for many of its processes are clearly not over. The United States' role as a global superpower and its war in Iraq, the fate of democracy in Latin America and Africa, the rise of China and India as economic giants, the position of Islam in Turkey and Iran—all of these are unfinished stories, their outcomes unknown and unknowable. In dealing with such matters, historians write from the middle of the stream, often uncomfortably, rather than from the banks, where they might feel more at ease.

In part, that discomfort arises from questions about the future that such issues inevitably raise. Can the spread of nuclear weapons be halted? Will democracy flourish globally? Are Islamic and Christian civilizations headed for a global clash? Can African countries replicate the economic growth experience of India and China? Historians in particular are uneasy about responding to such questions because they are so aware of the unexpectedness and surprising quality of the historical process. Yet those questions about the future are legitimate and important, for as the nineteenth-century Danish philosopher Søren Kierkegaard remarked: "Life can only be understood backward, but it is lived forward." History, after all, is the only guide we have to the possible shape of that future. So, like everyone before us, we stumble on, both individually and collectively, largely in the dark, using analogies from the past as we make our way ahead.

These vast uncertainties about the future provide a useful reminder that although we know the outcomes of earlier human stories—the Asian and African struggles for independence, for example—those who lived that history did not. Such awareness can perhaps engender in us a measure of humility, a kind of sympathy, and a sense of common humanity with those whose lives we study. However we may differ from our ancestors across time and place, we share with them an immense ignorance about what the future holds.

Second Thoughts

What's the Significance?

decolonization

Indian National Congress

Mahatma Gandhi

satyagraha

Muslim League

Muhammad Ali Jinnah

African National Congress

Nelson Mandela

Black Consciousness

Soweto

democracy in Africa

economic development

Kemal Atatürk

Ayatollah Khomeini

To assess your mastery of the material in this chapter, visit the **Student Center** at bedfordstmartins.com/strayer.

Big Picture Questions

1. In what ways did the colonial experience and the struggle for independence shape the agenda of developing countries in the second half of the twentieth century?

2. To what extent did the experience of the former colonies and developing countries in the twentieth century parallel that of the earlier "new nations" in the Americas in the eighteenth and nineteenth centuries?

3. How would you compare the historical experiences of India and China in the twentieth century?

4. From the viewpoint of the early twenty-first century, to what extent had the goals of nationalist or independence movements been achieved?

Next Steps: For Further Study

Chinua Achebe, *Anthills of the Savannah* (1989). A brilliant fictional account of postindependence Nigeria by that country's foremost novelist.

Fredrick Cooper, *Africa since 1940* (2002). A readable overview of the coming of independence and efforts at development by a leading historian of Africa.

Ramachandra Guha, *India after Gandhi: The History of the World's Largest Democracy* (2007). A thoughtful account of India's first six decades of independence.

John Isbister, *Promises Not Kept* (2006). A well-regarded consideration of the obstacles to and struggles for development in the Global South.

Nelson Mandela, *Long Walk to Freedom: The Autobiography of Nelson Mandela* (1995). Mandela's account of his own amazing life as nationalist leader and South African statesman.

W. David McIntyre, *British Decolonization, 1946–1997* (1998). A global history of the demise of the British Empire.

Complete site on Mahatma Gandhi, http://www.mkgandhi.org. A wealth of resources for exploring the life of Gandhi.

For Web sites and additional documents related to this chapter, see **Make History** at bedfordstmartins.com/strayer.

Documents

Considering the Evidence:
Debating Development in Africa

Nowhere were the expectations for national independence greater than in Africa during the 1950s through the 1970s as country after country broke free from colonial rule. "We shall achieve in a decade what it took others a century," declared Kwame Nkrumah, who had led Ghana to freedom in 1957 as black Africa's first independent country. "[W]e shall not rest content until we demolish these miserable colonial structures and erect in their place a veritable paradise."[9] But nowhere have the disappointments of the postindependence era been more acute than in Africa. Despite some scattered successes, Africa after independence experienced the slowest rate of economic growth among the various regions of the developing world. Famine, civil war, genocide, failed states, endemic corruption, the AIDS epidemic, massive poverty, frequent military coups—all of this and more accompanied, and surely contributed to, the economic disappointments of the past half-century.

Such conditions have generated a sharp debate about development among African political and intellectual leaders as well as among disillusioned citizens. Why have African nations performed so poorly in improving the living standards of their impoverished people? What strategies should African states adopt in their continuing search for development? The documents presented here offer a sample of African thinking about development.

Document 23.1

The Colonial Legacy for Modern Development

The starting point for much discussion about African development is the legacy of colonial rule. How well or how poorly had the colonial experience prepared these new countries for modern economic development? To varying degrees, most recent African assessments have been highly critical, even while acknowledging some positive developments. One such account comes from the well-known Ghanaian historian A. Adu Boahen. He recognized some benefits of colonial rule: a measure of "peace and stability" for a time; "an infrastructure of roads, railways, harbors"; the "spread of cash crop agriculture...and western education"; and opportunities for social mobility. But the overall thrust of his judgment was negative.

- What were Boahen's chief criticisms of the colonial economy?

- What problems or challenges did the colonial economic legacy present to newly independent states?

- How might European defenders of colonial rule respond to Boahen's critique?

- How does Boahen's assessment of colonial rule in Africa compare to that of Indian critics of colonial rule as reflected in Documents 20.3, 20.4, and 20.5?

A. ADU BOAHEN
African Perspectives on Colonialism
1987

Had African states been in control of their own destinies—as say, Japan was…—there is no reason why…they could not also have followed the Japanese model, as indeed some of their educated sons…were advocating…. It is in this loss of sovereignty and the consequent isolation from the outside world that one finds one of the most pernicious impacts of colonialism on Africa and one of the fundamental causes of its present underdevelopment and technological backwardness….

The transportation and communication infrastructure that was provided [by colonial rule] was not only inadequate but was also very unevenly distributed…. The roads and railways were by and large constructed to link areas with the potential for cash crops and mineral deposits with the sea or the world commodity market. [They] were meant to facilitate the exploitation of natural resources, but not to promote…the development of all regions of the colony. The outcome…has been uneven regional economic development….

[T]he colonial system led to the delay of industrial and technological developments in Africa…. One of the typical features of the colonial political economy was the total neglect of industrialization and of the processing of locally produced raw materials and agricultural products in the colonies…. [P]reexisting industries were almost all eradicated by the importation of cheap and even better substitutes from Europe and India…. This…further explains Africa's present technological backwardness….

[C]olonialism saddled most colonies with monocrop economies…. Each colony was made to produce a single cash crop or two, and no attempts were made to diversify the agricultural economy…. The other consequence of this concentration on the production of cash crops for export was the neglect of the internal sector of the economy and, in particular, of the production of food for internal consumption. Thus, during the colonial period, Africans were encouraged to produce what they did not consume and to consume what they did not produce, a clear proof of the exploitative nature of the colonial political economy….

Colonialism also put an end to inter-African trade…. The new artificial boundaries not only divided peoples but also blocked the centuries-old transregional and regional caravan routes…. The flow of trade in each colony was now oriented to the relevant metropolitan country….

[A]ll the colonial currencies were tied to those of the metropolitan countries, and all their foreign exchange earnings were kept in the metropolitan countries and not used for internal development.

Source: A. Adu Boahen, *African Perspectives on Colonialism* (Baltimore: The Johns Hopkins University Press, 1987), pp. 99–108.

The expatriate commercial banks and companies were also allowed to repatriate their deposits, savings, and profits instead of reinvesting them in the colonies for further development. The consequence of all this was that at the time of independence, no African state apart from the Union of South Africa had the strong economic or industrial base needed for a real economic takeoff....

[I]t was the colonial system that initiated the gap that still exists between the urban and rural areas. All of the modern facilities—schools, hospitals, street lights, radio, postal services—and above all most of the employment opportunities were concentrated in the urban centers. The combination of modern life and employment pulled rural dwellers, especially the young one and those with schooling, in the direction of the cities.

[T]he social services provided by colonialism were grossly inadequate and unevenly distributed.... University education was totally ignored in all the colonies until the 1940s, and only one university was subsequently established for each colony.... In practically every colony only a very small percentage of school-age children could gain admission into schools....

The effects of colonial education were really unfortunate.... Because of its inadequacy, large numbers of Africans remained illiterate.... The elite produced by these colonial educational institutions were with few exceptions people who were alienated from their own society in terms of their dress, outlook, and tastes in food, music, and even dance. They were people who worshiped European culture and looked down on their own culture....

Another negative social impact of colonialism was the downgrading of the status of women in Africa.... [T]here were far fewer facilities for girls than for boys. Women could not therefore gain access into the professions.... The colonial world was definitely a man's world, and women were not allowed to play any meaningful role in it except as petty traders and farmers.

The colonial administrators and their allies, the European missionaries, condemned everything African in culture—African names, music, dance, art, religion, marriage, the system of inheritance—and completely discouraged the teaching of these things in their schools and colleges....

[This has resulted in] the creation of a colonial mentality among educated Africans in particular and also among the populace in general. This mentality manifests itself in the condemnation of anything traditional, in the preference for imported goods to locally manufactured goods (since independence), and in the style of dress—such as the wearing of three piece suits in a climate where temperatures routinely exceed eighty degrees Farenheit. Above all, it manifests itself in the belief...that government and all public property and finance belong, not to the people, but to the colonial government, and could and should therefore be taken advantage of at the least opportunity, a belief which leads to the often reckless dissipation and misuse of public funds and property.

Document 23.2

Development and African Unity

One of the most important legacies of the colonial era was the African continent's division into more than fifty separate countries, many of them quite small. And yet the common experience of colonial rule and the sharp racial divisions of the colonial era had also given rise to the notion of an overall African identity, especially among educated people. As independence dawned across the continent, some leaders sought to translate that pan-African ideal into a concrete political and economic union. The chief spokesman for that idea in the early years of independence was Ghana's nationalist leader and its first president, Kwame Nkrumah. He was convinced that only in union could the African continent achieve genuine and substantial economic development. Nkrumah's pan-African ideal has achieved some very modest successes in the form of several regional groupings of African states trying to coordinate their economic policies and in an African Union in which all African states seek to address common problems. But nothing approaching the kind of larger economic and political union that Nkrumah envisaged has emerged.

- Why did Nkrumah think that union was so essential? What benefits would it bring to Africa in its efforts at development?

- What kind of union did Nkrumah seek?

- What challenges does Nkrumah identify to his soaring vision of a United States of Africa? Which of these do you think was most daunting?

- Why do you think the thirteen separate colonies of British North America were able to form a United States of America in the late eighteenth century while their twentieth-century counterparts in Africa have not created a more substantial union?

Kwame Nkrumah
Africa Must Unite
1963

There are those who maintain that Africa cannot unite because we lack the three necessary ingredients for unity, a common race, culture, and language. It is true that we have for centuries been divided. The territorial boundaries dividing us were fixed long ago, often quite arbitrarily, by the colonial powers. Some of us are Moslems, some Christians; many believe in traditional, tribal gods. Some of us speak French, some English, some Portuguese, not to mention the millions who speak only one of the hundreds of different African languages. We have acquired cultural differences which affect our outlook and condition our political development....

In the early flush of independence, some of the new African states are jealous of their sovereignty and tend to exaggerate their separatism in a historical

period that demands Africa's unity in order that their independence may be safeguarded....

[A] united Africa—that is, the political and economic unification of the African Continent—should seek three objectives:

Firstly, we should have an overall economic planning on a continental basis. This would increase the industrial and economic power of Africa. So long as we remain balkanized, regionally or territorially, we shall be at the mercy of colonialism and imperialism. The lesson of the South American Republics vis-à-vis the strength and solidarity of the United States of America is there for all to see.

The resources of Africa can be used to the best advantage and the maximum benefit to all only if they are set within an overall framework of a continentally planned development. An overall economic plan, covering an Africa united on a continental basis, would increase our total industrial and economic

Source: Kwame Nkrumah, *Africa Must Unite* (London: Heinemann, 1963), 132, 148, 218–21.

power. We should therefore be thinking seriously now of ways and means of building up a Common Market of a United Africa and not allow ourselves to be lured by the dubious advantages of association with the so-called European Common market....

Secondly, we should aim at the establishment of a unified military and defense strategy....

For young African States, who are in great need of capital for internal development, it is ridiculous—indeed suicidal—for each State separately and individually to assume such a heavy burden of self-defense, when the weight of this burden could be easily lightened by sharing it among themselves....

The third objective: [I]t will be necessary for us to adopt a unified foreign policy and diplomacy to give political direction to our joint efforts for the protection and economic development of our continent.... The burden of separate diplomatic representation by each State on the Continent of Africa alone would be crushing, not to mention representation outside Africa. The desirability of a common foreign policy which will enable us to speak with one voice in the councils of the world, is so obvious, vital and imperative that comment is hardly necessary....

Under a major political union of Africa there could emerge a United Africa, great and powerful, in which the territorial boundaries which are the relics of colonialism will become obsolete and superfluous, working for the complete and total mobilization of the economic planning organization under a unified political direction. The forces that unite us are far greater than the difficulties that divide us at present, and our goal must be the establishment of Africa's dignity, progress, and prosperity.

Document 23.3

Development, Socialism, and Self-Reliance

In the early postindependence decades, a number of African states expressed their plans for development in terms of socialism. After all, capitalism was associated with a despised colonial rule, and the communist countries of the Soviet Union and China had made significant economic progress within a socialist framework. One of the most prominent expressions of this socialist approach to development came from Tanzania, in East Africa. There Julius Nyerere, the country's nationalist leader and its first president, articulated a distinctly African and non-Marxist version of socialism, known as *ujamaa* ("familyhood" in the Swahili language). Ujamaa found expression in the nationalization of businesses and rental housing in the cities, while in the countryside socialist villages were supposed to encourage the cooperative working of the land and the creation of small local manufacturing industries. Document 23.3 presents excerpts from the Arusha Declaration of 1967, which spelled out the basic principles of ujamaa socialism.

- What kind of development does the declaration foresee for Tanzania?

- What criticisms does it make about other formulas for development?

- What is socialist about the Arusha Declaration? How does it differ from Marxist socialism (see Documents, Chapter 18, pp. 855–66)?

In an economic sense, ujamaa socialism in Tanzania was largely a failure and was later abandoned. Farmers herded into communal villages did not have much personal incentive to produce, and state-run businesses were inefficient and badly managed.

■ What features of the Arusha Declaration might have contributed to this failure?

JULIUS NYERERE

The Arusha Declaration
1967

We are trying to overcome our economic weakness by using the weapons of the economically strong—weapons which in fact we do not possess.... It is stupid to rely on money as the major instrument of development when we know only too well that our country is poor. It is...even more stupid, for us to imagine that we shall rid ourselves of our poverty through foreign financial assistance rather than our own financial resources....

We are mistaken when we imagine that we shall get money from foreign countries, firstly because, to say the truth, we cannot get enough money for our development and, secondly, because even if we could get it, such complete dependence on outside help would have endangered our independence and the other policies of our country.

We have put too much emphasis on industries.... The mistake we are making is to think that development *begins* with industries. It is a mistake because we do not have the means to establish many modern industries in our country. We do not have either the necessary finances or the technical know-how.... And even if we could get the necessary assistance [from foreigners], dependence on it could interfere with our policy of socialism. The policy of inviting a chain of capitalists to come and establish industries in our country might succeed in giving us all the industries we need, but it would also succeed in pre-

venting the establishment of socialism unless we believe that without first building capitalism, we cannot build socialism.

Our emphasis on money and industries has made us concentrate on urban development.... The largest proportion of the [foreign] loans will be spent in, or for, the urban areas, but the largest proportion of the repayment will be made through the efforts of the farmers [through the sale of their agricultural products].... We must not forget that people who live in towns can possibly become the exploiters of those who live in the rural areas....

A great part of Tanzania's land is fertile and gets sufficient rains. Our country can produce various crops for home consumption and for export. We can produce food crops such as maize, rice, wheat, beans, and groundnuts. And we can produce such cash crops as sisal, cotton, coffee, tobacco, pyrethrum, and tea. Our land is also good for grazing cattle, goats, sheep, and for raising chickens; we can get plenty of fish from our rivers, lakes, and from the sea.... [O]ur purpose must be to increase production of these agricultural crops. This is in fact the only road through which we can develop our country....

Everybody wants development, but not everybody understands and accepts the basic requirements for development. The biggest requirement is hard work.... In towns, for example, the average paid worker works...for 45 hours a week in 48 to 50 weeks a year.

For a country like ours, these are really quite short working hours.... By starting with such short

Source: From "The Policy of Self-Reliance: Excerpts from the Arusha Declaration of February 5, 1967," *Africa Report* (March 1967): 11–13.

working hours and asking for even shorter hours, we are in fact imitating the more developed countries....

It would be appropriate to ask our farmers, especially the men, how many hours a week and how many weeks a year they work. Many do not even work for half as many hours as the wage-earner does. The truth is that in the villages the women work very hard. At times they work for 12 or 14 hours a day. They even work on Sundays and public holidays. Women who live in the villages work harder than anybody else in Tanzania. But the men who live in villages (and some of the women in towns) are on leave for half of their life. The energies of the millions of men in the villages and thousands of women in the towns which are at present wasted in gossip, dancing, and drinking, are a great treasure which could contribute more toward the development of our country than anything we could get from rich nations....

The second condition of development is the use of intelligence. Unintelligent hard work would not bring the same good results as the two combined. Using a big hoe instead of a small one; using a plough pulled by oxen instead of an ordinary hoe; the use of fertilizers; the use of insecticides; knowing the right crop for a particular season or soil; choosing good seeds for planting; knowing the right time for planting, weeding, etc.; all these things show the use of knowledge and intelligence. And all of them combine with hard work to produce more and better results.

The money and time we spend on passing on this knowledge to the peasants are better spent and bring more benefits to our country than the money and the great amount of time we spend on other things which we call development....

None of this means that from now on we will not need money or that we will not start industries or embark upon development projects which require money.... What we are saying, however, is that from now on we shall know what is the foundation and what is the fruit of development. Between *money* and *people* it is obvious that the people and their *hard work* are the foundation of development, and money is one of the fruits of that hard work.... This is the meaning of self-reliance.

Document 23.4

Development and Women

When deliberate planning for African economic development began in earnest following independence, it was focused almost wholly on men, for women had little presence in the modern sector of the economy toward which development was aimed. By the 1980s and 1990s, however, that was changing as scholars and policymakers alike focused more attention on the role of women in the modern development of African countries. In part, this was a consequence of international feminism, which turned the spotlight on issues of gender in all fields of study and practice. Furthermore, the importance of agriculture, in which African women were centrally involved, became increasingly apparent. This new perspective on development is reflected in a 1981 essay written by Mildred Malineo Tau from Lesotho in southern Africa, who was then her country's ambassador to the United States, Mexico, and Brazil.

■ What obstacles to women's active participation in economic development does this document emphasize? How does Ambassador Tau understand the sources of sexual inequality?

- Why does Ambassador Tau believe that development planning should focus explicitly on the needs of women? How would attention to women alter the priorities of development planning?

- What features of Ambassador Tau's development plan might coincide with the priorities of the Arusha Declaration? In what respects might they differ?

- What do the visions of development laid out by Ambassador Tau and the Arusha Declaration tell us about the lives of women in modern Africa? Are these issues unique to Africa or are they common to women everywhere?

MILDRED MALINEO TAU
Women: Critical to African Development
1981

Women, especially rural women, are the core of development in most African countries. Most of them are faced with a disproportionate level of responsibility for which they are ill prepared. Development efforts have had the tendency to "plan *for* instead of *with* women."

Recognition of the role of women in development is critical. There are many efforts to introduce women into the process of development, but these efforts must not be mere gestures to make them appear useful....

One striking characteristic of African women is their multiplicity of roles. African women's contribution to an active involvement in subsistence farming and wage activities, their critical presence in marketing, food distribution networks, and their continued responsibilities as wives and mothers combine to make their role in the survival of the family and the community most important....The majority of African women are engaged in agriculture.

Several factors have mitigated against developmental programs having a positive impact on these women. First, development planning has been based largely on male conceptualizations of life, which most often fail to take into account the activities of, and socioeconomic pressures impinging upon, women. Second, they are often designed from an urban viewpoint rather than from an understanding of the dynamics of rural life.

The heavy dependence in Africa on subsistence agriculture, which is largely the province of women, makes policies affecting land, its distribution, and ownership critical to development....Assuming that men were the primary factors in agricultural production, improved technology and training were offered to men, but not to women....

[T]he increasing monetization of economies in developing countries puts an extra demand on women to raise cash for food, transportation, shelter, school fees, and household supplies. The opportunities for women's entry into the cash economy are severely limited, but it is they who need the cash since incidental cash earned by men is less likely to go into the basic needs of the family than that earned by women....Improving their productive capacity even within these spheres of activity has been limited by their lack of access to training, intermediate and advanced technology, and capital resources.

...The long hours African women labor and the near impossibility of cutting out any of this work

Source: Mildred Malineo Tau, "Women: Critical to African Development," *Africa Report* (March/April, 1981): 4–6.

which is so necessary for daily survival, hinder their ability to participate in development activities, take advantage of training, health services, political forums, etc.

Environmental conditions present in many African countries have imposed heavy burdens on women. Fetching water and collecting fuel can consume a large portion of a woman's time each day. Improving the productive capacity of women as a means of enhancing general development gains will need to include attention to access to water and fuel....

Among the potential resources for development in Africa are a strong tradition of cooperative work and diverse and often strong women's organizations, both formal and informal....

[W]omen may be denied credit as a policy of the bank although by law discrimination is prohibited.

We need support for projects which analyze existing legislation, monitor implementation, or disseminate information and education to grass-roots women on their legal rights and responsibilities.

The issue of women's access to wage work and other sources of cash income in the African continent is more than one of equity. It goes beyond the question of equal rights for women to become one of economic survival for them and their children. Because women in Africa are not secondary earners, neither ideologically nor in reality as are many women in Latin America, for example, but are providers of food, clothing, and shelter, their increased dependence on the monetary economy may have a more immediate negative impact on African women. If their role as main provider continues to go unacknowledged in development planning, the consequences could be serious.

Document 23.5

Development, Elites, and the State

In the aftermath of independence, many African explanations for the continent's mounting economic problems focused on external factors such as the colonial legacy and an unjust world economy dominated by the rich countries. Many argued that the solution to these problems lay in state control or direction of the economy. By the 1980s and 1990s, however, many African economies had deteriorated badly in sharp contrast to the growth patterns of Asian countries, such as South Korea, China, India, and Indonesia. In this context, a number of African intellectuals and some political leaders began to rethink the task of development with a more self-critical focus on the continent's internal problems and with a greater appreciation for the possibilities of private enterprise. Document 23.5, drawn from two of the writings by prominent Ghanaian economist George Ayittey in the 1990s, represents this line of thinking.

■ How does Ayittey understand the major obstacles to development in Africa?

■ How does he view the role of post-independence African elites and the states they govern?

■ What prescriptions for African development are stated or implied in this document?

■ In what ways might Ayittey's prescriptions for development be seen as a rejection of the ideas contained in the first three selections in this feature? To what extent does his thinking build upon, or evolve from, those earlier ideas?

GEORGE B. N. AYITTEY

Africa Betrayed

1992

Africa in Chaos

1998

By the beginning of the 1990s economic and political conditions in Africa had become intolerable....

It is easy for African leaders to put the blame somewhere else; for example, on Western aid donors or on an allegedly hostile international economic environment,... but in my view the internal factors have played far greater roles than the external ones.

True freedom never came to much of Africa after independence. Despite the rhetoric and vituperations against colonialism, very little changed in the years immediately following independence. For many countries independence meant only a change in the color of the administrators from white to black. The new leaders began to act in the same manner as the colonialists. In fact in many places they were worse than the colonialists.

Inchoate democratic structures, hastily erected by the departing colonialists, were perceived by the new leaders as "Western." They were quickly uprooted and replaced with systems that were, in many cases, far more repressive than the hated colonial system....

In most African countries, the elites as a group make up less than 10 percent of the population. Yet they regard political power as their prerogative and government as their property. Political power is not to be shared with the "backward masses," who are too uneducated to understand such esoterica as "constitutional rights." The elites deem it the responsibility of the government to provide and care for themselves. The government must provide them not only jobs but also everything from houses, cars, refrigerators, television sets, to even their own funerals at subsidized rates. Naturally, to win their political support, African governments have been obliged to grant many of these demands. Moreover, governments themselves are run by the elites. Therefore, providing perks and subsidies to one section of the elite class enables the super elites to grab an even larger piece of the pie for themselves....

Dishonesty, thievery, and speculation pervade the public sector. Public servants embezzle state funds; high-ranking ministers are on the take. The chief bandit is the head of state himself. President Mobutu Sese Seko of Zaire was not satisfied with his personal fortune of $10 billion; he stole an entire gold-mining region, Kilo-motor, which covers 32,000 square miles and reportedly has reserves of 100 tons of gold....

[I]n Africa, government officials do not serve the people. The African state has been reduced to a mafia-like bazaar, where anyone with an official designation can pillage at will. In effect, it is a "state" that has been hijacked by gangsters, crooks, and scoundrels. They have seized and monopolized both political and economic power to advance their own selfish and criminal interests, not to develop their economies. Their overarching obsession is to amass

Source: George B. N. Ayittey, *Africa Betrayed* (New York: St. Martin's Press, 1992), 100, 335–36; George B. N. Ayittey, *Africa in Chaos* (New York: St. Martin's Press, 1998), 120–21, 150–52, 248, 343–44.

personal wealth, gaudily displayed in flashy automobiles, fabulous mansions, and a bevy of fawning women. Helping the poor, promoting economic growth, or improving the standard of living of their people is anathema to the ruling elites. "Food for the people!" "People's power!" "Houses for the masses!" are simply empty slogans that are designed to fool the people and the international community. . . .

. . . [V]irtually all the internal problems emanate from two deadly diseases: sultanism° and statism.° While acknowledging that the state or government has a role to play in the development process, the state, as it is conventionally understood, does not exist in Africa. Rather what exists in many African countries is a vampire state—a government hijacked by gangsters, con artists, and scrofulous bandits. . . . Its driving motivation is self-perpetuation in power and self-aggrandizement. Poverty reduction and promotion of economic growth are the least among its priorities. It operates by extracting resources from the productive sections of the population (the peasant majority) and spends it in the urban areas and on the elites—a non-productive, parasitic class.

In country after country, the state has been captured or monopolized by one tiny group—an ethnic group, professional (soldiers), or a religious group—and the instruments of state power and government machinery have been used to advance the economic interests of the ruling group. . . .

In other words, the state vehicle that currently exists in many African countries cannot take Africans on the "development journey" into the twenty-first century. . . .

In the postcolonial period, African governments . . . arrogated onto themselves the power to intervene in almost every conceivable aspect of their economies, ostensibly for "national development" and [to] protect the New African nations against "foreign exploitation." Subsequently, state controls were used for the benefit of a tiny ruling elite. State hegemony in the economy became pervasive. The bureaucracy swelled with payrolls padded with government/party supporters. State controls created shortages and opportunities for illicit enrichment by the elites and bred a culture of bribery and corruption. In addition, they killed off the incentive to produce. The state sector became grotesquely inefficient and wasteful. The rot at the government house propelled the military to intervene in politics. . . .

The pervasive control African governments wield over their economies needs to be rolled back. Peasants who produce foodstuffs and cash crops should be allowed to keep a larger portion of their proceeds. Countries that move away from a state-controlled economy toward greater reliance on the private sector generally do better economically. . . .

Privatization (economic reform) seeks to place the vehicle in the hands of the people or the private sector for the simple reason that it would be better taken care of. Evidence for this fact abounds in Africa. In West Africa some of the privately owned "mammy lories,"° called *trotros* in Ghana and *mutates* in East Africa, that regularly ply the roads, have been in operation for the past 40 years. By contrast, brand-new buses ordered by African governments barely last six months. . . .

[T]here are a number of ways that aid resources Africa desperately needs can be found in Africa itself. . . .

First, in 1989 Africa was spending $12 billion annually to import arms and to maintain the military. Second, the elites illegally transferred from Africa at least $15 billion annually during the latter part of the 1980s. Third, at least $5 billion annually could be saved if Africa could feed itself. Foreign exchange saved is foreign exchange earned. Fourth, another $5 billion could be saved from waste and inefficiencies in Africa's 3,200-odd state enterprises. This might entail selling off some of them or placing them under new management. Fifth, the civil wars raging in Africa exact a heavy toll in lost output, economic development, and destroyed property.

°**sultanism:** one-man rule.

°**statism:** government control of the economy.

°**mammy lories:** mini-buses.

Using the Evidence:
Debating Development in Africa

1. **Defining a controversy:** Based on these documents, identify the major issues that constitute the development debate in post-independence Africa. How do these documents define "development"?

2. **Explaining African economic performance:** What alternative explanations for Africa's poor economic performance over the past half-century are apparent in these documents? To what extent are those explanations at odds with one another? How might you combine them into a single comprehensive understanding of Africa's post-independence economic difficulties? What other factors, not mentioned in these documents, might have contributed to those difficulties?

3. **Comparing prescriptions:** What different policy suggestions or overall approaches to African development are suggested or implied by these documents? How might critics challenge the effectiveness or feasibility of these proposals?

4. **Noticing change:** What differences do you see between Documents 23.2 and 23.3, written during the 1960s and 1970s, and the last two documents, composed in the 1980s and 1990s? How would you explain the changes in tone and emphasis?

Visual Sources

Considering the Evidence: Representing Independence

For millions of people in Africa and Asia, the achievement of political independence from European or American domination marked a singular moment in their personal and collective histories. That moment represented a triumph against great odds and an awakening to the possibility of building new lives and new societies. In the words of India's nationalist leader and first prime minister, Jawaharlal Nehru, it was a "tryst with destiny." Both during the struggle and after, the various meanings attributed to independence found visual expression in a proliferation of poster art. Such images served to inspire and mobilize large numbers of people for the tasks ahead, to articulate a vision of the future, and sometimes to celebrate success. Those grand hopes became a baseline from which future generations measured the realities of the post-independence period.

India's independence movement, embodied in the Congress Party and led by the iconic figure of Mahatma Gandhi, was among the first to achieve success as it broke the hold of British colonialism in 1947. It subsequently became an inspiration and a model for many others all across the colonial world and beyond. That success, however, was the product of long decades of hard struggle against British repression, for the colonial power was reluctant to fully accommodate the increasingly forceful demands of the movement. The Indian nationalist struggle was likewise accompanied by serious internal divisions and controversies, and the moment of its greatest victory also witnessed its greatest tragedy—the bloody partition of the country into two states: a Muslim Pakistan and a largely Hindu India (see pp. 1089–90).

Visual Source 23.1 shows a Congress Party poster from the early 1930s in support of Gandhi's policy of nonviolence and noncooperation with British authorities. In "reading" this richly detailed image, it will be useful to notice a number of its major features. In the center is the Tree of Noncooperation; slightly to the right, a British soldier is trying to shake Gandhi's followers out of the tree using a rope labeled "Policy of Repression" with a British colonial jail prominent in the upper right. In the tree are two rival groups of Gandhi's followers, one labeled the "Swarajya (Independence) Party" and the other called the "No-Change Party," a critical reference to those who thought Gandhi was moving too rapidly and aggressively. Two bridges cross the "Gulf of Differences" at left. One leads to the Council Chamber, representing cooperation with British-created political institutions, while the other leads to the Swarajya Ashram, a center for training young freedom fighters in Gandhi's philosophy of noncooperation. At the bottom left are several blood-stained and quarreling figures labeled "Hindu-Mohammedan friction," while at the upper left three earlier figures in India's nationalist movement overlook the scene below from the clouds.

In the lower right, the female figure labeled Bharat Mata (Mother India) is a Hindu goddess image widely used in Congress Party circles to represent the Indian nation. Her male companion is Krishna, a major Hindu deity, shown pointing toward Gandhi. The quotation above Krishna's head comes from a famous speech that the god made, as recorded in the sacred Hindu text known as the Bhagavad Gita:

> The virtuous people to protect, and to destroy the sinful ones,
> To set up firmly righteousness, from age to age, I enter birth.

Finally, the red-clad Goddess of Unity in the Tree of Noncooperation seeks to hold together the several factions of Gandhi's movement.

- How does the poster portray British colonial authorities in relationship to Gandhi's movement?

- What kinds of divisions within India's nationalist movement does the poster suggest?

- What does the poster disclose about the role of religion, and particularly Hinduism, in the Indian nationalist movement? How might Muslims have responded to the Hindu religious imagery of the poster?

- How does the poster portray Gandhi and his wife, Kasturbai, the woman in white sitting in front of the small red house? According to the poster, what kind of India was Gandhi seeking after independence?

The freedom struggle in South Africa was led by the African National Congress (ANC), a political organization that was founded in 1912 and finally came to power in 1994. Over those decades, its strategy evolved from polite elite protest to confrontational mass campaigns and from a commitment to open and peaceful means to a selective embrace of underground organization and armed struggle. Throughout its history, the ANC held generally to the goal of a democratic and multiracial society. Visual Source 23.2, an undated ANC poster, shows the organization's flag and various symbols of its long struggle. The colors of the flag depict South Africa's resources: black for the vast majority of its population, green for its rich land, and yellow for the gold that had long provided a basis for the country's wealth.

- Does the poster reflect the ANC's earlier, more peaceful and elite-based politics or its later, more aggressive posture? On what do you base your conclusion?

Visual Source 23.1 *Non-Co-operation Tree and Mahatma Gandhi* (© British Library Board, PIB 170/2)

- How might you understand the wheel, the fist, the spear, and the shield shown on the poster? Why do you think the poster used these traditional weapons rather than modern rifles?

- Notice the mass march that provides the background to the poster's primary images. What message does this convey?

- Pay attention to the several red flags, representing the South African Communist Party, among the crowd. What posture toward communism is suggested by these flags? Keep in mind that the Communist Party was a longtime ally of the ANC.

- How might white, Indian, and mixed-race ("colored") supporters of the ANC react to this poster? How might white advocates of apartheid respond to it?

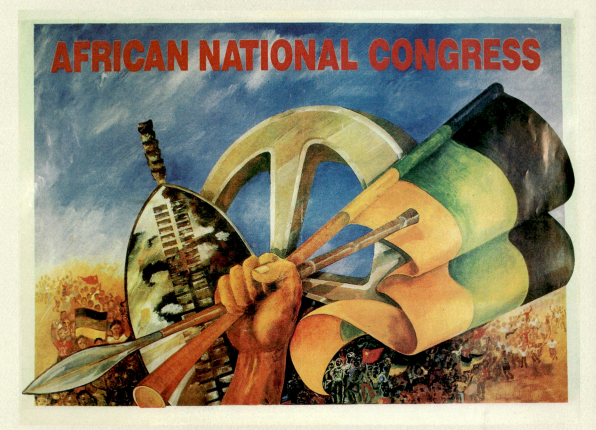

Visual Source 23.2 African National Congress (Special Collections, Senate House Library, University of London)

In Vietnam, the struggle for independence was a prolonged process and took place against a variety of enemies. French colonial rule had prompted various kinds of resistance since the late nineteenth century. Then Japanese occupation of the country during World War II stimulated the formation of a nationalist party known as the Viet Minh, dominated by a communist party and led by Ho Chi Minh. After Japan's defeat in World War II, that movement continued as an effort to oust the French, which succeeded by 1954. At that point, Vietnam was divided between the communist-dominated North Vietnam and the U.S.-backed South Vietnam. What followed was a twenty-year effort by North Vietnam and communist supporters in the south to reunify their country and to drive out the American military forces, which numbered over a half million by the mid-1960s.

By 1975, the North Vietnamese had succeeded (see Map 23.1, p. 1084). It was a stunning reversal for the American superpower and an equally stunning triumph for the small Southeast Asian country. While the reasons for this

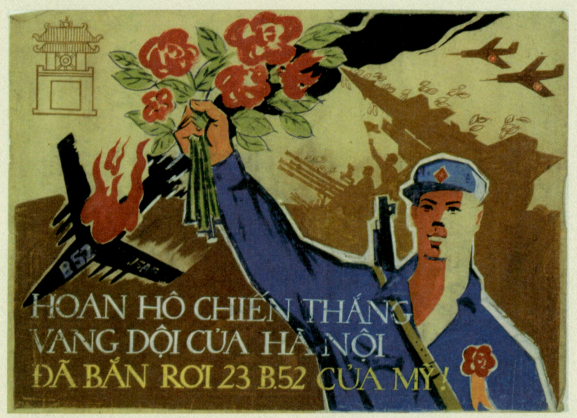

Visual Source 23.3 Vietnamese Independence and Victory over the United States (Laurie Steelink/Track16/ SmartArt, Inc.)

surprising turn of events have been debated ever since, it was clearly of enormous significance for Vietnamese understandings of their national independence. Visual Source 23.3 presents a Vietnamese poster, dating from somewhere between 1965 and 1975, that celebrates one aspect of that unlikely achievement. The caption reads: "Bravo for Hanoi's Tremendous Victory When 23 B-52s Were Shot Down!"

■ How does this poster present the struggle against the United States?

■ In what way does it anticipate or celebrate the victory over the United States? What meaning does it attach to that victory? How might you understand the flowers that the soldier is holding and the small pagoda in the upper left?

■ What other perspectives on this victory for national independence can you imagine? Consider various viewpoints within the United States as well as those of the anticommunist elements in Vietnamese society.

The establishment of the independent state of Israel in 1948 marked an enormous victory for Jewish people that took on rich meaning for them in many contexts. The most historically significant context no doubt lay in the return of widely scattered Jewish people to the ancient biblical homeland from which so many Jews had fled or been expelled by various foreign rulers—Babylonian, Assyrian, Roman, Byzantine, and Crusader European. Since the first century C.E., the majority of the world's Jews had lived in diaspora in the Middle East, North Africa, or Europe, with smaller numbers retaining a Jewish presence in what was then called Palestine. For those whose families had long lived in exile, the opportunity to return to an authentically Jewish state in the area comprising the ancient Land of Israel must have seemed miraculous.

A more immediate context for the establishment of Israel was that of the Zionist movement, formally initiated in Europe in 1897 with the goal of creating a "home for the Jewish people in Palestine." It was a response to the racism and anti-Semitism of European culture, and it drew upon currents of nationalist thinking then surging across Europe. A major expression of Zionism lay in growing Jewish emigration to their ancient homeland, especially during the 1920s and 1930s and even more so in the several years following World War II. During that war some 6 million Jews perished in Nazi death camps as Hitler sought to rid Europe of a Jewish presence. Many among those who survived the Holocaust sought refuge and security in a land of their own.

Two major obstacles confronted these Jewish emigrants. One was British control of Palestine, granted to Great Britain as a mandate of the League of Nations following World War I. While the British favored the eventual creation of a Jewish state, they also feared antagonizing their Arab allies by allowing unfettered Jewish immigration. The second obstacle was opposition from the Arab majority of Palestine, who feared not only the loss of their land as Jewish settlers bought up growing amounts of it but also the loss of their cultural identity as Muslims in what they feared would become a Jewish land. The creation of Israel in 1948, with support from the United Nations, marked the triumph of Zionism and a victory over both British imperialism and Arab resistance.

Visual Source 23.4 shows a Zionist poster created around 1940 and intended to encourage emigration to the Land of Israel and to persuade donors to contribute money for the purchase of land in Palestine. It was titled "Redeem the Land," a reference to the Zionist goal of using up-to-date farming techniques to provide the agricultural basis for a modern society.[10]

- What features of the poster contributed to the Zionists' message?

- Why do you think the land is shown without any people?

- How do you understand the contrast between the richly plowed land and the adjacent barren areas? What image of the new Israel does this poster project?

Visual Source 23.4 Winning a Jewish National State (The Central Zionist Archives, Jerusalem)

■ The fruits on the left side of the poster reflect the biblical description of "promised land" as recorded in Deuteronomy 8:7–10. What is their function in the poster?

If the establishment of Israel as an independent state was a great triumph for Jewish nationalism, it was a disaster for Arabs in general and Palestinian Arabs in particular. In the decades that followed, Israel and various Arab states (Egypt, Jordan, and Syria, for example) went to war repeatedly. The so-called Six Day War of 1967 brought under Israeli control additional Palestinian land, including the West Bank, the Gaza Strip, and East Jerusalem, areas now known as the Palestinian Territories.

At the same time, the Arabs of Palestine, both within Israel and in the adjacent territories, were developing a distinct national identity of their own. Many of them had lost their land and had lived for several generations as refugees in overcrowded camps in neighboring countries or territories where they were dependent on services provided by the United Nations. Almost all Palestinians felt oppressed, constrained, or discriminated against by Israeli authorities. Their emerging national identity found expression in the Palestinian Liberation Organization (PLO), founded in 1964. Initially the PLO called for the complete liberation of Palestine from Zionist colonialism, but by the late 1980s the organization had implicitly recognized the right of Israel to exist and sought a "two-state solution" with an independent Palestine and Israel living side by side.

Achieving even a limited Palestinian state, however, has proved extraordinarily difficult. In pursuit of their national goals, Palestinians have conducted raids, suicide bombing missions, and rocket attacks on Israel from camps in neighboring territories and on several occasions have organized large-scale violent resistance movements known as *intifada*. For its part, Israel has launched highly destructive large-scale military actions in the Palestinian territories, imposed economic blockades that have brought immense suffering to Palestinians, built walls and fences that have disrupted the normal movement of Palestinians, and continued to enlarge the Jewish settlements, especially in the West Bank. Both sides have presented their actions as largely defensive and reactive to the provocations of the other. They have also engaged in periodic negotiations with each other, but those efforts have thus far foundered on unbridgeable differences as to the size and nature of a future Palestinian state, the status of Jerusalem, and the right of Palestinian refugees to return to their lands in Israel. Divisions among Palestinians have also hampered their movement, particularly the recent rivalry between the PLO and Hamas, an Islamic organization with both welfare and political/military functions.

Like other peoples seeking an independent state, Palestinians have represented their struggles in posters such as Visual Source 23.5, created by the Palestinian artist Abdel Rahman Al Muzain in 1984. Featuring a Palestinian

يوم الأرض ٣٠ آذار مارس

Visual Source 23.5 A Palestinian Nation in the Making (Palestine Poster Project Archives/ Visual Connection Archive)

farmer, it was undertaken to commemorate Land Day, an annual observance of the occasion in 1976 when six Palestinians were killed in demonstrations against Israeli confiscation of their land.[11]

■ How might you read this poster as a response to the Israeli poster in Visual Source 23.4?

■ What significance would you attach to the posture and the traditional clothing of the farmer? Why do you think the artist depicted him with a pickax rather than a rifle?

■ What message is conveyed by the rows of traditional houses on the hillside behind the farmer?

■ What expectations for the future does the poster imply? Consider the meaning of the doves between the feet and on the shoulder of the farmer as well as the sun's swirling rays that seem to link the earth and sky.

Using the Evidence:
Representing Independence

1. **Making comparisons:** Movements of national independence can be defined by the conditions they were opposing as well as the kind of future they were seeking. With these two criteria in mind, what similarities and what differences can you identify among these visual sources and the movements they represented?

2. **Defining points of view:** How would you identify the point of view that each of these visual sources conveys? Can you imagine a visual source with an alternative point of view for each of them?

3. **Seeking meaning in visual sources:** How do visual sources such as these help to illuminate the meaning of national independence? In what ways are they limited as sources of evidence for historians?

Accelerating Global Interaction

SINCE 1945

"I think every Barbie doll is more harmful than an American missile," declared Iranian toy seller Masoumeh Rahimi in early 2002. To Rahimi, Barbie's revealing clothing, her shapely appearance, and her close association with Ken, her longtime unmarried companion, were "foreign to Iran's culture." Thus Rahimi warmly welcomed the arrival of Sara and Dara, two Iranian Muslim dolls meant to counteract the negative influence of Barbie and Ken, who had long dominated Iran's toy market. Sara and her brother, Dara, depicted eight-year-old twins. Sara came complete with a headscarf to cover her hair in modest Muslim fashion and a full-length white chador enveloping her from head to toe. They were described as helping each other solve problems, while looking to their loving parents for guidance, hardly the message that Barbie and Ken conveyed.[1]

The widespread availability of Barbie in Muslim Iran provides one small example of the power of global commerce in the world of the early twenty-first century. The creation of Sara and Dara illustrates resistance to the cultural values associated with this American product. Still, Sara and Barbie had something in common: both were manufactured in China. This triangular relationship of the United States, Iran, and China neatly symbolized the growing integration of world economies and cultures as well as the divergences and conflicts that this process generated. Those linked but contrasting patterns are the twin themes of this final chapter.

DURING THE TWENTIETH CENTURY, AN INCREASINGLY DENSE WEB OF POLITICAL RELATIONSHIPS, economic transactions, and

One World: This NASA photograph, showing both the earth and the moon, reveals none of the national, ethnic, religious, or linguistic boundaries that have long divided humankind. Such pictures have both reflected and helped create a new planetary consciousness among growing numbers of people. (Image created by Reto Stockli, Nazmi El Saleous, and Marit Jentoft-Nilsen, NASA GSFC)

cultural influences cut across the world's many peoples, countries, and regions, binding them together more tightly, but also more contentiously. By the 1990s, this process of accelerating engagement among distant peoples was widely known as globalization.

Although the term was relatively new, the process was not. From the viewpoint of world history, the genealogy of globalization reaches far into the past. The Arab, Mongol, Russian, Chinese, and Ottoman empires; the Silk Road, Indian Ocean, and trans-Saharan trade routes; the spread of Buddhism, Christianity, and especially Islam—all of these connections had long linked the societies of the Eastern Hemisphere, bringing new rulers, religions, products, diseases, and technologies to many of its peoples. Later, in the centuries after 1500, European maritime voyages and colonizing efforts launched the Columbian exchange, incorporating the Western Hemisphere and inner Africa firmly and permanently into a genuinely global network of communication, exchange, and often exploitation. During the nineteenth century, as the Industrial Revolution took hold and Western nations began a new round of empire building in Asia and Africa, that global network tightened further, and its role as generator of social and cultural change only increased.

These were the foundations on which twentieth-century globalization was built. A number of prominent developments of the past century, explored in the previous three chapters, operated on a global scale: the world wars, the Great Depression, communism, the cold war, the end of empire. But global interaction, while continuing earlier patterns, vastly accelerated its pace after World War II. Those contacts and interactions among geographically and culturally distant peoples gave rise to a world more densely connected and converging than ever before, but also to a world deeply divided, unequal, conflicted, and violent. To illustrate this accelerating globalization, this chapter examines four major processes: the transformation of the world economy, the emergence of global feminism, the confrontation of world religions with modernity, and the growing awareness of humankind's enormous impact on the environment.

The Transformation of the World Economy

■ **Change**
What factors contributed to economic globalization during the twentieth century?

When most people speak of globalization, they are referring to the immense acceleration in international economic transactions that took place in the second half of the twentieth century and has continued into the twenty-first. Many have come to see this process as almost natural, certainly inevitable, and practically unstoppable. Yet the first half of the twentieth century, particularly the decades between the two world wars, witnessed a deep contraction of global economic linkages as the aftermath of World War I and then the Great Depression wreaked havoc on the world economy. International trade, investment, and labor migration dropped sharply as major states turned inward, favoring high tariffs and economic autonomy in the face of a global economic collapse.

The aftermath of World War II was very different. The capitalist victors in that conflict, led by the United States, were determined to avoid any return to such

Depression-era conditions. At a conference in Bretton Woods, New Hampshire, in 1944, they forged a set of agreements and institutions (the World Bank and the International Monetary Fund) that laid the foundation for postwar globalization. This "Bretton Woods system" negotiated the rules for commercial and financial dealings among the major capitalist countries, while promoting relatively free trade, stable currency values linked to the U.S. dollar, and high levels of capital investment.

Technology also contributed to the acceleration of economic globalization. Containerized shipping, huge oil tankers, and air express services dramatically lowered transportation costs, while fiber-optic cables and later the Internet provided the communication infrastructure for global economic interaction. In the developing countries, population growth, especially when tied to growing economies and modernizing societies, further fueled globalization as dozens of new nations entered the world economy.

What kind of economic globalization was taking shape? In the 1970s and after, major capitalist countries such as the United States and Great Britain abandoned many earlier political controls on economic activity as their leaders and businesspeople increasingly viewed the entire world as a single market. Known as neo-liberalism, this approach to the world economy favored the reduction of tariffs, the free global movement of capital, a mobile and temporary workforce, the privatization of many state-run enterprises, the curtailing of government efforts to regulate the economy, and both tax and spending cuts. Powerful international lending agencies such as the World Bank and the International Monetary Fund imposed such free-market and pro-business conditions on many poor countries if they were to qualify for much-needed loans. The collapse of the state-controlled economies of the communist world only furthered such unrestricted global capitalism. In this view, the market, operating both globally and within nations, was the most effective means of generating the holy grail of economic growth. By the end of the twentieth century, as economic historian Jeffrey Frieden put it, "capitalism was global and the globe was capitalist."[2]

A World Economy
Indian-based call centers that serve North American or European companies and customers have become a common experience of globalization for many. Here employees in one such call center in Patna, a major city in northeastern India, undergo voice training in order to communicate more effectively with their English-speaking callers. (Indiapicture/Alamy)

Reglobalization

These were the foundations for a dramatic quickening of global economic transactions after World War II, a "reglobalization" of the world economy following the contractions of the 1930s. This immensely significant process was expressed in the accelerating circulation of goods, capital, and people.

■ **Connection**

In what ways has economic globalization linked the world's peoples more closely together?

Map 24.1   Globalization in Action: Foreign Direct Investment in the Late Twentieth Century Investment across national borders has been a major expression of globalization. This map shows the global distribution of investment inflows as of 1998. Notice which countries or regions were receiving the most investment from abroad and which received the least. How might you account for this pattern? Keep in mind that some regions, such as the United States, Western Europe, and Japan, were major sources of such investment as well as recipients of it.

World trade, for example, skyrocketed from a value of some $57 billion in 1947 to well over $13 trillion in 2007. Department stores and supermarkets around the world stocked their shelves with goods from every part of the globe. Twinings of London marketed its 120 blends of tea in more than 100 countries, and the Australian-based Kiwi shoe polish was sold in 180 countries. In 2005, about 70 percent of Walmart products reportedly included components from China. And the following year, Toyota replaced General Motors as the world's largest auto maker with manufacturing facilities in at least eighteen countries.

Money as well as goods achieved an amazing global mobility in three ways. The first was "foreign direct investment," whereby a firm in, say, the United States opens a factory in China or Mexico (see Map 24.1 and Visual Source 24.1, p. 1181). Such investment exploded after 1960 as companies in the rich countries sought to take advantage of cheap labor, tax breaks, and looser environmental regulations in the developing countries. A second form of money in motion has been the short-term movement of capital, in which investors annually spent trillions of dollars purchasing foreign currencies or stocks likely to increase in value and often sold them quickly thereafter, with unsettling consequences. A third form of money movement involved the personal funds of individuals. By the end of the twentieth century, international

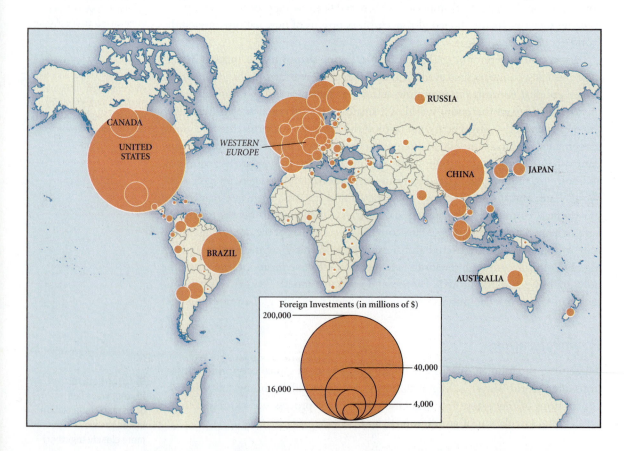

credit cards had taken hold almost everywhere, allowing for easy transfer of money across national borders. In 2003, MasterCard was accepted at some 32 million businesses in 210 countries or territories.

Central to the acceleration of economic globalization have been huge global businesses known as transnational corporations (TNCs), which produce goods or deliver services simultaneously in many countries. For example, Mattel Corporation produced Barbie, that quintessentially American doll, in factories located in Indonesia, Malaysia, and China, using molds from the United States, plastic and hair from Taiwan and Japan, and cotton cloth from China. From distribution centers in Hong Kong, more than a billion Barbies were sold in 150 countries by 1999. Burgeoning in number since the 1960s, those TNCs, such as Royal Dutch Shell, Sony, and General Motors, often were of such an enormous size and economic clout that they dwarfed many countries. By 2000, 51 of the world's 100 largest economic units were in fact TNCs, not countries. In the permissive economic circumstances of recent decades, such firms have been able to move their facilities quickly from place to place in search of the lowest labor costs or the least restrictive environmental regulations. Nike, for example, during one five-year period closed twenty factories and opened thirty-five others, often thousands of miles apart.

More than ever workers too were on the move in a rapidly globalizing world economy. Examples included South Asians and West Indians seeking work and a better life in Great Britain; Algerians and West Africans in France; Yugoslavs in Germany and Switzerland; Mexicans, Cubans, and Haitians in the United States. By 2003, some 4 million Filipino domestic workers were employed in 130 countries. Young women by the hundreds of thousands from poor countries have been recruited as sex workers in wealthy nations, sometimes in conditions approaching slavery. Many highly educated professionals—doctors, nurses, engineers, computer specialists—left their homes in the Global South in a "brain drain" that clearly benefited the Global North. These migrating workers often represented a major source of income to their home countries. They also provided an inexpensive source of labor for their adopted countries, even as their presence generated mounting political and cultural tensions (see Visual Source 24.3, p. 1184). Beyond those seeking work, millions of others sought refuge in the West from political oppression or civil war at home, and hundreds of millions of short-term international travelers and tourists joined the swelling ranks of people in motion.

Growth, Instability, and Inequality

What was the impact of these tightening economic links for nations and peoples around the world? That question has prompted enormous debate and controversy. Amid the swirl of contending opinion, one thing seemed reasonably clear: economic globalization accompanied, and arguably helped generate, the most remarkable spurt of economic growth in world history. On a global level, total world output grew from a value of $7.1 trillion in 1950 to $55.9 trillion in 2003 and on a per capita basis

■ Connection

What new or sharper divisions has economic globalization generated?

Snapshot   **Indicators of Reglobalization**[3]

Telephone lines	from 150 million in 1965 to 1.5 billion in 2000
Mobile telephones	from 0 in 1978 to more than 1 billion in 2004
Internet users	from 0 in 1985 to 934 million in 2004
International air travelers	from 25 million in 1950 to 400 million in 1996
Export processing zones	from 0 in 1957 to 3,000 in 2002
Daily foreign exchange turnover	from $15 billion in 1973 to $1.9 trillion in 2004
International bank loans	from $9 billion in 1972 to $1.465 trillion in 2000
World stock of foreign direct investment	from $66 billion in 1960 to $7.1 trillion in 2002
Value of international trade	from $629 billion in 1960 to $13.6 trillion in 2007
Number of transnational companies	from 7,000 in the late 1960s to 65,000 in 2001

from $2,835 to $8,753.[4] This represents an immense, rapid, and unprecedented creation of wealth with a demonstrable impact on human welfare. Life expectancies grew almost everywhere, infant mortality declined, and literacy increased. The UN Human Development Report in 1997 concluded that "in the past 50 years, poverty has fallen more than in the previous 500."[5]

Far more problematic have been the stability of this emerging world economy and the distribution of the wealth it has generated. Amid overall economic growth, periodic crises and setbacks have likewise shaped recent world history. Soaring oil prices contributed to a severe stock market crash in 1973–1974 and especially great hardship for many developing countries. Inability to repay mounting debts triggered a major financial crisis in Latin America during the 1980s and resulted in a "lost decade" in terms of economic development. Another financial crisis, this time in Asia during the late 1990s, resulted in the collapse of many businesses, widespread unemployment, and political upheaval in Indonesia and Thailand.

But nothing since the Great Depression more clearly illustrated the unsettling consequences of global connectedness in the absence of global regulation than the worldwide economic contraction that began in 2008. When an inflated housing market, or "bubble," in the United States collapsed—triggering millions of home foreclosures, growing unemployment, the tightening of credit, and declining consumer spending—the results rippled around the world. Iceland's rapidly growing economy collapsed almost overnight as three major banks failed, the country's stock market dropped by 80 percent, and its currency lost more than 70 percent of its value—all in a single week. In Africa, reduced demand for exports threatened to halt a promising decade of economic progress. In Sierra Leone, for example, some 90 percent of the country's diamond-mine workers lost their jobs. The slowing of China's once-booming economy led to unemployment for one in seven of the country's urban migrants, forcing them to return to already overcrowded rural areas. Impoverished Central American and Caribbean families, dependent on money sent home by family members working abroad, suffered further as those remittances dropped sharply. Calls for both protectionism and greater regulation suggested that the wide-open capitalist world economy of recent decades was perhaps not as inevitable as some had thought. Whatever the overall benefits of the modern global system, economic stability and steady progress were not among them.

Nor was equality. Since Europe's Industrial Revolution took hold in the early nineteenth century, a wholly new division appeared within the human community—between the rich industrialized countries, primarily in Europe and North America, and everyone else. In 1820, the ratio between the income of the top and bottom 20 percent of the world's population was three to one. By 1991, it was eighty-six to one.[6] The accelerated economic globalization of the twentieth century did not create this global rift, but it arguably has worsened the North/South gap and certainly has not greatly diminished it. Even the well-known capitalist financier and investor George Soros, a billionaire many times over, acknowledged this reality in 2000: "The global capitalist system has produced a very uneven playing field. The gap between the rich and the poor is getting wider."[7] That gap has been evident, often tragically, in great disparities in incomes, medical care, availability of clean drinking water, educational and employment opportunities, access to the Internet, and dozens of other ways. It has shaped the life chances of practically everyone (see Map 24.2 and Visual Source 24.5, p. 1186).

These disparities were the foundations for a new kind of global conflict. As the East/West division of capitalism and communism faded, differences between the rich nations of the Global North and the developing countries of the Global South assumed greater prominence in world affairs. Highly contentious issues have included the rules for world trade, availability of and terms for foreign aid, representation in international economic organizations, the mounting problem of indebtedness, and environmental and labor standards. Such matters surfaced repeatedly in international negotiations during the last half of the twentieth century and into the twenty-first. In the 1970s, for example, a large group of developing countries joined together to demand a "new international economic order" that was more favorable to the poor countries. Not much success attended this effort. More recently, developing countries have contested protectionist restrictions on their agricultural exports imposed by the rich countries seeking to protect their own politically powerful farmers.

Beyond active resistance by the rich nations, a further obstacle to reforming the world economy in favor of the poor lay in growing disparities among the developing countries themselves (see Chapter 23). The oil-rich economies of the Middle East had little in common with the banana-producing countries of Central America. The rapidly industrializing states of China, India, and South Korea had quite different economic agendas than impoverished African countries. These disparities made common action difficult to achieve.

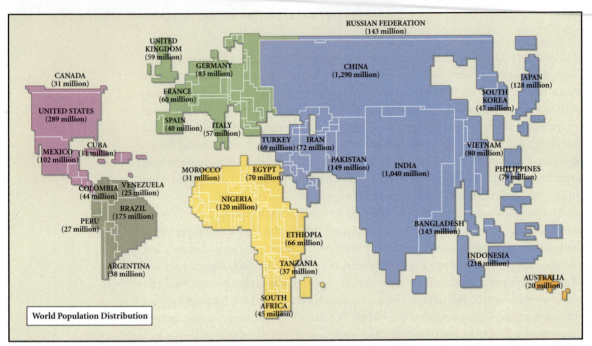

World Population Distribution

RUSSIAN FEDERATION (143 million)
UNITED KINGDOM (59 million)
GERMANY (83 million)
CHINA (1,290 million)
JAPAN (128 million)
FRANCE (60 million)
SOUTH KOREA (47 million)
CANADA (31 million)
UNITED STATES (289 million)
SPAIN (40 million)
ITALY (57 million)
TURKEY (69 million)
IRAN (72 million)
VIETNAM (80 million)
MEXICO (102 million)
CUBA (11 million)
PAKISTAN (149 million)
INDIA (1,040 million)
PHILIPPINES (79 million)
MOROCCO (31 million)
EGYPT (70 million)
COLOMBIA (44 million)
VENEZUELA (25 million)
NIGERIA (120 million)
BRAZIL (175 million)
PERU (27 million)
BANGLADESH (143 million)
ETHIOPIA (66 million)
INDONESIA (218 million)
TANZANIA (37 million)
ARGENTINA (38 million)
AUSTRALIA (20 million)
SOUTH AFRICA (45 million)

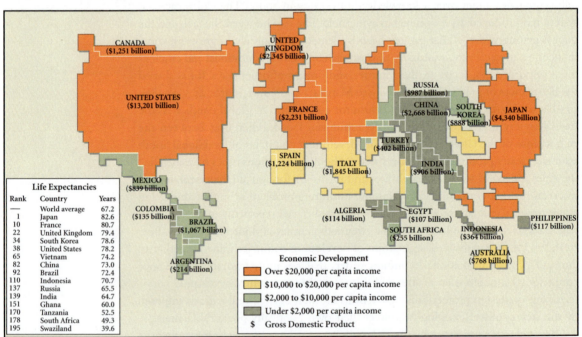

CANADA ($1,251 billion)
UNITED KINGDOM ($2,345 billion)
UNITED STATES ($13,201 billion)
RUSSIA ($987 billion)
FRANCE ($2,231 billion)
CHINA ($2,668 billion)
SOUTH KOREA ($888 billion)
JAPAN ($4,340 billion)
SPAIN ($1,224 billion)
TURKEY ($402 billion)
ITALY ($1,845 billion)
INDIA ($906 billion)
MEXICO ($839 billion)
COLOMBIA ($135 billion)
BRAZIL ($1,067 billion)
ALGERIA ($114 billion)
EGYPT ($107 billion)
PHILIPPINES ($117 billion)
SOUTH AFRICA ($255 billion)
INDONESIA ($364 billion)
AUSTRALIA ($768 billion)
ARGENTINA ($214 billion)

Life Expectancies		
Rank	**Country**	**Years**
—	World average	67.2
1	Japan	82.6
10	France	80.7
22	United Kingdom	79.4
34	South Korea	78.6
38	United States	78.2
65	Vietnam	74.2
82	China	73.0
92	Brazil	72.4
110	Indonesia	70.7
137	Russia	65.5
139	India	64.7
151	Ghana	60.0
170	Tanzania	52.5
178	South Africa	49.3
195	Swaziland	39.6

Economic Development

- 🟧 Over $20,000 per capita income
- 🟨 $10,000 to $20,000 per capita income
- 🟩 $2,000 to $10,000 per capita income
- ⬛ Under $2,000 per capita income
- $ Gross Domestic Product

Map 24.2 Global Inequality: Population and Economic Development
These two maps illustrate in graphic form the global inequalities of the early twenty-first century. The first shows the relative size of the world's population by region and country; the second shows the size of the economy measured by total gross domestic product and per capita income. Illustrating yet another indication of the global economic divide are figures for overall life expectancy, an indicator that has narrowed more sharply than have others.

Economic globalization has generated inequalities not only at the global level and among developing countries but also within individual nations, rich and poor alike. In the United States, for example, a shifting global division of labor required the American economy to shed millions of manufacturing jobs. With recent U.S. factory wages perhaps thirty times those of China, many companies moved their manufacturing operations offshore to Asia or Latin America. This left many relatively unskilled American workers in the lurch, forcing them to work in the low-wage service sector, even as other Americans were growing prosperous in emerging high-tech industries. Even some highly skilled work, such as computer programming, was outsourced to lower-wage sites in India, Ireland, Russia, and elsewhere.

Globalization divided Mexico as well. The northern part of the country, with close business and manufacturing ties to the United States, grew much more prosperous than the south, which was largely a rural agricultural area and had a far more slowly growing economy. Beginning in 1994, southern resentment boiled over in the Chiapas rebellion, which featured a strong antiglobalization platform. Its leader, Subcomandante Marcos, referred to globalization as a "process to eliminate that multitude of people who are not useful to the powerful."[8] China's rapid economic growth likewise fostered mounting inequality between its rural households and those in its burgeoning cities, where income by 2000 was three times that of the countryside. Economic globalization may have brought people together as never before, but it also divided them sharply.

The hardships and grievances of those left behind or threatened by the march toward economic integration have fueled a growing popular movement aimed at criticizing and counteracting globalization. Known variously as an antiglobalization, alternative globalization, or global justice movement, it emerged in the 1990s as an international coalition of political activists, concerned scholars and students, trade unions, women's and religious organizations, environmental groups, and others, hailing from rich and poor countries alike. Thus opposition to neo-liberal globalization was itself global in scope. That opposition, though reflecting a variety of viewpoints, largely agreed that free-trade, market-driven corporate globalization had lowered labor standards, fostered ecological degradation, prevented poor countries from protecting themselves against financial speculators, ignored local cultures, disregarded human rights, and enhanced global inequality, while favoring the interests of large corporations and the rich countries.

This movement appeared dramatically on the world's radar screen in late 1999 in Seattle at a meeting of the World Trade Organization (WTO) (see Visual Source 24.4, p. 1185). An international body representing 149 nations and charged with negotiating the rules for global commerce and promoting free trade, the WTO had become a major target of globalization critics. "The central idea of the WTO," argued one such critic, "is that *free trade*—actually the values and interests of global corporations—should supersede all other values."[9] Tens of thousands of protesters—academics, activists, farmers, labor union leaders from all over the world—descended on Seattle in what became a violent, chaotic, and much-publicized protest. At the city's harbor, protest organizers created a Seattle Tea Party around the slogan "No globalization without representation," echoing the Boston Tea Party of 1773. Subsequent meetings of the WTO and other high-level international economic gatherings were likewise greeted with large-scale protest and a heavy police presence. In 2001, alternative globalization activists created the World Social Forum, an annual gathering to coordinate strategy, exchange ideas, and share experiences, under the slogan "Another world is possible." It was an effort to demonstrate that neo-liberal globalization was not inevitable and that the processes of a globalized economy could and should be regulated and subjected to public accountability.

Globalization and an American Empire

For many people, opposition to this kind of globalization also expressed resistance to mounting American power and influence in the world. An "American Empire," some have argued, is the face of globalization (see Map 24.3), but scholars, commentators, and politicians have disagreed about how best to describe the United States' role in the postwar world. Certainly it has not been a colonial territorial empire such as that of the British or the French in the nineteenth century. Americans generally, seeking to distinguish themselves from Europeans, have vigorously denied that they are an empire at all.

In some ways, the U.S. global presence might be seen as an "informal empire," similar to the ones that Europeans exercised in China and the Middle East during the nineteenth century. In both cases, economic penetration, political pressure, and periodic military action sought to create societies and governments compatible with the values and interests of the dominant power, but without directly governing large populations for long periods. In its economic dimension, American dominance has been termed an "empire of production," which uses its immense wealth to entice or intimidate potential collaborators.[10] Some scholars have emphasized the United States' frequent use of force around the world, while others have focused attention on the "soft power" of its cultural attractiveness, its political and cultural freedoms, the economic benefits of cooperation, and the general willingness of many to follow the American lead voluntarily.

With the collapse of the Soviet Union and the end of the cold war by the early 1990s, U.S. military dominance was now unchecked by any equivalent power. When the United States was attacked by Islamic militants on September 11, 2001, that power was unleashed first against Afghanistan (2001), which had sheltered the al-Qaeda instigators of that attack, and then against Iraq (2003), where Saddam Hussein allegedly had been developing weapons of mass destruction. In the absence of the Soviet Union, the United States could act unilaterally without fear of triggering a conflict with another major power. Although the Afghan and Iraqi regimes were quickly defeated, establishing a lasting peace and rebuilding badly damaged Muslim countries have proved difficult tasks. Thus, within a decade of the Soviet collapse, the United States found itself in yet another global struggle, an effort to contain or eliminate Islamic terrorism.

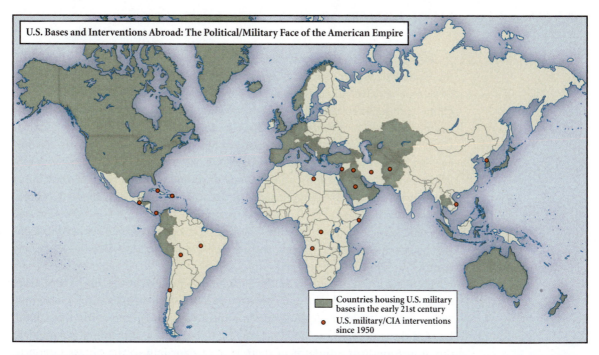

U.S. Bases and Interventions Abroad: The Political/Military Face of the American Empire

Countries housing U.S. military bases in the early 21st century

U.S. military/CIA interventions since 1950

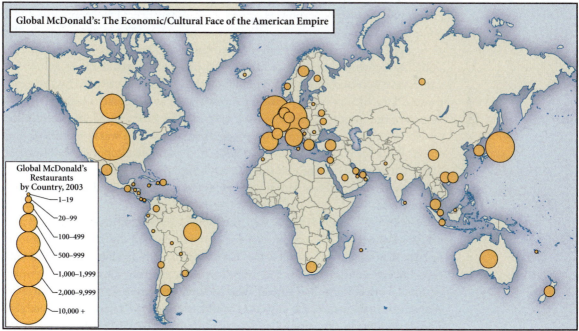

Global McDonald's: The Economic/Cultural Face of the American Empire

Global McDonald's Restaurants by Country, 2003

1–19
20–99
100–499
500–999
1,000–1,999
2,000–9,999
10,000 +

Map 24.3   Two Faces of an "American Empire"

Those who argue that the United States constructed an empire in the second half of the twentieth century point both to its political/military alliances and interventions around the world and to U.S. economic and cultural penetration of many countries. The distribution of U.S. military bases, a partial indication of its open and covert interventions, and the location of McDonald's restaurants indicates something of the scope of America's global presence in the early twenty-first century.

In the final quarter of the twentieth century, as its relative military strength peaked, the United States faced growing international economic competition. The recovery of Europe and Japan and the emergent industrialization of South Korea, Taiwan, China, and India substantially reduced the United States' share of overall world production from about 50 percent in 1945 to 20 percent in the 1980s. By 2008 the United States accounted for just 8.1 percent of world merchandise exports. Accompanying this relative decline was a sharp reversal of the country's trade balance as U.S. imports greatly exceeded its exports. Once the world's leading creditor, the United States now became its leading debtor. Lee Iacocca, president of Chrysler Corporation, registered the dismay that many Americans felt at this turn in their fortunes: "We send Japan low-value soybeans, wheat, corn, coal, and cotton. They send us high-value autos, motorcycles, TV sets, and oil well casings. It's 1776 and we're a colony again."[11]

However it might be defined, the exercise of American power, like that of many empires, was resisted abroad and contested at home. In Korea, Vietnam, Cuba, Iraq, and elsewhere, armed struggle against U.S. intervention was both costly and painful. During the cold war, the governments of India, Egypt, and Ethiopia sought to diminish American influence in their affairs by turning to the Soviet Union or playing off the two superpowers against each other. Even France, resenting U.S. domination, withdrew from the military structure of NATO in 1967 and expelled all foreign-controlled troops from the country. Many intellectuals, fearing the erosion of their own cultures in the face of well-financed American media around the world, have decried American "cultural imperialism." By the early twenty-first century, the United States' international policies—such as its refusal to accept the jurisdiction of the International Criminal Court; its refusal to ratify the Kyoto protocol on global warming; its doctrine of preemptive war, which was exercised in Iraq; and its apparent use of torture—had generated widespread opposition. However, when Barack Obama became the country's first African-American president in 2009, promising a different global posture, his election was greeted warmly in much of the world.

Within the United States as well, the global exercise of American power generated controversy. The Vietnam War, for example, divided the United States more sharply than at any time since the Civil War. It split families and friendships, churches and political parties. The war provided a platform for a growing number of critics, both at home and abroad, who had come to resent American cultural and economic dominance in the post-1945 world. It stimulated a new sense of activism among students in the nation's colleges and universities. Finally, the Vietnam War gave rise to charges that the cold war had undermined American democracy by promoting an overly powerful, "imperial" presidency, by creating a culture of secrecy and an obsession with national security, and by limiting political debate in the country. Not a few came to see America itself as an imperialist power. A similar set of issues, protests, and controversies followed the American invasion of Iraq in 2003.

The Globalization of Liberation: Comparing Feminist Movements

More than goods, money, and people traversed the planet during the twentieth century. So too did ideas, and none was more powerful than the ideology of liberation. Communism promised workers and peasants liberation from capitalist oppression. Nationalism offered subject peoples liberation from imperialism. Advocates of democracy sought liberation from authoritarian governments.

The 1960s in particular witnessed an unusual convergence of protest movements around the world, suggesting the emergence of a global culture of liberation. Within the United States, the civil rights demands of African Americans and Hispanic Americans; the youthful counterculture of rock music, sex, and drugs; the prolonged and highly divisive protests against the war in Vietnam—all of this gave the 1960s a distinctive place in the country's recent history. Across the Atlantic, swelling protests against unresponsive bureaucracy, consumerism, and middle-class values likewise erupted, most notably in France in 1968. There a student-led movement protesting conditions in universities attracted the support of many middle-class people, who were horrified at the brutality of the police, and stimulated an enormous strike among some 9 million workers. France seemed on the edge of another revolution. Related but smaller-scale movements took place in Germany, Italy, and elsewhere.

The communist world too was rocked by protest. In 1968, the new Communist Party leadership in Czechoslovakia, led by Alexander Dubcek, initiated a sweeping series of reforms aimed at creating "socialism with a human face." Censorship ended, generating an explosion of free expression in what had been a highly repressive regime; unofficial political clubs emerged publicly; victims of earlier repression were rehabilitated; secret ballots for party elections were put in place. To the conservative leaders of the Soviet Union, this "Prague Spring" seemed to challenge communist rule itself, and they sent troops and tanks to crush it. Across the world in communist China, another kind of protest was taking shape in that country's Cultural Revolution (see Chapter 22).

In the developing countries, a substantial number of political leaders, activists, scholars, and students developed the notion of a "third world." Their countries, many of which had only recently broken free from colonial rule, would offer an alternative to both a decrepit Western capitalism and a repressive Soviet communism. They claimed to pioneer new forms of economic development, of grassroots democracy, and of cultural renewal. By the late 1960s, the icon of

Che Guevara
In life, Che was an uncompromising but failed revolutionary, while in death he became an inspiration to third-world liberation movements and a symbol of radicalism to many in the West. His image appeared widely on T-shirts and posters, and in Cuba itself a government-sponsored cult featured schoolchildren chanting each morning "We will be like Che." This billboard image of Che was erected in Havana in 1988. (Tim Page/Corbis)

this third-world ideology was Che Guevara, the Argentine-born revolutionary who had embraced the Cuban Revolution and subsequently attempted to replicate its experience of liberation through guerrilla warfare in parts of Africa and Latin America. Various aspects of his life story—his fervent anti-imperialism, cast as a global struggle; his self-sacrificing lifestyle; his death in 1967 at the hands of the Bolivian military, trained and backed by the American CIA—made him a heroic figure to third-world revolutionaries. He was popular as well among Western radicals, who were disgusted with the complacency and materialism of their own societies.

No expression of the global culture of liberation held a more profound potential for change than feminism, for it represented a rethinking of the most fundamental and personal of all human relationships—that between women and men. Feminism had begun in the West in the nineteenth century with a primary focus on suffrage and in several countries had achieved the status of a mass movement by the outbreak of World War I (see pp. 800–803). The twentieth century, however, witnessed the globalization of feminism as organized efforts to address the concerns of women took shape across the world. Communist governments—in the Soviet Union, China, and Cuba, for example—mounted vigorous efforts to gain the support of women and to bring them into the workforce by attacking major elements of older patriarchies (see pp. 1039–40). But feminism took hold in many cultural and political settings, where women confronted different issues, adopted different strategies, and experienced a range of outcomes.

Feminism in the West

■ Comparison

What distinguished feminism in the industrialized countries from that of the Global South?

In the West, organized feminism had lost momentum by the end of the 1920s, when most countries had achieved universal suffrage. When it revived in the 1960s in both Western Europe and the United States, it did so with a quite different agenda. In France, for example, the writer and philosopher Simone de Beauvoir in 1949 had published *The Second Sex*, a book arguing that women had historically been defined as "other," or deviant from the "normal" male sex. The book soon became a central statement of a reviving women's movement. French feminists dramatized their concerns publicly in the early 1970s when some of them attempted to lay a wreath at the tomb of the unknown soldier in Paris, declaring, "Someone is even more unknown than the soldier: his wife." They staged a counter–Mother's Day parade under the slogan "Celebrated one day; exploited all year." To highlight their demand to control their own bodies, some 343 women signed a published manifesto stating that they had undergone an abortion, which was then illegal in France.

Across the Atlantic, millions of American women responded to Betty Friedan's book *The Feminine Mystique* (1963), which disclosed the identity crisis of educated women who were unfulfilled by marriage and motherhood. Some adherents of this second-wave feminism took up the equal rights agenda of their nineteenth-century predecessors, but with an emphasis now on employment and education rather than voting rights.

A more radical expression of American feminism took shape from the experience of women who had worked in other kinds of radical politics, such as the civil rights movement. Widely known as "women's liberation," this approach took broader aim at patriarchy as a system of domination, similar to those of race and class. One manifesto from 1969 declared:

> We are exploited as sex objects, breeders, domestic servants, and cheap labor. We are considered inferior beings, whose only purpose is to enhance men's lives.... Because we live so intimately with our oppressors, we have been kept from seeing our personal suffering as a political condition.[12]

Thus liberation for women meant becoming aware of their own oppression, a process that took place in thousands of consciousness-raising groups across the country. Many such women preferred direct action rather than the political lobbying favored by equal rights feminists. They challenged the Miss America contest of 1968 by tossing stink bombs in the hall, crowning a live sheep as their Miss America, and disposing of girdles, bras, high-heeled shoes, tweezers, and other "instruments of oppression" in a Freedom Trashcan. They also brought into open discussion issues involving sexuality, insisting that free love, lesbianism, and celibacy should be accorded the same respect as heterosexual marriage.

Yet another strand of Western feminism emerged from women of color. For many of them, the concerns of white, usually middle-class, feminists were hardly relevant to their oppression. Black women had always worked outside the home and so felt little need to be liberated from the chains of homemaking. Whereas white women might find the family oppressive, African American women viewed it as a secure base from which to resist racism. Solidarity with black men, rather than separation from them, was essential in confronting a racist America. Viewing mainstream feminism as "a family quarrel between White women and White men," many women of African descent in the United States and Britain established their own organizations, with a focus on racism and poverty.[13]

Feminism in the Global South

As women mobilized outside of the Western world during the twentieth century, they faced very different situations than did white women in the United States and Europe. For much of Asia, Africa, and Latin America, the predominant issues— colonialism, racism, the struggle for independence, poverty, development, political oppression, and sometimes revolution—were not directly related to gender. Women were affected by and engaged with all of these efforts and were welcomed by nationalist and communist leaders, mostly men, who needed their support. Once independence or the revolution was achieved, however, the women who had joined those movements often were relegated to marginal positions.

The different conditions within developing countries sometimes generated sharp criticism of Western feminism. To many African feminists in the 1970s and beyond, the concerns of their American or European sisters were too individualistic, too focused on sexuality, and insufficiently concerned with issues of motherhood, marriage, and poverty to be of much use. Furthermore, they resented Western feminists' insistent interest in cultural matters such as female genital mutilation and polygamy, which sometimes echoed the concerns of colonial-era missionaries and administrators. Western feminism could easily be seen as a new form of cultural imperialism. Moreover, many African governments and many African men defined feminism of any kind as "un-African" and associated with a hated colonialism.

Women's movements in the Global South took shape around a wide range of issues, not all of which were explicitly gender based. In the East African country of Kenya, a major form of mobilization was the women's group movement. Some 27,000 small associations of women, which were an outgrowth of traditional self-help groups, had a combined membership of more than a million by the late 1980s. They provided support for one another during times of need, such as weddings, births, and funerals; they took on community projects, such as building water cisterns, schools, and dispensaries; in one province, they focused on providing permanent iron roofing for their homes. Some became revolving loan societies or bought land or businesses. One woman testified to the sense of empowerment she derived from membership in her group:

> I am a free woman. I bought this piece of land through my group. I can lie on it, work on it, keep goats or cows. What more do I want? My husband cannot sell it. It is mine.[14]

Elsewhere, other issues and approaches predominated. In the North African Islamic kingdom of Morocco, a more centrally directed and nationally focused feminist movement targeted the country's Family Law Code, which still defined women as minors. In 2004, a long campaign by Morocco's feminist movement, often with the help of supportive men and a liberal king, resulted in a new Family Law Code, which recognized women as equals to their husbands and allowed them to initiate divorce and to claim child custody, all of which had previously been denied.

In Chile, a women's movement emerged as part of a national struggle against the military dictatorship of General Augusto Pinochet, who ruled the country from 1973 to 1990. Because they were largely regarded as "invisible" in the public sphere, women were able to organize extensively, despite the repression of the Pinochet regime. From

Mothers of Missing Children

This group of Brazilian mothers in Rio de Janeiro gathered every week during the mid-1990s to bring pressure on the government to find their missing children, generally believed to have been seized by criminal gangs engaged in child prostitution and illegal adoption. Often seeking loved ones who probably were executed by government or paramilitary death squads, such "mothers of the disappeared" have been active in many Latin American countries. (AP Images/Diego Guidice)

this explosion of organizing activity emerged a women's movement that crossed class lines and party affiliations. Human rights activists, most of them women, called attention to the widespread use of torture and to the "disappearance" of thousands of opponents of the regime, while demanding the restoration of democracy. Poor urban women by the tens of thousands organized soup kitchens, craft workshops, and shopping collectives, all aimed at the economic survival of their families. Smaller numbers of middle-class women brought more distinctly feminist perspectives to the movement and argued pointedly for "democracy in the country and in the home." This diverse women's movement was an important part of the larger national protest that returned Chile to democratic government in 1990.

In South Korea as in Chile, women's mobilization contributed to a "mass people's movement" that brought a return to democracy by the late 1980s, after a long period of highly authoritarian rule. The women's movement in South Korea drew heavily on the experience of young female workers in the country's export industries. In those factories, they were poorly paid, were subjected to exhausting working conditions and frequent sexual harassment, and lived in crowded company dormitories, often called "chicken coops." Such women spearheaded a democratic trade union movement during the 1970s, and in the process many of them developed both a feminist and a class consciousness.

International Feminism

Perhaps the most impressive achievement of feminism in the twentieth century was its ability to project the "woman question" as a global issue and to gain international recognition for the view that "women's rights are human rights."[15] Like slavery and empire before it, patriarchy lost at least some of its legitimacy during this most recent century, although clearly it has not been vanquished.

Feminism registered as a global issue when the United Nations, under pressure from women activists, declared 1975 as International Women's Year and the next ten years as the Decade for Women. The United Nations also sponsored a series of World Conferences on Women over the next twenty years. By 2006, 183 nations had ratified a UN Convention to Eliminate Discrimination against Women, which committed them to promote women's legal equality, to end discrimination, to actively encourage women's development, and to protect women's human rights. Clearly this international attention to women's issues was encouraging to feminists operating in their own countries and in many places stimulated both research and action.

This growing international spotlight on women's issues also revealed sharp divisions within global feminism. One issue was determining who had the right to speak on behalf of women at international gatherings—the official delegates of male-dominated governments or the often more radical unofficial participants representing various nongovernmental organizations. North/South conflicts also surfaced at these international conferences. In preparing for the Mexico City gathering in 1975, the United States attempted to limit the agenda to matters of political and civil rights for women, whereas delegates from third-world and communist countries wanted to include issues of economic justice, decolonization, and disarmament. Feminists from the South resented the dominance and contested the ideas of their Northern sisters. One African group highlighted the differences:

> While patriarchal views and structures oppress women all over the world, women are also members of classes and countries that dominate others and enjoy privileges in terms of access to resources. Hence, contrary to the best intentions of "sisterhood," not all women share identical interests.[16]

Nor did all third-world groups have identical views. Some Muslim delegates at the Beijing Conference in 1995 opposed a call for equal inheritance for women, because Islamic law required that sons receive twice the amount that daughters inherit. In contast, Africans, especially in non-Muslim countries, were aware of how many children had been orphaned by AIDS and felt that girls' chances for survival depended on equal inheritance.

Beyond such divisions within international feminism lay a global backlash among those who felt that its radical agenda had undermined family life, the proper relationship of men and women, and civilization generally. To Phyllis Schlafly, a prominent American opponent of the Equal Rights Amendment, feminism was a "disease" that brought in its wake "fear, sickness, pain, anger, hatred, danger, violence, and all manner of ugliness."[17] In the Islamic world, Western-style feminism, with its claims of gender equality and open sexuality, was highly offensive to many and fueled movements of religious revivalism that invited or compelled women to wear the veil and sometimes to lead highly restricted lives. The Vatican, some Catholic and Muslim countries, and at times the U.S. government took strong exception to aspects of global feminism, particularly its emphasis on reproductive rights, including access to abortion and birth control. Thus feminism was global as the twenty-first century dawned, but it was very diverse and much contested.

Religion and Global Modernity

Beyond liberation and feminism, a further dimension of cultural globalization took shape in the challenge that modernity presented to the world's religions. To the most "advanced" thinkers of the past several hundred years—Enlightenment writers in the eighteenth century, Karl Marx in the nineteenth, socialist intellectuals and secular-minded people in the twentieth—supernatural religion was headed for extinction in the face of modernity, science, communism, or globalization. In some places—Britain, France, the Netherlands, and the Soviet Union, for example—religious belief and practice had declined sharply. Moreover, the spread of a scientific culture around the world persuaded small minorities everywhere, often among the most highly educated, that the only realities worth considering were those that could be measured with the techniques of science. To such people, all else was superstition, born of ignorance. Nevertheless, the far more prominent trends of the last century have been those that involved the further spread of major world religions, their resurgence in new forms, their opposition to elements of a secular and global modernity, and their political role as a source of community identity and conflict. Contrary to earlier expectations, religion has played an unexpectedly powerful role in this most recent century.

Buddhism, Christianity, and Islam had long functioned as transregional cultures, spreading far beyond their places of origin. That process continued in the twentieth century. Buddhist ideas and practices such as meditation found a warm reception in the West, as did yoga, originally a mind-body practice of Indian origin. Christianity of various kinds spread widely in non-Muslim Africa and South Korea and less extensively in parts of India. By the end of the century, it was growing even in China, where perhaps 7 to 8 percent of China's population—some 84 to 96 million people—claimed allegiance to the faith. No longer a primarily European or North American religion, Christianity by the early twenty-first century found some 62 percent of its adherents in Asia, Africa, and Latin America. In some instances missionaries from those regions have set about the "re-evangelization" of Europe and North America. Moreover, millions of migrants from the Islamic world planted their religion solidly in the West. In the United States, for example, a substantial number of African Americans and smaller numbers of European Americans engaged in Islamic practice. For several decades the writings of the thirteenth-century Islamic Sufi poet Rumi have been bestsellers in the United States. Religious exchange, in short, has been a two-way street, not simply a transmission of Western ideas to the rest of the world. More than ever before, religious pluralism characterized many of the world's societies, confronting people with the need to make choices in a domain of life previously regarded as given and fixed.

Fundamentalism on a Global Scale

Religious vitality in the twentieth century was expressed not only in the spread of particular traditions to new areas but also in the vigorous response of those traditions to the modernizing and globalizing world in which they found themselves. One such response has been widely called "fundamentalism," a militant piety—defensive, assertive, and exclusive—that took shape to some extent in every major religious tradition. Many features of the modern world, after all, appeared threatening to established religion. The scientific and secular focus of global modernity directly challenged the core beliefs of supernatural religion. Furthermore, the social upheavals connected with capitalism, industrialization, and globalization thoroughly upset customary class, family, and gender relationships that had long been sanctified by religious tradition. Nation-states, often associated with particular religions, were likewise undermined by the operation of a global economy and challenged by the spread of alien cultures. In much of the world, these disruptions came at the hands of foreigners, usually Westerners, in the form of military defeat, colonial rule, economic dependency, and cultural intrusion.

■ **Change**
In what respect did the various religious fundamentalisms of the twentieth century express hostility to global modernity?

To such threats, fundamentalism represented a religious response, characterized by one scholar as "embattled forms of spirituality…experienced as a cosmic war between the forces of good and evil."[18] Although fundamentalisms everywhere have looked to the past for ideals and models, their rejection of modernity was selective, not wholesale. What they sought was an alternative modernity, infused with particular religious values. Most, in fact, made active use of modern technology to communicate their message and certainly sought the potential prosperity associated with modern life. Extensive educational and propaganda efforts, political mobilization of their followers, social welfare programs, and sometimes violence ("terrorism" to their opponents) were among the means that fundamentalists employed.

The term "fundamentalism" derived from the United States, where religious conservatives in the early twentieth century were outraged by critical and "scientific" approaches to the Bible, by Darwinian evolution, and by liberal versions of Christianity that accommodated these heresies. They called for a return to the "fundamentals" of the faith, which included the literal truthfulness of the scriptures, the virgin birth and physical resurrection of Jesus, and a belief in miracles. After World War II, American Protestant fundamentalism came to oppose political liberalism and "big government," the sexual revolution of the 1960s, homosexuality and abortion rights, and secular humanism generally. Many fundamentalists saw the United States on the edge of an abyss. For one major spokesman, Francis Schaeffer (1912–1984), the West was about to enter

> an electronic dark age, in which the new pagan hordes, with all the power of technology at their command, are on the verge of obliterating the last strongholds of civilized humanity. A vision of darkness lies before us. As we leave the shores of Christian Western man behind, only a dark and turbulent sea of despair stretches endlessly ahead…unless we fight.[19]

And fight they did! At first, fundamentalists sought to separate themselves from the secular world in their own churches and schools, but from the 1970s on, they entered the political arena as the "religious right," determined to return America to a "godly path." "We have enough votes to run this country," declared Pat Robertson, a major fundamentalist evangelist and broadcaster who ran for president in 1988. Conservative fundamentalist Christians, no longer willing to restrict their attention to personal conversion, had emerged as a significant force in American political life well before the end of the century.

In the very different setting of independent India, another fundamentalist movement—known as Hindutva (Hindu nationalism)—took shape during the 1980s. Like American fundamentalism, it represented a politicization of religion within a democratic context. To its advocates, India was, and always had been, an essentially Hindu land, even though it had been overwhelmed in recent centuries by Muslim invaders, then by the Christian British, and most recently by the secular state of the postindependence decades. The leaders of modern India, they argued, and particularly its first prime minister, Jawaharlal Nehru, were "the self-proclaimed secularists who…seek to remake India in the Western image," while repudiating its basically Hindu religious character. The Hindutva movement took political shape in an increasingly popular party called the Bharatiya Janata Party (BJP), with much of its support coming from urban middle-class or upper-caste people who resented the state's efforts to cater to the interests of Muslims, Sikhs, and the lower castes. Muslims in particular were defined as outsiders, potentially more loyal to a Muslim Pakistan than to India. The BJP became a major political force in India during the 1980s and 1990s, winning a number of elections at both the state and national levels and promoting a distinctly Hindu identity in education, culture, and religion.

Creating Islamic Societies: Resistance and Renewal in the World of Islam

The most prominent of the fundamentalisms that emerged in the late twentieth century was surely that of Islam, which was permanently etched in Americans' memory in the image of Osama bin Laden and the destruction of the World Trade Center on September 11, 2001. However, this violent event was only one expression of a much larger phenomenon—an effort among growing numbers of Muslims to create a new religious/political order centered on a particular understanding of Islam.

■ **Change**
From what sources did Islamic renewal movements derive?

Emerging strongly in the last quarter of the century, this Islamic renewal gained strength from the enormous disappointments that had accumulated in the Muslim world by the 1970s. Political independence had given rise to major states—Egypt, Iran, Algeria, and others—that pursued essentially Western and secular policies of nationalism, socialism, and economic development, often with only lip service to an Islamic identity. These policies, however, were not very successful. A number of endemic problems—vastly overcrowded cities with few services, widespread unemployment, pervasive corruption, slow economic growth, a mounting gap between the rich and poor—flew in the face of the great expectations that had accompanied the struggle against European domination. Despite independence from a century or more of humiliating Western imperialism, foreign intrusion still persisted. Israel, widely regarded as an outpost of the West, had been reestablished as a Jewish state in the very center of the Islamic world in 1948. In 1967, Israel inflicted a devastating defeat on Arab forces in the Six-Day War and seized various Arab territories, including the holy city of Jerusalem. Furthermore, broader signs of Western cultural penetration—secular schools, alcohol, Barbie dolls, European and American movies, scantily clad women—appeared frequently in the Muslim world.

This was the context in which the idea of an Islamic alternative to Western models of modernity began to take hold (see Document 24.2, pp. 1169–71). The intellectual and political foundations of this Islamic renewal had been established earlier in the century. Its leading figures, such as the Indian Mawlana Mawdudi and the Egyptian Sayyid Qutb, insisted that the Quran and the *sharia* (Islamic law) provided a guide for all of life—political, economic, and spiritual—and a blueprint for a distinctly Islamic modernity not dependent on Western ideas. It was the departure from Islamic principles, they argued, that had led the Islamic world into decline and subordination to the West, and only a return to the "straight path of Islam" would ensure

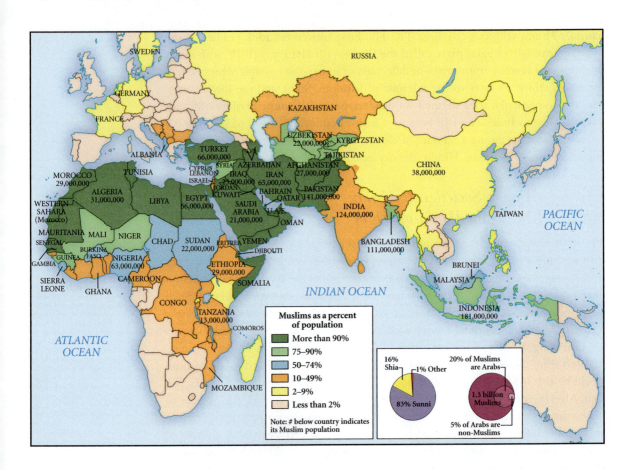

Map 24.4   The Islamic World in the Early Twenty-first Century
An Islamic world of well over a billion people incorporated much of the Afro-Asian landmass but was divided among many nations and along linguistic and ethnic lines as well. The long-term split between the majority Sunnis and the minority Shias also sharpened in the new millennium.

a revival of Muslim societies. That effort to return to Islamic principles was labeled *jihad*, an ancient and evocative religious term that refers to "struggle" or "striving" to please God. In its twentieth-century political expression, jihad included the defense of an authentic Islam against Western aggression and vigorous efforts to achieve the Islamization of social and political life within Muslim countries. It was a posture that would enable Muslims to resist the seductive but poisonous culture of the West. Sayyid Qutb had witnessed that culture during a visit to the United States in the late 1940s, and was shocked by what he saw:

> Look at this capitalism with its monopolies, its usury…at this individual free-dom, devoid of human sympathy and responsibility for relatives except under force of law; at this materialistic attitude which deadens the spirit; at this behavior like animals which you call "free mixing of the sexes"; at this vulgarity which you call "emancipation of women"; at this evil and fanatical racial discrimination.[20]

■ **Comparison**

In what different ways did Islamic renewal express itself?

Such ideas soon echoed widely all across the Islamic world and found expression in many ways. At the level of personal life, many people became more religiously observant, attending mosque, praying regularly, and fasting. Substantial numbers of women, many of them young, urban, and well educated, adopted modest Islamic dress and the veil quite voluntarily. Participation in Sufi mystical practices increased. Furthermore, many governments sought to anchor themselves in Islamic rhetoric and practice. Under pressure from Islamic activists, the government of Sudan in the 1980s adopted Quranic punishments for various crimes (such as amputating the hand of a thief) and announced a total ban on alcohol, dramatically dumping thousands of bottles of beer and wine into the Nile. During the 1970s, President Anwar Sadat of Egypt claimed the title of "Believer-President," referred frequently to the Quran, and proudly displayed his "prayer mark," a callus on his forehead caused by touching his head to the ground in prayer.

All over the Muslim world, from North Africa to Indonesia, Islamic renewal movements spawned organizations that operated legally to provide social services— schools, clinics, youth centers, legal-aid centers, financial institutions, publishing houses—that the state offered inadequately or not at all. Islamic activists took leadership roles in unions and professional organizations of teachers, journalists, engineers, doctors, and lawyers. Such people embraced modern science and technology but sought to embed these elements of modernity within a distinctly Islamic culture. Some served in official government positions or entered political life where it was possible to do so. The Algerian Islamic Salvation Front was poised to win elections in 1992, when a frightened military government intervened to cancel the elections, an action that plunged the country into a decade of bitter civil war. In Turkey, Egypt, Jordan, Iraq, Palestine, and Lebanon, Islamic parties made impressive electoral showings in the 1990s and the early twenty-first century.

Hamas in Action

The Palestinian militant organization Hamas, founded in 1987 as an offshoot of Egypt's Muslim Brotherhood, illustrates two dimensions of Islamic radicalism. On the one hand, Hamas repeatedly sent suicide bombers to target Israeli civilians and sought the elimination of the Israeli state. A group of would-be suicide bombers are shown here in white robes during the funeral of colleagues killed by Israeli security forces in late 2003. On the other hand, Hamas ran a network of social services, providing schools, clinics, orphanages, summer camps, soup kitchens, and libraries for Palestinians. The classroom pictured here was part of a school founded by Hamas. (Andrea Comas/Reuters/Corbis; Abid Katib/Getty Images)

Another face of Islamic renewal, however, sought the violent overthrow of what they saw as compromised regimes in the Muslim world. One such group, the Egyptian Islamic Jihad, assassinated President Sadat in 1981, following Sadat's brutal crackdown on both Islamic and secular opposition groups. One of the leaders of Islamic Jihad explained:

> We have to establish the Rule of God's Religion in our own country first, and to make the Word of God supreme....There is no doubt that the first battlefield for jihad is the extermination of these infidel leaders and to replace them by a complete Islamic Order.[21]

Two years earlier in Mecca, members of another radical Islamic group sought the overthrow of the Saudi government. They despised its alliance with Western powers, the corrupt and un-Islamic lifestyle of its leaders, and the disruptive consequences of its oil-fueled modernization program. They even invaded the Grand Mosque, Islam's most sacred shrine. In Iran (1979), Afghanistan (1996), parts of Northern Nigeria (2000), and a section of Pakistan (2009), Islamic movements succeeded in coming to power and began to implement a program of Islamization based on the sharia. (See pp. 1105–08 in Chapter 23 for Iran and Documents 24.2 and 24.3, pp. 1169–73.)

Islamic revolutionaries also took aim at hostile foreign powers. Hamas in Palestine and Hezbollah in Lebanon, supported by the Islamic regime in Iran, targeted Israel with popular uprisings, suicide bombings, and rocket attacks in response to the Israeli occupation of Arab lands. For some, Israel's very existence was illegitimate. The Soviet invasion of Afghanistan in 1979 prompted widespread opposition aimed at liberating the country from atheistic communism and creating an Islamic state. Sympathetic Arabs from the Middle East flocked to the aid of their Afghan compatriots.

Among them was the young Osama bin Laden, a wealthy Saudi Arab, who created an organization, al-Qaeda (meaning "the base" in Arabic), to funnel fighters and funds to the Afghan resistance. At the time, bin Laden and the Americans were on the same side, both opposing Soviet expansion into Afghanistan, but they soon parted ways. Returning to his home in Saudi Arabia, bin Laden became disillusioned and radicalized when the government of his country allowed the stationing of "infidel" U.S. troops in Islam's holy land during and after the first American war against Iraq in 1991. By the mid-1990s, he had found a safe haven in Taliban-ruled Afghanistan, from which he and other leaders of al-Qaeda planned their now infamous attack on the World Trade Center and other targets. Although they had no standing as Muslim clerics, in 1998 they issued a *fatwa* (religious edict) declaring war on America:

> [F]or over seven years the United States has been occupying the lands of Islam in the holiest of places, the Arabian Peninsula, plundering its riches, dictating to its rulers, humiliating its people, terrorizing its neighbors, and turning its bases in the Peninsula into a spearhead through which to fight the neighboring Muslim peoples.... [T]he ruling to kill the Americans and their allies—civilians and military—is an individual duty for every Muslim who can do it in any country in which it is possible to do it, in order to liberate the al-Aqsa Mosque in Jerusalem

and the holy mosque (in Mecca) from their grip, and in order for their armies to move out of all the lands of Islam, defeated and unable to threaten any Muslim.[22]

Elsewhere as well—in East Africa, Indonesia, Great Britain, Spain, Saudi Arabia, and Yemen—al-Qaeda or groups associated with it launched scattered attacks on Western interests. At the international level, the great enemy was not Christianity itself or even Western civilization, but irreligious Western-style modernity, U.S. imperialism, and an American-led economic globalization so aptly symbolized by the World Trade Center. Ironically, al-Qaeda itself was a modern and global organization, many of whose members were highly educated professionals from a variety of countries. Despite their focus on the West, the struggles undertaken by politicized Islamic activists were as much within the Islamic world as they were with the external enemy. If Islamic fundamentalism represented a clash of cultures or civilizations, that collision took place among different conceptions of Islam at least as sharply as with the outlook and practices of the modern West.

Religious Alternatives to Fundamentalism

Militant revolutionary fundamentalism has certainly not been the only religious response to modernity and globalization within the Islamic world. Many who shared a concern to embed Islamic values more centrally in their societies have acted peacefully and within established political structures. Considerable debate among them has raised questions about the proper role of the state, the difference between the eternal law of God (sharia) and the human interpretations of it, the rights of women, the possibility of democracy, and many other issues (see Documents 24.4 and 24.5, pp. 1173–78). Some Muslim intellectuals and political leaders have called for a dialogue between civilizations; others have argued that traditions can change in the face of modern realities without losing their distinctive Islamic character. In 1996, Anwar Ibrahim, a major political and intellectual figure in Malaysia, insisted that

> [Southeast Asian Muslims] would rather strive to improve the welfare of the women and children in their midst than spend their days elaborately defining the nature and institutions of the ideal Islamic state. They do not believe it makes one less of a Muslim to promote economic growth, to master the information revolution, and to demand justice for women.[23]

And in many places Sufi devotionalism stands as a strong alternative to a legalistic Islamic fundamentalism.

Within other religious traditions as well, believers found various ways of responding to global modernity. More liberal or mainstream Christian groups spoke to the ethical issues arising from economic globalization. Many Christian organizations, for example, were active in agitating for debt relief for poor countries. Pope John Paul II was openly concerned about "the growing distance between rich and poor, unfair competition which puts the poor nations in a situation of ever-increasing inferiority." "Liberation theology," particularly in Latin America, sought a Christian basis for action in the areas of social justice, poverty, and human rights, while viewing Jesus as liberator as well as savior. In Asia, a growing movement known as "socially engaged Buddhism" addressed the needs of the poor through social reform, educational programs, health services, and peacemaking action during times of conflict and war. The Dalai Lama has famously advocated a peaceful resolution of Tibet's troubled relationship with China. Growing interest in communication and exchange among the world's religions was expressed at a World Peace Summit in 2000, when more than 1,000 religious and spiritual leaders met to explore how they might more effectively confront the world's many conflicts. In short, religious responses to global modernity were articulated in many voices.

The World's Environment and the Globalization of Environmentalism

Even as world religions, fundamentalist and otherwise, challenged global modernity on cultural or spiritual grounds, burgeoning environmental movements in the 1960s and after did so with an eye to the human impact on the earth and its many living creatures, including ourselves. Among the distinctive features of the twentieth century, none has been more pronounced than humankind's growing ability to alter the natural order and the mounting awareness of this phenomenon. When the wars, revolutions, and empires of this most recent century have faded from memory, environmental transformation and environmental consciousness may well seem to future generations the decisive feature of that century.

The Global Environment Transformed

■ Change
How can we explain the dramatic increase in the human impact on the environment in the twentieth century?

Underlying the environmental changes of the twentieth century were three other factors that vastly magnified the human impact on earth's ecological systems far beyond anything previously known.[24] One was the explosion of human numbers, an unprecedented quadrupling of the world's population in a single century. Another lay in the amazing new ability of humankind to tap the energy potential of fossil fuels—coal in the nineteenth century and oil in the twentieth. Hydroelectricity, natural gas, and nuclear power added to the energy resources available to our species. These new sources of energy made possible a third contribution to environmental transformation—phenomenal economic growth—as modern science and technology immensely increased the production of goods and services. None of this occurred evenly across the planet. An average North American in the 1990s, for example, used 50 to 100 times more energy than an average Bangladeshi. But almost everywhere—in capitalist, communist, and developing countries alike—the idea of economic growth as something possible and desirable took hold as a part of global culture.

These three factors were the foundations for the immense environmental transformations of the twentieth century. Human activity had always altered the natural order, usually on a local basis, but now the scale of those disruptions assumed global

Snapshot   **World Population Growth, 1950–2005**[25]

The great bulk of the world's population growth in the second half of the twentieth century occurred in the developing countries of Asia, Africa, the Middle East, and Latin America.

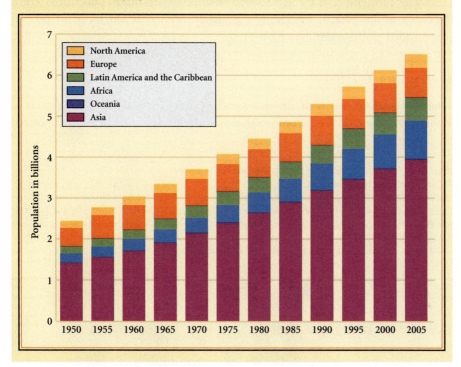

proportions. The growing numbers of the poor and the growing consumption of the rich led to the doubling of cropland and a corresponding contraction of the world's forests and grasslands. With diminished habitats, numerous species of plants and animals either disappeared or were threatened with extinction. The human remaking of the environment also greatly increased the population of cattle, pigs, chickens, rats, and dandelions.

The global spread of modern industry, which was heavily dependent on fossil fuels, created a pall of air pollution in many major cities. By the 1970s, traffic police in Tokyo frequently wore face masks. In Mexico City, officials estimated in 2002 that air pollution killed 35,000 people every year. Industrial pollution in the Soviet Union rendered about half of the country's rivers severely polluted by the late 1980s, while fully 20 percent of its population lived in regions defined as "ecological disasters." The release of chemicals known as chlorofluorocarbons thinned the ozone layer, which protects the earth from excessive ultraviolet radiation.

The most critical and intractable environmental transformation was global warming. By the end of the twentieth century, a worldwide scientific consensus had emerged that the vastly increased burning of fossil fuels, which emit heat-trapping greenhouse gases, as well as the loss of trees that would otherwise remove carbon dioxide from the air, had begun to warm the atmosphere significantly. Although considerable disagreement existed about the rate and likely consequences of this process, concern about melting glaciers and polar ice caps, rising sea levels, thawing permafrost, extreme hurricanes, further species extinctions, and other ecological threats punctuated global discussion of this issue. It was clearly a global phenomenon and, for many people, it demanded global action (see Map 24.5).

Green and Global

Environmentalism began in the nineteenth century as Romantic poets such as William Blake and William Wordsworth denounced the industrial era's "dark satanic

Map 24.5   Carbon Dioxide Emissions in the Twentieth Century
The source of carbon dioxide emissions, the chief human contribution to global warming, was distributed quite unevenly across the planet. Although the industrialized countries have been largely responsible for those emissions during the twentieth century, India and China in particular have assumed a much greater role in this process as their industrialization boomed in the early twenty-first century. The historically unequal distribution of those emissions has prompted much controversy between the countries of the Global North and the Global South about who should make the sacrifices required to address the problem of global warming.

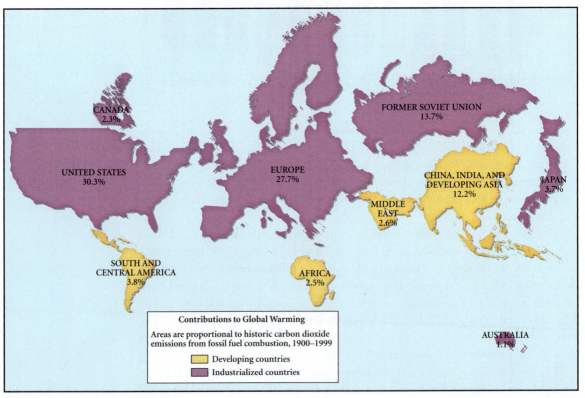

mills," which threatened the "green and pleasant land" of an earlier England. The "scientific management" of nature, both in industrializing countries and in European colonies, represented another element of emerging environmental awareness among a few. So did the "wilderness idea," which aimed to preserve untouched areas from human disruption,[26] as, for example, in the U.S. national parks. None of these strands of environmentalism attracted a mass following or provoked a global response. Not until the second half of the twentieth century, and then quite rapidly, did environmentalism achieve a worldwide dimension, although it was expressed in many quite different ways.

This second-wave environmentalism began in the West with the publication in 1962 of Rachel Carson's *Silent Spring*, an exposure of the chemical contamination of the environment that threatened both human health and the survival of many other species. She wrote of a "strange stillness" in a world where the songs of birds might no longer be heard. The book touched a nerve, generating an enormous response and effectively launching the environmental movement in the United States. Here, as virtually everywhere else, the impetus for action came from the grass roots and citizen protest. By the early 1990s, some 14 million Americans, one in seven adults, had joined one of the many environmental organizations—national or local—that aimed much of their effort at lobbying political parties and businesses. In Europe, the Club of Rome, a global think tank, issued a report in 1972 called *Limits to Growth*, which warned of resource exhaustion and the collapse of industrial society in the face of unrelenting economic growth. The German environmental movement was distinctive in that its activists directly entered the political arena as the Green Party, which came to have a substantial role in German national politics. One of the Greens' main concerns was opposition to nuclear energy. Beyond addressing environmental pollution, Western activists focused much attention on wilderness issues, opposing logging, road building, and other development efforts in remaining unspoiled areas.

Quite quickly, during the 1970s and 1980s, environmentalism took root in the developing countries as well. There it often assumed a different character: it was more locally based and had fewer large national organizations than in the West; it involved poor people rather than affluent members of the middle class; it was less engaged in political lobbying and corporate strategies; it was more concerned with issues of food security, health, and basic survival than with the rights of nature or wilderness protection; and it was more closely connected to movements for social justice.[27] Thus, whereas Western environmentalists defended forests where few people lived, the Chikpo, or "tree-hugging," movement in India sought to protect the livelihood of farmers, artisans, and herders living in areas subject to extensive deforestation. A massive movement to prevent or limit the damming of India's Narmada River derived from the displacement of local people; similar anti-dam protests in the American Northwest were more concerned with protecting salmon runs.

Western environmentalists often called on individuals to change their values by turning away from materialism toward an appreciation of the intricate and fragile web of life that sustains us all. In the Philippines, by contrast, environmental activists

■ **Comparison**

What differences emerged between environmentalism in the Global North and that in the Global South?

Environmentalism in Action These South Korean environmental activists are wearing death masks and holding crosses representing various countries during an anti-nuclear protest in Seoul in 1996, exactly ten years after a large-scale nuclear accident at Chernobyl in the Soviet Union. The lead protester holds a placard reading "Don't forget Chernobyl!" (AP Images/Yun Hai-Huoung)

confronting the operation of foreign mining companies have sought fundamental changes in the political and social structure of their country. There, environmental protest has overlapped with other movements seeking to challenge established power structures and social hierarchies. Coalitions of numerous local groups—representing various religious, women's, human rights, indigenous peoples', peasant, and political organizations—frequently mobilized large-scale grassroots movements against the companies rather than seeking to negotiate with them. These movements have not been entirely nonviolent; occasionally they have included guerrilla warfare actions by "green armies." Such mass mobilization contributed to the decision of the Australian-based Western Mining Corporation in 2000 to abandon its plans for developing a huge copper mine in Mindanao.

By the late twentieth century, environmentalism had become a matter of global concern. That awareness motivated legislation aimed at pollution control in many countries; it pushed many businesses in a "green" direction; it fostered research on alternative and renewable sources of energy; it stimulated UN conferences on global warming; it persuaded millions of people to alter their way of life; and it generated a number of international agreements addressing matters such as whaling, ozone depletion, and global warming.

The globalization of environmentalism also disclosed sharp conflicts, particularly between the Global North and South. Both activists and governments in the developing countries have often felt that Northern initiatives to address atmospheric pollution and global warming would curtail their industrial development, leaving the North/South gap intact. "The threat to the atmospheric commons has been building over centuries," argued Indian environmentalist Vandana Shiva, "mainly because of industrial activity in the North. Yet…the North refuses to assume extra responsibility for cleaning up the atmosphere. No wonder the Third World cries foul when it is asked to share the costs." A Malaysian official put the dispute succinctly: "The developed countries don't want to give up their extravagant lifestyles, but plan to curtail our development."[28] Western governments argued that newly industrializing countries such as China and India must also sharply curtail their growing emissions if further global warming is to be prevented. Such deep disagreements between industrialized and developing countries contributed to the failure of the United Nations Copenhagen climate conference in late 2009 to reach legally binding agreements to substantially reduce greenhouse gas emissions.

Beyond these and other conflicts, global environmentalism, more than any other widespread movement, came to symbolize "one-world" thinking, a focus on the common plight of humankind across the artificial boundaries of nation-states. It also marked a challenge to modernity itself, particularly its consuming commitment to endless growth. The ideas of sustainability and restraint, certainly not prominent in any list of modern values, entered global discourse and marked the beginnings of a new environmental ethic. This change in thinking was perhaps the most significant achievement of global environmentalism.

Final Reflections: Pondering the Uses of History

The end of a history book is an appropriate place to ask the fundamental question: just what is it good for, this field of study we call history? What, in short, are the uses of the past, and particularly of the global past?

At one level, philosophers, scholars, and thoughtful people everywhere have long used history to probe the significance of human experience. Does an examination of the past disclose any purpose, meaning, or pattern, or is it "just one damned thing after another"? Some sages, of course, have discerned divine purpose in the unfolding of the human story. To Saint Augustine, an early Christian thinker and writer, that purpose was the building of the "heavenly city," while events in this world were but steps in God's great plan. Chinese thinkers often viewed history as the source of moral lessons and related the behavior of rulers to the rise and fall of their dynasties. Europeans and others operating within the Enlightenment tradition have seen history in secular terms as a record of progress toward greater freedom or rationality in human affairs. Karl Marx viewed the past as a succession of economic changes and class struggles culminating in the creation of socialism, a secular utopia that would forever banish war, inequality, and social conflict.

Most contemporary historians are skeptical of such grand understandings of the human past, especially those that depend on some unseen hand directing the course of history to a defined end or those that reflect a particular set of values. But if "purpose" is hard to detect in the human story, some general "directions" over the long run are perhaps more evident.

One such trend lies in growing human numbers, which are linked to greater control over the natural environment as our ways of living moved from gathering and hunting, to agriculture, and most recently to industrial societies. Accompanying this broad direction in world history has been the growing complexity of human societies. Small hunting bands of a few dozen people gave way to agricultural villages of several thousands, to cities populated by tens or hundreds of thousands, to states and empires consisting of many millions. As the scale of human communities enlarged, so too did the pace of change in human affairs. In recent centuries, change has become both expected and valued in ways that would surely seem strange to most of the world's earlier inhabitants. A final possible direction in world history has been toward greater connection among the planet's diverse cultures and peoples. To early links among neighboring settlements or villages were later added networks of exchange and communication that operated among distant civilizations, across whole hemispheres, and after 1500 on a genuinely global level.

A word of caution, however, about finding direction in world history. None of this happened smoothly, evenly, or everywhere, and all of it was accompanied by numerous ups and downs, reversals, and variations. Furthermore, the notion of direction in history is quite different from that of progress. It is an observation rather than a judgment. One might consider growing populations, control over nature, increasing complexity, more rapid change, and global integration as great achievements and evidence of human "success." Alternatively, one might regard them as a burden or a curse, more of a disease than a triumph. We do well in studying the past to separate as much as possible our descriptions about what happened from our opinions about those events and processes.

In addition to discovering meaning or, even more modestly, direction in history, the uses of the past have long included efforts by political authorities to inculcate national, religious, civic, patriotic, or other values in their citizens. Furious debates in recent decades about history curricula in the schools of the United States, Japan, China, and elsewhere testify to the continuing impulse to use history in this way. In democratic societies, many people also express the hope that grounding in history will generate wiser public policies and more informed and effective participation by citizens. It is not always easy to find evidence for such outcomes of historical study, for the lessons of the past are many, varied, and conflicting, and the world, as always, hovers on the knife edge of possibility and disaster. Nonetheless, advocates for historical study continue to believe that probing the past enhances public life.

On a more personal level, many people have found in the study of history endless material for musing, for pondering those matters of the heart and spirit that all of us must confront as we make our way in the world. Consider, for example, the question of suffering. History is, among other things, a veritable catalog of the varieties of human suffering. It provides ample evidence, should we need it, that suffering is a common and bedrock human experience—and that none of us is exempt. But the study of history also highlights the indisputable fact that much of human suffering has come at our own hands in the shape of war, racism, patriarchy, exploitation, inequality, oppression, and neglect.

Is it possible that some exposure to the staggering sum of human suffering revealed in the historical record can soften our hearts, fostering compassion for our own suffering and that of others? In short, can the study of history generate kindness, both at the level of day-to-day personal interactions and at the wider level of acting to repair the brokenness of the world?

For those who choose to practice kindness or to seek justice in public life— overcoming global poverty, promoting equality between men and women, seeking understanding among religious traditions, encouraging environmental sustainability— history offers some encouragement. For one thing, it provides a record of those who have struggled long, hard, and on occasion with some success. Abolitionists contributed to the ending of slavery. Colonized peoples broke free of empire. Women secured the vote and confronted patriarchy. Socialists and communists challenged the inequities of capitalism, while popular protest brought repressive communist regimes to their knees in the Soviet Union and Eastern Europe. Brave people have spoken truth to power. In short, things changed, and sometimes people changed things.

There is yet another way in which history might assist our personal journeys through life. We are, most of us, inclined to be insular, to regard our own ways as the norm, to be fearful of difference. Nor is this tendency largely our own fault. We all have limited experience. Few of us have had much personal encounter with cultures beyond our own country, and none of us, of course, knows personally what life was like before our birth. But we do know that a rich and mature life involves opening up to a wider world. If we base our understanding of life only on what we personally experience, we are impoverished indeed.

In this task of opening up, history in general and world history in particular have much to offer. They provide a marvelous window into the unfamiliar. They confront us with the whole range of human achievement, tragedy, and sensibility. They give context and perspective to our own limited experience. They allow us some modest entry into the lives of people far removed from us in time and place. They offer us company for the journeys of our own lives. If we take it seriously, historical study can assist us in enlarging and enriching our sense of self. In helping us open up to the wider experience of "all under heaven," as the Chinese put it, history can assist us in becoming wiser and more mature people. What more might one ask from any field of study?

Second Thoughts

What's the Significance?

To assess your mastery of the material in this chapter, visit the **Student Center** at bedfordstmartins.com/strayer.

neo-liberalism	Prague Spring	Islamic renewal
reglobalization	Che Guevara	Osama bin Laden/al-Qaeda
transnational corporations	second-wave feminism	global warming
North/South gap	fundamentalism	environmentalism
antiglobalization	Hindutva	

Big Picture Questions

1. To what extent did the processes discussed in this chapter (economic globalization, feminism, fundamentalism, environmentalism) represent something new in the twentieth century? In what respects did they have roots in the more distant past?
2. In what ways did the global North/South divide find expression in the twentieth and early twenty-first centuries?
3. What have been the benefits and drawbacks of globalization since 1945?
4. Do the years since 1914 confirm or undermine Enlightenment predictions about the future of humankind?
5. "The twentieth century marks the end of the era of Western dominance in world history." What evidence might support this statement? What evidence might contradict it?
6. To what extent do you think the various liberation movements of the twentieth and early twenty-first centuries—communism, nationalism, democracy, feminism, internationalism—have achieved their goals?
7. Based on material in Chapters 21, 22, and 24, how might you define the evolving roles of the United States in the twentieth and early twenty-first centuries?

For Further Study

For Web sites and additional documents related to this chapter, see **Make History** at bedfordstmartins.com/strayer.

Karen Armstrong, *The Battle for God* (2000). A comparison of Christian, Jewish, and Islamic fundamentalism in historical perspective.

Nayan Chanda, *Bound Together: How Traders, Preachers, Adventurers, and Warriors Shaped Globalization* (2007). An engaging, sometimes humorous, long-term view of the globalization process.

Jeffrey Frieden, *Global Capitalism: Its Fall and Rise in the Twentieth Century* (2006). A thorough, thoughtful, and balanced history of economic globalization.

Michael Hunt, *The World Transformed* (2004). A thoughtful global history of the second half of the twentieth century.

J. R. McNeill, *Something New under the Sun: An Environmental History of the Twentieth Century World* (2001). A much-acclaimed global account of the rapidly mounting human impact on the environment during the most recent century.

Bonnie Smith, ed., *Global Feminisms since 1945* (2000). A series of essays about feminist movements around the world.

"No Job for a Woman," http://www.iwm.org.uk/upload/package/30/women/index.htm. A Web site illustrating the impact of war on the lives of women in the twentieth century.

Documents

Considering the Evidence: Contending for Islam

L ike all religious traditions, Islam has never been a single body of thought and practice. Various legal traditions, leadership issues, rituals, under- standings of the Quran, attitudes toward human reason, and more have long divided the Islamic world. Other divisions arose as Muslims confronted the growing intrusion of Western imperialism and modern secular culture. Which ideas and influences flowing from the West could Muslims safely utilize and which should they decisively reject? In the twentieth century, and especially during its second half, the issue prompted acute and highly visible controversy among Muslims as they debated the meaning of Islam and its implications for social and political life (see pp. 1153–57). The documents that follow illustrate something of the sharp controversies and variations in the understanding of Islam during the past century.

Document 24.1

A Secular State for an Islamic Society in Turkey

Modern Turkey emerged from the ashes of the Ottoman Empire after World War I and adopted a distinctive path of modernization, Westernization, and secularism under the leadership of Mustafa Kemal Atatürk (see pp. 1103–05). Such policies sought to remove Islam from any significant role in public life and included abolition of the caliphate, by which Ottoman rulers had claimed leadership of the entire Islamic world. In a speech delivered in 1927, Atatürk explained and justified these policies, which went against the grain of much Islamic thinking.

- On what grounds did Atatürk justify the abolition of the caliphate?

- What additional actions did he take to remove Islam from a public or political role in the new Turkish state?

- What can you infer about Atatürk's view of Islam?

- How did Atatürk's conception of a Turkish state differ from that of Ottoman authorities? In what ways did he build upon Ottoman reforms of the nineteenth century? (See pp. 891–94 in Chapter 19.)

Mustafa Kemal Atatürk

Speech to the General Congress of the Republican Party

1927

[Our Ottoman rulers] hoped to unite the entire Islamic world in one body, to lead it and to govern it. For this purpose, [they] assumed the title of Caliph.°...It is an unrealizable aim to attempt to unite in one tribe the various races existing on the earth, thereby abolishing all boundaries....There is nothing in history to show how [such] a policy of Pan-Islamism could have succeeded....

If the Caliph and the Caliphate were to be invested with a dignity embracing the whole of Islam,...a crushing burden would be imposed on Turkey....I gave the people to understand that neither Turkey nor the handful of men she possesses could be placed at the disposal of the Caliph so that he might fulfill the mission attributed to him, namely, to found a state comprising the whole of Islam....

[Furthermore], will Persia or Afghanistan, which are [Muslim] states, recognize the authority of the Caliph in a single matter? No, and this is quite justifiable, because it would be in contradiction to the independence of the state, to the sovereignty of the people.

[The current constitution] laid down as the first duty of the Grand National Assembly that "the prescriptions of the Shari'a° should be put into force...." [But] if a state, having among its subjects elements professing different religions and being compelled to act justly and impartially toward all of them..., it is obliged to respect freedom of opinion and conscience....The Muslim religion includes freedom of religious opinion....Will not every grownup person in the new Turkish state be free to select his own religion?...When the first favorable opportunity arises, the nation must act to eliminate these superfluities [the enforcement of sharia] from our Constitution....

Under the mask of respect for religious ideas and dogmas, the new Party [in opposition to Atatürk's reformist plans] addressed itself to the people in the following words: "We want the re-establishment of the Caliphate; we are satisfied with the religious law; we shall protect the Medressas,° the Tekkes,° the pious institutions, the Softahs,° the Sheikhs,° and their disciples....The party of Mustapha Kemal, having abolished the Caliphate, is breaking Islam into ruins; they will make you into unbelievers...they will make you wear hats." Can anyone pretend that the style of propaganda used by the Party was not full of these reactionary appeals?...

Gentlemen, it was necessary to abolish the fez,° which sat on our heads as a sign of ignorance, of fanaticism, of hatred to progress and civilization, and to adopt in its place the hat, the customary headdress of the whole civilized world, thus showing that no difference existed in the manner of thought between the Turkish nation and the whole family of civilized mankind....[Thus] there took place the closing of the Tekkes, of the convents, and of the mausoleums, as well as the abolition of all sects and all kinds of [religious] titles....

Could a civilized nation tolerate a mass of people who let themselves be led by the nose by a herd of Sheikhs, Dedes, Seids, Tschelebis, Babas, and Emirs°....Would not one therewith have committed the greatest, most irreparable error to the cause of progress and awakening?

°**Caliph:** successor to the prophet Muhammad.

°**Shari'a:** Islamic law.

Source: *A Speech Delivered by Ghazi Mustapha Kemal, October 1927* (Leipzig: K. F. Koehler, 1929), 377–79, 591–93, 595–98, 717, 721–22.

°**Medressas:** Islamic schools.

°**Tekkes:** places for Sufi worship.

°**Softahs:** students in religious schools.

°**Sheikhs:** Sufi masters.

°**fez:** a distinctive Turkish hat with no brim.

°**Sheikhs...Emirs:** various religious titles.

Document 24.2

Egypt's Muslim Brotherhood

While Kemal Atatürk was building a secular state in a largely Muslim Turkey, an Egyptian organization known as the Muslim Brotherhood sought to move in precisely the opposite direction. Founded in 1928 by an impoverished schoolteacher named Hassan al-Banna (1906–1949), the Muslim Brotherhood believed that Egypt's many problems—poverty, political factionalism, social unrest— derived from the neglect of Islamic principles that followed from British colonial rule and the penetration of Western values. The solution was a return to the original prescriptions of Islam. The Muslim Brotherhood quickly attracted a mass following, including many poor urban residents recently arrived from the countryside. In 1936, the organization spelled out the kind of reforms that it sought for Egypt.

- How did the Muslim Brotherhood understand the proper role of government as well as the appropriate relationship of individuals and the state?

- What problems in Egyptian society did the Muslim Brotherhood seek to correct?

- How does this document understand the proper relationship of the sexes?

- What aspects of Western and modern culture did the Muslim Brotherhood reject and which might it have embraced?

- How might Atatürk (Document 24.1) have responded to the Muslim Brotherhood's vision of a good society?

HASSAN AL-BANNA

Toward the Light

1936

The following are chapter headings for a reform based upon the true spirit of Islam:

I. In the political, judicial, and administrative fields:

   1st. To prohibit political parties and to direct the forces of the nation toward the formation of a united front;

Source: Robert G. Landon, ed., *The Emergence of the Modern Middle East* (New York: Van Nostrand Reinhold, 1970), 261–64; translated, probably by the editor, from Hasan al-Banna, *Nahw al-Nur* (*Toward the Light*) (Cairo: 1936), 38–48.

   2nd. To reform the law in such a way that it will be entirely in accordance with Islamic legal practice;

   3rd. To build up the army, to increase the number of youth groups; to instill in youth the spirit of holy struggle, faith, and self-sacrifice;

   4th. To strengthen the ties among Islamic countries and more particularly among Arab countries which is a necessary step toward serious examination of the question of the defunct "Caliphate";

5th. To propagate an Islamic spirit within the civil administration so that all officials will understand the need for applying the teachings of Islam;

6th. To supervise the personal conduct of officials because the private life and the administrative life of these officials forms an indivisible whole;...

9th. Government will act in conformity to the law and to Islamic principles; the carrying out of ceremonies, receptions, and official meetings, as well as the administration of prisons and hospitals should not be contrary to Islamic teachings. The scheduling of government services ought to take account of the hours set aside for prayer....

II. In the fields of social and everyday practical life:...

2nd. To find a solution for the problems of woman, a solution that will allow her to progress and which will protect her while conforming to Islamic principles....

3rd. To root out clandestine or public prostitution and to consider fornication as a reprehensible crime, the authors of which should be punished;

4th. To prohibit all games of chance (gaming, lotteries, races, golf);

5th. To stop the use of alcohol and intoxicants—these obliterate the painful consequences of people's evil deeds;

6th. To stop attacks on modesty, to educate women, to provide quality education for female teachers, school pupils, students, and doctors;

7th. To prepare instructional programs for girls; to develop an educational program for girls different than the one for boys;

8th. Male students should not be mixed with female students—any relationship between unmarried men and women is considered to be wrong until it is approved;...

10th. To close dance halls; to forbid dancing;

11th. To censor theater productions and films; to be severe in approving films;

12th. To supervise and to approve music;

13th. To approve programs, songs, and subjects before they are released, to use radio to encourage national education;

14th. To confiscate malicious articles and books as well as magazines displaying a grotesque character or spreading frivolity;...

16th. To change the hours when public cafés are opened or closed, to watch the activities of those who habituate them—to direct these people toward wholesome pursuits, to prevent people from spending too much time in these cafés;

17th. To use the cafés as centers to teach reading and writing to illiterates, to seek help in this task from primary school teachers and students;...

19th. To bring to trial those who break the laws of Islam, who do not fast, who do not pray, and who insult religion;...

21st. Religious teaching should constitute the essential subject matter to be taught in all educational establishments and faculties;

22nd. To memorize the Koran in state schools—this condition will be essential in order to obtain diplomas with a religious or philosophical specialty—in every school students should learn part of the Koran;...

24th. Interested support for teaching the Arabic language in all grades—absolute priority to be given to Arabic over foreign languages (primary teaching);

25th. To study the history of Islam, the nation, and Muslim civilization;

26th. To study the best way to allow people to dress progressively and in an identical manner;

27th. To combat foreign customs (in the realm of vocabulary, customs, dress, nursing) and to Egyptianize all of these (one finds these customs among the well-to-do members of society);

28th. To orient journalism toward wholesome things, to encourage writers and authors who should study specifically Muslim and Oriental subjects;

29th. To safeguard public health through every kind of publicity—increasing the number of hospitals, doctors, and out-patient clinics;

30th. To call particular attention to the problems of village life (administration, hygiene, water supply, education, recreation, morality).

III. The economic field:

1st. Organization of the "zakat tax" according to Islamic precepts, using zakat proceeds for welfare projects such as aiding the indigent, the poor, orphans; the zakat should also be used to strengthen the army;

2nd. To prevent the practice of usury, to direct banks to implement this policy; the government should provide an example by giving up the "interest" fixed by banks for servicing a personal loan or an industrial loan, etc.;

3rd. To facilitate and to increase the number of economic enterprises and to employ the jobless there, to employ for the nation's benefit the skills possessed by the foreigners in these enterprises;

4th. To protect workers against monopoly companies, to require these companies to obey the law, the public should share in all profits;

5th. Aid for low-ranking employees and enlargement of their pay, lowering the income of high-ranking employees; . . .

7th. To encourage agricultural and industrial works, to improve the situation of the peasants and industrial workers;

8th. To give special attention to the technical and social needs of the workers, to raise their level of life and aid their class;

9th. Exploitation of certain natural resources (unworked land, neglected mines, etc.).

Document 24.3

The Ideas of the Ayatollah Khomeini

While the Muslim Brotherhood was never able to seize control of the state in Egypt, an Islamic Revolution in Iran brought to power in 1979 a government committed to the thorough Islamization of public life (see the map on p. 1154, and see pp. 1105–08). That revolution had been inspired and led by the Ayatollah Khomeini (1902–1989), an Iranian religious scholar, who became the rallying point for those opposed to the regime of the Shah of Iran, which was strongly backed by the United States. Document 24.3 provides the flavor of Khomeini's thinking. As the Supreme Leader of Iran during the 1980s, he was in a position to put many of those ideas into practice.

■ How does Khomeini define the enemies of Islam?

■ How would you summarize his case against European imperialism and the Shah's government?

■ In what ways does Khomeini seek to apply Islamic principles in the public life of Iran? What is his view of Iranian popular culture? How do his prescriptions for an Islamic society compare with those of Hassan al-Banna in Document 24.2?

■ What kind of government does Khomeini foresee for Iran? Why does he believe that a proper Islamic government "cannot be totalitarian or despotic but is constitutional and democratic"?

■ To whom might Khomeini's views be most appealing?

AYATOLLAH KHOMEINI

Sayings of the Ayatollah Khomeini

1980

Islam is a religion of those who struggle for truth and justice, of those who clamor for liberty and independence. It is the school of those who fight against colonialism.

Islamic faith and justice demand that within the Muslim world, anti-Islamic governments not be allowed to survive.... Any nonreligious power, whatever form or shape it may take, is necessarily an atheistic power, the tool of Satan;... [W]e have no recourse other than to overthrow all governments that do not rest on pure Islamic principles.... That is not only our duty in Iran, but it is also the duty of all Muslims in the world, in all Muslim countries, to carry the Islamic political revolution to its final victory....

The homeland of Islam, one and indivisible, was broken up by the doings of the Imperialists and despotic and ambitious leaders.... And when the Ottoman Empire struggled to achieve Islamic unity, it was opposed by a united front of Russian, English, Austrian, and other imperialist powers, which split it up among themselves.

Western missionaries, carrying out secret plans drawn up centuries ago, have created religious schools of their own within Muslim countries.... These missionaries infiltrated our villages and our countrysides, to turn our children into Christians or atheists!

The Islamic movement met its first saboteur in the Jewish people, who are at the source of all the anti-Islamic libels and intrigues current today. Then came the turn of those even more damnable repre-

sentatives of Satan, the imperialists. Within the last three centuries or more, they have invaded every Muslim country, with the intention of destroying Islam.

Their plan is to keep us in our backward state, to preserve our backward state, to preserve our pathetic way of life, so they can exploit the tremendous wealth of our underground resources, of our land, and our manpower. They want us to stay destitute, distracted by niggling day-to-day problems of survival, our poor living in misery, so that we will never become aware of the laws of Islam—which contain the solution to misery and poverty! All of this they have done so they can sit in their big palaces, living their stupid shallow lives!

Many of these corruptions have their origin in the gang that is in power, and in the family of a despotic and capricious ruler [the Shah of Iran]. These are the rulers who create hotbeds of lust, prostitution, and drugs, who devote the revenues of the mosque to building cinemas!

What do you understand of the harmony between social life and religious principles? And more important, just what is the social life we are talking about? Is it those hotbeds of immorality called theaters, cinemas, dancing, and music? Is it the promiscuous presence in the streets of lusting young men and women with arms, chests, and thighs bared? Is it the ludicrous wearing of a hat like the Europeans or the imitation of their habit of wine drinking? We are convinced that you have been made to lose your ability to distinguish between good and evil, in exchange for a few radio sets and ludicrous Western hats. Your attention has been attracted to the disrobed women to be seen on thoroughfares and in swim-

Source: *Sayings of the Ayatollah Khomeini* (New York: Bantam Books, 1980), 3–4, 7–12, 15–17, 29–30, 35–36.

ming pools. Let these shameful practices come to an end, so that the dawn of a new life may break!

We [clergy] forcefully affirm that refusal to wear the veil is against the law of Allah and the Prophet, and a material and moral affront to the entire country. We affirm that the ludicrous use of the Western hat stands in the way of our independence and is contrary to the will of Allah. We affirm that coeducational schools are an obstacle to a wholesome life; they are a material and moral affront to the country and contrary to the divine will. We affirm that music engenders immorality, lust, and licentiousness, and stifles courage, valor, and the chivalrous spirit; it is forbidden by Qur'anic law and must not be taught in the schools. Radio Tehran, by broadcasting Western, Oriental, and Iranian music, plays a nefarious role by introducing immorality and licentiousness into respectable families.

An Islamic government cannot be totalitarian or despotic, but is constitutional and democratic. In this democracy, however, the laws are not made by the will of the people, but only by the Qur'an and the Sunnah° of the Prophet. The constitution, the civil code, and the criminal code should be inspired only by Islamic laws contained in the Qur'an and transcribed by the Prophet. Islamic government is the government of divine right, and its laws cannot be changed, modified, or contested....

It is often proclaimed that religion must be separated from politics, and that the ecclesiastical world should keep out of affairs of state. It is proclaimed that high Muslim clerical authorities have no business mixing into the social and political decisions of the government. Such proclamations can come only from atheists; they are dictated and spread by imperialists....Think of it—a political clergy! Well, why not? The Prophet was a politician!...

Islam has precepts for everything that concerns man and society....There is no subject upon which Islam has not expressed judgment.

The Islamic republic is a government according to the Law and the wise men and theological experts of the clergy are therefore responsible for it. It is they who must watch over all aspects of administration and planning. In administering the laws of God in such matters as taxes and property for example, they must be trusted.... If the punitive laws of Islam were applied for only one year, all the devastating injustices and immoralities would be uprooted. Misdeeds must be punished by the law of retaliation: cut off the hands of the thief; kill the murderer instead of putting him in prison; flog the adulterous woman or man....

We have a duty to create an Islamic republic and to that end our first obligation is the creation of a system of propaganda.... Radio and television are allowed if they are used for the broadcasting of news or sermons, for the spreading of good educational material for publicizing the products and curiosities of the planet; but they must prohibit singing, music, anti-Islamic laws, the lauding of tyrants, mendacious words, and broadcasts which spread doubt and undermine virtue.

°**Sunnah:** traditions.

Document 24.4

A Liberal Viewpoint from an Islamic Woman

Islamic renewal movements such as the Muslim Brotherhood and Islamic governments in Iran and even more radically in Taliban-governed Afghanistan have sought to impose sharp restrictions on the public activities and private behavior of women as well as maintaining their seclusion from and subordination to men. For them, this was a crucial element of an effort to bring society into alignment with Islamic law. Yet this element of Islamic thought and practice has been sharply contested. While Iran was implementing a largely male-dominated Islamic society during the last two decades of the twentieth century, the Muslim country of Pakistan twice selected the same woman, Benazir Bhutto, as prime minister. Both times she was removed from power on charges of corruption and spent many years in exile. During her third attempt to achieve the political leadership of Pakistan in 2007, she was assassinated. In 1985, Bhutto gave an address at Radcliffe College in the United States in which she laid out an argument for women's equality within an Islamic context.

- On what basis does Bhutto argue that "Islam provides justice and equality for women"?

- How does she account for the manifest inequality of women in so many Muslim societies?

- How do you think Kemal Atatürk, Hasan al-Banna, and the Ayatollah Khomeini might respond to her ideas?

BENAZIR BHUTTO
Politics and the Muslim Woman
1985

I think one of the first things that we must appreciate about the religion of Islam is that there is no one interpretation to it....

I would describe Islam in two main categories: reactionary Islam and progressive Islam. We can have a reactionary interpretation of Islam which tries to uphold the status quo, or we can have a progressive interpretation of Islam which tries to move with a changing world, which believes in human dignity, which believes in consensus, and which believes in giving women their due right....

I believe that Islam within it provides justice and equality for women, and I think that those aspects of Islam which have been highlighted by the *mullas* [religious scholars] do not do a service to our religion.... Christianity has a clergy. Islam does not have a clergy. The relationship between a Muslim and God is direct. There is no need for somebody to intervene. The *mullas* try to intervene. The *mullas*

give their own interpretation. But I think there are growing movements, as more and more people in Muslim countries, both men and women, achieve education and begin to examine the Qur'an in the light of their education, they are beginning not to agree with the *mullas* on their orthodox or reactionary version of Islam.

Let us start with the story of the Fall. Unlike Christianity, it is not Eve who tempts Adam into tasting the apple and being responsible for original sin. According to Islam—and I mention this because I believe that Islam is an egalitarian religion—both Adam and Eve are tempted, both are warned, both do not heed the warning, and therefore the Fall occurs.

As far as opportunity is concerned, in Islam there is equal opportunity for both men and women. I refer to the Sura *Ya Sin* [Sura 36, Verses 34–35], which says: "We produce orchids and date gardens and vines, and we cause springs to gush forth, that they may enjoy the fruits of it." God does not give fruits, orchids, or the fruit of the soil just for men to enjoy or men to plow; he gives it for both men and women. What, in terms of income and opportunity, is avail-

Source: Benazir Bhutto, "Politics and the Muslim Woman," transcript of audio recording, April 11, 1985, in Charles Kurzman, ed., *Liberal Islam: A Sourcebook* (New York: Oxford University Press, 1998), 107–11.

able, is available to both man and woman. Sura *an-Nisa* [Sura 4, Verse 32]: "To men is allotted what they earn, and to women what they earn."...

The references [in the Quran] are to men and women. The references are not to men as being characteristic of certain qualities and separate qualities for women. It is not a reference to the male sex as being endowed with some superior attributes and to the woman as being endowed with inferior attributes. The attributes are the same. Both are the creatures of God. Both have certain rights. Both have certain duties. Both have certain obligations. If they want to go to Heaven, thay have to behave in a special manner. If they want to do good in this earth, they have to give alms to the needy, they have to help orphans—the behavior is applicable to both men and women. It is not religion which makes the difference. The difference comes from man-made law. It comes from the fact that soon after the Prophet died, it was not the Islam of the Prophet that remained. What took place was the emergence or the reassertiveness of the partiarchal society, and religion was taken over to justify the norms of the tribal society, rather than the point that the Prophet had made in replacing the tribal society with a religion that aimed to cut across narrow loyalties and sought to create a new community, or *umma*, on the basis of Islam and the message of God.

[About] the right of divorce and polygamy. It is often said that Islam provides for four wives for a man. But in my interpretation of this, and in the interpretation of many other Muslims, that is simply not true.

What the Qur'an does say, and I quote: "Marry as many women as you wish, wives two or three or four. If you fear not to treat them equally, marry only one. [...] I doubt you will be able to be just between your wives, even if you try" [Sura 4, Verses 3 and 129]. So if God Himself and His message says that He doubts that you can be equal, I don't know how any man can turn around and say that "God has given me this right to get married more than once."

I would like to say that within Islamic history there are very strong roles for women. For instance, the Prophet's wife, Bibi Khadija, was a woman of independent means. She had her own business, she traded, she dealt with society at large, she employed the Prophet Muhammad, peace be upon him, when he was a young boy, and subsequently, Bibi Khadija herself sent a proposal [of marriage] to the Prophet. So she is the very image of somebody who is independent, assertive, and does not conform to the passive description of women in Muslim societies that we have grown accustomed to hearing about....

[T]here is Bibi 'A'isha [wife of the Prophet, circa 614–678], who is also put forward as a politically astute woman, who, after the death of the Prophet, was responsible for many of the Traditions that have been handed down to us, who was the one who proposed the caliphate of Hazrat 'Uthman, and held out the shirt of the Prophet Muhammad, and said that, "Even before this shirt has decayed, you have to ordain someone like Hazrat 'Uthman." She made her views known. She was an extremely bold person. Not only did she make her views known; when she opposed something, she went to the battlefield and fought against it.

So when we have such powerful role models of women...then one must ask, why is it that today in Muslim countries, one does not see that much of women? One does not hear that much of women. Why is it that women are secluded? Why is it that women are subject to social control? Why is it that women are not given their due share of property?... It has got nothing to do with the religion, but it has got very much to do with material or man-made considerations....

Before I conclude on this aspect of the powerful role within Islam of women, I would like to quote from the Qur'an, the Sura "The Ant" [Sura 27, Verse 23]: "I found a woman ruling over them, and she has been given abundance of all things, and hers is a mighty throne." It is not Islam which is averse to women rulers, I think—it is men.

Document 24.5

Islam and 9/11

In the early twenty-first century, the international face of an assertive Islamic fundamentalism was that of Osama bin Laden, whose al-Qaeda organization launched the attacks on the United States on September 11, 2001, and called for the overthrow of compromised governments in Saudi Arabia and elsewhere in the Islamic world (see pp. 1156–57). Substantial numbers of Muslims no doubt shared bin Laden's outrage at the sorry state of many Muslim societies as well as his opposition to heavy U.S. backing for the state of Israel and to American military interventions in Iraq and Afghanistan. Addressing fellow Muslims, bin Laden lashed out against those who interacted with American economic interests: "The money you pay to buy American goods will be transformed into bullets and used against our brothers in Palestine."

But bin Laden and his followers were certainly not the only voices laying claim to Islam in the aftermath of 9/11. All across the Islamic world, others argued that Muslims could retain their distinctive religious sensibility while embracing democracy, women's rights, technological progress, freedom of thought, and religious pluralism. Just a month after the 9/11 attacks, the well-known Malaysian intellectual and political figure Anwar Ibrahim pondered the meaning of those attacks: "One wonders how, in the twenty-first century, the Muslim world could have produced an Osama bin Laden. In the centuries when Islam forged civilizations, men of wealth created pious foundations supporting universities and hospitals, and princes competed with one another to patronize scientists, philosophers, and men of letters."[29] Muslims like Anwar Ibrahim were following in the tradition of nineteenth-century Islamic modernism (see pp. 891–94), even as they recalled earlier centuries of Islamic intellectual and scienific achievement and religious tolerance. That viewpoint was expressed in a pamphlet composed by a leading American Muslim scholar, translator, and Sufi teacher, Sheikh Kabir Helminski, in 2009.

- Against what charges does Sheikh Kabir seek to defend Islam? How does this document reflect the experience of 9/11?

- In what ways are Sheikh Kabir's views critical of radical or "fundamentalist" ideas and practices?

- How does this document, together with Document 24.4, articulate the major features of a more progressive or liberal Islam? What kinds of arguments are employed to make their case?

- To whom might these arguments appeal? What obstacles do they face in being heard within the Islamic world?

■ How might the Muslim Brotherhood (Document 24.2), Ayatollah Khomeini (Document 24.3), or Osama bin Laden respond to the arguments in this document? In what ways does this vision of a "liberal" or "moderate" Islam differ from those of Kemal Atatürk (Document 24.1)?

KABIR HELMINSKI
"Islam and Human Values"
2009

If the word "Islam" gives rise to fear or mistrust today, it is urgent that American Muslims clarify what we believe Islam stands for in order to dispel the idea that there is a fundamental conflict between the best values of Western civilization and the essential values of Islam....

Islamic civilization, which developed out of the revelation of the Qur'an in the seventh century, affirms the truth of previous revelations, affirms religious pluralism, cultural diversity, and human rights, and recognizes the value of reason and individual conscience....

[One issue] is the problem of violence.... Thousands of Muslim institutions and leaders, the great majority of the world's billion or more Muslims, have unequivocally condemned the hateful and violent ideologies that kill innocents and violate the dignity of all humanity....

Islamic civilizations have a long history of encouraging religious tolerance and guaranteeing the rights of religious minorities. The reason for this is that the Qur'an explicitly acknowledges that the diversity of religions is part of the Divine Plan and no religion has a monopoly on truth or virtue....

Jerusalem, under almost continuous Islamic rule for nearly fourteen centuries, has been a place where Christians and Jews have lived side by side with Muslims, their holy sites and religious freedom preserved. Medieval Spain also created a high level of civilization as a multi-cultural society under Islamic rule for several centuries. The Ottoman Empire, the longest lived in history, for the more than six centuries of its existence encouraged ethnic and religious minorities to participate in and contribute to society. It was the Ottoman sultan who gave sanctuary to the Jews expelled from Catholic Spain. India was governed for centuries by Muslims, even while the majority of its people practiced Hinduism....

[T]he acceptance of Islam must be an act of free will. Conversion by any kind of coercion was universally condemned by Islamic scholars....

There are many verses in the Qur'an that affirm the actuality and even the necessity of diversity in ways of life and religious belief: [For example] *O mankind, truly We [God] have created you male and female, and have made you nations and tribes that ye may know one another.* [Surah 49:13]....

In general, war is forbidden in Islam, except in cases of self-defense in response to explicit aggression. If there is a situation where injustice is being perpetrated or if the community is being invaded, then on a temporary basis permission is given to defend oneself. This principle is explained in the following verses: *And fight in God's cause against those who war against you, but do not commit aggression—for, verily, God does not love aggressors.* [Surah 2:190]

The general principle established throughout the Qur'an is that the relationship between Muslims and non-Muslims should be based on peace and fairness. So that there is no ambiguity, it clearly and unequivocally states: *Allah does not forbid you from dealing kindly and justly with those who do not fight you for (your) Faith nor drive you out of your homes: for Allah loves those who are just.* [Surah 60:8]

Source: Selections from Kabir Helminski, "Islam and Human Values," unpublished pamphlet, 2009.

[I]n recent decades... an intolerant ideology has been unleashed. A small minority of the world's one and a half billion Muslims has misconstrued the teachings of Islam to justify their misguided and immoral actions. It is most critical at this time for Muslims to condemn such extreme ideologies and their manifestations. It is equally important that non-Muslims understand that this ideology violates the fundamental moral principles of Islam and is repugnant to the vast majority of Muslims in the world.... So-called "suicide-bombers" did not appear until the mid-1990s. Such strategies have no precedent in Islamic history. The Qur'an says quite explicitly: *Do not kill yourselves.* [4:29]...

Muslims living in pluralistic societies have no religious reasons to oppose the laws of their own societies as long as they are just, but rather are encouraged to uphold the duly constituted laws of their own societies.... Islam and democracy are compatible and can coexist because Islam organizes humanity on the basis of the rule of law and human dignity.

The first four successors to the Prophet Muhammad were chosen by the community through consultation, i.e., a representative democracy. The only principle of political governance expressed in the Qur'an is the principle of Consultation (Shura), which holds that communities will "*rule themselves by means of mutual consultation.*" [Surah 42:38]

Following the principles of the Qur'an, Muslims are encouraged to cooperate for the well-being of all. The Qur'an emphasizes three qualities above all others: peace, compassion, and mercy. The standard greeting in Islam is "As-Salam alaykum (Peace be with you)."

An American Muslim scholar, Abdul Aziz Sachedina, expresses it this way: "Islam does not encourage turning God into a political statement since humans cannot possess God. They can simply relate themselves to God by emulating God's compassion and forgiveness."...

[T]here is nothing in the Qur'an that essentially contradicts reason or science.... Repeatedly the Qur'an urges human beings to "reflect" and "use their intelligence."

Islam is not an alien religion. It does not claim a monopoly on virtue or truth. It follows in the way of previous spiritual traditions that recognized One Spirit operating within nature and human life. It continues on the Way of the great Prophets and Messengers of all sacred traditions.

Using the Evidence:
Voices of Islam

1. **Understanding the uses of history:** How does each of these authors use history to make his or her arguments? To what different historical contexts do they appeal?

2. **Identifying "fundamentalist" themes:** What common emphases do you see in the two more "fundamentalist" authors represented here in Documents 24.2 and 24.3? To what extent do they reflect or diverge from themes articulated in the mid-eighteenth century by Abd al Wahhab (Document 16.4, pp. 756–57)?

3. **Comparing Islamic modernists:** How do you think Kemal Atatürk would respond to later Islamic modernists such as Benazir Bhutto and Sheikh Kabir?

4. **Imagining an Islamic conversation:** Construct a dialog between the Islamic fundamentalists and the Islamic moderates. Can you identify any points of contact or similarity on which they might be able to agree? On which points would they probably never agree?

5. **Considering religion and politics:** How does each of these documents understand the relationship of religion and political life? How do they view the division between the public and private spheres of life?

Visual Sources

Considering the Evidence: Experiencing Globalization

Although a few people in the world of the early twenty-first century may remain untouched by globalization, surely they are not many. For most of humankind, the pervasive processes of interaction among distant peoples has shaped the clothing we wear, the foods we eat, the products we consume, the ways we work, the music we listen to, the religions we practice, and the identities we assume. Globalization has bound the various peoples of the planet more tightly together and in some respects has made us more alike. Almost all of us, for example, live in nation-states and seek the wealth and prosperity that modern science and technology promise. And yet in other ways we are very different, divided, and conflicted. The enormous gap in wealth between the rich countries of the Global North and the poor nations of the Global South represents a sharp and quite recent rift in the human community. The visual sources that follow illustrate just a few of the ways in which the world's peoples have experienced globalization in recent decades and have responded to it.

Among the common experiences of globalization for some people living in Asia, Africa, or Latin America has been that of working in foreign-owned production facilities. Companies in wealthier countries have often found it advantageous to build such facilities in places where labor is less expensive or environmental regulations are less strict. China, Vietnam, Indonesia, Bangladesh, the Philippines, Mexico, Brazil, and various African states are among the countries that have hosted foreign-owned manufacturing operations. The worst of them—in terms of child labor, low pay, few benefits, and dangerous working conditions—have been called "sweatshops." Such abuses have generated an international movement challenging those conditions. Visual Source 24.1 illustrates an interesting twist on this common feature of a globalized world economy—a Chinese-owned company producing Western-style blue jeans in Lesotho, a small country in southern Africa.

■ Why might China, itself the site of many foreign-owned factories, place such a factory in Africa? What does this suggest about the changing position of China in the world economy? What is the significance of the blue jeans for an understanding of contemporary globalization?

■ Does this photograph conform to your image of a sweatshop? Why or why not?

Visual Source 24.1 Globalization and Work (brianafrica/Alamy)

■ Why might many developing countries accept foreign-owned production facilities, despite the criticisms of the working conditions in them?

■ Why do you think most of the workers in this photo are women? How might you imagine their motivations for seeking this kind of work? Keep in mind that the unemployment rate in Lesotho in the early twenty-first century was 45 percent.

■ What differences can you observe between the workers in this assembly factory and those in the Indian call center shown on page 1135? What similarities might you identify?

If globalization offered employment opportunities—albeit in often wretched conditions—to some people in the developing countries, it also promoted a worldwide culture of consumerism. That culture placed the accumulation of material goods, many of them of western origin, above older values of spiritual attainment or social responsibility. Nowhere has this culture of consumerism been more prominent than in China, where the fading of Maoist communism, the country's massive economic growth, and its new openness to the wider world combined to generate an unabashed materialism in the late twentieth and early twenty-first centuries. A popular slogan suggested that life in modern

China required the "eight bigs": color TV, refrigerator, stereo, camera, motorcycle, a suite of furniture, washing machine, and an electric fan. Visual Source 24.2 illustrates this culture of consumerism as well as one of the "eight bigs" in a poster from the post-Mao era. The photograph on page 1053 in Chapter 22 provides further illustration of Chinese consumerism, as does Visual Source 22.5 on page 1078.

■ In what ways might these images be used to illustrate Westernization, modernization, globalization, and consumerism?

■ How might the young people on the motorcycle and those in the KFC restaurant understand their own behavior? Do you think they are conscious of behaving in Western ways or have these ways become Chinese? What is the significance of a Chinese couple riding a Suzuki motorcycle, a Japanese product probably manufactured in China under a license agreement?

■ Beyond consumerism, how does this poster reflect changes in relationships between men and women in China after Mao? Is this yet another face of globalization or does it remain a distinctly Western phenomenon?

■ How might these images be read as a celebration of Chinese success? How might they be used to criticize contemporary Chinese society?

Beyond changes in the working lives and consumption habits of individuals, globalization in the second half of the twentieth century reversed earlier patterns of global migration. In the nineteenth century, Europeans had moved in huge numbers to the Americas, Australia, New Zealand, and South Africa. That flow largely stopped by the 1920s, replaced by a massive movement of people from the so-called third world to the West. Pakistanis, Indians, and West Indians moved to Great Britain; Algerians and West Africans to France; Filipinos, Koreans, Mexicans, and Haitians to the United States. These new patterns of migration disrupted the lives of many, both in their countries of origin and in their new homelands. A poem by a young Moroccan wife whose husband left for work in Europe during the 1970s reflects the pain of separation:

> With you he stays one year, with me just one month,
> to you he gives his health and sweat,
> to me he only comes to recuperate.
> Then he leaves again to work for you, to beautify
> you as a bride, each day anew.
> And I, I wait; I am like a flower that
> withers, more each day....
> I ask you: give him back to me.[30]

入勤春早

Visual Source 24.2 Globalization and Consumerism (Coll. SL [Stefan Landsberger]/IISH)

Visual Source 24.3 Globalization and Migration (Owen Franken/Corbis)

North African migrants to France, almost all of them Muslims, have injected new controversies in their adopted country. One of them has been the issue of girls wearing headscarves in school. A French law passed in 2004 forbade the practice on the grounds that it compromised the secularism of French education and represented the repression of women. But many Muslim women strongly objected to that law, arguing that it undermined their freedom of religion and violated their cultural traditions. Visual Source 24.3 captures one such protest. The first line of the large banner in the front reads: "The veil is a choice," but the second line is more ambiguous, for "frace" is not a word in the French language. Does it contain a misspelling of "France" with the letter "n" omitted? If so, it could be translated as "France is my right." Or is it a pun on "face" or "race," both of which are French words that carry the same meaning as their English equivalents? If so, perhaps it implies that the protesters have a right to their facial appearance or to the culture of their racial or ethnic group. Or does it contain a deliberate double or triple meaning?

■ How might different readings of "la frace" convey different meanings of the poster? On what principles do you think this protest is based? Do they derive from France or from the world of Islam?

■ The smaller sign behind the banner says, "The ignorance of people is the door that undermines our freedom." How might you understand this statement?

■ In what respect do these young women seem to be "French" or "European" and in what ways are they Muslim and North African?

■ What groups of people might find the demands of these protesters unacceptable? How might such critics have responded to the protesters?

■ What outcomes and tensions of globalization does this image reflect?

During the last several decades of the twentieth century, the process of economic globalization spawned various movements of resistance and criticism (see pp. 1141–42). In dozens of developing countries, protesters demonstrated or rioted against government policies that removed subsidies, raised prices on essential products, froze salaries, or cut back on social services. Because such policies were often required by the World Bank or the International Monetary Fund as a condition for receiving much-needed loans, protesters often directed their anger at these international financial institutions. In the wealthier countries of the world as well, activists have mounted large-scale protests against what they see as the abuses of unregulated corporate power operating in the world economy. Visual Source 24.4 shows a display of this anger that occurred during the protests in Seattle that coincided with the 1999 gathering of the World Trade Organization in that city.

Visual Source 24.4 Globalization and Protest (Michael McGuerty)

■ How does this image reflect the concerns of globalization's many critics? What political message does it convey? Do you think it expresses more clearly the political agenda of the Global North or the Global South?

Visual Source 24.5 Globalization: One World or Many? (NASA/GSFC Digital Archive)

■ Why have these criticisms come to focus so heavily on the activities of the World Trade Organization?

■ To what groups of people might such images be most compelling? How might advocates of corporate globalization respond to these protesters?

Visual Source 24.5, a composite satellite photograph of the world at night taken in late 2000, reflects three aspects of the globalization process. The first is the growing consciousness of the earth as a single place, the common home of humankind. Such thinking has been fostered by and expressed in those many remarkable images of the earth taken from space or from the moon (see the photo on p. 1132). In such photographs no artificial boundaries of state or nation are visible; just a single solitary planet cast against the immeasurable vastness of space. Second, this photograph shows the globalization of electricity, a central feature of modern life, which has taken place since the late nineteenth century. Finally, this image discloses sharp variations in modern development across the planet as the twenty-first century dawned.

■ To what extent has your thinking about the earth and its inhabitants been shaped by images such as this?

■ Based on the electrification evident in this photo, what does this image show about the economic divisions of the world in the early twenty-first century?

■ Does this image support or contradict Map 24.2, page 1140? What features of this image do you find surprising?

Using the Evidence:
Experiencing Globalization

1. **Defining differences:** Based on these visual sources and the text of Chapter 24, in what different ways have various groups of people experienced globalization since the end of World War II?

2. **Noticing change:** Based on these visual sources and those in the text of Chapter 24 as well, in what respects does contemporary globalization differ from that of earlier times? What continuities might you observe? Consider in particular the question of who is influencing who. Does recent globalization represent largely the impact of the West on the rest of the world or is it more of a two-way street?

3. **Making assessments:** Opinions about contemporary globalization depend heavily on the position of observers—their class, gender, or national locations. How might you illustrate this statement from the visual sources in this chapter?

4. **Seeking further evidence:** What additional visual sources might add to this effort to illustrate visually the various dimensions of globalization? What visual sources do you think might be added to it fifty or a hundred years from now?

Notes

Chapter 13

1. Brian Fagan, *Ancient North America* (London: Thames and Hudson, 2005), 503.

2. Quoted in Charles C. Mann, *1491: New Revelations of the Americas before Columbus* (New York: Alfred A. Knopf, 2005), 334.

3. Louise Levanthes, *When China Ruled the Seas* (New York: Simon and Schuster, 1994), 175.

4. Niccolò Machiavelli, *The Prince* (New York: New American Library, 1952), 90, 94.

5. Frank Viviano, "China's Great Armada," *National Geographic*, July 2005, 34.

6. Quoted in John J. Saunders, ed., *The Muslim World on the Eve of Europe's Expansion* (Englewood Cliffs, N.J.: Prentice Hall, 1966), 41–43.

7. Leo Africanus, *History and Description of Africa* (London: Hakluyt Society, 1896), 824–25.

8. Quoted in Craig A. Lockhard, *Southeast Asia in World History* (Oxford: Oxford University Press, 2009), 67.

9. Quoted in Patricia Risso, *Merchants and Faith* (Boulder, Colo.: Westview Press, 1995), 49.

10. Quoted in Stuart B. Schwartz, ed., *Victors and Vanquished* (Boston: Bedford/St. Martin's, 2000), 8.

11. Quoted in Michael E. Smith, *The Aztecs* (London: Blackwell, 2003), 108.

12. Smith, *The Aztecs*, 220.

13. Miguel Leon-Portilla, *Aztec Thought and Culture*, translated from the Spanish by Jack Emory Davis (Norman: University of Oklahoma Press, 1963), 7; Miguel Leon-Portilla, *Fifteen Poets of the Aztec World* (Norman: University of Oklahoma Press, 1992), 80–81.

14. Terence N. D'Altroy, *The Incas* (London: Blackwell, 2002), chaps. 11, 12.

15. For a summary of this practice among the Aztecs and Incas, see Karen Vieira Powers, *Women in the Crucible of Conquest* (Albuquerque: University of New Mexico Press, 2005), chap. 1.

16. Ibid., 25.

17. Louise Burkhart, "Mexica Women on the Home Front," in *Indian Women of Early Mexico*, edited by Susan Schroeder et al. (Norman: University of Oklahoma Press, 1997), 25–54.

18. The "web" metaphor is derived from J. R. McNeill and William H. McNeill, *The Human Web* (New York: W. W. Norton, 2003).

19. Graph from David Christian, *Map of Time* (Berkeley: University of California Press, 2004), 343.

20. Andrew Spicer and Sarah Hamilton, eds., *Defining the Holy: Sacred Space in Medieval and Early Modern Europe* (Farnham, U.K.: Ashgate Publishing, 2006), Chap. 1.

21. Oleg Grabar, "The Umayyad Dome of the Rock in Jerusalem," in Eva R. Hoffman, ed., *Late Antique and Medieval Art of the Mediterranean World* (London: John Wiley and Sons, 2007), 166.

22. Ibid., 161.

23. Trudy Ring, ed., *International Dictionary of Historic Places*, vol. 4, *Middle East and Africa* (Chicago: Fitzroy Dearborn, 1994–96), 444.

24. Francisco Alvarez, *The Prester John of the Indies* (Cambridge: Hakluyt Society, 1961), 226.

Part Four

1. Victor Lieberman, "Transcending East–West Dichotomies," *Modern Asian Studies* 31 (1997): 463–546; John Richards, *The Unending Frontier* (Berkeley: University of California Press, 2003), 22–24.

Chapter 14

1. *Taipei Times*, October 11, 1999, http://uyghuramerican.org/articles/145/1/Fight-for-East-Turkestan/Fight-for-East-Turkestan.html.

2. Winona LaDuke, "We Are Still Here: The 500 Year Celebration," *Sojourners Magazine*, October 1991.

3. Quoted in Thomas E. Skidmore and Peter H. Smith, *Modern Latin America* (New York: Oxford University Press, 2001), 15.

4. George Raudzens, ed., *Technology, Disease, and Colonial Conquest* (Boston: Brill Academic, 2003), xiv.

5. Alfred W. Crosby, "The Columbian Voyages, the Columbian Exchange, and Their Historians," in *Islamic and European Expansion*, edited by Michael Adas (Philadelphia: Temple University Press, 1993), 160.

6. Quoted in Noble David Cook, *Born to Die: Disease and the New World Conquest* (Cambridge: Cambridge University Press, 1998), 202.

7. Quoted in ibid., 206.

8. Quoted in Charles C. Mann, *1491* (New York: Alfred A. Knopf, 2005), 56.

9. Felipe Fernandez-Armesto, "Empires in Their Global Context," in *The Atlantic in Global History*, edited by Jorge Canizares-Esguerra and Erik R. Seeman (Upper Saddle River, N.J.: Prentice-Hall, 2007), 105.

10. Quoted in Anthony Padgen, "Identity Formation in Spanish America," in *Colonial Identity in the Atlantic World, 1500–1800*, edited by Nicholas Canny and Anthony Padgen (Princeton, N.J.: Princeton University Press, 1987), 56.

11. Quoted in Marjorie Wall Bingham, *An Age of Empire, 1200–1750* (Oxford: Oxford University Press, 2005), 116.

12. Derived from Skidmore and Smith, *Modern Latin America*, 25.

13. Quoted in James Lockhart and Stuart B. Schwartz, *Early Latin America* (Cambridge: Cambridge University Press, 1983), 206.

14. From Kevin Reilly et al., eds., *Racism: A Global Reader* (Armonk, N.Y.: M. E. Sharpe, 2003), 136–37.

15. Felipe Fernandez-Armesto, *The Americas: A Hemispheric History* (New York: Modern Library, 2003), 58–59.

16. Willard Sutherland, *Taming the Wild Fields: Colonization and Empire on the Russian Steppe* (Ithaca, N.Y.: Cornell University Press, 2004), 223–24.

17. Quoted in Michael Khodarkovsky, *Russia's Steppe Frontier* (Bloomington: Indiana University Press, 2002), 216.

18. Andreas Kappeler, *The Russian Empire* (New York: Longman, 2001), 115–17, 397–99.

19. Khodarkovsky, *Russia's Steppe Frontier*, 222.

20. Geoffrey Hosking, "The Freudian Frontier," *Times Literary Supplement*, March 10, 1995, 27.

21. Peter Perdue, *China Marches West: The Qing Conquest of Central Eurasia* (Cambridge: Harvard University Press, 2005), 10–11.

22. Quoted in Stephen F. Dale, "The Islamic World in the Age of European Expansion," in *The Cambridge Illustrated History of the Islamic World*, edited by Francis Robinson (Cambridge: Cambridge University Press, 1996), 80.

23. Quoted in Stanley Wolpert, *A New History of India* (New York: Oxford University Press, 1993), 160.

24. Jane I. Smith, "Islam and Christendom," in *The Oxford History of Islam*, edited by John Esposito (Oxford: Oxford University Press, 1999), 342.

25. Charles Thornton Forester and F. H. Blackburne Daniell, *The Life and Letters of Ogier Ghiselin de Busbecq* (London: C. Kegan Paul & Co., 1881), 1:405–6.

26. Jean Bodin, "The Rise and Fall of Commonwealths," chap. 7, http://www.constitution.org/bodin/bodin_4.htm.

27. Lord Wharncliffe, ed., *The Letters and Works of Lady Mary Wortley Montagu* (London: Henry G. Bohn, 1861), 1:298–300.

28. Quoted in Stuart B. Schwartz, ed., *Victors and Vanquished* (Boston: Bedford/St. Martin's, 2000), 31.

29. Schwartz, *Victors and Vanquished*, 29.

30. Quoted in ibid., 164.

31. Miguel Leon-Portilla, *The Broken Spears* (Boston: Beacon Press, 1992), 80–81.

Chapter 15

1. Jacob Wheeler, "From Slave Post to Museum," *Christian Science Monitor*, December 31, 2002.

2. Quoted in Paul Lunde, "The Coming of the Portuguese," *Saudi Aramco World*, July–August 2005, 56.

3. Philip Curtin, *Cross Cultural Trade in World History* (Cambridge: Cambridge University Press, 1984), 144.

4. Quoted in Patricio N. Abinales and Donna J. Amoroso, *State and Society in the Philippines* (Lanham: Rowman and Littlefield, 2005), 50.

5. Anthony Reid, *Southeast Asia in the Age of Commerce, 1450–1680* (New Haven: Yale University Press, 1993), 2:274, 290.

6. Anthony Reid, *Charting the Shape of Early Modern Southeast Asia* (Chiang Mai: Silkworm Books, 1999), 227.

7. Andre Gunder Frank, *ReOrient: Global Economy in the Asian Age* (Berkeley: University of California Press, 1998), 131.

8. Quoted in Richard von Glahn, "Myth and Reality of China's Seventeenth Century Monetary Crisis," *Journal of Economic History* 56, no. 2 (June 1996): 132.

9. Kenneth Pomeranz and Steven Topik, *The World That Trade Created* (Armonk, N.Y.: M. E. Sharpe, 2006), 151–54.

10. Dennis O. Flynn and Arturo Giraldez, "Born with a 'Silver Spoon,'" *Journal of World History* 6, no. 2 (Fall 1995): 210.

11. Quoted in Mark Elvin, *The Retreat of the Elephant* (New Haven: Yale University Press, 2004), 37.

12. Quoted in Robert Marks, *The Origins of the Modern World* (Lanham: Rowman and Littlefield, 2002), 81.

13. See John Richards, *The Endless Frontier* (Berkeley: University of California Press, 2003), part 4. Much of this section is drawn from this source.

14. Elspeth M. Veale, *The English Fur Trade in the Later Middle Ages* (Oxford: Clarendon Press, 1966), 141.

15. Quoted in Richards, *The Endless Frontier*, 499.

16. Richards, *The Endless Frontier*, 504.

17. Quoted from "The Iroquois Confederacy," Portland State University, 2001, http://www.iroquoisdemocracy.pdx.edu/html/furtrader.htm.

18. These figures derive from the Trans-Atlantic Slave Trade Database, http://www.slavevoyages.org/tast/assessment/estimates.faces.

19. David Brion Davis, *Challenging the Boundaries of Slavery* (Cambridge, Mass.: Harvard University Press, 2003), 13.

20. Quoted in Bernard Lewis, *Race and Slavery in the Middle East* (New York: Oxford University Press, 1990), 52–53.

21. Audrey Smedley, *Race in North America* (Boulder, Colo.: Westview Press, 1993).

22. Kevin Reilly et al., eds., *Racism: A Global Reader* (Armonk, N.Y.: M. E. Sharpe, 2003), 131.

23. Quoted in Donald R. Wright, *The World and a Very Small Place in Africa* (Armonk, NY: M. E. Sharpe, 1997), 109–10.

24. John Thornton, *Africa and Africans in the Making of the Atlantic World* (Cambridge: Cambridge University Press, 1998), 72.

25. Thomas Phillips, "A Journal of a Voyage Made in the Hannibal of London in 1694," in *Documents Illustrative of the History of the Slave Trade to America*, edited by Elizabeth Donnan (Washington, D.C.: Carnegie Institute, 1930), 399–410.

26. Erik Gilbert and Jonathan T. Reynolds, *Africa in World History* (Upper Saddle River, N.J.: Pearson, 2004), 160.

27. Trans-Atlantic Slave Trade Database, http://www.slavevoyages.org/tast/assessment/estimates.faces.

28. Paul Adams et al., *Experiencing World History* (New York: New York University Press, 2000), 334.

29. Anne Bailey, *African Voices in the Atlantic Slave Trade* (Boston: Beacon Press, 2005), 153–54.

30. The present-day state of Benin is where the earlier kingdom of Dahomey once was. The ancient kingdom of Benin was located within present-day Nigeria.

31. Erik Gilbert and Jonathan Reynolds, *Trading Tastes: Commodity and Cultural Exchange to 1750* (Upper Saddle River, N.J.: Pearson Prentice Hall, 2006), 9.

32. Alex Szogyi, ed., *Chocolate: Food of the Gods* (Santa Barbara: Greenwood Press, 1997), 166.

33. James Grehan, "Smoking and 'Early Modern' Sociability: The Great Tobacco Debate in the Ottoman Middle East (Seventeenth to Eighteenth Centuries)," *The American Historical Review*, December 2006, http://www.historycooperative.org/journals/ahr/111.5/grehan.html.

34. Uzi Baram and Lynda Carroll, eds., *A Historical Archeology of the Ottoman Empire* (New York: Springer, 2000), 172–74.

Chapter 16

1. Andrew Rice, "Mission from Africa," *New York Times Magazine*, April 8, 2009; "African Missionaries Take Religion to the West," *Church Shift*, August 7, 2006, (http://www.churchshift.org).

2. Dr. Peter Hammond, "The Reformation," http://www.frontline.org.za/articles/thereformation_lectures.htm.

3. Glenn J. Ames, *Vasco da Gama: Renaissance Crusader* (New York: Pearson Education, 2005), 50.

4. Cecil Jane, ed. and trans., *Selected Documents Illustrating the Four Voyages of Columbus* (London: Hakluyt Society, 1930–1933), 2:2–18.

5. Kenneth Mills, *Idolatry and Its Enemies* (Princeton, N.J.: Princeton University Press, 1997), chap. 9.

6. Quoted in U.S. Library of Congress, "Country Studies: Peru," http://countrystudies.us/peru/5.htm.

7. Quoted in Nicolas Griffiths, *The Cross and the Serpent* (Norman: University of Oklahoma Press, 1996), 263.

8. See James Lockhart, *The Nahuas after Conquest* (Stanford, Calif.: Stanford University Press, 1992), chap. 6.

9. Quoted in Joanna Waley-Cohen, *The Sextants of Beijing* (New York: W. W. Norton, 1999), 76–77.

10. Richard M. Eaton, "Islamic History as Global History," in *Islamic and European Expansion*, edited by Michael Adas (Philadelphia: Temple University Press, 1993), 25.

11. Robert Bly and Jane Hirshfield, trans., *Mirabai: Ecstatic Poems* (Boston: Beacon Press, 2004), ix–xi.

12. Quoted in Steven Shapin, *The Scientific Revolution* (Chicago: University of Chicago Press, 1996), 66.

13. This section draws heavily on Toby E. Huff, *The Rise of Early Modern Science* (Cambridge: Cambridge University Press, 2003), 48, 52, 76.

14. Huff, *The Rise of Early Modern Science*, 87, 288.

15. Jerome Cardano, *The Book of My Life*, translated by Jean Stoner (London: J. M. Dent, 1931), 189.

16. Quoted in Shapin, *The Scientific Revolution*, 28.

17. Quoted in ibid., 61.

18. Quoted in ibid., 33.

19. Quoted in ibid., 68.

20. Stillman Drake, trans., *Discoveries and Opinions of Galileo* (Garden City, N.Y.: Doubleday, 1957).

21. H. S. Thayer, ed., *Newton's Philosophy of Nature: Selections from His Writings* (New York: Hafner Library of Classics, 1953), 42.

22. Immanuel Kant, "What Is Enlightenment?" translated by Peter Gay, in *Introduction to Contemporary Civilization in the West* (New York: Columbia University Press, 1954), 1071.

23. Voltaire, *A Treatise on Toleration* (1763), chap. 22, http://www.constitution.org/volt/tolerance.htm.

24. Quoted in Margaret C. Jacob, *The Enlightenment* (Boston: Bedford/St. Martin's, 2001), 103.

25. Quoted in Jonathan Spence, *The Search for Modern China* (New York: Norton, 1999), 104.

26. Waley-Cohen, *The Sextants of Beijing*, 105–14.

27. Benjamin A. Elman, *On Their Own Terms: Science in China, 1550–1900* (Cambridge, Mass.: Harvard University Press, 2005).

28. Quoted in David R. Ringrose, *Expansion and Global Interaction, 1200–1700* (New York: Longman, 2001), 188.

29. Ekmeleddin Ihsanoglu, *Science, Technology, and Learning in the Ottoman Empire* (Burlington, Vt.: Ashgate, 2004).

30. Quoted in Sergiusz Michalski, *The Reformation and the Visual Arts* (New York: Routledge, 1993), 7.

31. Quoted in Angela Vanhalaen, "Iconoclasm and the Creation of Images in Emanuel de Witte's Old Church in Amsterdam," *The Art Bulletin* (June 2005): 5.

32. David Brett, *The Plain Style* (Cambridge: Letterworth Press, 2004), 61–62.

33. Gauvin Alexander Bailey, *Art on the Jesuit Missions in Asia and Latin America* (Toronto: University of Toronto Press, 1999), 102–4.

34. John W. O'Malley et al., *The Jesuits* (Toronto: University of Toronto Press, 1999), 381.

Part Five

1. Quoted in Ross Dunn, *The New World History* (Boston: Bedford/St. Martin's, 2000), 17.

2. William H. McNeill, "*The Rise of the West* after 25 Years," *Journal of World History* 1, no. 1 (Spring 1990): 7.

Chapter 17

1. Quoted in Keith M. Baker, "A World Transformed," *Wilson Quarterly* (Summer 1989): 37.

2. Quoted in Thomas Benjamin et al., *The Atlantic World in the Age of Empire* (Boston: Houghton Mifflin, 2001), 205.

3. Jack P. Greene, "The American Revolution," *American Historical Review* 105, no. 1 (February 2000): 96–97.

4. Quoted in ibid., 102.

5. Quoted in Susan Dunn, *Sister Revolutions* (New York: Faber and Faber, 1999), 11, 12.

6. Quoted in ibid., 9.

7. Quoted in Lynn Hunt et al., *The Making of the West* (Boston: Bedford/St. Martin's, 2003), 625.

8. From James Leith, "Music for Mass Persuasion during the Terror," a collection of texts, tapes, and slides, copyright James A. Leith, Queen's University Kingston.

9. Franklin W. Knight, "The Haitian Revolution," *American Historical Review* 105, no. 1 (February 2000): 103.

10. Quoted in David P. Geggus, *Haitian Revolutionary Studies* (Bloomington: Indiana University Press, 2002), 27.

11. John C. Chasteen, *Born in Blood and Fire* (New York: Norton, 2006), 103.

12. Peter Winn, *Americas: The Changing Face of Latin America and the Caribbean* (Berkeley: University of California Press, 2006), 83.

13. Quoted in Thomas E. Skidmore and Peter H. Smith, *Modern Latin America* (New York: Oxford University Press, 2001), 33.

14. James Walvin, "The Public Campaign in England against Slavery," in *The Abolition of the Atlantic Slave Trade*, edited by David Eltis and James Walvin (Madison: University of Wisconsin Press, 1981), 76.

15. Michael Craton, "Slave Revolts and the End of Slavery," in *The Atlantic Slave Trade*, edited by David Northrup (Boston: Houghton Mifflin, 2002), 200.

16. Joseph Dupuis, *Journal of a Residence in Ashantee* (London: Henry Colburn, 1824), 162–64

17. Eric Foner, *Nothing but Freedom* (Baton Rouge: Louisiana State University Press, 1983).

18. Quoted in Daniel Moran and Arthur Waldron, eds., *The People in Arms: Military Myth and National Mobilization since the French Revolution* (Cambridge: Cambridge University Press, 2003), 14.

19. Barbara Winslow, "Feminist Movements: Gender and Sexual Equality," in *A Companion to Gender History*, edited by Teresa A. Meade and Merry E. Weisner-Hanks (London: Blackwell, 2004), 186.

20. Bonnie S. Anderson, *Joyous Greetings: The First International Women's Movement, 1830–1860* (Oxford: Oxford University Press, 2000).

21. Quoted in Claire G. Moses, *French Feminism in the Nineteenth Century* (Albany: SUNY Press, 1984), 135.

22. See Lynn Hunt, ed., *The French Revolution and Human Rights* (Boston: Bedford/St. Martin's, 1996), 1–31.

23. Quoted in "The Rights of Women," http://www.pinn.net/~sunshine/book-sum/gouges.html.

24. Jean-Denis Lanjuinais, "Discussion of Citizenship under the Proposed New Constitution" in *The French Revolution and Human Rights*, edited by Lynn Hunt (Boston: Bedford/St. Martin's, 1996), 133.

25. Quoted in Lynn Hunt, *Politics, Culture, and Class in the French Revolution* (Berkeley: University of California Press, 2004), 35.

26. Modern History Sourcebook, "Ca ira," http://www.fordham.edu/halsall/mod/caira.html.

Chapter 18

1. "Mahatma Gandhi on Industrialization," http://www.tinytechindia.com/gandhi3.htm#1.

2. Edmund Burke III and Kenneth Pomeranz, eds., *The Environment and World History* (Berkeley: University of California Press, 2009), 41.

3. David Christian, *Maps of Time* (Berkeley: University of California Press, 2004), 346–47.

4. Joel Mokyr, *The Lever of Riches* (New York: Oxford University Press, 1990), 40–44.

5. Lynda Shaffer, "Southernization," *Journal of World History* 5, no. 1 (Spring 1994): 1–21.

6. Kenneth Pomeranz, *The Great Divergence* (Princeton, N.J.: Princeton University Press, 2000). See also Jack Goldstone, *Why Europe? The Rise of the West in World History* (Boston: McGraw-Hill, 2009).

7. Pier Vries, "Are Coal and Colonies Really Crucial?" *Journal of World History* 12, no. 2 (Fall 2001): 411.

8. Christian, *Maps of Time*, 390.

9. E. L. Jones, *The European Miracle* (Cambridge: Cambridge University Press, 1981), 119.

10. Quoted in Mokyr, *The Lever of Riches*, 188.

11. Quoted in Prasannan Parthansaranthi, "Rethinking Wages and Competitiveness in the Eighteenth Century," *Past and Present* 158 (February 1998): 79.

12. Maxine Berg, *Luxury and Pleasure in Eighteenth-Century Britain* (Oxford: Oxford University Press, 2005), 79–84.

13. Peter Stearns, *The Industrial Revolution in World History* (Boulder, Colo.: Westview Press, 1998), 36.

14. Goldstone, *Why Europe?* Ch. 8.

15. Eric Hopkins, *Industrialization and Society* (London: Routledge, 2000), 2.

16. Mokyr, *The Lever of Riches*, 81.

17. Eric Hobsbawm, *Industry and Empire* (New York: New Press, 1999), 58. This section draws heavily on Hobsbawm's celebrated account of British industrialization.

18. Lynn Hunt et al., *The Making of the West* (Boston: Bedford/St. Martin's, 2009), 656.

19. Samuel Smiles, *Thrift* (London: John Murray, 1875), 30–40.

20. Hobsbawm, *Industry and Empire*, 65.

21. Peter Stearns and John H. Hinshaw, *Companion to the Industrial Revolution* (Santa Barbara: ABC-CLIO, 1996), 150.

22. Workers' Liberty, http://www.workersliberty.org/node/view/3359?PHPSESSID=93d.

23. Hobsbawm, *Industry and Empire*, 171.

24. Derived from Paul Kennedy, *The Rise and Fall of the Great Powers* (New York: Random House, 1987), 149.

25. John Charles Chasteen, *Born in Blood and Fire* (New York: W. W. Norton, 2006), 181.

26. Peter Bakewell, *A History of Latin America* (Oxford: Blackwell, 1997), 425.

27. Michael Adas, *Machines as the Measure of Men* (Ithaca, N.Y.: Cornell University Press, 1990).

28. Ibid., 133.

29. Quoted in Francis D. Klingender, *Art and the Industrial Revolution* (New York: Augustus M. Kelley Publishers, 1968), 139.

30. See Kathryn J. Summerwill, "Eyre Crowe A.R.A. (1824–1910)," http://www.geocities.com/eyre_crowe/1874.html.

31. "*The Dinner Hour: Wigan*, Eyre Crowe," Images of the Industrial Revolution, http://www.netnicholls.com/neh2000/paper/pages/txt07.htm#.

32. "Child Labor in America: Photographs of Lewis W. Hine, 1908–1912," The History Place, http://www.historyplace.com/unitedstates/childlabor/.

33. Quoted in Albert Boime, *Art in an Age of Bonapartism, 1800–1815* (Chicago: University of Chicago Press, 1990), 120–21.

Chapter 19

1. People's Daily, April 6, 2001, http://english.peopledaily.com.cn/english/200104/06/eng20010406_66955.html.

2. Quoted in Heinz Gollwitzer, *Europe in the Age of Imperialism* (London: Thames and Hudson, 1969), 136.

3. Robert Knox, *Races of Man* (Philadelphia: Lea and Blanchard, 1850), v.

4. Quoted in Ralph Austen, ed., *Modern Imperialism* (Lexington, Mass.: D. C. Heath, 1969), 70–73.

5. Quoted in Julian Burger, "Echoes of History," *New Internationalist*, August 1988, http://www.newint.org/issue186/echoes.htm.

6. Dun J. Li, ed., *China in Transition, 1517–1911* (New York: Van Nostrand Reinhold, 1969).

7. Quoted in Jonathan D. Spence, *The Search for Modern China* (New York: W. W. Norton, 1999), 169.

8. Hsin-Pao Chang, ed., *Commissioner Lin and the Opium War* (New York: Norton, 1970), 226–27.

9. Barbara Hodgson, *Opium: A Portrait of the Heavenly Demon* (San Francisco: Chronicle Books, 1999), 32.

10. Quoted in Teng Ssu and John K. Fairbanks, eds. and trans., *China's Response to the West* (New York: Atheneum, 1963), 69.

11. Quoted in Magali Morsy, *North Africa: 1800–1900* (London: Longman, 1984), 79.

12. Quoted in M Sukru Hanioglu, *The Young Turks in Opposition* (New York: Oxford University Press, 1995), 17.

13. Marius B. Jansen, *The Making of Modern Japan* (Cambridge, Mass.: Harvard University Press, 2002), 33.

14. Quoted in Carol Gluck, "Themes in Japanese History," in *Asia in Western and World History*, edited by Ainslie T. Embree and Carol Gluck (Armonk, N.Y.: M. E. Sharpe, 1997), 754.

15. Quoted in S. Hanley and K. Yamamura, *Economic and Demographic Change in Pre-Industrial Japan* (Princeton, N.J.: Princeton University Press, 1977), 88–90.

16. Quoted in Harold Bolitho, "The Tempo Crisis," in *The Cambridge History of Japan*, vol. 5, *The Nineteenth Century*, edited by Maurice B. Jansen (Cambridge: Cambridge University Press, 1989), 230.

17. Kenneth Henshall, *A History of Japan* (New York: Palgrave, 2004), 67.

18. Quoted in James L. McClain, *Japan: A Modern History* (New York: W. W. Norton, 2002), 177.

19. Selcuk Esenbel, "Japan's Global Claim to Asia and the World of Islam," *American Historical Review* (October 2004), par. 1, 9, http://www.historycooperative.org/journals/ahr/109.4/esenbel.html.

20. Jonathan Spence, *The Search for Modern China* (New York: W. W. Norton, 1999), 154.

21. Ibid., 159.

22. Quoted in Marius B. Jensen, *The Making of Modern Japan* (Cambridge: Harvard University Press, 2000), 460.

23. Quoted in Julia Meech-Pekarik, *The World of the Meiji Print: Impressions of a New Civilization* (New York: Weatherhill, 1986), 182.

24. Quoted in Oka Yoshitake, Prologue to Marlene Mayo, ed., *The Emergence of Imperial Japan* (Lexington: Heath, 1970).

Chapter 20

1. Quoted in Robert Strayer, *The Making of Mission Communities in East Africa* (London: Heinemann, 1978), 89.

2. Quoted in John Iliffe, *Africans: The History of a Continent* (Cambridge: Cambridge University Press, 1995), 191.

3. Quoted in Nicholas Tarling, "The Establishment of Colonial Regimes," in *The Cambridge History of Southeast Asia*, edited by Nicholas Tarling (Cambridge: Cambridge University Press, 1992), 2:76.

4. R. Meinertzhagen, *Kenya Diary* (London: Oliver and Boyd, 1957), 51–52.

5. Quoted in Neil Jamieson, *Understanding Vietnam* (Berkeley: University of California Press, 1993), 49–57.

6. Quoted in Donald R. Wright, *The World and a Very Small Place in Africa* (Armonk, N.Y.: M. E. Sharpe, 2004), 170.

7. Quoted in Scott B. Cook, *Colonial Encounters in the Age of High Imperialism* (New York: HarperCollins, 1996), 53.

8. D. R. SarDesai, *Southeast Asia: Past and Present* (Boulder, Colo.: Westview Press, 1997), 95–98.

9. Quoted in G. C. K. Gwassa and John Iliffe, *Records of the Maji Maji Rising* (Nairobi: East African Publishing House, 1967), 1: 4–5.

10. Michael Adas, "Continuity and Transformation: Colonial Rice Frontiers and Their Environmental Impact…," in *The Environment and World History*, edited by Edmund

Burke III and Kenneth Pomeranz (Berkeley: University of California Press, 2009), 191–207.

11. Iliffe, *Africans*, 216.

12. Quoted in Basil Davidson, *Modern Africa* (London: Longmans, 1983), 79, 81.

13. This section draws heavily on Margaret Jean Hay and Sharon Stichter, eds., *African Women South of the Sahara* (London: Longmans, 1984), especially chaps. 1–5.

14. Quoted in Robert A. Levine, "Sex Roles and Economic Change in Africa," in *Black Africa*, edited by John Middleton (London: Macmillan, 1970), 178.

15. Elizabeth Schmidt, *Peasants, Traders, and Wives: Shona Women in the History of Zimbabwe, 1870–1939* (Portsmouth, N.H.: Heinemann, 1992), chap. 4.

16. Derived from Adam McKeown, "Global Migration, 1846–1940," *Journal of World History* 15, no. 2 (June 2004): 156.

17. Josiah Kariuki, *Mau Mau Detainee* (London: Oxford University Press, 1963), 5.

18. Quoted in Harry Benda and John Larkin, *The World of Southeast Asia* (New York: Harper and Row, 1967), 182–85.

19. William Theodore de Bary, *Sources of Indian Tradition* (New York: Columbia University Press, 1958), 619.

20. Quoted in Edward W. Smith, *Aggrey of Africa*, (London: SCM Press, 1929).

21. C. A. Bayly, *The Birth of the Modern World* (Oxford: Blackwell, 2004), 343.

22. de Bary, *Sources of Indian Tradition*, 652.

23. Nirad Chaudhuri, *Autobiography of an Unknown Indian* (London: John Farquharson, 1968), 229.

24. Edward Blyden, *Christianity, Islam, and the Negro Race* (Edinburgh: Edinburgh University Press, 1967), 124.

25. John Iliffe, *A Modern History of Tanganyika* (Cambridge: Cambridge University Press, 1979), 324.

26. British Museum, http://ww.britishmuseum.org/explore/highlights/ highlight_objects/aoa/b/the_battle_of_adwa, _painting.aspx.

Part Six

1. J. R. McNeill, *Something New under the Sun* (New York: W. W. Norton, 2000), 3–4.

Chapter 21

1. "Scotland's Oldest Man Turns 107," *Scotsman*, June 25, 2003, http://www.aftermathww1.com/oldestscot.asp; MSNBC, November 21, 2005, http://www.msnbc.msn.com/id/10138446/

2. Quoted in John Keegan, *The First World War* (New York: Vintage Books, 1998), 3.

3. Adapted from Lynn Hunt et al., *The Making of the West: Peoples and Cultures* (Boston: Bedford/St. Martin's, 2001), 1024.

4. Stanley Payne, *History of Fascism, 1914–1945* (Madison: University of Wisconsin Press, 1995), 208.

5. Richard Bessel, ed., *Fascist Italy and Nazi Germany: Comparisons and Contrasts* (Cambridge: Cambridge University Press, 1996), 8.

6. Quoted in Laurence Rees, *The Nazis: A Warning from History* (New York: New Press, 1997), 62.

7. James L. McClain, *Japan: A Modern History* (New York: W. W. Norton, 2002), 378.

8. Quoted in ibid., 414.

9. Bernd Martin, *Japan and Germany in the Modern World* (Providence: Berghahn Books, 1995), 155–81.

10. Quoted in Marius B. Jansen, *The Making of Modern Japan* (Cambridge, Mass.: Harvard University Press, 2000), 607.

11. Quoted in ibid., 639.

12. Quoted in John Keegan, *The Second World War* (New York: Viking Penguin, 1989), 186.

13. John Lewis Gaddis, *We Now Know: Rethinking Cold War History* (Oxford: Oxford University Press, 1997), 52.

14. Adam Gopnik, "The Big One: Historians Rethink the War to End All Wars," *The New Yorker*, August 23, 2004, 78.

Chapter 22

1. BBC, "On this Day," November 9, 1989, http:// news.bbc.co.uk/onthisday/hi/witness/november/9/newsid_ 3241000/3241641.stm.

2. Quoted in Ronald Suny, *The Soviet Experiment* (Oxford: Oxford University Press, 1998), 357.

3. Yuan-tsung Chen, *The Dragon's Village* (New York: Penguin Books, 1980), 85.

4. Such figures are often highly controversial. See Maurice Meisner, *Mao's China and After* (New York: Free Press, 1999), 413–25; Roderick MacFarquhar, ed., *The Politics of China* (Cambridge: Cambridge University Press, 1997), 243–45.

5. Quoted in Richard Rusk, *As I Saw It* (New York: Norton, 1990), 245.

6. Quoted in John L. Gaddis, *The Cold War: A New History* (New York: Penguin Press, 2005), 57.

7. Ronald Steel, *Pax Americana* (New York: Viking Press, 1970), 254.

8. Quoted in Donald W. White, *The American Century* (New Haven: Yale University Press, 1996), 164.

9. David Potter, *People of Plenty* (Chicago: University of Chicago Press, 1954), 139.

10. Quoted in John M. Thompson, *A Vision Unfulfilled* (Lexington, Mass.: D. C. Heath, 1996), 383.

11. Deng Xiaoping, "The Necessity of Upholding the Four Cardinal Principles in the Drive for the Four Modernizations," in *Major Documents of the People's Republic of China* (Beijing: Foreign Language Press, 1991), 54.

12. Mikhail Gorbachev, *Perestroika: New Thinking for Our Country and the World* (New York: Harper and Row, 1987), 64.

13. Quoted in Abraham Brumberg, *Chronicle of a Revolution* (New York: Pantheon Books, 1990), 225–26.

14. Quoted in *Chinese Propaganda Posters* (Koln: Taschen, 2003), 5.

15. Quoted in ibid., 10.

Chapter 23

1. Nelson Mandela, "I Am Prepared to Die," statement at the Rivonia trial, April 20, 1964, http://www.anc.org.za/ ancdocs/history/rivonia.html.

2. Quoted in Jim Masselos, *Nationalism on the Indian Subcontinent* (Melbourne: Nelson, 1972), 122.

3. Mohandas Gandhi, *Hind Swaraj*, 1909, http://www.mkgandhi-sarvodaya.org/hindswaraj.htm.

4. Quoted in Stanley Wolpert, *A New History of India* (Oxford: Oxford University Press, 1993), 331.

5. This information is drawn from the World Bank, *World Development Report 2009* (Oxford: Oxford University Press, 2008), Tables 1, 2.

6. Quoted in Bernard Lewis, *The Emergence of Modern Turkey* (London: Oxford University Press, 1968), 268–69.

7. Quoted in Patrick B. Kinross, *Ataturk: A Biography of Mustafa Kemal* (New York: Morrow, 1965), 390.

8. Sandra Mackey, *The Iranians* (New York: Penguin, 1998), 306.

9. Kwame Nkrumah, *Ghana: An Autobiography* (London: Nelson, 1957), 34.

10. Liberation Graphics, "Palestine Poster Project," http:// www.liberationgraphics.com/ppp/Redeem_the_Land.html.

11. Ibid., http://www.liberationgraphics.com/ppp/ landday.html.

Chapter 24

1. BBC News, March 5, 2002, http://news.bbc.co.uk/ 2/hi/middle_east/1856558.stm.

2. Jeffrey Frieden, *Global Capitalism* (New York: W. W. Norton, 2006), 476.

3. Jan Aart Scholte, *Globalization: A Critical Introduction* (New York: Palgrave, 2005), 117.

4. Based on constant 2004 U.S. dollars. Earth Policy Institute, "Eco-Economy Indicators," http://www.earth-policy.org/ Indicators/Econ/Econ_data.htm.

5. United Nations, *Human Development Report, 1997*, 2, http://hdr.undp.org/reports/global/1997/en.

6. Michael Hunt, *The World Transformed* (Boston: Bedford/ St. Martin's, 2004), 442.

7. Quoted in Frieden, *Global Capitalism*, 408.

8. Quoted in Manfred B. Steger, *Globalization: A Very Short Introduction* (Oxford: Oxford University Press, 2003), 122.

9. Quoted in Frieden, *Global Capitalism*, 459.

10. Charles S. Maier, *Among Empires: American Ascendancy and Its Predecessors* (Cambridge, Mass.: Harvard University Press, 2006), chap. 5.

11. Quoted in Donald W. White, *The American Century: The Rise and Decline of the United States as a World Power* (New Haven: Yale University Press, 1996), 395.

12. Quoted in Sarah Shaver Hughes and Brady Hughes, *Women in World History* (Armonk, N.Y.: M. E. Sharpe, 1997), 2:268.

13. Susan Kent, "Worlds of Feminism," in *Women's History in Global Perspective*, edited by Bonnie G. Smith (Urbana: University of Illinois Press, 2004), 1:305–6.

14. Quoted in Wilhelmina Oduol and Wanjiku Mukabi Kabira, "The Mother of Warriors and Her Daughters: The Women's Movement in Kenya," in *Global Feminisms since 1945*, edited by Bonnie Smith (London: Routledge, 2000), 111.

15. Elisabeth Jay Friedman, "Gendering the Agenda," *Women's Studies International Forum* 26, no. 4 (2003): 313–31.

16. Quoted in Mary E. Hawkesworth, *Globalization and Feminist Activism* (New York: Rowman and Littfield, 2006), 124.

17. Phyllis Schlafly, *The Power of the Christian Woman* (Cincinnati: Standard, 1981), 117.

18. Karen Armstrong, *The Battle for God* (New York: Alfred A. Knopf, 2000), xi.

19. Quoted in Armstrong, *The Battle for God*, 273.

20. Quoted in John Esposito, *Unholy War* (Oxford: Oxford University Press, 2002), 57.

21. Quoted in ibid., 63.

22. "Fatwah Urging Jihad against Americans," http://www .ict.org.il/articles/fatwah.htm.

23. Anwar Ibrahim, "The Ardent Moderates," *Time*, September 23, 1996, 24.

24. See J. R. McNeill, *Something New under the Sun: An Environmental History of the Twentieth Century World* (New York: Norton, 2001).

25. Adapted from Lynn Hunt et *al., The Making of the West: Peoples and Cultures* (Bedford/St. Martin's, 2009), 968.

26. Ramachandra Guha, *Environmentalism: A Global History* (New York: Longman, 2000), part 1.

27. Timothy Doyle, *Environmental Movements in Minority and Majority Worlds: A Global Perspective* (New Brunswick, N.J.: Rutgers University Press, 2005).

28. Quoted in Shiraz Sidhva, "Saving the Planet: Imperialism in a Green Garb," *The UNESCO Courier*, April 2001, 41–43.

29. Anwar Ibrahim, "Who Hijacked Islam?" *Time Magazine*, October 8, 2001.

30. *Bulletin of the Committee of Moroccan Workers in Holland*, 1978, quoted in *Third World Lives of Struggle*, edited by Hazel Johnson and Henry Bernstein (London: Heinemann, 1982), 173-74.

Acknowledgments

Chapter 13

Miguel Leon-Portilla. "Like a painting, we will be erased." From *Fifteen Poets of the Aztec World* by Miguel Leon-Portilla, editor and translator. Copyright © 1992 by the University of Oklahoma Press, Norman. Reprinted by permission.

Chapter 15

Mark Elvin. "Rarer too their timber grew." Excerpt (4 lines) from *Retreat of the Elephants* by Mark Elvin. Copyright © 2004 by Mark Elvin. Used by permission of Yale University Press.

Chapter 16

Mirabai. "What I paid was my social body...." From *Mirabai: Ecstatic Poems* by Robert Bly and Jane Hirshfeld. Copyright © by Robert Bly and Jane Hirshfield. Reprinted by Beacon Press, Boston.

Chapter 20

Neil Jamieson. "Fine wine but no good friends." From *Understanding Vietnam* by Neil Jamieson, translator. Copyright © 1993 by University of California Press. Reproduced with permission of University of California Press in the format Textbook via Copyright Clearance Center.

Chapter 24

Map 24.3 (bottom) is adapted from http://www.princeton.edu/~ina/infographics/starbucks.html (2003).

Index

Note: Names of individuals are in **boldface** and: (f) figures, including charts and graphs; (i) illustrations, including photographs and artifacts in the narrative portion of the book only, not in the docutext sections; (m) maps; (t) tables; (v) visual sources, including all illustrations in the docutext portion of the book; (d) documents in the docutext portion of the book